NISEI LINGUISTS

Japanese Americans in the Military Intelligence Service during World War II

by
James C. McNaughton

DEPARTMENT OF THE ARMY
WASHINGTON, D.C., 2006

Published by Books Express Publishing
Copyright © Books Express, 2011
ISBN 978-1-1780390-43-7

Books Express publications are available from all good retail
and online booksellers. For publishing proposals and direct
ordering please contact us at: info@books-express.com

Foreword

From long experience, U.S. Army leaders have found that success in sustained land operations has often required extremely sophisticated linguistic skills. In many cases, such abilities are unique to narrow sections of the nation's civilian populace. Nevertheless, where intelligence gathering, coalition building, and military government are concerned, the ability to understand the languages of the nation's allies and opponents can spell the difference between victory and defeat.

When America entered the war against Japan in 1941, the need for this skill was imperative. A deep understanding of both Japanese culture and the Japanese language would be necessary for American intelligence efforts to succeed. However, with the exception of about 300,000 Japanese immigrants and their American-born children living on the West Coast and in Hawaii, few Americans were familiar with the enemy's language and culture. The atmosphere of outrage and fear that followed the attack on Pearl Harbor complicated matters. Most Americans wanted little to do with anything Japanese, particularly their fellow citizens of Japanese origin. Even so, the War Department's General Staff recognized the necessity of mastering both the culture and the language of their Asian opponent in order to pursue the war effort effectively and efficiently. In response, they turned to the nation's second-generation Japanese Americans, or *Nisei*, in the hopes that they would be willing and able to fill that void.

Initially, these wartime leaders had to address a number of the same questions facing today's Army. How well did these second-generation Americans actually speak the complex language of their forebears? Could those that did be trusted? What was the best way to integrate them into the various tactical and strategic intelligence organizations that could benefit from their services? That it took only two years to answer these questions bears witness not only to the effectiveness of the innovative programs that the War Department created, but also to the willingness of America's loyal Japanese to ignore the distrust of their fellow citizens and give their best to the war effort. The end result contributed heavily to Allied victory in the Pacific by making possible the rapid exploitation of information from captured enemy documents, intercepted radio communications, and prisoners of war.

To supplement the Center of Military History's works covering the exploits of the Japanese American 442d Regimental Combat Team in Europe, this volume chronicles the establishment and achievements of the organization that trained and employed these uniformed Japanese American linguists, the U.S. Army Military Intelligence Service. Although often overlooked, the entire experience provides valuable lessons to U.S. Army officers both present and future. In fact, the Global War on Terrorism underlines the need for similar capabilities and programs as the Army girds itself for the sustained struggle ahead.

Washington, D.C.   JEFFREY J. CLARKE
2 September 2006   Chief of Military History

The Author

James C. McNaughton serves as command historian for the U.S. European Command. He received his B.A. from Middlebury College, Vermont, and M.A. and Ph.D. in history from The Johns Hopkins University, Baltimore, Maryland. He has served in the U.S. Army in several components: Active Army, National Guard, Army Reserve, and civilian sector. He has worked as command historian for the Defense Language Institute Foreign Language Center and for U.S. Army Pacific.

Preface

This book tells the story of an unusual group of American soldiers in World War II, second-generation Japanese Americans (*Nisei*) who served as interpreters and translators in the Military Intelligence Service. It describes how the War Department recruited soldiers from an ethnic minority and trained them in a secret school to use the Japanese language. Months before the Japanese attack on Pearl Harbor, the Fourth Army Intelligence School was established on the Presidio of San Francisco with sixty students. After the attack the Western Defense Command removed all persons of Japanese ancestry from the West Coast. The War Department transferred the school with its Nisei instructors and students to the Midwest. For the rest of the war the renamed Military Intelligence Service Language School operated in Minnesota at Camp Savage from 1942 to 1944 and then at Fort Snelling from 1944 to 1946. By the spring of 1946 the school had graduated nearly 6,000 military linguists in the Japanese language.

The book also describes how these Nisei served with every major unit and headquarters in the Pacific war. Their courage, skill, and loyalty helped win the war sooner and at lower cost to the United States than would otherwise have been possible. During the American occupation of Japan they helped turn bitter enemies into friends, thus securing the victory and serving as a bridge between the two cultures.

During the decades after the war little was publicly known about the Nisei linguists due to continued secrecy about wartime intelligence activities. Meanwhile, other Nisei who served in the 100th Infantry Battalion and 442d Regimental Combat Team in Italy and France received widespread recognition. This changed in the late 1970s through the efforts of one man, Joseph D. Harrington. A retired Navy journalist, Harrington contacted hundreds of veterans to assemble their stories into the first book ever to describe their exploits in detail. He called them Yankee Samurai to symbolize their blend of American and Japanese traits and values. My own work is indebted to him on almost every page.

The 1980s and 1990s witnessed a flood of Nisei veterans' memories and writings. Many veterans felt that a more comprehensive overview was needed. In 1994 U.S. Senator Daniel K. Akaka and several other members of Congress called on the Secretary of the Army to publish an official history of the Nisei linguists. Dr. Jeffrey J. Clarke, then chief historian, invited me to undertake this task. At the time I was serving as command historian for the Defense Language Institute Foreign Language Center at the Presidio of Monterey, California, the direct descendent of the wartime Military Intelligence Service Language School. I began research with support from a Secretary of the Army Research and Study Fellowship. During this time I also served as research director for the Asian American Medal of Honor

Review from 1996 until 1998. I am grateful for the commandants and chiefs of staff under whom I served who recognized the value of these two projects.

I completed the manuscript while serving at Headquarters U.S. Army Pacific at Fort Shafter, Hawaii, from 2001 to 2005. I thank the commanding generals and chiefs of staff there who supported my work. In 2003 the Center of Military History convened a review panel for the manuscript. I am grateful to the panel members whose recommendations resulted in a much improved final product. I completed revisions while serving as command historian at Headquarters U.S. European Command, Patch Barracks, Germany. Although U.S. European Command is on the other side of the world from the Pacific, the Global War on Terrorism reminds Americans everywhere of the continuing need for courage, loyalty, and language skills for members of our armed forces in war and peace.

Many people helped me write this book; they have waited far too long to see it completed. My deepest regret is that my father, Col. George C. McNaughton, U.S. Marine Corps, Ret., did not live to see the final result. A combat veteran with the 1st Marine Division in World War II, Korea, and Vietnam, he encouraged me in the book's early stages but sadly passed away before its completion. As time went on, the Nisei veterans became my adoptive uncles. This book could not have been completed without their generous assistance, especially through veterans associations, including the Military Intelligence Service Association of Northern California, the Military Intelligence Service Veterans of Hawaii, the Military Intelligence Service Veterans of Southern California, the Japanese American Veterans of America, and the Military Intelligence Service Northwest Association.

In particular I want to thank those individuals whose assistance over many years was above and beyond the call of duty: Jeffrey J. Clarke, Stanley L. Falk, Shigeya Kihara, Harry K. Fukuhara, Richard K. Hayashi, S. Phil Ishio, Stephen M. Payne, Thomas T. Sakamoto, James T. Stensvaag, John A. Tagami, Ted T. Tsukiyama, Warren M. Tsuneishi, and Roy T. Uyehata.

For research assistance, my special thanks to the staff at the Combined Arms Research Library, Hoover Institution, Japanese American National Museum, MacArthur Memorial, Military History Institute, National Archives, and National Japanese American Historical Society. I must also thank the Publishing Division staff at the Center of Military History, including Diane M. Donovan, who carefully reviewed the text, and S. L. Dowdy, who translated my vague notions of geography into proper maps.

Special thanks go to my family who watched this project evolve, and especially to my wife, without whose constant support and encouragement this book would never have been completed.

I am solely responsible for all interpretations and conclusions, as well as any errors that may appear. The views expressed in this book are mine and do not necessarily reflect the official policy or position of the Department of the Army, the Department of Defense, or the U.S. Government.

I have been privileged to meet so many men and women of the "greatest generation" who served their country so loyally during such trying times. To them all I owe a great debt. Traditional Japanese culture distinguishes between two kinds of obligations. *Giri* is a simple obligation one incurs in exchange for favors, gifts, goods, or services. *On* is a more complex and demanding obligation, such as the debt you owe your parents for bringing you into the world and raising you to adulthood. According to the *Encyclopedia of Japanese American History*, *"on* is so profound that it can never be completely repaid in one's lifetime." My debt is of the latter kind; I can only hope that my friends will accept this book as a partial repayment of their trust, patience, and many kindnesses.

Stuttgart-Vaihingen, Germany
15 August 2006

JAMES C. McNAUGHTON
Command Historian
U.S. European Command

Contents

Tables

Charts

Maps

Illustrations

      Illustrations courtesy of the following sources: cover, 83, 105, 169, 171, 177,
237, 253, 266, 280, 290, 343, 353, 360, 363, 364, 367, 374, 385, 393, 407, 408,

443, 455, National Archives; 10, 13, 38, 95, 109, 111 (*top*), 219, 263, 301, 303, 421, Defense Language Institute Foreign Language Center; 24, 36, 39, 75, 112, 113, 117, 118, 213, 312, 317, 319, 327, 409, *Military Intelligence Service Language School Album, 1946*; 46, Library of Congress; 57, 128, 435, Bancroft Library, University of California at Berkeley; 111 (*bottom*), 127, Stone Ishimaru; 149, 431, Fordham University Press; 217, 249, 439, 445, Military Intelligence Service Veterans Club of Hawaii; 232, *Fort Ord Panorama*; 251, 345, Military Intelligence Service Association of Northern California/National Japanese American Historical Society; 243, Vantage Press; 261, 354, Pettigrew Enterprises; 334, Henry E. Suzuki Family; 427, *Collier's* magazine; 441, National Japanese American Historical Society. All other illustrations from U.S. Army files.

NISEI LINGUISTS

Japanese Americans in the
Military Intelligence Service
during World War II

1

The U.S. Army and the Nisei before Pearl Harbor

On 7 December 1941, the United States was plunged into a war with Japan. Bitter fighting throughout East Asia, Southeast Asia, and the Pacific ended almost four years later with the defeat and occupation of Japan. The U.S. Army needed soldiers who could read and speak Japanese to serve as translators, interpreters, and interrogators. In an unprecedented experiment, the Army turned to an ethnic group it had previously distrusted—American citizens of Japanese ancestry known as *Nisei* (second generation)—and trained thousands for the Military Intelligence Service (MIS). While their brothers were fighting in Italy and France with the famous 100th Infantry Battalion and 442d Regimental Combat Team (RCT), the MIS Nisei fought in secret using the language of their parents' homeland to help win the war against Japan for America, the land of their birth. In this way they overcame racial prejudice and proved their loyalty, skill, and valor. After the war, the Military Intelligence Service Language School grew into the Defense Language Institute Foreign Language Center, an enduring legacy of the Nisei's service to the nation.

The Nisei Enter the U.S. Army, 1940–1941

America did not begin preparing for war in earnest until 1939, by which time the war was already raging around the world. Germany had conquered Austria, Czechoslovakia, and Poland, quickly adding France and other countries and attacking Britain by air and sea. In the Far East, Japan had clashed with the Soviet Union, was waging war in China, and threatened Europe's Southeast Asian colonies. America's diverse ethnic groups all followed the fighting with concern, none more so than Japanese immigrants and their American-born children. Like other Americans who could trace their ancestry to lands engulfed in war, Japanese Americans hoped that America could avoid open conflict with Japan. If Japan and America went to war, they would have much to lose.[1]

In September 1940 the U.S. Congress approved the first peacetime draft. The Selective Service System began to affect all Americans, as local boards across America registered 16 million men between the ages of twenty-one and thirty-six. That December the boards sent out the first induction notices, and fresh manpower soon began to swell the Army's ranks. Draft notices reached into every corner of America, whether black or white, rich or poor, even to groups that had not yet fully shared in American society. On the West Coast and in the Territory of Hawaii, they reached into the homes of the 284,000 Japanese immigrants and their families.[2]

Japanese American communities responded with pride. In late 1940 and into 1941 they held festive ceremonies for their Nisei sons being inducted into the U.S. Army. (Most of the parents, known as *Issei* [first generation] had come to America before 1924, when Congress had closed the door to further immigration from Japan. Their children, the Nisei, were citizens by birth.) The Nisei and their parents hoped that military service would dispel any lingering questions of their loyalty to America.

When the day came for the young men to report for induction, many towns hoisted the Stars and Stripes alongside the Rising Sun, symbolizing the Nisei's dual heritage. The festivities featured patriotic speeches by community leaders, group photographs, and traditional songs in Japanese and English. Prominent families hosted banquets in local restaurants. Some families gave their sons traditional Japanese *sennin bari* (thousand-stitch belts) into which female family members and friends each had sewn one stitch for good luck. Some Issei mothers wept openly; others remained silent. Issei fathers swelled with pride, often recalling their own service in the Japanese Army many years before. Now their sons would finally gain recognition as true Americans; they could be Yankees *and* Samurai.[3] The Issei parents told their sons that it was now their duty possibly to die for their country. Above all, they must never disgrace the family: "No bring shame!"

---

[1] For responses of American ethnic groups to the war, see John M. Blum, *V Was for Victory: Politics and American Culture during World War II* (New York: Harcourt Brace Jovanovich, 1976), pp. 147–81, and Ronald Takaki, *Double Victory: A Multicultural History of America in World War II* (Boston: Little, Brown, 2000). James C. McNaughton, "Japanese Americans and the U.S. Army: A Historical Reconsideration," *Army History* (Summer/Fall 2003): 4–15.

[2] George Q. Flynn, *The Draft, 1940–1973* (Lawrence: University Press of Kansas, 1993), pp. 9–52. In the year before Selective Service began, the Army expanded through voluntary enlistments but allowed no Nisei to enlist, except for a few who enlisted in National Guard units.

[3] The pairing of "Yankees" and "Samurai" was first popularized in Foster R. Dulles, *Yankees and Samurai: America's Role in the Emergence of Modern Japan* (New York: Harper & Row, 1965). In 1979 Joseph D. Harrington titled his book *Yankee Samurai: The Secret Role of Nisei in America's Pacific Victory* (Detroit: Pettigrew Enterprises, 1979).

Cheers rang out: in Japanese, *"Banzai!"* (Ten thousand years!) and in English, "Good luck!"[4]

The Nisei were following in the footsteps of other American minority groups that had used military service to obtain recognition and citizenship. During the Civil War, Frederick Douglass had described the progression in vivid terms: "Let the black man get upon his person the brass letters U.S.; let him get an eagle upon his buttons and a musket on his shoulder, and bullets in his pocket, and there is no power on the earth which can deny that he has earned the right to citizenship."[5] For the Nisei, military service was an important sign of acceptance into the mainstream of American society. The Nisei, like Chinese Americans and other immigrant groups from Asia before them, had grown up under the shadow of racial prejudice reinforced by American fears of Japanese militarism. The Japanese invasion of China in 1937 had raised some Americans' fear and hatred of Japan to new heights.

Donning U.S. Army uniforms was the culmination of the Nisei generation's rise to recognized citizenship. When the Japanese American Citizens League (JACL) held its national convention in August 1940, President Walter Tsukamoto proclaimed his support for Selective Service and "call[ed] upon every American of Japanese ancestry to offer his life if necessary in defense of his country." Tsukamoto himself set the example, holding a commission in the Officers' Reserve Corps. His successor as president stated the political calculus even more bluntly in February 1941: "The number that we send into the army is one of the best evi-

---

[4] Elliott R. Thorpe, *East Wind, Rain: An Intimate Account of an Intelligence Officer in the Pacific, 1939–49* (Boston: Gambit, 1969), pp. 7–8; Daisuke Kitagawa, *Issei and Nisei: The Internment Years* (New York: Seabury Press, 1967), pp. 31–33; Masako M. Yoshioka, "Just Remembering My Brother Yukitaka Mizutari," Remarks at a Ceremony, Defense Language Institute, 9 May 80, copy at Defense Language Institute Foreign Language Center (DLIFLC), Monterey, Calif.; "Caught between Two Worlds, He Chose, and Fought Well," *San Jose Mercury-News*, 7 Mar 99; Thomas T. Sakamoto autobiography, p. 1, Unpubl Ms, 1 Nov 96, copy in author's files; John A. Rademaker, *These Are Americans: The Japanese Americans in Hawaii in World War II* (Palo Alto, Calif.: Pacific Books, 1951), p. 12.

In Japanese villages, the departure ceremony for new conscripts had been traditional since the 1870s. See Warren J. Clear, "Close Up of the Jap Fighting Man," *Infantry Journal* (November 1942): 16–23; John F. Embree, *Suye Mura: A Japanese Village* (Chicago: University of Chicago Press, 1939), pp. 109, 197–201; Hillis Lory, *Japan's Military Masters: The Army in Japanese Life* (New York: Viking, 1943), pp. 12, 15–31; Ruth Benedict, *The Chrysanthemum and the Sword: Patterns of Japanese Culture* (Boston: Houghton Mifflin, 1989), p. 311.

Some Japanese emigration to America before 1924 resulted from Japan's conscription laws. Yamato Ichihashi, *Japanese in the United States: A Critical Study of the Problems of the Japanese Immigrants and Their Children* (Stanford, Calif.: Stanford University Press, 1932), pp. 87–88; David J. O'Brien and Stephen S. Fugita, *The Japanese American Experience* (Bloomington: Indiana University Press, 1991), p. 11; Paul R. Spickard, *Japanese Americans: The Formation and Transformations of an Ethnic Group* (New York: Twayne, 1996), p. 12.

[5] Quote from Arthur E. Barbeau and Florette Henri, *The Unknown Soldiers: Black American Troops in World War I* (Philadelphia: Temple University Press, 1974), p. xii.

dences as to where our loyalty lies."[6] In the spring of 1941 a Nisei political activist from Salt Lake City, Mike Masaoka, wrote a summons to patriotism, which the JACL published as the "Japanese American Creed." Masaoka called on each Japanese American to defend America "against all enemies, foreign or domestic," and "to actively assume [his] duties and obligations as a citizen, cheerfully and without any reservations whatsoever."[7]

The Issei felt pride at seeing their sons in uniform but could scarcely conceal their anxiety that these American-born soldiers might have to fight against Japan. They could take comfort that President Franklin D. Roosevelt promised in 1940 not to send American boys into any foreign wars and that the Army's stated role was limited to hemispheric defense. Issei hoped that America and Japan could avoid a war that would place their sons in an impossible position.

Because the U.S. Navy, Marines, and Air Corps refused to accept most Nisei enlistments, the Army Ground Forces took the Nisei selectees. By the spring of 1941 more than a thousand at Schofield Barracks in Hawaii and a similar number in Army camps on the West Coast were in basic training. Together with hundreds of thousands of other young American men, they were learning the basics of soldiering.[8]

Thomas Tokio Sakamoto from San Jose, California, was the oldest son of eleven children. When he turned sixteen, his Issei parents sent him to Japan for schooling. After four years of studying at a Japanese high school, Sakamoto returned to America in 1938 to help his parents start a 43-acre fruit and vegetable farm. When he was drafted on 26 February 1941, a large crowd of Japanese Americans from the local community came to bid farewell to him and several other Nisei draftees: "As the train slowly moved from the then–Santa Clara train station," he recalled, "the families waved both the U.S. and Japanese flags, shouting *banzai* over and over. The echoes of *banzai* stayed with me for a long time, as we rode the train with mixed feelings. As the oldest son, I worried about leaving my parents and the farm, wondering just how my parents would get along without

[6] Bill Hosokawa, *JACL in Quest of Justice: The History of the Japanese American Citizens League* (New York: William Morrow, 1982), p. 106. Walter Tsukamoto was an ROTC graduate of the University of California. An attorney, he held a reserve commission in the Judge Advocate General's Corps. For other evidence on JACL support for Selective Service in 1940–1941, see *Pacific Citizen*, Oct 40; Mutsuye Kawanami, "A Nisei Couple Faces the Draft Problem: Goodbye—For Just a Year," *Pacific Citizen*, Dec 40; Saburo Kido, "The President's Corner," *Pacific Citizen*, Feb 41. For the overall dilemma facing the Nisei, see Saburo Kido, "Situation of Japanese in United States Today," *Pacific Citizen*, Jul 41.

[7] "Japanese American Creed," *Pacific Citizen*, Apr 41, p. 1. In Mike Masaoka, *They Call Me Moses Masaoka: An American Saga* (New York: William Morrow, 1987), p. 50, the word "any" is omitted from the last phrase. This error is commonly repeated.

[8] For the exclusion of persons of Asian descent by the Army Air Corps at this time, see the Henry H. Arnold Papers, Air Force Historical Research Agency, Maxwell Air Force Base, Alabama. The Army Air Corps accepted a few Nisei in 1941–1942, perhaps inadvertently. For the Navy's racial exclusion policies in World War II, see Morris J. MacGregor, Jr., *Integration of the Armed Forces, 1940–1965* (Washington, D.C.: U.S. Army Center of Military History, 1981), pp. 58–122.

my help." Sakamoto took his basic training at Fort Lewis, Washington, and was then assigned to an antitank company.[9]

Born on Maui in 1919, Hoichi Kubo had attended public schools in Hawaii and then enrolled at the University of Hawaii, majoring in agriculture. Both his grand-fathers had fought in the Russo-Japanese War. He was drafted on 30 June and took basic training at Schofield Barracks, where he was assigned to the medical section of the 298th Infantry.[10]

Although the interwar Army permitted no Nisei enlistments, thousands attended colleges offering the Reserve Officer Training Corps (ROTC). By 1941 several hundred Nisei were enrolled at the University of Hawaii, where they were allowed to join ROTC and earn reserve commissions. Another 500 Nisei were enrolled at the University of California at Berkeley, where they were not allowed in the ROTC. When the Army called most reserve officers to active duty in the autumn of 1940, few Nisei were included.[11]

By the summer of 1941 about 3,000 Nisei wore "the brass letters U.S." They represented the intersection of two stories: how the Japanese came to America and how the U.S. Army prepared for war with Japan, the war that would eventually bring these stories together in previously unimagined ways.

Japanese in America, 1885–1941

For over fifty years immigrants from Japan had been coming to Hawaii and the mainland and staying to raise families. They began arriving in Hawaii in 1885 to work on the plantations and grew in number to comprise over half of Hawaii's agricultural labor force within a few years. Some moved onward to the mainland through Seattle, San Francisco, and Los Angeles to work as farmers, fishermen, and shopkeepers. These "strangers from a different shore" were not eligible for

---

[9] Interv, author with Thomas Sakamoto, 16 Nov 87; Thomas Sakamoto, "Original Japanese Student Reflects on MISLS Language Training," *DLIFLC Globe* (December 1996): 12–13; Saka-moto autobiography, 1 Nov 96; "Caught between Two Worlds."

[10] Hoichi Kubo, "Military Biography," Unpubl Ms, 1996, copy in author's files; Interv, author with Hoichi Kubo, 30 Oct 87.

[11] In 1939 a War Department (WD) General Staff officer addressed the problem of the growing numbers of Nisei reserve officers in Hawaii by proposing a special reserve unit to be composed solely of these Nisei. The G–2 concurred, but Lt. Col. Rufus Bratton of the Far Eastern Section dis-agreed, saying their loyalty could never be trusted. If the Army did not plan to use them, he recom-mended instead that they simply not be allowed to enroll in advanced ROTC. Memo, R. S. Bratton for Chief, Intelligence Br, G–2, sub: Hawaiian Dept. Reserve Officers of Japanese Extraction, 4 Feb 39, unmarked folder; Security-Class Gen Corresp, 1926–1946, Far Eastern Br, Ofc of the Dir of Intel G–2, Record Group (RG) 165, National Archives and Records Administration (NARA).

In the summer of 1940 the Army called several Nisei reserve officers to active duty in Hawaii along with non-Nisei. Sixteen Nisei reserve officers shipped out with the 100th Infantry Battalion in June 1942. In November 1942 the Hawaiian Department reported it had three Nisei reserve offi-cers remaining on active duty and thirty-two as yet uncalled. Some of these were called to active duty in 1943 to serve with the 442d RCT. Thomas D. Murphy, *Ambassadors in Arms* (Honolulu: University of Hawaii Press, 1954), pp. 65, 67, 107.

citizenship. The 1900 census counted 85,393 Japanese living in America, of whom 72 percent lived in Hawaii.[12]

Like the Chinese before them, the Japanese encountered racial prejudice in the New World. The Chinese had endured prejudice against "Orientals" that began during the California Gold Rush and culminated in the Chinese Exclusion Act of 1882. Japan's dramatic 1905 victory over Russia inflamed anti-Japanese prejudice in America. The California state legislature and the U.S. Congress further restricted Japanese immigration. The Japanese government acted to protect its citizens and in 1907–1908 negotiated a "gentleman's agreement" with the United States that restricted further immigration to family members. In 1913 California passed an "alien land law" that prohibited individuals "ineligible for citizenship" from purchasing land. Other states soon followed suit. The Japanese persisted but lived under a cloud of suspicion, prejudice, and legal restrictions on the part of their non-Asian neighbors.[13]

Despite the discrimination, hundreds of Issei served in the U.S. Navy from the 1890s until 1907, usually as mess men and cooks. When the USS *Maine* blew up in Havana Harbor in 1898, seven Issei on board lost their lives. During the First World War, over a thousand Issei, mostly from Hawaii, served in the U.S. Army. After the war these veterans sought to become naturalized citizens. In 1925 the U.S. Supreme Court ruled against them on the basis of race, but in 1935 the U.S. Congress reversed the decision and granted them naturalization rights in exchange for their military service.[14]

By 1920 the population of Japanese descent living on the mainland United States and Hawaii had risen to 220,122. By the time Congress slammed the door to further immigration from Japan in 1924, the Issei had already established families and continued to grow in number. The 1940 census counted 284,731 persons of Japanese descent living in Hawaii and on the mainland. By this time more than half were citizens by birth in a land that did not fully accept them.[15] Most Japanese

[12] For overviews of Japanese American history, see Harry H. L. Kitano, *Japanese Americans: The Evolution of a Subculture*, 2d ed. (Englewood Cliffs, N.J.: Prentice-Hall, 1976); David J. O'Brien and Stephen S. Fugita, *The Japanese American Experience* (Bloomington: Indiana University Press, 1991); Spickard, *Japanese Americans*; Ronald Takaki, *Strangers from a Different Shore: A History of Asian Americans* (Boston: Little, Brown, 1989).

[13] Roger Daniels, *The Politics of Prejudice: The Anti-Japanese Movement in California and the Struggle for Japanese Exclusion*, 2d ed. (Berkeley: University of California Press, 1977); Gary Y. Okihiro, *Cane Fires: The Anti-Japanese Movement in Hawaii, 1865–1945* (Philadelphia: Temple University Press, 1991).

[14] Bill Hosokawa, *Nisei: The Quiet Americans* (New York: William Morrow, 1969), p. 394. For one Issei World War I veteran, see Eileen Sunada Sarasohn, *The Issei, Portrait of a Pioneer: An Oral History* (Palo Alto, Calif.: Pacific Books, 1983), pp. 71–74.

[15] For a perceptive description of Japanese Americans before the war, see Roger Daniels, "Japanese America, 1930–1941: An Ethnic Community in the Great Depression," *Journal of the West* (October 1985): 35–49. For more recent detailed studies, see Eileen H. Tamura, *Americanization, Acculturation, and Ethnic Identity: The Nisei Generation in Hawaii* (Urbana: University of Illinois Press, 1994), and David K. Yoo, *Growing Up Nisei: Race, Generation, and Culture among Japanese Americans of California, 1924–1949* (Urbana: University of Illinois Press, 2000).

Americans were still strangers to their neighbors. The average American could see only an alien presence within the American melting pot. In Hawaii, Japanese Americans comprised more than a third of the population and formed thriving communities within that multiracial society. They were moving out of the plantations into other sectors of the economy, but they remained under the domination of the white oligarchy. Nevertheless, in the 1940 elections thirteen Nisei were elected to the territorial legislature.[16] On the West Coast, Japanese Americans made up a much smaller percentage of the population. They worked as farmers or as keepers of small shops. Many lived in the "Japantowns" or "Little Tokyos" of Los Angeles, San Francisco, and Seattle.

In Hawaii and on the mainland, the Issei raised families and built the institutions of the immigrant community, including schools, churches, temples, and civic organizations. Some were Buddhist, and some were Christian. As the years passed, some Issei returned to Japan; most abandoned the dream of returning. The Japanese government remained solicitous of its subjects residing in America and maintained consulates in Honolulu and the major West Coast port cities. The Imperial Japanese Navy periodically sent training vessels to call at American ports, where the local Japanese communities always greeted them warmly. The Issei sent their children after regular school hours to Japanese-language schools. They hoped their children would remain connected to their ancestral homeland. But they could see that for all America's faults, it was a far better place than Japan for their families to live. Although they were denied citizenship, the Issei had made their lives in America, a country that held great promise for their children.

The Nisei had an outlook very different from their parents. Born and raised in America between 1910 and 1940, the Nisei attended public schools and spoke English or, in Hawaii, pidgin Hawaiian, among their friends. The parents sometimes sent their children to Japan to visit relatives or attend school. But American and Japanese observers were unanimous that at heart the Nisei were growing up as American boys and girls. The lure of American society and culture proved far stronger than the distant call of their parents' homeland.

The Nisei were a problematic generation from the beginning, an object of concern for their Issei parents and scholars alike.[17] Like most children of immigrants, they grew up between two worlds. "The Nisei lived in two societies," wrote one sociologist at the University of Hawaii: "The home, the language school, and the Japanese community formed one. Surrounding this smaller world was the rest of American Hawaii. Much of what the children learned in one society they were

---

[16] Lawrence H. Fuchs, *Hawaii Pono, "Hawaii the Excellent": An Ethnic and Political History* (Honolulu: Bess Press, 1961), p. 136. For a vivid portrait of Hawaiian plantation life in the 1930s, see the novel by Milton Murayama, *All I Asking for Is My Body* (Honolulu: University of Hawaii Press, 1988). Murayama served with the MIS in the China-Burma-India Theater.

[17] For example, see Yamato Ichihashi, "The Problem of the Second-Generation Japanese," in *Japanese in the United States* (New York: Arno Press, 1969), and Edward K. Strong, *The Second-Generation Japanese Problem* (Stanford, Calif.: Stanford University Press, 1934).

John F. Aiso

expected to forget or disregard in the other."[18] The pull of assimilation was strong. From their classmates they learned the stuff of American popular culture: music, movies, slang, and sports. From their schools they learned the civic culture of interwar America: Washington, Jefferson, and Lincoln; the pledge of allegiance; and an intense loyalty to their country.[19]

On the West Coast, the best known of the Nisei generation was John Fujio Aiso, born in 1909 in Hollywood, California, where his father worked as a gardener.[20] His parents stressed academic achievement and patriotism. His mother hung pictures of Washington, Lincoln, and Jesus in the family parlor to inspire her children.

Encountering prejudice early in life, Aiso responded by studying harder. In 1922 he ran for student body president of his junior high school; when he won, the principal dissolved the student government rather than permit a Japanese boy to take office. When this incident was publicized, Aiso became the iconic Nisei; in the 1920s and 1930s Issei parents in southern California pressed his example on their children.[21]

Aiso was his high school class valedictorian, having achieved the highest academic ranking. A skillful debater, he nevertheless was denied a top spot on his school's team in the national championships in 1926. The publisher of the *Los Angeles Times* sponsored Aiso to accompany the winners to Washington, D.C.,

---

[18] Murphy, *Ambassadors in Arms*, p. 11.

[19] For example, see Fuchs, *Hawaii Pono*, pp. 263–98. For a nuanced study of the Americanization campaign in Hawaii and the Nisei, see Tamura, *Americanization, Acculturation, and Ethnic Identity*, pp. 45–88.

[20] Kiyoshi Yano, "Participating in the Mainstream of American Life amidst Drawback of Racial Prejudice and Discrimination," in *John Aiso and the M.I.S.: Japanese-American Soldiers in the Military Intelligence Service, World War II*, ed. Tad Ichinokuchi (Los Angeles: Military Intelligence Service Club of Southern California, 1988), pp. 4–32; Interv, Loni Ding and Eric Saul with John F. Aiso, 10 Jan 86, National Japanese American Historical Society (NJAHS), San Francisco, Calif.; Interv, author with John F. Aiso, 30 Oct 87; John F. Aiso, "Observations of a California Nisei," Interv by Marc Landy, University of California at Los Angeles, 1971. For a personal appreciation, see James Oda, *Secret Embedded in Magic Cables* (Northridge, Calif.: J. Oda, 1993), pp. 113–24.

[21] See, for example, Tad Ichinokuchi, "John Aiso and the M.I.S.," in Ichinokuchi, *John Aiso and the M.I.S.*, pp. 1–3.

where he was introduced to the Japanese ambassador. After a year of Japanese-language study in Japan, he entered Brown University on a Japanese government scholarship. He followed this with a law degree from Harvard in 1934 and then worked in New York (1934–1936) and Japan and Manchuria (1936–1939), practicing American and Japanese commercial law. He returned to California in 1939, passed the state bar exam, and set out to practice law in Los Angeles.

In April 1941 Aiso was inducted into the Army. When the 31-year-old private, first class, reported to D Company, 69th Quartermaster Battalion (Light Maintenance), at Camp Haan, Riverside, California, a Regular Army master sergeant snarled, "Just what we need, another goddamned lawyer." He sent Aiso to the motor pool to be a parts clerk. The exemplary Nisei, talented and overeducated, became just another soldier in the rapidly expanding Army.

As war approached, many Americans became increasingly suspicious of the loyalty of the Nisei regardless of the evidence of assimilation of American values. Many white Americans found support for their suspicions in the tangle of U.S. and Japanese laws that left many Nisei with dual citizenship, claiming this as proof of loyalty to the emperor. The truth was more complicated. Until 1924 Japan automatically extended citizenship to children born abroad of Japanese nationals. After 1924 the parents had to register their children with the local consulate for Japanese citizenship. Many Issei, denied U.S. citizenship themselves, took this simple step for their children. Realizing that their antagonists could use dual citizenship as propaganda, Nisei leaders seized the issue as yet another way to demonstrate their loyalty. They encouraged and assisted Nisei to file with Japanese consulates the necessary paperwork to revoke their Japanese citizenships. Nevertheless, the War Department was sufficiently concerned about the issue that in the spring of 1941 the Military Intelligence Division (MID) recommended that Congress allow individuals to clarify their status simply by swearing an oath of allegiance to the United States in naturalization court.[22]

Moreover, some suspected that Japan was conscripting American-born Nisei to serve in the Imperial Japanese Army. In 1940 Senator Guy M. Gillette (D-Iowa) even charged that Japan was conscripting Nisei for espionage, which the JACL vigorously protested. Nisei visiting Japan in the 1930s indeed risked conscription

---

[22] Frank F. Chuman, *The Bamboo People: The Law and Japanese Americans* (Chicago: Japanese American Citizens League, 1981), pp. 167–68; Murphy, *Ambassadors in Arms*, pp. 17–24; "Dual Citizenship," in *Encyclopedia of Japanese American History*, rev. ed., ed. Brian Niiya, (New York: Facts on File, 2001); Okihiro, *Cane Fires*, pp. 201–04; Tamura, *Americanization, Acculturation, and Ethnic Identity*, pp. 84–88. For War Department memos on the issue of dual citizenship in 1941, see Security-Class Gen Corresp, 1926–1946, Far Eastern Br, Ofc of the Dir of Intel G–2, RG 165, NARA. To avoid complications, some Nisei renounced their Japanese citizenship before they traveled to Japan. Richard Sakakida's mother did this in the summer of 1941 on behalf of her son after he secretly enlisted in the Army and was sent to the Philippines. Richard Sakakida and Wayne S. Kiyosaki, *A Spy in Their Midst* (Lanham, Md.: Madison Books, 1995), pp. 137–38.

while in Japan, but there is no evidence that Nisei in Hawaii or on the mainland were being conscripted. Nevertheless, this accusation circulated widely.[23]

For the U.S. government and most white Americans, Nisei loyalty remained an open question. In the autumn of 1941 the White House secretly dispatched an investigator to make an independent assessment of the "Japanese problem." After conferring with Army and Navy intelligence and the Federal Bureau of Investigation, Curtis B. Munson reported that the Nisei were "approximately ninety-eight percent loyal." "The Nisei," he concluded, "are pathetically eager to show this loyalty. They are not Japanese in culture. They are foreigners to Japan."[24]

Another aspect of the Nisei culture that raised suspicion was their Japanese-language schools. Like other immigrants, Issei parents set up private language schools so their children could learn something of the Japanese language and culture. Typically these schools held classes one hour each afternoon after the public schools let out, as well as on Saturday mornings. Caucasian Americans pointed to these schools as one more example of how even the children of Japanese immigrants were being indoctrinated into Japanese culture and loyalty to the emperor.[25] In fact, these schools did little to inculcate Japanese values in the Nisei and even less in teaching the language. For most Nisei it reinforced their sense of

---

[23] *Pacific Citizen*, Jan 41, p. 1. For a discussion of Nisei serving in the Japanese Army before the war, see John J. Stephan, *Hawaii under the Rising Sun: Japan's Plans for Conquest after Pearl Harbor* (Honolulu: University of Hawaii Press, 1984), pp. 35–37, 44; and John J. Stephan, "Hijacked by Utopia: American Nikkei in Manchuria," *Amerasia Journal* 23, no. 3 (Winter 1997–1998): 23–24, note 168.

During the Russo-Japanese War of 1904–1905, a number of Issei returned home from Hawaii to serve in the Imperial Japanese Army and Navy, which may have been the source of white American concerns in 1940–1941. See Stephan, *Hawaii under the Rising Sun*, p. 15; Franklin Odo and Kazuko Sinoto, *A Pictorial History of the Japanese in Hawaii, 1885–1924* (Honolulu: Bishop Museum, 1985), p. 206.

For the autobiography of a California-born Nisei who was conscripted into the Japanese Army, see Iwao Peter Sano, *One Thousand Days in Siberia: The Odyssey of a Japanese-American POW* (Lincoln: University of Nebraska Press, 1997). Some Nisei who had served in the Japanese Army in the 1930s subsequently returned to the United States, even though foreign military service cost them their U.S. citizenship. One was Terry Takeshi Doi, who regained his U.S. citizenship and earned the Silver Star as an interpreter with the 3d Marine Division on Iwo Jima. John Weckerling, "Japanese Americans Play Vital Role in United States Intelligence Service in World War II" (1946), first printed in *Hokubei Mainichi*, 27 Oct–5 Nov 71, reprinted as a pamphlet. Harrington, *Yankee Samurai*, p. 276. Another was Karl Yoneda, who was born in California and sent to Japan, where he was conscripted into the Japanese Army. In 1927 he escaped and returned to America. He volunteered for the MIS and later served in China-Burma-India.

[24] Murphy, *Ambassadors in Arms*, pp. 31–32; Greg Robinson, *By Order of the President: FDR and the Internment of Japanese Americans* (Cambridge, Mass.: Harvard University Press, 2001), pp. 65–72.

[25] "Japanese-language Schools," in *Encyclopedia of Japanese American History*; Murphy, *Ambassadors in Arms*, pp. 8–11; Okihiro, *Cane Fires*, pp. 153–56; Toyotomi Morimoto, *Japanese Americans and Cultural Continuity: Maintaining Language and Heritage* (New York: Garland, 1997).

themselves as American, not Japanese.[26] Carey McWilliams, California journalist and editor of *The Nation*, downplayed the schools: "The fact of the matter is that these schools were never successful." The typical Japanese youngster, he wrote, spent a "precious hour and one-half tossing spit balls at his classmates and calling his teacher names in American slang which she pretended not to understand. Physically he was in school; mentally he was making a run around left end for another touchdown. He was restless. He counted the minutes. At the gong, he dashed to freedom."[27]

John Weckerling

Some Nisei did pay attention and acquired a working knowledge of the Japanese language, but they were the exceptions. Brig. Gen. John Weckerling, who established the Fourth Army Intelligence School in 1941, later concluded that "Japanese language schools created and encouraged by the Japanese government before the war to maintain ties with the homeland had not achieved the results with which they were generally credited."[28]

Some went to experience Japan for themselves. Inexpensive steamship fares made travel between the United States and Japan relatively easy. Many Issei made the return trip or sent their children to stay with relatives. Other groups such as Chinese and Filipinos periodically traveled back to their homelands or sent their children. By one estimate, 50,000 Nisei visited Japan before the war. Perhaps 20,000 had returned to the United States by the autumn of 1941.[29] Some went to

[26] For example, see Daniel K. Inouye, *Journey to Washington* (Englewood Cliffs, N.J.: Prentice-Hall, 1967), pp. 35–38.

[27] Carey McWilliams, *Prejudice: Japanese-Americans, Symbol of Racial Intolerance* (Boston: Little, Brown, 1944), pp. 121–23. Tamura also minimizes the effect of the schools in Hawaii: Tamura, *Americanization, Acculturation, and Ethnic Identity*, pp. 146–61. As early as 1932 Ichihashi declared the language schools a failure. Ichihashi, *Japanese in the United States*, pp. 326–33.

[28] Weckerling, "Japanese Americans Play Vital Role."

[29] Spickard, *Japanese Americans*, pp. 89–90. Spickard gives the number of Kibei as 10,000, but this applies only to the mainland. According to the War Relocation Authority, of the 101,278 persons in camps in 1942, 9,892 were Kibei. Spickard, *Japanese Americans*, p. 167; War Relocation Authority, *The Evacuated People: A Quantitative Description* (Washington, D.C.: Government Printing Office, 1946), tables 27–34. Nisei from Hawaii may have traveled to Japan in even larger numbers. See also McWilliams, *Prejudice*, pp. 321–22, and Jacobus tenBroek et al., *Prejudice, War, and the Constitution* (Berkeley: University of California Press, 1954), pp. 279–82.

Japan for schooling. For others the trip resulted from a family emergency such as
the death of a parent.

Nisei who visited Japan and then returned became known as *Kibei* (returned
to America).[30] Many Americans feared that the Kibei had been exposed to the
"bacillus" of Japanese militarism. The effects were usually quite the opposite.
Upon arriving in Japan, the Nisei were often ostracized for their funny speech,
manners, and dress. Munson reported: "Many of those who visited Japan subsequent to their early American education come back with added loyalty to the
United States. In fact it is a saying that all a Nisei needs is a trip to Japan to make
a loyal American out of him. The American educated Japanese is a boor in Japan
and treated as a foreigner."[31]

While studying in Japan, Kibei often were exposed to compulsory military
training in Japanese middle and high schools. Thomas Sakamoto took such training while attending high school in Japan. When he graduated in 1938, a Japanese
Army major offered him a commission in the Army. Sakamoto declined because
he was an American citizen. He recalled that the Japanese officer became agitated
and waved his sword and called the young man a traitor to his homeland. Sakamoto returned soon afterward to his real home, California.[32]

As diplomatic tensions rose in the autumn and winter of 1940–1941, the U.S.
embassy in Tokyo contacted Nisei visiting in Japan and urged them to return home.
Those who had been in Japan the longest suffered the most, some having almost
completely lost their ability to speak English. Now they were cast adrift in Hawaii
or on the West Coast with little chance of finding work. Those who enrolled in
American high schools were older than most other students. They sometimes found
themselves rejected by both worlds. John Aiso described the Kibei's experience,
"With over twenty years of close infighting against prejudice and discrimination
heaped upon him by chauvinistic elements in both the United States and Japan, he
was by 1941 already a mentally and morally battle-conditioned veteran."[33]

In the impending crisis, the Army would come to prize the Kibei for their language skill. Who better to translate or interpret that difficult language? But often

---

[30] The War Relocation Authority reserved the term Kibei for Nisei who had spent three or more
years in Japan. See Alexander H. Leighton, *The Governing of Men: General Principles and Recommendations Based on Experience at a Japanese Relocation Camp* (Princeton: Princeton University Press, 1945), pp. 79–80; Spickard, *Japanese Americans*, pp. 89–90; Brian Masaru Hayashi,
Democratizing the Enemy: The Japanese American Internment (Princeton, N.J.: Princeton University Press, 2004), pp. 45–48, 161–63.

[31] *Pearl Harbor Attack: Hearings before the Joint Committee on the Investigation of the Pearl
Harbor Attack*, 39 parts (Washington, D.C: Government Printing Office, 1946), pt. 6, p. 2685.

[32] "Caught between Two Worlds."

[33] John F. Aiso, "Tribute to Nisei in G–2," Arlington National Cemetery, 2 Jun 63, printed in
"Tributes to Japanese American Military Service in World War II," *Congressional Record* (11 Jun
63), p. 7. In October 1940 and again in February 1941, the U.S. embassy advised all U.S. citizens to
leave Japan. *Foreign Relations of the United States, 1940*, vol. 4, *The Far East* (Washington, D.C.:
Government Printing Office, 1955), pp. 930–55; *Foreign Relations of the United States, 1941*, vol.
5, *The Far East* (Washington, D.C.: Government Printing Office, 1962), pp. 397–453.

the same Kibei felt most keenly the anguish of the two countries' going to war, for, as Aiso put it, "those best qualified for G–2 service were those whose sentimental heartstrings for relatives and close friends tugged the strongest."[34]

The Military Intelligence Division Prepares for War with Japan, 1940–1941

The War Department's Military Intelligence Division was ill prepared for war with Japan or any other country. War Plan ORANGE called for the Army to defend the Philippine Islands in the event of war with Japan, but the Navy would wage the decisive campaign.[35] MID itself had dwindled in size during the interwar years. Combat units lacked intelligence personnel and the specialized schools to train them, and few officers valued intelligence as a career. One exception, Col. Rufus S. Bratton, headed MID's Far Eastern Branch after 1937. A West Point graduate, he had served three tours in Japan.[36]

The Signal Intelligence Service (SIS) fared little better in apprehending Japanese plans. It had radio intercept stations targeting Japan from Fort Shafter, Hawaii, and Fort McKinley in the Philippines. In Washington, D.C., a handful of officers, enlisted men, and civilians had been decrypting and translating Japanese diplomatic messages since August 1940. However, with the low volume of messages intercepted and decrypted, the Army needed only a handful of translators.[37]

By early 1941 it was clear that the Military Intelligence Division had to prepare for a possible conflict with Japan. If the U.S. and Japanese Armies should meet on some future battlefield, combat intelligence would be critical. This would require soldiers who could read and speak Japanese. The War Department needed

---

[34] Aiso, "Tribute to Nisei in G–2," p. 7.

[35] Louis Morton, *Strategy and Command: The First Two Years*, U.S. Army in World War II (Washington, D.C.: Office of the Chief of Military History, 1962), pp. 21–127; Brian M. Linn, *Guardians of Empire: The U.S. Army and the Pacific, 1902–1940* (Chapel Hill: University of North Carolina Press, 1997).

[36] Bruce W. Bidwell, *History of the Military Intelligence Division, Department of the Army General Staff: 1775–1941* (Frederick, Md.: University Publications of America, 1986); John P. Finnegan and Romana Danysh, *Military Intelligence*, Army Lineage Series (Washington, D.C.: U.S. Army Center of Military History, 1998), pp. 41–60; David Kahn, "The United States Views Germany and Japan in 1941," in *Knowing One's Enemies: Intelligence Assessment before the Two World Wars*, ed. Ernest R. May (Princeton: Princeton University Press, 1984), pp. 476–501; Ladislas Farago, *The Broken Seal: "Operation Magic" and the Secret Road to Pearl Harbor* (New York: Random House, 1967), pp. 279–92.

[37] Ronald Lewin, *The American Magic: Codes, Ciphers and the Defeat of Japan* (New York: Farrar Straus Giroux, 1982); Diane T. Putney, "The U.S. Military Intelligence Service: The Ultra Mission," in *Ultra and the Army Air Forces in World War II*, ed. Lewis F. Powell (Washington, D.C.: Office of Air Force History, 1987), pp. 65–103; James L. Gilbert and John P. Finnegan, eds., *U.S. Army Signals Intelligence in World War II: A Documentary History*, U.S. Army in World War II (Washington, D.C.: U.S. Army Center of Military History, 1993); Ronald Spector, ed., *Listening to the Enemy: Key Documents on the Role of Communications Intelligence in the War with Japan* (Wilmington, Del.: Scholarly Resources, 1988); "History of Special Branch, MIS, WD, 1942–1944," SRH–035, Records of the National Security Agency/Central Security Service, RG 457, NARA.

speakers of European languages as well, but these were easier to find, having been required in previous wars. Maj. Gen. Charles A. Willoughby, General MacArthur's chief of intelligence during the war, later commented that "linguist requirements for the European theater of war could have been met without leaving the sidewalks of New York City, but there was a vastly different story in the Far East."[38]

From January through March 1941 the United States and Britain held their first staff talks in Washington to coordinate their defense plans in the Far East.[39] Soon after, MID sent a former language attaché, Lt. Col. Moses W. Pettigrew, to the Far East to assess the overall intelligence posture against Japan. He met with American and allied intelligence officers in Honolulu, Manila, Hong Kong, Chunking, Singapore, and elsewhere and returned with a great sense of urgency. As a result, the Army published a handbook on Japanese military forces in July 1941. The Army also decided to establish a Japanese-language training program.[40]

The War Department possessed one valuable resource: a small group of Regular Army officers such as Bratton and Pettigrew who had learned Japanese through the language attaché program. In Tokyo, the U.S. embassy had operated a joint language-training program for the Army, Navy, and State Department since before the First World War. In the 1920s the embassy hired Naoe Naganuma as a language instructor. Naganuma developed a set of textbooks and readers with which all the language attachés became familiar.[41] Each year between the wars MID sent two officers to Japan for four years of language training and service as assistant military attachés. Language attachés took intensive language classes in Tokyo

[38] Maj. Gen. Charles A. Willoughby, Remarks to Japanese American Citizens League, reprinted in 90th Cong., 1st sess., *Congressional Record* 113, No. 22 (15 Feb 67).

[39] Morton, *Strategy and Command*, pp. 86–90; Ray S. Cline, *Washington Command Post: The Operations Division* (Washington, D.C.: Office of the Chief of Military History, 1951), pp. 58–60.

[40] Bidwell, *History of the Military Intelligence Division*, pp. 435–36. Pettigrew's recommendations were printed in *Pearl Harbor Attack*, pt. 18, pp. 3436–39; Classified Material for 1941, Jap [*sic*] Empire File, Security-Class Gen Corresp, 1926–1946, Far Eastern Br, Ofc of the Dir of Intel G–2, RG 165, NARA.

Technical Manual 30–480, *Handbook on Japanese Military Forces* (Washington, D.C.: War Department, July 1941), was revised and expanded as the war progressed. MID sent page proofs to the Philippine and Hawaiian Departments in early June 1941.

In August MID sent Maj. Warren J. Clear, U.S. Army, Retired, to recommend a War Department secret intelligence system in the Far East. He submitted his recommendations on 3 November 1941, but they were never implemented. Bidwell, *History of the Military Intelligence Division*, pp. 438–40.

[41] "Reminiscences of Rear Admiral Arthur H. McCollum, U.S. Navy Retired," 2 vols., pp. 254–55, Unpubl Ms, 1970–1971, Naval Historical Center, Washington, D.C.; Office of the Chief of Naval Operations, "School of Oriental Languages," pp. 5–12, Unpubl Ms, Naval Historical Center, Washington, D.C. Naoe Naganuma, *Hyojun Nihongo Tokuhon* [*Standard Japanese Readers*] (Tokyo: various publishers and editions). Each year the State Department trained one or two Foreign Service officers in the Japanese program. John K. Emmerson was a student in 1936–1939. See John K. Emmerson, *The Japanese Thread: A Life in the U.S. Foreign Service* (New York: Holt, Rinehart and Winston, 1978). Naganuma was a local employee of the U.S. embassy, not a U.S. citizen. After the war, he resumed teaching for the U.S. Army. His textbooks continued to be published into the 1980s.

and often were subsequently sent to Japanese Army units as observers. They came away with a firsthand appreciation of the Japanese Army, its soldiers, leaders, tactics, equipment, and spirit. When then–First Lieutenant Weckerling returned from Japan in 1932, he published an article in the *Cavalry Journal* describing his tour and urging other officers to volunteer.[42] By 1941 MID had a pool of more than forty officers who could speak at least some Japanese. However, not all were available by then, many being "retired, incapacitated or . . . beyond the age and rank of interpreters," Weckerling later explained.[43] The Office of Naval Intelligence (ONI) had a similar number of language-qualified officers.[44]

Army and Navy intelligence officers were also responsible to protect U.S. territories against espionage and sabotage. MID and ONI coordinated their efforts with the Federal Bureau of Investigation (FBI). The Japanese populations on the West Coast and in Hawaii were prime suspects, as were the Japanese communities in Mexico, Panama, and the Philippines. Stunning German victories in Europe since 1939 greatly increased American fears of a "fifth column" inside their own country.[45]

MID, ONI, and the FBI developed active surveillance programs directed at Japanese communities in the United States and its territories.[46] In 1933 the G–2 of

---

[42] 1st Lt. John Weckerling, "The Japanese Language Detail," *Cavalry Journal* (May–June 1932): 31–34. First Lt. Harold Doud spent 1933–1935 learning Japanese. "Six Months with the Japanese Infantry," *Infantry Journal* (January–February 1937).

[43] Weckerling, "Japanese Americans Play Vital Role." List of Japanese-Qualified Officers, 27 Mar 41, Security-Class Gen Corresp, 1926–1946, Far Eastern Br, Ofc of the Dir of Intel G–2, RG 165, NARA. Of the three full colonels on the list, by 1942 two were retired and the third was military attaché to Australia. Another graduate, Maj. Maxwell D. Taylor (Tokyo, 1935–1939), who later commanded the 101st Airborne Division and served as Army Chief of Staff, never served in MID. Maxwell D. Taylor, *Swords and Plowshares* (New York: W. W. Norton, 1972), pp. 31–36. See also Sidney F. Mashbir (Tokyo, 1920–1923), *I Was an American Spy* (New York: Vantage, 1953), pp. 59–161.

John T. Greenwood, "The U.S. Army Military Observers with the Japanese Army during the Russo-Japanese War (1904–1905)," *Army History* (Winter 1996): 1–14, 16; Bidwell, *History of the Military Intelligence Division*, pp. 379–94; Scott A. Koch, "The Role of U.S. Army Military Attachés between the World Wars," *Studies in Intelligence* (Winter 1994): 53–57; John F. Votaw, "United States Military Attachés, 1885–1919: The American Army Matures in the International Arena," Ph.D. Diss., Temple University, 1991. The British Army had a similar program for training language attachés. M. D. Kennedy, *The Military Side of Japanese Life* (Boston: Houghton Mifflin, 1923).

[44] Memo, Naval Attachés, Assistant Naval Attachés, and Language Officers Attached to American Embassy, Tokyo, Dec 38 [updated through 1941], in Henri H. Smith-Hutton Papers, Box 1, Hoover Institution Archives, Stanford University, Stanford, Calif. For a similar list, see Wyman H. Packard, *A Century of U.S. Naval Intelligence* (Washington, D.C.: Office of Naval Intelligence/ Naval Historical Center, 1996), pp. 367–71; Lewin, *American Magic*, pp. 29–31.

[45] John A. Herzig, "Japanese Americans and Magic," *Amerasia Journal* 11, no. 2 (Fall/Winter 1984): 47–65; Bob Kumamoto, "The Search for Spies: American Counterintelligence and the Japanese American Community, 1932–1941," *Amerasia Journal* 6 (1979): 45–75; Francis MacDonnell, *Insidious Foes: The Axis Fifth Column and the American Home Front* (New York: Oxford University Press, 1995), pp. 82–90; *Personal Justice Denied: Report of the Commission on Wartime Relocation and Internment of Civilians* (Seattle: University of Washington Press, 1997), pp. 51–60, 471–78.

[46] Okihiro, *Cane Fires*. For firsthand accounts, see Thorpe, *East Wind, Rain*, pp. 3–30; Ellis M. Zacharias, *Secret Missions: The Story of an Intelligence Officer* (New York: G. P. Putnam's Sons,

Ninth Corps Area at the Presidio of San Francisco gave a reserve commission to David Swift, a Japanese-speaking customs inspector born in Japan. Swift reported to G–2 what he found out about Japanese visitors to the busy port. The 12th Naval District intelligence officer retained John Anderton, a San Francisco lawyer who had learned Japanese and knew the local Japanese community, to be a translator.[47] When Capt. Frederick P. Munson returned in 1937 from his tour as a language attaché in Tokyo, he was assigned to Ninth Corps Area Headquarters in San Francisco. The headquarters "wanted a Japanese-speaking person," he recalled, "particularly to work with the Navy and FBI on Japanese relations in San Francisco because we had a lot of Japanese going through there and they were doing all kinds of things." In 1939 the War Department assigned then-Major Weckerling to the Panama Canal Zone to keep an eye on the substantial Japanese population there. MID also posted Japanese-speaking officers to the Hawaiian and Philippine Departments.[48] Growing concerns led the FBI to reopen its office in Honolulu in August 1939.[49]

Local Army, Navy, and FBI offices hired a few trusted Nisei as translators, interpreters, even as undercover informants. As early as 1931 the Hawaiian Department G–2 recruited Gero Iwai to monitor the local Japanese; he was one of the first Nisei to receive a reserve commission through the University of Hawaii ROTC. In 1937 the 14th Naval District intelligence officer recruited Douglas T. Wada, a graduate of the University of Hawaii.[50] In other ways, intelligence officials

1946), pp. 136–212. ONI began offering reserve commissions to Japanese-speaking Caucasians in the mid-1930s. Mashbir, *I Was an American Spy*, p. 223.

[47] David W. Swift, Sr., *Ninety Li a Day*, ed. David W. Swift, Jr., Social Life Monographs, vol. 69 (Taipei: Chinese Association for Folklore, 1975), pp. 265–68. For Anderton, see Harrington, *Yankee Samurai*, pp. 44–45; Memo, 12th Naval District to Chief of Naval Operations (CNO), 7 Jan 36, sub: Japanese Translators, Folder A8–2/P11–5, Translators (5), Commandant's Ofc, Gen Corresp (Declass), 12th Naval District, RG 181, NARA–Pacific Region, San Bruno, Calif.

[48] Interv, Frederick P. Munson, 5 Mar 75, in Frederick P. Munson Papers, Hoover Institution Archives. Munson returned to the Far East in 1938 as assistant military attaché in Peking under Col. Joseph W. Stilwell. He later transferred to Tokyo, where he was the military attaché when the war began. The Army's Hawaiian Department was authorized one Japanese language officer, but the incumbent left in the summer of 1941 without a replacement. Memos, Col. R. S. Bratton for AGO [Adjutant General's Office], 11 Jul 41, and Lt. Col. Ralph C. Smith for AGO, 22 Jul 41, both in Security-Class Gen Corresp, 1926–1946, Far Eastern Br, Ofc of the Dir of Intel G–2, RG 165, NARA. According to historian Gary Okihiro, as late as July 1940 the ONI office in Hawaii had one Japanese translator and one undercover operator and the Hawaiian Department G–2 had the same. Okihiro, *Cane Fires*, p. 178. Memo, G–2 to TAG [The Adjutant General], sub: Assignment of Major John Weckerling, 19 Jun 41, Security-Class Gen Corresp, 1926–1946, Far Eastern Br, Ofc of the Dir of Intel G–2, RG 165, NARA.

[49] Tom Coffman, *The Island Edge of America: A Political History of Hawaii* (Honolulu: University of Hawaii Press, 2003), pp. 43–44; Murphy, *Ambassadors in Arms*, pp. 27–30; Okihiro, *Cane Fires*, pp. 178–79.

[50] Ted T. Tsukiyama et al., eds., *Secret Valor: M.I.S. Personnel, World War II Pacific Theater, Pre–Pearl Harbor to Sept. 8, 1951* (Honolulu: Military Intelligence Service Veterans Club of Hawaii, 1993), pp. 31–33; Interv, Ted Tsukiyama with Douglas T. Wada, 21 Mar 02, copy of tape in author's files.

obtained the quiet cooperation of Nisei community leaders who provided information on Issei and Nisei. In the spring of 1940 FBI officials in Hawaii organized Nisei advisory committees. In Los Angeles, on 21 March 1941, Nisei leaders held a meeting with "representatives of the Naval Intelligence, the Army, the County government, the Chamber of Commerce and the metropolitan press." At the meeting, the 11th Naval District intelligence officer, Lt. Cmdr. Kenneth D. Ringle, and other military and local officials reaffirmed their belief in the loyalty of the Nisei and rejected any accusations of disloyalty.[51]

Nevertheless, intelligence officials had some cause for concern about the Japanese government. In January 1941 Tokyo urged its consulates in Hawaii and the West Coast to step up efforts to gather information, using "U.S. citizens of foreign extraction (other than Japanese), aliens (other than Japanese), communists, Negroes, labor union members, and anti-Semites." As for the Issei and Nisei, the Japanese foreign ministry advised, "In view of the fact that if there is any slip in this phase, our people in the U.S. will be subjected to considerable persecution...the utmost caution must be exercised."[52] However, Japanese espionage efforts brought few rewards beyond what was freely available in the daily newspapers. American surveillance of the Issei was tightened in the autumn of 1940, when Congress directed the registration of all alien residents, allowing government agencies to open investigative files on all Issei. In the spring of 1941 the FBI broke into the Japanese consulate in Los Angeles and photographed documents that detailed Japanese espionage operations on the West Coast. In June 1941 the FBI broke up an espionage ring of Japanese military officers but found no evidence of Nisei involvement.[53]

The War Department was also concerned about Japanese fifth-column activity in the Philippines, where Japanese residents numbered over 20,000. In late 1940 the Philippine Department G–2 asked the Hawaiian Department to send two reliable Nisei to infiltrate the Japanese community in Manila. In March 1941 the Hawaiian Department G–2 selected Arthur S. Komori and Richard M. Sakakida. Neither had ever set foot in Japan, but both spoke excellent Japanese. The department

---

[51] "Intelligence Officers Invite SCDC [Southern California District Council] Members to Dinner Meeting, Express Faith in Loyalty of Nisei Citizens," *Pacific Citizen*, Apr 41, p. 1.

[52] Msg no. 44, Tokyo to Washington, 30 Jan 41, in *The "Magic" Background of Pearl Harbor*, 5 vols. (Washington, D.C.: Department of Defense, 1977), vol. 1. Memo, WD Gen Staff G–2 to Chief, Counter Intelligence Br, 12 Feb 41, sub: Reorganization of Japanese Intelligence Service in the United States, Classified Material for 1941, RG 165, NARA.

[53] *Pacific Citizen*, Jan 41. The Alien Registration Act of 1940 called for all resident aliens to be registered and fingerprinted between 27 August and 26 December 1940. MacDonnell, *Insidious Foes*, pp. 82–85; *New York Times*, 10 Jun 41, p. 3; *Time* (23 June 1941): 17.
On the effectiveness of prewar Japanese intelligence about the United States, see Michael A. Barnhart, "Japanese Intelligence before the Second World War: 'Best Case' Analysis," in May, *Knowing One's Enemies*, pp. 424–55; Pedro A. Loureiro, "Japanese Espionage and American Countermeasures in Pre–Pearl Harbor California," *Journal of American–East Asian Relations* 3, no. 3 (Fall 1994): 197–210; Stephen C. Mercado, "Japanese Army Intelligence Activities against the United States, 1921–1945," *Studies in Intelligence* 38, no. 2 (Summer 1994): 49–55.

G–2 secretly enlisted the two young men into the Corps of Intelligence Police (later redesignated the Counter Intelligence Corps) and sent them undercover by steamer to Manila in April. There, they infiltrated the Japanese business and diplomatic community and soon began reporting valuable information to the Philippine Department G–2. Sakakida found work as a desk clerk at a hotel favored by Japanese visitors and began to win their trust. That summer, when the U.S. government froze all Japanese assets, Sakakida helped Japanese businessmen fill out their declaration forms, carefully remembering any information they asked him not to write down, which he later passed to his superiors.[54]

Despite the use of individual Nisei in sensitive assignments and considerable success in countering Japanese espionage, American officials remained uncertain of the loyalty of American-born Nisei before the war. No amount of Nisei cooperation or fervent declarations of patriotism such as the "Japanese American Creed" could allay white suspicions that at least some Nisei might prove disloyal. Nisei leaders worked hard to dispel these fears. They even feared their expressions of patriotism might backfire and make whites more suspicious than ever.[55] Intelligence officials searched for a formula that would tell them what they wanted to know. Could they trust the Nisei, but not the Issei? Were Christian Japanese more trustworthy than Buddhists? Could they trust Nisei who had never visited Japan but not those who had? Could they trust only Nisei who seemed more "Americanized" and took no part in Japanese community organizations?

Put this way, the question was unanswerable. How could an outsider evaluate participation in sports clubs, language schools, community-sponsored events, or even Japanese government–sponsored study tours to Japan and Manchuria? How to weigh having relatives in Japan? Absent any explicit evidence of disloyalty, how could Army, Navy, or FBI officials look into the hearts of the young Nisei men in particular, many of them still in their teens or twenties, and predict the future? The Nisei would have to demonstrate their loyalty in action under the most difficult circumstances, but first they would have to be given the chance to do so.

A "Master Stroke": Establishing a Japanese-Language School, April–October 1941

If the U.S. Army were to defeat the Japanese Army, it would need not just a few dozen officers, but hundreds and possibly thousands of interrogators and translators. On 24 March 1941, without specifically mentioning the Nisei, MID directed the Fourth Army G–2 to survey its ranks for Japanese-speaking soldiers: "In the event of a major emergency involving Japan, there will be a great demand for Japanese speaking men in intelligence units of many combatant troops and for

---

[54] Ann Bray, "Undercover Nisei," in *Military Intelligence: Its Heroes and Legends* (Arlington Hall Station, Va.: U.S. Army Intelligence and Security Command, 1987), pp. 29–45; Sakakida and Kiyosaki, *A Spy in Their Midst*, pp. 62–64; Duval A. Edwards, *Spy Catchers of the U.S. Army in the War with Japan* (Gig Harbor, Wash.: Red Apple Publishing, 1994), pp. 15–21.

[55] Kido, "Situation of Japanese."

certain duties under the War Department. It would appear desirable, therefore, to have readily available some record of this personnel, together with such information as to probable loyalty and ability as is obtainable."[56]

Fourth Army, headquartered on the Presidio of San Francisco, was the Army's area command on the West Coast. That spring the headquarters was consumed by the mobilization of Regular Army and National Guard divisions in training camps stretching from the 3d Division at Fort Lewis, Washington, to the 7th Division at Fort Ord, California, to the 40th Division at Camp San Luis Obispo, California. As an indication of the seriousness of the mobilization, on 17 March the War Department designated Fourth Army as the Western Defense Command (WDC) under Lt. Gen. John L. DeWitt, one of the Army's most senior generals. (*See Map 1.*) By the summer of 1941 Fourth Army counted over 100,000 soldiers, including 1,000 Nisei. Even so, it soon became clear that the Fourth Army's ranks would not yield enough proficient Japanese-speakers to meet requirements. The Army needed a training program. The former language attachés knew that Japanese took longer to learn than did most European languages. The training would take at least six months, but the War Department had few alternatives. Weckerling later wrote: "Those few who realized the language difficulties involved in prosecuting a war against the Japanese were alarmed by the lack of our preparations in this regard."[57]

In April Maj. Carlisle C. Dusenbury, a former language attaché then in the Far Eastern Branch, suggested using Nisei soldiers as linguists.[58] Some Nisei, he thought, already spoke Japanese and would need training only in the military aspects of the language. He discussed his idea with Maj. Wallace H. Moore, who had been born in Japan of missionary parents and had taught at the University of California before being called to active duty. Together Dusenbury and Moore sold the idea to their branch chief, Colonel Bratton. After the war school officials esteemed their idea as a "master stroke."[59]

At that time the War Department had no schools for training in foreign languages or in combat intelligence. The Signal Corps operated a small school at

---

[56] Draft Ltr, WD G–2 to G–2, Fourth Army, 24 Mar 41, Security-Class Gen Corresp, 1926–1946, Far Eastern Br, Ofc of the Dir of Intel G–2, RG 165, NARA. Related correspondence alluded to a subsequent letter, dated 5 May 1941, on the same subject. Fourth Army declined to conduct the survey, recommending instead that its subordinate commands maintain these files. Memo, HQ, Fourth Army, to TAG, 14 May 41, sub: Personnel Familiar with Japanese, Far Eastern Br, Ofc of the Dir of Intel G–2, RG 165, NARA.

[57] Weckerling, "Japanese Americans Play Vital Role."

[58] By December 1941 Dusenbury was chief of the Japanese subsection of the Far Eastern Section. He had served as a language officer in Japan in 1929–1933 and in China under Stilwell in 1935–1937. Bidwell, *History of the Military Intelligence Division*, p. 454.

[59] Weckerling, "Japanese Americans Play Vital Role." The phrase "master stroke" first appeared in a MISLS press release of 22 October 1945. Japanese Evacuation Research Study (JERS), pt. 2, sec. 2, reel 20, frame 0037, Bancroft Library, University of California, Berkeley. Bidwell, *History of the Military Intelligence Division*, p. 225, dates the decision in April 1941. Weckerling says Dusenbury first proposed it in June, when the correspondence from MID to Fourth Army begins. MID apparently did not consider directing the Hawaiian Department to organize such a school.

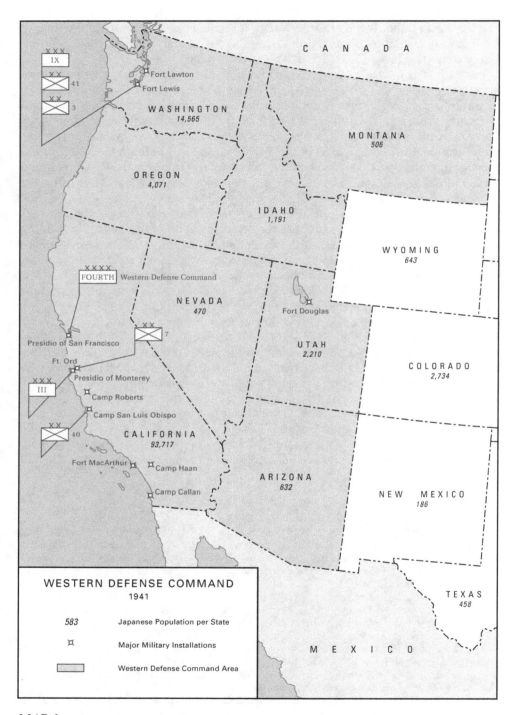

XXX
IX

XX
41

XX
3

Fort Lawton
Fort Lewis

C A N A D A

WASHINGTON
14,565

MONTANA
506

OREGON
4,071

IDAHO
1,191

WYOMING
643

XXXX
FOURTH   Western Defense Command

NEVADA
470

Fort Douglas

UTAH
2,210

COLORADO
2,734

XX
7

Presidio of San Francisco
Ft. Ord

XXX
III

Presidio of Monterey
Camp Roberts
Camp San Luis Obispo

XX
40

CALIFORNIA
93,717

ARIZONA
632

NEW   MEXICO
186

Fort MacArthur
Camp Haan

Camp Callan

TEXAS
458

M E X I C O

WESTERN DEFENSE COMMAND
1941

583   Japanese Population per State

⌗   Major Military Installations

Western Defense Command Area

MAP 1

Fort Monmouth, New Jersey, for radio intelligence. In November 1941 the Corps of Intelligence Police established its own training school in Chicago. MID itself was neither staffed nor organized to supervise a school, so the logical choice was to assign the task to Fourth Army, the command nearest to potential instructors and students.

In June 1941 the Far Eastern Branch got to work on the problem. On 19 June it requested that Major Weckerling be reassigned to Fourth Army to organize the school. On 23 June Colonel Bratton asked the G–2 to direct Fourth Army to establish a school with a minimum of fifty Nisei students. As he envisioned it, the program would consist of "3 months' intensive review of the language (mostly oral), 2 months' study of military terminology, 1 month's instruction in application of the language to Combat Intelligence (specifically examination of prisoners and duties of interpreters in the field)."[60] The Adjutant General's Office provided data on the number of Japanese Americans in uniform, reporting that as of March 1941 there were 1,690 Nisei in the service divided roughly equally between Hawaii and the mainland.[61] Hundreds more were being inducted each month. The Far Eastern Branch also asked Colonel Munson, the military attaché in Tokyo, to purchase and send to Fourth Army some Japanese dictionaries.[62]

On 1 July the War Department directed Fourth Army to establish an intelligence school "to train combat intelligence personnel for work as translators and interpreters of the Japanese language."[63] The directive came just in time. That month relations between America and Japan plunged deeper into crisis when Japan occupied French Indochina and the United States froze all Japanese assets, imposed an oil embargo, and recalled General Douglas MacArthur from retirement to establish a new command, U.S. Army Forces in the Far East. The Office of Naval Intelligence withdrew its naval officers studying Japanese in Tokyo, but the Army language attachés remained in place.[64]

The United States was ill prepared for war in almost every respect, not the least in the languages of the Far East. In early 1941 the Rockefeller Foundation

---

[60] Memo, Bratton to Assistant Chief of Staff (ACS), G–2, 23 Jun 41, sub: Intelligence School Fourth Army, Security-Class Gen Corresp, 1926–1946, Far Eastern Br, Ofc of the Dir of Intel G–2, RG 165, NARA.

[61] Memo, TAGO for Bratton, 1 Jul 41, Security-Class Gen Corresp, 1926–1946, Far Eastern Br, Ofc of the Dir of Intel G–2, RG 165, NARA. TAGO reported the following figures for Nisei enlistments by month: November 1940, 6; December 1940, 397; January 1941, 128; February 1941, 208; March 1941, 906. During the same period another forty-five Nisei joined the National Guard.

[62] Memo, WD Gen Staff G–2 to ACS, G–2, Ninth Corps Area, 23 Jun 41, sub: Japanese Dictionaries, Security-Class Gen Corresp, 1926–1946, Far Eastern Br, Ofc of the Dir of Intel G–2, RG 165, NARA.

[63] Memo, TAG to CG [Commanding General], Fourth Army, 1 Jul 41, sub: Intelligence School, Fourth Army, AG 352.01, cited in MISLS, "Training History of the Military Intelligence Service Language School," ann. 10, Personnel Procurement Office, sec. IV.A., p. 1, Unpubl Ms, 1946, U.S. Army Center of Military History (CMH).

[64] For some reason the Navy language attachés lacked diplomatic immunity and were thus at more risk than those of the Army. "Reminiscences of Rear Admiral Arthur H. McCollum," pp. 298–99.

Kai E. Rasmussen

awarded a $100,000 grant to the Amer-
ican Council of Learned Societies for
"the development of intensive instruction in foreign languages." The "scientific" linguists at several universities
proposed to begin methodically with
a descriptive analysis of each selected
language before moving on to preparing instructional materials.[65]

In July 1941 Cornell University
sponsored a three-day conference of
Japanese-language teachers from seven
American universities; representatives
of MID, ONI, and the FBI attended. The
officers found the results sorely disappointing. They learned that only sixty
Caucasian students nationwide were
enrolled in college-level Japanese-language courses, mostly "from a purely
literary, artistic, or philological point of
view," according to one participant. "It
became obvious to all concerned that
the teaching methods and techniques"
then in use "were in a state of unmitigated confusion." On the conference's last
day the War Department representative, Maj. Wallace H. Moore, stood up and
delivered a harsh assessment: "Well, gentlemen, you haven't got a thing that's any
use to the government at all." The Army and Navy officers "left the conference
determined to do the job [them]selves."[66]

The Army realized several advantages in having its own Japanese-language
school at the Presidio of San Francisco, among them Capt. Kai E. Rasmussen, a
coast artillery officer then commanding harbor defenses for San Francisco Bay.[67]
Rasmussen had emigrated from Denmark to the United States in 1922 and enlisted
in the Army. He was selected for the U.S. Military Academy class of 1929. He later
spent four years in Japan learning the language and observing the Japanese Army.
He returned to the States in 1940; but instead of using his language skills, the
Army assigned him to command Battery E, 65th Coast Artillery, guarding the
Golden Gate. By the spring of 1941 Rasmussen was serving on the Fourth Army

[65] Paul F. Angiolillo, *Armed Forces Foreign Language Teaching: Critical Evaluation and
Implications* (New York: Vanni, 1947), p. 23.

[66] Office of the Chief of Naval Operations, "School of Oriental Languages," pp. 2–3; "Reminiscences of Rear Admiral Arthur H. McCollum," pp. 280–82.

[67] The most important sources for the origins of the school are: "Training History"; Ibid., ann. 1,
Academic Training, 20 Feb 46; *MISLS Album* (Minneapolis: Military Intelligence Service Language
School, 1946); and Weckerling, "Japanese Americans Play Vital Role."

staff overseeing the harbor defenses. The Army would soon have great need for his language skills.[68]

Building a Japanese-language school presented a daunting challenge. Rasmussen could hardly expect to screen all the Nisei soldiers himself. To help out, MID sent another language attaché, Capt. Joseph K. Dickey, who had been serving in the U.S. embassy in Tokyo. Dickey sailed for San Francisco in August. To lead the effort to build a school, the War Department dispatched a more senior officer, Lt. Col. John Weckerling (promoted that summer). He arrived in San Francisco in September. A 44-year-old infantry officer, Weckerling had enlisted in 1917 and subsequently earned a commission. As a language attaché in Tokyo from 1928 to 1932, he had watched as the Imperial Japanese Army occupied Manchuria in 1931. Returning to Tokyo as the assistant military attaché from 1935 to 1938, he had watched as the Japanese Army attacked China in 1937. After a total of eight years' duty in Japan, he was well versed in the Japanese threat. Since late 1939 he had served in Panama, searching for possible Japanese subversion, espionage, or sabotage directed against the canal. Now he would be searching for Americans of Japanese ancestry and recruiting them for language training.[69] These three former language attachés, Rasmussen, Dickey, and Weckerling, worked together to assemble students and instructors.

That summer the Western Defense Command held the largest maneuvers ever seen on the West Coast. All Regular Army and National Guard units under DeWitt's command remained in the field for several weeks, enduring long hikes, choking dust, and stifling tents. In the intervals between marches and training exercises, a strange scene played out hundreds of times in various camps: an Army officer appeared wearing civilian clothes and carrying secret orders. At the camp headquarters, he presented his credentials and asked to meet every Nisei soldier in the camp. When each soldier reported to him, the mysterious officer showed him a Japanese Army manual and asked him to read a few passages.[70]

---

[68] George W. Cullum, *Biographical Register of the Officers and Graduates of the U.S. Military Academy at West Point, New York, Since Its Establishment in 1802*, vol. 7, supplement, 1920–1930, ed. William H. Donaldson (Chicago: Lakeside Press, 1931); Kai E. Rasmussen, speech, DLIFLC, 25 Jun 77, printed in *DLIFLC Forum* (November 1977); "In Memoriam, Kai E. Rasmussen, 1902–1988," memorial service booklet, 1988; Norman Y. Mineta, "Tribute to Col. Kai E. Rasmussen," *Congressional Record* (3 May 1988). Rasmussen was promoted to major on 10 October 1941.

[69] John Weckerling, Personnel File, National Military Records Center, St. Louis, Mo.; Weckerling, "Japanese Language Detail." The War Department requested his reassignment from Panama to Fourth Army on 19 June 1941. Memo, WD G–2 to TAG, 19 Jun 41, sub: Assignment of Major John Weckerling, Security-Class Gen Corresp, 1926–1946, Far Eastern Br, Ofc of the Dir of Intel G–2, RG 165, NARA. He arrived on or about 5 September.
From July 1941 to February 1942, the Fourth Army G–2 was Lt. Col. Donald A. Stroh; Weckerling was his assistant. Shigeya Kihara recalls that when he became an instructor in October 1941, Weckerling was the Fourth Army G–2 (personal communication to author, May 99). Weckerling's personnel file indicates he did not replace Stroh until March 1942.

[70] "Training History," ann. 10, sec. IV.A., gives details.

Captain Rasmussen found Pvt. Thomas Sakamoto assigned to an antitank unit on maneuvers at Fort Hunter Liggett, California. Sakamoto remembered a man wearing civilian clothes and speaking with a Scandinavian accent. The Danish-born Rasmussen took Sakamoto into a field tent, pulled a Japanese field manual from his coat pocket, and asked him to translate some passages. "Since I graduated from the Japanese high school in 1938, reading and translating this textbook wasn't difficult." Sakamoto recalled that Rasmussen mentioned the chance of a commission if he would volunteer for the school. Sakamoto soon received orders for the Presidio.[71]

Captain Dickey visited the 40th Division at Camp San Luis Obispo and interviewed Pvt. Masaji Gene Uratsu, a Kibei who as a child had lived five years in Japan. Uratsu was ordered without explanation to report to division headquarters, "scared and apprehensive to say the least." Dickey "produced several Japanese field manuals and requested that I read and translate portions of the manuals. The whole procedure, which lasted about thirty minutes, seemed like an eternity to me. Upon conclusion of the interview, the officer stated that I would be hearing from him again, and he warned me, in no uncertain terms, that this interview was not to be revealed or discussed with anyone." Two months later, Uratsu and three other Nisei from the camp received orders to report to the G–2, Fourth Army.[72]

For most Nisei, the interviews proved embarrassing. One of the books the officers used was the Imperial Japanese Army field service regulations, *Sakusen Yōmurei*. Another was the Japanese military academy textbook on applied tactics, *Ōyō Senjutsu*. Even if the Nisei had paid attention to their lessons, none knew the complicated Japanese military terminology, *heigo*. Perhaps their fathers could have read these materials, but the Nisei could not. The Nisei probably recalled all those boring afternoons spent in the Japanese-language school while their non-Japanese friends were already on the baseball diamond. When tested, even if some could speak a few words of simple Japanese, most could not translate even the simplest sentences.

From July to October 1941 Rasmussen, Dickey, and Weckerling interviewed all 1,300 Nisei soldiers on the West Coast.[73] For reasons of time, or perhaps not

---

[71] Thomas Sakamoto, speech, DLIFLC, 1 Nov 87; Sakamoto, "Original Japanese Student Reflects"; Interv, author with Sakamoto, 16 Nov 87; "Caught Between Two Worlds"; Sakamoto autobiography, 1 Nov 96. Arthur M. Kaneko also was promised a commission in 1941, when he was selected for language training. David W. Swift, Jr., ed., "First Class," p. 15, Unpubl Ms, 2000, copy in author's files. Not all Nisei recruited that summer for language training recall being promised commissions.

[72] Gene Masaji Uratsu, Biography, Military Intelligence Service Club of Northern California (this and similar biographies hereafter cited as MISNorCal Bios).

[73] Some sources, such as the MISLS press release of 22 October 1945 and the *MISLS Album*, give the number of Nisei soldiers interviewed at this time as 3,700. Other sources do not necessarily bear this out. For example, Weckerling uses 1,300 in his letter of 31 December 1941. "Training History," ann. 1 (dated December 1945), uses 1,300; "Training History" (dated April 1946) uses 1,200. After 7 December 1941, an unknown number of Nisei were discharged, but others were still being drafted as late as February 1942. That month the Western Defense Command reported transferring

wishing to cross command lines, no one screened the Nisei serving in Hawaii. In December Weckerling reported to the War Department: "The general impression gained by Rasmussen and me in our interviews with these men was an excellent one. The majority seemed eager to serve although the nature of the school, classified by the War Department as secret at that time, could not be fully explained. Many thought that it was to be organized along F.B.I. lines but their eagerness to serve still remained high. Only a few were obviously sullen and uncommunicative." [74]

The officers then tried to determine the loyalty of each Nisei candidate based on the interview and security questionnaires, which they used for background investigations. In addition to the few malcontents, about 30 percent of the Nisei had a parent or sibling living in Japan, an automatically disqualifying factor. [75] For the remaining candidates, the officers questioned families, neighbors, and teachers; in some cases they searched the candidates' homes. Many "were 'blackballed' by the investigators simply because of racial prejudice or because the person being investigated had made a trip to Japan or had belonged to a Japanese athletic club." [76]

Weckerling reported that "only 40 men were sufficiently qualified linguistically to pursue a six months course in the Japanese language." Of all Nisei screened, only 3 percent could be rated "accomplished," 4 percent "proficient," and 3 percent "fair." Of the Nisei interviewed, Weckerling reported, "only 17 men spoke, read and wrote Japanese proficiently, indicating a gradual moving away from the influence of the first generation Japanese." [77]

The Army officers were especially interested in Kibei like Sakamoto and Uratsu. Ironically, some Kibei spoke *English* so poorly that they were of little use to the Army. Weckerling identified about half who "had lived in Japan only for a short period of time and whose outlook is essentially American, or, who as a result of their visit to Japan were embittered against the Japanese by treatment received

---

1,211 Nisei soldiers from the West Coast. Memo, TAGO to Commanding General, Western Defense Command & Fourth Army, 3 Mar 42, Sub: Enlisted Personnel of Japanese Extraction (AG 220.31); Enemy Aliens File, Box 23, General Robert C. Richardson, Jr., Papers, Hoover Institution Archives. The Selective Service later reported that 3,188 Nisei were drafted up to 1 November 1941. Selective Service System, *Special Groups*, Special Monograph no. 10 (Washington, D.C.: Selective Service System, 1953), p. 114. Of these, perhaps 2,000 were from Hawaii. War Department estimates for the summer of 1942 range from 3,000 to 4,600. The figure 3,700 may represent an estimate of the total number of Nisei soldiers in December 1941, but it is too high for the total in the WDC. Another report gives a much higher figure. "Training History," ann. 10, sec. IV.A., p. 2. This cites 5,700 "Presidio of San Francisco interviews" and states that this was the number interviewed for the first class. A footnote adds "but only about 1,500 personal history statements on file."

[74] Ltr, Weckerling to Dusenbury, 31 December 1941, Trng Grp, Ofc of the Dir of Intel G–2, RG 165, NARA; Weckerling, "Japanese Americans Play Vital Role."

[75] "Training History," ann. 4, Intelligence Section.

[76] "Training History," p. 5. Some Nisei initially disqualified were accepted for the school after the war began.

[77] Ltr, Weckerling to Dusenbury, 31 December 1941; Weckerling, "Japanese Americans Play Vital Role." Rasmussen later gave slightly different figures, 3 percent as "fully qualified" and another 8 percent as "potential students after a long training period." Rasmussen, speech, DLIFLC, 25 Jun 77.

there." The other half had attended school in Japan and lived there for a longer time. "During this stay it is probable that, while in Japan at any rate, the thought of those who returned to Japan at a very early age was predominantly Japanese. In many cases the influence of Japan had disappeared since their return." [78] The Kibei proved to be the most valuable of all. A few even had personal knowledge of the Japanese Army from having served as conscripts.[79] Weckerling deemed 5 percent or less of the Kibei completely unsuitable for military service, describing them as "those unassimilated elements who have, or believe they have, cause to hate the United States, those whose parents have maintained a very close tie with the old country, those who went to Japan as infants and only returned within the last year or two—their outlook being wholly Japanese." [80]

The War Department also searched for Caucasian soldiers who spoke Japanese, to little avail. Many claimed an ability to speak Japanese that far surpassed their facility with the language. Only two Caucasian enlisted men were selected for the first class. Both had lived in Japan for a time and spoke some colloquial Japanese.[81]

Weckerling later concisely described how "the selection of Nisei of unquestioned loyalty reasonably qualified in the Japanese language became the primary task." [82] In four months of searching, the Army officers found fifty-eight Nisei who met these two criteria.

The Office of Naval Intelligence Prepares for War with Japan, 1940–1941

ONI was making its own preparations for the coming conflict with Japan. For decades the U.S. Navy had been rehearsing War Plan Orange. ONI used radio intercept stations to monitor the Japanese Fleet. District intelligence officers kept watch over local Japanese communities on the West Coast and in Hawaii.[83] In Washington, the ONI Far East Section employed a handful of Japanese translators. The section chief, Lt. Cmdr. Arthur H. McCollum, had been stationed in Tokyo in 1922–1925 and again in 1928–1930 and spoke Japanese. In 1940 he happened

---

[78] Ltr, Weckerling to Dusenbury, 31 December 1941.

[79] Masaharu Ano, "Loyal Linguists: Nisei of World War II Learned Japanese in Minnesota," *Minnesota History* 45, no. 7 (Fall 1977): 273–87, includes a discussion of the special role of the Kibei.

[80] Ibid.

[81] Some Caucasians who spoke Japanese, such as Faubion Bowers, were overlooked at the time, particularly if they were assigned outside Fourth Army. Stanley L. Falk and Warren M. Tsuneishi, eds., *MIS in the War against Japan* (Washington, D.C.: Japanese American Veterans Association, 1995), pp. 11–12, 94. The two Caucasians selected for the first class were Dempster Dirks and Victor V. Belousoff, a Russian immigrant who later changed his last name to Bell. Neither was proficient enough to graduate with the first class.

[82] Weckerling, "Japanese Americans Play Vital Role."

[83] For naval intelligence against Japan before 7 December 1941, see Alan H. Bath, *Tracking the Axis Enemy: The Triumph of Anglo-American Naval Intelligence* (Lawrence: University Press of Kansas, 1998), pp. 135–68; Lewin, *American Magic*, pp. 16–48.

upon Glenn W. Shaw, an acquaintance who had taught English in Japan and had published translations of modern Japanese plays and novels. McCollum made him chief of the Translation Section.[84]

The Navy had its own small pool of officer-linguists using the same program at the U.S. embassy in Tokyo. Several former naval language attachés worked in the Far East Section and understood the urgent need for more Japanese linguists. Several were already attacking the Japanese naval and diplomatic codes; the effort would soon require many more.

In the autumn of 1940, as the Navy began calling reserve officers to active duty, Albert E. Hindmarsh, a professor of international law at Harvard University, obtained a commission and approached the Far Eastern Branch to offer his services. While spending a year as an exchange professor at the Imperial University in Tokyo, he had learned some Japanese. In December 1940 McCollum gave Hindmarsh and Shaw the task of developing a Japanese-language program for the Navy. In the spring of 1941 they conducted a survey of college students and found fifty-six who had some potential to learn the language.[85] The Navy could not draw upon the services of Nisei as easily as the Army for one simple reason: As the Navy rapidly expanded in 1940–1941 it had continued its traditional racial exclusion policies against Asians. Filipinos were allowed to serve, but only as cooks and mess stewards. If the Navy wanted Japanese linguists, it would have to train them from scratch.

In July 1941 McCollum and Hindmarsh attended the disappointing language conference at Cornell University. Upon returning to Washington, Hindmarsh recommended that the Navy establish its own language program through contracts with leading universities. At Harvard University, he secured the services of one of the leading Japanese scholars in the country, Russian émigré Professor Serge Elisséeff. Elisséeff was a world authority on Japanese art and theater and taught the Japanese language. He and his younger protégé, Edwin O. Reischauer, had just published a two-volume textbook for the Japanese language.[86] While visiting California, Hindmarsh chose Florence Walne, an unknown language instructor at the University of California. Walne had been born in Nagasaki, the historic seat of Christianity in Japan, and was raised by missionary parents. In 1931 she left Japan for the United States and graduate studies. While completing her doctorate, she

---

[84] "Reminiscences of Rear Admiral Arthur H. McCollum," pp. 260–61. In September the naval attaché in Tokyo sent all ten naval language attachés out of the country.

[85] "School of Oriental Languages"; "Reminiscences of Rear Admiral Arthur H. McCollum," pp. 282–83. See also key Navy documents from this period reproduced in Scott E. Nadler, *The Evolution of Foreign Language Training in the Armed Forces* (Washington, D.C.: Defense Language Institute, 1972).

[86] Serge Elisséeff and Edwin O. Reischauer, *Elementary Japanese for University Students* (Cambridge, Mass.: Harvard-Yenching Institute, 1941). Elisséeff also coedited with Hugh Borton and Edwin O. Reischauer *A Selected List of Books and Articles on Japan in English, French, and German* (Washington, D.C.: Committee on Japanese Studies, American Council of Learned Societies, ca. 1940). Donald Keene describes Elisséeff in *On Familiar Terms: A Journey across Cultures* (New York: Kodansha, 1994), pp. 10–11, 87–90.

supported herself by teaching Japanese. The personable "Miss Walne" counted many Nisei among her students.[87]

McCollum and Hindmarsh narrowed their list of potential students to forty-eight, "all native-born United States citizens, white, male, and anxious to serve the Navy; most of them had lived and studied in Japan or China, had university degrees, and were in the age bracket of twenty to thirty." All were promised reserve commissions upon graduation. Instruction began on 1 October 1941, with twenty-seven students at Harvard and twenty-one at the University of California at Berkeley.[88] Meanwhile, in July 1941 the U.S. Marine Corps sent twelve reserve officers to a separate program at the University of Hawaii to learn Japanese.[89]

For textbooks McCollum had the naval attaché in Tokyo send copies of the Naganuma readers; fifty complete sets arrived in September. Hindmarsh then designed a practical course of instruction that crammed the three-year Naganuma course into one. The final course objectives were vague. "We didn't have anything specific in mind," he later recalled, "but we thought it would be useful to have some people who could handle the language."[90]

At Harvard, Professor Elisséeff did not like naval officers telling him how to teach Japanese. The Navy directed him to use the Naganuma readers, but he preferred his own textbook. Hindmarsh visited in November and wrote a sternly worded report that demanded changes in the curriculum, which Elisséeff ignored. Meanwhile, things were much more to the Navy's liking on the West Coast, where Miss Walne had fewer preconceptions about the "right" way to teach the language and her students were making steady progress.[91]

As Army officers interviewed prospective students, a "delay in the establishment of the school was barely averted," Weckerling recalled, as MID wavered on whether to open a Japanese-language school at all.[92] Some argued it would be better to open a centralized intelligence school. That summer a group of mili-

---

[87] The U.S. Navy had identified Walne as a potential intelligence asset in 1935, shortly after she enrolled at the University of California: Memo, 12th Naval District to CNO, 7 Jan 36, sub: Japanese Translators, Folder A8–2/P11–5, Translators (5), Commandant's Ofc, Gen Corresp (Declass), 12th Naval District, RG 181, NARA–Pacific Region.

[88] "School of Oriental Languages," p. 2. See also Bureau of Navigation, "Organization and Contents of an Intensive Course in the Japanese Language for Naval Students," [ca. Aug 41], in Folder P16/P11–5 (12), Course in Japanese Language, Box 12, Commandant's Ofc, Gen Corresp (Declass), 12th Naval District, RG 181, NARA–Pacific Region.

[89] Roger Pineau, "World War II Japanese Language School for Marines," Unpubl Ms, author's files; Roger V. Dingman, "Language at War: U.S. Marine Corps Japanese Language Officers in the Pacific War," *Journal of Military History* 68 (July 2004): 856–57. One Marine officer who trained at the University of Hawaii was Gerald Holtom, born in Japan to missionary parents. He was assigned to the 2d Marine Raider Battalion and died on Makin in August 1942. "Palo Alto Marine Finally Comes Home," *Palo Alto Daily News*, 2 Dec 00.

[90] "Reminiscences of Rear Admiral Arthur H. McCollum," p. 56.

[91] Elisséeff's 28 November 1941 response to Hindmarsh's criticisms is reproduced in part in Nadler, *Evolution of Foreign Language Training*, pp. 112–14.

[92] Weckerling, "Japanese Americans Play Vital Role." See also Rasmussen's comments in *Minnesota Morning Tribune*, 23 Oct 45.

tary intelligence officers visited Britain and were impressed by the British Army's interrogator-training school. When they returned to Washington, D.C., in July, they recommended that MID establish a similar school. One of the observers was the Fourth Army G–2, Lt. Col. Donald A. Stroh, who agreed with the British approach. But his assistant G–2 in San Francisco, Weckerling, disagreed, as did the officers in the Far Eastern Branch. They argued that the psychology of captured Asian personnel was quite different from that of captured Germans. Hence the need for a separate school that would teach only Japanese and interrogation techniques appropriate to Japanese prisoners of war.[93] At the end of August the Far Eastern Branch won out and MID directed Fourth Army to proceed with establishing their school "as soon as practicable."[94]

Another threat to the school came from a new Army organization, General Headquarters (GHQ), responsible for the supervision and direction of Army training. In June 1941 GHQ moved to block MID's plans for intelligence training. In July Fourth Army requested GHQ's permission to start a Japanese-language school. MID endorsed Fourth Army's request but conceded that "the question of training translators and interrogators is only one phase of combat intelligence training." MID recommended that "a War Department study should be made to determine the needs of all task forces for translators, interpreters and interrogators for all required languages, rather than only Japan." GHQ then approved Fourth Army's request and allowed the school to proceed. The General Staff scheduled a meeting for 8 December to decide which War Department staff section would control language and intelligence training. The meeting would never happen.[95]

By October 1941 Fourth Army had assembled sixty students to begin Japanese-language training at Crissy Field on the Presidio of San Francisco. Across the San Francisco Bay at the University of California, the Office of Naval Intelligence had begun training Caucasian officer candidates and had a similar program at Harvard University.

---

[93] The perceived differences in the "psychology" of interrogating Asians vs. Caucasians persisted during the war and after. In 1946–1947 the basic intelligence officers course taught at the Intelligence School, Fort Riley, Kansas, had two separate blocks of instruction based on wartime experiences, labeled "Interrogation Techniques, Caucasian," 28 Feb 47, and "Interrogation Techniques, Oriental," 20 Feb 47, both in Trng Grp, Ofc of the Dir of Intel G–2, RG 165, NARA.

[94] Weckerling, "Japanese Americans Play Vital Role"; Memo, Fourth Army G–2 to WD G–2, 18 Aug 41, sub: Fourth Army Language and Intelligence School; Ltr, MID to Fourth Army, 30 Aug 41. Both in Security-Class Gen Corresp, 1926–1946, Far Eastern Br, Ofc of the Dir of Intel G–2, RG 165, NARA. Colonel Stroh was a military observer in England from May through July 1941.

[95] Kent Roberts Greenfield et al., *The Army Ground Forces: The Organization of Ground Combat Troops* (Washington, D.C.: Historical Division, Department of the Army, 1947), pp. 32–55; Bidwell, *History of the Military Intelligence Division*, pp. 366–67; Weckerling, "Japanese Americans Play Vital Role." Weckerling and Rasmussen were aware of the Navy's language training in Berkeley. Memo, CG, Fourth Army, to ACS, G–2, WD, 17 Sep 41, sub: Navy and Marine Japanese Language Schools, in Security-Class Gen Corresp, 1926–1946, Far Eastern Br, Ofc of the Dir of Intel G–2, RG 165, NARA.

2

Fourth Army Intelligence School,
November 1941–May 1942

As diplomatic tensions with Japan increased during 1941, the War Department Military Intelligence Division (MID) quietly turned to its Nisei soldiers to train a carefully selected few for special duty as interpreters and translators. Several officers who had studied Japanese in Tokyo in the 1930s were assigned to Fourth Army at the Presidio of San Francisco; they selected sixty students from among the roughly 1,300 Nisei from the western states who had been enlisted through Selective Service over the previous year.

"Your Country Needs You"

It was difficult to find Nisei students proficient in both English and Japanese who could pass a security check; finding qualified instructors was even more so. Pfc. Arthur Masaji Kaneko and Pfc. John Fujio Aiso, interviewed at Camp Haan, California, seemed especially promising. Kaneko had been born in Riverside and had spent ten years attending school in Japan before returning to California for high school. In March 1941 he was studying architecture at Los Angeles Junior College when he received his Selective Service notice. Because of his drafting skills, the Army assigned him to the Coast Artillery. Though Kaneko's Japanese and English skills were excellent, he felt unqualified to teach Japanese. Aiso tried to persuade him, but Kaneko joined the school as a student.[1]

---

[1] John Weckerling, "Japanese Americans Play Vital Role in United States Intelligence Service in World War II" (1946), first printed in *Hokubei Mainichi*, 27 Oct–5 Nov 71, reprinted as a

Aiso, the Harvard-trained lawyer now working as a parts clerk, had his doubts too. At the Presidio of San Francisco, he reported to Maj. John Weckerling in his office in the Fourth Army headquarters building. Aiso was the most promising of all the Nisei the officers had identified. In addition to speaking excellent English and Japanese, he was more mature than most. Weckerling offered Aiso the job of chief instructor.

Aiso thought for a moment. It was clear that relations between the United States and Japan were deteriorating sharply. Who knew how all that would turn out? In Washington, the two governments were engaged in tense negotiations; but most American newspaper readers remained hopeful that a conflict could be avoided. Aiso had no intention of staying in uniform. In fact, he was already on his way out of the Army. About this time the War Department changed its age rules for selectees: those over twenty-eight years old would be released (he was thirty-two). In Los Angeles, his fiancée was waiting for him; he was planning to marry and resume his law practice.

Aiso declined Weckerling's offer, and what happened next surprised him. Weckerling came out from behind his desk, put his hand on Aiso's shoulder, and said, "John, your country needs you." This caught Aiso off guard. He paused for only a moment and then responded: "Yes, sir, I will take the job." The encounter was a turning point in his life, Aiso later recalled. "No American person had ever told me that America was my country." [2]

Weckerling felt it would not be right for the chief instructor to be a junior enlisted man. Aiso was too old for a direct commission, so Weckerling decided to make him a War Department civilian. He had Aiso discharged from the Enlisted Reserve Corps and hired as a civilian "with the understanding that if he should sever his connection with the school he would be recalled to active duty as an enlisted man." Now that Aiso was no longer a soldier, he and his fiancée set as their wedding date his birthday, 14 December, just before the Christmas holidays. [3]

---

pamphlet; Interv, author with Arthur M. Kaneko, 23 Aug 95; Joseph D. Harrington Papers, National Japanese American Historical Society (NJAHS), San Francisco, Calif. After Kaneko's class graduated in May 1942, he was held back as an enlisted instructor for two years. Similar in age and upbringing to most Nisei, Kaneko was a rare *Sansei* (third-generation Japanese American). His grandfather had immigrated to the United States in 1893, so his father was a Nisei.

[2] This story is recounted in various sources: John F. Aiso, "Observations of a California Nisei," Interv by Marc Landy, University of California at Los Angeles, 1971; Interv, author with John F. Aiso, 30 Oct 87; Joseph D. Harrington, *Yankee Samurai: The Secret Role of Nisei in America's Pacific Victory* (Detroit: Pettigrew Enterprises, 1979), pp. 20–21; Shigeya Kihara, "Remembering General John Weckerling," Unpubl Ms, Dec 92, author's files; Interv, Stephen A. Haller with Shigeya Kihara, 21 Jan 94, pp. 15–16; Kiyoshi Yano, "Participating in the Mainstream of American Life amidst Drawback of Racial Prejudice and Discrimination," in *John Aiso and the M.I.S.: Japanese-American Soldiers in the Military Intelligence Service, World War II*, ed. Tad Ichinokuchi (Los Angeles: Military Intelligence Service Club of Southern California, 1988), p. 15. The meeting probably took place in late September or early October 1941.

[3] MISLS, "Training History of the Military Intelligence Service Language School," ann. 1, Academic Training, p. 4, Unpubl Ms, 1946, U.S. Army Center of Military History (CMH). See also

The search for qualified instructors continued. Capt. Kai E. Rasmussen crossed the San Francisco Bay to Berkeley to see Florence Walne, who was already working for the Navy's Japanese-language program. Walne knew many Nisei students at the University of California but also knew that most were not interested in working for the War Department. Rumors had spread that the Army's school would train informers to spy on the Japanese American community.

Walne suggested that Rasmussen speak with two of her recent students, Akira Oshida and Shigeya Kihara. Oshida had graduated from Berkeley High School and Meiji University in Tokyo. Most recently he had worked in the Japan pavilion at the Golden Gate International Exhibition. Oshida received a phone call from an Army officer with "a thick German accent" (the Danish-born Rasmussen) inviting him for an interview at the Presidio of San Francisco. After some questions about his schooling and work experience, the officer "threw a book on the table and asked me if I knew what it was. I said, "Yes," Oshida replied, "I used to carry one in my back pocket" (during his military training at Meiji University). After the interview, the officer told Oshida he was in. "In what?" Oshida asked. Only then did he learn the nature of the job.[4]

Kihara had earned a bachelor's degree in political science and a master's degree in international relations at the University of California. In October 1941 he had just returned from a short trip to Japan and began working in his father's grocery store. His experiences in Japan convinced him that a conflict would soon break out between the two countries. Kihara was interviewed but was not given a reading test. If he had, he later reflected, he probably would not have done very well. In any event, Walne's recommendation was good enough for Weckerling to offer him a job.[5]

Tetsuo Imagawa was selected as the fourth instructor. Although he had a bachelor's degree in economics from the University of California, he could find work only as a salesman for a liquor company. Imagawa was the only instructor with firsthand experience teaching at a Japanese-language school.[6]

On Monday morning, 20 October 1941, Weckerling assembled the four Nisei instructors in a basement room of the Fourth Army headquarters for their first meeting. Piled on an orange crate was Rasmussen's personal collection of textbooks from Tokyo: the Naganuma readers (eight volumes), Creswell's Japanese-English military dictionary, various Japanese and American training manuals, Ueda's *Daijiten* (a voluminous compendium of *kanji*, or Chinese characters), and

---

Aiso, "Observations of a California Nisei"; Harrington, *Yankee Samurai*, p. 32; Yano, "Participating in the Mainstream," p. 16.

   [4] "Akira Oshida: DLI's 'Living History,'" *DLI Globe* (13 March 1980).

   [5] Intervs, Haller with Kihara, 21 Jan 94, and Lt. Cmdr. Donald McCabe with Shigeya Kihara, 19 Jul 91.

   [6] Harrington Papers; Biographies, Military Intelligence Service Club of Northern California (hereafter cited as MISNorCal Bios); Weckerling, "Japanese Americans Play Vital Role"; Shigeya Kihara, autobiography, Unpubl Ms, NJAHS; Intervs, McCabe with Kihara, 21 Jan 91, and Haller with Kihara, 19 Jul 94.

Three of the instructors at Crissy Field take a lunch break. Shigeya Kihara is in the center.

several other books.[7] Weckerling suggested they go to the school building. A ten-minute walk took them down toward the bay across some railroad tracks to a shabby warehouse, a converted hangar that was a relic of the days when Crissy Field had been an active airfield.[8] There were no desks or chairs, only two old Army cots. One side would serve as classrooms, the other as the sleeping area.

"Sixty Nisei soldiers will report here in two weeks on November 1," Weckerling told them. "Be prepared to start training them." He then turned on his heel and walked out. The new instructors looked at each other for a minute, not sure where to begin. After a moment, Aiso took charge and began giving them their assignments. They had no time to lose.[9]

---

[7] Kihara, "Remembering General John Weckerling." Though 15 and 16 October have both been given for the first meeting, Kihara recalls it as a Monday (personal communication to author). That would make the date 13 or 20 October 1941. The confusion may have arisen in later years because the four new civilian instructors were placed on the payroll at the beginning of the mid-month pay period, i.e., 16 October.

[8] Crissy Field was established in 1921, the hangar erected in 1921–1922 for the Air Mail Service. Originally Bldg. 907, sometime after 1942 the hangar was renumbered as Bldg. 640. In 1928 it was converted into barracks for ROTC summer camp. In 1936 the airfield was closed. Stephen A. Haller, *The Last Word in Airfields: A Special History Study of Crissy Field, Presidio of San Francisco, California* (San Francisco: National Park Service, 1994); Mary Grassick, *Fourth Army Intelligence School: Historic Furnishings Report* (Harpers Ferry, W.Va.: National Park Service, 1999).

[9] Harrington, *Yankee Samurai*, p. 21; Interv, Haller with Kihara, 19 Jul 94.

Aiso laid down the daily schedule: classes from 0800 to 1130, a lunch break, then back into the classroom from 1300 to 1630, five days a week. Supervised study hours would be four evenings a week from 1900 to 2100. Saturday mornings from 0900 to 1200 were spent on review and examinations.[10] The school was to be all work, for students and instructors alike.

The curriculum was based on Naganuma's and *Hyojun Nihongo Tokuhon*, standard Japanese readers, which had to be reprinted as soon as possible. The books came with a set of flash cards that showed the kanji characters on one side and English on the reverse. Oshida had the best handwriting, so he was assigned to write the kanji on stencils for mimeographing. The curriculum covered reading, translation, interpretation, grammar, and military terminology. For military terminology the instructors used the same Japanese field manuals that Rasmussen and Capt. Joseph K. Dickey had used to screen prospective students. Weckerling also gave them Lt. Col. Moses W. Pettigrew's new technical manual on the Japanese military. Using Creswell's military dictionary, the instructors laboriously translated Pettigrew's manual into Japanese. Meanwhile, other instructors scoured San Francisco's Little Tokyo for print shops that could reproduce Japanese-language materials. With the start of classes barely two weeks away, they wasted precious hours soliciting multiple bids on each print job as required by government contracting rules. From Washington, MID requested that the U.S. military attaché in Tokyo ship more dictionaries to the school directly from Japan.[11]

The school needed money as well as instructors. There had been no requirement for an intelligence school in the Fourth Army budget when the new fiscal year began on 1 July. Nevertheless, Weckerling obtained $2,000 from the Fourth Army quartermaster. Carpenters erected partitions to make three classrooms on one side and offices and barracks space on the other. During the last weeks of October, the Nisei students trickled into the hangar and waited for the school to begin.

On the morning of Monday, 3 November, classes began.[12] Fifty-eight Nisei and two Caucasians sat down in three makeshift classrooms in the hangar, almost in the shadow of the Golden Gate Bridge.[13] Kihara, Oshida, and Imagawa each

[10] "Training History," ann. 1, para. 9a.; Interv, McCabe with Kihara, 19 Jul 91, pp. 18–20.

[11] Weckerling, "Japanese Americans Play Vital Role." Intervs, author with Kaneko, 23 Aug 95; McCabe with Kihara, 21 Jan 91; Haller with Kihara, 19 Jul 94. *MISLS Album* (Minneapolis: Military Intelligence Service Language School, 1946), pp. 30–31. The military attaché in Japan shipped the requested dictionaries, but they made it only as far as Manila, where they fell into Japanese hands when the war broke out. "Training History"; General Records, 1943–1945, Military Intelligence [Service] Language School, Fort Snelling, Minn., Records of the Army Staff, Record Group (RG) 319, National Archives and Records Administration (NARA), p. 4.

[12] The Fourth Army Intelligence School was formally activated on 1 November 1941, the date commonly used to denote the school's origin. However, classes did not begin until the following Monday, 3 November. The four students from San Luis Obispo were ordered to travel by rail to the Presidio of San Francisco starting on the afternoon of Friday, 31 October. Gene Masaji Uratsu, MISNorCal Bio.

[13] No official list of the students who started the class has been found. Forty-two graduates are listed in *MISLS Album*, p. 125. The two Caucasians, Dempster Dirks and Victor Belousoff, who

Classroom inside Crissy Field hangar, late 1945

took one class.[14] They covered reading, Japanese-to-English translation, conversation, and interpreting and tested the students' memorization skills by drilling them daily on kanji, with the top section learning fifty to sixty kanji each day. John Aiso became the unquestioned leader, and the instructors and students looked to him to run the school.[15]

Aiso and his instructors intended the course as a refresher, because the students were supposed to have a good grasp of Japanese already. This assumption turned out to be mistaken. They soon found out that only the top twenty or so students could handle the language with ease. For the rest, "the process was one of learning anew rather than merely refreshing up on knowledge previously acquired but presently dormant."

---

began with the fifty-eight Nisei, graduated later than the Nisei in the first class. "Training History," ann. 1, states that the first class was composed of fifty-seven Nisei and three Caucasians (para. 6, p. 5). The third Caucasian name might be that of S.Sgt. George Spence, who began as the supply sergeant and later attended training. Grassick, *Fourth Army Intelligence School*, p. 26.

[14] The basic sources for the first class are "Training History," *MISLS Album*, and Weckerling, "Japanese Americans Play Vital Role." See also Uratsu, MISNorCal Bio. Intervs, author with John F. Aiso, 30 Oct 87; McCabe with Kihara, 21 Jan 91; Haller with Kihara, 19 Jul 94; author with Thomas Sakamoto, 16 Nov 87.

[15] The school's opening was supposed to be secret, but Aiso recalled that the Japanese *Dōmei* radio service mentioned the school on the air and identified the instructors by name. Yano, "Participating in the Mainstream," p. 16; Aiso, "Observations of a California Nisei."

Nisei students in front of Chinatown YMCA in San Francisco

The Japanese language was notoriously difficult for English speakers to learn. Written Japanese uses a mixture of kanji and letters of the Japanese syllabary (*kana*, or *-gana*). Kanji may be written in block print or in cursive (*sōsho*, also known as grass writing). Two types of kana, *katakana* and cursive *hiragana*, must also be learned. Additionally, Japanese may be written using the Latin alphabet (*rōmaji*). Its spoken form has several dialects. Nationalists in Japan boasted of this complexity and assured the Japanese people that few foreigners could master their language. American commentators also stressed its complexity but as if this was somehow additional evidence of the perversity and cunning of the Japanese mind.[16]

Inside the hangar, the students worked hard day and night. Many wished they had paid more attention in Japanese school. But all preferred this to being on summer maneuvers or driving a truck. One of the Kibei students later recalled: "There I was, a farm boy turned soldier, studying a language I already knew, in the wonderful city of San Francisco. It was the happiest six months of my entire

---

[16] Weckerling, "Japanese Americans Play Vital Role"; Sidney F. Mashbir, *I Was an American Spy* (New York: Vantage, 1953); Francis S. Wickware, "The Japanese Language," *Life* (7 September 1942). Warren Tsuneishi assisted the author with this explanation.

life!" Their parents would be proud that their sons were finally buckling down to learn the language. After hours a popular place to study was the latrine, where the lights stayed on all night. The intensive instruction soon revealed where each student stood; after a few weeks the students were redivided into four sections by skill level.[17]

Meanwhile, on the weekends the students found San Francisco a congenial city. Several had families or other relatives living in the Bay Area. San Francisco had a thriving Little Tokyo with over 6,000 inhabitants, which gave the students plenty to do with their off-duty time. Shops, bars, and restaurants welcomed Nisei soldiers; and several students owned cars.

Weckerling visited the school once or twice each day but left the day-to-day administration to Aiso.[18] After several weeks, Lt. Gen. John L. DeWitt visited the school just down the hill from his headquarters at the Western Defense Command. When Aiso was introduced as the chief instructor, DeWitt patted him on the shoulder and said "John, you're doing a good job. If there is anything I can do for you, come and see me." It was Friday, 5 December.[19]

"Now the Time Has Come To Prove Your Loyalty"

On the morning of 7 December the students slowly awoke in their hangar-barrack at Crissy Field. Sunday was their day off, so they had no reason to hurry. Five weeks had passed since classes began, and they had fallen into a routine. Some skipped breakfast to sleep late. The quiet was broken when Captain Dickey walked into the building and someone yelled, "Attention!" Dickey somberly announced: "I have just received the bad news: Japan bombed Pearl Harbor."

The Nisei were stunned. Before they could recover, Colonel Weckerling appeared and they all gathered in a classroom. "Well men, you have just heard the bad news. I sincerely sympathize with you boys on your peculiar predicament. I was in the same spot when World War I broke out, as I happen to be of German

---

[17] Harrington, *Yankee Samurai*, p. 24; Grassick, *Fourth Army Intelligence School*, pp. 26–27; "Training History," ann. 1, pp. 5–6; Ltr, Weckerling to Dusenbury, 31 December 1941.

[18] Some sources report that Dickey was the commandant between November and December 1941 and in the spring of 1942. In fact, Weckerling was the commandant and Dickey the deputy. After assisting with student selection, Rasmussen had no formal connection with the school until May 1942. Dickey and Rasmussen apparently alternated recruiting and supervision duties. See Grassick, *Fourth Army Intelligence School*, p. 8; *The Army Almanac* (Washington, D.C.: Department of the Army, 1950), p. 383.

[19] Aiso, "Observations of a California Nisei," p. 72. Intervs, Loni Ding with John F. Aiso, 1986, NJAHS; author with Aiso, 30 Oct 87. Harrington claims DeWitt made this remark to Roy Kawashiri, another student in the class, but he is probably mistaken. Harrington, *Yankee Samurai*, pp. 25–26; Roy Kawashiri autobiography, in David W. Swift, Jr., ed., "First Class," p. 15, Unpubl Ms, 2000, copy in author's files. Quote from James Matsumura, Harrington Papers.

The USS Shaw *explodes during the Japanese attack on the U.S. Pacific Fleet at Pearl Harbor.*

descent. You are free to leave if you so desire, but now the time has come to prove your loyalty and I expect each and everyone's utmost." [20]

The Nisei hardly knew what to think. Some were angry, others confused and frightened. The country of their birth was now at war with their parents' home country. How would America treat its Nisei soldiers? Their reaction, Weckerling wrote to the War Department a few weeks later, "was not unlike that of other Americans, one of surprise and shocked amazement.... [They] reacted as any American would." [21]

---

[20] Harrington, *Yankee Samurai*, p. 29; Interv, Haller with Kihara, 19 Jul 94, p. 21; Aiso, "Observations of a California Nisei," p. 73. According to the recollection of one student, Kazuo Kozaki, Weckerling did not address the students until the following Monday morning. Swift, "First Class," p. 127.

[21] Ltr, Weckerling to Dusenbury, 31 December 1941.

John Aiso, the chief instructor, left his apartment that morning for the main telegraph office. He and his fiancée were to wed the following Sunday, and he was sending her one last telegram about the arrangements. When he boarded a streetcar to return to his apartment, a woman began to scream: "Kill him! He's a Jap!" She became hysterical and shouted again and again to the other men on the streetcar: "Kill him!" No one took up her challenge, but Aiso was grateful when the streetcar stopped at the gates to the Presidio and he escaped to the relative safety of the post.[22]

The entire West Coast had flown into panic; the Western Defense Command commenced frantic preparations against air attack and sabotage. San Francisco was blacked out. Almost daily, enemy aircraft and submarines were reported to be approaching the coast. The War Department rushed troops and aircraft westward to protect the mainland.

The attack shocked Americans everywhere. Even though tensions had been growing, it came as a total surprise. Americans were quick to label it a "sneak attack." On 10 December the *Chicago Tribune* published an editorial cartoon calling for "War without Mercy on a Treacherous Foe," reflecting the emotional response of most Americans.[23]

For Japanese Americans the attack was doubly devastating. Any hope of reconciling their dual heritage was shattered, replaced by an overwhelming sense of fear and shame. A young Nisei in Hawaii later wrote: "It was like watching your older brother whom you'd believed in and loved now running wild committing murders."[24] One Nisei stationed at Fort Ord, California, recalled his feelings of "shock, bewilderment, anger, shame and sorrow. But mostly, I felt deep anguish and despair because the land that I had been taught to honor by my parents had committed an act of war against the country that I loved."[25]

The Nisei students at Crissy Field were deeply affected. Would the Army close the school? Would they be arrested or discharged? One Kibei took John Aiso aside and asked, "*Sensei* [teacher], why don't we run away now, while we have a chance?" Aiso simply told him, "We'll have to be patient."[26]

[22] Harrington, *Yankee Samurai*, p. 29; see also sources on Aiso in note 2, above. In the 1987 interview, Aiso described the woman's words differently: "There's a Jap there! Why don't you get after him? Are you people yellow or something?" Interv, author with Aiso, 30 Oct 87.

[23] Quote from John W. Dower, *War without Mercy: Race and Power in the Pacific War* (New York: Pantheon, 1986), p. 181. See also Emily S. Rosenberg, *A Date Which Will Live: Pearl Harbor in American Memory* (Durham, N.C.: Duke University Press, 2003), pp. 11–33.

[24] Milton Murayama, *All I Asking for Is My Body* (Honolulu: University of Hawaii Press, 1988), p. 83.

[25] Akiji Yoshimura, who later joined the MIS, fought in Burma with Merrill's Marauders and earned a battlefield commission. Quote from Bill Hosokawa, *Nisei: The Quiet Americans* (New York: William Morrow, 1969), pp. 229, 420.

[26] Aiso, "Observations of a California Nisei"; John F. Aiso, in *The Color of Honor*, documentary film, Loni Ding, prod., Vox Productions, 1987; Harrington, *Yankee Samurai*, p. 29; Shigeya Kihara, in *Unsung Heroes: The Military Intelligence Service, Past-Present-Future* (Seattle: MIS-Northwest Association, 1996), p. 63. The student, Kazuo Kozaki, remained at the school and went

Compounding the Nisei's fear and anger was the sense of shame. When they had been inducted into the Army, many of their Issei parents told them to bring no shame to the family. Now they could feel the angry stares of their fellow Americans. They were innocent of any crime, yet the accusations remained. If they were innocent, why were the newspapers full of the wildest rumors? How could they prove their accusers wrong? [27]

In Hawaii, as the attack continued, Nisei soldiers rushed to defend the skies and beaches. A seventeen-year-old high school student, Daniel K. Inouye, hurried through the streets of Honolulu to his civil defense station; "choking with emotion [he] looked up into the sky and called out, 'You dirty Japs!'" Hoichi "Bob" Kubo, assigned to the 298th Infantry medical section, saw the Japanese aircraft flying low over Schofield Barracks and shooting up Wheeler Field. He threw open the locker of medical supplies and began dispensing plasma, bandages, and medicines as fast as he could. The governor activated the Territorial Guard, mostly ROTC cadets at the University of Hawaii, including over 160 Nisei. The next morning at first light two Nisei soldiers spotted a Japanese midget submarine caught on a reef on Oahu's eastern shore. A story was told of two local soldiers who were manning a machine gun on a beach in Hawaii shortly after the attack. One soldier of Hawaiian ancestry asks his companion of Japanese ancestry, "If dey come, who you shoot? Dem or me?" The Nisei replies, "Who you t'ink, stupid? Me as good American as you!" [28]

The Federal Bureau of Investigation (FBI) joined with Army and Navy counterintelligence officials to seize all Japanese diplomatic and commercial personnel in Hawaii and on the mainland, together with hundreds of Japanese Association leaders, language school teachers, newspaper editors, Buddhist priests, and anyone with close ties to Japanese consulates. J. Edgar Hoover and the attorney general were confident they had headed off any threat of sabotage or espionage. Within a week the Justice Department had about 3,000 Japanese aliens in custody.[29] Out of

---

on to fight with the Australian 9th Division at Lae in New Guinea, where he became the first Nisei to receive the Silver Star.

[27] Many observers identify *haji*, or shame, as central to Japanese American culture. See Tom Kawaguchi, quoted in John Tateishi, *And Justice for All: An Oral History of the Japanese American Detention Camps* (New York: Random House, 1984), pp. 182–83. Ruth Benedict made much of the culture of shame in Japanese society based on her wartime study of Issei and Nisei. Ruth Benedict, *The Chrysanthemum and the Sword: Patterns of Japanese Culture* (Boston: Houghton Mifflin, 1989), pp. 222–27, 270–72.

[28] Hoichi Kubo, "Military Biography," Unpubl Ms, [1996], copy in author's files; Interv, author with Hoichi Kubo, 30 Oct 87. Kubo later joined the MIS and was awarded the Distinguished Service Cross in 1944. Daniel K. Inouye, *Journey to Washington* (Englewood Cliffs, N.J.: Prentice-Hall, 1967), p. 56. Inouye later served with the 442d Regimental Combat Team; after the war, he served in the U.S. House of Representatives and the U.S. Senate. Thomas D. Murphy, *Ambassadors in Arms* (Honolulu: University of Hawaii Press, 1954), frontispiece.

[29] For the initial reactions of law enforcement, see Jacobus tenBroek et al., *Prejudice, War, and the Constitution* (Berkeley: University of California Press, 1954), p. 298; Stetson Conn, "Japanese Evacuation from the West Coast," in Stetson Conn, Rose E. Engelman, and Byron Fairchild, *Guarding the United States and Its Outposts*, U.S. Army in World War II (Washington, D.C.: Office

fear, thousands of Issei burned or buried their personal papers, books, or family heirlooms, anything the local authorities might consider suspicious. Typical of the arrests was Yasuyuki Mizutari, a Japanese-language school principal and *kendo* fencing instructor in Hilo, Hawaii. His oldest son, Yukitaka Terry Mizutari, had been inducted on 12 November and was taking basic training at Schofield Barracks. The elder Mizutari was shipped to a detention center on the mainland; his son remained at Schofield Barracks.[30]

The wave of arrests did not defuse public anger directed against persons of Japanese descent living in America. The question of their loyalty, citizens or not, emerged with renewed virulence and became linked with the search for answers to the disaster. Secretary of the Navy Frank Knox flew to Hawaii and declared on 15 December, "I think the most effective Fifth Column work of the entire war was done in Hawaii with the possible exception of Norway," which the German Army had invaded in April 1940. He urged that all Japanese be removed from Oahu to one of the smaller Hawaiian Islands.

At the Fourth Army Intelligence School, classes continued with a grim new determination. Aiso considered canceling his wedding; but Captain Dickey counseled him: "John, this is going to be a long war. A man has to get married sometime." Aiso despaired how he, a Japanese American, could travel to Los Angeles. Dickey had an answer for that also. He drew up official orders so Aiso could travel to Los Angeles for "recruiting purposes." With a knowing look he added, "If you decide to get married on your leisure time, that's your business."[31]

Weckerling and Dickey knew that the Army needed their Nisei students more than ever. Weckerling was determined to protect his students and instructors alike from the wave of anger and suspicion. He had come to know these Nisei well, and he respected and trusted them. In late December the Military Intelligence Division requested his assessment of the loyalty of the Nisei soldiers in the school, telling him to "make exhaustive studies on the subject utilizing some Japanese of known loyalty." They wanted to know: "What is the loyalty of the soldier of Japanese extraction? How much can he be depended upon? Can he be entrusted with tasks other than general infantry or non-combatant services? Is he a liability in the army today and would it be far better to discharge him and not use him at all?"[32]

On New Year's Eve Weckerling sat down to compose his reply. The three weeks since Pearl Harbor had been perfectly awful for his students and himself. Worst of all was the students' agony. Since his own arrival at Fourth Army in

---

of the Chief of Military History, 1964), p. 116; "ABC List" and "Internment Camps," in *Encyclopedia of Japanese American History*, rev. ed., ed. Brian Niiya (New York: Facts on File, 2001). Roger Daniels gives the figure 3,000 in "The Forced Migrations of West Coast Japanese Americans, 1942–1946: A Quantitative Note," in *Japanese Americans: From Relocation to Redress*, rev. ed., ed. Roger Daniels et al. (Seattle: University of Washington Press, 1991), pp. 72–74.

[30] Yukitaka Mizutari was later transferred to the MIS. He was killed in action in New Guinea in June 1944 and posthumously awarded the Silver Star.

[31] Hosokawa, *Nisei*, p. 96.

[32] Ltr, Weckerling to Dusenbury, 31 December 1941.

September, he wrote, he had made an "exhaustive study" of Japanese-American soldiers, a study that was "practical rather than academic," while rushing to establish the school. As for the loyalty of the Nisei soldiers, he answered emphatically in the affirmative. Based on personal interviews and "close supervision of, and association with," the Nisei students, "as well as I could judge, I believe all to be loyal Americans, anxious and willing to serve in any task in the armed forces." [33]

But larger forces were at work. In late January 1942 Supreme Court Justice Owen J. Roberts released a report that implied that the Japanese attack may have been aided by a fifth column. Two weeks later Walter Lippmann published a widely read article entitled "The Fifth Column on the West Coast," declaring that "the Pacific Coast is in imminent danger of a combined attack from within and without." [34] Some private employers and state and local governments dismissed their Japanese American employees. On 9 February the War Department sent the Western Defense Command a telegram: "You are hereby directed to suspend all civilian employees of Japanese ancestry in your establishments, . . . and to refuse to employ any such person hereafter until further orders. . . . All passes and badges shall be removed from such employees and they shall be barred from the post, camp, or station until further notice." The Western Defense Command agreed, but asked for an exception for their Nisei instructors: "Graduates of this school will provide only available personnel for interpreters, translators and interrogators in Japanese language. Continued operation of school extremely desirable. School cannot continue present operations without Japanese civilian instructors." On 16 February the War Department agreed to allow Fourth Army to keep its instructors. [35]

Public pressure on West Coast military and civilian leaders to do something about the Japanese population became unbearable. General DeWitt, who had visited the school before the attack on Pearl Harbor, decided that nothing short of complete removal of all persons of Japanese ancestry, including the Nisei soldiers under his command, would adequately protect the region. On 19 February President Franklin D. Roosevelt signed Executive Order 9066, authorizing military commanders to designate military areas "from which any or all persons may be excluded." The provost marshal general, responsible for internal security, sent the head of the Aliens Division, Lt. Col. Karl R. Bendetsen, to the Western Defense Command to plan and supervise the evacuation of all persons of Japanese ancestry from the West Coast. [36]

---

[33] Ibid.

[34] Quote from Ronald Takaki, *Strangers from a Different Shore: A History of Asian Americans* (Boston: Little, Brown, 1989), p. 388.

[35] Folder 5, Entry 147, RG 407/360, NARA. Memo, The Adjutant General's Office (TAGO) to CG, Western Defense Command, et al., 9 Feb 42, sub: Civilian Employees of Japanese Ancestry (AG 291.2), Misc Class Material for 1942, Far Eastern Br, Ofc of the Dir of Intel G–2, RG 165, NARA.

[36] For the Army's involvement in the evacuation decision, see Stetson Conn, "Japanese Evacuation from the West Coast," in Conn, Engelman, and Fairchild, *Guarding the United States*, pp. 115–49. The War Department (WD) published the Western Defense Command (WDC) history of the evacuation in 1943 as *Final Report: Japanese Evacuation from the West Coast, 1942* (Wash-

The San Francisco Examiner
*announces the imminent removal
from the West Coast of all Japanese
Americans.*

By March the Western Defense Command began removing over 110,000 Japanese civilians from their mainland homes and packing them into temporary assembly centers at fairgrounds or racetracks. Contractors began hasty construction of ten "war relocation centers" in remote inland areas. The War Department had no interest in becoming the caretaker for such a large displaced population, so the federal government established the War Relocation Authority (WRA) to administer these camps to which all evacuees were transported that summer and autumn.[37]

For persons of Japanese ancestry in Hawaii, the situation was quite different. The commanding general declared martial law on 7 December, which historian Gary Okihiro considers "fundamentally an anti-Japanese act," one that "had been planned and was subsequently executed specifically to contain the 'Japanese problem.'" Over a thousand subversion suspects were rounded up and interned. Navy Secretary Knox urged the Army to remove all Japanese from the Hawaiian Islands, or at least from Oahu, where they numbered about 118,000, over one-third of the population. Army officials dragged their feet; the size of the affected group, combined with the acute lack of shipping, made such a move

---

ington, D.C.: Government Printing Office, 1943). *Final Report* caused controversy even within the War Department and should be used with caution in its claims of "military necessity." Peter Irons, *Justice at War: The Story of the Japanese American Internment Cases* (New York: Oxford University Press, 1983), pp. 206–18. See also Forrest C. Pogue, *George C. Marshall*, 4 vols. (New York: Viking, 1963–1987), 3: 139–47. For more recent discussions, see Roger Daniels, *Prisoners without Trial: Japanese Americans in World War II* (New York: Hill and Wang, 1993); Greg Robinson, *By Order of the President: FDR and the Internment of Japanese Americans* (Cambridge, Mass.: Harvard University Press, 2001).

[37] The appropriate term for these camps remains a matter of controversy. The WRA called them war relocation centers; however, many people today consider "relocation" a dangerous euphemism. During the war, government officials sometimes referred to them as concentration camps, a term that later became associated with the Nazi extermination camps. The Department of Justice established internment camps for enemy aliens and diplomatic personnel; many people today use that term to refer both to the camps established by the War Relocation Authority and to those established by the Department of Justice. Wherever possible, I simply use the term camps for the WRA centers, as most Japanese Americans did (and still do). For further discussion, see "Assembly Centers," "Concentration Camps," and "Internment Camps" in *Encyclopedia of Japanese American History*.

impossible.[38] In fact, about 2,000 Nisei soldiers were helping to guard Hawaii's beaches and critical facilities.

Their commanders remained wary. The Nisei ROTC cadets who had been mobilized on 7 December with the Territorial Guard were suddenly dismissed on 19 January 1942. The Nisei requested to be allowed to serve in some other capacity: "Hawaii is our home; the United States our country. We know but one loyalty and that is to the Stars and Stripes. We wish to do our part as loyal Americans in every way possible and we hereby offer ourselves for whatever service you may see fit to use us." The Army relented and organized them into a labor service unit. The 169 Nisei called themselves the Varsity Victory Volunteers and for the next year performed construction projects and general labor on the islands for the Army engineers.[39]

The threat of a Japanese attack on Midway finally provoked Army authorities to action. On 5 June more than 1,400 Nisei soldiers from two National Guard regiments were shipped to the mainland. Sgt. Hoichi Kubo, who had seen the Japanese planes attack Wheeler Field, went along, as did Pvt. Terry Mizutari, whose father had been arrested. The Hawaiians moved by rail to Camp McCoy, Wisconsin, where they began training as the 100th Infantry Battalion (Separate).[40]

On the mainland, many Nisei rushed to enlist after the Pearl Harbor attack. Many were turned away, but some were successful. In Nebraska, Ben Kuroki asked his Issei father, a potato farmer, what he should do. His father replied, "Enlist in the Army, Ben. America is your country. You fight for it." Ben and his brother drove 150 miles to the nearest recruiting station but were turned away. A few weeks later a new recruiting station opened at North Platte, and there Kuroki was enlisted into the Air Corps.[41] In Washington, Spady A. Koyama promised his mother he would not enlist until after the Christmas holidays. In early January 1942 he marched into a recruiting station. When the recruiters turned him away,

[38] Conn, "Japanese Evacuation," pp. 206–14; Gary Y. Okihiro, *Cane Fires: The Anti-Japanese Movement in Hawaii, 1865–1945* (Philadelphia: Temple University Press, 1991), pp. 195–252. Quote from p. 209.

[39] Yutaka Nakahata and Ralph Toyota, "Varsity Victory Volunteers: A Social Movement," *Social Process in Hawaii* (November 1943): 29–35; Murphy, *Ambassadors in Arms*, pp. 52–54; Franklin S. Odo, *No Sword To Bury: Japanese Americans in Hawai'i during World War II* (Philadelphia: Temple University Press, 2004); Ted T. Tsukiyama, in *We Remember Pearl Harbor: Honolulu Civilians Recall the War Years, 1941–1945*, ed. Lawrence R. Rodriggs (Newark, Calif.: Communications Concepts, ca. 1991), pp. 243–56.

[40] Murphy, *Ambassadors in Arms*, pp. 59–72; Masayo Umezawa Duus, *Unlikely Liberators: The Men of the 100th and 442nd* (Honolulu: University of Hawaii Press, 1987), pp. 11–23.

[41] Ben Kuroki earned two Distinguished Flying Crosses while flying over Europe as a B–24 gunner; he later flew missions against Japan. Ralph G. Martin, *Boy from Nebraska: The Story of Ben Kuroki* (New York: Harper & Row Brothers, 1946); "Ben Kuroki, American," *Time* (7 February 1944): 76–77; Hosokawa, *Nisei*, p. 227. Assistant Secretary of War John J. McCloy later recalled that in the first few weeks after the attack many Nisei wrote to the War Department requesting to serve. John J. McCloy, "Speech at Japanese American Dinner for Dillon S. Myer, [WRA Director]," 22 May 46; John J. McCloy Papers, Amherst College, Amherst, Mass.

he threatened to give their names to the local newspaper. Only then did they relent; he was sworn in on 8 January.[42]

Another Nisei, Dye Ogata, enlisted at Helena, Montana, in February. He had studied in Japan from 1938 to 1940 and spoke excellent Japanese. After enlisting, he heard about the language school from a friend and wrote directly to Captain Dickey, who offered him a space at the school.[43] Frank Tadakazu Hachiya, a 21-year-old college student from Hood River, Oregon, was inducted on 7 January. Hachiya had been born and raised in Oregon; but when his father inherited the family farm in Japan, his parents took him there and enrolled him in school. When his father brought him back to Oregon in February 1940, his mother and younger brother stayed behind in Japan. Hachiya completed high school and enrolled in a local college. In the autumn of 1941 he wrote a freshman essay:

I really now think and believe that living in Japan four years has done me one great good. The appreciation of America or the love of one's country. Now I don't mean I don't like Japan, but will never get so that I like her as well as America. As I was born and reared here, I am an American, though I was born of Japanese parents.... I read where some people stated that they did not fully appreciate their country until they traveled abroad. And I, too, after living across the sea, realize it now.

When asked about his mother and little brother still in Japan, he replied, "The only way I can help them is to aid in freeing Japan of the military party."[44]

In the first few weeks after Pearl Harbor, each Selective Service board made its own decisions. In Hawaii, local boards stopped inducting Nisei at once. Some boards on the mainland, particularly in the interior, continued to accept Nisei to fill their rapidly expanding quotas. In January the director of Selective Service, Brig. Gen. Lewis B. Hershey, publicly declared his intent to continue drafting Nisei and highlighted the "pressing need for solidarity."[45]

Confusion still reigned as to whether the Army would accept the Nisei. On 16 February one division commander on his own authority discharged all Nisei under his command to the Enlisted Reserve.[46] The Selective Service headquarters protested, but the War Department declined to overrule the local commander. Soon

[42] Interv, author with Spady A. Koyama, 2 Nov 87; Spady A. Koyama, MISNorCal Bio.

[43] Interv, author with Dye Ogata, 30 Oct 87; Dye Ogata, MISNorCal Bio.

[44] Hachiya later served with the MIS; he was killed in action on Leyte in January 1945 and received the Silver Star posthumously. His teacher later published his essay. Martha F. McKeown, "Frank Hachiya: He Was an American at Birth—And at Death," *Sunday Oregonian*, 20 May 45. Lyn Crost, *Honor by Fire: Japanese Americans at War in Europe and the Pacific* (Novato, Calif.: Presidio Press, 1994), pp. 207–08, cites wording that differs slightly from that in McKeown's own notes for her remarks at Hachiya's funeral on 11 September 1948.

[45] *Pacific Citizen*, Jan 42, p. 3. For example, Hiro Nishimura was drafted in February 1942. Hiro Nishimura, *Trials and Triumphs of the Nikkei* (Mercer Island, Wash.: Fukuda Publishers, 1993), p. 51.

[46] Selective Service System, *Special Groups*, Special Monograph no. 10 (Washington, D.C.: Selective Service System, 1953), p. 117.

after the evacuation was approved, the War Department directed that all Nisei soldiers be shipped out of the Western Defense Command. The Nisei soldiers were removed from their units; collected at Fort Lewis, Fort Ord, and other camps; and then shipped to army service commands in the interior. Fort Lewis alone shipped almost four hundred.[47]

At the end of March the War Department notified Selective Service that it would no longer accept "for service with the armed forces, Japanese or persons of Japanese extraction, regardless of citizenship status or other factors." On 30 March Selective Service headquarters sent out a confidential telegram to all state directors "to the effect that no more registrants of Japanese extraction would be accepted by the Army for induction. Local boards were therefore to discontinue deliveries for such purpose." The local boards reclassified all Nisei registrants and placed them into the category that seemed to best fit their circumstances, IV–C, or "enemy aliens." This was especially galling to the Nisei, who were citizens and certainly not the enemy. They considered the designation a personal insult, but under the circumstances they had little choice.[48]

Another obstacle arose in early 1942, when the War Department issued a new directive that no Japanese American soldiers were to be sent overseas. Weckerling later remarked that "the implementation of this policy would have vitiated the only feasible plan to provide qualified interpreters and translators for the Pacific theatre and would have thoroughly frustrated the efforts of the field intelligence agencies." Colonel Pettigrew in the Military Intelligence Division obtained a special exemption for the students at the Fourth Army Intelligence School. What was the point of giving them the training if they could not be sent overseas? [49]

---

[47] Stanley L. Falk and Warren M. Tsuneishi, eds., *MIS in the War against Japan* (Washington, D.C.: Japanese American Veterans Association, 1995), pp. 134–35. For discussions between December 1941 and March 1942 of what to do with Nisei soldiers on the mainland, see Enemy Aliens File, Box 23, General Robert C. Richardson, Jr., Papers, Hoover Institution Archives, Stanford University. Richardson was then commanding the Northern California Sector and U.S. Army VII Corps.

[48] Selective Service System, *Selective Service as the Tide of War Turns*, Third Report of the Director of Selective Service, 1943–1944 (Washington, D.C.: Selective Service System, 1945), pp. 241–43; Selective Service System, *Special Groups*, p. 117. Col. Pettigrew reported in November 1942 that "their induction and enlistment was stopped March 31, 1942." Murphy, *Ambassadors in Arms*, p. 108. On 14 September Selective Service headquarters finally issued a clear directive that mandated the use of Class IV–C for all registrants who were "not acceptable to the armed forces because of nationality or ancestry." Selective Service System, *Special Groups*, p. 118.

In his office files, Assistant Secretary of War McCloy, who oversaw all Japanese American issues, kept all documents dealing with Japanese Americans, including those serving in the Army, under the file label "Enemy Aliens." See Ser. 8, McCloy Papers.

Official publications of the Selective Service System identified categories by Roman numeral and letter, such as IV–C. Some later authors have used an Arabic numeral and letter, such as 4–C. I have used the former. George Q. Flynn, *The Draft, 1940–1973* (Lawrence: University Press of Kansas, 1993).

[49] Weckerling, "Japanese Americans Play Vital Role."

"Shikata Ga Nai," December 1941–May 1942

At Crissy Field, the students and instructors plunged into their work and reached deep inside themselves for the spirit to go on. John Aiso later recalled those hours: "Seldom in history has a generation of young men been so confronted with the necessity of self-examination, self-restraint, self-discipline, moral courage, and intellectual honesty. We asked ourselves ... what is the meaning of loyalty measured by legal, political, and moral criteria? Where lies the proper choice between rational decision and heartbreaking human affections?" [50] How could they go on, with such an uncertain future? They found the answer in the traditional Japanese phrase, *"Shikata ga nai."* (It cannot be helped.) With quiet resolution they buckled down to their studies with an intensity that would have surprised their Japanese-language schoolteachers in quieter days.

San Francisco was now a city at war. At night the windows were blacked out and troop convoys slipped out silently under the Golden Gate Bridge. The Nisei went into town less and less often. One evening, as two of the instructors were driving off the Presidio, a nervous young guard at the gate stopped their car. With his .45-caliber pistol drawn, he ordered them out of the car with their hands in the air. He then directed them to place their identification cards on the ground and step back. Only when he verified that they were indeed War Department civilians did he allow them to proceed. Incidents of this sort had a chilling effect. [51]

In the classrooms, the instructors knew their mission but were uncertain as to the ultimate purpose. Weckerling could not describe the duties of their graduates, because he himself did not know. He could only tell them that "it was vaguely connected with usage of Japanese in connection with American military operations in the Pacific." [52] They only knew that the course had to be intensified. They introduced some new subjects, such as sōsho, the difficult "grass writing" that turned kanji characters into mysterious scratchings. [53] About fifteen students "were relieved because of their inability to learn Japanese or their failure to receive a favorable loyalty recommendation." [54]

While the instructors continued to teach their classes, Weckerling found more instructors. When the local authorities shut down all Japanese-language newspapers, he hired two former reporters, Thomas N. Tanimoto and Tsutomu "Paul" Tekawa. Satoshi "Bud" Nagase, formerly a California-based reporter for the *Dōmei*

---

[50] Aiso, speech to veterans' reunion, 6 Sep 64, author's files.

[51] Interv, Haller with Kihara, 19 Jul 94, p. 27.

[52] "Training History," ann. 1, p. 5.

[53] Some accounts claim that originally the course was designed to be twelve months but was shortened to six after Pearl Harbor. Harrington, *Yankee Samurai*, pp. 36, 44; Thomas Sakamoto, "Original Japanese Student Reflects on MISLS Language Training," *DLIFLC Globe* (December 1996): 12. The evidence does not support this claim. One key document calls for a six-month course. Memo, Col. Rufus S. Bratton to Asst C/S [Assistant Chief of Staff], G–2, 23 Jun 41, sub: Intelligence School Fourth Army, Security-Class Gen Corresp, 1926–1946, Far Eastern Br, Ofc of the Dir of Intel G–2, RG 165, NARA.

[54] "Training History," p. 2.

radio news service, would teach a course on how to read Japanese kana radio messages. Toshio G. Tsukahira, another Kibei, had graduated the University of California at Los Angeles with a bachelor's degree in history and political science and a master's in history.[55] Tadao Yamada, a graduate of Meiji University, would develop a course on Japanese geography. After a short while, another one of the new instructors was dropped for lack of language proficiency. Although he had graduated from an American university and had made a short trip to Japan, he had not studied the language well enough to teach it.[56] Security officers also removed Bud Nagase, the former radio reporter, because of suspicions about his previous employment.[57] Weckerling built a solid group of eight civilian Nisei instructors. All were U.S. citizens with excellent Japanese-language skills and university graduates committed to preparing their students to serve in the war against Japan.

Weckerling knew that Nisei linguists alone could not meet the needs of future battlefields. Even before the war began, the Military Intelligence Division recognized that "In time of war, in many cases, officers will obtain better results in the interrogation of prisoners than enlisted personnel." With few Japanese-speaking officers and no plans to commission the Nisei enlisted men, the War Department had to train more. The Military Intelligence Division declared that "efforts should be initiated immediately for the use of every qualified Regular, Reserve, or National Guard officer who can be released from his present assignment for the course in the Japanese language." The first step was "to determine the capacity of officers who claim a knowledge of the Japanese language" and assign them to the course.[58] After Pearl Harbor, the Military Intelligence Division concluded that a Caucasian officer had to lead each team of Nisei sent to the field.[59]

In the highly charged atmosphere of suspicion, Weckerling foresaw that white commanders might have difficulty entrusting their Nisei soldiers with sensitive intelligence tasks, such as interrogating prisoners and translating captured documents on the battlefield:

Despite my confidence in the loyalty of the enlisted students enrolled in the Intelligence School, I fully realize that, when the course is completed and the students assigned as translators, interpreters or interrogators at division, corps and army headquarters, many commanders will look upon these men with suspicion, whether justified or not. I can fully sympathize with the feelings of such commanders, because the translator will be in a prime position to do great harm in the event that he is, as a matter of fact, disloyal. In the absence of white officers or soldiers, with at least a smattering of Japanese, in a position to check their actions, the G–2 will be at their mercy.

[55] Falk and Tsuneishi, *MIS in the War against Japan*, pp. 9–10, 130–31.

[56] "Training History," ann. 1, p. 4; Grassick, *Fourth Army Intelligence School*, pp. 14–21.

[57] Nagase was later rehired; he then enlisted in the Army, rose to master sergeant, and won appointment as a warrant officer in 1945. "Training History," ann. 4, Intelligence Section, p. 2.

[58] Draft Memo, MID to AG [Adjutant General], Fourth Army, 2 Dec 41, sub: Fourth Army Intelligence School, Trng Grp, Ofc of the Dir of Intel G–2, RG 165, NARA.

[59] Kai E. Rasmussen, speech, DLIFLC, Monterey, Calif., 25 Jun 77, printed in *DLIFLC Forum* (November 1977).

It is for this reason that I have been so anxious to enroll white Americans, particularly officers, in the school. Upon their graduation such personnel, of unquestioned loyalty, will be available to assign to the headquarters of divisions, corps and army. Their presence there would serve to check the actions of the Japanese translators, and relieve commanders of their apprehensions on being double-crossed by the latter. [60]

The War Department looked for white officers to serve as team leaders over the Nisei, and this policy remained in effect until almost the end of the war. Beginning in December, eighteen National Guard and Reserve officers "drifted in at odd times." Some showed promise, but most did not. One had listed on his personnel questionnaire that he had studied Japanese. Upon closer examination, he admitted that his exposure was limited to six weeks of classes, one hour per week, at the Young Men's Christian Association (YMCA). Two Chinese American reserve officers were sent to the school, but they spoke Cantonese, not Japanese.[61]

Of all these officers, only two graduated with their class. Capt. David W. Swift, son of an English teacher at Tokyo Imperial University, had been born and raised in Japan. Since 1933 he had worked as a customs inspector in the Port of San Francisco and was a captain in the Military Intelligence Reserve. After Pearl Harbor, Fourth Army loaned him for a time to Naval Intelligence for "locating certain citizens of Japanese ancestry." He was then sent to Southern California for censorship duties. On 28 December the 45-year-old reservist was ordered to the Presidio of San Francisco for a refresher course in Japanese.[62]

Capt. John A. Burden, a 41-year-old medical doctor, came from Hawaii. Burden had been born in Japan, where his American parents had both been teachers. He grew up with Japanese playmates and spoke the Tokyo dialect better than many Japanese. When he graduated from medical school during the Depression, there was little work to be found even for doctors, so he joined the Medical Reserve Corps, where he could earn $250 each summer on active duty. He soon found a job as a plantation doctor on Maui, where he served the predominantly Japanese work force. In January 1942 he received orders to the Presidio of San Francisco for a refresher language course.[63]

---

[60] Ltr, Weckerling to Dusenbury, 31 December 1941.

[61] "Training History," ann. 1, pp. 1–3. Two Caucasian officers, Burden and Swift, graduated from Crissy Field. Six others continued on to Camp Savage. Headquarters Western Defense Command and Fourth Army, Special Orders no. 127, 7 May 42, "Training History," ann. 10, Personnel Procurement Office, encl. 4. The Chinese American reserve officers were 1st Lt. Robert F. Pang and 2d Lt. Won Loy Chan. One Nisei reserve officer, 2d Lt. Roy M. Hirano, also arrived at the school during this period.

[62] David W. Swift, Sr., *Ninety Li a Day*, ed. David W. Swift, Jr., Social Life Monographs, vol. 69 (Taipei: Chinese Association for Folklore, 1975), pp. 270–73.

[63] Interv, author with John A. Burden, 5 Dec 94; Burden autobiographical notes, author's files; Interv, Loni Ding et al. with John A. Burden, 30 Sep 86, NJAHS; Harrington, *Yankee Samurai*, pp. 85–86; Arnold T. Hiura, "John Alfred Burden," *Hawaii Herald*, 2 Jul 93; Ted T. Tsukiyama, "Dr. Alfred J. [*sic*] Burden, Col.," in *Secret Valor: M.I.S. Personnel, World War II Pacific Theater, Pre–Pearl Harbor to Sept. 8, 1951*, ed. Ted T. Tsukiyama et al. (Honolulu: Military Intelligence

Second Lt. Lawrence P. Dowd had lived in Japan for three years and had studied the language. He had earned his master's degree in Oriental Studies from the University of Hawaii in 1938 and was teaching at the University of Washington.[64]

The school's leaders looked high and low for Caucasian students. When Major Dickey visited Fort Bragg, North Carolina, he interviewed Pvt. Faubion Bowers, a Julliard graduate who taught music at Hosei University before the war. Dickey welcomed him with the Japanese greeting, "*Ohayō gozai masu.*" ("Good morning.") Bowers "immediately answered in astonishment, rather homesick for the language and the country I had come to love." [65]

Other Caucasians who claimed to speak Japanese rushed to Washington, D.C., to apply for direct commissions on the basis of their language skills. The War Department commissioned some and sent them straight to Crissy Field for a refresher course. Many proved utterly incompetent in the language and caused considerable trouble for their instructors. One reserve major from Hawaii could speak some "pidgin" Japanese but didn't take his studies very seriously. An instructor finally chewed him out. "Don't talk to me like that," the student protested, "I'm a major." The instructor responded in heavily accented English, but his meaning was clear: "I don care you major, you general—I am shibirian [civilian]!" The major was soon removed from the course.[66]

The evacuation of all persons of Japanese ancestry from the West Coast made the school's location untenable. But where could they go, and who would be in charge? Colonel Weckerling stepped up to become G–2 for the Western Defense Command on 12 March, leaving Captain Rasmussen in charge of the school. Rasmussen was soon scouting for a new site. He considered moving the school to Salt Lake City, Utah, still inside the boundaries of the Western Defense Command but outside the exclusion zone.[67] At the same time, the Army was looking for places to send the evacuees. On 7 April Lt. Col. Karl R. Bendetson from the Western Defense Command and Milton Eisenhower, newly appointed director of the War Relocation Authority, met in Salt Lake City with representatives of ten western states to discuss possible sites for relocation centers. The response was overwhelmingly hostile. Almost no one was willing to accept these Japanese Americans, whether citizens or resident aliens. If the War Department wanted to move the Japanese population away from the coast, most governors felt strongly that they should not

---

Service Veterans Club of Hawaii, 1993), pp. 52–54. See also Dr. John A. Burden Papers, Hoover Institution.

[64] Dowd remained at the school for the rest of the war as adjutant. Grassick, *Fourth Army Intelligence School*, p. 12.

[65] Falk and Tsuneishi, *MIS in the War against Japan*, pp. 11–12, 94.

[66] Swift, *Ninety Li a Day*, p. 272.

[67] Memo, MID to Army Chief of Staff, 3 Apr 42, sub: Japanese Language School (352.11), Trng Grp, Ofc of the Dir of Intel G–2, RG 165, NARA.

be burdened with them. In consequence the War Relocation Authority selected ten sites, most on government property, such as Indian reservations.[68]

Since Salt Lake City was out of the question as a site for the language school, Rasmussen traveled to the Seventh Corps Area in the upper Midwest, where he met the governor of Minnesota, Harold E. Stassen. Stassen was eager to help the war effort, but his state had only one Army base, Fort Snelling in Minneapolis–St. Paul. The busy reception center was already filled to capacity. Stassen suggested a former Civilian Conservation Corps camp near the small town of Savage, about a dozen miles from Fort Snelling. The state still used the camp as a home for indigent men, but he offered to remove them. Stassen assured Rasmussen that all Minnesotans would accept the Nisei soldiers, since the state had no history of prejudice toward "Orientals." (The 1940 census counted only fifty-one residents of Japanese descent in the entire state.) Rasmussen later said the area "not only had to have room physically, but room in the people's hearts." The War Department directed the Seventh Corps Area on 7 April to provide facilities for the school, and Rasmussen hurried back to San Francisco to prepare for the move.[69]

With the change of location came a change of command alignment. Before the war began, the War Department directed the Western Defense Command to establish the school because the Military Intelligence Division could not do so itself. By the spring of 1942 the division had expanded and had its own training branch to supervise both the language school and the new Military Intelligence Training Center, which opened at Camp Ritchie, Maryland, in June 1942. Consequently, the language school would report directly to the General Staff, not to General Headquarters (GHQ) or the Western Defense Command.[70]

Another reason to move the school was to facilitate its expansion. Many more graduates would be needed. In the six months after the Pearl Harbor attack, Weckerling and his officers recruited another 150 Nisei, over twice as many as they had selected for the first class. This feat was all the more remarkable because the Selective Service System stopped accepting Nisei after February 1942 and Fourth

---

[68] War Relocation Authority, *WRA: A Story of Human Conservation* (Washington, D.C.: Government Printing Office, 1946), pp. 28–30; Conn, "Japanese Evacuation," pp. 141–42; Hosokawa, *Nisei*, pp. 338–39.

[69] Theodore C. Blegen, *Minnesota: A History of the State* (Minneapolis: University of Minnesota Press, 1963), pp. 539–49. Stassen was an anti-isolationist Republican. In March 1942 he obtained a naval reserve commission; in April 1943 he stepped down to become a naval aide to Admiral William F. Halsey. *Current Biography 1948* (New York: Wilson, 1948). In October 1945 Rasmussen told Minneapolis reporters how he selected Camp Savage. "Minnesota-Trained Nisei Act as Pacific 'Eyes, Ears' for U.S.," *Minneapolis Star-Journal*, 22 Oct 45; "Snelling's Jap Language School Proves Army Opposition Wrong," *Minneapolis Morning Tribune*, 23 Oct 45. See also Kihara's comments in Interv, Haller with Kihara, 19 Jul 94, pp. 23–24. Memo, Adjutant General to Assistant Chief of Staff (ACS), G–2, 7 Apr 42, sub: Japanese Language School (352), Trng Grp, Ofc of the Dir of Intel G–2, RG 165, NARA.

[70] For intelligence schools during World War II, see *Federal Records of World War II*, 2 vols. (Washington, D.C.: Government Printing Office, 1951), 2: 142–45; John P. Finnegan and Romana Danysh, *Military Intelligence*, Army Lineage Series (Washington, D.C.: U.S. Army Center of Military History, 1998), pp. 66–68.

Army removed all Nisei soldiers from the West Coast. Rasmussen and Dickey frantically combed the Army camps in January and February 1942, before the Nisei soldiers were removed.

At Fort Ord, Dickey interviewed Pfc. Richard Kaoru Hayashi from Stockton, California. Hayashi's eleven years in Japanese-language classes made him a good candidate, but soon after the interview all Nisei soldiers were shipped under guard from Fort Ord to Fort Leavenworth, Kansas. Two weeks later Hayashi was transferred to Camp Crowder, Missouri. In May he was ordered to Camp Savage.[71]

Dickey also interviewed Pvt. Satsuki Fred Tanakatsubo of Sacramento, California, at Fort Lewis, where the Nisei were pulling kitchen police and garbage details. Tanakatsubo refused to volunteer for language training and walked out of the interview, "since I felt the anger of being kicked around and I was not motivated to serve my obligation for this country in any shape or form." He also was shipped to Camp Crowder but a few months later received orders to Camp Savage, "though none of us knew why." [72]

In March 1942 Pfc. Roy T. Uyehata of Gilroy, California, was shipped with the other Nisei from Fort Ord to Camp Wolters, Texas, where they were assigned to garbage details, replacing the prisoners from the post stockade in the unpleasant job. In May he too was ordered to Camp Savage.[73]

Just as Rasmussen and Dickey had discovered the previous summer, most Nisei had meager Japanese-language skills. In search of language-qualified Nisei, Rasmussen even visited some of the temporary assembly centers. At the Puyallup Fairgrounds in Washington State, he interviewed Seattle-born Bill Hosokawa, a graduate of the University of Washington who had spent 1938–1941 as a journalist in the Far East. "I thought I could boast a fair speaking knowledge of the language," Hosokawa later recalled, "but he quickly proved me completely inadequate in other respects." He remembered how the colonel ended the interview "with ill-concealed disgust," saying, "Hosokawa, you'd make a helluva Jap." [74]

By the summer of 1942 Rasmussen and his officers would feel that they had exhausted the available pool of Japanese-speaking Nisei. Without authorization to recruit Nisei directly from the new internment camps, there would be no more Japanese linguists available. The War Department would have to meet the growing requirements in some other way.

In the spring of 1942 some Army commanders were removing Nisei soldiers and others were begging for Japanese linguists for their units deploying to the South Pacific. The first request came on 28 March, when the Military Intelligence Division sent an urgent radiogram to the Fourth Army G–2: "A soldier [from] your

---

[71] Richard Kaoru Hayashi, MISNorCal Bio.

[72] Satsuki Fred Tanakatsubo, MISNorCal Bio.

[73] Interv, author with Roy T. Uyehata, 16 Nov 87; Roy T. Uyehata, MISNorCal Bio.

[74] Bill Hosokawa, "Our Own Japanese in the Pacific War," *American Legion Magazine* (July 1964): 45. See also Bill Hosokawa, "The Uprooting of Seattle," in Daniels et al., *Japanese Americans: From Relocation to Redress*, pp. 18–20. Hosokawa was in the Puyallup assembly center from May to August 1942.

intelligence school of Japanese ancestry is needed to be sent with a task force to the Pacific area. Recommend name[,] organization[,] rank." [75] On 3 April MID offered the 37th Division a language team composed of "one officer (white) and 5 enlisted men (American citizens of Japanese ancestry) who will have finished a specialized course in military Japanese, interrogation and translation of Japanese documents." [76] On 7 April the War Department lifted the overseas ban for Nisei "whose loyalty is attested to by the Commanding Officer of the school after suitable investigation." Shortly afterward the school sent one of the best Kibei students, Masanori Minamoto, straight to the South Pacific, where he joined the 102d Infantry on Bora Bora.[77]

On 1 May the Fourth Army Intelligence School held a small graduation ceremony. About forty Nisei graduated, along with two Caucasian reserve officers, Swift and Burden. Because of the shortage of instructors, the best ten students were held back as instructors. Within days all others were on their way to overseas assignments.[78]

During these difficult months, over 100,000 persons of Japanese ancestry on the West Coast were being forced from their homes, including the families of all the Nisei students and instructors. In the last weeks before graduation there was "total confusion and disaster," one of the instructors recalled, with "total chaos" for Japanese communities up and down the coast.[79] Families were trying to sell their furniture and cars, close their shops, and put their property in storage. Fourth Army ordered all Japanese in San Francisco to report to collection centers in early May, just days after the school's graduation, for transport to the assembly center at Tanforan Racetrack.

All this upheaval caused considerable confusion and frustration. One Issei farmer whose Nisei son was serving in the Army told a reporter: "They took my boy to the army, and now they take my other children to a concentration camp." A Nisei soldier told another reporter: "They are evacuating all the Japanese from the Coast and even trying to take away our citizenship. I don't know why I am in

---

[75] Radiogram, Kroner, MID, to ACS, G–2, Fourth Army, 28 Mar 42, Restricted, Secret and Confidential Msgs—Outgoing, Security-Class Gen Corresp, 1926–1946, Far Eastern Br, Ofc of the Dir of Intel G–2, RG 165, NARA.

[76] Memo, MID to ACS, G–2, 37th Division, 3 Apr 42, sub: Japanese Interrogators and Translators (350.03), Trng Grp, Ofc of the Dir of Intel G–2, RG 165, NARA.

[77] Memo, Adjutant General to ACS, G–2, 7 Apr 42, sub: Japanese Language School (352), Trng Grp, Ofc of the Dir of Intel G–2, RG 165, NARA. See also Interv, author with Kaneko, 23 Aug 95. Harrington incorrectly identifies Kiyoshi Kaye Sakamoto as an early graduate, perhaps confusing him with Minamoto. Harrington, *Yankee Samurai*, pp. 31, 70–71; Swift, "First Class," pp. 273–75. Some sources give Minamoto's first assignment as Tongatabu.

[78] Sources differ on the number of Nisei graduates, but most researchers agree on 40 as most likely. *MISLS Album* lists 40 Japanese names (p. 125), although the text says 43, not counting the 2 Caucasian officers (p. 9). "Training History" says 36 (p. 2), probably omitting the 10 held over as instructors. A few pages later (p. 16) a table says 45. "Training History," ann. 1, p. 5, para. 6, says 45. Swift, who has conducted the most detailed research, can identify only 40. Swift, "First Class."

[79] Interv, Haller with Kihara, 19 Jul 94, pp. 22–23, 26–27.

A Nisei soldier on leave from Camp Leonard Wood, Missouri, has returned to California to help his mother prepare for removal.

the Army. I want to see democracy as it is supposed to be, but this is getting just as bad as Hitler." Another Nisei soldier was taking basic training when one of his tent mates, an Italian American, told him: "If they did that to my family, I wouldn't serve in this god-damn army."[80]

Meanwhile, the Navy was having its own problems training Caucasian officer candidates in Japanese at Harvard and Berkeley. After Pearl Harbor, Navy commanders began begging for linguists, so the Office of Naval Intelligence began planning to double its language training program. But the expansion would take time. The Marine Corps demanded Japanese linguists, but the Office of Naval Intelligence responded that all the students were already earmarked for naval assignments. The best they could offer was sixty linguists from the class that would graduate in June 1943, more than a year away.[81]

---

[80] Alexander H. Leighton, *The Governing of Men: General Principles and Recommendations Based on Experience at a Japanese Relocation Camp* (Princeton: Princeton University Press, 1945), p. 27; Moffett Ishikawa, in Harrington Papers.

[81] For the Navy language programs, see "Reminiscences of Rear Admiral Arthur H. McCollum, U.S. Navy Retired," 2 vols., Unpubl Ms, 1970–1971; Office of the Chief of Naval Operations (CNO),

In February 1942 Lt. Comdr. Albert E. Hindmarsh and Glenn W. Shaw traveled to Berkeley and Cambridge to inspect their two contract programs. At the University of California they were pleased with Florence Walne's classes. But at Harvard, despite the onset of war, Serge Elisséeff frustrated any attempts to change his teaching methods. The officers complained of "a continuing reluctance to recognize the practical needs of the Naval Service and constant underhanded criticism of the whole idea of intensified training because it did not conform to the usual academic set-up as exemplified in the leisurely and highly theoretical teaching of Professor Elisséeff." [82]

Deciding to put all his eggs in one basket, Hindmarsh sent the next batch of forty-seven students to the University of California, where they arrived on 22 February. Walne quickly hired additional instructors, including some Korean Americans who spoke Japanese with a distinctive Korean accent (Korea had been under Japanese rule since 1910), and pressed forward with her practical, rapid-fire program. When the University of Washington closed its Japanese department that spring, she absorbed three of the instructors.[83]

The Navy's program in Berkeley faced the same problem as the Army's at Crissy Field. Though the students were Caucasian, many of their instructors were Nisei. When the Western Defense Command announced the evacuation of Japanese from the West Coast, the Office of Naval Intelligence first requested through the War Department Military Intelligence Division to allow their school to move a short distance, "as close as possible to Berkeley," so the University of California could continue to operate the program. By this point Walne had eight Nisei teachers on staff and the school was continuing to expand. That spring Hindmarsh and Shaw recruited over 150 more Caucasian students and Walne identified 20 more Japanese Americans as instructors.[84] But Fourth Army insisted that no person of Japanese ancestry could remain in the exclusion areas, even for important defense work. Thus, at the end of May, Hindmarsh visited the University of Colorado at Boulder. The university already had a Naval ROTC program, and a few weeks earlier Colorado's governor had been the only western governor to agree to accept

---

"School of Oriental Languages," Unpubl Ms. Both at Naval Historical Center, Washington, D.C.

   [82] Office of the CNO, "School of Oriental Languages," p. 13. The two programs differed in cost as well: Harvard charged the Navy $900 per year per student, the University of California $600. The Navy sent no more students to Harvard and let the contract expire in September 1942.

   [83] Ibid. "Reminiscences of Rear Admiral Arthur H. McCollum," p. 286. Several students who studied Japanese at Berkeley in 1941–1942, such as Otis Cary, Donald Keene, and William T. De Bary, later became leading Japan scholars. See Otis Cary, ed., *From a Ruined Empire: Letters—Japan, China, Korea 1945–46* (New York: Kodansha, 1975); Donald Keene, *On Familiar Terms: A Journey across Cultures* (New York: Kodansha, 1994), pp. 14–20.

   [84] Memo, Vice CNO to Bureau of Naval Personnel, 21 May 42, sub: Transfer of Navy Japanese Language Course out of Military Area No. 1 to Military Area No. 2, California, in Scott E. Nadler, *The Evolution of Foreign Language Training in the Armed Forces* (Washington, D.C.: Defense Language Institute, 1972), pp. 123–24. This states that eight of the eleven instructors were Japanese, as does a telegram from OP–16–F–2 dated 28 May 1942 (p. 121); "American Born Japanese Teach at Navy School," *Pacific Citizen*, 9 Jul 42, p. 2.

Japanese evacuees. The university president immediately agreed to accept the Navy school. On 23 June the students and staff moved to Colorado. The next group of 153 students arrived at Boulder on 1 July.[85]

Another government agency, William J. Donovan's Coordinator of Information (predecessor of the Office of Strategic Services), ran into similar problems. In May Donovan appealed to the Secretary of War for permission to keep six Nisei in San Francisco as translators and announcers for radio broadcasts directed at Japan. Assistant Secretary of War John J. McCloy rejected his appeal: "In concluding against exemptions, General DeWitt has removed his own Japanese-language school to the interior. He feels that language school teachers and Japanese-language broadcast translators can function as effectively behind the coastal frontier as they do in San Francisco or elsewhere along the coast." [86]

Disasters at Home and Overseas, Spring 1942

The world had changed dramatically since the Nisei began their classes. America was at war. The military and naval forces of Imperial Japan ranged at will to the south, east, and west, capturing the colonial possessions of Britain, France, the Netherlands, and the United States. Singapore, the linchpin of British defenses in the Far East, fell on 15 February. On 23 February President Franklin D. Roosevelt gave his first wartime "fireside chat" to the nation and recalled the Continental Army's dark days at Valley Forge. On the same day, as if to underscore the threat, a Japanese submarine shelled an oil refinery at Santa Barbara, California.

The Japanese seemed to be winning on all fronts as starving Filipino and American defenders of Bataan surrendered on 9 April. The two Nisei who had been sent from Hawaii to Manila one year earlier, Sgts. Arthur S. Komori and Richard M. Sakakida, fought valiantly on Bataan and then were transferred to Corregidor, where they translated captured documents, interrogated prisoners, and monitored radio transmissions. On 13 April Komori was evacuated by air to Australia, but Sakakida remained behind. When Corregidor surrendered on 6 May, he fell into Japanese hands.[87]

---

[85] Office of the CNO, "School of Oriental Languages," pp. 12–14; "Reminiscences of Rear Admiral Arthur H. McCollum," pp. 285–89, 458; "American Born Japanese Teach at Navy School."

[86] Ltr, John J. McCloy to William J. Donovan, 14 May 1942, reprinted in *American Concentration Camps: A Documentary History of the Relocation and Incarceration of Japanese Americans, 1941–1945*, 9 vols., ed. Roger Daniels (New York: Garland, 1989), vol. 5. See also Ltr, McCloy to Donovan, 23 May 1942, in which McCloy states "we are moving our own Japanese school to Denver." X-OSS, Class Ref Subj File, 1940–1947, Ofc of the Asst Sec of War, RG 107, NARA.

[87] Ann Bray, "Undercover Nisei," in *Military Intelligence: Its Heroes and Legends* (Arlington Hall Station, Va.: U.S. Army Intelligence and Security Command, 1987), pp. 34–37; Duval A. Edwards, *Spy Catchers of the U.S. Army in the War with Japan* (Gig Harbor, Wash.: Red Apple Publishing, 1994), pp. 51–54; Harrington, *Yankee Samurai*, pp. 65–67; Richard M. Sakakida and Wayne S. Kiyosaki, *A Spy in Their Midst: The World War II Struggle of a Japanese American Hero* (Lanham, Md.: Madison Books, 1995), pp. 67–115.

The Nisei who graduated from the Fourth Army Intelligence School in May 1942 faced a situation very different from six months earlier. Now their families were confined in guarded assembly centers. Many brothers and buddies with whom they had enlisted were pulling kitchen police and garbage details in far-off Army posts in the Midwest. The graduates quietly said their farewells, and about two dozen shipped off to points unknown.

Shortly after the graduation, the staff, instructors, and remaining graduates packed up and set out for Minnesota, most by automobile. Eleven officers, twenty-four enlisted men, and eight civilian instructors made the trip (some enlisted men traveled by train). The civilian instructors were allowed to bring their families, so John Aiso brought his wife of five months. Each automobile carrying Nisei was accompanied by a Caucasian officer for their protection.[88] A few weeks later the Western Defense Command declared to the public that all Nisei soldiers had been removed from the West Coast, "cautioning citizens to be on the alert for Japanese persons wearing U.S. Army uniforms in the Pacific Coast combat zone. General DeWitt noted that by then all American-born Japanese in the U.S. Army had been removed from the Western Defense Command and the Fourth Army and transferred to interior posts." [89] The Matson liner SS *Maui* slipped into port in Oakland, California, on 12 June, bearing the 1,400 Nisei of the Hawaiian Provisional Infantry Battalion. They were hurried onto blacked-out trains and spirited away to Camp McCoy, Wisconsin, with no public notice.

. . .

By June 1942 there was little cause for hope for Americans of Japanese ancestry. On the mainland, 117,000 people languished in the assembly centers awaiting transport to the camps. In Hawaii, only a few hundred were detained, but all others were placed under surveillance. With the exception of the 169 Varsity Victory Volunteers, all civilians of Japanese ancestry were barred from the war effort; though they remained a significant portion of the local labor force.

Two other bright spots remained, as yet out of the public eye. First, at Camp McCoy, the Nisei soldiers in the newly designated 100th Infantry Battalion began training to fight, not as a labor service unit, as they had feared, but as combat infantrymen. Second, at Camp Savage, 150 Nisei began Japanese-language classes in June. The Military Intelligence Service's Nisei were all citizens, and their loyalty had been carefully investigated. However, the question remained how well they would fight against the Japanese. Eventual success in the war against Japan and in their acceptance into the mainstream of American society hung in the balance.

---

[88] HQ, Western Defense Command and Fourth Army, Special Orders no. 127, 7 May 42, in "Training History," ann. 10, encl. 4.

[89] "Nisei Soldiers Removed from Western Zone," *Pacific Citizen*, 11 Jun 42.

3

MIS Nisei Pioneers,
May 1942–February 1943

Beginning in May 1942, Nisei graduates of the Fourth Army Intelligence School served in the early campaigns against Japanese forces from Alaska to Guadalcanal to Papua New Guinea. Until then, using Nisei as interpreters and translators against the Japanese was an untested concept. However, the initial results were so positive the War Department quickly increased the size of the school. Furthermore, the War Department decided to allow Nisei volunteers to serve in two all-Nisei combat units, the 100th Infantry Battalion and the 442d Regimental Combat Team (RCT), which saw action in Italy and France from 1943 to 1945.

On 1 May 1942, the Fourth Army Intelligence School held its first graduation ceremony at Crissy Field for forty Nisei enlisted men and two reserve officers who had completed the six-month course in Japanese. When the class began, their country was at peace. Now America was at war, and San Francisco was still blacked out as a precaution against air raids. The city's several thousand individuals of Japanese ancestry were waiting for the Western Defense Command to remove them to a temporary assembly area at the Tanforan racetrack.

The Nisei graduates did not know whether they would be sent to Tanforan or somewhere else. From December 1941 to May 1942, America had suffered a string of overseas disasters unprecedented in the nation's history. The Nisei's families faced an equally unprecedented series of disasters, culminating in their wholesale removal from the coast. What would be the fate of Nisei already in uniform? Would the Army place them in special camps or labor service units, or would they get a chance to prove themselves? If they turned their thoughts from their families to the world situation, there was still little to reassure them. Several weeks before graduation, one of their fellow students, Masanori Minamoto, shipped out and had not been heard from since. Shortly after graduation, orders arrived for most of the class; they boarded transports for destinations unknown.

In the Philippines, even America's best-known soldier, General Douglas MacArthur, could not hold back the Japanese onslaught. His air forces had been destroyed on the ground. The American and Filipino defenders of Bataan had surrendered in April; those on Corregidor would soon follow. The British, French, and Dutch empires had folded like houses of cards. Japanese forces threatened India and Australia and pressed toward U.S. territories in the Aleutian and Hawaiian island chains. Lt. Col. James H. Doolittle and Army Air Corps fliers had just staged a daring raid on Japanese cities on 18 April. Japanese retaliation was expected at any moment somewhere in Hawaii, Alaska, or the West Coast.

In the weeks ahead, America would narrowly win its first victories in the Battles of the Coral Sea and Midway. In both cases, a handful of Navy intelligence specialists would use their ingenuity to help turn the tide. These intelligence victories were won with only a handful of Japanese linguists, none of them Japanese Americans.

American commanders were desperate for reliable information on the enemy's next moves. Where would he strike next? What forces would he bring to bear? The Fourth Army Intelligence School's graduates, men who could help answer those questions, would amount to more than half of all Japanese linguists in the Army and Navy. They were ready to go wherever the need was greatest.

During the last weeks before graduation, staff officers in the Far Eastern Branch of the Military Intelligence Division (MID) allocated the precious graduates. Lt. Col. Moses W. Pettigrew offered the Nisei to various interested headquarters. In April MID offered one Caucasian language officer and five Nisei enlisted men to the 37th Division preparing for deployment to the South Pacific. MID assured the division, "All enlisted men have been checked for loyalty, and all come from families having no close relatives in Japan, and it is believed that they will be found both useful and trustworthy."[1]

MID was leery of promising too much, since it had barely three dozen graduates to dispatch. Of the fifty-eight Nisei selected for training, only forty completed the course. Caucasian students had fared even worse: Several dozen from the Regular Army, Officers' Reserve Corps, and National Guard came to Crissy Field claiming some knowledge of the language; but only two finished the course that spring. When the Western Defense Command ordered all Japanese removed from the West Coast, the school had to relocate. With ten graduates held back as enlisted instructors, only thirty Nisei remained available for field duty.

---

[1] Ltr, MID to Assistant Chief of Staff (ACS), G–2, 37th Div, 3 Apr 42, sub: Japanese Interrogators and Translators, MID 350.03, Trng Grp, Ofc of the Dir of Intel G–2, Record Group (RG) 165, National Archives and Records Administration (NARA).

Colonel Pettigrew and his Far Eastern Branch made tough choices based on their appreciation of the strategic situation in May 1942. No Nisei deployed to Hawaii, where the threat was greatest. Instead, they went to Alaska, Australia, and the South Pacific. Five Nisei went to the Alaska Defense Command. A Caucasian officer with eight Nisei went to Australia, where MacArthur was establishing General Headquarters (GHQ), Southwest Pacific Area. MID sent the rest to the South Pacific: an officer and three Nisei to Fiji with the 37th Infantry Division and six Nisei to New Caledonia. Their job was to help stop Japanese forces from cutting the tenuous lifeline from the United States to Australia and New Zealand.[2]

The shortage of Japanese-language specialists in the United States remained critical. *Life* magazine claimed in September 1942 that fewer than 100 Caucasians in America could speak or read Japanese. The author asserted: "One of the most troublesome war shortages faced by the U.S. since Pearl Harbor has been the acute lack of non-Japanese American citizens who understand the Japanese language. Various Government agencies have been combing the country for months trying to find men and women qualified to serve as interpreters, code-room assistants and censors. The results of this hunt have been depressing." Counting individuals "with full command of the language," the author reported that "the most optimistic estimates from Washington put the number at less than 100 persons." This number obviously did not include Americans of Japanese ancestry.[3] The outbreak of war precipitated a flood of popular literature about Japan that often stressed the difficulty of the language. "Our difficulties in [understanding the Japanese Army]," one such book declared, "are greatly increased by the inscrutable Jap language which, to all intents and purposes, denies us access to the Japanese military literature."[4]

Intelligence in Hawaii: Pearl Harbor to Midway

After the Crissy Field graduation, none of the Nisei linguists deployed to the point of greatest danger—Hawaii. In fact, in May 1942 the Hawaiian Department was planning to send away most of its Nisei soldiers. Army and Navy intelligence officers in Hawaii had worked out a division of effort: The Navy would defend against further external attack, while the Army would counter any internal threat of espionage or sabotage. Naval intelligence thus would focus on the Japanese fleet, while Army intelligence would focus on the local Japanese population. Neither requested Nisei for language work.

---

[2] Unless otherwise indicated, assignment information is based on Military Intelligence Service Language School (MISLS), Disposition of Graduates, Trng Grp, Ofc of the Dir of Intel G–2, RG 165, NARA.

[3] Francis S. Wickware, "The Japanese Language," *Life* (7 September 1942): 58–65. See also the letters in response published in the 28 September issue.

[4] Wickware, "Japanese Language"; Lt. Col. Paul W. Thompson et al., *How the Jap Army Fights* (Washington, D.C.: Infantry Journal Press, 1942).

Naval intelligence in Hawaii included a small signals intelligence capability, the Combat Intelligence Unit under Cmdr. Joseph J. Rochefort. Later renamed the Fleet Radio Unit, Pacific (FRUPAC), this unit was already working in the secret world of communications intelligence.[5] Both Rochefort and Lt. Cmdr. Edwin T. Layton, the Pacific Fleet intelligence officer, had previously studied in Tokyo as language attachés. Rochefort already had several naval officers in FRUPAC who could read Japanese messages, though the volume of intercepted messages was still low. Rochefort sent individual language officers to accompany early aircraft-carrier raids against Japanese naval bases, beginning with the raid on Kwajalein in the Marshall Islands on 1 February 1942. The 14th Naval District intelligence officer had one trusted Nisei on staff, Hawaii-born Douglas T. Wada, who worked in counterintelligence; but the Navy did not use him for combat intelligence. Among naval intelligence personnel were five Caucasian language officers who had been withdrawn from Tokyo in November 1941. More language officers were in training on the mainland, but the first would not arrive in Hawaii until February 1943, fourteen months after the Pearl Harbor attack.[6]

Army leaders in Hawaii were more inclined to trust the Hawaii Japanese, especially the Nisei. This may have been due in part to their positive experiences with Nisei soldiers drafted in Hawaii since 1940. Even before that, in the 1920s and 1930s, many Nisei boys trained in the ROTC program at McKinley High School in Honolulu and many others earned reserve commissions through the ROTC at the University of Hawaii. The Hawaiian Department G–2 employed one Nisei, Gero Iwai, in counterintelligence. Immediately after the start of the war, Selective Service boards in Hawaii suspended inductions of Nisei. By that point the Hawaiian Department already had 2,000 Nisei in uniform. After the attack, local commanders deployed their soldiers, including the Nisei, to guard landing sites and critical public facilities. However, when sufficient reinforcements arrived from the mainland over the next few months, the Hawaiian Department shipped more than 1,400 Nisei soldiers to the mainland on 5 June 1942 to form the 100th

---

[5] ACS for Intelligence, Commander in Chief, Pacific Ocean Area, Rpt of Intelligence Activities in the Pacific Ocean Areas, 15 Oct 45. Alan H. Bath, *Tracking the Axis Enemy: The Triumph of Anglo-American Naval Intelligence* (Lawrence: University Press of Kansas, 1998); W. J. Holmes, *Double-Edged Secrets: U.S. Naval Intelligence Operations in the Pacific during World War II* (Annapolis, Md.: Naval Institute Press, 1979); Edwin T. Layton, *"And I Was There": Pearl Harbor and Midway—Breaking the Secrets* (New York: William Morrow, 1985); Ronald Lewin, *The American Magic: Codes, Ciphers and the Defeat of Japan* (New York: Farrar Straus Giroux, 1982); Frederick D. Parker, *A Priceless Advantage: U.S. Navy Communications Intelligence and the Battles of Coral Sea, Midway, and the Aleutians*, United States Cryptologic History, ser. IV, World War II (Fort Meade, Md.: National Security Agency, 1993), vol. 5; John Prados, *Combined Fleet Decoded: The Secret History of American Intelligence and the Japanese Navy in World War II* (New York: Random House, 1995), pp. 223–335; Edward Van Der Rhoer, *Deadly Magic: A Personal Account of Communications Intelligence in World War II in the Pacific* (New York: Charles Scribner's Sons, 1978); John Winton, *Ultra in the Pacific: How Breaking Japanese Codes & Cyphers Affected Naval Operations against Japan, 1941–45* (Annapolis, Md.: Naval Institute Press, 1993).

[6] Holmes, *Double-Edged Secrets*, pp. 36–37, 57–58; Prados, *Combined Fleet Decoded*, pp. 287–88.

Infantry Battalion (Separate). The Nisei soldiers who remained in Hawaii worked in engineer and other noncombat units.

For more than a year after the Pearl Harbor attack, Army and Navy intelligence officers in Hawaii struggled to meet growing demands for Japanese-language work without using the thousands of Nisei citizens on the islands. When the Imperial Japanese Navy struck at Midway in June, FRUPAC played a critical role in the narrow victory with its brilliant cryptographers and a handful of Japanese linguists, none of them Nisei. During the battle, the U.S. Navy captured about thirty Japanese sailors and aviators whom Caucasian language officers interrogated.[7] Shortly afterward the Navy organized the Intelligence Center Pacific Ocean Areas, which included some Caucasian Japanese linguists but no Nisei.

Intelligence in Alaska: Defending the Aleutian Islands

The Western Defense Command, which directly controlled the Fourth Army Intelligence School, was an active theater of war. In the spring of 1942 Lt. Gen. John L. DeWitt and his staff were planning two major operations: the removal of all Japanese Americans from the West Coast and the defense of Alaska. The Western Defense Command requested five Nisei for the Alaska Defense Command. On 12 May Sgt. Yoshio Hotta led four other Nisei to Anchorage; from there, they dispersed to other bases in Alaska and the Aleutians. In early June a Japanese naval task force approached the Aleutians, and on 3 and 4 June Japanese aircraft raided Dutch Harbor, killing forty-three American soldiers and sailors. At least one Nisei linguist, Henry Suyehiro, witnessed the attack but was unhurt. One week later U.S. Navy reconnaissance aircraft discovered that the Japanese had landed on the fog-bound islands of Attu and Kiska, much farther to the west along the Aleutian chain.

The five Nisei sat out the next few months in Alaska, where their major task was keeping warm. They had no prisoners to interrogate and few documents to translate, including those confiscated from the handful of Japanese settlers in the region. Throughout the autumn and winter the Nisei waited for an enemy who never came. A few weeks later the Americans located a Japanese Zero fighter plane that had crash-landed near Dutch Harbor and called on Sergeant Hotta to help investigate the wreckage.[8] Meanwhile, the Western Defense Command removed all civilians of Japanese ancestry from Alaska, 230 in all, and about 900 Aleuts. American offensive operations had to wait until the following spring to drive the

---

[7] Prados, *Combined Fleet Decoded*, pp. 328, 495; Holmes, *Double-Edged Secrets*, pp. 122–23.

[8] Henry Suyehiro, in David W. Swift, Jr., ed., "First Class," Unpubl Ms, 2000, copy in author's files; Brian Garfield, *The Thousand Mile War: World War II in Alaska and the Aleutians* (Garden City, N.Y.: Doubleday, 1969), pp. 41–42; James S. Russell, "A Zero Is Found Bottom Up in a Bog," in *The Pacific War Remembered*, ed. John T. Mason (Annapolis, Md.: Naval Institute Press, 1986), pp. 108–11; Jim Rearden, *Cracking the Zero Mystery* (Harrisburg, Pa.: Stackpole, 1990); John Toland, *The Rising Sun: The Decline and Fall of the Japanese Empire, 1936–1945* (New York: Random House, 1970), p. 499.

Japanese from American soil. American reinforcements continued to pour into the region, including fifteen more Nisei enlisted graduates who arrived in December 1942 and January 1943 with three Caucasian language officers.

Intelligence in the South Pacific Area: The Guadalcanal Campaign

In the spring of 1942 the South Pacific was the point of greatest risk for the Allied cause, as the United States struggled to keep open the lines of communication with Australia and New Zealand. MID sent some of the first Nisei graduates to this region and to Australia. Naval intelligence officers were groping in the dark, hoping somehow to provide advance warning of the next Japanese attack. From aerial reconnaissance covering thousands of square miles of open ocean, they tracked the Imperial Japanese Navy. They gathered information about possible landing sites from travel literature and by interviewing former residents. They established a tenuous network of "coast watchers," Australian and New Zealand civilians who had worked in the region before the war. They relied on naval intelligence in Hawaii for radio intelligence. In May the Japanese landed forces on Tulagi and Guadalcanal in the Solomon Islands and began constructing airfields. This was the advance the Allies had feared. American commanders began planning for a counteroffensive.

In April 1942 the Fourth Army Intelligence School sent the first Nisei, Masanori Minamoto, to the South Pacific. Minamoto, who had spent many years in Japan before the war, went to the 102d Infantry (Bobcat Task Force) at Bora Bora. (*Map 2*) He found little in the way of any intelligence setup and little language work to do, with no prisoners to interrogate and no captured documents to translate. With no officer to give him assignments, he was detailed to drive a truck.[9]

After graduation, Sgt. Mac N. Nagata led five other Nisei to the South Pacific, departing San Francisco on 7 May. They joined the Americal Division at Noumea, New Caledonia, on 10 June. The colonial French port was rapidly becoming the hub of U.S. military operations in the region. In July the Commander, South Pacific (COMSOPAC), established his headquarters there. The sergeant who picked up the Nisei at the dock told them that the truck had to remain covered because their presence in New Caledonia had to remain secret. At first the Nisei had little to do except pull guard duty around division headquarters and watch the American movies each week. They translated occasional Japanese letters, magazines, and books confiscated from the handful of Japanese residents in the region. Their first prisoner was a downed Japanese pilot in June. That autumn Admiral William F. Halsey summoned two Nisei to interrogate six downed Japanese pilots. Their

---

[9] Joseph D. Harrington, *Yankee Samurai: The Secret Role of Nisei in America's Pacific Victory* (Detroit: Pettigrew Enterprises, 1979), pp. 31, 70–71; *The Pacific War and Peace: Americans of Japanese Ancestry in Military Intelligence Service, 1941 to 1952* (San Francisco: Military Intelligence Service Association of Northern California/National Japanese American Historical Society, 1991), p. 17. Harrington mistakes K. K. Sakamoto for Minamoto; Tateshi Miyasaki recalls that Minamoto was on Tongatabu.

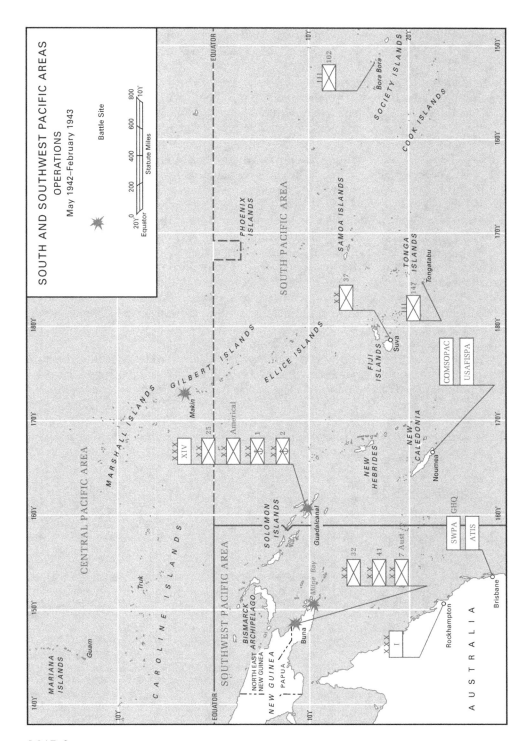

SOUTH AND SOUTHWEST PACIFIC AREAS

OPERATIONS

May 1942–February 1943

✳ Battle Site

Statute Miles

0 200 400 600 800

MAP 2

faces were badly burned, and only two could open their mouths enough to speak. The Nisei questioned the injured pilots but could find out only one or two of their names. Those who could talk would only whisper, "Kill me." Halsey was disappointed and unleashed his fury on the Nisei: "Goddamn you bastards; what in the goddamn hell did the government send you to school for?"[10]

The three Nisei assigned to the 37th Division had considerable trouble linking with their unit. The division was stationed at Fort Indiantown Gap, Pennsylvania, when the Nisei's orders arrived, so they took a train from San Francisco to Harrisburg, Pennsylvania, where a friendly military policeman gave them a ride to the post. When the Nisei arrived, the division had already left for the West Coast, so the Nisei were arrested for being absent without leave. The next day they convinced the authorities of their identities and took a train back to San Francisco, where they caught up with the division just in time to board the SS *President Coolidge*, departing on 25 May for the long, zigzag voyage to Fiji.[11]

Capt. John A. Burden, one of the first two Caucasian graduates of the school, accompanied the three Nisei overseas. Having been born in Japan, Burden spoke excellent Japanese.[12] In Fiji, as in New Caledonia, the linguists found no prisoners to interrogate and no captured documents to translate. Burden became the division counterintelligence officer and used the Nisei and ten other soldiers to help monitor the main telephone switchboard. He also assigned the Nisei to monitor Japanese shortwave-radio news broadcasts.[13]

At this point, Army and Navy intelligence officers were desperate for any scraps of information about the enemy. In August two submarines carried a marine raiding party to Makin in the Central Pacific to uncover Japanese intentions. Among the raiders who lost their lives in the effort was their Japanese-language officer, Capt. Gerald P. Holtom, a marine who had been born in Japan. The raiders returned to Hawaii with large quantities of captured documents, which

[10] Ltr, Roy Kawashiri to Joseph Harrington, 7 December 1977, Kawashiri File, Joseph D. Harrington Papers, National Japanese Historical Society (NJAHS), San Francisco, Calif.; Harrington, *Yankee Samurai*, pp. 31, 108–09; Ltr, Isao Kusuda to Joseph Harrington, [1977?], Harrington Papers; Shigeru Yamashita, Biography, Military Intelligence Service Club of Northern California (this and similar biographies hereafter cited as MISNorCal Bios). Jim Masaru Ariyasu, in Swift, "First Class," p. 12.

[11] Tateshi Miyasaki, MISNorCal Bio.

[12] Intervs, Joseph Harrington with John Burden, 11 Dec 77, Harrington Papers; Loni Ding, Eric Saul, and Shigeya Kihara with John Burden, 30 Sep 86, NJAHS; author with John Burden, 5 Dec 94. John Burden autobiography, Unpubl Ms, 1992, copy in author's files; Arnold T. Hiura, "MIS Profile: John Alfred Burden," *Hawaii Herald*, 2 Jul 93; Ted T. Tsukiyama, "Dr. Alfred J. [*sic*] Burden, Col.: MIS Pioneer," in Ted T. Tsukiyama et al., eds., *Secret Valor: M.I.S. Personnel, World War II Pacific Theater, Pre–Pearl Harbor to Sept. 8, 1951* (Honolulu: Military Intelligence Service Veterans Club of Hawaii, 1993), pp. 52–55; Lyn Crost, *Honor by Fire: Japanese Americans at War in Europe and the Pacific* (Novato, Calif.: Presidio Press, 1994), pp. 47–53; John Burden Papers, Hoover Institution Archives, Stanford University, Stanford, Calif.

[13] Harrington, *Yankee Samurai*, pp. 85–86; Miyasaki, MISNorCal Bio; Duval A. Edwards, *Spy Catchers of the U.S. Army in the War with Japan* (Gig Harbor, Wash.: Red Apple Publishing, 1994), pp. 59–60.

Caucasian language officers eagerly translated and studied. Capt. Ellis M. Zacharias, U.S. Navy, deputy director of Naval Intelligence, later called this "the first major haul as far as enemy documents were concerned." The materials included "plans, charts and battle orders, including one top-secret map which revealed the exact air defenses of all Japanese Pacific islands, the strength of the air forces stationed on them, their radius, methods of alert, types of planes used—and above all, operational plans for any future emergency."[14]

On 7 August the 1st Marine Division landed on Tulagi and Guadalcanal in the Solomon Islands. At the time the marines had only a handful of Japanese-speaking officers. A few officers and enlisted marines had taken a six-month course at San Diego, but they had no Nisei linguists. In any event, the marines took few prisoners on Guadalcanal and got little useful information from the ones they did.[15] Their unwillingness to take prisoners was reinforced early in the battle, on 12 August, when the division intelligence officer, Lt. Col. Frank B. Goettge, led a patrol behind Japanese lines. The Japanese ambushed the patrol, and survivors told of watching Japanese soldiers execute the wounded marines they had left behind. The story was widely told among American military personnel, who believed that it proved Japanese treachery.[16] This racial hatred soon spread to most Americans in the Pacific Theater.[17] Goettge died in the ambush, as did a marine language officer, 1st Lt. Ralph Cory. Until a just few months before, Cory had worked in OP–20–G, Navy signals intelligence, in Washington and thus was familiar with recent American cryptologic successes. Only a desperate shortage of linguists might explain why the marines allowed such an important intelligence officer to accompany a high-risk combat patrol. His capture might have alerted the Japanese that the Americans were reading their highest level diplomatic messages.[18]

Back in New Caledonia, the six Nisei supported the marines from a distance. They translated documents captured at the front, but the information was often

[14] Ellis M. Zacharias, *Secret Missions: The Story of an Intelligence Officer* (New York: G. P. Putnam's Sons, 1946), p. 318.

[15] Prados, *Combined Fleet Decoded*, pp. 377–78. In October 1942 a Navy language officer was assigned to a mobile radio intelligence unit at Henderson Field on Guadalcanal. The Navy may have used two Japanese-speaking Korean Americans to help with the language work on Guadalcanal. Ronald Takaki, *Strangers from a Different Shore: A History of Asian Americans* (Boston: Little, Brown, 1989), p. 366.

[16] For the impact of the Goettge incident, see George McMillan, *The Old Breed: A History of the First Marine Division in World War II* (Washington, D.C.: Infantry Journal Press, 1949), pp. 52–56; William Manchester, *Goodbye, Darkness: A Memoir of the Pacific War* (New York: Dell, 1980), pp. 219–20; E. B. Sledge, *With the Old Breed at Peleliu and Okinawa* (New York: Oxford University Press, 1990), pp. 33–34.

[17] For racism during the Pacific War, see John W. Dower, *War without Mercy* (New York: Pantheon, 1986). For more recent interpretations, see Eric Bergerud, *Touched with Fire: The Land War in the South Pacific* (New York: Penguin, 1996), pp. 403–25; John A. Lynn, *Battle: A History of Combat and Culture* (Boulder, Colo.: Westview Press, 2003), pp. 219–80; Peter Schrijvers, *The GI War against Japan: American Soldiers in Asia and the Pacific during World War II* (New York: New York University Press, 2002), ch. 9.

[18] Lewin, *American Magic*, p. 123.

long out of date. Nevertheless, their commanders valued the Nisei's work. MID directed the school to send out more graduates as early as possible. From September through November the school sent out six more Nisei and several more Caucasian officers. The Nisei translated documents, diaries, and letters. Most contained little of intelligence value, but some revealed a wealth of information. On Tulagi, the marines found a list of call signs and code names of all Imperial Japanese Navy ships and air bases. This was flown to Noumea, where the Nisei worked 24-hour shifts for several days to translate. Shigeru Yamashita, who had been born in California but had lived in Japan from age three to nineteen, considered the task a personal challenge: "Even though there were no officers bearing down on [the Nisei], they were determined to show their country that loyalty and honor were an integral part of the fabric they were made of and taking away their outer freedom didn't change that. They were acutely aware that the translation of this Japanese Navy book would be a significant triumph to their country and . . . to them as Japanese Americans as well."[19]

Some documents went immediately to Hawaii, where graduates from the Navy language school in Boulder, Colorado, translated them. Among the first of the Boulder graduates to arrive in Hawaii was Ens. Donald Keene, who noticed "a box filled with malodorous little books...and was informed that these were diaries taken from the bodies of dead Japanese soldiers and sailors. The odor was caused by the dried blood with which many of the diaries were stained." He related that he "gingerly selected a diary without any noticeable bloodstains, and began to read."[20]

In October the Americal Division sent an infantry regiment to reinforce the marines on Guadalcanal. The rest of the division followed in November, but the six Nisei stayed behind at COMSOPAC headquarters.[21] Meanwhile, in Fiji, Burden and his three Nisei continued to monitor the telephones and had no chance to help with the fight in Guadalcanal. At one point Takashi and Takeo Kubo interrogated a downed Japanese pilot; another time they interrogated a captured eighteen-year-old Japanese submariner.[22] This might have been the fate of all the Nisei, far from the action and relegated to lower level duties. It seemed that the war was passing them by.

Even Burden was feeling left out. One evening while pulling telephone duty, he overheard a message from Guadalcanal highlighting the urgent need for a

---

[19] Harrington, *Yankee Samurai*, p. 112; Yamashita, MISNorCal Bio; Kawashiri File, Harrington Papers; Ltr, Kusuda to Harrington, Harrington Papers; Ariyasu, in Swift, "First Class," p. 7. Shigeru Yamashita, in Swift, "First Class," p. 1. These may have been the materials recovered from the submarine I–1, sunk near Guadalcanal on 29 January 1943. See Richard B. Frank, *Guadalcanal* (New York: Random House, 1990), pp. 575–76 and note; Holmes, *Double-Edged Secrets*, pp. 124–25; Prados, *Combined Fleet Decoded*, pp. 400–402.

[20] Holmes, *Double-Edged Secrets*, pp. 123–24; Donald Keene, *On Familiar Terms: A Journey across Cultures* (New York: Kodansha, 1994), pp. 22–23.

[21] Yamashita, MISNorCal Bio.

[22] *Pacific War and Peace*, p. 32.

language officer. The next morning he went back to his room, packed his bag, and told his roommate he was going to Guadalcanal. But the call did not come. A few nights later he overheard a similar message, but still no orders came. One day in December Admiral Halsey visited the 37th Division headquarters. The division G–2 commented, "I understand you are looking for a Japanese language officer." Halsey replied, "They are driving me crazy for one, but I don't know where to find one." The G–2 introduced Burden to Halsey, who shook Burden's hand and told him to pack his bag and catch the next flight to New Caledonia. Burden arrived on Guadalcanal two days later.[23]

On Guadalcanal, Burden found two marine officers and five enlisted men working as interrogators. Only one had any real proficiency in Japanese. The others had taken a short class in Japanese in San Diego but were ineffective with prisoners or documents. "They would talk nothing but Japanese among themselves and thought they were pretty good," Burden later recalled. When he first arrived he assigned some prisoners to them for interrogation. At the end of the day they turned in a sheet of paper for each prisoner with only the prisoner's name and rank. "You talked to them for over two hours!" he exclaimed. "Is that all you got out of them?" The marines just responded, "They didn't know much." Finally, one admitted the truth: "They talked so much and so fast we couldn't understand what they were saying." Burden sent the interrogators back to the marines.[24]

The 25th Infantry Division joined the Americal Division to launch an offensive on 17 December. Burden noted reluctance on the part of many soldiers to take prisoners, just as the marines before them. Officers and enlisted men shared the attitude, as he later put it, that "the only good Jap is a dead Jap." Burden heard of one regimental commander who censured his men for bringing in prisoners, saying, "Don't bother to take prisoners, shoot the sons of bitches!"

Several times Burden heard from a front-line unit that had taken a prisoner; later he would learn that the prisoner had "died" en route to the rear. He was concerned for practical as well as ethical reasons. American soldiers appeared to have "no appreciation for the value of the information obtainable from prisoners or documents. . . . As a result documents were scattered and destroyed in the search for souvenirs." Burden frequently lectured commanders and units about the intelligence value of prisoners and documents and convinced the corps commander to offer a three-day pass and a serving of ice cream as rewards for bringing in live

---

[23] See sources on Burden cited above. Many years later Burden recalled that this meeting was with Admiral Chester W. Nimitz, not Admiral Halsey, and took place in October, not early December. Nimitz indeed visited Noumea in October, but Burden's after-action report clearly stated that Burden arrived on Guadalcanal in early December 1942, only a short time after his encounter with the senior naval officer. Nimitz apparently did not visit the South Pacific in late November or early December.

[24] This account of Burden's experiences on Guadalcanal from December 1942 until February 1943 is based primarily on John A. Burden, "The Work of the Language Section, Including a Summary of the Work Conducted on Guadalcanal and a Tentative Plan for the Future Conduct of Japanese Language Work in the South Pacific Area," 22 Jul 43, Folder 3, Burden Papers.

Captain Burden (center) *makes a broadcast to urge Japanese soldiers to surrender.*

prisoners. As the American offensive gathered momentum, over 200 prisoners had arrived at the stockade; Burden's small crew of marine interrogators began to work around the clock. Contrary to popular belief, they found the prisoners cooperative. Some would even obtain information from their fellow prisoners when they did not know the answer to a specific question.

Along with prisoners came a harvest of captured documents, an "astonishing . . . amount of information." Burden reported: "The Japanese seem to have a mania for putting things down on paper and hanging on to old documents. . . . disposition of troops, distribution of artillery units, casualties following engagements, hospital records, and numerous other points were found in large numbers."[25]

---

[25] Ibid. The Burden Papers contain copies of several translations.

Burden also used his language skill to encourage Japanese soldiers to surrender. The first, mass-produced, surrender leaflets used on Guadalcanal, prepared and printed in the United States, had little effect on Japanese soldiers. Burden made up his own leaflets on the spot to explain the hopelessness of their situation and to instruct them to approach American lines during certain hours, unarmed with their hands raised. One day, while Burden was looking through captured Japanese diaries, an entry caught his eye: "Went up to battalion headquarters to look at the surrender leaflets," the unknown Japanese soldier had written. "The handwriting was terrible!" Burden was amused to discover that his doctor's handwriting was no better in Japanese than English.[26]

Psychological warfare remained an important tool of war. Early in 1943, when the 25th Infantry Division faced determined Japanese resistance in the Gifu strong point, the division commander, Maj. Gen. J. Lawton Collins, summoned Burden to his command post on 15 January. He told him: "You said the Japanese would surrender if we could reassure them they would not be killed. Here is your chance to prove that. You can have broadcast equipment and we will give them two days to come out." Burden set up a loudspeaker and began to broadcast, but heavy rain and thick foliage weakened its power.

By the end of the third day, only thirteen Japanese soldiers had responded. Burden begged for one more day, but Collins refused: "That's not the way we fight a war—they were given an ultimatum, and the shelling starts tomorrow." The next day Burden watched in horror as the American artillery blasted the Japanese position. Most of the prisoners taken over the next two weeks were deafened and shell-shocked. Burden recommended repeating the experiment and equipping language sections with portable public address systems.[27]

Burden's experiences on Guadalcanal convinced him that doing translation and interrogation work far to the rear was not effective. He estimated that it took between three to six weeks for information to get back to Guadalcanal. Several times, he later wrote, "documents having important tactical information were overlooked and sent to Noumea, and the information from them was not received until after it had lost its value."[28] Burden pushed to bring his Nisei to Guadalcanal, where they would be more useful. He encountered great resistance based in large part on "a general distrust of all persons of Japanese extraction, . . . the result of the National hysteria which resulted following the attack on Pearl Harbor." When American soldiers first met the Nisei, they commonly thought they were Chinese

---

[26] Burden autobiography.

[27] Burden, "Work of the Language Section," pp. 12–13; Burden autobiography; Harrington, *Yankee Samurai*, p. 111; John Miller, jr., *Guadalcanal: The First Offensive* (Washington, D.C.: Department of the Army Historical Division, 1949), pp. 298–99. Burden was injured soon afterward in the crash of a liaison aircraft while disseminating leaflets. He was awarded the Silver Star for his service on Guadalcanal.

[28] Burden, "Work of the Language Section," p. 2.

Americans. "What small amount of prejudice that still exists," he wrote, "is wiped out as soon as the individuals become acquainted with the Nisei."[29]

Burden finally appealed directly to the XIV Corps commander, Maj. Gen. Alexander M. Patch, who gave his permission to send the Nisei into the forward area. Burden arranged for the three Nisei languishing on Fiji with the 37th Infantry Division to fly to New Caledonia. A fellow officer told Burden he had seen a Nisei soldier driving a jeep on Tonga. Burden guessed that the soldier must be Masanori Minamoto, so he brought him up as well. In January 1943 a fresh team of ten Nisei straight from the school arrived in New Caledonia.

As the American offensive gained strength, the flow of prisoners and documents grew rapidly. Two Nisei flew on 15 January to join the 2d Marine Division on Guadalcanal, where they met a marine sergeant "struggling with a pile of Japanese documents." As the Nisei began combing through the documents, one recalled, "the very first one that we worked on, a 'Jackpot,' was a thick bounded document (handwritten with brush), a 'Japanese General Staff Operational Plan: and Directives for the Combined Japanese Forces in the South Pacific Area.' . . . It was really a very 'hot' item."[30] Burden brought forward four more Nisei, who joined the XIV Corps language section on Guadalcanal on 22 January.[31] When the fighting ended in February 1943, the Americans held more than 300 prisoners and thousands of captured documents. Now that the fighting had ceased, Burden began to let his Nisei interrogate the prisoners. On 13 February another language officer arrived at XIV Corps with five more Nisei.[32]

Just as the battle for Guadalcanal was ending, dozens more Nisei graduates arrived in the South Pacific. Lt. Col. Frederick P. Munson arrived in New Caledonia shortly before Christmas with six more Nisei under Sgt. Tetsuo Hayashida of California. Munson had been among the diplomatic personnel exchanged on the SS *Gripsholm*. He took charge of the combat intelligence center in Noumea. The Nisei were assigned to Headquarters, U.S. Army Forces, in the South Pacific Area.[33] In January 1943 twenty more Nisei arrived, all graduates of the December 1942 class at Camp Savage. Ten each went to the 37th and 43d Infantry Divisions. Meanwhile, Burden and his small team transferred to the 25th Infantry Division.

---

[29] Ibid., p. 14.

[30] Ltr, Joe J. Yoshiwara to Roy Uyehata, 18 February 1993. His partner was Makoto Sakamoto. A few days later two more Nisei joined them. Harrington, *Yankee Samurai*, p. 132. Yoshiwara recalls flying to Guadalcanal on 15 January 1943, the date reflected on his award of the Bronze Star Medal. The cited document may have been "Japanese Army-Navy Central Agreement Concerning South Pacific Area Operations, with Supplement," 4 Jan 43, in Louis Morton, *Strategy and Command: The First Two Years*, U.S. Army in World War II (Washington, D.C.: Office of the Chief of Military History, 1962), app. G, pp. 624–26.

[31] Burden, "Work of the Language Section," and Burden autobiography; Harrington, *Yankee Samurai*, p. 89; Miyasaki, MISNorCal Bio; Yamashita, MISNorCal Bio. Roy Kawashiri says three Nisei eventually went to Guadalcanal, but he did not. Ltr, Kawashiri to Harrington, 7 December 1977.

[32] Roy T. Uyehata, MISNorCal Bio.

[33] Interv, Frederick P. Munson, 5 Mar 75, Frederick P. Munson Papers, Hoover Institution Archives; Tetsuo Hayashia, MISNorCal Bio.

G–2 Section, XIV Corps, February 1943. In front row, beginning fourth from left: *Shigeru Yamashita, Terno Odow, Roy T. Uyehata, and Isao Kusuda.*

The experiences of the MIS Nisei in the South Pacific replayed in other campaigns for the rest of the war. Commanders initially restricted the first to arrive from the combat zone. Only when their Caucasian language officer insisted could a few go forward to support the front-line units. Only then could they finally show the full range of their abilities.

By early 1943 enough Nisei were available for other tasks. Thirteenth Air Force began using interrogations of captured Japanese pilots to modify American aerial tactics.[34] Burden proudly wrote to the school that he was "glad to say that those who opposed the use of Nisei the most are now their most enthusiastic advocates." At first General Patch, who had commanded the Americal Division and then the XIV Corps, strongly opposed using the Nisei. According to a later report, when the first group arrived at his command, he "remarked that he didn't want any Japs" and only "begrudgingly tolerated them through a campaign." By the end of the campaign "he thought so much of them that he used to go personally to the transports and welcome each group as they came off the gangplank."[35]

With the Nisei's help, the Army learned some valuable language lessons from the Guadalcanal Campaign. Combat intelligence had to flow upward as forward

---

[34] Wesley F. Craven and James L. Cate, eds., *The Army Air Forces in World War II*, 7 vols. (Chicago: University of Chicago Press, 1950), 4: 215.

[35] "Nisei Linguists—Eyes and Ears of Allied Pacific Forces," Trng Grp, Ofc of the Dir of Intel G–2, RG 165, NARA. This appears to be a draft of the MISLS press release of 22 October 1945. Japanese Evacuation Research Study (JERS), pt. 2, sec. 2, reel 20, frame 0037, Bancroft Library, University of California, Berkeley. Patch's remarks were toned down in the final version. Patch later commanded Seventh Army and expressed pride in the 442d RCT that served under him in 1944. Crost, *Honor by Fire*, pp. 53, 237.

units grappled with the enemy. Without front-line intelligence, units could only blunder into the enemy. Commanders needed intelligence specialists who could interrogate prisoners and translate documents quickly and accurately. The Nisei learned that it was better to sort through captured documents quickly, rather than translate every one. They became adept at scanning large numbers of documents and picking out significant information that they could quickly translate into idiomatic English and proper American military terminology.

The Army also learned that its prewar doctrine of questioning a prisoner through an interpreter was impractical. In theory, an interpreter could simply relay questions and answers between an intelligence officer and a prisoner. However, the regimental S–2 or division G–2 seldom had time to interrogate prisoners in person.

The Nisei learned to use their knowledge of Japanese culture and psychology to elicit information through indirect questioning. They discovered that compassionate treatment worked wonders. Their captives, expecting torture and death, were at first astonished, then grateful. Any recalcitrant prisoner needed only to hear that authorities would notify his family through the International Committee of the Red Cross that he had been captured alive. The implied disgrace could usually convince him to cooperate.[36]

The Nisei also learned that American soldiers and marines needed constant reminders of the importance of bringing in prisoners and captured documents. Japanese soldiers, contrary to common belief, were worth more alive than dead.

Tactical psychological warfare had great potential. In most cases, Japanese soldiers would fight to the death rather than face capture. But when the situation was clearly hopeless and the message properly communicated, at least some would respond to surrender appeals.

When the fighting was over, Burden used captured documents and interrogation reports to compile a history of the campaign from the Japanese point of view. This gave American commanders unique insights into Japanese military psychology.[37]

Most important of all, the Nisei had demonstrated that they could be trusted to work near the front lines. Commanders and intelligence officers came to rely on the intelligence that only the Nisei could provide, as close to the front as possible. Other Japanese linguists were too few or too unskilled to provide the quality and timeliness of combat intelligence that ground commanders desperately needed.

---

[36] Maj. Sherwood F. "Pappy" Moran, a marine language officer on Guadalcanal, had lived in Japan and spoke excellent Japanese. *Hit the Beach: Your Marine Corps in Action* (New York: Wm. H. Wise, 1948), p. 53. His interrogation methods were later taught at the Military Intelligence Training Center, Camp Ritchie, Maryland. Division Intelligence Section, HQ, 1st Marine Division, Suggestions for Japanese Interpreters Based on Work in the Field, 17 Jul 43, at http://mysite.verizon.net/vze6kt7j/, last accessed 12 Feb 06. See also Stephen Budiansky, "Truth Extraction," *Atlantic Monthly* (June 2005): 32–35. Ulrich Straus, *The Anguish of Surrender: Japanese POWs of World War II* (Seattle: University of Washington Press, 2003).

[37] HQ, XIV Corps, Ofc of the ACS, G–2, "Enemy Operations on Guadalcanal (August 7, 1942 to February 9, 1943)," 24 Apr 43, Folder 2, Burden Papers. However, see Miller, *Guadalcanal*, comment in bibliographic note, p. 379.

These lessons circulated in various ways. From Guadalcanal, Burden wrote letters to the language school commandant, Col. Kai E. Rasmussen. The Medical Reserve doctor and the Regular Army officer had a deep mutual respect, perhaps because they were both outsiders. Burden, raised in Japan, had not set foot on American soil until he was sixteen, Rasmussen, born in Denmark, not until he was twenty. One went to medical school; the other joined the Army and won appointment to West Point. They shared a fluency in Japanese, an appreciation of the Nisei, and a commitment to defeat the common enemy. Burden prepared a report on the work of the XIV Corps language section in July 1943 and lectured to corps intelligence personnel. A few months later he returned to the language school to lecture on his experiences. Through these formal and informal channels, the work of the pioneering Nisei became known throughout the Army.[38]

During the Guadalcanal Campaign, the Nisei's direct contributions remained limited and usually confined to the tactical level. Even then, they mostly helped regiment, division, and corps commanders to know what was happening to their immediate front. Higher level commanders in New Caledonia and Hawaii relied on other sources such as radio intercepts, coast watchers, and aerial reconnaissance to determine Japanese movements, strengths, and intentions. But even these sources could miss important stories. For example, in February 1943 the Japanese evacuated their remaining troops from Guadalcanal without detection.[39]

After the fighting on Guadalcanal concluded, Burden visited Australia to see how Nisei were employed in the Southwest Pacific Area. He was impressed by what he saw at I Corps and General MacArthur's headquarters. MacArthur's headquarters had already established a single agency to control all language work in the theater. Burden recommended that linguists in both theaters combine into one super agency under the Southwest Pacific Command. But intertheater cooperation proved impossible at this stage. Nevertheless, in Australia, Burden witnessed a method of using the Nisei that contrasted sharply with their piecemeal employment in the South Pacific.[40]

Intelligence in the Southwest Pacific Area: The Allied Translator and Interpreter Section

General MacArthur arrived in Australia in March 1942 to establish his new command, the Southwest Pacific Area. His chief intelligence officer, Brig. Gen. Charles A. Willoughby, began building a joint U.S.-Australian intelligence architecture that would support MacArthur's plans to halt the Japanese in New Guinea, drive them back, and eventually liberate the Philippines.[41] In April the first such

---

[38] Burden, "Work of the Language Section," and lecture notes, Folder 3, Burden Papers.
[39] John Prados, "US Intelligence and the Japanese Evacuation of Guadalcanal, 1943," *Intelligence and National Security* 10 (April 1995): 294–305.
[40] Burden, "Work of the Language Section," pp. 15–21.
[41] *A Brief History of the G–2 Section, GHQ, SWPA and Affiliated Units*, Intelligence Series (Tokyo: Far East Command, 1948).

organization, the Central Bureau, was formed in Brisbane to break into Japanese codes. Over the next few months Willoughby organized other intelligence organizations, including the Allied Geographical Section for terrain intelligence, an Order of Battle Section to collate information on enemy units, and the Allied Intelligence Bureau to support resistance movements behind Japanese lines. These theater intelligence agencies grew to surpass in size anything the Army or Navy had established in the South Pacific.

In the early months of the war the Allies had lost many experienced intelligence personnel with the fall of Hong Kong, Singapore, and the Netherlands East Indies. Nevertheless, they could draw upon considerable Australian intelligence experience against the Germans and Italians in North Africa. The Australians were certainly aware of the need for Japanese linguists. In 1940 the Royal Australian Army Censorship School in Melbourne began Japanese-language training under Capt. John V. Shelton, a White Russian and superb Japanese linguist who had graduated from Waseda University in Tokyo. In early 1941 Australia's Eastern Command established a small Japanese-language intelligence section in Sydney. The Royal Australian Navy could find only one language-qualified civil servant at the time. In Melbourne, in January 1942 the Royal Australian Air Force established a prisoner of war section and the Royal Australian Army headquarters established a translation center. The Australian Army linguists later moved up to Australian Advance Land Headquarters in Brisbane. In early September the Australians established the Combined Services Detailed Interrogation Centre at the Indooroopilly Racetrack in Brisbane.[42]

On 19 June 1942, Capt. David W. Swift arrived in Brisbane with eight Nisei led by S.Sgt. Gary Tsuneo Kadani, a Kibei from California. Swift, Kadani, and the other Nisei were all Crissy Field graduates. Swift had jaundice from his yellow fever inoculation at the port of embarkation, so he was hospitalized immediately upon arrival. Kadani took charge of the team, which proceeded to Melbourne for assignment to the American counterintelligence officer, Col. Elliott R. Thorpe. They began counterintelligence training and studied Malay, the lingua franca of the Netherlands East Indies.[43]

---

[42] John Shelton, speech to Army Forces Far East Intelligence School, 1953, transcript in author's files. Shelton was born Ivan Shalfeieff, son of the last Imperial Russian military attaché in Tokyo and a Japanese mother. He changed his name upon arrival in Australia in 1940. George Kiyoshi [Yamashiro] Sankey, "Areya, Koreye [This and That]," p. 38, Unpubl autobiography, excerpted in *Hawaii Pacific Press* (1 Dec 94): 56; General Headquarters, Far East Command, *Operations of the Allied Translator and Interpreter Section, GHQ, SWPA*, Intelligence Series, vol. 5 (Tokyo: Far East Command, 1948), pp. 3–4, 59 (hereafter cited as ATIS History); Colin Funch, *Linguists in Uniform: The Japanese Experience* (Australia: Japanese Studies Centre, Monash University, 2003). Grant K. Goodman, *America's Japan: The First Year, 1945–1946* (New York: Fordham University Press, 2005), p. 52.

[43] David W. Swift, Sr., *Ninety Li a Day*, ed. David W. Swift, Jr., Social Life Monographs, vol. 69 (Taipei: Chinese Association for Folklore, 1975), pp. 273–76; Gary Tsuneo Kadani, in Swift, "First Class"; Harrington, *Yankee Samurai*, pp. 70, 73, 86; Funch, *Linguists in Uniform*, pp. 78–80.

Meanwhile, the Japanese continued their southward advance. On 26 August a Japanese naval landing force attacked the Australians and Americans guarding Milne Bay on the eastern tip of Papua. While repelling the attack, the Allies there captured their first Japanese documents, including a copy of the Japanese operations order. Although naval and air battles had been raging in the region for several months, only when the opposing ground forces made contact did the flow of captured documents and prisoners of war begin.[44]

On 19 September General Willoughby replaced the Australian Combined Services Detailed Interrogation Centre in Brisbane with an American-led organization, the Allied Translator and Interpreter Section (ATIS), "to co-ordinate and expedite the translation of captured enemy documents and prompt collation and distribution of the results."[45] Willoughby canvassed Australia for Japanese linguists: "There was nothing there, except a handful of scholarly Orientalists in Universities and some people with business experience in Japan."[46] The Australians sent fourteen officers and three enlisted men. The Americans contributed Swift and the eight Nisei. Willoughby named the military attaché to Australia, Lt. Col. Karl F. Baldwin, as coordinator. A board of three language officers (the Australian Shelton, the American Swift, and Lt. Donald Bartlett, U.S. Navy Reserve) tested the language proficiency of the first Nisei on 3 September. Six passed, but two were rated "ineffective" for their poor English skills, a common problem for Kibei.[47]

Baldwin organized ATIS into four units parallel to the major components of MacArthur's command: all the Nisei were assigned to GHQ; other sections included Allied Naval Forces, Allied Land Forces, and Allied Air Forces. All were housed near the Indooroopilly Racetrack in Tighnabruaich, a mansion suitable for barracks and office space. A few months later the Nisei enlisted men moved into tents at Camp Chelmer, across the Brisbane River. In the first month ATIS processed over 1,000 documents, translated and distributed 90 documents, and interrogated 7 prisoners.

On 6 October Col. Sidney F. Mashbir replaced Baldwin as the ATIS coordinator. Mashbir had begun his military intelligence career in 1916 and went to Tokyo as a language attaché before leaving active duty in 1923. He was recalled to active service after the outbreak of war; but, like many World War I veterans, he was too old for field service. After Mashbir spent eight months in Washington, the War Department G–2, Maj. Gen. George V. Strong, sent him to Australia to "head up

---

[44] ATIS History, p. 11.

[45] Memo, GHQ, South West Pacific Area (SWPA), sub: Directive Covering the Organization, Co-ordination and Operation of Allied Translator & Interpreter Section, 19 Sep 42, reproduced in ATIS History, app. 2.

[46] Charles A. Willoughby, "The Language Problem in War," in "Corregidor to the Yalu: MacArthur's Intelligence Service: 1941–1951," p. 190, Unpubl Ms, Box 3, Charles A. Willoughby Papers (copies from Gettysburg College), RG 23B, MacArthur Memorial, Library and Archives, Norfolk, Va.

[47] ATIS History; Sidney F. Mashbir, *I Was an American Spy* (New York: Vantage, 1953); Swift, *Ninety Li a Day*, pp. 273–93; Memo, ATIS, sub: Analysis of Linguistic Requirements, 27 Jun 44, author's files.

the language work at GHQ." When he arrived, ATIS "was a small—less than forty men—but polyglot unit, composed of Australian, Canadian and British army, air and navy men; Chinese, White Russians, East Indies Netherlanders and a handful of Americans.... We were a potpourri, not an organization." He immediately reorganized ATIS into functional sections, including a translation section headed by Shelton and an examination section for interrogating prisoners of war. Swift remained the officer in charge of all Nisei personnel.[48]

Three other American Nisei in Brisbane were assigned to other duties. One was Sgt. Arthur S. Komori, recruited by the Hawaiian Department before the war and sent to infiltrate the Japanese community in Manila. He had escaped Corregidor in April 1942 on one of the last flights. (His colleague, Sgt. Richard Sakakida, had remained behind and became a prisoner when the island fortress fell in May.) For several months after his arrival in Australia, Komori conducted routine counterintelligence tasks before being assigned to ATIS as the senior American noncommissioned officer from September until December 1942. He passed on the lessons he had learned fighting the Japanese in the Philippines.[49] Clarence Yamagata, an American Nisei who had been practicing law in Manila before the war, had left Corregidor on the same airplane as Komori. Yamagata joined the Central Bureau as a civilian employee and the only Nisei assigned to this code-breaking organization.[50] A third Nisei then in Australia, Yoshikazu Yamada, had been serving as an Army Air Corps medic at Del Monte Airfield in the southern Philippines. He had been studying chemistry at the University of Michigan when he was drafted in 1941 and assigned to the Philippines. In April 1942 he fell off a truck and injured his back. Evacuated to Australia, he spent two months recuperating in a U.S. Army hospital in Melbourne before being reassigned, first to the Japanese-language section in Allied Air Forces Headquarters, then to ATIS in September.[51]

These first few Japanese-language personnel, including the ten Nisei enlisted men from the school, began to work on the documents now starting to stream south from the battlefront. "Clotted with blood and body fat, they had been taken

---

[48] ATIS History, p. 2; Mashbir, *I Was an American Spy*, pp. 219–24; Interv, D. Clayton James with Mashbir, 1 Sep 71, RG 49, MacArthur Memorial.

[49] Memo, Komori to OIC [Officer in Charge], sub: The Philippine Theater of War, 1 Jul 42; Interv, Ann Bray with Arthur S. Komori, 1955; Interv, Joseph D. Harrington with Arthur S. Komori (notes), 10 Dec 77; all in Harrington Papers. Tsukiyama et al., *Secret Valor*, pp. 34–35. Komori told an interviewer in 1955 that during his first months in Australia he conducted counterintelligence investigations; Bray and Harrington later claimed that he was assigned as a vehicle driver. He may have done both.

[50] Clarence S. Yamagata, resume, 10 Feb 78, Harrington Papers; *The Quiet Heroes of the Southwest Pacific Theater: An Oral History of the Men and Women of CBB and FRUMEL* (Fort Meade, Md.: National Security Agency, 1996), p. 50. Yamagata was commissioned in the Signal Corps in July 1944.

[51] Yoshikazu Yamada, MISNorCal Bio; Yoshikazu Yamada, "My Wartime Experiences," in Tsukiyama et al., *Secret Valor*, pp. 84–85; Yoshikazu Yamada, "A Nisei in World War II," reprinted in *John Aiso and the M.I.S.: Japanese-American Soldiers in the Military Intelligence Service, World War II*, ed. Tad Ichinokuchi (Los Angeles: Military Intelligence Service Club of Southern California, 1988), pp. 138–39.

in New Guinea and flown to Brisbane," Mashbir recalled. "Australian Lt. Shelton read them aloud [while] our group made notes." The first prisoners of war arrived in Brisbane on 30 September. Corporal Kadani interrogated the first as Mashbir listened via a hidden microphone. ATIS released its first spot report on 1 November. By 27 December Allied units fighting in New Guinea had sent back 1,100 Japanese documents. ATIS completed 293 pages of translation in November, 601 pages in December, and 581 pages in January 1943.[52] Mashbir's top priority was to support the Australian and American forces in contact with the enemy and to assist the language teams that were soon assigned to regiments, divisions, and corps. ATIS also produced reports. The first one, on military service in Japan, was dated 31 December 1942. In January and February 1943 ATIS issued research reports on topics such as Japanese aircraft recognition, task force organization, shell identification, and landing craft armor.[53]

Other intelligence agencies were organized in Australia. In April 1942 Seventh Fleet, MacArthur's naval command, established a combined U.S.-British-Australian radio intelligence center, later renamed Fleet Radio Unit, Melbourne, or FRU-MEL. In November 1942 Navy Capt. Arthur H. McCollum became the Seventh Fleet intelligence officer and established a combat intelligence center. McCollum, the son of a Baptist missionary, had been born in Japan. He was a former Japanese-language attaché and had served as head of the Far Eastern Section in the Office of Naval Intelligence from 1939 until 1942; there, he had helped establish the Navy's Japanese-language training program for officers.[54]

Nisei language teams were soon committed to forward units. In the autumn of 1942, the U.S. I Corps headquarters arrived in Australia under the command of Maj. Gen. Robert L. Eichelberger. A group of fourteen Nisei under M.Sgt. Arthur K. Ushiro arrived in November and was assigned to the corps under two Caucasian lieutenants. The Nisei were the top students from Camp Savage and had needed only ninety days of training.[55] Upon arrival in Australia, T3g. Phil Ishio recalled,

---

[52] ATIS History, p. 11; Sidney F. Mashbir, "I Was an American Spy," *Saturday Evening Post* (10 April 1948): 28; "Analysis of Linguistic Requirements," Exhibit G. (Copies of early ATIS spot reports, nos. 1–194, can be found in RG 3, MacArthur Memorial.) ATIS History, p. 15; Harrington, *Yankee Samurai*, p. 109. ATIS Pub no. 6, "The Exploitation of Japanese Documents," 14 Dec 44 (included in ATIS History at tab 5, documentary appendix), states the Allies captured 268 documents at Kokoda and 1,349 at Buna.

[53] ATIS reports can be found in the Gordon W. Prange Collection, University of Maryland; MacArthur Memorial; "P" File (Security-Class Intel Reference Publications), ACS (G–2), Intel, RG 165, NARA, and the Combined Arms Research Library, Fort Leavenworth, Kansas. A nearly complete set is available on microfiche as *Wartime Translations of Seized Japanese Documents: Allied Translator and Interpreter Section Reports, 1942–1946* (Bethesda, Md.: Congressional Information Service, 1988). For a convenient listing of selected publications, see ATIS History, app. 9.

[54] "Reminiscences of Rear Admiral Arthur H. McCollum," in *The Pacific War Remembered*, ed. John T. Mason (Annapolis, Md.: Naval Institute Press, 1986), pp. 146–55; Prados, *Combined Fleet Decoded*, pp. 420–24; Edward J. Drea, *MacArthur's Ultra: Codebreaking and the War against Japan, 1942–1945* (Lawrence: University Press of Kansas, 1992), pp. 15–16.

[55] Interv, Sheryl Narahara with Tarao "Pat" Neishi, 1992, NJAHS; Harrington, *Yankee Samurai*, pp. 44–45, 100. Ushiro changed his surname to Castle during the war.

the corps G–2 "asked each of us individually whether we could read, speak, and write the Japanese language." Ishio, who had been born and raised in Salt Lake City, Utah, had studied economics for three years at Waseda University in Tokyo. "It was all we could do to keep from laughing out loud," he recalled. "After all, we were the special class, the elite at Camp Savage." They were further discouraged when they were demoted by one grade. At that time, enlisted men assigned to a new command could have their ranks adjusted depending upon the table of organization. The I Corps reduced all the Nisei from technician, third grade, to technician, fourth grade, with a predictable impact on their morale.[56]

Papua New Guinea, October 1942–February 1943

American ground combat units joined the fight for Papua New Guinea in October. Nisei enlisted men and Caucasian language officers were assigned to Headquarters, New Guinea Forces; I Corps; the Australian 7th Infantry Division; the U.S. 32d Division; and each American infantry regiment. At first, Allied tactical and operational intelligence was poor and radio intelligence was little help. Allied units frequently did not discover Japanese strong points until they stumbled upon them in the dense New Guinea jungle. When they succeeded in pinpointing Japanese locations, they frequently erred in their estimates of the enemy's strength. Accurate and timely combat intelligence became precious and promised to save many Allied lives.[57]

The Nisei "were never allowed forward of regimental command posts, for had they been captured they undoubtedly would have been tortured." However, in the close-in jungle fighting, division and regimental command posts were often within range of Japanese gunners and snipers. Ishio went forward from I Corps headquarters to visit a Nisei assigned to an infantry regiment near Buna and was shocked at front-line conditions. "When I called out his name, he crawled out of a vine-covered hut, unshaven and in dirty fatigues. If I had not known that he was one of us, I would have taken him for a Japanese soldier." Ishio himself had a "close shave" when a Japanese shell landed near his foxhole, collapsing the hole on top of him.[58]

---

[56] Stanley L. Falk and Warren M. Tsuneishi, eds., *MIS in the War against Japan* (Washington, D.C.: Japanese American Veterans Association, 1995), p. 27. See also Interv, author with Sunao Phil Ishio, 18 Apr 95; S. [Phil] Ishio, "The Nisei Contribution to the Allied Victory in the Pacific," *American Intelligence Journal* (Spring/Summer 1995): 59–67. On enlisted promotion policies, see Ernest F. Fischer, Jr., *Guardians of the Republic: History of the Noncommissioned Officer Corps of the U.S. Army* (New York: Ballantine, 1994), ch. 14.

[57] Radio intelligence from Central Bureau contributed little to the Papua Campaign from September 1942 to January 1943, according to Drea, *MacArthur's Ultra*, pp. 48–60.

[58] G–2 Rpt, ann. 2, Report of the Commanding General, Buna Forces, on the Buna Campaign, Dec. 1, 1942–Jan. 25, 1943, p. 58; "Nisei Officer [Phil Ishio] Lauds U.S. Army Spirit," *Salt Lake Tribune*, Apr 45, reprinted in War Relocation Authority, *Nisei in the War against Japan* (Washington, D.C.: Department of the Interior, 1945); Falk and Tsuneishi, *MIS in the War against Japan*, pp.

S. Phil Ishio and Arthur K. Ushiro (second and third from left) *interrogate a Japanese prisoner in Papua New Guinea, early 1943.*

After crossing the imposing Owen Stanley mountain range, the U.S. 32d and Australian 7th Infantry Divisions launched a slogging offensive against Japanese positions around Buna-Gona in mid-November. The fighting was bitter and exhausting, and many soldiers fell victim to disease in the malarial swamps. On 15 December T3g. James M. Tsumura became the first Nisei linguist to receive the Combat Infantryman Badge.[59]

In December ATIS sent two Nisei to join two Australian language officers already assigned to the Australian 7th Division. At first the Australians took few prisoners. When the Nisei offered three bottles of Coca Cola for each prisoner, more began to arrive. One day the Australians intercepted a Japanese messenger; from the papers he was carrying the Nisei discovered that the Japanese were planning to raid a battery of the Royal Australian Field Artillery. The battery got the

28–29; "Japanese with U.S. Army [Fred Nishitsuji] in [New] Guinea Has Bodyguard," United Press International, 25 Nov 42, in *Seattle Times*, 21 Dec 42.

[59] ATIS History, app. 2; Harrington, *Yankee Samurai*, p. 101.

alert just in time to repel the attack. This incident persuaded the Australians of the Nisei's value.[60]

A few weeks later another Nisei with the Australians learned from another captured Japanese messenger that 200 Japanese soldiers had withdrawn from a pocket to the Australian front the previous night. The division attacked through the area and cleared the roadblock within six hours of the interrogation. Two days later another wounded prisoner disclosed to a Nisei the existence of a previously unknown strong point. "He gave a detailed disposition of enemy troops and automatic weapons covering the approaches along the Soputa Track, the exact position of the enemy headquarters within the perimeter, and the enemy strength as well as the exact locations of all land mines planted on the track." The Nisei passed on this information, and the division adjusted its plan of attack. At dawn, just hours after receiving the fresh intelligence, Australian and American units captured the position with minimal losses.[61]

The U.S. 163d Infantry with three Nisei joined the Australian 7th Infantry Division in early January 1943.[62] Lt. George E. Aurell, who had been raised in Japan and had served as American vice consul in Yokohama, led a team of three other Nisei to I Corps headquarters in Port Moresby on 14 November. They soon moved to the Buna-Gona area, closer to the action. At first the Nisei saw few captured documents and even fewer prisoners, many of whom turned out to be not Japanese soldiers at all, but rather Korean laborers. Ishio went through the first batch of documents, including many diaries, and "listed all of the military units mentioned in them along with pertinent intelligence information on each." He recalled that "the order of battle officer was very excited by what I had compiled, saying that mine was the first report on any order of battle data that he had seen."[63]

As in the South Pacific, the ATIS language personnel in Brisbane were frustrated by the delays in bringing prisoners and documents back from the combat zone hundreds of air miles away. On 31 December Colonel Mashbir requested permission to establish an advance echelon to provide translation and interrogations closer to the front lines. Four weeks later he sent six officers and three Nisei to Headquarters, New Guinea Force. They arrived in Port Moresby on 28 January and completed their first translation and interrogation reports on 13 February.[64] By this time Allied forces had crushed Japanese resistance at Buna-Gona.

The Nisei had proven their value to tactical commanders. Eichelberger's G–2 praised them: "Throughout the campaign these American Japanese soldiers were

---

[60] ATIS History, p. 44; Willoughby, "Language Problem in War," p. 193; Harrington, *Yankee Samurai*, p. 110.

[61] ATIS History, p. 45; Willoughby, "Language Problem in War," pp. 193–94.

[62] Interv, Narahara with Neishi, 1992.

[63] Falk and Tsuneishi, *MIS in the War against Japan*, pp. 28–29; Harrington, *Yankee Samurai*, pp. 110, 182; "Aurell, George," in G. J. A. O'Toole, ed., *The Encyclopedia of American Intelligence and Espionage* (New York: Facts on File, 1988). The two Aurell brothers, George and Paul, both served as language officers in the Southwest Pacific.

[64] ATIS History, p. 24.

completely loyal, cheerful and competent. Their work, without exception, was excellent."[65] Eichelberger himself had become an avid reader of translations of captured Japanese diaries, which gave him a better sense of his opponents than any other sort of intelligence report.[66]

At the conclusion of this first clash of armies in the Southwest Pacific, General Willoughby asked the Military Intelligence Division to send him as many Nisei linguists as possible. MacArthur's chief of staff, Maj. Gen. Richard K. Sutherland, concurred in Willoughby's request. "He was slightly amused when I asked for a thousand to clean the barrel," Willoughby later wrote; "however, we had no reason ever to regret this decision." MID replied that it could provide a thousand Nisei "of high-school and university caliber," since "other services would not touch them in quantities without time-consuming security screening."[67]

War Department Decision To Form a Nisei Combat Unit

As the first Nisei linguists went into action against the Japanese in the summer and autumn of 1942, in Washington, leaders were making decisions that would have lasting consequences for all Japanese Americans, including whether to allow Nisei to serve in combat units. Brig. Gen. John Weckerling later wrote that "the impetus behind the organization of the two Nisei combat units [100th Infantry Battalion and 442d RCT] stemmed from the interpreter and translator problem."[68]

In the spring of 1942 Colonel Pettigrew in the Military Intelligence Division first suggested organizing a Nisei combat unit. According to Weckerling, Pettigrew "pursued his plans determinedly" through the rest of that year.[69] Milton

---

[65] G–2 Rpt, Buna Forces, p. 58.

[66] For example, see Robert L. Eichelberger, *Our Jungle Road to Tokyo* (New York: Viking, 1950), pp. 53–56; Jay Luvaas, ed., *Dear Miss Em: General Eichelberger's War in the Pacific, 1942–1945* (Westport, Conn.: Greenwood Press, 1972), pp. 108–19.

[67] Willoughby, "Language Problem in War," p. 190. Willoughby sent his request to the MID in March 1943. The War Department Operations Division set the SWPA requirement at about 400 Nisei. Memo, OPD, 2 Jul 43, sub: Future Requirements for Japanese Speaking Personnel, 350.03, Trng Grp, Ofc of the Dir of Intel G–2, RG 165, NARA.

[68] John Weckerling, "Japanese Americans Play Vital Role in United States Intelligence Service in World War II" (1946), first printed in *Hokubei Mainichi*, 27 Oct–5 Nov 71, reprinted as a pamphlet.

[69] Stuart Portner, "The Japanese-American Combat Team," *Military Affairs* (Fall 1943): 158–62; Masayo Umezawa Duus, *Unlikely Liberators: The Men of the 100th and 442nd* (Honolulu: University of Hawaii Press, 1987), pp. 50–58; Bill Hosokawa, *Nisei: The Quiet Americans* (New York: William Morrow, 1969), pp. 359–69; Mike Masaoka, *They Call Me Moses Masaoka: An American Saga* (New York: William Morrow, 1987), pp. 105–38; Thomas D. Murphy, *Ambassadors in Arms* (Honolulu: University of Hawaii Press, 1954), pp. 104–12; *Personal Justice Denied: Report of the Commission on Wartime Relocation and Internment of Civilians* (Seattle: University of Washington Press, 1997), pp. 185–91; Ted T. Tsukiyama, "The Origins of the 442nd," in *Go For Broke, 1943–1993* (Honolulu: n.p., 1993), pp. 11–15. Key documents are collected in Roger Daniels, ed., *American Concentration Camps: A Documentary History of the Relocation and Incarceration of Japanese Americans, 1941–1945*, 9 vols. (New York: Garland, 1989), vol. 9. Weckerling, "Japanese Americans Play Vital Role."

S. Eisenhower, the director of the War Relocation Authority from March to June 1942, took a broader approach and urged the War Department to reverse its decision and allow American-born Nisei to be eligible for Selective Service. On 18 May he wrote to Assistant Secretary of War John J. McCloy to plead the Nisei's case. McCloy forwarded his letter to Milton's older brother, Maj. Gen. Dwight D. Eisenhower, then serving in the War Department Operations Division. "I have felt for some time," McCloy added, "that it might be well to use our American citizen Japanese soldiers in an area where they could be employed against the Germans. I believe that we could count on these soldiers to give a good account of themselves against the Germans."[70]

In July the War Department General Staff formed a committee to consider the question. Col. Rufus S. Bratton and Colonel Pettigrew of the Far Eastern Branch recommended that the Army form a division of Japanese-American soldiers, and Pettigrew boldly asked for the honor of commanding the unit. "I have consistently believed and advocated that the overwhelming majority of the Nisei are unquestionably loyal," he wrote, "and that they would make the finest type of combat soldiers." The Western Defense Command and other army major commands were less enthusiastic than Bratton and Pettigrew. General DeWitt had already ordered the removal of all Nisei soldiers from his command and was removing over 110,000 persons of Japanese ancestry into camps. In September the committee concluded that the War Department should not use Nisei soldiers because of a "universal distrust" of them. The only exception would be for the intelligence work they were already doing.[71]

The Far Eastern Branch lobbied to overturn the board's recommendation with the help of overseas commands, the War Relocation Authority, and the Office of War Information. Supportive letters arrived from Alaska and the South Pacific, "the only two places in which [the Nisei] have had a chance to engage in action against the Japanese," Pettigrew pointed out. "While it may be argued that these recommendations are only straws, this Division believes that they are extremely important indications as to what may be expected of the entire group in question."[72] From the South Pacific came a radiogram: "Prisoners of war are being interrogated [and] many captured documents are being translated. . . . interpreters

---

[70] Memo, McCloy to Eisenhower, 20 May 42, Folder: D. D. Eisenhower, Box WD1, ser. 8; War Department (WD), John J. McCloy Papers, Amherst College Archives, Amherst, Mass.

[71] "The Military Utilization of United States Citizens of Japanese Ancestry," 14 Sep 42 (291.2), WD G–1 Decimal Files, RG 165, NARA. Ltr, Pettigrew to McCloy, sub: Key Personnel, Nisei Division, 17 Nov 42, ASW 020 ASW 014.311 W.D.C.: Segregation—Japs, Ofc of the Asst Sec of War, RG 107, NARA. Pettigrew was not selected to command the 442d RCT but remained in the Military Intelligence Division for the duration. John Weckerling may have been considered for command, but he remained the G–2 of Western Defense Command until after Attu and Kiska, when he transferred to the MID and was promoted to brigadier general.

[72] Memo, Pettigrew for WD Gen Staff, G–2, sub: Documents Dealing with Americans of Japanese Ancestry (hereafter referred to as Nisei), 10 Oct 42, Ofc of the Dir of Intel G–2, RG 165, NARA.

from the intelligence school are performing valuable services."[73] The coordinator of the Allied Translator and Interpreter Section in Australia wrote to ask MID to send more Nisei.[74] The Hawaiian Department G–2, Col. Kendall J. Fielder, "came to Washington and spent several weeks helping to convince high officials in the War Department that a change of policy was important and badly wanted by many Hawaiians of Japanese lineage."[75] The director of the Office of War Information, Elmer Davis, appealed directly to President Franklin D. Roosevelt to allow Nisei enlistments. Milton Eisenhower's successor at the War Relocation Authority, Dillon Myer, continued to push for Nisei enlistments.[76]

In October 1942 the naval district intelligence officer for Southern California, Comdr. Kenneth D. Ringle, published an article in *Harper's Monthly* defending the Nisei against charges of disloyalty.[77] In November the Japanese American Citizens League appealed to the War Department to allow Nisei to serve and to reinstate their eligibility for Selective Service. The organization's national secretary, Mike Masaoka, affirmed: "I have come to the inescapable conclusion that this matter of Selective Service is the cornerstone of our future in this country. . . . When the war is won, and we attempt to find our way back into normal society, one question which we cannot avoid will be, 'Say, Buddy, what did you do in the war?' If we cannot answer that we, with them, fought for the victory which is ours, our chance for success and acceptance will be small."[78]

The War Department already had several long-serving segregated units for African Americans, Puerto Ricans, and Filipinos and established several more during 1942. The Office of War Information saw propaganda value in having combat units of different nationalities. Thus during 1942 the War Department organized the 1st Filipino Infantry in California and battalion-size units of Norwegians, Austrians, and Greeks. In November 1942 Secretary of War Henry L. Stimson complained to Roosevelt about this pressure for special units, rather than integrating ethnic groups into the ranks, citing the need for "encouraging Americanization in the Army." Roosevelt agreed that "formation of such Battalions should be

[73] Memo, MID (908) to MISLS, sub: Paraphrased Extract from Radiogram, 25 Aug 42, "R (Confidential) Reference," Box 86, Class Ref Sub Files, 1940–1947, Ofc of the Asst Sec of War, RG 107, NARA.

[74] Memo, Colonel Pettigrew to Captain Zacharias, 18 Nov 42, Far Eastern Br, Security-Class Gen Corresp, 1926–1946, Ofc of the Dir of Intel G–2, RG 165, NARA.

[75] Dillon S. Myer, *Uprooted Americans: The Japanese Americans and the War Relocation Authority during World War II* (Tucson: University of Arizona Press, 1971), p. 146. Fielder played an important role in gaining War Department acceptance for the Nisei. After the war, he assisted in the first scholarly study of Nisei soldiers in World War II. Murphy, *Ambassadors in Arms*, acknowledgments, pp. 51, 105.

[76] Murphy, *Ambassadors in Arms*, pp. 105–06.

[77] [K. D. Ringle], "The Japanese in America," *Harper's Monthly* (October 1942): 489–97; Jacobus tenBroek et al., *Prejudice, War, and the Constitution* (Berkeley: University of California Press, 1954), pp. 298–99.

[78] Bill Hosokawa, *JACL in Quest of Justice: The History of the Japanese American Citizens League* (New York: William Morrow, 1982), p. 199; Masaoka, *They Call Me Moses Masaoka*, pp. 120–21.

strictly limited to cases where political advantages are to be gained," but refused to stop the practice, saying, "I must be the one to determine political advantages if any."[79]

At the end of November War Department leaders decided to form a Nisei regimental combat team, and the White House concurred.[80] With the November elections past and a new front opened in North Africa, the Roosevelt administration could afford to be less concerned about anti-Japanese hysteria in California. The public announcement came in late January 1943, and the White House released a widely publicized endorsement: "No loyal citizen of the United States should be denied the democratic right to exercise the responsibilities of his citizenship, regardless of his ancestry. The principle on which this country was founded and by which it has always been governed is that Americanism is a matter of the heart and mind; Americanism is not, and never was, a matter of race or ancestry."[81]

The first Nisei volunteers for the 442d RCT reported to Camp Shelby, Mississippi, for training in April 1943. The Nisei pioneers who began fighting in the Pacific almost one year earlier could take some credit for convincing the War Department to form this unit. The first graduates from Crissy Field convinced their Caucasian officers of their loyalty and effectiveness. "They were the test case," language school officials would announce at the war's end.[82]

The MIS Nisei and their Caucasian officers in turn convinced War Department leaders, the Office of War Information, the War Relocation Authority, and finally President Roosevelt, of the value of allowing Nisei to serve their country. They were fighting alongside American and Australian soldiers and marines, using their language skills to provide combat intelligence to front-line commanders. On Guadalcanal and New Guinea, they faced harsh battlefield conditions to lift the veil of ignorance that had plagued Allied commanders in the early months of the war. They exposed themselves to snipers, booby traps, artillery and mortar fire, and air attacks to help overcome fierce Japanese resistance. They had proven their loyalty, if anyone had lingering doubts.

The initial campaigns proved that the available numbers of Caucasian Japanese-speakers could not handle the volume of language work once ground units made contact, and it simply took too long to train new linguists to an adequate

[79] Memo, Franklin D. Roosevelt for Henry L. Stimson, 17 Nov 42, WD Folder 2–42, Roosevelt Library, in frame 82, reel 3, Commission on Wartime Relocation and Internment of Civilians (CWRIC) Papers, Bancroft Library, University of California, Berkeley. For correspondence about ethnic units, see Marshall File, ser. 8, McCloy Papers.

[80] On 20 November 1942, The Adjutant General instructed all Army commands to report all Nisei soldiers by name. Boxes 280–82, Ofc of the Dir of Intel G–2, RG 165, NARA. For an interpretation that stresses propaganda value, see T. Fujitani, "The Reischauer Memo: Mr. Moto, Hirohito, and Japanese American Soldiers," *Critical Asian Studies* 33, no. 3 (2001): 379–402.

[81] See entry for 1 February 1943 in *The Public Papers and Addresses of Franklin D. Roosevelt*, 13 vols., comp. Samuel I. Rosenman (New York: Random House, 1938–1950); Greg Robinson, *By Order of the President: FDR and the Internment of Japanese Americans* (Cambridge, Mass.: Harvard University Press, 2001), pp. 163–76.

[82] WD Press Release, 22 Oct 45.

level of proficiency. In contrast, many of these early Nisei were Kibei, having spent several years living in and attending school in Japan. Their knowledge of the Japanese language, as well as the culture and people, was priceless. Once Allied soldiers saw the value of capturing prisoners, they brought them in by the hundreds. These prisoners, treated with compassion, willingly gave their Nisei interrogators an astonishing amount of useful information. Captured documents proved even more valuable. The Nisei used these documents to re-create the workings of the Japanese armed forces in a way no other form of intelligence could. In the Southwest Pacific, a new organization had been invented, the Allied Translator and Interpreter Section, which could support the forces in contact and simultaneously support the theater commander with flexible and timely language and analytical support.

In April 1943 Captain Burden wrote from Guadalcanal to Camp Savage asking for a surgeon's position with the 442d RCT and urging that the unit be sent to the Pacific: "I just wish that they would bring them out this way and give them a chance to really clear the name of the Nisei. They would do it. However they will do plenty good work on the other side [in Europe] I'm sure." The commandant forwarded the letter to MID, which sent it on to Assistant Secretary of War McCloy.[83] In 1944 the 442d RCT deployed to the Mediterranean, not the Pacific, and fought there with distinction. Little did the Nisei in that unit realize that their opportunity to serve came from the little-heralded achievements of the first MIS Nisei in fighting against the Japanese in the Pacific.

---

[83] Memo, Asst Sec of War to Chief, Far Eastern Unit, MIS, 19 May 43, Trng Grp, Ofc of the Dir of Intel G–2, RG 165, NARA.

4

Camp Savage, 1942–1943

In May 1942 the Fourth Army Intelligence School dispatched its first graduates to Alaska and the Pacific, vacated the hangar at Crissy Field, and moved to Camp Savage, Minnesota. The school would need to reestablish itself in the new location, recruit more students and instructors, and train thousands of new linguists to meet the expanding needs of America's field commanders.

That same spring and summer the Western Defense Command was removing over 110,000 men, women, and children of Japanese ancestry from the West Coast into hastily constructed camps in the interior. (*See Map 3*.) The contradiction between the military necessity for Japanese speakers and widespread suspicion of anyone of Japanese ancestry was clear and for most Nisei students intensely personal. Shortly after graduation Cpl. Tsuneo Gary Kadani drove south to Salinas, where his parents were housed at the Salinas Rodeo Grounds:

This was the saddest day of my life: [the] trip to Salinas to say farewell to my parents. . . . I wasn't supposed to be there; they wouldn't let me into the camp. . . . My parents were sleeping in a horse stall! It smelled so bad they couldn't sleep, so my mother asked me to get all the Clorox I could find. And when she was asking me, my sister-in-laws and friends also asked, "Ah, Kadani-san, can you get some for me?" I . . . bought dozens of bottles of Clorox—they were only about nine cents a bottle in those days, 1942. I loaded them in the back of my Chevrolet trunk. I went back to the rodeo grounds and gave them to the people waiting at the gate. Then I went back to the Presidio after saying goodbye to everybody. And that was the saddest day of my life.[1]

---

[1] Kadani, in David W. Swift, Jr., ed., "First Class," Unpubl Ms, 2000, copy in author's files.

WASHINGTON

MONTANA

NORTH DAK

OREGON

IDAHO

Heart Mountain ▲

SOUTH DAK

Tule Lake ▲

Minidoka ▲

WYOMING

NEBRASK

NEVADA

Topaz ▲

UTAH

COLORADO

KAN

Manzanar ▲

Granada ▲

CALIFORNIA

ARIZONA

Poston ▲

NEW   MEXICO

OK

Gila River ▲

TEX

C   A

WAR RELOCATION CENTERS
1942–1946

MEXICO

MAP 3

Kadani soon sailed from San Francisco for Australia, where he arrived six weeks later.

In the days ahead the school's challenges would be to overcome these doubts of Nisei loyalty and to produce skilled military linguists needed to win the war against Japan. First the school had to relocate. In mid-May the eight civilian instructors, ten graduate-instructors, and a handful of other students and staff drove in private automobiles eastward out of the exclusion zone. The civilian instructors had permission to bring their wives to spare them internment. A Caucasian officer accompanied each carload in case there might be some trouble carrying Japanese Americans beyond the reach of the relocation orders. Together they drove through the Sierra Nevada and Rocky Mountains then deep into the Midwest, far from the West Coast exclusion areas.[2]

On 25 May 1942, they arrived at Fort Snelling, on the outskirts of Minneapolis. Their destination was ten miles down the road in a cluster of wooden buildings nestled under pine trees. Built in the early 1930s by the Civilian Conservation Corps, Camp Savage lay along a railroad line and state highway one-half mile from the Minnesota River. This would become the school's home for the next two years.[3]

The 132-acre post enjoyed several advantages. It was isolated and quiet, good for security and for studying. It already contained a few dozen simple, one-story wooden buildings that would become barracks and classrooms. The Nisei soldiers and civilian instructors could remain inconspicuous, yet the post was close to Fort Snelling, a busy reception center with a capacity of more than 3,000 men. The twin cities of Minneapolis–St. Paul were convenient for off-duty recreation.[4] Like the rest of America, Minnesota was still reeling from the war's opening months. A company of the Minnesota National Guard had been captured on Bataan; nevertheless, Minnesota had no history of anti-Asian prejudice. In 1940 the census counted only fifty-one persons of Japanese ancestry in the whole state.[5] State officials were

---

[2] HQ, Western Defense Command (WDC) and Fourth Army, Special Orders no. 127, 7 May 42, in MISLS, "Training History of the Military Intelligence Service Language School," ann. 10, Personnel Procurement Office, encl 4, Unpubl Ms, 1946, U.S. Army Center of Military History (CMH), and Gen Records, 1943–1945, Military Intelligence [Service] Language School, Fort Snelling, Minn., Records of the Army Staff, Record Group (RG) 319, National Archives and Records Administration (NARA); "Army School at Savage To Teach Jap Language," *Minneapolis Morning Tribune*, 26 May 42.

[3] Shunji Hamano, "Rocky Mountain MIS Veterans Club Autobiographies," pp. 16–19, Unpubl Ms, ed. Kent T. Yoritomo, [1989], author's files (this and similar biographies hereafter cited as Rocky Mountain Bios). Intervs, Dan Tompkins with Yoshio G. Kanegai, 11 Oct 94, and author with Yoshio G. Kanegai, 16 Sep 96. Pete Nakao, in *The Saga of the MIS*, videotaped presentation, Los Angeles, 11 Mar 89; Intervs, author with Kan Tagami, 7 Dec 94, and with Roy T. Uyehata, 16 Nov 87; Roy T. Uyehata, Biography, Military Intelligence Service Club of Northern California (this and similar biographies hereafter cited as MISNorCal Bios).

[4] The basic sources for Camp Savage are "Training History" with annexes and *MISLS Album* (Minneapolis: Military Intelligence Service Language School, 1946).

[5] Theodore C. Blegen, *Minnesota: A History of the State* (Minneapolis: University of Minnesota Press, 1963), pp. 521–49. Savage was too small to appear in *Minnesota: A State Guide*, American Guide Series (New York: Hastings House, 1954).

*Camp Savage, Minnesota, autumn 1942. The road and rail lines to Minneapolis
are visible at top.*

"extremely cooperative in arranging for this camp," Lt. Col. Kai E. Rasmussen
told local reporters, "and we hope the public will show the men every courtesy
due American soldiers." For his part, he assured them that "if anything untoward
occurs, officers of course will have to see that proper protection is provided." The
Minneapolis Morning Tribune urged local residents to "extend a cordial welcome
to this unique army encampment."[6] In time Minneapolis–St. Paul would become a
haven for the Nisei soldiers and other Japanese Americans from the West Coast.

About 150 additional Nisei soldiers collected that spring from Army camps
in the South and Midwest joined the small group from Crissy Field. Together they
turned Camp Savage into a proper Army post. In recent years the state had used
the camp to house indigents. White rocks at the entrance spelled out "Homeless

---

[6] "Army School at Savage," with editorial. The school's relocation to Minnesota was also mentioned in the *Pacific Citizen*, 2 Jul 42, which reported a small number of Nisei were "teaching the
Japanese language to intelligence officers, studying and analyzing Japanese propaganda, making
use of specialized training and aptitude so that the United Nations may emerge victorious." The
next issue mentioned a Nisei soldier who was "attending the Army's intelligence school at Savage,
Minnesota." "Evacuee Drowns in Kings River," *Pacific Citizen*, 9 Jul 42, p. 1.

Men's Camp," to the wry amusement of the first Nisei who arrived there. The previous occupants had left the place filthy; inside the buildings, the soldiers found garbage and human waste everywhere. They dragged straw mattresses into the open air and set fire to them, then scrubbed the buildings from top to bottom.

Some of the new students arrived angry and demoralized. After Pearl Harbor, they had been mistrusted, disarmed, and shipped from one post to another without explanation. Their families had been evicted and placed into internment camps. Some did not even learn they had been selected for Japanese-language training until they arrived.

One disgruntled Nisei, Sgt. George Kanegai, had been a high school football player in Gardena, California. Drafted in March 1941, by June 1942 he was ready for a fight. When he arrived, a corporal assigned him to a work detail, but Kanegai refused. "You're not going to get me to pull grass, when you got these guys sitting around the office doing nothing," he said. "Get their asses out there.... I earned my stripes and I'm not about to go out there and do menial jobs when you've got these guys in your office sitting on their butt." A compromise put Kanegai in charge of the detail as befitted his rank as a noncommissioned officer.[7]

Most of the new students were ready to learn the Japanese language, but many already knew the language very well. Sunao Phil Ishio, a Kibei, was born in Berkeley, California, and raised in Salt Lake City, Utah. After one year at the University of Utah, he went to Japan in 1939 to study economics at Waseda University in Tokyo. In 1941 he returned to finish his degree at Utah but was soon drafted. After Pearl Harbor, he was transferred to several Army posts before being selected for Camp Savage. Placed in an accelerated class, he graduated in only three months.[8]

For leadership the school had two Caucasian officers who had come out of the prewar language attaché program. The commandant, Rasmussen, had studied Japanese in Tokyo for four years, during which "he had only scratched the surface," he later told a reporter. "I'd say if a man stayed at it about 28 years he might be rated pretty fair."[9] He was a dedicated and capable Regular Army officer who would stand by the Nisei through the worst of times. Maj. Joseph K. Dickey, another former language attaché and Military Academy graduate as well as a native Minnesotan, became assistant commandant.[10]

Colonel Rasmussen sympathized with the Nisei's plight after Pearl Harbor:

In the emergency which had naturally arisen the abrupt manner in which they were removed from various organizations to which they had been originally assigned ... and

---

[7] Intervs, Tompkins with Kanegai, 11 Oct 94, and author with Kanegai, 16 Sep 96.

[8] Interv, author with Sunao P. Ishio, 18 Apr 95; Stanley L. Falk and Warren M. Tsuneishi, eds., *MIS in the War against Japan* (Washington, D.C.: Japanese American Veterans Association, 1995), pp. 26–31, 102–03.

[9] "Army School at Savage."

[10] See also "Training History," ann. 1, Academic Training, para. 4–j, p. 12. "In Memoriam: Kai E. Rasmussen, 1902–1988," memorial service booklet, 1988.

re-assigned to non-combat units had left them bewildered and skeptical of their future as individuals and as a minority group.

Then, too, the evacuation of their families from their homes to War Relocation Centers created a confusion of thoughts within each individual. Their morale was at this time at a low point, because their minds were confused by the complexities of the position in which they found themselves. Question after question arose in their minds either imaginarily created by rumors or by misinterpretation of the necessary restrictive measures that the particular situation imposed upon them.

When upon subsequent assignment to the Military Intelligence Service Language School the individuals concerned were not at first amenable to their assignment. However, after a few months of pursuing the course of study and training, and the careful application of discipline by the School Staff, the confusion of their minds brought on by previous conditions slowly dispelled itself.[11]

On Monday, 1 June 1942, classes began with 160 Nisei and thirty Caucasian students.[12] Eighteen Nisei instructors (eight civilians and ten enlisted men) taught the classes using the curriculum developed at Crissy Field based on the Naganuma readers. Until tables and chairs could be procured, the students sat on the floor.[13] The course work was hard and the instructors demanding. The instructors were almost as inexperienced as the students, so students and instructors often worked late into the night. After lights out, many students pored over their textbooks and flashcards in the latrines, where the lights remained on all night. Because the school now reported directly to the Military Intelligence Service and was no longer part of Fourth Army, on 26 June the War Department renamed it the Military Intelligence Service Language School (MISLS).[14]

---

[11] Memo, MISLS for Brig. Gen. Hayes A. Kroner, 25 May 43, sub: Publicity in Regard Activities of American Soldiers of Japanese Descent in the Army of the United States (352), Office of the Assistant Secretary of War, RG 107, NARA.

[12] Sources vary for the number of students that began with the first Savage class. "Training History," table, p. 16, reports 22 officers (2 Nisei, 18 Caucasians, 2 Chinese Americans) and 160 enlisted men (149 Nisei, 10 Caucasians, 1 Chinese American). "Training History," ann. 1, para. 6–2, p. 6, reports 9 officers and 174 enlisted men (no separate figures by race). "Training History," ann. 10, Personnel Procurement, sec. IV, p. 3, reports 12 officers (Caucasian) and 200 enlisted men (192 Nisei and 8 Caucasians). Other sources report 200 students. *MISLS Album*, p. 10, and "A History of the Military Intelligence Division, 7 December 1941–2 September 1945," p. 225, Unpubl Ms, n.d., CMH. The higher figures may include overhead personnel or students who reported after 1 June 1942. The figures reported in "Training History" seem the most reliable. One former student remembers that about 360 Nisei were selected but only 160 passed the background checks. Hamano, Rocky Mountain Bio, p. 16.

[13] Ronald Chagami, "Tidbits from the MISLS Instructor Corps," in *Sempai Gumi*, ed. Richard S. Oguro (Honolulu: MIS Veterans of Hawaii, [1981]), p. 35.

[14] Memos, The Adjutant General's Office (TAGO) to CG, Seventh Corps Area, 22 May 42, sub: Constitution and Activation of Military Intelligence Service Japanese Intelligence School (AG 352), and Chief, MIS, to TAG, 26 Jun 42, sub: Redesignation of Miltary Intelligence Service Japanese Intelligence School (MID 352), both in Ofc of the Dir of Intel G–2, War Department (WD) Gen and Special Staffs, RG 165, NARA. On 25 May 1942, MID renamed the school the Military Intelligence Service Japanese Intelligence School. However, on 26 June the name changed again

Soon after the beginning of classes came encouraging news that the U.S. Navy had defeated the Japanese Navy at Midway on 4–5 June. As American and Australian forces took the offensive in the Solomon Islands and New Guinea, field commanders demanded more Japanese linguists. On 8 September the school graduated a special class of fourteen Nisei after just ten weeks of training. Twelve of them were Kibei, including Ishio. Led by two Caucasian officers and M.Sgt. Arthur Katsuyoshi Ushiro, the team accompanied the I Corps staff to Australia.[15] Later that autumn six more Nisei went to the South Pacific before graduation. By the end of 1942 the Joint Chiefs of Staff had sent ten Army and two Marine divisions to the Pacific. They would need more Japanese linguists as fast as the school could produce them.

John F. Aiso as Technical Director

Although Caucasian officers remained in control of the school, a senior civilian Nisei ran its day-to-day operations. Colonel Rasmussen was the commandant, but John Aiso as the technical director set the tone for students and instructors alike. The school was similar to the Japanese-language schools that many Nisei had attended before the war, with two key differences. First, the U.S. Army, not Japanese community leaders, operated the school. Second, Nisei, not Issei, served as the principal and instructors. Aiso had been named senior instructor in October 1941 at Crissy Field. By the time the school arrived in Minnesota, the 32-year-old lawyer was the leader of the Nisei staff and worked well with Rasmussen. Rasmussen handled the school's relations with the War Department, while Aiso ruled over the school's internal affairs with an iron hand.[16]

When Nisei students arrived at Camp Savage, they were sometimes surprised to see Aiso. Those from Southern California had heard about him as they were growing up. Aiso had struggled during the 1920s to overcome racial prejudice in the public schools and made the front pages of the Japanese American press.

---

to the Military Intelligence Service Language School. The first name was mentioned in "Training History," pp. 5–6, and "History of the Military Intelligence Division," p. 225.

[15] Joseph D. Harrington, *Yankee Samurai: The Secret Role of Nisei in America's Pacific Victory* (Detroit: Pettigrew Enterprises, 1979), pp. 44–45, 83–84; Interv, author with Ishio, 18 Apr 95; Falk and Tsuneishi, *MIS in the War against Japan*, pp. 27–28; "Training History," ann. 1, para. 6–2, p. 6; Interv, Sheryl Narahara with Torao "Pat" Neishi, 1992, National Japanese American Historical Society (NJAHS), San Francisco, Calif.; Thomas Masaharu Takata, diary, Joseph D. Harrington Papers, NJAHS. The fourteen Nisei included twelve members of the special class and two graduates from Crissy Field. Two other special class graduates stayed back as instructors. The officers were John Anderton and George Aurell.

[16] John F. Aiso, "Observations of a California Nisei," Interv with Marc Landy, University of California at Los Angeles, 1971; Loni Ding and Eric Saul with John F. Aiso, 1986, NJAHS; author with John F. Aiso, 30 Oct 87; Kiyoshi Yano, "Participating in the Mainstream of American Life amidst Drawback of Racial Prejudice and Discrimination," in *John Aiso and the M.I.S.: Japanese-American Soldiers in the Military Intelligence Service, World War II*, ed. Tad Ichinokuchi (Los Angeles: Military Intelligence Service Club of Southern California, 1988), pp. 4–32.

"Wherever the Japanese newspapers went, the story of John F. Aiso's victories also went." One Nisei remembered how his mother admonished him to "study intensively like John Aiso and become a great orator and bring honor to the then-budding Japanese American community."[17] Aiso was drafted in early 1941.

At Camp Savage, he delivered a stern message to each incoming class: "You were brought here to [study]," a student summarized, "and if you don't [study] according to our expectation, we know where your parents are!" Another student recalled how in June 1942 Aiso warned incoming students not to protest or strike: "Whatever you do here will have a reaction against your parents.... You have direct relation to your parents, your brothers and sisters."[18]

Aiso had lived in the limelight all his life as an exemplary Nisei and held the other Nisei to the same high standards he set for himself. He had a brilliant mind honed by years of hard study. He was steeped in the American political tradition and fond of quoting Abraham Lincoln.[19] The Nisei of his generation "had 'talked to Lincoln' as often as he prayed to his God," he later remarked, "because the rail-splitter knew what it was like to be born and raised in a rural shack as so many of the older Nisei were."[20] In Aiso's mind the Nisei's American heritage did not have to conflict with their Japanese heritage. Instead he urged them to "live like the cherry trees in our nation's capital; of Japanese origin and symbol of its knightly lore, but taking root into the richness of American soil enhancing with beauty in their season the Washington, Lincoln and Jefferson Memorials."[21]

The removal of Japanese from the West Coast may have shaken Aiso's faith, but he responded characteristically by working even harder. Nevertheless, the anti-

---

[17] Tad Ichinokuchi, "John Aiso and the MIS," in Ichinokuchi, *John Aiso and the M.I.S.*, pp. 1–3. Carey McWilliams described the young Aiso as "a brilliant Nisei" in *Prejudice: Japanese-Americans: Symbol of Racial Intolerance* (Boston: Little, Brown, 1944), p. 101. See also Bill Hosokawa, *Nisei: The Quiet Americans* (New York: William Morrow, 1969), pp. 167–68. See also ch. 1, note 20.

[18] Ltr, Joe Yoshiwara to Roy Uyehata, 18 February 1993, author's files; Harrington, *Yankee Samurai*, pp. 65, 144; Interv, author with Tagami, 7 Dec 94. During the same period, the commanding officer of the 100th Infantry Battalion at Camp McCoy gave similar lectures to his Nisei soldiers: "Isn't this the most important time of your life? Every one of you is being watched. Don't forget that the future of your families rests on your shoulders." Masayo U. Duus, *Unlikely Liberators: The Men of the 100th and 442nd* (Honolulu: University of Hawaii Press, 1987), p. 27.

Camp McCoy was also the site for a Department of Justice internment camp. One scholar asserts "that *both* the Japanese American internees and the soldiers were prisoners of the state, incarcerated at Camp McCoy during a time in which the dominant racial order threatened to dehumanize these men" (emphasis in original). Peggy Choy, "Racial Order and Contestation: Asian American Internees and Soldiers at Camp McCoy, Wisconsin, 1942–1943," in *Asian Americans: Comparative and Global Perspectives*, ed. Shirley Hune et al. (Pullman: Washington State University Press, 1991), pp. 87–102.

[19] Aiso, remarks, 1985, cited in Ichinokuchi, *John Aiso and the M.I.S.*, pp. 5, 28. When he ran for student body president of his junior high school in 1922, he quoted Lincoln's Gettysburg Address (p. 5).

[20] John F. Aiso, remarks at Arlington National Cemetery, 2 Jun 63, reprinted in "Tributes to Japanese American Military Service in World War II," *Congressional Record* (11 Jun 63), p. 7.

[21] John F. Aiso, speech to MIS Veteran's Reunion, Honolulu, Hawaii, 6 Sep 64.

Japanese prejudice of the war's first year provoked him to write a letter to California Attorney General Earl Warren, who was running for governor in the autumn of 1942. As attorney general, Warren had played a key role in the evacuation and declared he did not want the Japanese to return after the war. Aiso wrote to say that "I thought, at heart, he was a very religious man," he recalled. "I wanted him to know that some of us so-called 'Japs' were in the United States Army. I felt that after the war was over he would change his mind and let us come back."[22]

The Nisei, citizens by birth, responded in various ways to the tragic situation. Two-thirds were still minors and went with their families into the camps. Many men of military age chose to stay in the camps to keep their families together. Some became embittered and angry. A handful even sought legal remedies, but the federal courts rejected their cases. Aiso offered a different path: proving Nisei loyalty through dedicated military service. In the face of overwhelming prejudice, Aiso urged the Nisei to study their Japanese heritage and learn the language of the hated enemy—and their own parents. He infused the school with his ethics of hard study, patriotism in the face of prejudice, and self-discipline. Many saw him as a stern, unbending taskmaster. The school's official history praised his "firm direction," but one student many years later recalled him as having been "pompous, officious, and conceited." Only years after the war did Aiso admit to having been a "martinet" and to having overlooked "personal comfort and welfare."[23]

One of the first to run afoul of Aiso, Sergeant Kanegai, had also come from Southern California but had a very different outlook. Upset about the government's treatment of the Japanese (his family was interned at a camp in Manzanar, California), Kanegai first refused a work detail, then refused to study. Eventually he was dropped from the class. However, because of Kanegai's rank, the post commander named him acting first sergeant without clearing it with Aiso. Aiso would not tolerate this challenge to his authority over the other Nisei. Kanegai, whose new wife was expecting their first child, soon received orders for Australia. He

---

[22] Aiso, "Observations of a California Nisei," p. 106. After the war Aiso resumed his law practice in Los Angeles; in 1953 Governor Warren appointed him to the municipal court of Los Angeles, making him the first Nisei to serve in the state judiciary on the mainland. When Warren became Chief Justice of the U.S. Supreme Court, many Nisei felt he was unrepentant for his role in the evacuation. However, Aiso urged the Nisei "to respect [Warren's] reluctance and display a little magnanimity" and argued "it would serve no purpose to press him further." Hosokawa, *Nisei: The Quiet Americans*, p. 494.

[23] "Training History," ann. 1, para. 5, p. 4; Aiso, speech, 6 Sep 64; Faubion Bowers, personal communication to author, 1999. Gene Uratsu, a student and enlisted instructor at Crissy Field and Camp Savage, recalled that "the autocratic Director was known as 'Der Hitler' among the students and instructors." Uratsu later referred to himself as having been "young, foolish, and reckless." He added, "As I assumed more and more responsible positions in the army [as a career officer after the war], I began to realize how difficult it must have been for Aiso to run the school under extreme wartime pressure. I guess somebody had to be the son-of-a-bitch." Gene Masaji Uratsu, MISNorCal Bio. See also similar comments about Aiso and the school by WO Gerald Kobayashi to a War Relocation Authority (WRA) field worker in January 1944. Memo, 2 Jan 44, sub: Free Association: Army and Registration, Milwaukee, Wis.; Microfilm, frame 552, reel 84, sec. 15, pt. 2, Japanese Evacuation Research Study, Bancroft Library, University of California, Berkeley.

departed in early 1943 in charge of a group of nongraduating Nisei. They were sent to the Allied Translator and Interpreter Section as "overhead": clerks, cooks, and supply personnel.[24]

During 1942–1943 Aiso was the senior Nisei in government service; and as time went on he brought in other older Nisei who could serve as a stabilizing influence on the younger Nisei. Some were too old for active duty but still able to render valuable stateside service. In March 1943 Capt. Walter T. Tsukamoto, a 38-year-old Sacramento lawyer, was assigned as the school's staff judge advocate. Before the war, Tsukamoto had served as president of the Japanese American Citizens League (JACL) from 1938 to 1940 and held a reserve commission.[25] From Hawaii came Masaji Marumoto, thirty-seven, a Honolulu attorney and Harvard Law School graduate. After the war broke out, Marumoto helped form the Emergency Service Committee as a liaison between law enforcement officials in Hawaii and the Japanese community. He had tried to enlist in early 1943 but could not pass the physical exam. A few months later he joined MISLS and soon became a master sergeant and Aiso's personal clerk.[26]

Aiso's stern philosophy and personal example were a blend of Japanese and American characteristics. All his life he had studied hard, and he expected his students to do the same. Respect and self-discipline were essential, and education was the key to future success. He was profoundly aware of the gravity of the Nisei's position. He knew full well how they were being treated with suspicion and that the evacuation had swept away two generations of toil by the Nisei and their Issei parents. He responded by bearing down harder to prove his loyalty. At Camp Savage, the War Department allowed the Nisei to serve. Perhaps in time the Military Intelligence Service (MIS) Nisei could redeem all Japanese Americans and restore them to a place of honor.

Aiso also knew that the MIS Nisei would face a special challenge in fighting against Japan. When the War Department considered forming a Nisei combat unit

---

[24] Intervs, Tompkins with Kanegai, 11 Oct 94, and author with Kanegai, 16 Sep 96; *Saga of the MIS*. Kanegai became first sergeant for the Nisei assigned to ATIS and later earned a commission through officer candidate school.

[25] *MISLS Album*, p. 66; "Training History," ann. 15a, Legal Assistance; Bill Hosokawa, *JACL in Quest of Justice: The History of the Japanese American Citizens League* (New York: William Morrow, 1982), pp. 104–07.

[26] Interv notes, Joseph D. Harrington with Masaji Marumoto, 1973, Harrington Papers; Duus, *Unlikely Liberators*, p. 62; Aiso, "Observations of a California Nisei," p. 75; Masaji Marumoto, "Okinawa Revisited: A Look at Past, Future," *Honolulu Star Bulletin & Advertiser*, 14 Feb 71. In May 1944 Rasmussen nominated Marumoto for the Judge Advocate General Department officer candidate school. Marumoto was commissioned in May 1945 and served in the occupation of Okinawa. After the war he was appointed a justice of the Hawaii Territorial Supreme Court. Another Emergency Service Committee leader, Dr. Katsumi Kometani, went to Italy in 1944 with the 442d RCT as the regimental "morale officer." Duus, *Unlikely Liberators*, p. 29; Thomas D. Murphy, *Ambassadors in Arms* (Honolulu: University of Hawaii Press, 1954), pp. 66–67; "Emergency Service Committee," in *Encyclopedia of Japanese American History*, rev. ed., ed. Brian Niiya (New York: Facts on File, 2001); Tom Coffman, *The Island Edge of America: A Political History of Hawaii* (Honolulu: University of Hawaii Press, 2003), pp. 63–65.

in the autumn of 1942, Assistant Secretary of War John J. McCloy recommended such a unit but wrote to the Secretary of War, "We need not use them against members of their own race, but we could use them for many useful purposes."[27] The Secretary of War agreed to forming the 442d Regimental Combat Team (RCT) but employing it only "in a theater where it will not be fighting Japanese troops." General George C. Marshall, Army Chief of Staff, later gave a similar reason for sending the 100th Infantry Battalion and 442d RCT to Italy: "I knew that it was quite unwise and quite unfair to send them to the Southwest Pacific where they would be in contact with their own people."[28] Whether from concern about their personal feelings or from lingering doubts about their loyalty, War Department leaders acknowledged that sending Nisei to fight Japanese soldiers would be placing a special burden on them.

MIS Nisei, especially those who still had friends or family living in Japan, felt this burden acutely. "It was the AJA in the MIS who faced and answered the greatest challenge to his generation," Aiso later declared. "Are Americans of Japanese ancestry loyal enough to fight in the defense of America directly against their own kith and kin?"[29] "There were certain instances," he later admitted, of students who expressed hesitancy to fight against the Japanese. But this did not keep them from their duty.[30]

Recruiting Students, June–December 1942

As the new students began class at Camp Savage, school officials looked for hundreds more for future classes. "The greatest problem which faced [the school] after its removal to Savage," declared the school's official history after the war, "was the recruitment of adequate numbers of students for the school to carry an expanded program."[31] School officials knew that those with no previous exposure to the Japanese language required at least a year and often longer to reach a useful level of proficiency. The MIS did not have that kind of time. The government had placed the largest pool of potential students, Nisei of military age on the West

[27] Ltr, John J. McCloy to Henry L. Stimson, 15 October 1942, Folder: Stimson, Box WD1, Ser. 8, McCloy Papers, Amherst College, Amherst, Mass. Quote cited in Murphy, *Ambassadors in Arms*, pp. 106–07. Forrest C. Pogue, *George C. Marshall*, 4 vols. (New York: Viking, 1963–1987), 3: 147.

[28] Memo, WDGS [War Department General Staff] G–3 for Chief of Staff, 16 Dec 42, sub: Organization of a Military Unit To Be Composed of American Citizens of Japanese Descent (WDGCT 320), copy in Drawer 1600, Research File, Microfilm reel 300, item 4523, George C. Marshall Research Library, Lexington, Va.

[29] Aiso, speech, 6 Sep 64. See also similar comments in 1985, cited in Ichinokuchi, *John Aiso and the M.I.S.*, pp. 29–30.

[30] Aiso, "Observations of a California Nisei." In response to the interviewer's question in 1970 about the Nisei's hesitancy to fight against the Japanese, he commented: "I think the time is not ripe for me to answer this question in its full ramifications."

[31] WD Press Release, 22 Oct 45. Japanese Evacuation Research Study (JERS), pt. 2, sec. 2, reel 20, frame 0037, Bancroft Library, University of California, Berkeley.

Coast, behind barbed wire. One year earlier, before Pearl Harbor, school officials had screened 1,300 Nisei to select the first fifty-eight students. In the first half of 1942 they had selected another 150. (*See Table 1.*) By that summer all other Nisei soldiers on the West Coast had been transferred to interior posts or discharged.

Despite these difficult conditions, Colonel Rasmussen was able to recruit the first class at Camp Savage; but the school's future looked bleak. The Military Intelligence Division directed Rasmussen to recruit twice as many Nisei for yet another class to begin in December. More than 1,000 remained in mainland Army posts, and about 400 had been discharged to the Enlisted Reserve Corps.[32] Rasmussen checked and rechecked these Nisei, finding some whom previous searches had overlooked. By September Rasmussen had selected another 150 Nisei for the school, well short of the number required. The school even accepted Nisei over the normal enlistment age. In Tule Lake, they enlisted a veteran of the First World War, John M. Tanikawa, age forty-one. In 1918 he had served in France with the American Expeditionary Forces and had earned the Purple Heart and Croix de Guerre.[33] The recruiters occasionally found Caucasian soldiers such as Joseph J. Milanowski, who had studied Japanese at the University of Washington.[34] But Caucasians who could speak Japanese were rare.

To meet his requirements Rasmussen would have to recruit Nisei from behind barbed wire. In July the Military Intelligence Division obtained permission for Rasmussen to recruit students from the assembly and relocation centers and he wrote to Fourth Army and all center directors to describe the characteristics he was seeking: "A fair amount of fluency in the spoken Japanese; possession of an elementary knowledge of written Japanese, preferably, however, the capacity of reading newspapers; a good scholastic background in English and Japanese. In respect to this requirement it has been found here at the school that the best students usually are *Chūgakkō* [middle school] graduates with subsequent secondary American schooling."[35] He was granted access to the camps, and on 6 August he interviewed ninety Nisei at Manzanar.[36]

---

[32] Memo, Pettigrew to McCloy, 17 Dec 42, sub: Nisei Division (ASW 342.18), RG 107, NARA.

[33] "45-Year-Old Nisei Veteran Reenlists for Duty in Japan," *Pacific Citizen*, 27 Apr 46; WD Press Release, 22 Oct 45; Harrington, *Yankee Samurai*, p. 114.

[34] Interv, author with Joseph J. Milanowski, 30 Oct 87; Joseph J. Milanowski, "Camp Savage Memories," *MIS Northwest Newsletter* (April 1986), reprinted in Ichinokuchi, *John Aiso and the M.I.S.*, pp. 54–58.

[35] Ltr, Kai E. Rasmussen to WRA Center Directors, 13 July 1942, reprinted in Roger Daniels, ed., *American Concentration Camps: A Documentary History of the Relocation and Incarceration of Japanese Americans, 1941–1945*, 9 vols. (New York: Garland, 1989), vol. 9. Colonel Bendetsen, a key planner in the evacuation, noted on his file copy: "Rasmussen should not have addressed center managers directly—his action in so doing is irregular."

[36] Karl G. Yoneda, *Ganbatte: Sixty-Year Struggle of a Kibei Worker* (Los Angeles: Asian American Studies Center, University of California at Los Angeles, 1983). For other sources on recruiting in the camps in the summer and autumn of 1942, see "Training History," ann. 10; Harrington, *Yankee Samurai*, pp. 105–06, 113–19.

TABLE 1—SUMMARY OF STUDENT PERSONNEL FOR MISLS ACADEMIC TERMS NOVEMBER 1941–FEBRUARY 1944[a]

Academic Term	Students Entered		Students Relieved[b]		Students Graduated			
	Officer	Enlisted	Officer	Enlisted	Officer	Date	Enlisted	Date
Presidio[c] (4th Army)	18[d] (6 AEA) (2 ACA)	60	4	15	2	1 May 42	45	1 May 42
Jun 42	22[e] (18 AEA) (2 ACA)	160 (10 AEA) (1 ACA)	0	4	22	1 Dec 42	149 6 1 156	1 Dec 42 18 Jun 43 2 Feb 43
Dec 42	22	442	10	46	2 1 9 12	19 Apr 43 24 Apr 43 18 Jun 43	2 2 61 1 1 329 396	16 Jan 43 23 Mar 43 10 Apr 43 15 Apr 43 30 May 43 18 Jun 43
Jul 43	22[f] (20 AEA) (2 ACA)	733 (53 AEA) (50 ACA)	12	76	8 2 10	15 Jan 44 25 Mar 44	357 238 51 2 9 657	15 Jan 44 25 Mar 44 10 Aug 44 29 Sep 44 18 Nov 44
Feb 44	7 (1 ACA)	683 (14 AEA) (18 ACA)	1	140	1 4 1 6	10 Jun 44 10 Aug 44 29 Sep 44	5 8 89 1 4 10 1 1 379 45 543	25 Mar 44 19 May 44 10 Aug 44 23 Aug 44 7 Sep 44 29 Sep 44 9 Oct 44 10 Oct 44 18 Nov 44 17 Feb 45
Feb 44 OCS	3 (2 AEA) (1 ACA)	107	0	0	3	10 Aug 44	107	10 Aug 44

ACA American of Chinese Ancestry
AEA American of European Ancestry

Source: MISLS, "Training History of the Military Intelligence Service Language School," pp. 16–18, Unpubl Ms, 1946, U.S. Army Center of Military History (CMH).

Notes
a All Americans of Japanese Ancestry unless otherwise indicated. Figures are from existing available records, and slight inaccuracies are unavoidable.
b Includes those relieved for special assignment, academic reasons, CDD (Certificate of Disability for Discharge), etc.
c Numbers for Presidio Class are approximate.
d Twelve officers transferred to the first class at Camp Savage in June 1942.
e Twelve officers formerly from Presidio.
f Number does not include ten Marine officers; does not include nine officers and seven enlisted men of the Canadian Army.

*Nisei in Granada (Amache) Camp, Colorado, volunteering for the Military
Intelligence Service, 12 December 1942*

Once identified, how could these Nisei enlist in the Army? In March 1942
the War Department had declared all Nisei "unacceptable for service." The War
Department G–2, Maj. Gen. George V. Strong, took the question directly to General Marshall on 31 August, recommending that the Army enlist 350 Nisei from
the camps. Marshall agreed, and the recruiting proceeded as planned.[37] On 3
October Colonel Rasmussen wrote to the War Relocation Authority, requesting
"approximately 250 Nisei and Kibei for use in the Military Intelligence Service."[38]
The volunteers most highly sought were Kibei who had proficiency in both Japanese and English and could pass a loyalty investigation.

The requirements frustrated some Nisei who wanted to enlist. When Dillon
S. Myer, the director of the War Relocation Authority, visited the camp in Gila

---

[37] Memo, Strong to Chief of Staff, 31 Aug 42, sub: Enlistment of Americans of Japanese Ancestry (MID 327.31), WD G–1 Decimal File (291.2), RG 165, NARA.

[38] Ltr, Kai E. Rasmussen to Acting Regional Director, WRA, 3 October 1942, RG 210,
NARA.

River, Arizona, that autumn, he overheard a conversation between two young Nisei: "One of them asked the other, 'Are you going to join the army?' The other boy replied 'Hell no! Nobody but a damned Kibei can get into this man's army.'" Myer related this story to Assistant Secretary of War McCloy "to help prove our point that many Nisei wanted very badly to have the opportunity to demonstrate their loyalty." He recalled that McCloy "was impressed and promised to redouble his efforts to secure a change in policy."[39]

When Rasmussen's recruiters visited the camps in November, they could not have come at a worse time. The atmosphere in the camps had moved from initial shock at the forced relocation to seething anger at the indefinite incarceration. Hostility and resistance appeared in the form of threats and violence against suspected informants and supporters of the camp administration. In November and December violence erupted in Poston and Manzanar. The recruiters often conducted interviews at night so potential recruits could evade watchful eyes. In November two Nisei instructors from Camp Savage went to Poston and smuggled out eight Nisei volunteers at night during a campwide strike.[40] Fourteen more were selected from Manzanar.

Volunteers inside some camps were threatened or beaten. Some Issei parents were so angered at the thought of their sons' volunteering to fight against Japan that they disowned them. To make matters worse, rumors spread that the War Department was using Japanese-speaking Nisei as spies inside the camps. Nevertheless, recruiters interviewed 439 Nisei in the camps that autumn and selected 66 for language training.[41]

Some volunteered for the MIS primarily to escape camp. "To be perfectly honest about it, I felt I was in a rut and just decaying in camp," Shoso Nomura recalled of his months in Gila River: "It wasn't a normal society like, as you expect just to be able to go into business or further your education. Those opportunities were all lost." He volunteered for MIS that November.[42] Some Issei parents supported their sons' decision to enlist. "Wars were just a short period in a man's life," Marshall M. Sumida's father told him. "The question of being a Japanese or American was a difficult one. What he considered important was that a man be a man—and do whatever a man must do."[43]

---

[39] Dillon S. Myer, *Uprooted Americans: The Japanese Americans and the War Relocation Authority during World War II* (Tucson: University of Arizona Press, 1971), pp. 145–46.

[40] Interv, author with Roy T. Takai, 30 Oct 87; Pat Nagano, MISNorCal Bio. Harrington, *Yankee Samurai*, p. 114. See also Elaine B. Yoneda, in *Only What We Could Carry: The Japanese American Internment Experience*, ed. Lawson Fusao Inada (Berkeley, Calif.: Heyday Books, 2000), pp. 164–70. Yoneda was married to Karl Yoneda, one of the Nisei recruited from Manzanar for MISLS in November 1942.

[41] Masaharu Ano, "Loyal Linguists: Nisei of World War II Learned Japanese in Minnesota," *Minnesota History* 45, no. 7 (Fall 1977): 279–80; Daisuke Kitagawa, *Issei and Nisei: The Internment Years* (New York: Seabury Press, 1967), pp. 109–11; "Training History," ann. 10, p. 4.

[42] Interv, author with Shoso Nomura, 10 Sep 96.

[43] Ano, "Loyal Linguists," p. 280.

Shortly afterward, the Foreign Broadcast Intelligence Service (FBIS) sent recruiters into the camps to look for Japanese-speaking Nisei. "Unfortunately, Colonel Rasmussen . . . visited all the projects about six weeks ago and did an excellent job of cream skimming," complained the agency's recuiter. "He has taken literally dozens of the best people and left very few." The recruiters interviewed 174 people in the camps; they considered only twenty-two well qualified. Of these, FBIS was able to hire only four.[44]

Another valuable source of students was the Hawaii Nisei soldiers transferred to Camp McCoy, Wisconsin, in June 1942.[45] The 100th Infantry Battalion contained many Kibei, but many could not speak English very well. Late in 1942 Lt. Col. Joseph K. Dickey and Akira Oshida, a civilian instructor, visited McCoy. Of the 1,400 Nisei stationed there, only ninety-two passed the screening test; about sixty were selected for the school.[46] Many did not want to leave their friends.

Hoichi Kubo objected strongly. Drafted in 1941, he had witnessed the Japanese air raid on Wheeler Field on 7 December 1941. His two grandfathers had both fought for Japan against Russia in 1904–1905, and he felt it was now his turn to fight for America. He wanted to fight, not sit at a desk. He deliberately failed the language test, even though his Japanese was excellent. But school officials saw through his ruse and selected him.[47]

Terry Mizutari was also selected, even though his father, a Japanese-language school principal and kendo instructor, was interned in the Department of Justice camp in Crystal City, Texas. Mizutari was a typical Hawaii Nisei, outgoing and popular. He played the ukulele and harmonica and thanks to his father was excellent in kendo.

Another Hawaii Nisei was Thomas Kiyoshi Tsubota, a platoon sergeant. Tsubota graduated from Waseda and Meiji Universities in Tokyo before returning to Hawaii, where he was drafted before the war. He was one of two Nisei soldiers who had spotted a beached Japanese midget submarine the day after the Pearl Harbor attack. He tried to refuse language training to stay with his friends but was selected anyway.[48]

The class that began on 15 December 1942 was composed of 444 Nisei, a mix of prewar draftees, volunteers from the camps, and Hawaii Nisei from the 100th Infantry Battalion. Many were over thirty, older than the Army usually enlisted. School officials had identified virtually every available potential student. Rasmus-

---

[44] Stephen C. Mercado, "FBIS against the Axis, 1941–1945," *Studies in Intelligence* 11 (Fall/ Winter 2001).

[45] Murphy, *Ambassadors in Arms*, pp. 73–90; Duus, *Unlikely Liberators*, pp. 24–39; Harrington, *Yankee Samurai*, pp. 120, 123–24. The 100th Infantry Battalion was transferred to Camp Shelby in January 1943 and then to the Mediterranean Theater in August. The MIS did not recruit Nisei directly from Hawaii until the summer of 1943.

[46] Sources vary on the number selected. See Oguro, *Sempai Gumi*, pp. iii, 158–76.

[47] Interv, author with Hoichi Kubo, 30 Oct 87; Hoichi Kubo, MISNorCal Bio.

[48] Oguro, *Sempai Gumi*, p. 21; Ted T. Tsukiyama et al., eds., *Secret Valor: M.I.S. Personnel, World War II Pacific Theater, Pre–Pearl Harbor to Sept. 8, 1951* (Honolulu: Military Intelligence Service Veterans Club of Hawaii, 1993), p. 69.

sen appealed directly to Nisei leaders on the mainland for their support. On 22 November he addressed a national conference of the Japanese American Citizens League held in Salt Lake City, Utah:

I want you to know that I believe the whole future of the Nisei lies with two groups—the JACL and the Nisei in the armed services. We must assure the rest of the country that you are not just Americans, but that you are superlative Americans, contributing more to the war effort at higher cost.... Let's forget about justice and confront conditions and find out how we can best improve and meet them. Keep improving your lot, and this can be done only with unselfish efforts. Upon your shoulders rests the success of your cause.[49]

The Nisei leaders at the conference came out strongly for the resumption of Selective Service. Two months later, in January 1943, the War Department called for volunteers for the 442d RCT. Hundreds were quietly diverted to the Military Intelligence Service.

Teaching and Learning at Camp Savage

Before the war most Americans regarded the Japanese language as notoriously difficult to learn, almost a secret weapon in itself. "The complexities of the Japanese language," Col. John Weckerling later wrote, "are almost beyond occidental comprehension."[50] For most Nisei it was not much easier. Based on the three-year Naganuma program that the U.S. Embassy in Tokyo had used before the war, the school improvised a curriculum crammed into six months. Its key feature was intensive study. The students at Camp Savage remained under tremendous pressure for academic performance and found the course exhausting and frustrating. After lights-out, the duty officer patrolled the latrines to prevent the students from staying up all night to cram for exams. (Many did anyway.) The instructors "were not handicapped by pre-conceived habits of leisurely peacetime teaching," according to the school's official history, "and did not tolerate student inefficiency on the plea that Japanese was 'a very difficult language.'"[51]

Added to military and academic discipline was a cultural factor, the high value that Japanese families placed on education. Students were to respect, honor, and obey their teachers. Each day the students attended seven hours of classes with two hours of mandatory evening study. Saturday mornings were reserved for weekly examinations. "They really meant business," a Hawaii Nisei recalled. "Boy, did they give it to us. No fool around kind."[52] School officials noticed "a rise

---

[49] Suppl no. 37, JACL Special Emergency National Conference, 17–24 Nov 42, frame 173, reel 84, sec. 14, pt. 2, Japanese Evacuation Research Study, Bancroft Library.

[50] John Weckerling, "Japanese Americans Play Vital Role in United States Intelligence Service in World War II" (1946), first printed in *Hokubei Mainichi*, 27 Oct–5 Nov 71, reprinted as a pamphlet.

[51] "Training History," p. 4.

[52] "Masao 'Harold' Onishi: Former Instructor Shares Memories," *Hawaii Herald*, 2 Jul 93.

Shoji Takimoto teaching Japanese tactics at Camp Savage

in the need for eyeglasses. . . . The reading of the intricate and involved characters running up and down the page instead of across the page as in English seems to put a strain on the eyes and the optic nerve. If it is continued for a protracted length of time and under poor lights, its damaging effects are pronounced."[53]

The instructors soon realized that classes had to start from the very beginning and had to provide more than mere refresher training. Some students advanced faster than others, so the instructors developed a classification examination to divide the students into sections by ability.[54] The instructors gradually improved upon and supplemented the Naganuma readers and other materials.[55] In addition to language instruction, special topics ranged from Japanese culture and history to military terminology. For example, during 1942 Aiso wrote a lecture on "Racial Characteristics of the Japanese"; Shigeya Kihara wrote on "History of Japan" and "Institutional Factors in Japanese Militarism"; and Toshio G. Tsukahira wrote on "Japanese Militarism, Past and Present."[56] The school also exposed the students to Japanese films, large quantities of which the U.S. government had seized when

---

[53] "Training History," ann. 1, para. 6, pp. 3–4.

[54] Ibid., para. 9–8, p. 6.

[55] Sample textbooks in Box 290, Ofc of the Dir of Intel G–2, WD Gen and Special Staffs, RG 165, NARA.

[56] "Training History," ann. 1, contains a thorough description of the curriculum as it evolved during the war. Background lectures: "Training History," ann. 1, para. 10c., pp. 11–12. See also other annexes to "Training History" and administrative memos in Box 321, Ofc of the Dir of Intel G–2, WD Gen and Special Staffs, RG 165, NARA.

the war began. As the war went on, the curriculum continued to evolve. Beginning with the December 1942 class, the instructors laid new stress on heigo, or military Japanese; in a few cases instructors tailored the course for special classes.[57]

School officials tried to balance military training with the language instruction. On Wednesday afternoons the director of military training sent the students on conditioning marches across the Minnesota countryside. Other military training and orientation programs were conducted during the week and occasionally on weekends. "But whatever were the ratings of the military training program on the popularity poll," the student album later acknowledged, "it was devised to keep the men as sharp physically as they would have to be linguistically." Instructors resented the time taken away from language instruction, which they felt "demoralized the students by diversity of command and [gave] those directing the training very little opportunity for coordination and integration. The military training tended to encroach on the academic training in disregard of the primary mission of the school."[58]

Responding to the needs of field commanders, the school added special instruction in prisoner of war interrogation. At first the instructors recommended harsh, aggressive interrogation techniques. "The students loved this approach," Kihara recalled, especially when the teacher played the "prisoner" and the students gleefully practiced shouting at him in Japanese: "Stupid! Don't lie! If you don't talk, we'll beat you!"[59] However, as time went on, reports from the field indicated that compassion and kind treatment tended to work better.

The school expanded its physical plant, adding a theater, a gymnasium, and other buildings to the Spartan CCC facilities. During the winter of 1942–1943, one student wrote directly to the War Department Inspector General, "stating his grievances of inadequate living quarters and sanitation facilities (showers, toilet bowls, and urinals) as well as other inadequacies."[60] Students and staff alike complained about the drafty camp buildings that proved no match for the Minnesota winters. That winter the thermometer fell to 40 degrees below zero, quite an ordeal for the Nisei from California and Hawaii. In the classrooms and barracks, those too close to the coal stoves were too hot, those too far away too cold. It was the first time many Nisei had seen snow.[61]

In spite of poor facilities, the students found a camaraderie and group identity at Camp Savage that had been sorely lacking since the war began. Like sol-

[57] *MISLS Album*, p. 10; "Training History," ann. 1, para. 4–c3.

[58] *MISLS Album*, p. 69; "Training History," ann. 1, para. 4–j, pp. 11–12. See also student paper, "Specialized Intelligence Personnel," 21 Jun 46, N–13775, U.S. Army Command and General Staff College, Fort Leavenworth, Kans. For other Army schools, see William R. Keast, "Service Schools of the Army Ground Forces," in *The Procurement and Training of Ground Combat Troops*, ed. Robert R. Palmer et al. (Washington, D.C.: Department of the Army, Historical Division, 1948), pp. 241–319.

[59] Shigeya Kihara, in *Unsung Heroes: The Military Intelligence Service, Past-Present-Future* (Seattle: MIS-Northwest Association, 1996), p. 64.

[60] Richard Kaoru Hayashi, MISNorCal Bio, p. 5.

[61] Ichinokuchi, *John Aiso and the M.I.S.*, p. 60; Oguro, *Sempai Gumi*, p. 138.

Temporary barracks at Camp Savage

Student outside barracks at Camp Savage. Minnesota's harsh winters came as a shock to Nisei from the West Coast and Hawaii.

*Military Intelligence Service
Language School emblem*

diers everywhere, at Camp Savage, the Nisei met old friends and made many new ones. In 1943 T.Sgt. Chris Ishii captured the school's spirit in a humorous logo. A graphic artist with Disney Studios before the war, he designed a buck-toothed Minnesota gopher wearing an Indian war bonnet. Although the gopher was the mascot of the University of Minnesota, no one could fail to notice the satirical reference to the caricature of the Japanese enemy.[62]

While the Nisei students enjoyed making fun of themselves, they also fought hard against the demonized image of the Japanese race that prevailed in wartime America. They considered the word "Jap" a racial slur. The JACL instead promoted a more dignified term: American of Japanese Ancestry. In 1943, when the 100th Infantry Battalion arrived at Camp Shelby, a staff officer asked the battalion commander, Lt. Col. Farrant L. Turner, "Did you get your Japs here all right?" Turner was said to have replied, "Sir, my men are not 'Japs.' That is a term of opprobrium we use for the enemy. My troops are Americans of Japanese ancestry serving in the American Army." In far-off Brisbane, Australia, M.Sgt. George Kanegai thought he heard an Australian officer address a group of American Nisei as Japs and took offense until someone explained that the officer was just trying to be friendly by asking them, "Where are you chaps from?"[63]

In Minnesota, the Nisei were pleased to find that local civilians viewed them simply as American soldiers far from home. On Saturday afternoons generous locals waited outside the gates to Camp Savage and as the Nisei left post on weekend pass invited them home to dinner. The Twin Cities offered all the attractions of a Midwestern metropolitan area for their off-duty time, even a few Chinese restaurants that served familiar fare. On weekends, hundreds of Nisei descended on Minneapolis–St. Paul to enjoy the Red Cross, YMCA, movie theaters, restaurants,

---

[62] *MISLS Album*, cover, p. 37. The album's art editor, M.Sgt. Tom Okamoto, had also worked at Disney before the war. *MISLS Album*, p. 84. The students wore a simple MISLS shoulder patch. The gopher remained an unofficial logo. In the 1990s MIS veterans groups stopped using the logo at the request of some Native Americans, who felt it perpetuated an offensive stereotype.

[63] Murphy, *Ambassadors in Arms*, pp. 91, 121; Interv, author with Kanegai, 16 Sep 96. The Hollywood film about the 442d RCT, *Go For Broke,* Metro-Goldwyn-Mayer, 1951, made a similar point about the Nisei's sensitivity to the slur.

Barracks poker, Camp Savage

and bars. In June 1943 the Young Women's Christian Association opened a special USO in Minneapolis for the Nisei soldiers.[64]

On occasion the Midwesterners were not sure what to make of the Nisei. Some bartenders mistook them for Native Americans and refused to serve them, because some states prohibited serving alcohol to Native Americans.[65] In another instance of mistaken identity, while on a recruiting trip to Camp Shelby, civilian instructor Shigeya Kihara encountered a tall, distinguished-looking stranger on the train platform in Hattiesburg, Mississippi: "I commanded the Marine Guard at the U.S. Embassy in Peking many years ago. I have a great admiration for the Chinese people," said the stranger, who added, "We're going to beat the hell out of the Japs, aren't we?" Kihara responded tactfully, "Yes, sir!"[66]

As the War Relocation Authority began to allow Nisei to leave the internment camps in 1943, Nisei women began to appear in Minneapolis–St. Paul in increas-

---

[64] Ichinokuchi, *John Aiso and the M.I.S.*, pp. 48–53. In the 1970s former Nisei students presented a Japanese garden to Minnesota in recognition of the people's generosity. Michael Albert, "The Japanese," in *They Chose Minnesota: A Survey of the State's Ethnic Groups*, ed. June D. Holmquist (St. Paul: Minnesota Historical Society Press, 1981), p. 568. The United Service Organization (USO) operated hundreds of service clubs in the States and overseas.

[65] "Masao 'Harold' Onishi: Former Instructor Shares Memories"; Spady Koyama, in Ichinokuchi, *John Aiso and the M.I.S.*, p. 165.

[66] Shigeya Kihara, "MIS Recruiting at Camp Shelby," in Tsukiyama et al., *Secret Valor*, p. 58.

ing numbers to seek jobs or schooling. Though the University of Minnesota could not accept Nisei students because of its large ROTC program, several other area colleges did accept them. By the end of the war, according to one report, "only Chicago had more Nisei students than the Twin Cities area."[67]

A number of Nisei students and instructors got married while stationed at Camp Savage. In the spring of 1943 Pat Nagano, a student from Morro Bay, California, visited a former college roommate studying at the University of Michigan. There he met Atsuko Ono, a Nisei from Fresno, California. They became engaged, Nagano recalled, "with the understanding that marriage would be deferred until I got back from duty overseas." Upon graduation Nagano was surprised to be held back as an enlisted instructor. His fiancée reminded him of his promise and, he recalled, "had all the arguments on her side." They were married in Chicago in November 1943.[68]

A more unpleasant aspect of life at the school was the constant surveillance for possible disloyalty. The Counter Intelligence Corps (CIC) kept close watch on the Nisei. Each was subject to a background investigation, which led to some being dropped from class. Others had to stay after graduation until their investigation could be completed. The school commandant sometimes had to overrule other government agencies when they denied security clearances to his students "merely because their parents now living in the United States had been born in Japan, or the person being investigated had visited Japan for a few months at a very early age, or he had deposited a small amount of money in a Japanese bank several years prior to the declaration of war."[69] On at least one occasion a student was denied a security clearance because his Issei father had requested repatriation to Japan rather than remain in an internment camp.[70]

Inside the school, students and staff alike cooperated with the CIC's counter-subversive program. This program recruited secret informants on the basis of one for every thirty soldiers throughout the Army. At Camp Savage, each barrack had two or three informants who reported secretly to the school's intelligence officer, Capt. Laurence P. Dowd. According to the school's official history, "this system worked very effectively and resulted in recommendations for relief and reassignment of several men."[71] In one case an informant's report followed a graduate all the way to New Caledonia, where the startled Nisei was called on the carpet for an unguarded remark he had made months earlier in the shower room at Camp

---

[67] Albert, "The Japanese," p. 560.

[68] Pat Nagano, MISNorCal Bio.

[69] "Training History," ann. 4, Intelligence Section, p. 1; John P. Finnegan and Romana Danysh, *Military Intelligence*, Army Lineage Series (Washington, D.C.: U.S. Army Center of Military History, 1998), pp. 72–76. The CIC also conducted close surveillance of other minority groups, such as African Americans, considered potential targets for German, Japanese, and Communist subversion. See Ulysses Lee, *The Employment of Negro Troops* (Washington, D.C.: Office of the Chief of Military History, 1966), pp. 361–62.

[70] Harrington, *Yankee Samurai*, p. 85.

[71] "Training History," ann. 4. Laurence P. Dowd remained on the MISLS staff throughout the war. The *MISLS Album* gives his first name incorrectly.

Savage. In early 1944 Captain Dowd called a student to account for writing a letter that mentioned poor student morale and called some of the Caucasian officers "unfit for regular duty."[72] Caucasian team leaders were secretly instructed to keep an eye on their Nisei enlisted men while overseas to make sure they were translating and interpreting accurately and not providing misleading or false information.[73] In overseas theaters, the CIC maintained an active surveillance program directed at all soldiers, including the Nisei.[74]

The Army's entire countersubversive program came under sharp criticism in 1943, and by year's end the War Department shut down the program within the continental United States and sharply reduced the Counter Intelligence Corps. In 1944 the War Department transferred most of its stateside functions to the Office of the Provost Marshal General. However, for the rest of the war, MISLS maintained its own surveillance program "to the extent that a few well-known and highly trusted enlisted men [were] asked to render confidential reports on any men who might come to their attention as not being suitable material for the school."[75] During 1943 about one student in ten was relieved for academic and nonacademic causes, some because of these background checks.[76]

Nevertheless, Rasmussen and his staff remained firm believers in the loyalty of their Nisei students and stood up to other government agencies on their behalf. In 1944 the school decided to send T5g. Terry Takeshi Doi overseas. Doi had been born in America, but his Issei parents took him to Japan at an early age. After schooling he was conscripted into the Imperial Japanese Army. After his discharge he returned home to California. According to U.S. law, by serving in the armed forces of a foreign state he had forfeited his citizenship. Nevertheless, MISLS accepted him. After graduation in the spring of 1943, he stayed at the school for another year. Finally, on 26 July 1944, he appeared before a U.S. district judge in St. Paul to apply for naturalization. "He wanted to meet the Japanese in combat," he told the judge, "so he could prove his loyalty to America." A Canadian woman refused naturalization at the same time, saying, "How can I be sworn in as an American citizen alongside a man who belonged to an army that's now killing our boys?" The judge took a different view. He reinstated Doi as a citizen

---

[72] Harrington, *Yankee Samurai*, p. 85; Hisashi Kubota, MISNorCal Bio, pp. 27–28. Kubota later served on Peleliu and Saipan and after the war worked as a chemist in Oak Ridge, Tennessee.

[73] Harrington, *Yankee Samurai*, pp. 62–63. Harrington's disclosure that Caucasian officers were instructed to keep watch over the Nisei enlisted men aroused controversy among MIS veterans. James Oda, "John Aiso and the MIS," *Pacific Citizen*, 1 Jan 89, reprinted in James Oda, *Secret Embedded in Magic Cables* (Northridge, Calif.: J. Oda, 1993), pp. 119–24.

[74] Elliott R. Thorpe, *East Wind, Rain: An Intimate Account of an Intelligence Officer in the Pacific, 1939–49* (Boston: Gambit, 1969); Duval A. Edwards, *Spy Catchers of the U.S. Army in the War with Japan* (Gig Harbor, Wash.: Red Apple Publishing, 1994).

[75] "Training History," ann. 4, p. 9.

[76] Some Nisei with unfavorable security determinations were reassigned to the 442d RCT. Pfc. George Gushiken, twenty-five, was removed from the top class for security reasons in October 1942. He later joined the 442d RCT and was killed in action in France on 7 November 1944. Hamano, Rocky Mountain Bio, p. 17.

and postponed the woman's case to a later date. Local newspapers reported the incident approvingly.[77]

Civilian instructors made up the core faculty. The eight original instructors from Crissy Field grew to twenty over the next two years.[78] Many, such as Yutaka Munakata, an electrical engineer hired in December 1942, were recruited from the camps. They averaged fifteen classroom hours per week and spent many additional hours grading tests and developing lessons. Aiso drew the civilian instructors close to him. They lived and worked together closely and kept separate from the enlisted instructors. The civilian instructors and their families formed a small, close-knit social group in a cluster of temporary wooden quarters known as Camp 7.[79] As the school expanded, civilian Nisei took over key jobs. When Aiso was commissioned in 1944 and appointed director of academic training, his closest associate, Paul T. Tekawa, a Kibei, replaced him as technical director. Akira Oshida became director of the Research and Liaison Section. Munakata became director of the Translation Section. Tsukahira became chair of the special division for students not of Japanese ancestry.

The faculty came mostly from the mainland, which caused some friction with Nisei from Hawaii. Moreover, while the Navy's school at Boulder used Nisei women as instructors, MISLS did not allow women instructors "because of inadequate administrative facilities," according to the school's official history, and "because it was believed that Military Japanese could best be taught by men."[80] In early 1944 Lt. Col. Moses W. Pettigrew in the Military Intelligence Division proposed to commission nine instructors and the school held a selection board for that purpose. But the War Department approved only one, Aiso, who received a direct commission to major in October 1944. At war's end the school's official history lamented that the Army had not commissioned more:

Problems of discipline among the student body would have been automatically solved. It would have added immeasurably to the prestige, dignity, and authority of the faculty. The instruction would have reflected this in increasing effectiveness and suasion. Classes

---

[77] WD Press Release, 22 Oct 45; and "Flayed by Skater, Doi 'Proved Loyalty,'" *St. Paul Dispatch*, 24 Oct 45; Harrington, *Yankee Samurai*, p. 276. Doi later served on Iwo Jima and earned the Silver Star. School officials helped other students obtain citizenship, including Ulrich Straus, a German Jew who had learned Japanese while his family lived in Tokyo from 1933 to 1940. Ulrich Straus, *The Anguish of Surrender: Japanese POWs of World War II* (Seattle: University of Washington Press, 2003), pp. x–xi; Falk and Tsuneishi, *MIS in the War against Japan*, pp. 76–78, 125–26; "Training History," ann. 10, sec. IV (2).

[78] All civilian instructors were Nisei except for Richard N. McKinnon, who was born in Japan to a Caucasian father and a Japanese mother. *MISLS Album*, pp. 47, 135. After the war he earned his Ph.D. in Japanese literature and joined the faculty of the University of Washington.

[79] *MISLS Album*, p. 39.

[80] "Training History," p. 14. MISLS may have tried to recruit Nisei women as instructors in early 1943, but none was hired. Brenda L. Moore, *Serving Our Country: Japanese American Women in the Military during World War II* (New Brunswick, N.J.: Rutgers University Press, 2003), p. 92. Shortly after the war's end, MISLS retained three graduates of the Women's Army Corps class as enlisted instructors.

Faculty at Camp Savage, early 1943. Second row, starting seventh from left:
Dickey, Rasmussen, and Aiso.

would always be characterized by the authority and compulsion of a military formation. Absences from or tardiness to class, poor performance, malingering would carry the seriousness of a dereliction of duty.[81]

To increase his cadre, Aiso retained many of the top students, as well as a few World War I veterans too old for overseas service.[82] He held over ten enlisted graduates from Crissy Field to be enlisted instructors and added a few more from each class. By the summer of 1944 their number had grown to several dozen. Most would have preferred overseas service, but the burgeoning enrollment gave school officials little choice.[83]

The need for new instructors intensified as instructors went to other assignments. In the summer of 1943 two Crissy Field graduates, S.Sgts. Thomas T. Sakamoto and Gene Uratsu, requested overseas assignment after a year as enlisted instructors. They got their wish and in September led sixty graduates to Australia. Within months Sakamoto was serving with the 1st Cavalry Division in the Admiralty Islands and Uratsu with the 158th RCT in New Guinea. By 1944 Aiso allowed other long-time enlisted instructors to go. In January 1944, M.Sgt. Joe Y. Masuda, a Crissy Field graduate, led a team to Vint Hill Farms, Virginia, for signals intelligence work. A few months later M.Sgt. Morio Nishita, another

---

[81] "Training History," ann. 1, para. 4–e, p. 5; Memo, Lt. Col. A. W. Stuart to Chief, Personnel Br, MIS, 18 Feb 44, Ofc of the Dir of Intel G–2, WD Gen and Special Staffs, RG 165, NARA.

[82] *MISLS Album*, p. 96 (photo).

[83] Intervs, author with Thomas Sakamoto, 16 Nov 87, and with Arthur M. Kaneko, 23 Aug 95; Takashi Matsui, "Teaching at the Military Intelligence Service Language School," in Falk and Tsuneishi, *MIS in the War against Japan*, pp. 4–8, 108–09; *MISLS Album*, pp. 46–47 (photo).

Top Class at Camp Savage, ca. 1943

Crissy Field graduate, replaced him. Kan Tagami, a November 1942 graduate who remained as an instructor for almost two years, left in July 1944 to join the 124th Cavalry in Burma. In September 1944 MISLS sent nine instructors to help set up the Pacific Military Intelligence Research Section (PACMIRS), a document-translation center in Maryland.

Through hard work and experience the instructors gradually learned how to teach Japanese. "None of us had any prior teaching experience, nor did we receive any kind of training on the artful management of teaching," Uratsu recalled. "I did not have the slightest idea how to conduct class at the beginning. . . . After several months of painful trials and tribulations, I blossomed into some sort of teacher or facsimile thereof. A life of a teacher was not a bed of roses. . . . I ruefully discovered that life was much easier to be a student than a teacher."[84]

The instructors had a firsthand knowledge of Japanese language and culture virtually unavailable anywhere else in the United States. S.Sgt. Takashi Matsui, a Kibei student in the first Savage class, had completed eleven years of schooling in Japan followed by the University of Washington. When he graduated from MISLS in December 1942, he was promoted to staff sergeant and stayed on as an instructor.[85] The instructors came to scorn those whose knowledge of Japanese

---

[84] Uratsu, MISNorCal Bio, p. 2.
[85] Falk and Tsuneishi, *MIS in the War against Japan*, pp. 4–8, 108–09.

was purely aesthetic or theoretical, such as Harold G. Henderson, an "Orientalist" on the faculty of Columbia University who had been active in the Japan Society, published translations of *haiku* poetry, and in 1943 published a handbook of Japanese grammar. When the 54-year-old Orientalist came to Camp Savage to give a lecture, his poor accent amused the Nisei faculty. Rasmussen appointed him director of academic training for a time, but he departed for Australia in mid-1944.[86]

During the school's stay at Camp Savage, change was constant, most visibly in the construction of barracks, classrooms, and other facilities. Key personnel changed as well. The assistant commandant, Colonel Dickey, who had helped select the first Nisei students in 1941, transferred to Chungking in 1943 as G–2 of U.S. Army Forces in China under Lt. Gen. Joseph W. Stilwell.[87] Lt. Col. Archibald W. Stuart, one of Americans who had been repatriated from Japan on the *Gripsholm* in 1942, replaced him.

In June 1943 Aiso completely reorganized the school. He divided it by ability (upper, middle, and lower) and formed two nonteaching sections: the Translation Section and the Military Research and Liaison Section.[88] In August he formed a special division for late-arriving students from Camp Shelby and for non-Nisei students. In January 1944 Aiso again reorganized the school, eliminating the ability groupings and forming four separate divisions. Under Yutaka Munakata the Translation Section became a graduate pool for Nisei waiting for assignment. (Munakata had formed the original section in November 1942.) As time went on, his students translated a variety of technical materials. While waiting for their orders (for weeks or sometimes months), the recent graduates labored over translating captured documents, partly for their intelligence value and partly to stay in practice.[89]

---

[86] Harold G. Henderson, *The Bamboo Broom: An Introduction to Japanese Haiku* (Boston: Houghton Mifflin, 1934); Harold G. Henderson, *Handbook of Japanese Grammar* (Boston: Houghton Mifflin, 1943). Henderson's grammar was used at MISLS. "Training History," ann. 1, para. 10c., pp. 14, 18. The *MISLS Album* lists Maj. Leon [*sic*] Henderson as director of academic training (p. 136), but he is otherwise unmentioned in the album or the official history. His departure in 1944 probably allowed Rasmussen to commission Aiso for the vacant position. See also "Former Academic Director Now General MacArthur Education Officer," *Yaban Gogai*, Nov 45, p. 11. Kihara, personal communication to author, 1999; James Oda, "John Aiso and the MIS," *Pacific Citizen*, 23–30 Dec 88, reprinted in Oda, *Secret Embedded*, pp. 119–24. After the war Henderson served as president of the Society of Japanese Studies and the Japan Society.

[87] *MISLS Album*, p. 22 (photo reversed).

[88] Ibid., p. 10; "Training History," ann. 1, para. 9d, p. 9. See also ann. 6, History of J.O.B. [Japanese Order of Battle], Research & Field Liaison Section, p. 13. MID apparently did not give MISLS a written mission statement until March 1944. Memo, ACS, G–2, to Commandant, MISLS, 22 Mar 44, sub: Policy Directive, Military Intelligence Service Language School, Ofc of the Dir of Intel G–2, WD Gen and Special Staffs, RG 165, NARA. For a summary of Rasmussen's expectations for the school as of April 1943, see Colonel Rasmussen, 29 Apr 43, Addenda for: Projects Contemplated at MIS Language School, Savage, Minnesota, during the Period May 1–August 1, 1943, Ofc of the Dir of Intel G–2, WD Gen and Special Staffs, RG 165, NARA.

[89] "Training History," ann. 13, Translation Section.

As the war continued, feedback from the field became more important than ever. Based on suggestions from the field, the school placed more stress on Japanese military terminology and authentic materials. English-language intelligence reports and "beautiful translations," the official history said, "are of no value to us except as reference." The history continued: "What we need most are the Japanese terms in Kanji. The original documents in Japanese are the very life and sustenance of our courses. The Army and Navy Readers put out in Japan for sale to the children have been of greater value as a source of teaching material than all the technical military translation we have stacked in our library."[90]

In August 1943 the school organized a Military Research and Liaison Section under Akira Oshida (later renamed the Japanese Order of Battle Section) to collect these sorts of materials.[91] That summer Capt. John A. Burden sent the school "three sacks of documents, diaries, and one bundle of maps" from the Solomon Islands. Colonel Rasmussen wrote back gratefully, saying "the maps are of particularly great interest to us here, as the Japanese terminology of various geographical locations is now being taught here in great detail."[92] Burden returned to the United States that autumn to give a course of lectures at the school.[93] M.Sgt. Arthur S. Komori, who had worked in the Counter Intelligence Corps, flew from Australia to visit the school for several weeks in late December 1943.[94]

Munakata encouraged the graduates to write back to the school about their experiences overseas, and by 1944 he was receiving a steady stream of letters from the field.[95] Wartime censorship prevented the Nisei from being very specific, but they commented freely on what had benefited them at the school. Some even found ways to ship back to the school captured Japanese documents, weapons, and other materials for classroom use. The school's official history commented at war's end that these letters "made it possible to revise, expand, or eliminate certain parts of the curriculum." The history concluded with the recommendation that "any similar schools set up in the future be given access to captured documents while they are still recent, to official reports and to the expertise of observers fresh from the combat area. It is also recommended that liaison officers be sent out into the field from time to time to determine the language training needs of the theater or theaters of operations on the spot."[96]

In early 1944 Colonel Rasmussen himself toured the Pacific to observe what his graduates were doing. In April he visited Bougainville, where a Nisei language

---

[90] Ibid., ann. 1, para. 4–g.

[91] Ibid., ann. 6.

[92] Ltr, Kai E. Rasmussen to John A. Burden, 10 August 1943, Box 1, John A. Burden Papers, Hoover Institution Archives, Stanford University, Stanford, Calif.

[93] Burden Papers, Hoover Institution Archives. Burden also smuggled a barrel of captured Japanese *shoyu* (soy sauce), which was hard to find in wartime Minnesota, for the instructors.

[94] Interv, Ann Bray with Arthur S. Komori, 1955, copy in Arthur S. Komori File, Harrington Papers; newspaper clipping, ca. Feb 44, author's files.

[95] Munakata preserved these letters, which can be found in the Harrington Papers. "Training History," p. 31.

[96] "Training History," p. 37.

team had just helped XIV Corps defeat the final Japanese assault. He also visited the Allied Translator and Interpreter Section in Australia.[97]

In 1943 a new problem threatened to interrupt the shipment of graduates overseas. The first students at Crissy Field all had completed basic training in 1941, before they joined the school. After graduation they were ready for immediate deployment overseas. In 1942 the school began enlisting Nisei directly from the camps with no previous military training. Upon graduation the school rushed some overseas with no additional training.[98] For example, Harry Fukuhara, twenty-two, a Kibei from Seattle, volunteered for MISLS from the Gila River camp in November 1942. He had graduated from a Japanese high school and was an excellent Japanese-speaker. He graduated from MISLS in April 1943 and was rushed straight to Australia and then on to New Guinea with I Corps headquarters with no basic military training.[99]

To alleviate this problem, in July the school sent 127 graduates to Camp Shelby for eight weeks of basic training. At Camp Shelby, the 442d RCT had already been training for several months. The Savage graduates were designated Company S, and the training officers and NCOs came from the 442d RCT. By now the trainees were all technical sergeants (technicians, 5th grade), not privates, and they were in poor physical shape after six months in the classroom. For eight weeks they learned how to be soldiers. The training was physically grueling in the summer heat: The linguists clambered over obstacle courses and made twenty-mile forced marches under the watchful eyes of the 442d RCT sergeants and training officers.[100] When they returned to Camp Savage in September, the first sixty went to Australia at once, the first large shipment in six months.

---

[97] Ltr, General Douglas MacArthur to Chief of Staff, 8 September 1943, sub: Allied Translator and Interpreter Section. This requested that a senior officer of MISLS be sent to the theater for liaison: "Specific problems which require discussion include the best type of training for translators and interpreters who are to be used in this theater." Interv, author with Roy T. Uyehata, 16 Nov 87; Uyehata, MISNorCal Bio, reprinted in *World War II Reminiscences*, ed. John H. Roush, Jr. (San Rafael, Calif.: Reserve Officers Association of the United States, 1995), pp. 257–60. Rasmussen's trip observations are summarized in "History and Description of the Military Intelligence Service Language School," pp. 32–33, Unpubl Ms, Military Intelligence Language School, Fort Snelling, Mich., Gen Records, 1943–1945, Records of the Army Staff, RG 319, NARA.

[98] This was also true of some Caucasian officer candidates from the program at the University of Michigan (see below), such as Benjamin H. Hazard, who had studied Japanese for four years at the University of California at Los Angeles followed by six months at Michigan. After six more months at Camp Savage, he was commissioned and sent to the Central Pacific in early 1944 with no further military training. Hazard, remarks at San José State University, 18 Mar 00.

[99] Intervs, John P. Finnegan with Harry K. Fukuhara, 5 Jun 90, U.S. Army Intelligence and Security Command, Fort Belvoir, Va., and Eric Saul and Loni Ding with Harry K. Fukuhara, 7 Jan 86, NJAHS; "US Officer Feared Worst for Family Living in Japan," *San Francisco Chronicle*, 5 Aug 95; Falk and Tsuneishi, *MIS in the War against Japan*, pp. 97–98. Fukuhara received a direct commission in 1945; he retired in 1971 as a colonel without ever having received basic combat training.

[100] "Training History," ann. 1, para. 6–3, p. 7; Orville C. Shirey, *Americans: The Story of the 442d Combat Team* (Washington, D.C.: Infantry Journal Press, 1946), p. 21. For personal accounts, see Nob Yamashita, "Fighting My Ancestors: The Autobiography of a Nisei," p. 5, Unpubl Ms, n.d.;

Graduates of later classes went to eight weeks of basic training at infantry replacement training centers at Camp Blanding, Florida; Fort McClellan, Alabama; and Fort Leonard Wood, Missouri. The resumption of Selective Service for the Nisei in early 1944 alleviated the recruitment problem. Henceforth MISLS could recruit from soldiers who had completed basic training. Thus the school's graduates could deploy overseas immediately without additional training. As the war continued, the War Department lengthened basic combat training to seventeen weeks. But the Military Intelligence Division successfully argued that its students were urgently needed in the field and required only eight weeks of basic training.

Colonel Rasmussen and Director Aiso built a unique military language school that melded civilian and enlisted instructors, created an intensive curriculum, and trained a diverse student body to meet field commanders' urgent needs for Japanese linguists. From its humble beginnings in 1941, MISLS had grown into a dynamic language school that graduated hundreds of Nisei soldier-linguists each year.

Forming Language Teams

After each group of students completed training, the school's leaders formed the graduates into teams to meet the requirements of field commanders. The process began when different theaters and headquarters requested Japanese-language personnel. These requests would flow into the Military Intelligence Division, where the Training Branch controlled school operations. This office, which never numbered more than four officers, also oversaw the Military Intelligence Training Center at Camp Ritchie, Maryland.[101] From time to time the division would send MISLS a message that field commanders required a certain number of graduates. Aiso would then convene his closest advisers to handpick men for each team. The selection committee was usually composed of Aiso, Munakata, Oshida, and Tekawa.[102]

Graduates normally received a thirty-day furlough before going overseas. Some waited for months for assignment. Others were rushed overseas without delay. Students from the mainland could visit their parents in the camps or brothers and sisters who had been released for employment or schooling elsewhere in the country.[103] In the summer of 1943, when Roy T. Takai graduated from MISLS, he traveled to Santa Fe, New Mexico, where his father, a Sacramento furniture

---

Interv, author with Takai, 30 Oct 87. The Navy did not require its Caucasian students at Boulder to complete basic combat training.

    [101] Trng Br Admin Records: Boxes 280–325, Ofc of the Dir of Intel G–2, WD Gen and Special Staffs, RG 165, NARA. "Disposition of Graduates," the working list of MISLS assignments is in Box 287.

    [102] "Training History," ann. 2, Admin Section.

    [103] Uratsu, MISNorCal Bio. Before April 1943 Nisei soldiers may have been restricted from visiting the four camps located within the WDC.

store owner, was in a Department of Justice camp. Takai was not allowed inside the camp and instead had to talk to his father through the barbed-wire fence.[104]

The Western Defense Command did not allow any Nisei soldiers to enter the exclusion zone until April 1943. When two students, Satsuki Fred Tanakatsubo and Mamoru Noji, applied to see their parents in Tule Lake in November 1942, permission was denied. In protest Tanakatsubo refused to take the final exam; nevertheless, he was assigned to the 7th Infantry Division for the assault on Attu in May 1943. Noji joined the 43d Infantry Division in the Solomon Islands.[105] In January 1943, when Sergeant Kanegai was waiting to go overseas, he requested permission to visit his father and family in Manzanar, where there had been rioting only a few weeks before. The officer refused, saying, "If I let you go, you'll never come back." Kanegai protested, but the officer stood his ground: "The machine guns are pointing inward. When you go there you're going to notice that and you're going to get bitter. They are going to be wearing the same uniform, and you're not going to like it."[106]

As the teams traveled by train from Fort Snelling to the port of embarkation, usually San Francisco or Los Angeles, they would occasionally be confused for Japanese prisoners of war. When Kanegai's team arrived at Angel Island in San Francisco Bay in January 1943, a suspicious Army officer asked, "Where'd ya learn your English?" Kanegai replied, "Hell, I'm from California."[107]

During 1942 the school sent out graduates in small groups as they became available. By 1943 the Military Intelligence Division fixed the team organization at ten Nisei and one officer. Usually led by a technical sergeant, teams included three each of translators, interpreters, and interrogators. School officials put together Kibei strong in Japanese and other Nisei strong in English.[108] Later in the war, teams sometimes included Nisei veterans reassigned from other theaters. Until 1944 the War Department deployed teams to each combat division and separate regiment, as well as corps and army headquarters. Each division received a team of ten Nisei led by a Caucasian officer. During the first half of 1944 the War Department sent to the Central and Southwest Pacific Areas seven new divisions. After that, no fresh combat units deployed there; but the demand for Nisei linguists to serve with different headquarters and for other special requirements continued unabated.[109] Soon after the language school arrived at Camp Savage, it dispatched a group of fourteen Nisei and three Caucasian officers who left in

---

[104] Roy T. Takai, MISNorCal Bio. In contrast, when Yoshiaki Fujitani visited the same Santa Fe camp in 1944, his father was allowed to leave the barbed-wire compound for the meeting. Yoshiaki Fujitani, "*Kuni no On*: Gratitude to My Country," in *Japanese Eyes, American Heart: Personal Reflections of Hawaii's World War II Nisei Soldiers* (Honolulu: Tendai Educational Foundation, 1998), pp. 98–99.
[105] Satsuki Fred Tanakatsubo, MISNorCal Bio.
[106] Interv, author with Kanegai, 16 Sep 96.
[107] *Saga of the MIS*; Interv, author with Kanegai, 16 Sep 96.
[108] "Training History," ann. 2, pp. 3–7.
[109] The last division sent to the Pacific was the 96th Infantry Division, which arrived in Hawaii in July 1944 and fought on Leyte in October.

CHART 1—DISPOSITION OF ENLISTED NISEI MISLS GRADUATES, 1942–1944

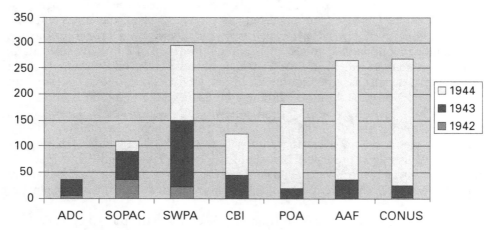

ADC	Alaska Defense Command
SOPAC	South Pacific
SWPA	Southwest Pacific Area
CBI	China-Burma-India
POA	Pacific Ocean Areas
AAF	Army Air Forces
CONUS	Continental United States

Source: Military Intelligence Service Language School, Disposition of Graduates, Trng Grp, Ofc of the Dir of Intel G–2, RG 165, NA.

August 1942 with only three months of training. This group was divided between the Southwest Pacific and the South Pacific. When the remainder of the first Camp Savage class graduated in December 1942, it was parceled out to the three active theaters of war: 26 to the Southwest Pacific, 26 to the South Pacific, and 15 to Alaska (approximately). (*Chart 1*)

The largest customer was General Douglas MacArthur's command, the Southwest Pacific Area. In June 1942 Capt. David Swift had led the first eight Crissy Field graduates to Australia. Another fourteen Nisei arrived with I Corps in September. In January 1943 twenty-six more left for Australia. Not satisfied, MacArthur's headquarters demanded forty more Nisei as soon as possible. These demands from the field presented school officials with difficult choices. They had to balance the demands with the need to retain instructors for future school expansion. In this case, they decided to hold back the first two sections, which eventually provided 27 enlisted instructors. Sections 3 and 4, forty graduates in all, graduated on 10 April after four months of instruction and rushed to the Southwest Pacific.[110] The school sent seventy more in January 1944. By the summer of 1944 MISLS had sent about 300 Nisei to the Southwest Pacific.

The South Pacific took graduates as well. Captain Burden led the first team to the theater in June 1942. By March 1943 the school had sent another thirty-six Nisei. By January 1944 over fifty Nisei graduates were serving in the South Pacific. However, as the war moved away from the region, the South Pacific Area was dissolved later that year and the Nisei linguists were reassigned.

The Alaska Defense Command took five graduates from the first class at Crissy Field in May 1942. After that, the school sent thirty-five more Nisei, with the last group leaving in July 1943 in time for the invasion of Kiska. The Alaska campaign effectively ended by the autumn of 1943, and most of the Nisei came back to the school. Some were reassigned to the South Pacific, while others remained as instructors.

In the Central Pacific, the island-hopping campaign did not begin until November 1943, when the 2d Marine Division assaulted Tarawa and the Army's 27th Infantry Division assaulted Makin. The 7th Infantry Division prepared to assault Kwajalein in January 1944. MISLS sent twenty Nisei in the summer of 1943 for the two Army divisions. After that, requirements grew by leaps and bounds. During 1944 the school sent 181 more Nisei to the Central Pacific, including the translation annex of the Joint Intelligence Center Pacific Ocean Areas formed in early 1944.

Although the War Department did not commit major ground forces to China or Burma, in November 1942 MISLS sent one graduate, Lt. Won-Loy Chan, a Chinese American, to serve as a liaison officer for General Stilwell.[111] In the spring of 1943 MISLS sent Maj. Sheldon M. Covell and ten Nisei to the Air Intelligence School at Harrisburg, Pennsylvania, and from there to India. In July MISLS sent ten more Nisei directly to New Delhi. In August the Joint Chiefs of Staff committed to provide American air and ground support to the British campaign to recapture Burma.

In August the school received a special requirement for fourteen enlisted men to form a special team to support the first American ground force for Southeast Asia, Project GALAHAD (later known as Merrill's Marauders). For the team chief Rasmussen selected 1st Lt. William A. Laffin, born in Japan to an American father and Japanese mother. He grew up in Japan and was repatriated to the United States in 1942 on the *Gripsholm*. He accepted an Army commission and went to MISLS. Akiji Yoshimura recalled that Laffin "began asking me rather personal questions about the state of my health, marital status, language proficiency, interests, etc." Soon after, "he offered the opportunity to volunteer for a secret and hazardous

[110] "Training History," ann. 1, para. 6–2, p. 6. Interv, author with Harry T. Kubo, 11 Sep 96; *Saga of the MIS*. These teams were assigned one each to the 32d and 41st Infantry Divisions and two to Sixth Army Headquarters.
    [111] Won-Loy Chan, *Burma: The Untold Story* (Novato, Calif.: Presidio Press, 1986).

mission." Howard Furumoto recalled that Colonel Rasmussen told them only that it would hazardous and the unit was expected to take 70 percent casualties. "To a man, everyone said, Yes."[112] Chosen as team sergeant was S.Sgt. Edward Mitsukado, a court reporter in Honolulu before the war who had come to Savage by way of the 100th Infantry Battalion at Camp McCoy.

In November 1943 the Army Air Forces requested one Nisei to help the 1st Air Commando Group intercept Japanese radio transmissions. Shojiro Tom Taketa, twenty-two, was selected. Born and raised near Sacramento, California, Taketa was a junior college graduate who had volunteered for MISLS from Tule Lake.[113] Dozens more Nisei were assigned to the Southeast Asia Translation and Interrogation Center in New Delhi. By early 1944 Assistant Commandant Dickey, as well as Majors Burden and Swift (the only two Caucasian graduates of the first class), were all in China.

When the Office of War Information (OWI) launched a psychological warfare program in the China-Burma-India Theater in 1943, MISLS organized a special ten-man team that included journalists, artists, and men with labor-organizing experience. Chris Ishii, the graphic artist who designed the MISLS gopher emblem, was selected. Also selected was Kenny Yasui, a 1935 graduate of Waseda University in Japan, as well as Karl Yoneda, a 38-year-old Kibei. Yoneda had been born in Southern California but raised in Japan. While attending high school in Hiroshima in the early 1920s, he had become a passionate Marxist. In 1926 he returned to Los Angeles, joined the Communist Party (changing his name from Gozo to Karl), and became a journalist and labor organizer. He was stunned when the Communist Party of the United States of America suspended its few Japanese American members after Pearl Harbor. But this hardly dampened his ardor to fight fascism. In November 1942 he volunteered from Manzanar for MISLS, where he excelled in the classroom and was the honor graduate in June 1943. He was held back at first as an enlisted instructor because, Colonel Rasmussen told him, "it's our policy not to send a known Communist overseas." But then Rasmussen placed him on the OWI team.[114]

Also selected for the OWI team was another labor activist, Koji Ariyoshi, twenty-nine. He had been raised on a Hawaiian coffee farm and in the late 1930s

---

[112] Akiji Yoshimura, "Fourteen Nisei and the Marauders," *Pacific Citizen*, 25 Dec 59, reprinted in MISNorCal Bios; Oguro, *Sempai Gumi*, pp. 85–96; Ichinokuchi, *John Aiso and the M.I.S.*, pp. 85–94. Interv, author with Howard Furumoto, 8 Dec 94; "A Kibei in the Burma Jungle," *Hawaii Herald*, 6 Nov 81, reprinted in Oguro, *Sempai Gumi*, pp. 97–105; Thomas Tsubota, "From the 100th Battalion to Merrill's Marauders," in Tsukiyama et al., *Secret Valor*, p. 69.

[113] Harrington, *Yankee Samurai*, pp. 167, 224–25; "Volunteer from Relocation Camp Reported Fighting in Burma in First U.S. Air Commando Unit," *Pacific Citizen*, 22 Apr 44; Tom Taketa File, Harrington Papers.

[114] Karl G. Yoneda, *Ganbatte*; "Yoneda, Karl Goso," in *Japanese American History*, pp. 362–63; Harrington, *Yankee Samurai*, p. 142; Yoneda, in *Saga of the MIS*. Several members of the OWI team later received field commissions, but Yoneda was told his paperwork was lost. Another MISLS student, James Oda, also recalls being investigated while at the school for his progressive political activities.

Colonel Rasmussen at Camp Savage with five Nisei who had just graduated from airborne training. The five were sent to the 11th Airborne Division.

drifted to San Francisco, where he became a militant member of the San Francisco longshoreman's union under Harry Bridges, the famous leader of the 1934 longshoreman's strike.[115] By the summer of 1944 MISLS had sent 150 Nisei graduates to the China-Burma-India Theater for Project GALAHAD, the Office of War Information, the Army Air Forces, and other assignments.

Another specialized team was formed for the 11th Airborne Division. Although the division needed only ten Nisei, the school selected twenty-five volunteers for airborne training, thinking that more than half would wash out. The team leader, T.Sgt. Charles Tatsuda, had been born and raised in Alaska and graduated from the University of Washington. In February 1944 he led his large team to Fort Benning, Georgia, where they had four weeks of tough physical conditioning culminating in

---

[115] Koji Ariyoshi, *From Kona to Yenan: The Political Memoirs of Koji Ariyoshi*, ed. Alice M. Beechert and Edward D. Beechert (Honolulu: University of Hawaii Press, 2000); Hugh Deane, ed., *Remembering Koji Ariyoshi: An American GI in Yenan* (Los Angeles: U.S.-China Peoples Friendship Association, 1978); Koji Ariyoshi, "Let Truth Live in Action," *Hawaii Herald*, 11 Nov 71, reprinted in Oguro, *Sempai Gumi*, pp. 223–34; "Ariyoshi, Koji," in *Japanese American History*. James Oda, a Nisei Leftist journalist and labor activist, remained for the duration of the war at MISLS, where he taught a course on propaganda writing.

Kazuo Yoshida (left) *and Clarence Ota visit the Heart Mountain camp in April 1944, after graduating from the language school and airborne training.*

five jumps. One Nisei weighed only ninety pounds, and his buddies joked that they had to put rocks in his pack so his parachute would open. In the end twenty-three Nisei pinned on jump wings.[116]

One of the new paratroopers, Mitsuo Usui, who had volunteered from the camp in Amache, traveled to Colorado to visit his father there before going overseas. When he walked into the camp, his starched uniform and smartly bloused boots left the school children awestruck. But his Issei father was not impressed: "You, stupid son. First you volunteered, then you went into the paratroops. You're sure sticking your neck out," his father told him. "But as you go, I say, give them hell and come back fighting."[117]

When all the team members returned from their furloughs in September 1944, Tatsuda led eleven to join the 11th Airborne Division in New Guinea. Usui led the

---

[116] "Training Branch File, Paratroops," Ofc of the Dir of Intel G–2, WD Gen and Special Staffs, RG 165, NARA. See also "Pfc. Bud Tsuyuki Now Member of Parachute Troops," *Pacific Citizen*, 4 Mar 44; "23 Nisei Soldiers Qualify for Army's Paratroop Unit," *Pacific Citizen*, 27 May 44; *MISLS Album*, p. 52 (photo). Jim Mita and Mitsuo Usui, both in *Saga of the MIS*; Interv, author with Mits Usui, 9 Sep 96; George T. Ito, "Linguist-Paratroopers," *The Voice of the Angels* (July 1996); Harrington, *Yankee Samurai*, pp. 186 (photo), 202–03. *MISLS Album* says twenty-four Nisei attended airborne training (p. 10). In December 1943 the War Department activated another segregated airborne unit, the 555th Parachute Company, composed of African American soldiers. This was later expanded to a battalion.

[117] Ano, "Loyal Linguists," p. 280.

others to Hawaii, where they joined Tenth Army headquarters for the invasion of Okinawa.[118]

In January 1944 the Signal Intelligence Service (SIS) asked for Nisei to do translation work near Washington, D.C. In response, enlisted instructor M.Sgt. Joe Y. Masuda led a team of twenty-five to Vint Hill Farms, Virginia. However, SIS security officers screened out Masuda and half the group. The school quickly sent out replacements and in June sent yet another thirty Nisei to Vint Hill Farms.

Also in January the A–2 of Army Air Forces demanded sixty graduates to help intercept radio traffic from Japanese aircraft. Air Staff planners requested at least 275 enlisted men for new units called "radio squadrons, mobile," including "as many Caucasians as possible." MISLS responded by sending 109 Nisei graduates over the next six months. Many attended voice intercept training at Camp Pinedale in Fresno, California, before joining the squadrons in the Pacific.[119]

Senior War Department leaders well understood the importance of these teams and showed their appreciation as often as they could. General Strong, the War Department G–2, visited Camp Savage to speak to the more than 300 graduating Nisei on 18 June 1943. He had served in Japan as early as 1908, and the school used his book on sōsho, or "grass writing" script. After Pearl Harbor, General Marshall had called him to Washington to take over the Military Intelligence Division. Strong addressed the Nisei with an "inspiring speech" and wished them "great success."[120] Joseph C. Grew, the former ambassador to Tokyo, visited more than once. "The importance of such visits as these to the students, who for reasons of wartime security had to do their jobs out of the spotlight of publicity and who nevertheless needed to be impressed with the essentiality of those jobs, cannot be calculated," the school's history later commented.[121]

Another key leader in Washington was the school's founder, Colonel Weckerling. In September 1943 Weckerling was called from the Western Defense Command to become Strong's deputy for Intelligence and acting chief of the MIS, where he could watch over his creation behind the scenes. The most senior War Department civilian official to take an active interest in the school was Assistant Secretary of War McCloy. McCloy's portfolio encompassed two issues that intersected with the MIS Nisei, intelligence and ethnic minorities. Throughout the war he was the War Department's point man for Japanese American issues such as the

---

[118] Interv, author with Usui, 9 Sep 96; *Saga of the MIS*. Neither team made any combat jumps.

[119] Memo, Enlisted Br, Ofc, Asst Ch of Air Staff, Pers, HQ, Army Air Forces, to Asst Ch of Staff, G–2, 8 Jan 44, sub: Transfer and Assignment to the Army Air Forces of Enlisted Men Qualified in Speaking and/or Translating the Japanese Language, Ofc of the Dir of Intel G–2, WD Gen and Special Staffs, RG 165, NARA. "Army Announces U.S. Soldiers of Japanese Ancestry Assigned to Central California Camp," *Pacific Citizen*, 26 Aug 44.

[120] Strong's speech was used for recruiting in the camps. "An Appeal," "Training History," ann. 10, encl 10.

[121] *MISLS Album*, p. 11. See also the photographs on pp. 18 and 52.

West Coast evacuation in 1942 and forming the 442d RCT in 1943, as well as all issues relating to African Americans.[122]

Forming language teams led to another sore point for the Nisei students. The Military Intelligence Division wanted an officer to lead each team, but the War Department would not award direct commissions to the Nisei graduates. Instead Caucasian officers, when available, were appointed to lead the teams. The first two Caucasian officers who graduated from Crissy Field in May 1942 each led a team into the Pacific. Because no more Caucasian officers were available, a third team went to Alaska under a Nisei sergeant. Three more Caucasian officers graduated with the special class in September, and the first large group of officers with seventeen Caucasians and two Chinese Americans graduated in December. During all of 1943 the school produced only twelve more Caucasian officer graduates.[123] (See Table 1.)

One solution was to commission Caucasian enlisted students. In the autumn of 1942 Rasmussen secured direct commissions for Charles H. Fogg and Faubion Bowers; both went overseas as second lieutenants. "I was the first person in the United States Army," Bowers later recalled, "who was ever commissioned on the basis of linguistic ability."[124] But Rasmussen and the Nisei instructors knew well that few Caucasian students could keep up with the Nisei in class. To meet this shortcoming, Rasmussen organized a preparatory course for Caucasian officer candidates that began in January 1943 at the University of Michigan.

This discrimination rankled the Nisei. From their point of view, the War Department did not trust them enough to grant them commissions as second lieutenants. It was especially grating for the college Nisei, who felt they met all the qualifications for commissioning but one—race. Their chances for commission diminished further when the War Department sharply reduced overall officer accessions after 1942.[125]

One day in the autumn of 1942 the Nisei were attending a lecture-demonstration on interrogation techniques. At one point the instructor suggested, "If the prisoner is a sergeant, borrow lieutenant bars and put them on so as to outrank the prisoner." Roy Yoshio Ashizawa, a cocky 23-year-old from San Francisco, yelled out from the back of the hall: "Give us the bars!" "A hush fell over those assembled," Ashizawa recalled. "One could hear a pin drop." Aiso hurried out of the building and returned a few minutes later with Rasmussen, who told the

---

[122] Kai Bird, *The Chairman: John J. McCloy, The Making of the American Establishment* (New York: Simon & Schuster, 1992); Alan Brinkley, "Minister without Portfolio," *Harper's* (February 1983): 31–46; Thomas P. Wolf, "McCloy, John Jay, Jr.," in *American National Biography*, ed. John A. Garraty and Mark C. Carnes (New York: Oxford University Press, 1999).

[123] See Maj. William P. Jones Papers, Oberlin College, Ohio.

[124] Falk and Tsuneishi, *MIS in the War against Japan*, pp. 11–13. Interv, D. Clayton James with Faubion Bowers, 18 Jul 71, D. Clayton James Collection, MacArthur Memorial, Library and Archives, Norfolk, Va.

[125] Palmer et al., *Procurement and Training of Ground Combat Troops*, pp. 104–30; Samuel A. Stouffer et al., *The American Soldier*, vol. 1, *Adjustment during Army Life* (Princeton, N.J.: Princeton University Press, 1949), ch. 6.

students "in his Danish accent": "I am goink to Vashington zis Zunday to zee about r-r-ratings for you boys." Some time later Rasmussen announced only that graduates would be promoted to technician, 5th grade; no lieutenant's bars were forthcoming.[126]

In May 1943 Rasmussen raised the issue with McCloy and asked for authority to commission a small number of Nisei from each class. McCloy concurred, as did General Strong; but Rasmussen's initiative went no further.[127] Rasmussen floated the idea again in February 1944 with Strong's successor, Maj. Gen. Clayton Bissell, and requested commissions for Aiso and his top civilian instructors. As a result, Aiso was awarded his direct commission to major in October 1944. There were still no commissions for Nisei students, even for top graduates.[128]

Rasmussen was not able to obtain direct commissions for the Nisei graduates. However, by the autumn of 1944 he obtained quotas for selected Nisei at the officer candidate school (OCS). In October 1944 nine Nisei graduates, including three Merrill's Marauders veterans, attended OCS at Fort Benning, Georgia. Most Caucasian graduates of language training were routinely awarded commissions without having to attend officer candidate school.[129]

.   .   .

In the first year at Camp Savage, Colonel Rasmussen and his administrators had built perhaps the largest Japanese-language school ever organized in America. The Nisei staff and instructors recruited hundreds of prospective students, mostly Nisei, drilled them in an intensive language training program, and formed them into balanced teams to meet the insatiable demands of field commanders. The MIS Nisei who served overseas carried with them the imprint not only of the training they had received, but also of the school's spirit.

---

[126] When Ashizawa graduated in December 1942, he was sent to Alaska, where he remained for the next two-and-a-half years. Roy Y. Ashizawa, MISNorCal Bio, p. 4.

[127] Memo, Brig. Gen. Hayes A. Kroner to McCloy, 10 May 43, ASW 352, Army Schools and Colleges, Class Ref Sub Files, 1940–1947, Ofc of the Asst Sec of War, RG 107, NARA. Memo, Lt. Col. A. W. Stuart to Ch, Pers Br, MIS, 18 Feb 44, Ofc of the Dir of Intel G–2, WD Gen and Special Staffs, RG 165, NARA. Aiso recalled that the school tried twice to obtain commissions for civilian and enlisted instructors before he received his. Ichinokuchi, *John Aiso and the M.I.S.*, p. 17.

[128] Ichinokuchi, *John Aiso and the M.I.S.*, p. 17. Aiso later credited Bissell with authorizing commissions for many MIS Nisei by the war's end. Aiso, "Observations of a California Nisei," p. 77.

[129] Interv, author with Wallace S. Amioka, 8 Dec 94. Several other MIS Nisei earned commissions through the American officer candidate school in Australia. One Nisei from the 100th Infantry Battalion may have been selected for OCS in August 1943, but he went overseas with his unit before he could attend. Murphy, *Ambassadors in Arms*, p. 117.

5

Camp Savage, 1943–1944

Recruiting Students, 1943–1944

War Department policy toward Nisei enlistment took a dramatic turn in January 1943, when the War Department announced the formation of an all-volunteer Nisei combat unit, the 442d Regimental Combat Team (RCT). The War Department did not mention that many of the volunteers would be assigned not to the 442d RCT but to the Military Intelligence Service (MIS). Hawaii Nisei greeted the announcement with great enthusiasm. War Department planners hoped for 1,500 volunteers, but 10,000 rushed to enlist. Grown men wept when turned away for medical reasons or age. The Hawaiian Department raised the quota to 2,500, the maximum local authorities would allow given Hawaii's manpower shortage, and agreed to permit 20 percent of Nisei soldiers serving in noncombat units in Hawaii to volunteer. Eventually 2,686 Hawaii Nisei enlisted and sailed for the mainland with great fanfare on 4 April 1943.[1]

In the mainland camps, the story was quite different. For months the War Relocation Authority (WRA) had been discussing how to grant selected individuals "leave clearance" to leave the camps for work or education, so long as they did not return to the West Coast. At the same time, the War Department needed a way to screen Nisei men in the camps for military service. Thus each adult inmate would register by means of a four-page questionnaire about his background, education,

---

[1] Thomas D. Murphy, *Ambassadors in Arms* (Honolulu: University of Hawaii Press, 1954), pp. 110–12; Masayo Umezawa Duus, *Unlikely Liberators: The Men of the 100th and 442nd* (Honolulu: University of Hawaii Press, 1987), pp. 58–62; Franklin S. Odo, *No Sword To Bury: Japanese Americans in Hawai'i during World War II* (Philadelphia: Temple University Press, 2004), pp. 222–28.

activities, and the like. A joint Army-Navy-FBI board would review the questionnaires and decide who was eligible for leave or military service. The Military Intelligence Service Language School (MISLS) provided ten senior Nisei sergeants to assist the War Department teams in conducting the registration.

When the camps erupted in anger and confusion, the War Relocation Authority and War Department were caught by surprise. Emotions that had been building since the beginning of the evacuation boiled over in tense public meetings and demonstrations inside the camps. Much of the anger focused on the last two questions on the questionnaire:

27. Are you willing to serve in the armed forces of the United States on combat duty, wherever ordered?
28. Will you swear unqualified allegiance to the United States of America and faithfully defend the United States from any or all attack by foreign or domestic forces, and forswear any form of allegiance or obedience to the Japanese emperor, or any other foreign government, power, or organization?[2]

These questions were addressed to every adult male, regardless of citizenship or age. How should a 50-year-old Issei answer number 27? Would a simple "no" be interpreted as disloyal? How should a citizen Nisei answer number 28? Would a simple "yes" mean an admission that he had once held allegiance to the Japanese emperor? What would happen if parents and their children gave different answers?

The camps were thrown into turmoil. "Terrified parents of draft-age youths," an observer later related, "immediately saw the entire proceeding as part of a plot to rob them of the only earthly possession left to them—their precious, obedient, gently brought-up sons, on whom they had pinned all their hopes and dreams."[3] "People walked the roads, tears streaming down their troubled faces, silent and suffering," a Nisei woman recalled. "The little apartments were not big enough for the tremendous battle that waged in practically every room."[4] One Issei father composed a dignified haiku to express his inner turmoil:

> Son joined the army
> Walked great distance
> Alone in the sagebrush[5]

---

[2] Three slightly different questionnaires were administered. The questions above appeared on Selective Service Form DSS 304a (1–23–43) for male citizens. Jacobus tenBroek et al., *Prejudice, War, and the Constitution* (Berkeley: University of California Press, 1954), pp. 149–50.

[3] Michi Weglyn, *Years of Infamy: The Untold Story of America's Concentration Camps* (New York: Morrow Quill, 1976), p. 141.

[4] Quote from Ibid. An extensive literature exists on the registration crisis. See Bill Hosokawa, *Nisei: The Quiet Americans* (New York: William Morrow, 1969), pp. 359–78; *Personal Justice Denied: Report of the Commission on Wartime Relocation and Internment of Civilians* (Seattle: University of Washington Press, 1997), pp. 191–97.

[5] Sho Nakashima, untitled poem translated from the Japanese, in *Only What We Could Carry: The Japanese American Internment Experience*, ed. Lawson F. Inada (Berkeley, Calif.: Heyday Books, 2000), p. 178.

The War Department's Bureau of Public Relations played a key role in managing the resulting crisis, led by veteran newsman Lt. Col. S. L. A. Marshall. Marshall scrambled to coordinate the registration and cope with all the problems. He would come to remember that time as "the roughest I had ever spent in the army, and far more trying than combat. I was dealing with mass hysteria, with thousands of sadly hurt people."[6] The ten Nisei sergeants from MISLS were thrown into the thick of the turmoil. All ten received commendations that read: "Your assignment, no doubt, at times was very difficult and trying and required you to exercise the utmost of your ability in understanding and judgement [sic] in working towards the objective of your team's mission."[7]

The recruiters had little success. Of the Nisei men in the camps, 28 percent answered "no" to both questions. Only 6 percent, or 1,181 male citizens of military age in the camps, volunteered. Of these, 805 were accepted. Most joined the volunteers from Hawaii in Camp Shelby to begin basic training in April.[8] Despite the turmoil, MISLS recruited several hundred more students from the camps, as the War Department gave the language school highest priority for Nisei recruits. More Nisei men were eligible than in the previous year, because in November 1942 Congress had lowered the minimum age for military service from twenty-one to eighteen. MISLS recruiters returned to the camps more than once in 1943.

Although the language school had priority, the preferences of the Nisei themselves affected its ability to bring in new recruits. Few Nisei wanted to prove their loyalty by volunteering for what they perceived to be a desk job. If they were going to fight, they wanted to fight as infantrymen. They wanted to carry rifles, not dictionaries. For more than a year, Nisei could volunteer only for intelligence. Now they could join a combat outfit. Others told recruiters that their parents refused to allow them to volunteer. Going against their parents' wishes was impossible. However, they told the recruiters, if the War Department reinstated Selective Service for the Nisei, it would be a different matter.

Robert K. Sakai, twenty-three, volunteered from a camp. A University of California student when the war broke out, Sakai had been evacuated to the camp in Poston, Arizona, where he was married in October 1942. In March 1943 he volunteered for the Military Intelligence Service (MIS). In June he and his bride

---

[6] S. L. A. Marshall, *Bringing Up the Rear: A Memoir*, ed. Cate Marshall (San Rafael, Calif.: Presidio Press, 1979), pp. 53–54; Joseph D. Harrington, *Yankee Samurai: The Secret Role of Nisei in America's Pacific Victory* (Detroit: Pettigrew Enterprises, 1979), pp. 95–98. Marshall subsequently visited the 442d RCT at Camp Shelby and later encountered MIS Nisei on Makin Island. See *The Capture of Makin, 20–24 November 1943* (Washington, D.C.: War Department, Historical Division, 1946), p. 121.

[7] Harrington, *Yankee Samurai*, p. 97.

[8] War Relocation Authority, *WRA: A Story of Human Conservation* (Washington, D.C.: Government Printing Office, 1946), pp. 57, 202; tenBroek et al., *Prejudice, War, and the Constitution*, p. 168. The figure 805 includes all volunteers accepted for service from camps before Selective Service resumed in January 1944. See also Robert W. O'Brien, *The College Nisei* (New York: Arno Press, 1978), pp. 92–108. No camp exceeded 9.9 percent for the rate of induction of eligible male citizens; the median was 4.8 percent.

were released from camp; with $200 collected from friends and family, they took a train to Minneapolis and found a tiny apartment. Sakai's draft board in Berkeley delayed his paperwork, so he was not officially enlisted until September; by that time the couple had almost exhausted their funds. Their first child arrived a few weeks later.[9]

The enlistment of Nisei volunteers and an expanded leave clearance program for Nisei to leave the camps for employment as well as education necessitated a new agency to administer loyalty reviews. The War Department set up the Japanese American Joint Board in Washington under Assistant Secretary of War John J. McCloy's direct control. Representatives of the War Relocation Authority, FBI, Military Intelligence Division (MID), Provost Marshal General, and the Office of Naval Intelligence checked each questionnaire and other information about each detainee. The board eventually accumulated investigative files on 50,000 Japanese Americans.[10] On 1 July 1943, the MID Counter Intelligence Group established a Japanese Section "devoted to the solution of all intelligence problems concerning military personnel of Japanese ancestry within the Army."[11] The War Department directed the Hawaiian Department to establish a similar program. In May 1944 the interagency board and Counter Intelligence Group were consolidated under the Office of the Provost Marshal General as the Japanese American Branch, which moved to San Francisco in December 1944 to prepare for the return of Japanese Americans to their homes on the West Coast.

Determined to add Nisei to the war effort, the War Department took pains to counter the perception of disloyalty. The War Department's press release of 28 January 1943, under the headline, "Loyal Americans of Japanese Ancestry To Compose Special Unit in Army," used the word *loyal* or *loyalty* four times in a 300-word statement. President Franklin D. Roosevelt's letter of 1 February drafted by the Office of War Information used the word *loyal* six times in four paragraphs.

Lt. Gen. John L. DeWitt on the West Coast remained a staunch advocate of exclusion. Public opinion supported his stance, as evidenced by the November 1942 election of Earl Warren as governor of California. In April 1943, as the 442d RCT

---

[9] Robert K. Sakai, "From Relocation Camp to Military Service," in *Japanese Eyes, American Heart* (Honolulu: Tendai Educational Foundation, 1998), pp. 121–34, 429–30. After the war, Sakai earned his Ph.D. in Asian history from Harvard and became professor of history at the University of Hawaii.

[10] Japanese-American Branch, Office of the Provost Marshal General, "History of Japanese Program, 20 January 1943 to 1 September 1945," Unpubl Ms, n.d., U.S. Army Center of Military History (CMH) files; Office of the Provost Marshal General, "World War II: A Brief History," pp. 289–310, Unpubl Ms, n.d., CMH files; tenBroek et al., *Prejudice, War, and the Constitution*, pp. 142–60; *Personal Justice Denied*, pp. 197–204. From January 1943 until May 1944, the board's executive secretary reported directly to McCloy. Memo, McCloy, 17 May 44, Folder: Adjutant General, Box WD1, Ser. 8: War Department, John J. McCloy Papers, Amherst College Archives, Amherst, Mass.

[11] Office of the Provost Marshal General, "History of Military Clearance Program (Screening of Alien Japanese and Japanese American Citizens for Military Service)," p. 23, Unpubl Ms, n.d., CMH files; Office of the Provost Marshal General, "World War II," pp. 247–88.

began training, a congressional committee called DeWitt to justify the removal and exclusion. Newspapers reported his blunt testimony, which made clear his underlying rationale: "A Jap's a Jap. They are a dangerous element, whether loyal or not. There is no way to determine their loyalty.... It makes no difference whether he is an American; theoretically he is still a Japanese and you can't change him ... by giving him a piece of paper."[12]

DeWitt's unrepentant remarks aroused a storm of controversy inside and outside the camps. At Camp Savage, students and staff alike were stunned, recalling that originally the school had been established within DeWitt's own headquarters.[13] Dan Nakatsu, a Hawaii Nisei who came to Camp Savage from the 442d RCT in July 1943, spoke for many when he recalled: "These stinging words of contempt were *seared into the minds of Nisei in uniform* and became symbolic of the racial hate and prejudice they would have to overcome" [emphasis in original]. The saying, "'We'll have to make him eat those words,'" Nakatsu wrote, "was not an uncommon thought as the Nisei went overseas, to Europe and the Pacific."[14]

Assistant Secretary of War McCloy worked to undercut DeWitt. A few weeks after DeWitt made his remarks, McCloy sent his executive officer and Col. Kai E. Rasmussen to speak to a Senate committee investigating the camps. Rasmussen was introduced as "an organization commander who has had [Nisei soldiers] for 2 years; he knows them better than any officer in the United States Army." Rasmussen assured the senators, "Their record for loyalty, in my opinion, is unquestioned." He did admit that he had found it necessary to separate 4–5 percent of the Nisei students. "Of the people who came to me from the camps, some of them were sullen and surly. After a couple months of Army treatment, they started straightening up. After 3 or 4 months, I considered them enthusiastic; they had regained their sense of perspective, and were well-conducted loyal soldiers."[15]

---

[12] *Los Angeles Times*, 14, 19 Apr 43, cited in Allan R. Bosworth, *America's Concentration Camps* (New York: Bantam, 1968), p. 166. See also Carey McWilliams, *Prejudice: Japanese-Americans, Symbol of Racial Intolerance* (Boston: Little, Brown, 1944), p. 251. The phrase "A Jap's a Jap" does not appear in the transcript of DeWitt's testimony but was apparently made in a separate press conference and widely reported at the time. McWilliams, *Prejudice*, p. 116; *Personal Justice Denied*, pp. 221–22.

[13] The draft of the MISLS Press Release at the end of the war noted that the Nisei students were "stunned" at DeWitt's remarks, but the phrase was removed from the version released on 22 October 1945. Compare draft Press Release, sec. 2, p. 3, Ofc of the Dir of Intel G–2, Record Group (RG) 165, National Archives and Records Administration (NARA), p. 5, and final Press Release, Japanese Evacuation Research Study (JERS), pt. 2, sec. 2, reel 20, frame 0037, Bancroft Library, University of California, Berkeley.

[14] Tad Ichinokuchi, ed., *John Aiso and the M.I.S.: Japanese-American Soldiers in the Military Intelligence Service, World War II* (Los Angeles: Military Intelligence Service Club of Southern California, 1988), p. 83.

[15] U.S. Senate, Committee on Military Affairs, *Japanese War Relocation Centers: Report of the Subcommittee on Japanese War Relocation Centers to the Committee on Military Affairs* (Washington, D.C.: Government Printing Office, 1943), pp. 13–14; also quoted in Galen M. Fisher, "What Race-Baiting Costs America," *The Christian Century* (8 September 1943).

With the decision to accept volunteers for the 442d RCT, MISLS began recruiting from Hawaii. In March 1943 the assistant commandant, Lt. Col. Archibald W. Stuart, flew to Hawaii to screen the volunteers. There, he met with Col. Kendall J. Fielder, the G–2 for Headquarters, Army Forces Pacific Ocean Areas, and other officials who supported using Nisei in intelligence work.[16] Because the Military Intelligence Service could waive physical and age limitations, it could enlist Nisei previously rejected for military service. The MISLS recruiters signed about 250 Nisei, or about 10 percent of the March 1943 volunteers from Hawaii.[17] One recruit, Honolulu attorney Yoshio Shitabata, thirty-four, who had tried unsuccessfully for the 442d RCT, now told a reporter, "I welcomed this opportunity to get into the fight." Others had served in the Varsity Victory Volunteers.[18] A few fathers and sons enlisted together, like Benjamin M. Tashiro, forty-five, an attorney and World War I veteran who signed up with his seventeen-year-old son.[19]

Two Hawaii Nisei had experience in broadcasting. Another volunteer, Masao H. Onishi, twenty-five, had worked as a Japanese-language radio announcer. When he heard the Army was looking for Nisei who could speak Japanese, he took a written language exam, "just like in Japanese school. I liked Japanese so much I passed the test with flying colors."[20] The Hawaii Nisei well understood that they would have to fight against Japan, where many had family ties. Kenichi Murata, thirty-four, told a reporter he already had one brother in the U.S. Army, but also another brother "on the other side of the fence," working as a radio broadcaster in Tokyo: "I'm ashamed to admit that I have a brother dishing out Jap propaganda. But both Jack, who's in Louisiana, and I will try to wipe out that shame by our record in the army. We're going to shove all that propaganda back down the throats of Tojo and the emperor and their militarists."[21]

Takejiro Higa, twenty, had been born in Hawaii but had been raised by relatives in Okinawa from age two to sixteen. His English-language skills were minimal, but he volunteered nonetheless, despite what he later recalled as "terrific

[16] Andrew Lind, *Hawaii's Japanese: An Experiment in Democracy* (Princeton: Princeton University Press, 1946); John A. Rademaker, *These Are Americans: The Japanese Americans in Hawaii in World War II* (Palo Alto, Calif.: Pacific Books, 1951).

[17] Accounts vary from 243 to 270 for the Nisei selected for MISLS from Hawaii at this time. MISLS, "Training History of the Military Intelligence Service Language School," ann. 10, Personnel Procurement Office, encl 4, Unpubl Ms, 1946, in CMH files, reports about 250 (p. 6). Lind, *Hawaii's Japanese*, p. 155, reports that a total of 600 students were selected in June and November 1943.

[18] Odo, *No Sword To Bury*; Yutaka Nakahata and Ralph Toyota, "Varsity Victory Volunteers: A Social Movement," *Social Process in Hawaii* 8 (November 1943): 29–35; Lind, *Hawaii's Japanese*, pp. 128–67.

[19] John F. Aiso, "Observations of a California Nisei," Interv with Marc Landy, University of California at Los Angeles, 1971, pp. 74–75.

[20] "Masao 'Harold' Onishi: Former Instructor Shares Memories," *Hawaii Herald*, 2 Jul 93.

[21] "243 Inducted Here into Interpreter Unit," *Honolulu Advertiser*, 14 Jun 43; "Japanese Translator List Issued by Army," *Honolulu Advertiser*, 3 Jul 43.

turmoil, psychologically," to think he might come face-to-face with someone he knew, a relative or classmate.[22]

On 12 June 1943, the Army held a ceremony at Schofield Barracks for the 243 Hawaii Nisei chosen for language training. They left Honolulu for the mainland three days later on a Matson liner, the SS *Lurline*. This group made up half the class that started at Camp Savage in July 1943. The Hawaii Nisei, most of whom had never visited the mainland, brought a special flavor to the language school. However, tensions quickly arose between Hawaii and mainland Nisei. The Hawaii Nisei considered the mainlanders too quiet and reserved, calling them kotonks. The mainlanders considered the Hawaii Nisei too boisterous and quick to fight, calling them Buddhaheads. These tensions had diverse sources, ranging from the Hawaii Nisei's pidgin English to their cocky self-confidence. Most mainlanders had grown up in quite different circumstances and had suffered the internment experience.[23]

The Hawaii Nisei made a different impression on the local Minnesotans as well. On their first weekend pass, some of the Hawaii Nisei went into a Minneapolis restaurant and ordered *sashimi*, a Japanese delicacy. Once they explained to the chef that they really did want thinly sliced raw fish, he complied. The following Monday school officials ordered them to stop ordering the delicacy, explaining that freshwater fish might harbor parasites.[24]

In November 1943 MISLS sent five Hawaii Nisei back to the islands for another recruiting trip, led by T.Sgt. Edwin I. Kawahara of Waipahu, Oahu. The team's star recruiter was Masaji Marumoto. The Honolulu attorney had enlisted in June 1943, telling a reporter, "In volunteering for active duty as an interpreter and translator, every young patriotic American of Japanese ancestry can make an individual contribution of loyalty and skill to America."[25] Before that, Marumoto had served as a confidential liaison between the Japanese community and law enforcement. When Kawahara returned in Hawaii in November, Army intelligence officers asked him to help interrogate some prisoners of war held there. Also held in a nearby compound were hundreds of Japanese Issei whom authorities had detained after the Pearl Harbor attack. One, whom Kawahara recognized as the principal of his Japanese-language school, had languished behind barbed wire for two years. Kawahara obtained the man's release, saying "he was an ally, not an enemy," who should be given credit for the "numerous qualified Japanese-language specialists

---

[22] "Takejiro Higa: An Okinawan Caught in the Battle of Okinawa," *Hawaii Herald*, 2 Jul 93, p. A–24; Interv, author with Takejiro Higa, 7 Dec 94.

[23] Murphy, *Ambassadors in Arms*, pp. 113–16; Tamotsu Shibutani, *The Derelicts of Company K: A Sociological Study of Demoralization* (Berkeley: University of California Press, 1978), pp. 81–83.

[24] "Masao 'Harold' Onishi."

[25] "More Volunteers for Active Duty as Interpreters and Translators Sought by Army" and "Service Station Manager and Taxi Driver Volunteer," *Honolulu Star-Bulletin*, [15 Nov 43?].

from Hawaii" now serving in the MIS.[26] On 3 January 1944, the Army swore in over 300 Hawaii Nisei for language training, including sixty students at the University of Hawaii.[27]

Although Army and Navy intelligence agencies in Hawaii needed Japanese linguists, they were unwilling to use Nisei in more than a limited capacity. Neither the local Army, Navy, nor Admiral Chester W. Nimitz's Pacific Ocean Areas headquarters used Nisei in any significant intelligence capacity until much time had passed. Not until the spring of 1944 did the Joint Intelligence Center, Pacific Ocean Areas, accept a group of Nisei as translators.[28]

Now that the Nisei could volunteer for the 442d RCT, language school recruiters encountered a new form of reluctance to join. Many Nisei were interested only in combat duty, not in some "rear echelon" job as a translator. However, the Military Intelligence Service had top priority over all Japanese American manpower and even authorized the school to choose students from the volunteers in training for the 442d RCT at Camp Shelby, Mississippi. In July 1943 Colonel Rasmussen personally led the recruiting team to Mississippi accompanied by civilian instructors Shigeya Kihara and Tetsuo Imagawa.

Some Nisei at Camp Shelby resisted the recruiters. Hawaii Nisei Daniel Inouye, nineteen, passed the qualifying exam but pleaded with the Nisei recruiting sergeant not to force him into language training. He was allowed to stay with his friends in the 442d RCT. Another Hawaii Nisei, Ted T. Tsukiyama, twenty-three, had been a student at the University of Hawaii when the war broke out. Like the other ROTC cadets, he was called into the Hawaii Territorial Guard. When the Territorial Guard dismissed all Nisei, he helped form the Varsity Victory Volunteers. In March 1943 he volunteered for the 442d RCT. When the MISLS recruiters came to Camp Shelby, he "purposely flunked the test they gave me because I didn't want to leave my group," Tsukiyama recalled; "but they took me anyway." The MISLS laid claim to about 250 Nisei, nearly 10 percent of the 442d RCT's strength; the class from Camp Shelby was activated at Camp Savage on 23 August.[29]

---

[26] Ted T. Tsukiyama et al., eds., *Secret Valor: M.I.S. Personnel, World War II Pacific Theater, Pre–Pearl Harbor to Sept. 8, 1951* (Honolulu: Military Intelligence Service Veterans Club of Hawaii, 1993), pp. 59–60.

[27] Sources vary on the number recruited on this trip. "Training History," ann. 10, sec. IV, p. 7, says about 340; other sources range from 280 to 330. Ltr, Masao Tanino to Joseph Harrington, 24 March 1978, in Ishizo Tanimura File, Joseph D. Harrington Papers, National Japanese Historical Society (NJAHS), San Francisco, Calif.

[28] During the war, an unknown number of Hawaii Nisei worked for the Army, Navy, and FBI in counterintelligence and censorship activities to monitor the Japanese population in Hawaii; but little is known about this group.

[29] Ted T. Tsukiyama, in *We Remember Pearl Harbor: Honolulu Civilians Recall the War Years, 1941–1945*, ed. Lawrence R. Rodriggs (Newark, Calif.: Communications Concepts, ca. 1991), pp. 243–56; Daniel K. Inouye, *Journey to Washington* (Englewood Cliffs, N.J.: Prentice-Hall, 1967), pp. 92–93. The regimental history does not mention this recruitment. Orville Shirey, *Americans* (Washington, D.C.: Infantry Journal Press, 1946), pp. 20–21. The movie version, *Go For Broke*, Metro-Goldwyn-Mayer, 1951, alludes briefly to MISLS recruitment at Camp Shelby.

The Military Intelligence Service was not the only military agency recruiting from Camp Shelby. In November 1943 the Office of Strategic Services (OSS) sent Daniel C. Buchanan, the OSS Japan desk officer.[30] Looking for men of high intelligence and athletic ability, he selected four Nisei lieutenants and fifty enlisted men. Of these, four officers and twenty enlisted men were selected in January 1944, among them 1st Lt. Ralph T. Yempuku, a University of Hawaii graduate and athletic instructor. The OSS was willing to overlook the fact that his entire family, including three brothers, was living in Japan. All the officers and ten enlisted men completed the OSS training program, which included communications training, a special Japanese-language course at MISLS, and commando training on Catalina Island off the California coast. In October 1944 they flew to India.[31]

Recruitment of Nisei for the Military Intelligence Service remained a challenge. In June 1943 the MISLS sent Nisei sergeants back into the internment camps to seek new students, instructing them to spread "a true and undistorted picture of the school."[32] School officials prepared a pamphlet in English and Japanese, "An Appeal to All Americans of Japanese Ancestry and Their Parents," which explained to the Issei parents that MISLS was not a "spy school."[33]

Nisei soldiers continued to endure suspicion and hostility despite positive news coverage of the 442d RCT. When President Franklin D. Roosevelt made a grand tour across the country in April 1943 to visit military bases and defense plants, he stopped at Fort Riley, Kansas. On the day of his visit, Easter Sunday, the post commander confined all Nisei soldiers, about two hundred, to their barracks. The Nisei were outraged, but they could do little. The following year at Fort McClellan, Alabama, Nisei recruits undergoing basic training complained of discrimination

---

[30] Anthony C. Brown, ed., *The Secret War Report of the OSS* (New York: Berkley Publishing, 1976), pp. 111–13, 119–33. See also the documents in Commission on Wartime Relocation and Internment of Civilians (CWRIC) Papers, reel 1, frame 816, and reel 4, frames 745–46, Bancroft Library. Buchanan was an authority on Eastern religions and had authored a study on a major Shinto deity. Daniel C. Buchanan, *Inari: Its Origin, Development, and Nature* (Tokyo: Asiatic Society of Japan, 1935).

[31] Shirey, *Americans*; Rademaker, *These Are Americans*, p. 68; Tomi Kaizawa Knaefler, *Our House Divided: Seven Japanese American Families in World War II* (Honolulu: University of Hawaii Press, 1991), pp. 88–95; "Ralph Yempuku," *Hawaii Herald*, 2 Jul 93, p. A–27; Ralph Yempuku, "OSS Detachment 101, CBI Theater," in Tsukiyama et al., *Secret Valor*, p. 75; Interv, Andrew Cox with Ralph Yempuku, n.d., author's files; Fumio Kido, Biography, Military Intelligence Service Club of Northern California (this and similar biographies hereafter cited as MISNorCal Bios).

James Y. Tanabe was also recruited directly from Camp Shelby in 1943. After completing training in counterintelligence at Havre de Grace, Maryland, and in signals intelligence at Fort Monmouth, New Jersey, in September 1943 he was shipped to the South Pacific, where he served as a warrant officer with the Australian Army and the U.S. Marine Corps in tactical signals intelligence, translating, and interpreting. Stanley L. Falk and Warren M. Tsuneishi, eds., *MIS in the War against Japan* (Washington, D.C.: Japanese American Veterans Association of Washington, D.C., 1995), pp. 32–33, 127–28.

[32] MISLS Ltr, 21 June 1943, in Gene Uratsu File, Harrington Papers.

[33] "An Appeal to All Americans of Japanese Ancestry and Their Parents," 23 Jun 43, and Press Release, 2 Jul 43, in "Training History," ann. 10, p. 6, encls. 10, 11. See also reel 20, sec. 2, pt. 2, frames 35–36, 49, JERS, Bancroft Library.

and harassment. Finally, on 20 March 1944, more than two dozen refused an order to report for training. Twenty-eight were eventually court-martialed.[34]

The existence of the 442d RCT at Camp Shelby had a noticeable effect on student morale at Camp Savage. For some Nisei, the risk of being sent to the infantry spurred them to study harder. (One former student remembers that John Aiso threatened to transfer him to the 442d RCT unless he improved his grades.)[35] Other students wanted nothing better than a transfer. T.Sgt. Sadao S. Munemori, a Kibei from Los Angeles, enlisted for language training from Manzanar in November 1942. When the 442d RCT was formed, he repeatedly asked for a transfer. At first Aiso refused and assigned him to menial jobs. But Munemori persisted and finally got his wish, taking a reduction in grade from technical sergeant to private, first class. He accompanied the 442d RCT to Italy and France, where he fought in an infantry squad for ten months. On 5 April 1945, during the final assault on the German defenses in northern Italy, he threw himself onto a German hand grenade to protect two comrades. He was posthumously awarded the Medal of Honor as the only member of the 442d RCT to be so honored at the time.[36]

From time to time the Army would send Chinese Americans to the MISLS for Japanese-language training. The first class at Crissy Field included two Chinese American reserve lieutenants, Won-Loy Chan and Robert F. Pang. Officers in the Military Intelligence Service hoped that their knowledge of written Chinese would help them learn Japanese kanji. In January 1943 MISLS began planning for more Chinese American students. The special class began in July 1943 with fifty-two students, but the experiment was not judged successful. The school's official history noted "that although a knowledge of the Chinese was some aid in assimilation of the Japanese, it also carried with it . . . great psychological obstacles which in the case of most of the [Chinese American] students whose scholastic ability was generally low made it very difficult if not impossible." Eventually, most were placed into separate sections. Fewer than half graduated with their Nisei classmates, and

---

[34] McCloy directed the War Department Inspector General to investigate the Fort Riley incident and on 23 September 1943 expressed his displeasure to the War Department G–3: Folder Assistant Secretary of War (ASW) 342.18, "Enlistment, J. A. (Divisions)," Ofc of the ASW, RG 107, NARA; McWilliams, *Prejudice*, p. 218; Shibutani, *Derelicts of Company K*, pp. 96–97; Loni Ding, prod., *The Color of Honor*, documentary film, Vox Productions, 1987; James Omura, "Japanese American Journalism during World War II," *Frontiers of Asian American Studies*, ed. Gail M. Nomura et al. (Pullman: Washington State University Press, 1989), pp. 71–77. After the war, President Harry S. Truman pardoned the Fort McClellan rebels.

[35] Akira Nakamura, MISNorCal Bio. Nakamura responded by studying harder, "to prove he was not malingering." He graduated in December 1944, "after nine months of gruesome studying and training," and served on Okinawa.

[36] War Department Bureau of Public Relations, Press Release, "Japanese-American Awarded Medal of Honor Posthumously," 17 Mar 46; "Nation's Highest Honor Given Japanese American Who Gave Life To Save Comrades in Italy" and Editorial, *Pacific Citizen*, 16 Mar 46; Hosokawa, *Nisei: The Quiet Americans*, pp. 412–13. In 2000 President William J. Clinton awarded the Medal of Honor to twenty other soldiers of the 100th Infantry Battalion and 442d RCT by upgrading their previous awards of the Distinguished Service Cross and Silver Star.

some required up to twelve additional months before they could graduate.[37] The February 1944 class included nineteen more Chinese Americans.[38]

Another source of Japanese speakers was the 9,000 Korean immigrants and their families living in Hawaii and the West Coast when war broke out. Most educated Koreans spoke Japanese because Korea had been under Japanese occupation since 1910. Before the war the U.S. government treated Korean immigrants as Japanese nationals; but after Pearl Harbor, the United States quickly reversed its position. Korean immigrants became a small but important source of Japanese speakers for the Army and Navy.[39]

Using Korean Americans as military linguists or even as instructors had some shortcomings. Korean immigrants often spoke Japanese with a distinct accent, and many Nisei exhibited the traditional Japanese disdain for Koreans and the Korean language. The Nisei instructors at MISLS were amused to hear the Korean-accented Japanese sometimes used by Caucasian officers who had begun their studies at Berkeley, Boulder, or Michigan with Korean instructors. Nevertheless, in the spring of 1943 the MISLS began recruiting Korean American students through Korean community groups in Hawaii and the mainland. The exiled Korean nationalist leader Syngman Rhee nominated sixty Korean Americans to serve in the OSS, but he urged the War Department not to place Korean American students in classes with Japanese American instructors. "The enmity that the Koreans feel for the Japanese and vice versa," he wrote, "is so ingrained that it is beyond their control."[40] By the summer of 1943 two Korean American officers and ten enlisted men were studying Japanese at Camp Savage. In 1944 MISLS provided seven Korean American graduates for Army Air Forces mobile radio squadrons.

Nisei women, many of whom spoke excellent Japanese, offered another source of students. As soon as the War Department allowed male Nisei to volunteer, the director of the Women's Army Corps (WAC), Col. Oveta C. Hobby, asked Assistant Secretary McCloy to allow Nisei women to volunteer. McCloy told her there was "no reason it could not be done" and agreed to look into the matter. In March 1943 Hobby sent recruiting teams to the camps, hoping to find 500 women volunteers. Her teams were just as disappointed as those looking for Nisei men. Most Issei parents were reluctant to give up their sons; they resisted even more allowing their daughters to serve.[41]

---

[37] "Training History," para. 6–4, p. 8, and ann. 10, sec. IV.(6).

[38] The February 1944 class included Lim P. Lee, who had been born in Hong Kong. When he was eight months old, his parents brought him to San Francisco. He served as postmaster of San Francisco from 1967 to 1980. Thomas W. Chinn, *Bridging the Pacific: San Francisco Chinatown and Its People* (San Francisco: Chinese Historical Society of America, 1989), pp. 258–60.

[39] Memo, The Adjutant General to CG Army Ground Forces (AGF), 23 Apr 42, sub: Soldiers of Korean Parentage, AG 014.311, Folder: AGF 291.2, Races (Restricted), Rcds of HQ AGF, RG 337, NARA. Takaki, *Strangers from a Different Shore*, pp. 363–67.

[40] "Training History," ann. 10, sec. IV, p. 6.

[41] McCloy Diary, 16 Jan 43, File "1943: III–11, Enemy Aliens," Ser. 2, WD Diaries, McCloy Papers; Mattie E. Treadwell, *The Women's Army Corps*, U.S. Army in World War II (Washing-

When MISLS recruiters visited the camps in 1943, Nisei women expressed an interest in attending the language school. Indeed, many of their brothers were already serving in the 442d RCT or the MIS. When Eleanor Roosevelt visited the Gila River camp in April 1943, some Nisei women approached her to ask how they could join the WAC. A recruiter from MISLS took the next step: "Knowing that their chances were remote at that time, yet curious to check on their qualifications, I [gave] several of them examinations, and each one passed with flying colors. They were better qualified for this school than many of the boys we accepted." In the spring of 1943 MISLS recruiters accepted several Nisei women as civilian translators for the Army Map Service in Cleveland, Ohio, after a two-week orientation at Camp Savage. Sergeant Kawahara made a recruiting trip to Hawaii in October 1943 and reported that "a number of inquiries were received from women of Japanese ancestry in regard to their acceptability as interpreters. They indicated a keen awareness of the important part they could play and were very anxious to be accepted for service in the [Women's Army Corps]. In many cases the inquiries were from college graduates, for the most part engaged in teaching or employed in business firms." Many Nisei men could remember how the girls had often outperformed the boys in Japanese-language schools before the war.[42]

The War Department dragged its feet, so this enthusiasm among some Nisei women did not immediately translate into many volunteers. Not until November 1943 did the War Department finally allow Nisei women to enlist, and then "only thirteen could be obtained in the first six months of enlistment, and negligible numbers thereafter."[43] At Camp Savage, school officials remained reluctant to accept women either as instructors or as students. In February 1944 Maj. Gen. Clayton Bissell directed the MISLS to look into accepting women. More than a year was to pass before the first Nisei women began training in May 1945.[44]

---

ton, D.C.: Office of the Chief of Military History, 1954), p. 589; Brenda L. Moore, *Serving Our Country: Japanese American Women in the Military during World War II* (New Brunswick, N.J.: Rutgers University Press, 2003).

[42] MISLS, Memorandum on the Question of Nisei WACS, 8 Jun 44, "Training History," ann. 10, sec. IV.3, pp. 1–5, and encl. 55. Eleanor Roosevelt, "To Undo a Mistake Is Always Harder Than Not To Create One Originally," [May 1943], printed in Jeffery F. Burton et al., *Confinement and Ethnicity: An Overview of World War II Japanese American Relocation Sites*, Publications in Anthropology 74 (Tucson: Western Archeological and Conservation Center, National Park Service, 1999), pp. 19–24. According to Misao Sakamoto, a group of Hawaii Nisei women wrote to Colonel Rasmussen sometime in 1943 to ask for permission to enlist. They received no reply. Misao Sakamoto, personal communication to author, 19 Oct 94.

[43] Treadwell, *Women's Army Corps*, p. 435. One Nisei woman who enlisted earlier, Yaye Furutani (Herman), enlisted in the WAC at Fort Bliss in 1942 while studying at the University of Texas; she was not inducted until November 1944. Yaye F. Herman, "The WAC-MIS Experience," in *Unsung Heroes: The Military Intelligence Service, Past-Present-Future* (Seattle: MIS-Northwest Association, 1996), pp. 5–8.

[44] Ltr, Lt. Col. A. W. Stuart to Personnel Branch, MIS, 18 February 1944, Ofc of the Dir of Intel G–2, RG 165, NARA. "Training History," ann. 10, contains materials on WAC students, as does reel 84, sec. 14, pt. 2, frames 00542–, JERS, Bancroft Library. "History of Military Clearance Program," pp. 23–29.

The Canadian government became interested in Japanese-language training as the war progressed. Canada had lost two battalions with the fall of Hong Kong in December 1941, and a joint U.S.-Canadian force had assaulted Kiska in the Aleutians in August 1943. Beyond that, Canada's commitment to the war against Japan was strictly limited until the defeat of Nazi Germany. However, in 1943 the Canadian government sent nine officers and seven enlisted men to the MISLS.[45] Several thousand Japanese immigrants and Nisei had lived in British Columbia before the war. After Pearl Harbor, the Canadian government had interned them and did not allow them in the armed forces. Canada took longer than the United States to decide to trust its Nisei for sensitive military service.

MISLS continued to find new students and assemble them into classes at Camp Savage. The class that began in February 1944 was the largest ever, with 651 Nisei students. But these increased numbers came at a cost. The new students on average did not look as promising as their predecessors. The better-qualified Nisei had already been either selected or definitively rejected for military service. Many of the new students had only turned eighteen the previous year. Though the MISLS extended the course length from six to nine months beginning with this class, the washout rate rose from 10 to 20 percent. Some of the nongraduates were assigned to language duties nonetheless, working with military police on prisoner of war processing teams.[46]

Over the winter of 1943–1944 the combat losses in the 100th Infantry Battalion in Italy became a heavy drain on Nisei manpower. The human cost of the war was affecting the Japanese American community as never before. The 100th Infantry Battalion entered combat near Salerno in September 1943 and a few months later joined the bruising fight for Monte Cassino. It was beginning to look like it was a "suicide battalion" after all. By January 1944 the 100th Infantry Battalion had lost more than 580 casualties, including 142 killed or missing. This was over 40 percent of its assigned strength. Because the battalion was racially segregated, the Army could not use regular replacements and voluntary enlistments alone could not fill the demand. In January the 442d RCT, still at Camp Shelby, was levied for ten officers and 165 enlisted men as immediate replacements.[47]

The War Department and the Japanese American Citizens League (JACL) both came to the conclusion that restoring eligibility for Selective Service was the logical next step. President Roosevelt had declared that "no loyal citizen of the United States should be denied the democratic right to exercise the responsibility of his citizenship." The JACL actively lobbied for the move. In the autumn of 1943 General DeWitt stepped down from the Western Defense Command, removing another stubborn opponent to Nisei service. On 18 November 1943, the War Department

---

[45] "Training History," p. 16; *MISLS Album* (Minneapolis: Military Intelligence Service Language School, 1946), p. 10.

[46] Attrition rates computed from table of graduates in "Training History," ann. 1, Academic Training, para. 6–5, pp. 12–13.

[47] Shirey, *Americans*, p. 26; Office of the Provost Marshal General, "World War II: A Brief History"; "History of Military Clearance Program," pp. 265–67.

formally changed its stance. After more than a year classified as IV–C, enemy aliens, Nisei became eligible for Selective Service.[48]

Selective Service proved a less than perfect process of bringing Nisei into the Army. Each Nisei still required special War Department approval before a local board could induct him. Often the Nisei were far removed from their local boards. For example, what if a Nisei had first registered in Los Angeles in 1941, was evacuated to Manzanar in 1942, and then left camp in 1943 for a job in Chicago? Moreover, some local boards in California may have stalled or tried to thwart the process. All this resulted in months-long delays in inducting Nisei. In Hawaii, the process was somewhat simpler but still slow. From the point at which the MISLS selected a Nisei to attend language training, the MIS took up to six months to get him through the clearance process and inducted. The first Nisei selectees were not inducted until July. They then had to attend eight weeks of basic training before arriving at the language school.[49]

The resumption of Selective Service caused another unexpected crisis in the mainland camps, similar to the registration crisis of early 1943. Some Nisei, still angry at the forced incarceration of themselves and their families, considered conscription the last straw. The government was denying them their constitutional rights: now that same government wanted to induct them against their will. Hundreds decided to resist the draft; eventually 265 were tried and convicted. But most Nisei willingly accepted the call to service.[50]

The resumption of Selective Service made a large difference for the MISLS. It stimulated a flood of applications from Nisei who would rather volunteer for language training than wait for the draft and automatic assignment to the 442d RCT.[51] The school no longer had to recruit from the camps or wait for volunteers. As more Nisei were drafted, the school could have its pick of the Nisei soldiers in basic training. By the summer of 1944 the problem of numbers was on the way to being solved.

---

[48] Selective Service reinstated the induction of Japanese Americans on 13 December 1943. "Training History," ann. 10, sec. IV.D., p. 10. Selective Service headquarters amended Local Board Memorandum no. 179 on 14 January 1944, but Nisei still had to be reviewed and reclassified on a case-by-case basis. Selective Service System, *Selective Service as the Tide of War Turns*, Third Report of the Director of Selective Service, 1943–1944 (Washington, D.C.: Selective Service System, 1945), pp. 241–43; *Special Groups*, Special Monograph no. 10, 2 vols. (Washington, D.C.: Selective Service System, 1953), 1: 113–42. The slow loosening of restrictions from 1943 to 1946 can be traced in the bulletins and policy directives collected in *Special Groups*, vol. 2. See especially Local Board Release nos. 112 and 179, with changes. The War Department did not drop the requirement for preclearance of Nisei selectees until 4 March 1946 (p. 23).

[49] "Training History," ann. 10, sec. IV.D., p. 12.

[50] Eric L. Muller, *Free To Die for Their Country: The Story of the Japanese American Draft Resisters in World War II* (Chicago: University Press of Chicago, 2001). In 1947 President Truman pardoned all individuals convicted of violating the Selective Service Act during the war, but reconciliation within the Japanese American community was long in coming. See also the novel by John Okada, *No-No Boy* (Rutherford, Vt.: Tuttle, 1957).

[51] "Training History," ann. 10, sec. IV.D., pp. 10–11.

Army Intensive Japanese Language School, University of Michigan, 1942–1944

At the outset of the war the Military Intelligence Division had established a strict policy: whenever possible, enlisted MIS Nisei would serve under Caucasian language officers. "The main purpose of this," Colonel Rasmussen recalled, "was to have an unmistakably Caucasian officer associated with Oriental faces in order not to have some trigger-happy G.I. pop a gun."[52] The difficulty with this policy was that the War Department did not have enough Japanese-speaking Caucasians. The few language attachés trained before the war were already in critical assignments or were too senior to serve as team leaders. Before the war Rasmussen had begun searching for Caucasian officers and enlisted men who spoke Japanese. Dozens of National Guard and Reserve officers, some of whom had experience in Japan before the war, had come to the school after Pearl Harbor. Two graduated in May 1942 and eighteen more in December. It later became more difficult to find Caucasian men who could keep up in class, not to mention those with any experience with the Japanese language.[53]

The War Department might have chosen to activate Nisei reserve officers, graduates of prewar ROTC commissioning programs at the University of Hawaii and elsewhere. A handful were already serving with the 100th Infantry Battalion, but the War Department declined to call up other Nisei reserve officers until the formation of the 442d RCT. Or the War Department might have awarded direct commissions to Nisei enlisted men for the language teams. Given the prejudice against Japanese Americans, even American-born Nisei, the War Department was not ready for this step. In fact, when Rasmussen began recruiting Nisei from the camps in the midst of the evacuations in the autumn of 1942, he told WRA officials that "all successful applicants will hold non-commissioned officers rank." But he made War Department policy clear: "None of these men will be commissioned into the Service as officers, however."[54]

Rasmussen was left with little choice but to find Caucasians able to learn Japanese. The Office of Naval Intelligence already had a year's head start, having begun recruiting Caucasian students in the summer of 1941. Rasmussen decided to begin a similar Army program. Most Caucasians needed a one-year preparatory course before attending regular classes at Camp Savage. To establish this, Rasmussen selected Professor Joseph K. Yamagiwa, a Japanese-language instruc-

---

[52] Kai E. Rasmussen, speech, Defense Language Institute Foreign Language Center (DLIFLC), Monterey, Calif., 25 Jun 77, printed in *DLIFLC Forum* (November 1977).

[53] The War Department encountered difficulties in procuring junior officers of all types in 1942–1943. In early 1943 it cut back on the number of soldiers sent to officer candidate schools. See Robert R. Palmer and William R. Keast, "The Procurement of Officers," and William R. Keast, "The Training of Officer Candidates," in *The Procurement and Training of Ground Combat Troops*, ed. Robert R. Palmer et al. (Washington, D.C.: Department of the Army, Historical Division, 1948), pp. 87–163, 321–64.

[54] Ltr, Kai E. Rasmussen to E. M. Rowalt, 3 October 1942, Rcds of the WRA, RG 210, NARA.

tor at the University of Michigan who had recently published a textbook of modern conversational Japanese. Rasmussen signed a contract with the university and appointed Yamagiwa as educational director. The university agreed to accept 150 students for forty-nine weeks of instruction to begin on 5 January 1943. Yamagiwa agreed to use the Naganuma readers, supplemented by his own textbook.[55]

Rasmussen then selected twenty-one instructors. The University of Michigan, unlike the MISLS, was free to hire Issei and women. Like the MISLS instructors, few had any previous teaching experience. Most came directly from the camps and were housed together with their families in a former fraternity house near campus. "At first some did not dare even to go to a church, let alone a movie theatre," Yamagiwa wrote. "The work in Ann Arbor was new, and the duties heavy. The staff room was small. As others joined the staff, with stories of their experiences in various assembly centers and in the WRA camps, some assumed for a time a certain cautiousness in their dealings with people in and around the campus."[56]

Finding qualified students offered an even greater challenge. Rasmussen sought college men of the highest caliber and contacted the national headquarters of Phi Beta Kappa. The academic honor society had already provided the Navy with hundreds of member names, but they gave more names to Rasmussen. Some, referred to as "BIJ," had been born in Japan. Others had taken Japanese-language classes or simply had demonstrated academic potential.[57] The Army recruited from Yale Law School a student who had attended a few sessions of an introductory Japanese course and was surprised to be accepted. "We are counting on you Phi Betes," the recruiting officer explained, "not to let us down."[58]

---

[55] Joseph K. Yamagiwa, *Modern Conversational Japanese* (New York: McGraw-Hill, 1942); "Army Japanese Language School," p. 2; Joseph K. Yamagiwa, "The Japanese Language Programs at the University of Michigan during World War II," ch. 2, Unpubl Ms, 1946, Ann Arbor, Mich.; "Training History," pp. 11–12; Robert J. Matthew, *Language and Area Studies in the Armed Services: Their Future Significance* (Washington, D.C.: American Council on Education, 1947), pp. 43–52.

[56] Yamagiwa, "Japanese Language Programs," p. 44. Nisuke Mitsumori, an Issei instructor at Michigan, was a World War I veteran who had been wounded in France. Eileen Sunada Sarasohn, ed., *The Issei: Portrait of a Pioneer, An Oral History* (Palo Alto, Calif.: Pacific Books, 1983), pp. 285–86.

[57] Donald M. Richardson, "Random Recollections of the Second Class, AIJLS [Army Intensive Japanese Language School]," Unpubl Ms, Sep 88, author's files; John A. Rappin, "Non-Nikkei MIS," and Allen H. Meyer, "MIS: Non-Nikkei," in *Unsung Heroes*, pp. 9–14, 97–104; "Scholars in Uniform," *Ann Arbor Observer* (August 1990): 2–7; Herbert Passin, *Encounter with Japan* (San Francisco: Kodansha, 1982). Passin, a professor of social anthropology at Northwestern University, became an AIJLS student in May 1944. Grant K. Goodman, *America's Japan: The First Year, 1945–1946* (New York: Fordham University Press, 2005), pp. 9–17. Goodman became an AIJLS student in May 1943. See also the papers of Irwin Hersey, Alfred H. Marks, and George H. Marshall, U.S. Army Military History Institute (MHI), Carlisle Barracks, Pa.

[58] Frank L. Hammond, Ltr to Editor, *The Key Reporter* (Spring 1992); Samuel J. Jacobs, Ltr to Editor, *The Key Reporter* (Autumn 1999): 9–10. Rasmussen also recruited two African American college students.

A Nisei instructor (left) *teaches Caucasian students at the Army Intensive Japanese Language School, Ann Arbor, Michigan, 1943.*

On 5 January 1943, the first classes began for the Army Intensive Japanese Language Course (later renamed the Army Intensive Japanese Language School). Students were in class twenty-four hours a week, followed by supervised study halls. Each section had seven or eight students. The university granted thirty semester hours of credit for the course and conferred bachelor's degrees on those who had sufficient credits from another school. Yamagiwa made a special point of showing Japanese movies. These movies, typically costume dramas of the Samurai style popular in Japan during the 1930s, were "extremely valuable in showing the social contexts in which particular language forms are used," Yamagiwa wrote. "The value of movies in increasing knowledge as to customs and institutions cannot be overstressed."[59] The students plunged into their studies. It felt strange to be attending language classes on a university campus while their friends were serving overseas, but they knew their time would come. Meanwhile, the academic pressures were intense.[60]

---

[59] Yamagiwa, "Japanese Language Programs," p. 23.

[60] Several students attempted suicide; some succeeded. Goodman, *America's Japan*, p. 21. The Royal Australian Air Force's Japanese-language program experienced a similar problem among its students: "There were not many of us, yet two had essayed suicide, one successfully, and two others had gone insane." The War Department removed five students in April 1944 for what it

The demand for Caucasian team leaders was also intense. As the first class was under way, Rasmussen decided that he could not wait for the year-long course to finish. In May 1943 he directed Yamagiwa to pick his best students for accelerated training. The top forty graduated after six months, on 19 June 1943, and went straight to Camp Savage to begin training at the MISLS, where they graduated in January 1944. Their classmates at Michigan graduated on schedule in late 1943 and reported to Camp Savage in February 1944. From that point on, all students stayed for the entire twelve-month course, followed by six months at the MISLS. These students became eligible for commissions upon completion of their MISLS training, except for a few who already had commissions before entering the program. Meanwhile, in early 1943 Rasmussen identified the next 150 Caucasians, as well as another 16 instructors, for another class that began on 24 May. In July the school also admitted sixteen Canadian students, nine of them officers. New classes began in January 1944, May 1944, January 1945, and May 1945, each class having 150–200 students. The faculty grew to about fifty Issei and Nisei. By the end of the war, Yamagiwa and his instructors had graduated 789 Caucasian students as language team leaders for the Nisei.

Navy Japanese Language School, University of Colorado at Boulder, 1942–1944

While the War Department was establishing a special Japanese-language training program for Caucasian officer candidates, the Office of Naval Intelligence continued at the University of Colorado at Boulder its program founded in the autumn of 1941 at Harvard and the University of California. On 1 July 1942, 153 Caucasian students arrived at the Navy School of Oriental Languages in Boulder, where they joined sixty-seven students who had started at the University of California.[61]

Cmdr. Albert E. Hindmarsh and Professor Florence Walne based the program on the Naganuma readers. Up to 150 Japanese Americans, many recruited directly from the camps, served as instructors under Assistant Director Susumu Nakamura, who had taught Japanese at the University of California before the war. Because the instructors were employees of the University of Colorado, the school was free

---

termed "effeminacy which leads to open suspicion." Ltr, 25 March 1944, Folder: Trng B4 Files, MISLS—Gen, 1945, Ofc of the Dir of Intel G–2, RG 165, NARA.

[61] "Reminiscences of Rear Admiral Arthur H. McCollum, U.S. Navy Retired," 2 vols., Unpubl Ms, 1970–1971, Naval Historical Center, Washington, D.C.; Office of the Chief of Naval Operations, "School of Oriental Languages," Unpubl Ms, Naval Historical Center, Washington, D.C. The first contract between the Navy Department and the University of Colorado, dated 1 July 1942, is reproduced in Scott E. Nadler, *The Evolution of Foreign Language Training in the Armed Forces* (Washington, D.C.: Defense Language Institute, 1972), pp. 103–04, 115–20. See also the U.S. Navy Japanese Language School Project and Roger Pineau Papers at the University of Colorado at Boulder.

to hire women as well as men.[62] Students were in class fourteen hours a week for fourteen months, and the course demanded extensive memorization. Each section had no more than four or five students to allow for practicing conversational skills. In December 1942 Hindmarsh boasted:

A large number of competent educators have characterized the course as having revolutionized the practical teaching of foreign languages in the United States. . . . It is a fact that today . . . the Navy standards of efficiency, practical fluency, and competency in the teaching and study of the Japanese language are approached in no university in this country and possibly nowhere in the world outside Japan. This evaluation is based on the experience of hard-boiled observers both within the course and in the use of the products of our course.[63]

Hindmarsh believed that the quality of students was key to the program's success. He insisted upon college men who had been born in Japan, had studied Japanese or Chinese for at least six months, or showed exceptional academic talent. Phi Beta Kappa nominated many of them.[64] Hindmarsh's vigorous recruiting caused some friction with Army recruiters in the autumn of 1942. "It seems clear that the Army Representative is deliberately staging rallies in each and every city to which I am going, and that these rallies are arranged so as to precede my arrival by four or five days," Hindmarsh complained, "Considerable pressure is being brought to bear on the students, particularly the first rate students." Rasmussen denied the charges but added that he felt "that in view of the common War Aim it might be well to propose a merger of Personnel Selection Boards for the purpose of future canvassing." Separate recruiting continued nevertheless.[65]

The Navy program continued to grow. By the end of 1942 there were 300 students in training. In 1943 Hindmarsh began to recruit college women as well; in June and July he interviewed 600 women nationwide. By the end of the year about seventy female students had enrolled as WAVES (Women Accepted for Volunteer Emergency Service). Over the winter of 1943–1944 the Royal Navy sent ten junior officers. During 1943 the school added courses in Russian, Malay,

[62] "American Born Japanese Teach at Navy School," *Pacific Citizen*, 9 Jul 42, p. 2; D. Daté and Dick Inokuchi Files, Harrington Papers; Jessica Arntson, "Journey to Boulder: The Japanese American Instructors of the Navy Japanese Language School, 1942–1946," Master's Thesis, University of Colorado, [2003?]; Pauline S. McAlpine, *Diary of a Missionary* (Decatur, Ga.: Presbyterian Church in America, 1986). McAlpine and her husband were Japanese instructors who followed the school from Berkeley to Boulder and then to Stillwater, Oklahoma, in 1945. Another instructor, Ensho Ashikaga, restarted the Japanese-language program at the University of California at Berkeley after the war.

[63] Memo, Hindmarsh to Dir of Naval Intel, 24 Dec 42, in "School of Oriental Languages," pp. 15–18 (quote from p. 18).

[64] *The Key Reporter* announced the program in its winter 1942–1943 issue. In the summer of 1943 the same newsletter published a firsthand description of the course, reprinted in *The Key Reporter* (Autumn 1991): 2.

[65] "School of Oriental Languages," p. 15. See the exchange of correspondence in Box 291, Ofc of the Dir of Intel G–2, RG 165, NARA.

and Chinese (Mandarin and several other dialects) and changed its name to the Navy School of Oriental Languages. By August 1944 the school had produced about 600 graduates.[66] The tremendous pressure took its toll on students and staff alike: ill health forced Florence Walne to resign in September 1944.[67]

Most graduates were commissioned in the Naval Reserve and shipped directly to the Pacific. The Marine Corps sent ten graduates to Camp Savage for follow-on training in the summer of 1943, but this was an exception. From early 1943 Boulder graduates began to pour into the Pacific. The first group of twenty arrived in Hawaii in February 1943. During the battle for Attu in May 1943, some were assigned to Army units, where they commanded enlisted Nisei linguists. Others served at the Naval Communications Intelligence Center in Washington, D.C. The "Boulder Boys" had a very different experience from that of the Army Nisei.[68]

Other Japanese-Language Programs, 1942–1944

To place in perspective the Army's programs at Camp Savage and the University of Michigan and the Navy's program at the University of Colorado, it is useful to examine other Japanese-language programs in the United States during the war. (*See Map 4.*) Several other military organizations, government agencies, and universities started or expanded their Japanese and Far Eastern programs; all competed for instructors and students. Assistant Secretary McCloy expressed his dismay to the War Department G–3 in June 1943: "At the present time there appears to be several agencies e.g. Military Intelligence, Signal Corps, Provost Marshal General's department, and Army Specialist Training Division, who are either now interested in or planning to become engaged in Japanese language." He called for "some overall agency [to] have the responsibility for co-ordinating the requirements of the various War Department agencies in this matter." This

---

[66] "School of Oriental Languages," p. 22. One WAVES student was Helen Craig (McCullough), a Phi Beta Kappa graduate of the University of California. After the war, she served in the Allied Translator and Interpreter Section (ATIS) from 1946 to 1950, earned her doctorate, and returned to the University of California as a professor of Japanese literature. See University of California: In Memoriam, 1998, http://sunsite.berkeley.edu/uchistory/archives_exhibits/in_memoriam/, accessed 27 Feb 04.

[67] Florence Walne married Samuel T. Farquhar in December 1944; she never regained her health and died on 14 October 1946. See Name Index, Farquhar, Florence Walne, University of California: In Memoriam, 1946, http://sunsite.berkeley.edu/uchistory/archives_exhibits/in_memoriam/, accessed 27 Feb 04.

[68] Roger V. Dingman, "Language at War: U.S. Marine Corps Japanese Language Officers in the Pacific War," *Journal of Military History* 68 (July 2004): 853–83; Pedro Loureiro, "'Boulder Boys': Naval Japanese Language School Graduates," in *New Interpretations in Naval History*, ed. Randy C. Balano and Craig Symonds (Annapolis, Md.: Naval Institute Press, 2001), pp. 366–88. Several went on to academic careers as Japan specialists. Otis Cary, ed., *From a Ruined Empire: Letters—Japan, China, Korea 1945–46* (San Francisco: Kodansha, 1975); Donald Keene, *On Familiar Terms* (New York: Kodansha, 1994). Two wrote novels of their wartime experiences. John Ashmead, *The Mountain and the Feather* (Boston: Houghton Mifflin, 1961); Kenneth Lamott, *The Stockade* (Boston: Little, Brown, 1952).

responsibility fell to the War Department G–3 Organization and Training Division, but the task was hopeless.[69]

Before the war Japanese-language instruction was rare in the United States, apart from community-based Japanese-language schools in Hawaii and on the West Coast. Only a few universities offered Japanese, most often for the study of Japanese art and literature. A linguistic scholar complained in 1943:

Most learning of Oriental languages has been disfigured by bad teaching and bad implements of instruction.... Most grammars and other paraphernalia of studying an Oriental language have been written by persons without the slightest technical linguistic competence.... Without proper analysis and implements, instruction in a language, particularly one which offers at every step the widest departures from the student's own linguistic experience, cannot but be inefficient, time-consuming, and impractical.[70]

Before the war a handful of scholars had set out to overcome these problems. The American Council of Learned Societies established the Intensive Language Program in the spring of 1941 at eighteen universities. Within a year the program had grown to 700 students and twenty-six languages, including several never before taught in the United States. For most languages the instructors had to develop entirely new curricular materials.[71] This program was designed to produce students with conversational skills through rapid and intense training based on the theories of anthropologists and scientific linguists such as Franz Boas, Edward Sapir, and Leonard Bloomfield. After the outbreak of war, publishers brought out a flood of textbooks, dictionaries, and readers for Japanese, some developed through the Intensive Language Program, most reprints of older materials. Few were written with any regard to modern pedagogy or military requirements.[72]

In the autumn of 1942 the leaders of American higher education prevailed upon President Roosevelt to use their campuses for military training programs. The Navy responded with the V–12 precommissioning program. The Army Ground Forces protested this as drain of skilled manpower, for the program eventually diverted 150,000 high-test-score enlisted men to college campuses across the nation.[73] The War Department's Military Government Division urged the inclu-

---

[69] Memo, Exec Asst to ASW to ACS, G–3, 16 Jun 43, Class Ref Sub Files, 1940–1947, Ofc of the ASW, RG 107, NARA.

[70] Mortimer Graves, "Intensive Language Study," *Far Eastern Survey* (22 March 1943): 63–64.

[71] Paul F. Angiolillo, *Armed Forces' Foreign Language Teaching: Critical Evaluation and Implications* (New York: Vanni, 1947), pp. 15–29; William G. Moulton, "Linguistics and Language Teaching in the United States, 1940–1960," in *Trends in European and American Linguistics, 1930–1960*, ed. Christine Mohrmann, Alf Sommerfelt, and Joshua Whatmough (Utrecht, Netherlands: Spectrum, 1963), pp. 82–109.

[72] Mortimer Graves, "Wartime Instruction in Far Eastern Languages," *Far Eastern Survey* (27 March 1946): 92–93.

[73] Louis E. Keefer, *Scholars in Foxholes: The Story of the Army Specialized Training Program in World War II* (Jefferson, N.C.: McFarland, 1988); Louis E. Keefer, "Birth and Death of the Army Specialized Training Program," *Army History* (Winter 1995): 1–7; V. R. Cardozier, *Colleges and*

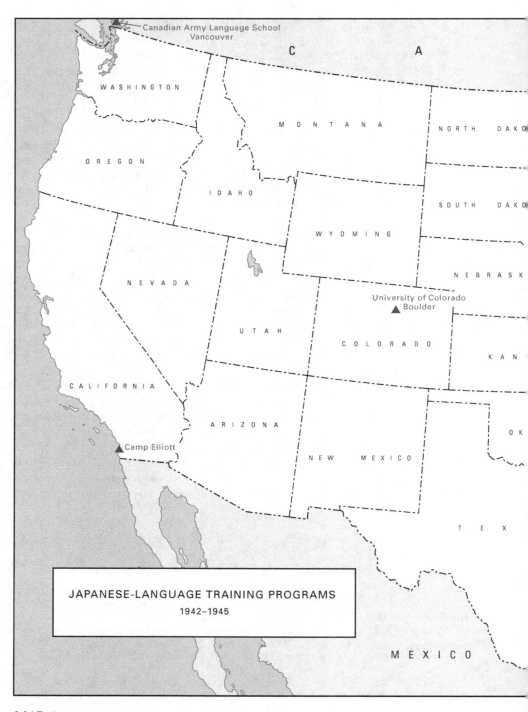

Canadian Army Language School
Vancouver

C A

WASHINGTON

MONTANA

NORTH DAKO

OREGON

IDAHO

SOUTH DAKO

WYOMING

NEBRASK

NEVADA

University of Colorado
▲ Boulder

UTAH

COLORADO

KAN

CALIFORNIA

ARIZONA

O K

▲ Camp Elliott

NEW MEXICO

T E X

JAPANESE-LANGUAGE TRAINING PROGRAMS
1942–1945

MEXICO

MAP 4

sion of foreign-area and language training, and the Office of the Provost Marshal General developed requirements for language and area studies for up to 2,000 soldiers. The Military Government Division then persuaded Army Specialized Training Program (ASTP) organizers to include the Foreign Area and Language Program. Other War Department branches added their needs; before long, stated foreign-language requirements had jumped to 15,000 soldiers.[74]

In the spring and summer of 1943, fifty-five colleges and universities set up ASTP programs in thirty-four languages, often with only a few weeks' notice. (The Navy's V–12 program never included foreign languages.) In some cases, the students didn't know what language they were to study until they arrived on campus. For example, in June 1943 the Army sent 125 enlisted men to the University of Washington for European language and area studies. "Two days before the official start of the program," wrote the program's director, "we learned that we were not to teach a European but an entirely Far Eastern program, with training in Japanese, Mandarin Chinese, and Korean languages and areas." This, he commented, "was a serious handicap in the organization of the staff and the development of the material."[75] In all, twelve universities eventually offered ASTP programs in Japanese-language and area studies.[76]

In most cases the Japanese ASTP courses built upon small, prewar Japanese-language programs at these schools. At the University of Michigan, beginning in October 1943, Professor Yamagiwa operated a Japanese ASTP program alongside the Army Japanese Language School.[77] He hired nineteen additional instructors just for the ASTP. Eventually, the Michigan program trained 264 ASTP students in addition to the 975 students in the Army Japanese Language School.

Normally, faculty members called scientific linguists directed ASTP courses. The director was assisted by native speakers called drillmasters or informants. For example, the University of Minnesota used as a scientific linguist Ganna M. Syro-Boyarsky, a woman of Danish-Russian heritage who had been educated in Japan. Several Nisei drillmasters assisted her.[78]

Across America, colleges and universities scrambled to design and provide language instruction. One of the program's founders later commented that the ASTP language program "was beset by all the difficulties and inefficiencies which

---

Universities in World War II (Westport, Conn.: Praeger, 1993). The War Department established a junior version of ASTP, called the Army Specialized Training Reserve Program (ASTRP), for youths under age eighteen.

[74] Frederick B. Agard et al., *A Survey of Language Classes in the Army Specialized Training Program* (New York: Commission on Trends in Education, Modern Language Association, 1944); Angiolillo, *Armed Forces' Foreign Language Teaching*; Matthew, *Language and Area Studies*; Mario A. Pei, *Languages for War and Peace*, 2d ed. (New York: Vanni, 1945).

[75] Franz H. Michael, "Civilians and Soldiers Study Pacific," *Far Eastern Survey* (23 August 1944): 158–61.

[76] Matthew, *Language and Area Studies*, pp. 177–78.

[77] Yamagiwa, "Japanese Language Programs."

[78] "She Teaches GIs To Say It in Japanese [Ganna M. Syro-Boyarsky]," unidentified newspaper clipping, [1943?].

armies and navies are able to devise; selection and assignment troubles kept morale low. . . . The Army and Navy programs were afflicted with all the ills that arise from hasty improvisation, paucity of trained personnel, lack of teaching materials, divided direction, and red tape."[79]

Before the program finished its first year, the War Department terminated it. Most language and area study courses were cancelled by March 1944, and the students were sent off to become individual replacements. The War Department made little effort to assign foreign-language graduates to duty positions requiring these languages. Indeed, at that point in the war the U.S. government had little need of military government specialists, the training of which was the ostensible purpose of the ASTP language and area studies program. Only a few students subsequently transferred to the Army Japanese-language course at the University of Michigan and from there to the MISLS. Enlisted students who had been promised commissions found themselves in combat units with neither stripes nor commissions, serving under sergeants with much less education.[80] Over 1,400 soldiers who had been studying Italian went to work with former Italian prisoners of war. The Signal Corps took 1,357 students of several languages. The MIS took 568 former students of all languages. However, of those who had studied Japanese few ever went on to use the language. According to one report, the Army sent to Normandy "infantrymen who had been beautifully trained to speak Japanese."[81] One student who had spent nine months studying Japanese at the University of Minnesota later admitted, "about the only recognizable residual is the fact that I can say in Japanese, 'Which is faster, the street car or the bus?' Nothing else."[82] Some ASTP graduates did go into appropriate intelligence assignments; but overall, the program contributed little toward the Army's pressing requirement for Japanese linguists.[83]

The Army Service Forces took a different approach. Instead of establishing full-time instruction, it produced and disseminated self-study materials and dictionaries in forty languages through its Information and Education Division. The pocket-size Japanese phrase books and handbooks were published in the

---

[79] Graves, "Wartime Instruction," p. 93.

[80] Keefer, "Birth and Death," describes the broken promise of commissions for ASTP graduates: "Even fifty years later, many former ASTPers harbor the feeling that the Army lied to them about their futures" (p. 4).

[81] "Science Comes to Languages," *Fortune* (August 1944): 135, cited in Angiolillo, *Armed Forces' Foreign Language Teaching*, p. 166.

[82] Keefer, "Birth and Death," p. 113. Another student who attended the ASTP Japanese program at the University of Michigan in 1943–1944 was assigned directly to the Signal Intelligence Service at Arlington Hall. Bill Leary, World War II questionnaire, MHI.

[83] The ASTP was the first federal experiment with a national program for foreign language and area studies and had significant impact on language-teaching methods after the war. Not until the National Defense Education Act of 1958 did the federal government again provide funding and direction on this scale to American colleges and universities for foreign language and area studies.

spring of 1943.[84] In a similar effort, the U.S. Armed Forces Institute in Madison, Wisconsin, produced a series of innovative self-study language guides that used simple textbooks and phonograph records. The Japanese basic course for the Armed Forces Institute was written by Yale Professor Bernard Bloch, a scientific linguist who had no previous experience with the Japanese language, together with Eleanor H. Jorden.[85]

The OSS also had Japanese-language requirements and sent a team of Nisei to MISLS for language training in 1944. These Nisei were handpicked from soldiers in training with the 442d RCT at Camp Shelby. For its morale operations propaganda unit, the OSS also recruited other Nisei and even Issei with excellent language skills, including some whom the War Department had previously deemed unacceptable. As the OSS planned for expanded operations against Japan in 1945, it established six-month courses in Japanese and Korean at the University of Pennsylvania.[86]

As the Army's signals intelligence effort against Japan expanded, the Signal Intelligence Service (SIS) needed Japanese linguists to translate the growing volume of radio message traffic but remained reluctant to use Nisei. In early 1943 the SIS recruited Edwin O. Reischauer from Harvard to set up a small Japanese-language school at Arlington Hall for Caucasian officers.[87]

In addition to the MISLS, the War Department G–2 operated the Military Intelligence Training Center at Camp Ritchie, Maryland, for general intelligence training. This center provided Japanese-language classes, some taught by T5g. Frances Nichols, WAC. Nichols was born and raised in Japan, where her father served as the Episcopal bishop of Kyoto from 1926 to 1940.[88]

Many universities established their own programs in Far Eastern languages and area studies in addition to the various military programs. The University of Washington reported over 1,500 students enrolled in Far Eastern courses during the 1943–1944 academic years.[89] However, none of these military or civilian Japanese-language programs approached MISLS in size or effectiveness. To the contrary, each new program drained off resources such as skilled instructors and qualified students at a time when the Army and Navy needed to concentrate their efforts.

---

[84] Technical Manual (TM) 30–275, *Japanese Phrase Book* (Washington, D.C.: War Department, 1943); TM 30–341, *Japanese: A Guide to the Spoken Language* (Washington, D.C.: War Department, 1943).

[85] Bernard Bloch and Eleanor H. Jorden, *Spoken Japanese*, 2 vols. (Silver Spring, Md.: United States Armed Forces Institute/Linguistic Society of America, 1945–1946). See also "Nisei Girls Teach Japanese Language [Yale]," *Pacific Citizen*, 9 Sep 44.

[86] Anthony C. Brown, *Secret War Report*, p. 132.

[87] Edwin O. Reischauer, *My Life Between Japan and America* (New York: Harper & Row, 1986), pp. 91–101.

[88] Nichols was the daughter of Shirley H. Nichols. MISLS, Memo on the Question of Nisei WACS, 8 Jun 44, "Training History," ann. 10, encl. 55; Ltr, Maj. Paul F. Rusch to Lt. Col. Mathewson, sub: American Born Japanese WACS & Caucasians Born in Japan, 13 October 1945, 091–300.6, Gen Corresp, 1944–1945, OCCIO, G–2, GHQ Southwest Pacific Area, RG 338, NARA.

[89] Michael, "Civilians and Soldiers Study Pacific."

Military government training occasionally included Japanese-language instruction because Army and Navy planners could see the need for language-trained personnel to help occupy Japanese-held territories and eventually Japan proper. Anthropologist John F. Embree, who had done field work in rural Japan before the war, declared, "It is essential that military government officers for Asia acquire a thorough grounding in Japanese language, culture and history."[90]

The Navy Department established the Navy School of Military Government and Administration at Columbia University in the summer of 1942. The students, commissioned directly from civilian life, studied the lands and peoples of the Pacific. During the nine-month course, students took 480 hours of conversational Malay, Japanese, or Chinese. Several hundred naval officers graduated from the course. In October 1944 the Navy established an abbreviated course at Princeton University that shortened the program and eliminated all language instruction.[91]

At the University of Virginia in 1942, the War Department established a similar school, the School of Military Government, to train staff officers. Hugh Borton, a Japan expert at Harvard, advised on the school's Far Eastern curriculum.[92] To train junior military government personnel, the Provost Marshal General set up Civil Affairs Training Schools (CATS) at ten universities in the autumn of 1943. Six universities conducted training for the Far Eastern area, including conversational Chinese or Japanese.[93] Their students were commissioned directly from civilian life and tended to be older than the ASTP students and already established in their professions or businesses. The different universities hired Nisei to conduct the language instruction. The language curriculum followed that of the ASTP but for a shorter period. At the University of Michigan, in August 1944 Professor Yamagiwa established a CATS Japanese-language program alongside the earlier MISLS officer candidate course begun in January 1943 and the ASTP course begun in October 1943. One observer praised the CATS language instruction and deemed it "a thoroughly excellent program in which another thousand Americans acquired a useful competence in Japanese." In his opinion, "certainly no such groups ever learned more Japanese in six months."[94] However, assessing the success of the various Japanese-language programs is difficult, especially

---

[90] John F. Embree, "Military Occupation of Japan," *Far Eastern Survey* (20 September 1944): 173–76.

[91] Matthew, *Language and Area Studies*, pp. 27–42, 91–99. One of the Nisei instructors at Columbia was Miya S. Kikuchi. Eriko Yamamoto, "Miya Sannomiya Kikuchi: A Pioneer Nisei Woman's Life and Identity," *Amerasia Journal* 23, no. 3 (1997): 73–101.

[92] Hugh Borton wrote several works on Japan, including *Japan Since 1931: Its Political and Social Developments* (New York: Institute for Pacific Relations, 1940).

[93] Ofc of the Provost Marshal General, "World War II: A Brief History," pt. 5, pp. 642–710. Universities that taught the Far Eastern curriculum were Chicago, Harvard, Michigan, Northwestern, Stanford, and Yale.

[94] Graves, "Wartime Instruction," p. 93. In addition, the Civil Affairs Holding and Staging Area at Fort Ord and the Presidio of Monterey used several Nisei MISLS graduates for Japanese-language training in 1944–1945.

since many students never used the language and were demobilized or reassigned at the end of the war.

Other commands established Japanese programs as needed. In June 1942 the Marine Corps mobilized two University of Oregon faculty members, Harold J. Noble and Paul S. Dull, both Marine Corps Reserve officers, to start a program at Camp Elliott in southern California for the 2d Marine Division.[95] They established the three-month Enlisted Marine Japanese Language School that continued even after the 2d Marine Division left for the South Pacific. In 1944 the school moved to Camp Pendleton and graduated over 150 marines.

Marine commanders were desperate for Japanese linguists, so much so that they sometimes made mistakes. When the 29th Marines sailed from San Diego in 1944, the regiment directed that all officers and staff noncoms receive Japanese training while embarked. The instructor was a marine who had grown up among the Nisei in southern California and claimed to speak Japanese. For weeks as they crossed the ocean he taught simple phrases and characters to his shipmates. When the regiment arrived in Guadalcanal and began to take Japanese prisoners of war, the instructor tried to interrogate some but had little success. On one occasion, his regimental commanding officer observed while he questioned a prisoner. When the instructor could extract no useful information, he explained that the prisoner was afraid to speak because he knew they were U.S. marines. Incidences of this sort went on for several more months. Finally, when his regiment went to Okinawa, he complained of a back injury and was evacuated to a hospital ship. There, a Navy language officer (a Boulder graduate) overheard his story and at last exposed him as a charlatan. He had invented the whole affair, including the phrases and made-up characters that the marines had so diligently memorized.[96]

Other Allied governments also needed Japanese-language expertise. In Southeast Asia, British Commonwealth forces urgently needed Japanese linguists. Before the war the Royal Army and Navy had trained a small number of language officers through the British embassy in Tokyo, just as the Americans did. When the war broke out many of these officers fell into Japanese hands in Tokyo, Hong Kong, and Singapore. In London, before the war the School of Oriental and African Studies (SOAS) taught Japanese to small numbers of scholars; but with the collapse of the British Empire in the Far East, something more had to be done. The school began a new class in May 1942 with thirty schoolboys age seventeen and

---

[95] Before the war, Harold J. Noble published "Recent Administration in Korea," *Amerasia* (April 1941): 84–90. See also Ltr to Editor, Capt. Harold J. Noble, U.S. Marine Corps Reserve, *Life* (28 September 1942): 11; Roger Pineau, "WW II Japanese Language Schools for Marines," Unpubl Ms, 1990, Roger Pineau Papers, Japanese Language School Project, Archives, University of Colorado at Boulder Libraries; and materials Calvin W. Dunbar provided to the author.

[96] This story was recounted by William Manchester, who served in the regimental intelligence and reconnaissance platoon. William Manchester, "The Man Who Could Speak Japanese," *American Heritage* (December 1975): 36–39, 91–95; William Manchester, *Goodbye, Darkness: A Memoir of the Pacific War* (New York: Dell, 1980), pp. 163–64.

eighteen. Twenty-eight completed the course in October 1943.[97] Other classes followed, usually taught by Japanese citizens who had stayed in Britain and by Canadian Nisei. The courses were generally fifteen months long. At first, classes for translators and interrogators were taught separately, but by June 1944 they were combined when the school started a new general-purpose course for ninety-two servicemen. During the war about 277 students completed full-length courses; another 371 completed specialized or refresher courses.

At Bletchley Park, the Government Communications Headquarters, counterpart to the U.S. Army's Signal Intelligence Service, was concerned about the slow pace of the SOAS courses and established its own Japanese-language courses at Bedford in February 1942. These were directed by two Japanese speakers: a senior Royal Army cryptographer, Col. John Tiltman, and a retired Royal Navy officer, Capt. Oswald Tuck.[98]

Other British Commonwealth nations started their own Japanese-language programs. The Australian Army established a school in Melbourne as early as 1940 and the Royal Australian Air Forces in Sydney in 1944. British authorities in India conducted Japanese-language training in Karachi.[99] As Canada began planning to enter the war against Japan, the Canadian Army set up its own Japanese-language school in early 1945 for Canadians of Japanese ancestry.

The Pacific War led to a profusion of Japanese-language programs in the United States and elsewhere. The MISLS trained the largest number of military linguists, who often worked alongside or under graduates of the other programs. Throughout the war the school's Nisei graduates proved indispensable in meeting the urgent language requirements.

.   .   .

By the summer of 1944 the MISLS had outgrown Camp Savage. From November 1941 to August 1944, about 1,300 Nisei enlisted men and about 200 Caucasian officers graduated. More than 550 others were in training, and another 630 were expected for classes to start in August and September. John Aiso directed a faculty of twenty-seven civilian and sixty-five enlisted instructors. The reception center at nearby Fort Snelling had closed, and Colonel Rasmussen decided to move his school onto the post. Because War Department planners expected the war with Japan to last at least two more years, it made good sense to move the school onto a permanent post that offered room for further expansion.

---

[97] Sadao Oba, *The "Japanese" War*, trans. Anne Kaneko (Sandgate, U.K.: Japan Library, 1995).

[98] Alan Stripp, *Codebreaker in the Far East* (New York: Oxford University Press, 1995), pp. 3–12, 139–44. Tuck had served before the war as the British assistant naval attaché in Tokyo.

[99] Interv, author with Henry Kuwabara, 12 Sep 96; Henry Kuwabara, "Japanese-Burmese Beauty," in *John Aiso and the M.I.S.*, p. 171. The Karachi intelligence school apparently used several Japanese nationals as instructors.

Despite the MISLS's size, it remained unknown to most Americans. The call for Japanese American volunteers in early 1943 garnered much public interest. By 1944, when Nisei soldiers entered combat in Italy, most Americans knew that Japanese American soldiers were fighting with the U.S. Army. In fact, the War Department, Office of War Information, and War Relocation Authority collaborated to publicize the exploits of the 442d Regimental Combat Team.[100] In May 1943 Assistant Secretary McCloy questioned whether this publicity might extend to Nisei in the Military Intelligence Service, but Rasmussen argued against it.[101] "A limited amount concerning the activities could be divulged to the public," he suggested, "but not to any degree by which his present value to the Army would be lessened in the intelligence field."

The value of the language graduates lie[s] in not disclosing their present activity as a part of the Army Combat Intelligence. . . . If the enemy learns to what degree that training in Japanese Intelligence is being conducted there is no question that their present means of communicating, writing, issuance of orders, and other phases of Japanese combat strategy would be changed from the written Japanese . . . to some other form so as not to give any indication of their moves. It goes without saying that the value of the captured Japanese material lies in the information acquired by translation and in insight into their training and strategy.

Rasmussen proposed that "the disciplinary record, War Bond subscription, Red Cross participation, high morale, and recreation activities" at Camp Savage were suitable topics for press coverage but that "no publicity regarding the training program or the course of study pursued at the Military Intelligence Service Language School be considered as material for publicity." The War Department G–2, Maj. Gen. George V. Strong, agreed, and McCloy yielded. The Adjutant General issued a confidential action notice to all Army commands on 14 August 1943, directing that "all necessary steps be taken to prevent publicity regarding Intelligence Personnel of Japanese extraction, the Military Intelligence Service Language Schools [sic], the assignment of graduates thereof or the type of work carried on by them." All photographs showing the school and its graduates were henceforth classified confidential.[102]

Henceforth the school and its graduates received little public notice until war's end, although the blackout was far from total. *Time* mentioned in December 1943

---

[100] Murphy, *Ambassadors in Arms*, pp. 196–202; Patricia A. Curtin, "Press Coverage of the 442nd Regimental Combat Team (Separate-Nisei): A Case Study in Agenda Building," *American Journalism Review* 12, no. 3 (Summer 1995): 225–41.

[101] Memo, MISLS for General Kroner, sub: Publicity in Regard [to] Activities of American Soldiers of Japanese Descent in the Army of the United States, 25 May 43 (352), Ofc of the ASW, RG 107, NARA.

[102] Memo, McCloy for Gen Kroner, 8 Jun 43 (ASW 352), Class Ref Sub Files, 1940–1947, Ofc of the ASW, RG 107, NARA; Memo, The Adjutant General's Office (TAGO), sub: Publicity Regarding Intelligence Personnel of Japanese Extraction, 14 Aug 43, Ofc of the Dir of Intel G–2, RG 165, NARA. See related correspondence in CWRIC Papers, reel 6, frame 485.

that "hundreds [of Nisei] serve in Military Intelligence in the South Pacific." In the summer of 1944 California journalist Carey McWilliams published an exposé of the government's treatment of Japanese Americans. He mentioned in passing: "Some [Nisei] have served as intelligence officers in the Southwest Pacific with distinction and courage. . . . Several hundred Nisei are with the British and American forces in India as intelligence officers. . . . [Lt. Col.] Karl Gould has described the Nisei as playing an 'indispensable role in the war' as interpreters."[103] The *Pacific Citizen* on occasion mentioned individual soldiers serving in the Pacific, as did the Honolulu newspapers. On 12 August 1944, the *Pacific Citizen* revealed that six Nisei had won the Bronze Star during the battle for Saipan but gave no specifics.[104] These brief notices received little attention. Consequently, during the war and for many years after, Americans learned little about the Nisei who used their language skills to fight against Japan.

---

[103] "Race: Inquisition in Los Angeles," *Time* (20 December 1943); McWilliams, *Prejudice*, p. 287. Gould was the MISLS director of personnel procurement in 1942–1943. McWilliams also briefly mentioned Nisei fighting in the Pacific in a network radio broadcast. *Pacific Citizen*, 5 Aug 44, p. 5. *The Washington Post* published an editorial in September 1944 to urge the closing of the internment camps and complained: "There has been virtually complete silence from the War Department concerning the valor of the Nisei in the Far East. We believe their story should be told—not merely in Hawaii, whence many of them entered the Army, but here in the continental United States, where some Americans still have to learn that devotion to democracy is not an inherited characteristic." In April 1945 the War Relocation Authority distributed a compilation of news stories about the MIS Nisei. War Relocation Authority, *Nisei in the War against Japan* (Washington, D.C.: Department of the Interior, 1945).

[104] "Six Nisei Soldiers Win Citation on Saipan," *Pacific Citizen*, 12 Aug 44.

6

MIS Nisei in the Campaigns of 1943

The year 1943 marked the turning point in the war between the United States and Japan. The Allies halted and then reversed Japanese advances in the Aleutian Islands, the Central Pacific, the Solomon Islands, and Papua New Guinea. Scores of Nisei linguists served in these campaigns. Other Nisei were in training for combat in Europe with the 100th Infantry Battalion and 442d Regimental Combat Team (RCT), partly because of the contributions of the Military Intelligence Service (MIS) Nisei in earlier stages of the war. American commanders in the Pacific were requesting hundreds more Nisei linguists. The War Department G–2, Maj. Gen. George V. Strong, visited the Military Intelligence Service Language School (MISLS) in June 1943 to thank the students and staff for their contributions. By that time the school had already graduated 552 Nisei enlisted men and thirty-four Caucasian officers.

Nisei linguists added important elements to the overall intelligence picture. Allied commanders had access to a wide variety of intelligence, such as communications intelligence, aerial photography, submarine reconnaissance, and reports from coast watchers. However, when Allied soldiers and marines clashed with Japanese forces in ground combat, intelligence requirements shifted rapidly. Tactical information then became critical: commanders wanted to know the enemy's location, strength, and plans. Good battlefield intelligence could make the difference between victory and defeat and between high casualties and easy victory. During 1943 the Nisei played an important role, especially at the tactical level.

The Aleutians

In the North Pacific, Japanese soldiers had dug into the tundra of the Aleutian Islands. Since June 1942 soldiers and sailors from Japan and America had faced off in that dismal island chain. Through the difficult winter of 1942–1943, the U.S. Army Alaska Defense Command and U.S. Army Corps of Engineers prepared for renewed fighting while the Eleventh Air Force and U.S. Navy patrolled the sea and sky.

The Military Intelligence Division (MID) rushed five Nisei graduates of the first language class to Alaska in May 1942. In December 1942 another five arrived with a Caucasian language officer. With other theaters clamoring for the Nisei, MID could spare no more. By early 1943 the Army had sent altogether nearly 100,000 soldiers to the region, of whom barely ten could understand the Japanese language. Gaining intelligence about the Japanese forces was especially difficult in the Aleutians. Commanders relied mostly on radio intelligence and photoreconnaissance. During the first half of 1943, radio intercepts from the area were decrypted and translated in Hawaii or Washington, where Nisei were not employed. Photoreconnaissance was unreliable because of poor weather conditions. The Nisei had no prisoners of war to interrogate or captured documents to translate. Some Nisei did translate letters that a Japanese immigrant family in Seward, Alaska, had received from relatives in Japan before the war.[1]

For the American counterstroke in the Aleutians, the Army's main strike force was the 7th Infantry Division. The division's language team of ten Nisei and two Caucasian officers traveled by rail from Minnesota to Seattle, then onward by ship to Anchorage. Upon arrival the team learned that the 7th Division was still completing its training in California. So the team retraced its steps to Seattle and from there went south to Fort Ord, where it finally found the division. The 7th Infantry Division departed San Francisco in April 1943 with its assigned Nisei language team.[2] Over 10,000 U.S. soldiers sailed to Attu, where 3,000 Japanese soldiers waited. Like the other American soldiers, the Nisei prepared themselves for their introduction to battle. (*Map 5*) Unlike the others, the Nisei feared that their fellow soldiers would mistake them for the enemy. Most Nisei had bodyguards. T5g. Satsuki Fred Tanakatsubo took a direct approach, telling his Caucasian comrades, "Take a good look, and *remember me*, because I'm going in with you!"[3]

---

[1] Joseph D. Harrington, *Yankee Samurai: The Secret Role of Nisei in America's Pacific Victory* (Detroit: Pettigrew Enterprises, 1979), p. 87.

[2] Nobuo Furuiye, Pete Nakao, and Don C. Oka, in *The Saga of the MIS*, videotaped presentation, Los Angeles, 11 Mar 89; Don C. Oka, Biography, Military Intelligence Service Club of Northern California (this and similar biographies hereafter cited as MISNorCal Bios); Nobuo Furuiye, "Rocky Mountain MIS Veterans Club Autobiographies," pp. 12–15, Unpubl Ms, ed. Kent T. Yoritomo, [1989], author's files (this and similar biographies hereafter cited as Rocky Mountain Bios). The 7th Infantry Division removed hundreds of Nisei from its ranks in March 1942 and sent them to inland posts.

[3] Harrington, *Yankee Samurai*, pp. 146–47 (emphasis in original). Weckerling reported that some Nisei were assigned to accompany the Attu landing force but noted cryptically that they

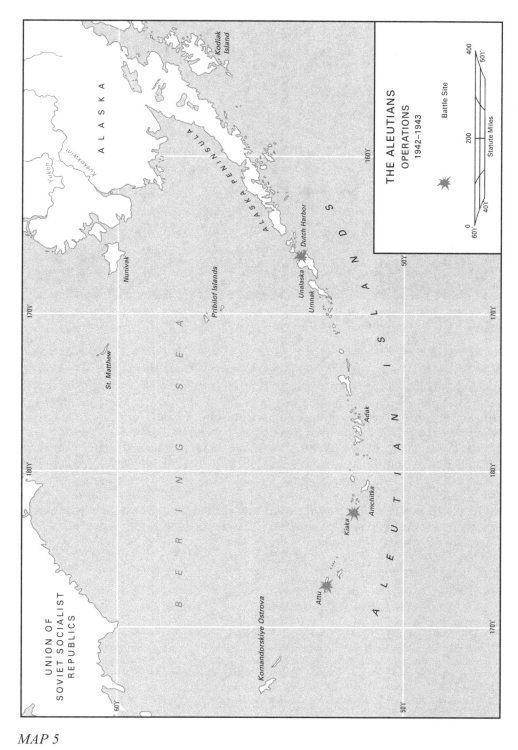

THE ALEUTIANS
OPERATIONS
1942–1943

✳ Battle Site

Statute Miles
0   200   400

MAP 5

Interrogation, *Aleutians, by Edward R. Laning, 1943*

Shortly before the landing on fog-bound Attu, several Navy language officers, recent graduates of the Navy school in Boulder, Colorado, were assigned as team leaders for the Nisei. The Nisei were unhappy to serve under them, judging the officers' language proficiency inferior to that of most Nisei, especially the Kibei. Moreover, the officers had commissions; the Nisei did not and were quick to see this as evidence of racial prejudice. In March 1943 two Navy language officers, Donald Keene and Otis Cary, were assigned to the 7th Infantry Division. The Nisei resented them, Keene recalled, because they "had been informed that the Navy interpreters and translators were all incompetent." Keene and Cary "felt obliged to prove that this was not true" and earned the trust of their Nisei team members. Not all Navy language officers were as successful. When one Navy language officer on Attu ordered a Nisei enlisted man to dig a foxhole for him, the Nisei refused. The officer threatened a court-martial, but the Nisei merely told him, "Dig your own foxhole!"[4]

"were not allowed to accompany the convoy because it was feared that reception [of the Nisei?] aboard ship might disclose location of the force." Col. John Weckerling, "Report of Attu Operation between 2 May and 15 May, 1943," 11 Jun 43, para. 12, Records of Fourth U.S. Army and Western Defense Command, Record Group (RG) 338, National Archives and Records Administration (NARA).

[4] Donald Keene, *On Familiar Terms: A Journey across Cultures* (New York: Kodansha, 1994), pp. 27; Harrington, *Yankee Samurai*, p. 146.

The 11 May landing was followed by nineteen days' fighting in the damp and bitter cold against stubborn Japanese resistance. During the same period 275,000 German and Italian soldiers surrendered in North Africa; in contrast, only twenty-eight Japanese soldiers surrendered on Attu. About sixteen MIS linguists served on the island during the fighting, interrogating prisoners and translating captured documents. Their work was stressful and exhausting. Some entered caves to persuade enemy soldiers to surrender. Others prepared psychological warfare leaflets, which the team leader dropped from a small airplane. Some remained aboard ship to monitor Japanese radio transmissions.[5]

Nisei soldier (left) *questioning Japanese prisoners, Attu, May 1943*

The Nisei and their language officers showed great bravery. Lt. Gordon S. Jorgensen, S.Sgt. Yasuo Sam Umetani, and S.Sgt. George T. Hayashida crawled into caves looking for Japanese survivors. "All I had was a flashlight and a .45," Hayashida recalled, "so when about ten [Japanese] agreed to surrender after prolonged discussions, I breathed a lot easier." The experience of combat could be nightmarish. One evening S.Sgt. Shigeo Ito and a language officer sought shelter under some large rocks only to find the bodies of three Japanese soldiers, which they pushed aside before lying down to sleep. Through the night Ito worried that the dead Japanese would come alive and kill them. "It was a long night with fear," he recalled, "and never thought I [would] come out alive." The next day he conducted his first interrogation on a Japanese soldier whose buttocks had been shot away; the wound was crawling with maggots. "I though about the Camp Savage training and I put all my effort and technology [*sic*], but didn't work," Ito recalled. "I couldn't get any information from him. I failed badly." Umetani translated the diary of a Japanese Army

---

[5] "Japanese-American [Sgt. Nakao] Fought Nips on Attu," *Denver Post*, 13 Oct 43; "Commanding General Reveals Japanese Americans Took Part in Capture of Kwajalein Atoll," *Pacific Citizen*, 4 Mar 44; "Notes on the Japanese—From Their Documents," in Military Intelligence Division, *Intelligence Bulletin* 2, no. 2 (October 1943): 52–60; Sylvia K. Kobayashi, "I Remember What I Want To Forget," in *Alaska at War, 1941–1945: The Forgotten War Remembered*, ed. Fern Chandonnet (Anchorage: Alaska at War Committee, 1995), pp. 285–88; Otis Hays, Jr., *Alaska's Hidden Wars: Secret Campaigns on the North Pacific Rim* (Fairbanks: University of Alaska Press, 2004).

doctor who described killing his patients who were too weak to kill themselves. The Nisei "wept bitterly" as he translated the tragic document.[6]

On the night of 29 May the remaining Japanese soldiers, many armed only with bayonets or hand grenades, threw themselves on American lines in a suicidal rush. They poured through the American positions and penetrated into the rear areas, where they rushed through a field hospital, killing many of the wounded Americans in their beds. T4g. Kunihiro Pete Nakao avoided certain death by rolling under his bed just in time. When the surviving Japanese attackers were finally surrounded, they committed collective suicide with hand grenades. That marked the end of the battle. Americans were left stunned at the ferocity of the Japanese attack and the Japanese willingness to fight to the death.[7] In less than three weeks of fighting, over 500 American soldiers had died; 3,000 more were out of action from wounds, trench foot, or illness.

The Army and Navy began preparations at once for the next assault on the island of Kiska. This time the Allies would employ twice as many troops, including 5,500 Canadian soldiers. The U.S. and Royal Canadian Armies had formed the 1st Special Service Force the previous summer: Kiska would be its first test. The War Department sent two more teams of twenty Nisei with two officers, giving local commanders about forty Nisei to support the assault. One Colorado Nisei, Nobuo Furuiye, the first MIS Nisei to be attached to the Canadian Army, served with the Canadian Grenadiers.[8]

As the assault date approached, the Nisei prepared for action; some were assigned to monitor Japanese radio transmissions at Kiska.[9] The first assault waves landed on 15 August to find the island empty.[10] Allied intelligence had failed to detect the Japanese withdrawal from the island two weeks earlier. However, the Nisei did not come away empty-handed. The Japanese had abandoned large stocks of equipment and supplies on the island; the Nisei were happy to seize Japanese rations, including large sacks of rice, cans of bamboo shoots, and kegs of soy sauce, all in short supply through U.S. Army commissary channels.[11]

---

[6] Harrington, *Yankee Samurai*, pp. 145–47; Joseph D. Harrington, "Yankee Samurai," *Ex-CBI Roundup* (February 1979): 13; Shigeo Ito, MISNorCal Bio; Brian Garfield, *The Thousand Mile War: World War II in Alaska and the Aleutians* (Garden City, N.Y.: Doubleday, 1969), p. 252.

[7] Harrington, *Yankee Samurai*, p. 147; *The Pacific War and Peace: Americans of Japanese Ancestry in Military Intelligence Service, 1941 to 1952* (San Francisco: Military Intelligence Service Association of Northern California/National Japanese American Historical Society, 1991), p. 28; Keene, *On Familiar Terms*, pp. 28–29.

[8] Furuiye, Rocky Mountain Bio, pp. 12–15; Yoshio Morita, "The Kiska Campaign," in *Secret Valor: M.I.S. Personnel, World War II Pacific Theater, Pre–Pearl Harbor to Sept. 8, 1951*, ed. Ted T. Tsukiyama et al. (Honolulu: Military Intelligence Service Veterans Club of Hawaii, 1993), p. 63.

[9] Nobuo Furuiye monitored Japanese radio transmissions near Kiska shortly before the invasion. Furuiye, Rocky Mountain Bio, p. 12. However, Roy Y. Ashizawa claims that the Army did not begin intercepting Japanese communications in the Aleutians until after the Attu and Kiska landings. Roy Y. Ashizawa, MISNorCal Bio, pp. 7–8.

[10] Galen R. Perras, *Stepping Stones to Nowhere: The Aleutian Islands, Alaska, and American Military Strategy, 1867–1945* (Toronto: UBC Press, 2003), pp. 151–57.

[11] Harrington, *Yankee Samurai*, pp. 157–58.

Umetani (left) *and Cpl. George Sadaji Tsukichi, Kiska, August 1943*

The MIS Nisei in the Aleutian Islands Campaign made a good impression on their fellow soldiers. In the serious business of close combat, they had proved their worth. "In the beginning the Caucasian boys were somewhat reserved," one newspaper reported, "but a couple of good 'bull' sessions broke the ice completely, and they have become warm buddies ever since." One veteran of the Aleutians wrote a California newspaper to protest the continuing prejudice against Japanese Americans at home:

We have gone into battle with loyal Americans of Japanese ancestry and they have acquitted themselves with honor and glory. Imagine the risk such a man takes when he volunteers and joins the army. Not only must he be careful of enemy fire, but he must take caution that he is not mistaken by his own troops as an enemy. We soldiers glory in the fact that these Japanese boys are with us giving their full measure of devotion, while their brothers and sisters, in some cases, are in relocation camps.[12]

---

[12] "Nisei Veterans from Aleutians Visit Center," *Pacific Citizen*, 20 Nov 43, p. 3; Capt. Ralph T. Lui, Ltr to the Editor, *Sacramento Bee*, 14 Jan 44, reprinted in War Relocation Authority, *What We're Fighting For* (Washington, D.C.: U.S. Department of the Interior, 1944), pp. 10–11.

After the Kiska landings, the Nisei interrogated the remaining prisoners from Attu and translated captured documents. As the months dragged on, they made an uneasy truce with the Navy language officers. Conversely, the weather remained a constant hazard. In the winter of 1943–1944 on Kiska, an avalanche smashed into the Quonset hut in which T4g. Hiromu Bill Wada was living. Two of the ten soldiers sleeping inside were killed, but Wada crawled out unharmed.[13]

The Joint Chiefs of Staff shelved plans for further offensive action in the North Pacific, and the War Department dissolved the Alaska Theater. Most Nisei in Alaska were reassigned between October 1943 and January 1944, with several becoming instructors at Camp Savage. In 1944 the school deployed eleven Alaska veterans to the South Pacific and five to Hawaii, environments very different from Alaska. By March 1944 only about ten Nisei remained in Alaska and by late 1944 only two, both of whom remained until the end of the war.[14] Despite the absence of a single consolidated intelligence center and despite the friction with the Navy's Boulder graduates, the Nisei showed their worth in developing intelligence from prisoners, captured documents, and tactical radio intercepts. The lessons learned in the Aleutians would be repeated many times over in other parts of the Pacific.

South Pacific Area

Other MIS Nisei were serving under Admiral William F. Halsey in the South Pacific. When the battle for Guadalcanal ended, U.S. Army Forces in the South Pacific Area (USAFISPA) had over thirty MIS Nisei, most of them concentrated in Noumea on New Caledonia. They had gained valuable combat experience in January and February 1943, interrogating Japanese prisoners and translating piles of captured documents. The new year would give many more the chance to experience combat, first on New Georgia, then on Vella Lavella and Bougainville.(Map 6) Col. Frederick P. Munson, the army attaché in Tokyo who was repatriated in 1942, was the officer in charge of the Combat Intelligence Center in Noumea.[15] Noumea was also headquarters for the Thirteenth Air Force, which established an air combat intelligence center that combined technical intelligence, interrogation, and interpretation.[16] In early 1943 the Army Air Forces asked for Japanese linguists. In January 1943 MISLS sent 10 Nisei to the Thirteenth Air Force, 10 to the Fifth Air Force in the Southwest Pacific, and 10 four months later to the Tenth AirForce in India. S.Sgt. Shunji Hamano, twenty-nine, led the Thirteenth

---

[13] Bill Wada, MISNorCal Bio, p. 4; *MISLS Album* (Minneapolis: Military Intelligence Service Language School, 1946), pp. 106–07; Richard S. Oguro, ed., *Sempai Gumi* (Honolulu: MIS Veterans of Hawaii, ca. 1981), pp. xx–xxvii; *Pacific War and Peace*, pp. 27–29.

[14] Bill Wada, "My Two Year Experiences," Unpubl Ms, n.d., author's files.

[15] Interv, D. Clayton James with Frederick P. Munson, 3 Jul 71, RG 49, MacArthur Memorial, Library and Archives, Norfolk, Va.

[16] John F. Kreis ed., *Piercing the Fog: Intelligence and Army Air Forces Operations in World War II* (Washington, D.C.: Air Force History and Museums Program, 1996), p. 256.

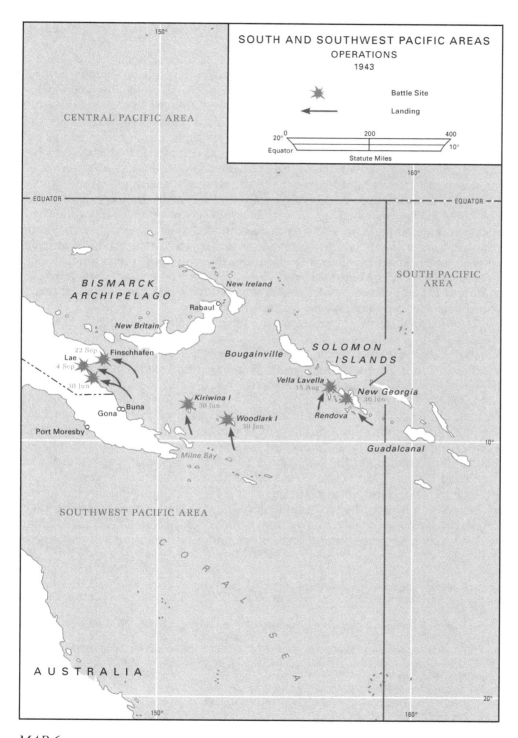

SOUTH AND SOUTHWEST PACIFIC AREAS
OPERATIONS
1943

Battle Site

Landing

0   200   400

Statute Miles

CENTRAL PACIFIC AREA

EQUATOR

EQUATOR

SOUTH PACIFIC
AREA

BISMARCK
ARCHIPELAGO

New Ireland

Rabaul

New Britain

SOLOMON
ISLANDS

Bougainville

22 Sep   Finschhafen
Lae
4 Sep

Vella Lavella
15 Aug

New Georgia
30 Jun

30 Jun

Kiriwina I
30 Jun

Rendova

Buna

Gona

Woodlark I
30 Jun

Port Moresby

Milne Bay

Guadalcanal

SOUTHWEST PACIFIC AREA

C O R A L

S E A

AUSTRALIA

MAP 6

Air Force team. He was born in Los Angeles but had spent eight years attending school in Japan.[17]

The Nisei still did not have the acceptance of some of their fellow Americans, who regarded them with suspicion. One Nisei remembered bitterly how he required a marine escort for each trip to the latrine. But Susumu Toyoda remembered how the Nisei from the Combat Intelligence Center often swam at the same beach as Admiral Halsey. "The admiral would always stop and say, how's the weather, boys," Toyoda recalled. "We'd say wonderful, Admiral, come and join us. He was such a friendly person." Halsey was often accompanied to the beach by his aide, Harold Stassen, now a Navy Reserve lieutenant and the former governor of Minnesota who in 1942 had offered the language school a new home.[18]

The Nisei could not avoid suspicions even in a combat theater. In early 1943 Colonel Munson questioned Sgt. Tetsuo Hayashida about a remark Hayashida had made while attending MISLS: "Did you make the statement while you were taking a shower back at Camp Savage in Minnesota that if you had the choice of bearing arms or not bearing arms against the Japanese, that you would prefer not to?" The astonished Nisei told Munson that although he respected and admired Japanese culture, if called upon he would certainly be willing to bear arms against them. Munson decided not to pursue the matter further.[19]

This constant scrutiny, combined with the geographical distance from home, made the Nisei feel very isolated. Furthermore, most of their families were in relocation camps, which made communication with them slow and difficult. When Sgt. Joe J. Yoshiwara returned to Noumea from Guadalcanal in February 1943, a colonel informed him that his mother had died three months earlier in the Amache relocation camp. His commander offered to let him return, but Yoshiwara declined.[20] The strain overwhelmed one Nisei when discouraging letters arrived from his family in the relocation camp at Tule Lake, California. According to one report, the unidentified Nisei "requested relief from duty, based on his own belief that he could not support the war effort. . . . He was relieved and was returned to the United States."[21] Most endured as best they could.

In June 1943 Halsey struck the Japanese at New Georgia with the 43d Infantry Division, supported by ten Nisei under Capt. Eugene A. Wright. In the thick jungle, the Japanese fought savagely from well-hidden positions. During the night of 17–18, July a Japanese counterattack overran the division command post where

---

[17] Hamano recalled that his team was first assigned to Army Air Forces headquarters in Hawaii, but upon arrival they were redirected to the South Pacific. Shunji Hamano, Rocky Mountain Bio, pp. 16–19.

[18] Ltr, Roy T. Uyehata, 21 October 1990, author's files; Interv, author with Susumu Toyoda, 12 Sep 96.

[19] Tetsuo Hayashida, MISNorCal Bio; MISLS, "Training History of the Military Intelligence Service Language School," ann. 4, Intelligence Section, p. 2, Unpubl Ms, 1946, U.S. Army Center of Military History (CMH).

[20] Ltr, Joe J. Yoshiwara to Roy Uyehata, 18 February 1993.

[21] "History and Description of the Military Intelligence Service Language School," [May 1944], p. 32, Gen Rcds, 1943–1945, Military Intelligence [Service] Language School, RG 319, NARA.

the language team was located. Sgt. Shigeo Yasutake from Gardena, California, survived only by crouching low in his foxhole, where the land crabs kept him company. At that moment, he recalled, he was "thankful for those mean Regular sergeants of the 7th Division," where he had received his basic training before the war, "who made me dig a foxhole *deep!*"[22]

After two weeks the division was nearly combat ineffective, so Halsey sent in elements of the 37th and 25th Infantry Divisions. With the new units came another Nisei team led by two Caucasian lieutenants and S.Sgt. Kazuo Komoto, who remembered it as the "toughest fighting in the world." After a week with no sleep he "climbed out of his foxhole behind the front lines to rest." As he was standing in the open with several other Americans, a Japanese sniper opened fire with a machine gun, shattering his knee. He was evacuated to a hospital ship, where his commanding general presented him with the Purple Heart, the first awarded to an MIS Nisei. While recovering from his wound he visited his parents interned in the Gila River camp in Arizona.[23] In the closing days of the battle Capt. John A. Burden accompanied a patrol to intercept the withdrawing enemy. The Americans could not halt the Japanese evacuation; but when they swept into the abandoned Japanese headquarters, Burden found a large number of valuable documents the Japanese had abandoned in their haste.[24]

The bitter fighting gave rise to many myths about the fighting capacity of the Japanese soldiers, often enlarging upon the stories from Guadalcanal. The American soldiers found it easy to exaggerate their enemy. The language teams tried to dispel beliefs that, for instance, many Japanese soldiers could speak English and they had mysterious powers to infiltrate and attack at night. After the battle, Captain Wright and another language officer, Lt. Michael Mitchell, a prewar newspaperman in Osaka, Japan, wrote an article entitled "The Jap Is Not Mysterious!" that was published in the *Infantry Journal*.[25]

The Allies found themselves guarding increasing numbers of Japanese prisoners of war (POWs). The United States transferred more than 850 POWs from the Solomon Islands to New Zealand in 1942–1943. The prisoners went to a camp at Featherston, about forty miles northeast of Wellington. On 25 February 1943, about

---

[22] Harrington, *Yankee Samurai*, pp. 159–60.

[23] Ibid., pp. 150, 160, 300; "Japanese Tells of Pacific War at Rivers [Gila River] Camp," *Baltimore Sun*, 20 Nov 43, reprinted in War Relocation Authority, *Nisei in the War against Japan* (Washington, D.C.: Department of the Interior, April 1945), p. 12; photo, *Pacific Citizen*, 8 Jan 44; John Weckerling, "Japanese Americans Play Vital Role in United States Intelligence Service in World War II" (1946), first printed in *Hokubei Mainichi*, 27 Oct–5 Nov 71, reprinted as a pamphlet. Komoto recovered from his wounds and served with the 11th Airborne Division in the Philippines. Harrington places him later in Burma with the Mars Task Force. Harrington, *Yankee Samurai*, p. 231.

[24] John Burden autobiography, pp. 16–17, Unpubl Ms, 1992, copy in author's files.

[25] Capt. Eugene A. Wright and Lt. Michael Mitchell, "The Jap Is Not Mysterious!" *Infantry Journal* (December 1943): 12–15; Harrington, *Yankee Samurai*, p. 87. The *New York Times*, 29 Aug 43, mentioned Wright's work as a language officer; the Army Service Forces published his photograph in the weekly news map for 9 August 1943.

250 Japanese prisoners at Featherston rioted and attacked their guards. The New Zealanders responded with fire, killing forty-eight Japanese POWs and wounding another seventy-four. One guard died, and another six were injured.[26]

The American soldiers were eager for souvenirs and had to be persuaded of the value of submitting captured documents and equipment to the intelligence section. After the fighting had ended, some Nisei exploited this desire for souvenirs and fabricated Japanese flags to sell to the gullible soldiers.[27]

The next move in the Solomons was Vella Lavella, where the 25th Infantry Division landed in August. Burden led ten Nisei including his right-hand man from Guadalcanal, Tateshi Miyasaki. By now they knew the routine: translating captured documents, interrogating the few prisoners captured alive, and trying to piece together the enemy's intentions. After several weeks the 3d New Zealand Division took over and continued to mop up the remaining Japanese defenders. Burden took several Nisei to the unit for language support. One day while in camp with the New Zealanders, Miyasaki was bending over a cooking fire stripped to the waist. Hearing a noise, he straightened up to see two or three New Zealand soldiers pointing their rifles at him. "I'm an American, don't shoot!" he yelled. At just that moment Burden returned. "He's okay," he said, "He's with me."[28]

By the end of 1943 about eighty Nisei were serving in the South Pacific. Since the first had arrived in May 1942 they had made many important contributions in combat operations and would prove their value again on Bougainville. By late 1943 many Nisei and their leaders had been overseas in the South Pacific for a year or more. Captain Burden returned to the language school in Minnesota for a number of weeks. Several Nisei were given the chance to earn commissions. In August 1943 Sgt. Richard Kaoru Hayashi interrogated a Japanese sailor who disclosed that he had been on the submarine *I–17* that had shelled oil storage tanks near Santa Barbara, California, in February 1942. The Office of Naval Intelligence expressed great interest in this special prisoner, so Hayashi escorted him to the United States. Instead of returning to the South Pacific, Hayashi was sent to Fort Benning, Georgia, for officer candidate school. In March 1944 he was commissioned and sent to the 442d RCT in Italy, thus becoming the first Nisei to fight in both the Pacific and Europe. T3g. Takeo Kubo also went to Fort Benning for officer candidate school in the summer of 1943 but was unable to complete the course due to recurring malaria attacks. He was reassigned to the 442d RCT at

---

[26] Colin Funch, *Linguists in Uniform: The Japanese Experience* (Australia: Monash University, 2003), pp. 181–83; Ulrich Straus, *The Anguish of Surrender: Japanese POWs of World War II* (Seattle: University of Washington Press, 2003).

[27] Harrington, *Yankee Samurai*, p. 161. Sample combat intelligence documents from the South Pacific can be found in the Judge Eugene A. Wright Papers, National Japanese American Historical Society (NJAHS), San Francisco, Calif., and the John A. Burden Papers, Hoover Institution Archives, Stanford University, Calif.

[28] Tateshi Miyasaki, in David W. Swift, Jr., ed. "First Class," Unpubl Ms, 2000, copy in author's files; Harrington, *Yankee Samurai*, pp. 189–90; Burden autobiography, p. 16–A.

Burden and two Nisei with the 25th Infantry Division question a Japanese prisoner, Vella Lavella, September 1943.

Camp Shelby, Mississippi, and later the language school at Fort Snelling.[29] Sergeant Yasutake, who had survived the attack on his division command post, was offered a battlefield commission or stateside officer candidate school. He chose officer candidate school, thinking "it would get me out of the muck and the dirt for at least a year, anyhow."[30]

Navajo Code Talkers

At the same time the Nisei served in the South Pacific, the U.S. Marine Corps employed another ethnic minority, Navajo Indians, whose story has many parallels. Two months after the Pearl Harbor attack, Philip Johnston approached Marine

---

[29] Richard K. Hayashi, MISNorCal Bio; Richard Hayashi Collection, NJAHS; Masayo Umezawa Duus, *Unlikely Liberators: The Men of the 100th and 442nd* (Honolulu: University of Hawaii Press, 1987), pp. 191; Takeo Kubo, in Swift, "First Class."

[30] Harrington, *Yankee Samurai*, p. 159; "Nisei Soldier Commended for Pacific Action," *Pacific Citizen*, 28 Oct 44, p. 1.

officials in San Diego with a suggestion. Johnston was a Caucasian who, having
been raised on a Navajo reservation, spoke the difficult language and was devoted
to their language and culture. He proposed that the Marine Corps recruit and train
young Navajo men to serve as radio operators. They could communicate with
each other in their native tongue, which few non-Navajos had mastered. During
the war, 45,000 American Indians served in all branches of the military. For many
the war presented an opportunity to show their patriotism and prove their warrior
spirit; four received the Medal of Honor.[31]

The Marine Corps recruited twenty-nine Navajo volunteers from the reservation in April 1942. The men took basic training and then learned a modified
version of their language that used over 400 common Navajo words to represent
military terms and letters of the alphabet. That autumn twenty-seven graduates
joined the 1st Marine Division on Guadalcanal; two others remained behind as
instructors for subsequent classes.

The Code Talkers sent and received messages over unencrypted voice radio
nets, using this natural "code" to prevent the Japanese from eavesdropping. The
Code Talkers were trained both as marines and in this special language. Like the
Nisei, they had to speak passable English as well as their own language; moreover,
the Marine Corps insisted on at least a tenth-grade education. Their service was
kept secret from their families. To most Caucasian Americans, the Navajo, like the
Nisei, "looked like the enemy" and risked being mistaken for Japanese and killed
by their fellow Americans. Like the Nisei, they often had Caucasian bodyguards
and were warned not to let themselves be captured.

At the beginning of the war one Navajo soldier (not a Code Talker) was captured on Bataan, where he was a member of the 200th Coast Artillery from the
New Mexico National Guard. After the war he described how he had convinced
his Japanese captors only with great difficulty that he was not an American Nisei.
They eventually brought him to Japan and made him listen to intercepted Code
Talker radio transmissions. He told his disappointed captors that he understood a
few of the words but not their meanings.[32]

On Guadalcanal, the Code Talkers proved highly successful, so the Marine
Corps expanded the program. By August 1943, 191 Navajo were serving as Code
Talkers. In contrast, the Army apparently did not use American Indians in this
way in the Pacific, nor did it borrow any from the Marine Corps. The Army did

[31] Margaret T. Bixler, *Winds of Freedom: The Story of the Navajo Code Talkers of World War II*
(Darien, Conn.: Two Bytes Publishing, 1992); Goode Davis, Jr., "Proud Tradition of the Marines'
Navajo Code Talkers," *Marine Corps League* (Spring 1990): 16–26; Lynn Escue, "Coded Contri-
butions: Navajo Talkers and the Pacific War," *History Today* (July 1991); Adam Jevec, "Semper
Fidelis, Code Talkers," *Prologue* 33, no. 4 (Winter 2001); Bruce Watson, "Navajo Code Talkers: A
Few Good Men," *Smithsonian* (August 1993): 34–43. The public first became aware of the Code
Talkers in the 1970s, about the same time as the MIS Nisei became more widely recognized.
[32] Davis, "Proud Tradition," p. 25; Escue, "Coded Contributions," p. 18; Watson, "Navajo Code
Talkers," p. 39.

later use smaller numbers of Choctaw and Comanche soldiers in a similar way in the European Theater.

Marine units began to include the Navajo radiomen in every operation, and the Navajo often worked at the battalion and regiment levels. Their usefulness came at a price. Two Code Talkers died on New Britain and three on Bougainville. Eventually more than 400 Navajo served as Code Talkers. Ten were killed in action. Like the Nisei, many of the Navajo families were confined to government-controlled reservations. The Code Talkers nevertheless used their language skills, which had set them apart from the white mainstream in civilian life, to help defeat the Japanese in battle.

Southwest Pacific Area

In the Southwest Pacific Area, the Allied Translator and Interpreter Section (ATIS) grew during 1943 from 5 officers and 22 Nisei enlisted men to 12 officers and 149 Nisei. Of all MISLS graduates sent overseas during 1943, the Southwest Pacific received the lion's share, about 40 percent.[33] The handful of Nisei who fought at Buna-Gona passed on their combat-tested techniques for translation and interrogation to each fresh group of Nisei. Australian "Diggers" and American GIs began to push Imperial Japanese forces back up the 1,500-mile New Guinea coast, fighting tough campaigns in the mountains, swamps, and jungles. Fifth Air Force fought to dominate the air, while intelligence officers worked night and day to achieve dominance over their dangerous foe. Teams of Nisei linguists accompanied each American and Australian division into battle, while others stayed in the rear to process the expanding torrent of captured documents and prisoners of war.

In Australia, Col. Sidney F. Mashbir had built ATIS at the Indooroopilly Racetrack on the outskirts of Brisbane, a provincial town on Australia's northeast coast. Mashbir was an ardent believer in the Nisei. He lamented the "war hysteria" that was affecting all Japanese Americans and told them he regarded their plight to be "as difficult as that of the Jews in Germany." He reminded them that "almost without exception, you are volunteers, [and] that you are doing a brave, courageous, and patriotic thing in volunteering for this service."[34] The Nisei repaid his trust with devoted service.

The senior Nisei under Mashbir, M.Sgt. Gary Tsuneo Kadani, had arrived in June 1942 with the original group. In February 1943 M.Sgt. George Kanegai brought nine more Nisei from Camp Savage to serve as support staff for the base camp. These Nisei were not MISLS graduates but had been sent overseas to serve as clerks, cooks, and supply personnel. Kadani had already developed a good

---

[33] General Headquarters, Far East Command, *Operations of the Allied Translator and Interpreter Section, GHQ, SWPA*, Intelligence Series, vol. 5 (Tokyo: Far East Command, 1948), pp. 3–4, 59 (hereafter cited as ATIS History), pp. 7–8; MISLS, Disposition of Graduates, Training Grp, Ofc of the Dir of Intel G–2, RG 165, NARA.

[34] Sidney F. Mashbir, *I Was an American Spy* (New York: Vantage, 1953), p. 243.

working relationship with Mashbir since September 1942, so he continued as the operations sergeant. Kanegai became first sergeant in charge of support functions such as mess and supply.[35]

To house the anticipated new personnel, in January 1943 ATIS established Camp Chelmer across the Brisbane River. The first ten pyramid tents were erected to hold 120 enlisted men.[36] On 4 March a new group of twenty-six Nisei linguists arrived from the school. The team leader, T.Sgt. Torao George Ichikawa, had been stationed at Fort Ord, California, when the war broke out. Also accompanying the group were two Caucasian lieutenants, Faubion Bowers and Paul Aurell, both having learned Japanese in Japan.[37] The new group was quickly indoctrinated into the ATIS way of doing business, a pattern repeated many times over in the months to come as MISLS sent evermore graduates to ATIS.

Nisei linguists learned and taught valuable lessons through their experiences in the Southwest Pacific Area. They learned firsthand that kindness and respect shown to Japanese prisoners yielded the best results during interrogations. Nisei learned to persuade American soldiers of the value of taking prisoners alive and turning over captured documents to intelligence personnel. They also learned that American and Australian commanders did not automatically accept them. "In the beginning, the Australians, like our own Navy, were loath to accept them at all," Mashbir recalled, "so I simply had to get tough about it and told the Aussies it was Nisei or nothing. There just weren't enough Caucasians capable of doing Intelligence work with the Australian division to go around."[38] Once the Nisei demonstrated what they could do—when an interrogation disclosed an impending attack or a translated map revealed enemy artillery positions—commanders quickly realized the Nisei were their most valuable source of reliable intelligence on the front lines.

ATIS became a more American organization as it grew, though a few Australian and other Commonwealth personnel remained, such as Maj. John V. Shelton of the Australian Imperial Forces. The Australian government also detailed many women to accomplish nonlinguist duties in ATIS. They served with the Women's Australian Air Force, Australian Women's Army Service, and the Women's Royal Australian Naval Service. However, the core group of translators and interpreters remained the American Nisei enlisted men.

The Nisei came to enjoy life in Australia, certainly as compared to conditions closer to the front lines, and settled down to become part of the local community. They worked hard during the day, especially during active campaigns when boxes and crates of captured documents would pour in. Off-duty Nisei enjoyed

---

[35] Interv, author with Yoshio George Kanegai, 13 Sep 96.

[36] ATIS History; Mashbir, *I Was an American Spy*, pp. 177–88; David W. Swift, Sr., *Ninety Li a Day*, ed. David W. Swift, Jr., Social Life Monographs, vol. 69 (Taipei: Chinese Association for Folklore, 1975), pp. 276–91.

[37] Stanley L. Falk and Warren M. Tsuneishi, eds., *MIS in the War against Japan* (Washington, D.C.: Japanese American Veterans Association, 1995), pp. 11–13, 94–95.

[38] Mashbir, *I Was an American Spy*, p. 247.

wartime Brisbane, which quickly became a soldiers' town. Local Australians treated the American Nisei with little prejudice: They saw the Nisei as "Yanks," not as Japanese. The Nisei spent their paychecks in local pubs and on weekend trips into town. A favorite spot was the Chinese restaurant incongruously named the Roma Cafe.[39]

At Camp Chelmer, the card games became legendary. One night in the spring of 1943, T.Sgt. George H. Goda lost a poker hand. One of his teammates, T.Sgt. Tarno H. Fudenna, commented that Goda had made a stupid move. Goda lost his temper, and Fudenna soon regretted his rash remark. The next morning ATIS received an urgent request for a single linguist to work at a remote airstrip in New Guinea. Fudenna found himself on the next plane out and would not see Brisbane again for six months.[40]

As more documents from the battlefront in New Guinea flowed into ATIS, it became apparent that Mashbir did not have enough translators to prepare a complete translation of every document. In July 1943 he established a scanning subsection with three officers and six enlisted men, some of his best translators, to scan the piles of documents and extract the most important information. Especially valuable were those who could read sōsho, the abbreviated grass writing that few but Kibei could decipher.[41]

During 1943 Mashbir became concerned that later Nisei graduates of the language school were not as proficient. "I was distressed to find that only a few were actually expert, and that as many as twenty-five percent out of every shipment were utterly unusable." He complained of "a steady diminution in the quality of the source of material, inasmuch as an ever decreasing percentage of effective linguists is reaching this theater." When sixty Nisei arrived in June 1943 for Sixth Army, Mashbir established a training section under Maj. David Swift, who directed a course "in forward interrogation and in the methods of using captured documents to aid prisoner examination."[42]

Some Nisei, especially Kibei like T4g. Harry K. Fukuhara, arrived with excellent language skills. Fukuhara had been born in Seattle in 1920. When his father died in 1933, his mother took her children back to her home in Hiroshima, where he attended a commercial high school. Fukuhara returned alone to the United States in 1938 to attend college. His mother remained in Hiroshima, as did three of his brothers who all later served in the Imperial Japanese Army.[43]

---

[39] Harrington, *Yankee Samurai*, pp. 94–95, 199–200; Edward J. Drea, "'Great Patience Is Needed': America Encounters Australia, 1942," *War & Society* (May 1993): 21–51.

[40] Tarno H. Fudenna, MISNorCal Bio. For the ATIS card games, see Interv, author with Kanegai, 13 Sep 96; Gene Masaji Uratsu, MISNorCal Bio.

[41] ATIS History, p. 12; Mashbir, *I Was an American Spy*, pp. 259–60.

[42] Mashbir, *I Was an American Spy*, pp. 224–25; Memo, ATIS, sub: Analysis of Linguistic Requirements, 27 Jun 44, author's files; ATIS History, pp. 21–22.

[43] Intervs, Eric Saul and Loni Ding with Harry K. Fukuhara, 7 Jan 86, NJAHS, and John P. Finnegan with Harry K. Fukuhara, 5 Jun 90, U.S. Army Intelligence and Security Command, Fort Belvoir, Va.; Falk and Tsuneishi, *MIS in the War against Japan*, pp. 97–98.

During 1943 arriving Nisei sometimes were assigned directly to individual divisions, corps, or Sixth Army headquarters. Mashbir fought to gain operational control over these teams. "The attached personnel were subject to withdrawal by their parent organizations without notice, a situation which caused considerable disruption in the development and organization of ATIS."[44] As 1943 went on, Mashbir gained control of the incoming teams so he could assign the Nisei as he saw fit. In this way he established a system for providing effective language support at all levels of each operation. The key to success, in his view, was "the pooling, to the extent permissible by circumstances, of all linguistic resources."[45]

Mashbir came to appreciate the Nisei and to understand their commitment and concerns. He soon learned of their unhappiness over the lack of promotions. Some even complained that commissions promised upon graduation from language training had never materialized. ATIS had no table of organization, thus the War Department would not allow Mashbir to promote or commission his soldiers. "At the end of two years and the conclusion of ten tough operations, not a single man had been promoted even one grade, solely because there were no legal vacancies." However, in August 1943 he found a way to promote three Nisei to warrant officer, telling them, "We couldn't get you 2d lieutenant bars but we'll get you warrant officers first and then we'll see what we can do after you get your warrant." Gary T. Kadani and Steve S. Yamamoto had come to Australia with the first group of Nisei; Sunao P. Ishio had come a few months later and served at Buna-Gona. Mashbir soon obtained quotas for the Nisei to attend the Army's officer candidate school at Camp Columbia outside Brisbane. The first Nisei graduates of this program received commissions in early 1944.[46]

ATIS began producing important intelligence reports and established in July 1943 a separate Production Section for editorial and printing work. During the year ATIS produced over 2,000 interrogation reports and translations of about seventy enemy publications, such as a Japanese manual on landing operations, the 1940 national census of Japan, and a Japanese analysis of American combat operations on Guadalcanal.[47] ATIS also published information bulletins, later designated research reports, on a wide variety of topics. These included such things as a profile of the Asahi Steel Works in Osaka, a description of Japanese booby traps,

---

[44] ATIS History, p. 7.

[45] Ibid., p. 2.

[46] Mashbir, *I Was an American Spy*, p. 222; "Intelligence Men Recount WW II Projects at Reunion," *Honolulu Star-Bulletin*, 2 Sep 68; James Oda, in *Pacific Citizen*, 23–30 Dec 88, p. E–3; Interv, author with S. Phil Ishio, 18 Apr 95. All three Nisei warrant officers received commissions in early 1944.

[47] ATIS History, pp. 20–21. Major ATIS publications are listed in ATIS History, app. IX. Copies are available at the National Archives, the MacArthur Memorial, and the University of Maryland. For an almost complete set, see *The History of Intelligence Activities under General Douglas MacArthur, 1942–50*, The Intelligence Series, G–2–USAFFE–SWPA–AFPAC–FEC–SCAP, S1657, 8 microfilm rolls (Wilmington, Del.: Scholarly Resources, 1984). The Japanese report on Guadalcanal was reprinted in John Miller, jr., *Guadalcanal: The First Offensive* (Washington, D.C.: Department of the Army, Historical Division, 1949), pp. 365–68.

and an analysis of Japanese military psychology. Mashbir took a special interest in gathering evidence on Japanese's decision for war and subsequent war crimes.[48]

During 1943 ATIS examined over 200 Japanese prisoners. Many were held in Camp Gaythorne, a POW compound on the outskirts of Brisbane. Several talked freely with the Americans, in part because the Imperial Japanese Army had never indoctrinated them in what to do if captured. Major Shelton personally handled one Japanese soldier whom the Australians captured in March 1943. The prisoner was a superior private in an artillery unit and had a photographic memory. He also was resentful that he had not been promoted to the Japanese equivalent of warrant officer. Over the next two years ATIS generated more than two dozen interrogation reports based on the variety of information he freely provided.[49]

Other prisoners were less helpful. Once during an interrogation in the autumn of 1943, Sergeant Yamamoto caught a prisoner in a lie. When Yamamoto confronted him, the prisoner "started telling the truth, which included a lot of useful information." Yamamoto, one of the Nisei just promoted to warrant officer, then took a few days' leave in Brisbane. Upon his return, he learned that the Japanese prisoner had committed suicide. He had left Yamamoto a note saying he thought the Nisei "was angry with him, and that made him so ashamed that he had to kill himself."[50]

In the spring of 1943 ATIS scored a coup that demonstrated that the Nisei could produce valuable strategic intelligence. Fifth Air Force was interdicting Japanese reinforcements and resupply for their forces in New Guinea. In March 1943 the Fifth Air Force, tipped off by Ultra, ambushed and destroyed a Japanese convoy ferrying troops to Lae on New Guinea's north coast in what became known as the Battle of the Bismarck Sea.[51] Several days later Allied troops discovered an abandoned lifeboat with a trunk of documents. Among these was the Japanese Army list, a register of every officer in the Imperial Japanese Army with unit of assignment as of 15 October 1942.

Since the war began, Allied intelligence specialists had been painstakingly piecing together the order of battle for the Japanese Army using prewar data. The Nisei's efforts yielded information about Japanese units the Allies encountered in Singapore, the Philippines, Guadalcanal, and New Guinea. Now intelligence officers could reconstruct every unit from company level to army headquarters. Given an officer's name, an American interrogator could deduce a prisoner's unit. A team of twenty Nisei and Caucasian linguists worked nonstop for weeks on the 40,000 names. The translation was tricky work because Japanese family names

---

[48] Mashbir, *I Was an American Spy*, pp. 234–37.

[49] ATIS History, p. 46; Harrington, *Yankee Samurai*, p. 149.

[50] Harrington, *Yankee Samurai*, p. 155; Steve S. Yamamoto, in Swift, "First Class," pp. 5–6; Ulrich Straus, *The Anguish of Surrender: Japanese POWs of World War II* (Seattle: University of Washington Press, 2004).

[51] Ronald Lewin, *The American Magic: Codes, Ciphers and the Defeat of Japan* (New York: Farrar Straus Giroux, 1982), pp. 185–87; Edward J. Drea, *MacArthur's Ultra: Codebreaking and the War against Japan, 1942–1945* (Lawrence: University Press of Kansas, 1992), pp. 61–74.

often can be rendered in more than one way. When the 683-page translation was published in May 1943, it was the first detailed, reliable profile of the Japanese Army in more than two years.[52]

Brig. Gen. Charles A. Willoughby kept direct control over the list and established a separate section in his headquarters for its exploitation. He sent an urgent request to MISLS for its best available translator. The language school sent M.Sgt. Taro Yoshihashi, a Kibei who had lived in Japan for five years as a teenager. Before the war, he had returned to the United States and earned a degree in psychology from the University of California at Los Angeles. In late May 1943 he left Minnesota for Brisbane, where he arrived in early June. He set to work at once maintaining the card file based on the officer list, together with Sgt. Ken Omura from Seattle. The order of battle section became one of the workhorses of intelligence in the theater for the rest of the war. In Washington, the Military Intelligence Division established a similar section to collate this data. Four Nisei were assigned to the Pentagon, the first Japanese Americans allowed into the new building since the War Department had moved in. For the remainder of the war, each time Allied soldiers captured an updated list, Yoshihashi and his counterparts in the Pentagon translated it and painstakingly updated their card files.[53]

Another organization in Willoughby's growing intelligence empire, Central Bureau, attacked Japanese radio traffic from its location at the Ascot Racetrack, five miles east of Brisbane. In the early months of the war Central Bureau required little translation work and used ATIS Nisei only sporadically. Clarence Yamagata, a Nisei civilian attorney who had been evacuated from the Philippines, was the only Nisei working for Central Bureau. Although the bureau succeeded in breaking into the Japanese Army's water transport code by April 1943, for the rest of the year it had little message traffic to translate.[54]

Fifth Air Force established its own network of radio intercept stations by early 1943 to provide advance warning of Japanese air attacks. One of these stations was the 138th Signal Radio Intercept Company with the Fifth Air Force advance headquarters near Port Moresby, New Guinea. The Australians operated a radio intercept station in Stuart Creek on Australia's northeast coast.[55] Air intelligence

---

[52] ATIS Publication no. 2 (May 43); ATIS History, p. 45; Willoughby, "The Language Problem in War," p. 194; Drea, *MacArthur's Ultra*, pp. 22, 73–74; Harrington, *Yankee Samurai*, pp. 133–34, 151–52. Intervs, author with Taro Yoshihashi, 22 Aug 95; author with Sunao P. Ishio, 18 Apr 95; D. Clayton James with Sidney F. Mashbir, 1 Sep 71, pp. 12–17, RG 49, MacArthur Memorial. George K. Sankey, *Areya, Koreya (This and That)*. Extracts reprinted in ATIS History, tab I, doc. app., pt. 1; *Reports of General MacArthur*, 4 vols., U.S. Army in World War II (Washington, D.C.: U.S. Army Center of Military History, 1994), 1: 112. See also S. Phil Ishio, "The Nisei Contribution to the Allied Victory in the Pacific," *American Intelligence Journal* (Spring/Summer 1995): 64; George Sankey, in *Saga of the MIS*.

[53] Interv, author with Taro Yoshihashi, 22 Aug 95.

[54] Drea, *MacArthur's Ultra*, pp. 61–93; ATIS History, pp. 64–65.

[55] Kreis, *Piercing the Fog*, pp. 57–109; Roger Pineau, "The Death of Admiral Yamamoto," *Naval Intelligence Professionals Quarterly* (Fall 1994): 1–5; Jack Bleakley, *The Eavesdroppers* (Canberra: AGPS Press, 1991).

officers developed an elaborate system to track Japanese aircraft. By one account, "when a Japanese pilot took off, intercept specialists listened to his radio call, recorded his aircraft's number, checked the aircraft's type and history of normal use (for example, it might be a transport that ordinarily flew between Rabaul and New Guinea), and predicted with good accuracy its probable destination and time of arrival." This information then could be checked against a card file of every Japanese aircraft in the region.[56]

The Army Air Forces also gained valuable information from "crash intelligence" from downed Japanese aircraft. According to one story, air intelligence officers estimated the production rate for Mitsubishi bombers by noting the serial numbers on the toilet seats. To translate the data plates and written materials found in the wreckage, at first Fifth Air Force borrowed Caucasian linguists from the Royal Australian Air Force and the British Army.[57] In January 1943 Fifth Air Force requested its own Nisei. In early April ten Nisei arrived from the United States led by Sergeant Goda, a Kibei who had two years of college in the United States.[58] Soon after their arrival, Fifth Air Force called for one to join the 138th Signal Radio Intercept Company at Seven Mile Strip on New Guinea. This was the request that led Goda to send the hapless Sergeant Fudenna to New Guinea the morning after their poker game. Fudenna was a Kibei who had grown up in Irvington, California. He had been in the Army since before Pearl Harbor and had graduated from the language school in one of the top sections.[59]

By this point in the war Nisei did not usually have access to the most sensitive ULTRA radio intelligence. However, they were allowed to monitor tactical frequencies such as those used for air-to-ground communications. The Japanese also sent some radio transmissions in a simple kana code, which American operators could write down and then have translated. On 13 April 1943, Army and Navy intercept stations in Hawaii and the West Coast picked up a Japanese message in the high-level JN–25 naval code. The large number of addressees attracted the code breakers' attention. Within hours they had most of the message decoded and translated. It told them that the commander of the Japanese Combined Fleet Command would

---

[56] Kreis, *Piercing the Fog*, pp. 247–96 (quote from p. 261).

[57] Mashbir, cited in "Intelligence Men Recount WW II Projects at Reunion," *Honolulu Star-Bulletin* (2 September 1968); Kreis, *Piercing the Fog*, p. 122; Funch, *Linguists in Uniform*, pp. 112–22.

[58] Walter Tanaka, MISNorCal Bio; Walter Tanaka, "Interrogation Experiences," in *World War II Reminiscences*, ed. John H. Roush, Jr. (San Rafael, Calif.: Reserve Officers Association of the United States, 1995), pp. 193–95.

[59] Harold Fudenna, "Harold Fudenna's Involvement in the Death of Admiral Yamamoto," MIS-NorCal Bio; Ltr, Walter Tanaka to Lyn Crost, 25 September 1993, copy in author's files; Lyn Crost, *Honor by Fire: Japanese Americans at War in Europe and the Pacific* (Novato, Calif.: Presidio Press, 1994), pp. 54–56. Fudenna refers incorrectly to Seventeen Mile Strip. For Seven Mile Strip, see George C. Kenney, *General Kenney Reports: A Personal History of the Pacific War* (New York: Duell, Sloan and Pearce, 1949). Fudenna also refers to First Radio Squadron, 138th Signal Corps; this was probably the 138th Signal Radio Intercept Company, which became the 1st Radio Squadron Mobile in August 1943. Kreis, *Piercing the Fog*, p. 258.

make an inspection tour of the South Pacific a few days hence. *Admiral Isoroku Yamamoto* was the planner of the Pearl Harbor attack and one of Japan's greatest wartime leaders. Admiral Chester W. Nimitz approved a plan to exploit the message and eliminate his Japanese counterpart.[60]

News of the intercepted message flashed around intelligence centers in the Pacific and Washington. Analysts worked feverishly to verify its authenticity and gather more information. Some even speculated that it might be a trap.[61] As might be expected, *Yamamoto*'s impending visit to the South Pacific sparked a flurry of new messages on Japanese radio nets. Because Japanese operational security practices tended to be poor and some messages were in less secure codes, Allied listeners intercepted and decrypted some messages.

The 138th Signal Radio Intercept Company at Seven Mile Strip intercepted one of these messages. Fudenna, the lone Nisei, translated one of these messages and passed it to his superiors. On the morning of 18 April the deputy commander of Fifth Air Force, Brig. Gen. Ennis Whitehead, spoke directly to Fudenna by telephone and asked him to verify the accuracy of his translation: "The sound that you hear," Fudenna recalled the general saying, "is coming from the P-38 fighter planes on Guadalcanal that are revving their engines prior to takeoff on a mission of intercepting and downing Admiral Yamamoto's plane over southern Bougainville." Whitehead asked the Nisei if his message had given any indication it might be a trap. Fudenna replied that it looked perfectly legitimate. Whitehead told him that if the mission failed "due to an error in the translated message," he would hold Fudenna personally accountable. Later that day American fliers successfully ambushed *Yamamoto*'s flight and destroyed his aircraft, killing the admiral. Whitehead visited Fudenna's tent to congratulate him for his role in the action.[62]

---

[60] Roger Pineau, "The Code Break," in *Lightning over Bougainville: The Yamamoto Mission Reconsidered*, ed R. Cargill Hall (Washington, D.C.: Smithsonian Institution Press, 1991), pp. 40–46; Pineau, "Death of Admiral Yamamoto"; Bleakley, *Eavesdroppers*, pp. 91–97; W. J. Holmes, *Double-Edged Secrets: U.S. Naval Intelligence Operations in the Pacific during World War II* (Annapolis, Md.: Naval Institute Press, 1979), pp. 135–36; David Kahn, *The Codebreakers: The Story of Secret Writing*, rev. ed. (New York: Scribner, 1996), pp. 595–601; Lewin, *American Magic*, pp. 187–91; John Prados, *Combined Fleet Decoded: The Secret History of American Intelligence and the Japanese Navy In World War II* (New York: Random House, 1995), pp. 459–62.

[61] In John Ashmead's novel about Navy language officers, his protagonist interrogates a captured Japanese Navy officer in Hawaii about *Yamamoto*'s habits and punctuality. John Ashmead, *The Mountain and the Feather* (Boston: Houghton Mifflin, 1961), pp. 62–68, 73–84.

[62] Fudenna, "Harold Fudenna's Involvement," MISNorCal Bio. Fifth Air Force played little or no role in this incident. The 138th Signal Radio Intercept Company may have confirmed information already obtained from other sources. A Navy language officer, Otis Cary, commented in November 1945 that "every man in every radio intelligence outfit from Noumea to Washington claimed himself responsible for Admiral Yamamoto's death." Otis Cary, ed., *From a Ruined Empire: Letters—Japan, China, Korea 1945–46* (San Francisco: Kodansha International, 1984), p. 185. Some writers have ascribed a more prominent role to Fudenna than the facts support. See, for example, *America's Superb Secret Human Weapon in World War II* (San Francisco, Calif.: Presidio Army Museum, 1981); "The Military Intelligence Service: A Brief History," in *Hawaii Herald*, 2

The Southwest Pacific was an infantryman's war: American and Australian soldiers waged a two-year campaign along 1,500 miles of New Guinea's northern coast. Small patrols and isolated detachments fought the enemy, the terrain, and the climate with equal tenacity.[63] In February 1943 ATIS established an advance echelon with the Australian headquarters of New Guinea Force at Maples, New Guinea, with six language officers and three enlisted men. During the year this grew to nineteen officer and enlisted linguists.[64]

The Sixth Army headquarters, renamed ALAMO FORCE, received two officers and twenty Nisei and launched its first offensive in June, landing regimental combat teams on Woodlark and Kiriwina Islands. At the same time, the 41st Infantry Division landed at Nassau Bay. Nisei accompanied the Allied units along the jungle tracks, doing on-the-spot translations and interrogations of the few prisoners. T3g. Albert Y. Tamura became the first Nisei awarded the Combat Infantry Badge for his service with the 41st Infantry Division in September 1943.[65] Some Nisei served with the Australians; Sergeant Kadani left Brisbane to support the Australian Army high in the Owen Stanley Mountains. In September 1943 Nisei accompanied American and Australian soldiers in landings near Lae on New Guinea's north coast. M.Sgt. Arthur K. Ushiro was attached to the 25th Australian Brigade. The Stanford University graduate had excelled at Camp Savage and had been with the group that started ATIS. T3g. Kazuhiko "Rocky" Yamada, a veteran of Buna with the 32d Division, and two other Nisei were assigned to the 9th Australian Division at Finschhafen. All three received Australian commendations. When the 3d Australian Division attacked Salamaua, the Diggers were armed with a Nisei translation of a captured Japanese map that showed the enemy's entire scheme of defense. During the battle, Nisei interrogated a Japanese prisoner and tricked him into thinking the town had already been captured. As a result, "13 important air targets in Salamaua were pinpointed and attacked by Allied aircraft within 24 hours."[66]

S.Sgt. Kazuo Kozaki also landed near Lae with the 9th Australian Division. Born in Salt Lake City, he was a Kibei and graduate of the first class at Crissy Field. Just before he landed, a flight of Japanese aircraft strafed the assault waves, killing over a hundred Australian and American soldiers and sailors. Kozaki hit the deck

Jul 93, pp. A–1, A–10, A–12; Mitzi Matsui in *Unsung Heroes: The Military Intelligence Service, Past, Present, Future* (Seattle: MIS-Northwest Association, 1996), p. xiii.

[63] For studies of soldiers' experiences, see Eric Bergerud, *Touched by Fire: The Land War in the South Pacific* (New York: Penguin, 1996); Gerald F. Linderman, *The World Within War: America's Combat Experience in World War II* (New York: Free Press, 1997); Peter Schrijivers, *The GI War Against Japan: American Soldiers in Asia and the Pacific during World War II* (New York: New York University Press, 2002).

[64] ATIS History, pp. 24–26.

[65] Interv, Sheryl Narahara with Torao "Pat" Neishi, 1992, NJAHS.

[66] ATIS History, pp. 24–26, 46; David Dexter, *Australia in the War of 1939–1945*, ser. 1, vol. 6, *The New Guinea Offensives* (Canberra: Australian War Memorial, 1961), p. 478; Harrington, *Yankee Samurai*, p. 163; Harrington, "Yankee Samurai," p. 13. For the 9th Australian Division commendations, see ATIS History, app. 12.

but was slightly wounded on the buttocks. "I didn't want anyone to know *where* I was wounded," he later recalled. After three days the pain became unbearable and he finally sought medical treatment. He was evacuated to an American field hospital in Milne Bay. Upon Kozaki's return to ATIS, General Willoughby presented him with the Silver Star, a first for the ATIS Nisei, which boosted morale considerably. From Camp Savage, where Kozaki had served as an enlisted instructor, the chief instructor, John Aiso, sent him a sympathy note about his wound. Kozaki treasured Aiso's note more than the Silver Star: "I kept that letter all through the New Guinea campaigns."[67]

During the Lae Campaign, Allied forces captured a record 1,562 Japanese documents. So large was the haul that ATIS was able to compile a complete history of the Japanese garrison from captured documents.[68] The Nisei proved once again their value and bravery while serving close to the front lines. Commanders and their intelligence officers quickly recognized the value of the intelligence the Nisei could provide, which could often spell the difference between victory and defeat.

In addition to the hazards and strains of battle, the Nisei continually risked falling victim to mistaken identity. Fudenna had an unpleasant reminder of this vulnerability in the spring of 1943 at the hands of some New Guinea natives. After the downing of *Yamamoto*'s plane, Fudenna remained near Port Moresby for several more months. One day he and three comrades borrowed a vehicle for an excursion to a native village. When the villagers noticed Fudenna's Japanese features, they seized him despite the protests of his Caucasian comrades. At that time the Australians were offering a reward for any Japanese stragglers, and the natives were eager to collect. Fudenna was rescued only by the timely arrival of an armed Australian patrol. The Australian sergeant freed Fudenna and told him: "Get your bloody arse out of here before you get into more trouble." Fudenna and his comrades complied in great haste.[69]

The U.S. Army had almost taken over Australia; by December 1943 the country was bursting with more than 300,000 Yanks. The U.S. Army employed 50,000 Australian civilians in construction, transportation, and other war-related duties. The Counter Intelligence Corps (CIC) protected this huge logistical base from espionage, subversion, and criminal activity. Col. Elliott R. Thorpe, G–2, U.S. Army Services of Supply, commanded the Southwest Pacific Area CIC.[70] Thorpe

---

[67] Harrington, *Yankee Samurai*, pp. 155–56; Mashbir, *I Was an American Spy*, pp. 240–41; "Army Silver Star Decoration Given to Nisei Soldier," *Pacific Citizen*, 29 Jan 44, p. 1; Kazuo Kozaki, in Swift, "First Class," pp. 13, 31–43; Faubion Bowers, in Falk and Tsuneishi, *MIS in the War against Japan*, p. 13. Kozaki was the first Nisei awarded the Silver Star in World War II; Nisei with the 100th Infantry Battalion in Italy began receiving the Silver Star a few weeks later.

[68] "The Exploitation of Japanese Documents," ATIS Publication no. 6, 14 Dec 44, in ATIS History, app. 5; ATIS History, p. 46.

[69] Fudenna, MISNorCal Bio.

[70] *Operations of the Counter Intelligence Corps in the Southwest Pacific Area*, Intelligence Series, vol. 8 (Tokyo: Far East Command, 1950); Elliott R. Thorpe, *East Wind, Rain: An Intimate Account of an Intelligence Officer in the Pacific, 1939–49* (Boston: Gambit, 1969), pp. 87–129; Interv, Lt. Col. J. H. Griffin with Elliott R. Thorpe, 1981, U.S. Army Military History Institute;

used carefully selected agents from ethnic minority groups to monitor and investigate American soldiers from these groups. As early as July 1942 two African American CIC agents arrived to help detect possible subversives among the thousands of African American service troops pouring into Australia.[71]

Thorpe already had one Nisei assigned to his command, Sgt. Arthur S. Komori, who served in a variety of assignments. In the autumn of 1942 he helped Colonel Mashbir set up ATIS in Brisbane, passing on to the Nisei newcomers his hard-won combat experience on Bataan. He conducted security and loyalty investigations and for a time even worked with aborigines in Australia's Northern Territory to aid in rescuing downed Allied aviators. At least one other Nisei worked with Komori in the CIC, Hawaii-born William T. Hiraoka, who arrived in Australia in December 1942.[72]

By the end of 1943 General Douglas MacArthur had built up a powerful fighting force in the Southwest Pacific Area. He had about 150 Nisei serving in the intelligence field, counting those serving with Allied fighting units and those serving in ATIS. MacArthur would need many more MIS Nisei for his unfolding campaign. In the first half of 1944 the Southwest Pacific Theater would add five new American divisions, each of which would go into combat with a team of MIS Nisei from ATIS. These Nisei brought skill, courage, and an understanding of their Japanese opponents. For example, in October 1943 M.Sgt. Thomas S. Kadomoto, a Kibei, brought a shipment of sixty Nisei from Minnesota to Brisbane. Kadomoto had been born in Phoenix, Arizona. When he was twelve years old his parents took the family to Japan. By the time Kadomoto arrived in Australia, his younger brother, who had remained in Japan, was serving in the Japanese Army.[73]

Dramatic breakthroughs such as the downing of *Admiral Yamamoto* and finding the Japanese Army list were rare. More often intelligence involved piecing together a picture of the enemy from many fragments of information. During 1943 ATIS developed the basic techniques and procedures for language work used during the rest of the war. The Nisei learned how to extract intelligence from prisoners of war and from captured documents of all descriptions. Just as important, ATIS had developed ways of sifting through this mountain of information and passing it to commanders in sufficient time for them to act on it. Mashbir and his staff understood the value of a centralized language center that could use

Duval A. Edwards, *Spy Catchers of the U.S. Army in the War with Japan* (Gig Harbor, Wash.: Red Apple Publishing, 1994), pp. 61–74, 103–08.

[71] Edwards, *Spy Catchers*, p. 73.

[72] Interv, Ann Bray with Arthur S. Komori, 1955; Ann Bray, "Undercover Nisei," in *Military Intelligence: Its Heroes and Legends* (Arlington Hall Station, Va.: U.S. Army Intelligence and Security Command, 1987), pp. 29–45; "Lone Hawaii Survivor of Bataan Epic Described 11th Hour Escape," *Honolulu Star-Bulletin*, 17, 18 Apr 44, and *Pacific Citizen*, 13 May 44. Two Hawaii Nisei, William T. Hiraoka and George Kiyoshi Yamashiro (Sankey), may have joined the CIC in Australia as early as December 1942. Harrington, *Yankee Samurai*, p. 245. Yamashiro was soon reassigned to ATIS. George Kiyoshi [Yamashiro] Sankey, "Areya, Koreye [This and That]," Unpubl autobiography.

[73] Folder, Tom Kadomoto, in Joseph D. Harrington Papers, NJAHS.

the Nisei to best advantage. The skill, bravery, and loyalty of these Nisei soldiers made possible many Allied victories on the battlefields of New Guinea and the Southwest Pacific.

Central Pacific Area

The situation was quite different in the Central Pacific, where communications intelligence provided Admiral Nimitz the most useful information on the Japanese Combined Fleet. American soldiers and marines did not meet the Japanese enemy in ground combat until November 1943, when Nimitz began his island-hopping campaign with amphibious assaults in the Gilbert Islands on Tarawa and Makin. Submarine and air reconnaissance provided little information on these islands. Nimitz's senior intelligence officer later described his challenge: "It is no exaggeration to say that for each person who had visited Tarawa prior to the war and was able to provide fragmentary intelligence of this tiny island, the intelligence officer in the European Theater would probably find a million persons who had visited the Normandy beaches and could provide intelligence thereof." [74]

Until Nimitz's forces began to meet their Japanese opponents on the ground, the amount of Japanese-language work to be done was limited. For the Japanese radio messages intercepted in 1942 and 1943 and the few prisoners and documents captured, the dozen or so Caucasian language officers in Hawaii were sufficient. During 1942 American forces in the Central Pacific captured only forty-nine Japanese sailors. [75] In February 1943 the first twenty graduates of the Navy language school in Boulder, Colorado, arrived in Hawaii.

Intelligence organizations in the Central Pacific grew rapidly during the first two years of the war. The Radio Intelligence Section, later renamed the Fleet Radio Unit, Pacific (FRUPAC), handled decoding and translating Japanese radio communications. The Intelligence Center, Pacific Ocean Areas, analyzed intelligence from all sources including aerial photography and geographic intelligence. [76] In September 1943 the center was renamed the Joint Intelligence Center, Pacific Ocean Areas (JICPOA). Brig. Gen. Joseph J. Twitty, the officer in charge who also served as Nimitz's J-2, had been a language attaché in Tokyo and was a topographic engineer. [77] JICPOA handled most language work from its location at Pearl

---

[74] Ltr, Joseph W. Twitty to Chief, Historical Section, Far East Command, 2 February 1948, copy in Folder 1, Box 17, RG–23, Willoughby Papers, MacArthur Memorial.

[75] Prados, *Combined Fleet Decoded*, p. 496.

[76] *Report of Intelligence Activities in the Pacific Ocean Areas* (Pearl Harbor: Assistant Chief of Staff for Intelligence, 1945); Wyman H. Packard, *A Century of U.S. Naval Intelligence* (Washington, D.C.: Office of Naval Intelligence/Naval Historical Center, 1996), pp. 396–402; Holmes, *Double-Edged Secrets*, pp. 120–21; Holmes, "Naval Intelligence in the War against Japan, 1941–45: The View from Pearl Harbor," in *New Aspects of Naval History*, ed. Craig L. Symonds et al. (Annapolis, Md.: Naval Institute Press, 1981), pp. 351–57; Edwin T. Layton, *"And I Was There!":* *Pearl Harbor and Midway—Breaking the Secrets* (New York: William Morrow, 1985).

[77] *Report of Intelligence Activities*; Holmes, *Double-Edged Secrets*, pp. 115, 145–46. In John Ashmead's novel, JICPOA became "JOKEPOA" and General Twitty became General "Waddleman."

Harbor, but sometimes Navy language officers deployed for specific operations, such as for Guadalcanal and the Aleutians. One Navy language officer spent eight months on Guadalcanal monitoring plain-text Japanese radio traffic.[78]

Military authorities in Hawaii remained concerned about the Japanese population in the islands. The Hawaiian Department commanding general had declared martial law on 7 December 1941; this remained in effect for three more years. Though the Army rejected calls for large-scale removal of Japanese from Hawaii as from the West Coast, about 1,450 Japanese aliens and American citizens of Japanese ancestry were interned. The Japanese remained critical to the local economy in Hawaii, where they constituted one-third of the labor force. The Navy took a firm stand and refused to allow persons of Japanese ancestry, even American citizens, to work on Navy bases. In contrast, Army officials led by Col. Kendall J. Fielder, the Hawaiian Department G–2, took a more positive approach and encouraged the cooperation of the local Japanese community. When 1,400 Nisei soldiers from the 298th and 299th Infantries were transferred to the mainland in June 1942, several hundred remained with service units and as civilian laborers in the Varsity Victory Volunteers. In January 1943, when the War Department announced the formation of a special combat unit of Japanese American volunteers, a wave of patriotism swept through Japanese communities in Hawaii. Ten thousand Nisei volunteered, of whom the Army accepted almost three thousand to form the 442d Regimental Combat Team. Other Nisei soldiers stayed back to form the 1399th Engineer Battalion, and the language school at Camp Savage began to recruit Nisei in Hawaii.

Suspicions of the Hawaii Japanese continued even as the 100th Infantry Battalion and 442d RCT went into combat in Italy and France. Those inclined to distrust the Nisei pointed out that in Italy the Nisei were fighting against Caucasians. The real test would be if the Nisei had to fight against "their own kind" in the Pacific. These critics did not know that the MIS Nisei were already doing just that.[79]

In 1943 Admiral Nimitz began his offensive drive with one marine division and two Army divisions. The 2d Marine Division attacked Tarawa in November, while the 27th Infantry Division was assigned to take Makin Atoll. The 7th Infantry Division, rebuilding after the Aleutian Islands Campaign, would be ready for its next battle by early 1944. In July 1943 U.S. Army Middle Pacific requested two teams of ten Nisei linguists each for the two Army divisions assigned for the coming campaigns. Twenty Nisei from Minnesota arrived in Hawaii in late September.[80] For some, like Sergeant Kubo, it was a homecoming. Kubo had been on

---

[78] Packard, *A Century of U.S. Naval Intelligence*, p. 409. Ashmead's novel mentions that a Navy language officer killed himself on Guadalcanal during this time, but the author does not know if he based this on an actual incident.

[79] Thomas D. Murphy, *Ambassadors in Arms* (Honolulu: University of Hawaii Press, 1954), pp. 191–202.

[80] U.S. Army Forces Middle Pacific (and Predecessor Commands), *History of G–2 Section, 7 December 1941–2 September 1945*, ch. 5, "Prisoner of War Interrogation & Translation Section," pp. 208–23, Richardson Papers, Hoover Institution Archives; Interv, author with Hoichi Bob Kubo,

active duty at Wheeler Field when the Japanese attacked in December 1941. He had gone to the mainland with the 100th Infantry Battalion and was recruited for the language school. For Nisei from the mainland, sailing to Hawaii was also laden with significance. T4g. Frank T. Hachiya, a 23-year old Kibei from Hood River, Oregon, told a friend just before leaving for Hawaii: "You know, we'll be fighting two wars out there—one against the Japanese, and the other against prejudice."[81]

On 20 November 1943, the 2d Marine Division assaulted Tarawa. In four days of savage fighting, the marines defeated the island's Japanese defenders at a terrible cost of 1,085 marines killed. Thousands of wounded marines filled the hospitals in Hawaii. Only seventeen Japanese survived, along with 129 Korean laborers.[82] The marines used no Nisei linguists during the battle, but JICPOA did assign a team of intelligence specialists that included one Caucasian language officer who conducted interrogations and translated captured documents. The marines who fought on Tarawa often overlooked captured documents as a source of intelligence. "Souvenir-hunters destroyed or 'liberated' more intelligence material than the [intelligence] teams could collect," one observer reported. "One sailor picked up a Japanese code book as a souvenir. That code remained in use in the Marshalls for several weeks after Tarawa fell, but much to [American code breakers'] disgust, it had been superseded by the time the code book was discovered in a barracks inspection back at Pearl Harbor." Several months later JICPOA sent Sgt. Nobuo Furuiye, a Colorado-born Nisei, to Tarawa "to observe and evaluate the evidence from documents and other items."[83]

The 27th Infantry Division landed on Makin on the same day the marines assaulted Tarawa, 20 November 1943. The 165th Infantry conducted the assault; Sgt. Nobue D. Kishiue led the regiment's three-man language team ashore with the assault waves. The Nisei scrambled down cargo nets to the rolling deck of a landing craft. When the landing craft ran aground a hundred yards from the beach, Kishiue and his team waded ashore through chest-deep water in full field gear while under enemy fire. On the first day they found no prisoners, only some Korean laborers. They did find some valuable documents at an enemy command

---

30 Oct 87; Nobuo D. Kishiue, "Island Hopping from Makin to Saipan to Okinawa," in Falk and Tsuneishi, *MIS in the War against Japan*, pp. 49–53; Nobuo D. Kishiue, MISNorCal Bio.

[81] Harrington, "Yankee Samurai," p. 20.

[82] When Charles Lindbergh visited Tarawa on 30 August 1944, he heard the story that a U.S. Navy officer had spared Japanese prisoners who could speak English but killed the rest. Charles A. Lindbergh, *The Wartime Journals of Charles A. Lindbergh* (New York: Harcourt Brace Jovanovich, 1970), pp. 914–15.

[83] Holmes, *Double-Edged Secrets*, pp. 150–51; Furuiye, Rocky Mountain Bio, p. 13. Harrington claims Frank Hachiya served on Tarawa, but this is unlikely. Harrington, *Yankee Samurai*, p. 170. John F. Aiso also suggested that Nisei may have served on Tarawa, perhaps based on Harrington's writings. Aiso's 1979 speech, reprinted in *Pacific Citizen* (December 1980), and in Oguro, *Sempai Gumi*, p. lxxxiv. Novelist John Ashmead describes a Navy language officer on Tarawa. Ashmead, *The Mountain and the Feather*, pp. 141–55.

post, but little else.[84] On the fourth day Cpl. Hoichi Kubo accompanied field historian Lt. Col. S. L. A. Marshall to the forward units in a jeep. As they drove down a sandy road, rifle fire erupted from the shrubbery less than twenty-five yards away and the driver gunned the engine. From the back seat Kubo cried out, "I'm hit!" The driver raced through the ambush, and Marshall turned around in his seat to ask, "Where are you hit?" Kubo grinned: "I'm all right. Nothing happened. I just wanted to make him move faster."[85]

When the battle had concluded, the division G–2 was very pleased with the Nisei: "We would have been twice as blind as we were on these islands without the Nisei. Without a doubt, our Nisei have saved many, many American lives."[86] The Nisei linguists had proven their worth in the Central Pacific as they had earlier in the South Pacific and Southwest Pacific. The 27th Infantry Division awarded to the three Nisei who fought on Makin the Combat Infantryman Badge.[87]

With the assaults on Tarawa and Makin, Admiral Nimitz's command had finally launched an offensive in the Central Pacific characterized by intense ground combat on a chain of heavily defended islands. That meant a large increase in captured documents and prisoners of war, some 500 during 1943 alone.[88] However, the Central Pacific still lagged behind other theaters in the use of Nisei. By the end of 1943 only 20 Nisei were serving in the theater, compared to over 100 in the South Pacific and 150 in the Southwest Pacific. Many more Nisei would serve in the Central Pacific in the months ahead.

· · ·

In early 1944 Col. Kai E. Rasmussen made his first inspection tour of the Pacific to observe how his graduates were performing. On Bougainville and elsewhere, he expressed his personal appreciation to the Nisei. His pride was well justified. It was "his considered opinion," he reported, "that graduates are contributing materially to the successful conduct of the war; their work is indispensable and cannot be done successfully by any other known agency." He reported that the Nisei were "being used very widely; units making use of them include the U.S. Army and Navy, Marine Corps, Australian, New Zealand and British units,

[84] Kishiue, in Falk and Tsuneishi, *MIS in the War against Japan*, pp. 49–53; Kishiue, MISNorCal Bio.

[85] S. L. A. Marshall, *Bringing Up the Rear: A Memoir*, ed. Cate Marshall (San Rafael, Calif.: Presidio Press, 1979), p. 72.

[86] Lt. Col. Van Antwerp, cited in "Use of Nisei Saved GI Lives in Pacific," *Pacific Citizen*, 29 Sep 45; *MISLS Album*, p. 115; Weckerling, "Japanese Americans Play Vital Role." Van Antwerp's comments referred to Makin as well as later 27th Infantry Division operations on Saipan and Okinawa.

[87] Kishiue, MISNorCal Bio; Kishiue, in Falk and Tsuneishi, *MIS in the War against Japan*, p. 51. The awards took eleven months to process, apparently because the Nisei were administratively assigned to division headquarters rather than the assault elements.

[88] Prados, *Combined Fleet Decoded*, p. 496.

and such quasi-military organizations as [the Office of War Information] and [the Office of Strategic Services], etc."[89]

The campaigns of the first two years of the war had proven the value of the MIS Nisei. Rasmussen returned to Minnesota determined to increase the supply by any means necessary. Poor utilization of Nisei in some areas compounded the problem of insufficient numbers. The Army had entered the war with no organization or doctrine for the use of translators and interpreters and precious few ideas about how to recruit and train them in numbers sufficient to meet urgent combat requirements. In addition, the Nisei often had to overcome prejudice and stereotypes before they could prove their worth. Rasmussen was critical of most theaters in this regard. "It is a necessity for the efficient operation of personnel sent from Camp Savage," he reported, "that units which make use of them accept and trust them." He further reported that "with the exception of the Southwest Pacific, full capabilities of this personnel are not generally realized and, in many ways, their use represents amateurish efforts compared to professional standards achieved in the Southwest Pacific." The services would have to learn how better to employ the Nisei if they did not want to see the fighting degenerate into bloody slugging matches such as took place on Tarawa.[90]

In the first three months of 1944 the language school would graduate another 565 Nisei, more than doubling the number available for overseas service. Rasmussen was doing all he could to increase the supply of qualified Nisei. Theater commanders and their intelligence officers had to learn how best to use them in future campaigns. The Nisei were indeed indispensable.

---

[89] "History and Description of the Military Intelligence Service Language School," [May 1944], p. 32, Unpubl Ms, 1943–1945, General Records, Military Intelligence [Service] Language School, RG 319, NARA; *Pacific War and Peace*, p. 33; Roy Uyehata, in Roush, *World War II Reminiscences*, pp. 257–60.

[90] "History and Description," pp. 32–33.

7

MIS Nisei Serving in the Continental United States, 1943–1945

Not all graduates of the Military Intelligence Service Language School served overseas. Many served in stateside intelligence assignments in out-of-the-way places such as Byron Hot Springs, California; Camp Ritchie, Maryland; and Vint Hill Farms, Virginia, using their language skills to help defeat Japan. (*See Map 7.*) During the early campaigns the greatest need was for linguists with frontline units and the theaters of operation. After 1943 these theater-level intelligence efforts were increasingly supplemented by national-level capabilities. In 1943–1944, intelligence centers sprang up in the continental United States to handle prisoners of war, translation, psychological warfare, signals intelligence, and miscellaneous tasks that required Japanese-language skills. Nisei were assigned to a broad range of these duties. Some assignments, such as technical translations and guarding Japanese prisoners of war, were valuable but routine. Others, such as translating signal intercepts or writing propaganda, were more sensitive and required greater skill. In the racially charged atmosphere of wartime America, Nisei soldiers serving in the United States continued to encounter prejudice and suspicion despite their citizenship and military service. The War Department continued to exclude them from its most sensitive operations and planning, such as signals intelligence. Nevertheless, the MIS Nisei who served in stateside intelligence assignments made important contributions to the war effort.

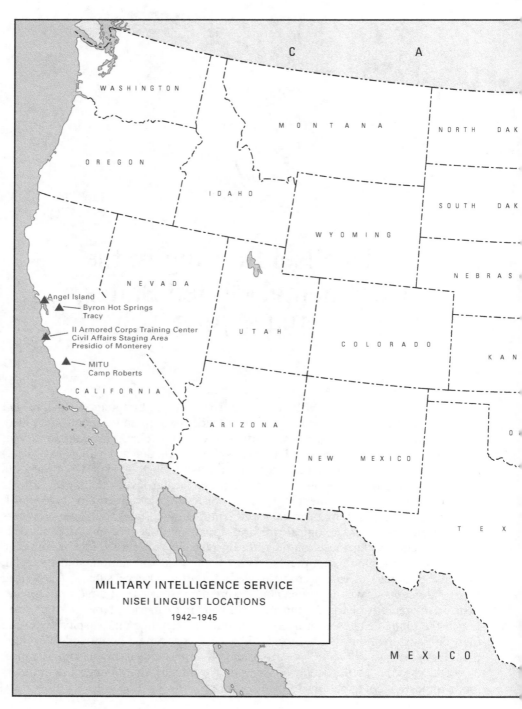

MILITARY INTELLIGENCE SERVICE
NISEI LINGUIST LOCATIONS
1942–1945

MAP 7

A   D   A

MAINE

NEW HAMPSHIRE

VERMONT

MASSACHUSETTS

MISLS
Fort Snelling
1944–1946

WISCONSIN

CONNECTICUT

RHODE ISLAND

vage
944

POW Camp
Camp McCoy

NEW YORK

POW Camp
Fort Custer

Manhattan Project
New York

W A

Army Map Service
Cleveland

PENNSYLVANIA

NEW JERSEY

MITU
Fort Meade

OW Camp
p Clarinda

INDIANA

OHIO

PACMIRS
Camp Ritchie

MARYLAND

DELAWARE

ILLINOIS

WEST
VIRGINIA

Signal Intelligence Service
Vint Hill Farms

War Department G-2
Pacific Order of Battle Section
FBIS
OSS/MO-FE
Office of War Information
Office of Naval Intelligence
Washington Document Center
Washington, DC

MISSOURI

KENTUCKY

VIRGINIA

NORTH CAROLINA

TENNESSEE

ARKANSAS

SOUTH
CAROLINA

MISSISSIPPI

GEORGIA

ALABAMA

Camp Shelby

LOUISIANA

The Military Intelligence Division after Pearl Harbor

The War Department's intelligence programs grew rapidly after Pearl Harbor. Although the War Department initially directed attention toward the North African landings and the subsequent campaigns in the Mediterranean and Northwestern Europe, the G–2 with its Far Eastern Branch did not completely neglect Japan.[1] In March 1942 Chief of Staff George C. Marshall selected Maj. Gen. George V. Strong, the Army's most senior Japan specialist, as assistant chief of staff for intelligence. Strong was a graduate of the U.S. Military Academy. He had traveled to the Far East to observe Japan's victory over Russia and returned to Tokyo in 1908 as a language attaché. In 1938 he succeeded Marshall as chief of the War Plans Division. According to General Dwight D. Eisenhower, who served with Strong on the General Staff, he possessed "a keen mind, a driving energy, and ruthless determination."[2]

In the spring of 1942 Strong reorganized the G–2 staff into the Military Intelligence Division (MID) and a much larger field operating arm, the Military Intelligence Service (MIS). Included in the MIS were all intelligence personnel under direct War Department control rather than organic to specific units such as divisions and regiments.[3] The Far Eastern Section grew quickly under Col. Rufus S. Bratton, who had been its chief since 1937. Bratton was a graduate of the U.S. Military Academy. He had served three tours in Japan and spoke the language fluently. Other Japanese-language officers in the section included Col. Thomas J. Betts, Col. Moses W. Pettigrew, and Lt. Col. Carlisle C. Dusenbury. The section also oversaw assignments of language-qualified officers.[4] The Far Eastern Branch itself produced little strategic, operational, or tactical intelligence in the early years; most was instead supplied by the combat theaters. However,

---

[1] Ronald H. Spector, *Eagle against the Sun* (New York: Free Press, 1985), pp. 445–77; James D. Marchio, "Days of Future Past: Joint Intelligence in World War II," *Joint Force Quarterly* (Spring 1996): 116–23.

[2] Dwight D. Eisenhower, *Crusade in Europe* (Garden City, N.Y.: Doubleday & Co., 1948), pp. 33–34; "George V. Strong" (obituary), *Assembly* (January 1947). While studying Japanese, Strong published a kanji handbook: *Common Chinese-Japanese Characters* (Yokohama, Japan: Kelly and Walsh, [1911]).

[3] John P. Finnegan and Romana Danysh, *Military Intelligence*, Army Lineage Series (Washington, D.C.: U.S. Army Center of Military History, 1998), pp. 61–84; "A History of the Military Intelligence Division, 7 December 1941–2 September 1945," Unpubl Ms, 1946 (hereafter cited as MID History), U.S. Army Center of Military History (CMH) files; Bruce W. Bidwell, "History of the Military Intelligence Division, Department of the Army General Staff," Unpubl Ms, 1959–1961, CMH files; Otto L. Nelson, Jr., *National Security and the General Staff* (Washington, D.C.: Infantry Journal Press, 1946), pp. 521–35.

[4] Bruce W. Bidwell, *History of the Military Intelligence Division, Department of the Army General Staff: 1775–1941* (Frederick, Md.: University Publications of America, 1986), pp. 435–36, 454. For prewar list of forty-six officers with varying degrees of language proficiency, see Plans & Training Branch, MID, "Japanese: R.A. Officers with Knowledge of Language," 27 Mar 41, Far Eastern Br, Ofc of the Dir of Intel G–2, Record Group (RG) 165, National Archives and Records Administration (NARA).

the branch did coordinate with the British, who were gaining valuable intelligence in Southeast Asia.[5]

Headquarters, Army Air Forces, in Washington had its own air intelligence staff. The Assistant Chief of Air Staff, Intelligence, or A–2, requested Nisei from the War Department G–2 as needed. In 1943 the A–2 requested some for technical air intelligence teams that were assigned to each numbered air force in the Pacific. In the summer of 1944 the Military Intelligence Service Language School (MISLS) sent ten more to work at the joint Army-Navy Technical Air Intelligence Center at Bolling Field in Anacostia, D.C.[6] The A–2 also wanted Nisei for tactical radio intercept duties. Beginning in February 1944, the Army Air Forces sent dozens of MISLS graduates to signals training at MacDill Field, Florida. The Nisei then joined mobile radio squadrons and were deployed to the Pacific.

The Office of Naval Intelligence had its own Far Eastern Section (OP–16–F) with a handful of Japanese-language officers under Cmdr. Arthur H. McCollum. In June 1942 Capt. Ellis M. Zacharias, a former Japanese-language attaché, became deputy director of Naval Intelligence.[7]

The Army and Navy, with their shortages of Japanese-language personnel, both turned to unlikely sources. In August 1942 the Swedish liner *Gripsholm* arrived in New York carrying over 2,000 Western diplomatic personnel and other civilians repatriated from Japan, including the staffs of the American and Canadian embassies in Tokyo.[8] Army and Navy intelligence officers had met them in Rio de Janeiro for debriefings. Several individuals proved of immediate value and gave a great boost to the American intelligence effort. Col. Frederick P. Munson, the Army attaché in Tokyo and a Japanese linguist, was sent to the South Pacific

---

[5] Richard J. Aldrich, *Intelligence and the War against Japan: Britain, America and the Politics of Secret Service* (Cambridge: Cambridge University Press, 2000); Alan H. Bath, *Tracking the Axis Enemy: The Triumph of Anglo-American Naval Intelligence* (Lawrence: University Press of Kansas, 1998).

[6] John F. Kreis, "Planning the Defeat of Japan: The A–2 in Washington, 1943–1945," in *Piercing the Fog: Intelligence and Army Air Forces Operations in World War II*, ed. John F. Kreis (Washington, D.C.: Air Force History and Museums Program, 1996), pp. 349–92; Joseph D. Harrington, *Yankee Samurai: The Secret Role of Nisei in America's Pacific Victory* (Detroit: Pettigrew Enterprises, 1979), p. 236.

[7] "Office of Naval Intelligence," United States Naval Administration in World War II, 16 parts in 4 vols., Unpubl Ms, n.d., U.S. Naval Historical Center, Washington, D.C.; Wyman H. Packard, *A Century of U.S. Naval Intelligence* (Washington, D.C.: Office of Naval Intelligence/Naval Historical Center, 1996); John Prados, *Combined Fleet Decoded: The Secret History of American Intelligence and the Japanese Navy in World War II* (New York: Random House, 1995); "Reminiscences of Rear Admiral Arthur H. McCollum, U.S. Navy Retired," 2 vols., Unpubl Ms, 1970–1971, Naval Historical Center, Washington, D.C.; Ellis M. Zacharias, *Secret Missions: The Story of an Intelligence Officer* (New York: G. P. Putnam's Sons, 1946), pp. 285–316; Jeffery M. Dorwart, *Conflict of Duty: The U.S. Navy's Intelligence Dilemma, 1919–1945* (Annapolis, Md.: Naval Institute Press, 1983), pp. 172–227.

[8] Max Hill, *Exchange Ship* (New York: Farrar & Rinehart, 1942); P. Scott Corbett, *Quiet Passages: The Exchange of Civilians between the United States and Japan during the Second World War* (Kent, Ohio: Kent State University Press, 1987).

in December 1942 to serve as Admiral Halsey's G–2. Capt. Henri H. Smith-Hutton, the naval attaché and a Japanese linguist, took over Admiral Ernest J. King's Operational Information Section. Claude Buss, the senior American Foreign Service officer in Manila and a Chinese linguist who while interned had taught himself to read some Japanese, took over the San Francisco branch of the Office of War Information.[9] Among the civilians was William Laffin, whose American father was a Ford Motor Company executive and mother was Japanese. Laffin accepted a commission and went to Camp Savage. He later led a team of Nisei with Merrill's Marauders in Burma. Lt. Col. Archibald W. Stuart became the language school's assistant commandant. The Signal Intelligence Service asked Harold E. Zaugg, son of a missionary, "to do some language work for them." James Hamasaki, a Nisei who had been an employee of the American embassy in Tokyo, took a civilian job in the Pentagon. Another former embassy employee, Mary Ogawa, a Nisei from Idaho, also went to work in Washington, D.C. In her off-duty time she volunteered at the USO, where she met her future husband, Sgt. Roger S. Obata, a Nisei from British Columbia serving in the Canadian Army and stationed at Camp Ritchie, Maryland.[10] An Army officer who returned on the *Gripsholm* wrote a study of Japanese land-combat operations through June 1942 based entirely on Japanese newspaper accounts he had read in confinement. "From competent observers who had returned to the United States on the first trip of the exchange ship *Gripsholm*, and from other intelligence sources," Zacharias later recalled, "we had put together a fairly accurate picture of the trend inside Japan."[11] These repatriated personnel were a windfall for Army and Navy intelligence, but they were also an indication of how desperate the military services had become for Japanese linguists.

Commanders in theaters of operations used MIS Nisei from 1942 onward for POW interrogation and document translation. In the continental United States, the War Department did not begin using MIS Nisei for intelligence duties until at least mid-1943. Naval Intelligence was even slower to begin using the Nisei.[12] Signals intelligence efforts against Japan in the early years used the limited number of Caucasian linguists. During the first two years it seemed that U.S.-based

[9] "Reminiscences of Rear Admiral Arthur H. McCollum," 2: 448–53; Interv, Frederick P. Munson, in Munson Papers, Hoover Institution Archives, Stanford University, Calif.; Interv, Henri H. Smith-Hutton, Smith-Hutton Papers, Hoover Institution Archives.

[10] Harrington, *Yankee Samurai*, pp. 129–30, 147; *MISLS Album* (Minneapolis: Military Intelligence Service Language School, 1946), p. 45; Harold E. Zaugg, *Sensei, the Ultra American: From Missionary Teacher to Wartime Translator* (Manhattan, Kans.: Sunflower University Press, 1995), pp. 109, 115; Roy Ito, *We Went to War* (Stittsville, Ontario: Canada's Wings, 1984), p. 252.

[11] *Japanese Land Operations (From Japanese Sources), December 8, 1941, to June 8, 1942*, MIS Campaign Study no. 3 (Washington, D.C.: War Department Military Intelligence Service, 1942); Zacharias, *Secret Missions*, p. 321; "Tokyo Raid, Gripsholm Interviews," HRC Geog V Japan 384.5, Archives, U.S. Army Center of Military History.

[12] One author concludes that the Navy similarly declined to use African American sailors in intelligence roles "because of their alleged ties to Japanese espionage." Dorwart, *Conflict of Duty*, p. 188.

intelligence efforts against Japan would carry on without those American soldiers best suited to the work. However, by 1943 these restrictive policies slowly began to change.

Pacific Order of Battle Section

The first Nisei to enter the War Department's recently completed headquarters building, the Pentagon, in the spring of 1943 were T.Sgt. Arthur Masaoki Kaneko and Pvt. Terry Takeshi Doi. The War Department was interested in interrogation methods, so the MISLS assistant commandant, Lt. Col. Joseph K. Dickey, brought the two Nisei to Washington. They stayed with his parents near Dupont Circle. The three staged demonstrations for War Department staff officers. Dickey asked questions and Kaneko translated them into Japanese while Doi played the part of a Japanese prisoner. Kaneko graduated in the first class at Crissy Field and became an enlisted instructor at Camp Savage. Born in 1912 in Riverside, California, he lost his parents when he was eight, so he was sent to live with relatives in Japan. He returned to California in 1930 to finish his education and was studying architecture at Los Angeles Junior College when he was drafted in early 1941. Though Doi had been born in the United States, he went to Japan as a child. He had been drafted into the Japanese Army, so he certainly had a firsthand knowledge of Japanese Army weapons, tactics, and fighting spirit. Doi "looked like a Japanese," recalled Kaneko, "I mean very strong and short, powerful looking, mean looking guy."[13]

These occasional demonstrations in the Pentagon and the Military Intelligence Training Center at Camp Ritchie, Maryland, soon gave way to long-term assignments for Nisei in the nation's capital, beginning with order of battle intelligence on Japanese units that officers in the Far Eastern Branch compiled from field reports. The goal was to piece together a detailed portrait of the Imperial Japanese Army. The painstaking work involved gathering and collating thousands of bits of information from battlefronts, Allies, signals intelligence, and all other sources. By early 1943 G–2 was publishing a weekly bulletin on Japanese order of battle and hosting periodic joint and inter-Allied conferences on the topic.

When American soldiers in New Guinea discovered the Japanese Army list with 40,000 officers' names in March 1943, the Order of Battle Section realized that it was now possible to build a comprehensive profile of the Japanese Army with greater accuracy than ever before. MacArthur's intelligence staff sent a photostatic copy with a preliminary translation to Washington.[14] When the list reached the War Department G–2, Colonel Pettigrew, by then chief of the Far Eastern Branch, and Lt. Col. Eric H. F. Svensson, Jr., another Japanese linguist, had been working alone, often late into the night, to assemble order of battle information.

---

[13] Interv, author with Arthur M. Kaneko, 23 Aug 95; Arthur M. Kaneko, in David W. Swift, Jr., ed., "First Class," p. 15, Unpubl Ms, 2000, copy in author's files. Kaneko's parents both had been born in the United States, so he was technically a Sansei, or third generation, not a Nisei.

[14] ATIS Publication no. 2 (May 1943).

At first Pettigrew requested and was denied additional Japanese linguists and typ-ists.[15] In June 1943 the G–2 held an Allied conference on Japanese order of battle in Washington, "attended by representatives from Washington, London, India, Chungking, Ottawa, Melbourne, and Brisbane." Allied intelligence staffs eagerly exchanged whatever scraps of information they could find about Japanese units in Burma, China, and the South Pacific.[16] Pettigrew could see that his office urgently needed additional staff to cope with the increasing amount of information. In July he requested help directly from the language school at Camp Savage.

In response the school sent T.Sgt. Jimmie M. Matsumura, a Kibei graduate of the first class at Crissy Field and then an enlisted instructor, together with three recent Nisei graduates. They quickly tackled the task of translating and filing the growing mountain of intelligence data. They carefully recorded names on index cards that eventually filled fourteen file drawers. Over the next two years, every time Allied troops captured new editions of the officer list or similar information, the Nisei updated their files. Often the names arrived from the field transliterated into rōmaji, so the Nisei had to figure out what the original kanji characters were. They also did other occasional translations for the War Department.[17]

At times the Nisei felt out of place in the Pentagon. One day someone noticed them at a coffee stand and asked if they were Indians. "That's right," Sgt. Kazuo E. Yamane, a Hawaii-born Nisei and graduate of Waseda University in Japan, replied. "What tribe?" asked the soldier. "Osaka," said Yamane, giving the name of Japan's second largest city. The Nisei enjoyed a good laugh at the Caucasian soldier's expense.[18]

In the autumn of 1943 Matsumura returned to the school and was replaced by M.Sgt. George M. Koshi, a Kibei from Colorado. He had attended school in Japan from age six to sixteen and upon his return to the United States had earned his bachelor's degree and then a law degree from the University of Denver. His draft board called him in March 1942, and he was sent to Camp Savage, where he became an instructor. The lawyer turned master sergeant took over the order of battle files, which became known as Koshi's files. A few weeks later the school sent six more Nisei on six months' temporary duty to assist.[19]

---

[15] James L. Gilbert and John P. Finnegan, eds., *U.S. Army Signals Intelligence in World War II: A Documentary History*, U.S. Army in World War II (Washington, D.C.: U.S. Army Center of Military History, 1993), p. 125; MID History, pp. 187–88.

[16] *Japanese Order of Battle Bulletin* no. 24 (1 July 1943); MID History, p. 191. The second con-ference was held in June 1944. *Japanese Order of Battle Bulletin* no. 73 (12 July 1944).

[17] Interv, author with Kazuo E. Yamane, 8 Dec 94; Ted T. Tsukiyama et al., eds., *Secret Valor: M.I.S. Personnel, World War II Pacific Theater, Pre–Pearl Harbor to Sept. 8, 1951* (Honolulu: Military Intelligence Service Veterans Club of Hawaii, 1993), pp. 104–05; Steve Lum, " Kazuo Yamane's Key Discovery," *Hawaii Herald*, 2 Jul 93; Richard S. Oguro, ed., *Sempai Gumi* (Hono-lulu: MIS Veterans of Hawaii, [1981]), pp. 106–13; Matsumura, in Swift, "First Class"; Harrington, *Yankee Samurai*, pp. 151–52.

[18] Harrington, *Yankee Samurai*, pp. 147–48.

[19] *Unsung Heroes: The Military Intelligence Service, Past, Present, Future* (Seattle: MIS-Northwest Association, 1996), pp. 25, 40–41; Richard Ishimoto, Harrington Papers, National

The Order of Battle Section opened the doors to a broader use of the Nisei in sensitive intelligence assignments. They may also have contributed to ending the exclusion policy and closing the wartime camps. In February 1944 Roosevelt placed the War Relocation Authority under the Department of the Interior, headed by Harold L. Ickes, a prominent New Dealer and an outspoken critic of the camps. Sometime over the winter of 1943–1944 he met with the Nisei serving in the Pentagon; Richard Ishimoto called this "the proudest moment of my six months duty at the Pentagon." In the spring of 1944 Ickes pressed the Roosevelt administration to reverse its exclusion policy. He wrote Roosevelt on 2 June, asking him to end the exclusion orders and close the camps. In November Roosevelt was reelected to an unprecedented fourth term, and in December the Supreme Court ruled against continued incarceration. Only then did Roosevelt agree to Ickes' request.[20]

Prisoner of War Interrogation

Americans took few prisoners of war in the Pacific compared to Allied forces fighting in Europe and North Africa. "It will be a long time before you hear of the surrender of a hundred thousand Japs as you have heard about the surrender of German and Italian troops," the I Corps commanding general, Lt. Gen. Robert L. Eichelberger, told a group of junior officers in Australia soon after the Axis surrenders in Tunisia. "The enemy you are going to meet is one you can count on fighting to the last."[21] In any event, most prisoners that the Americans did capture on Papua New Guinea and in the Solomons were transferred to Australia and New Zealand. As late as June 1943, America held only 62 Japanese prisoners. Six months later the number had risen to 297, of whom 116 were moved to the continental United States.[22] The only prisoners whom the Americans sent to Hawaii and the mainland

Japanese American Historical Society (NJAHS), San Francisco, Calif.; Oguro, *Sempai Gumi*, p. 57; Security-Classified Promotion and Transfer Lists of the Japanese Army, 1942–1945, RG 165, NARA.

[20] Oguro, *Sempai Gumi*, p. 57. Ishimoto was assigned to the Pentagon from about November 1943 until about April 1944. On Ickes and the internment camps, see Jacobus tenBroek et al., *Prejudice, War, and the Constitution* (Berkeley: University of California Press, 1954), pp. 171–73; Greg Robinson, *By Order of the President: FDR and the Internment of Japanese Americans* (Cambridge, Mass.: Harvard University Press, 2001); T. H. Watkins, *Righteous Pilgrim: The Life and Times of Harold L. Ickes, 1874–1952* (New York: Henry Holt, 1990), pp. 790–96; Michi Weglyn, *Years of Infamy: The Untold Story of America's Concentration Camps* (New York: Morrow Quill, 1976), pp. 218–24, 316. Ickes' letter can be found in Bill Hosokawa, *JACL in Quest of Justice: The History of the Japanese American Citizens League* (New York: William Morrow, 1982), pp. 252–53.

[21] Robert L. Eichelberger, *Our Jungle Road to Tokyo* (New York: Viking, 1950), p. 73. Many authors have observed how few Japanese surrendered to American troops. Eric Bergerud, *Touched with Fire: The Land War in the South Pacific* (New York: Penguin, 1996), pp. 403–25; John W. Dower, *War without Mercy: Race and Power in the Pacific War* (New York: Pantheon, 1986), pp. 33–73; Gerald F. Linderman, *The World within War: America's Combat Experience in World War II* (New York: Free Press, 1997), pp. 143–84.

[22] Arnold Krammer, "Japanese Prisoners of War in America," *Pacific Historical Review* (February 1983): 67–91; George G. Lewis, *History of Prisoner of War Utilization by the United States*

were those with high intelligence value, such as *Lt. Kazuo Sakamaki*, commander of the midget submarine captured in Hawaii after the Pearl Harbor attack. He was interrogated at Fort Shafter and sent to the mainland in February 1942.[23]

Japanese prisoners of war were brought into the United States through Angel Island in San Francisco Bay. Before the war, Angel Island had served as an immigration station for Chinese and Japanese immigrants. By the time the Japanese prisoners arrived there, any tactical intelligence they may have once possessed had grown stale, but they could still provide useful information. The Military Intelligence Service established two secret interrogation centers in the United States for strategic interrogations, one in Fort Hunt, Virginia, south of Washington, D.C., and the other a two-hour drive east of San Francisco near Tracy, California. Fourteen miles outside this small town, the Military Intelligence Service took over a resort hotel at Byron Hot Springs. Technicians installed hidden microphones in the prisoners' rooms and listening stations in the basement. The center opened in December 1942 with a capacity of forty-four prisoners. The intended guests were originally German and Italian prisoners of war; but Japanese prisoners, brought from Angel Island specifically for interrogation, came to predominate. The hotel was air-conditioned, a real advantage in California's hot central valley, and had amenities such as indoor swimming pools, tennis courts, a golf course, and mud baths. The American soldiers ate in the formal dining rooms and watched movies every night, but otherwise the work was so relentless they had little time to enjoy the hotel's other facilities.[24]

In the autumn of 1942 the G–2 directed the language school to send two Japanese interpreters. Because the Western Defense Command would not allow any persons of Japanese ancestry, even Nisei soldiers, into the region, the school sent two Caucasian linguists in December and two more the following March. One of these, T.Sgt. Dempster P. Dirks, had grown up in Southern California and had many Nisei friends. "Being of German heritage," he later wrote, "my family experienced prejudice during World War I—but considerably less probably than that

---

Army, 1776–1945 (Washington, D.C.: Government Printing Office, 1955); S. P. MacKenzie, "The Treatment of Prisoners of War in World War II," *Journal of Social History* 66, no. 3 (September 1994): 487–520; Ulrich Straus, *The Anguish of Surrender: Japanese POWs of World War II* (Seattle: University of Washington Press, 2003).

[23] Kazuo Sakamaki, *I Attacked Pearl Harbor*, trans. Toru Matsumoto (New York: Young Men's Christian Association Press, 1949). *Sakamaki*'s memoir is a rare first-person narrative in English by a Japanese prisoner of war.

[24] Lt. Col. Thomas C. Van Cleve, "Report on the Activities of Two Agencies of the CPM Branch, MIS, G–2, WDGS, the Interrogation Section, Fort Hunt, Virginia, Tracy, California, and the MIS-X Section, Fort Hunt, Virginia, 1 Aug 42–1 Aug 45," pp. 72–76, Unpubl Ms, n.d., copy in Combined Arms Research Library, Ft. Leavenworth, Kans.; MID History, pp. 99–107; "Office of Naval Intelligence," pp. 868–73; "Secret Center at Byron Hot Springs for Quizzing Japs, Germans Told," *Stockton Record*, 10 Jul 47; Captured Personnel and Materiel Branch-Misc-y, P.W. Camp Tracy, P.O. Box 651, RG 165, NARA, cited in Krammer, "Japanese Prisoners of War in America"; David W. Swift, *Ninety Li a Day*, ed. David W. Swift, Jr., Social Life Monographs, vol. 69 (Taipei: Chinese Association for Folklore, 1975), p. 293.

shown *Nikkei* [Japanese Americans] during World War II." After college he had traveled around the Far East working odd jobs such as playing the Wurlitzer organ in a Tokyo department store. Along the way he had picked up some of the Japanese-language. He had been hoping to go to officer candidate school when selected in 1941 for the language school at Crissy Field. "Don't worry," the assistant commandant told him, "because when you finish here, you'll be at least a captain— probably a major." Byron Hot Springs was his first assignment after graduation. "It was an interesting routine at the 'hotel,'" he recalled, with "twenty-four hour auditory surveillance of our 'guests.' When we weren't listening to the guests, we were monitoring *Dōmei* News."[25]

In April 1943 the War Department directed the Western Defense Command to allow Nisei soldiers to travel into and through the exclusion zone.[26] MISLS at once sent five Nisei to Byron Hot Springs, where they interrogated up to 175 prisoners each month. "It was touch-and-go in human relationships," recalled Ben I. Yamamoto, "and the day and night strain of interrogating people, then spending many hours reporting what they'd said, then repeating the process over and over again finally got to me." After a year at Byron Hot Springs, Yamamoto requested an overseas assignment.[27] Eventually, the Nisei were allowed to visit San Francisco on pass. At first they stayed in a small hotel in Chinatown, escorted by a husky Caucasian military policeman to forestall any incidents. One evening some of the Nisei were relaxing in a cocktail lounge when a Caucasian approached and bought them a round of drinks. "You're not fooling me," he said. "I had some good Japanese friends." There were no incidents.[28]

The number of Japanese prisoners of war held in the United States rose gradually; by December 1944 it had reached 2,629. The language school sent twenty-five

---

[25] Dempster Dirks, "Autobiography," in *MIS Club of Southern California Newsletter*, 1992; Stanley L. Falk and Warren M. Tsuneishi, eds., *MIS in the War against Japan* (Washington, D.C.: Japanese American Veterans Association, 1995), pp. 16–18, 95–96. Dirks remained a sergeant for the rest of the war.

[26] On 15 April 1943, General Marshall personally ordered the policy change to allow 2,700 Nisei volunteers to transit California from Hawaii en route to Camp Shelby, Mississippi, to form the 442d RCT. The War Department (WD) General Staff compiled a summary of DeWitt's resistance on this issue: "Dossier on General John L. DeWitt, August 22, 1942–April 29, 1943," in *American Concentration Camps: A Documentary History of the Relocation and Incarceration of Japanese Americans, 1941–1945*, ed. Roger Daniels, 10 vols. (New York: Garland, 1989), vol. 7.

[27] Yamamoto, in Oguro, *Sempai Gumi*, pp. 67–69; *Japanese Eyes, American Heart: Personal Reflections of Hawaii's World War II Nisei Soldiers* (Honolulu: Tendai Educational Foundation, 1998), pp. 178–79; Yamamoto, in Harrington Papers; Harrington, *Yankee Samurai*, p. 277; Roy T. Terada, in "Rocky Mountain MIS Veterans Club Autobiographies," pp. 62–63, Unpubl Ms, ed. Kent T. Yoritomo, [1989], author's files (this and similar biographies hereafter cited as Rocky Mountain Bios); Roy T. Terada, Biography, Military Intelligence Service Club of Northern California (this and similar biographies hereafter cited as MISNorCal Bios). Yamamoto was reassigned overseas and served with the Marine Corps on Iwo Jima.

[28] Ben I. Yamamoto, in Oguro, *Sempai Gumi*, pp. 67–77 (quote on p. 69). Terada recalls that Nisei soldiers in San Francisco on pass were "restricted to designated hotels and private residences." Yoritomo, Rocky Mountain Bio, p. 63.

other Nisei to Byron Hot Springs for longer or shorter periods. In 1944 alone they interrogated 1,077 Japanese prisoners confined there, sometimes searching for specific pieces of information. For example, in March 1945 Army Ground Forces sent a list of twenty-one questions for interrogators to ask "in connection with Intelligence Exploitation of the Philippines."[29]

On occasion, special prisoners were brought to Byron Hot Springs immediately after capture. In December 1944 American soldiers captured a Japanese soldier on Leyte who was familiar with the firebomb balloons the Japanese had just begun launching against the Pacific Northwest. Sgt. Kay I. Kitagawa escorted him to Byron Hot Springs for a detailed debriefing. Before the war Kitagawa had been a student at nearby Stanford University.[30]

Sometimes the Japanese prisoners arrived in large groups. For example, in March 1944 Haruo Sazaki escorted a group of 200 Japanese prisoners from New Caledonia to San Francisco. The Army held the growing numbers of Japanese prisoners of war at Camp Clarinda, Iowa; Fort Custer, Michigan; and Camp McCoy, Wisconsin. Each camp was operated by a military police POW-processing company. MISLS sent almost 100 Nisei to help administer these camps, selecting those who were better interrogators than translators. By August 1945 the number of Japanese prisoners being held in the United States reached 5,413, including 407 on Angel Island; 2,762 at Camp McCoy; and 1,055 at Camp Clarinda. Other Nisei joined military police POW-processing companies being sent overseas.[31]

The morale of the Japanese prisoners was a constant concern. A Japanese Navy commander captured at Midway attempted suicide upon arrival at Angel Island in July 1942. As the war went on and Japan's setbacks became clearer, the morale of the Japanese prisoners sank even lower. The Nisei who helped guard them became increasingly concerned, because the prisoners often stated to their captors that they could never return to Japan and face disgrace. "The Japanese POWs accumulated at the end of this war in the United States will create a problem which the United States must face," wrote T3g. Harold Nishimura, assigned to the 7th Infantry Division on Leyte, to Col. Kai E. Rasmussen in December 1944. "Steps should be taken to prevent them from committing mass suicides and putting them in a mood so that they will return to Japan. I suggest that we should send men with strong characters and an understanding of Japanese psychology to talk to them regularly at all Japanese POW camps, to stress upon them of their useful-

---

[29] Memo, Chief, Captured Personnel and Material Branch, to C.O., P.O. Box 651, Tracy, Calif., sub: Japanese Information Desired by the Army Ground Forces, 6 Mar 45, Security Class Gen Corresp, 1926–1946, Far Eastern Br, Ofc of the Dir of Intel G–2, RG 165, NARA.

[30] Harrington, *Yankee Samurai*, pp. 12, 349; Kay I. Kitagawa, in Harrington Papers; Kay I. Kitagawa Papers, Hoover Institution Archives.

[31] Harrington, *Yankee Samurai*, pp. 145, 160; "Nisei Interpreter [Cpl. Yukio Kajiyama] at PW Camp [Camp Clarinda]," *Pacific Citizen*, 14 Apr 45. Haruo Sazaki had an unusual career for a Nisei soldier. Drafted in California before Pearl Harbor, he was transferred to the Midwest. In 1943 he was assigned to a military police POW-processing company at Fort Custer and deployed with his unit to the South Pacific. Only after he returned in March 1944 as escort for this POW shipment was he enrolled in MISLS. Sazaki, in Harrington Papers.

ness to their country after the war." Similarly, *Lieutenant Sakamaki*, the Japanese submarine commander, visited Japanese POW camps to lecture his fellow prisoners not to kill themselves. By serving as interrogators and camp staff, these Nisei served the war effort and humanitarian ends as well.[32]

Psychological Warfare

America's first strategic propaganda broadcast to the Japanese people was sent from a shortwave radio transmitter in San Francisco on 10 February 1942. The broadcast, "Japan against Japan," was sponsored by the Coordinator of Information under William J. Donovan and was written and delivered by Yasuo Kuniyoshi, a Japan-born artist who had lived and worked in New York since 1910 and had volunteered his services to the fight against Japanese imperialism. He later made posters for the Office of War Information (OWI).[33] Meanwhile, on Bataan, tactical psychological warfare was being employed by two Nisei, Sgt. Richard M. Sakakida and Sgt. Arthur S. Komori. They wrote surrender appeals by hand and inserted them in short pipes, then used a crude slingshot to deliver their messages to attacking Japanese soldiers.[34]

These early psychological warfare efforts paid few dividends at first. There was no evidence that anyone actually received Kuniyoshi's broadcast. On Bataan, Sakakida recalled, the Japanese soldiers replied with more shells. But Kuniyoshi's efforts were the humble beginnings of what would grow into a major effort to influence Japanese soldiers, civilians, and government leaders. As the war progressed, the military services and other agencies gradually increased their efforts to persuade. Field commanders used portable loudspeakers and dropped leaflets from aircraft (the slingshot method was not repeated) to deliver tactical psychological warfare messages. The MIS Nisei, often paired with prisoners of war, played an important role in tactical efforts. At the national level, the military services and other government agencies developed a program of strategic psychological warfare they hoped would undercut Japanese morale and thus shorten the war. They learned that individuals were needed who could read, write, and speak Japanese

---

[32] James W. Hamilton and William J. Bolce, Jr., *Gateway to Victory* (Stanford, Calif.: Stanford University Press, 1946), pp. 145–56; Ltr, T3g. Harold Nishimura to Col. Kai Rasmussen, 15 December 1944, Trng Grp, Ofc of the Dir of Intel G–2, RG 165, NARA; Sakamaki, *I Attacked Pearl Harbor*, pp. 86–106; Krammer, "Japanese Prisoners of War in America," p. 87.

[33] Larry Tajiri, "Nisei USA," *Pacific Citizen*, 9 Jul 42; Japanese American Citizens League, "They Work for Victory," Unpubl Ms, 1945, JACL, San Francisco, Calif; "Kuniyoshi, Yasuo," in *Encyclopedia of Japanese American History*, rev. ed. (New York: Facts on File, 2001); "Kuniyoshi, Yasuo," *Dictionary of American Biography, Supplement 5: 1951–1955* (New York: C. Scribner's Sons, 1977).

[34] Harrington, *Yankee Samurai*, p. 66; Diane L. Hamm, *Military Intelligence: Its Heroes and Legends* (Arlington Hall Station, Va.: U.S. Army Intelligence and Security Command, 1987), p. 35; Richard Sakakida and Wayne S. Kiyosaki, *A Spy in Their Midst: The World War II Struggle of a Japanese American Hero* (Lanham, Md.: Madison Books, 1995), pp. 85–86.

convincingly. They often used Issei and Japanese prisoners of war as native speakers, but MIS Nisei often helped supervised the work.[35]

MIS Nisei played a much smaller role in strategic psychological warfare. When the Western Defense Command ordered the removal of all individuals of Japanese ancestry from the West Coast, the Coordinator of Information already had six Nisei employees in its San Francisco office. Donovan appealed to the secretary of war to let them remain, but the War Department refused. Assistant Secretary of War John J. McCloy reminded Donovan that the War Department was removing its own Japanese-language school from the Presidio of San Francisco. The Western Defense Command felt "that language school teachers and Japanese language broadcast translators," according to McCloy, "can function as effectively behind the coastal frontier as they do in San Francisco or elsewhere along the coast."[36]

In June 1942 OWI took over responsibility for strategic propaganda from Donovan and continued to use civilian Nisei to make radio broadcasts to Japan from the United States. China scholar Owen Lattimore became head of the Overseas Operations Branch, and George Taylor became chief of the Pacific Division. According to OWI official Archibald MacLeish, the agency could only find three white Americans other than the Nisei "with full command of the language." OWI did find some Korean immigrants who spoke Japanese and were glad to assist in the fight against Japan.[37] The San Francisco office continued to broadcast, even without its Nisei employees. Claude Buss, the Foreign Service officer whom the Japanese interned in Manila and later repatriated, headed the office. By the spring of 1944 OWI was broadcasting news and commentary in Japanese and twenty-three other Asia-Pacific languages using eleven powerful transmitters along the West Coast. Radio programs were written in San Francisco and translated into Japanese in Denver by a team of twenty-one Nisei under Takehiko Yoshihashi. After the Western Defense Command finally allowed persons of Japanese ancestry to return to the West Coast, OWI posted Nisei employees to San Francisco and

[35] Allison B. Gilmore, *You Can't Fight Tanks with Bayonets: Psychological Warfare against the Japanese Army in the Southwest Pacific* (Lincoln: University of Nebraska Press, 1998); Clayton D. Laurie, "The Ultimate Dilemma of Psychological Warfare in the Pacific: Enemies Who Don't Surrender and GIs Who Don't Take Prisoners," in *The U.S. Army and World War II: Selected Papers from the Army's Commemorative Conferences*, ed. Judith L. Bellafaire, U.S. Army in World War II (Washington, D.C.: U.S. Army Center of Military History, 1998), pp. 383–403; Stanley Sandler, *Cease Resistance, It's Good for You: A History of U.S. Army Combat Psychological Operations* (Fort Bragg, N.C.: U.S. Army Special Operations Command, 1996), pp. 164–231; Eleanor A. Sparagana, "The Conduct and Consequences of Psychological Warfare: American Psychological Warfare Operations in the War against Japan, 1941–1945," Ph.D. Diss., Brandeis University, 1990.

[36] Ltr, McCloy to Donovan, 14 May 1942, reprinted in Daniels, *American Concentration Camps*, vol. 5.

[37] Allan M. Winkler, *The Politics of Propaganda: The Office of War Information, 1942–1945* (New Haven, Conn.: Yale University Press, 1978); Francis S. Wickware, "The Japanese Language," *Life* (7 September 1942).

Portland in February 1945. By the spring of 1945 OWI employed twenty-one Nisei civilians who broadcast nine hours per day from San Francisco.[38]

In its attempt to recruit Nisei employees, OWI sometimes clashed with the War Department G–2, which fiercely protected its own Nisei linguists. However, the G–2 allowed its language school to give OWI occasional help with translation, research, and broadcasting.[39] When OWI sent psychological warfare teams to the China-Burma-India Theater in early 1944, MIS agreed to provide some Nisei language teams and later provided teams for the Philippines. For these teams, the language school selected Nisei students with backgrounds in newspapers, broadcasting, and commercial art, such as Chris Ishii, who had worked at Disney as a cartoonist and had designed the MISLS emblem. The school also selected Nisei with leftist political backgrounds, such as Koji Ariyoshi and Karl G. Yoneda. The school commandant, Colonel Rasmussen, told Yoneda that the Army was aware of his Communist affiliations, such as his having been editor of the official organ of the Japanese section of the American Communist Party, but that "his services were needed and appreciated." Yoneda was soon on his way to Burma.[40]

In contrast, OWI was not allowed to operate freely in the Central or Southwest Pacific. In July 1944 the OWI director accompanied President Roosevelt to Hawaii and requested access personally from Admiral Nimitz and General MacArthur. Soon after, OWI was able to establish a small office in Hawaii for the Pacific Ocean Areas but was never allowed into the Southwest Pacific Area.[41]

That summer OWI hired a Nisei in Hawaii, Paul Toda, who had been born in Hawaii but had spent many years growing up and attending school in Japan. He was deeply committed to the struggle against Japanese militarism. When the Army called for Nisei volunteers in January 1943, he and his two brothers answered. His brothers were accepted, but he was rejected on physical grounds. When OWI began hiring, he joined right away. Other Hawaii Nisei soon joined the OWI in Honolulu.[42]

---

[38] "War and Words—S.F. Office," *S.F. News*, 13 Apr 44, p. 11; "Civilian Nisei Specialists Aid Psychological War in Pacific," *Pacific Citizen*, 10 Feb 45; "Nisei Aid Psychological Warfare in Pacific," *Pacific Citizen*, 7 Apr 45; "OWI-MG [Military Government] Cooperation Is Told: Claude Buss, Famed Diplomat, Speaks at CASA," *CASALOG*, 16 May 45, p. 1; JACL, "They Work for Victory"; John F. Shelley, Speech, 11 Jun 63, *Congressional Record*, copy in author's files. Takehiko Yoshihashi also coauthored with Serge Elisséeff and Edwin O. Reischauer, *Elementary Japanese for College Students* (Cambridge, Mass.: Harvard University Press, 1941).

[39] Memo, MISLS, 29 Apr 43, Trng Grp, Ofc of the Dir of Intel G–2, RG 165, NARA.

[40] Harrington, *Yankee Samurai*, pp. 105–06, 142; Karl G. Yoneda, *Ganbatte: Sixty-Year Struggle of a Kibei Worker* (Los Angeles: Asian American Studies Center, University of California at Los Angeles, 1983); Hugh Deane, ed., *Remembering Koji Ariyoshi: An American GI in Yenan* (Los Angeles: U.S.-China Peoples Friendship Association, 1978); Koji Ariyoshi, *From Kona to Yenan: The Political Memoirs of Koji Ariyoshi*, ed. Alice M. Beechert and Edward D. Beechert (Honolulu: University of Hawaii Press, 2000).

[41] Zacharias, *Secret Missions*, p. 328.

[42] Bradford Smith, *Americans from Japan* (Philadelphia: J. B. Lippincott, 1948), p. 321.

In Washington, OWI had already recruited a Harvard psychiatrist, Dr. Alexander H. Leighton, to head the Foreign Morale Analysis Division. Leighton had spent more than a year in the Poston, Arizona, camp studying how persons of Japanese ancestry responded to the stress of incarceration.[43] OWI also sponsored other research into Japanese psychology. In June 1944 OWI recruited Ruth Benedict to prepare a study of the "Japanese mind." The pioneering cultural anthropologist used Issei as her research subjects for the study, which she published at war's end as *The Chrysanthemum and the Sword*. Similar studies were commissioned by other organizations such as the Smithsonian Institution, which published a booklet by anthropologist John Embree in January 1943.[44] Book publishers released many old and new titles, such as a revised edition of a cultural history by a leading Western scholar, Sir George Sansom.[45]

The War Department played a coordinating role in strategic psychological warfare against Japan. In October 1942 the G–2 established the Psychological Warfare Branch, which designed and distributed several Japanese-language leaflets; but the G–2 abolished the branch a few months later. After that, the G–2 worked with the Psychological Warfare Committee of the Joint Chiefs of Staff. In November 1943 the G–2 established the Propaganda Branch, but this section did not produce its own leaflets or radio broadcasts. Instead, it coordinated with the Navy, State, Joint Chiefs of Staff, and other agencies. OWI teams produced tactical materials in the field. The Office of Naval Intelligence had its own psychological warfare staff, OP–16–W, but this office concentrated on the German Navy, not the Japanese.[46]

The Office of Strategic Services (OSS) Morale Operations Branch established a Far Eastern Section in 1943 under Maj. Herbert S. Little, a Seattle lawyer who had lived in the Far East before the war. He visited the camps and in less than a year had recruited about fifty-five men. Two-thirds of the recruits were Issei, and most of the Nisei had lived in Japan, so they had excellent native-speaker language proficiency. Because the Army already had been scouring the camps for skilled Japanese-speakers, the OSS found mostly men who were over age or otherwise

[43] Alexander H. Leighton, *The Governing of Men: General Principles and Recommendations Based on Experience at a Japanese Relocation Camp* (Princeton, N.J.: Princeton University Press, 1945); Brian Masaru Hayashi, *Democratizing the Enemy: The Japanese American Internment* (Princeton: Princeton University Press, 2004), p. 24.

[44] Ruth Benedict, *The Chrysanthemum and the Sword: Patterns of Japanese Culture* (New York: Houghton Mifflin, 1946); Peter T. Suzuki, "Ruth Benedict, Robert Hashima and *The Chrysanthemum and the Sword*," *Research: Contributions to Interdisciplinary Anthropology* 3 (1985): 55–69; John Embree, *The Japanese*, Smithsonian Institution War Background Studies no. 7 (Washington, D.C.: Smithsonian Institution, 1943). Before the war, Embree had written the first study of Japanese life by a Western anthropologist. John Embree, *Suye Mura: A Japanese Village* (Chicago: University of Chicago Press, 1939). For the wartime role of social scientists and the study of the Japanese national character, see Alexander H. Leighton, *Human Relations in a Changing World* (New York: E. P. Dutton & Co., 1949); Dower, *War without Mercy*, pp. 118–46.

[45] George Sansom, *A Short Cultural History of Japan*, rev. ed. (New York: Appleton-Century, 1943).

[46] MID History, pp. 305–07; Sandler, *Cease Resistance*, pp. 45–55; Zacharias, *Secret Missions*, pp. 302–16.

unsuited for military service. Because the OSS was more willing than the War Department to enlist men with left-wing political backgrounds, at least 5 had been Communist Party members before the war, 10 or more had been active members of front organizations, and at least 6 had been union organizers.[47] These Issei and Nisei began producing print propaganda and simulated Japanese materials in 1944 from offices in New York City and Washington, D.C.; but they soon began to lobby to be deployed to the Far East. In April 1945 some of them moved to San Francisco, where they produced radio programs that were recorded on disks and flown to Saipan for broadcast to Japan.

The War Department G–2 was usually successful in resisting OSS requests for its Nisei linguists already in uniform, but in January 1944 MISLS did assign four recent graduates to OSS headquarters in Washington. When MISLS recruited fifty Nisei women for language training, the OSS diverted four to work in Washington. Unable to obtain enough Issei and Nisei for its propaganda work, the OSS contracted with the University of Pennsylvania in January 1945 for a six-month course in Japanese-language and area studies for Caucasian personnel.[48]

The OSS Research and Analysis Section also used Issei and Nisei along with several Caucasian experts on Japan. While not as extensive as the OSS Research and Analysis efforts directed toward Central Europe, this branch nevertheless produced some impressive results, foremost among them a series of research reports and area handbooks on Japan. This section produced 8 reports on Japan in 1942, 8 in 1943, about 40 in 1944, and many more in 1945.[49]

The U.S. government also listened to Japanese radio broadcasts. In 1941 the Federal Communications Commission established the Foreign Broadcast Intelligence Service (FBIS), which monitored radio from foreign countries, including the *Dōmei* shortwave news broadcasts that the Japanese government sent to overseas

---

[47] Howard Schonberger, "Dilemmas of Loyalty: Japanese Americans and the Psychological Warfare Campaigns of the Office of Strategic Services, 1943–45," *Amerasia Journal* 16, no. 1 (1990): 21–38; Anthony C. Brown, ed., *The Secret War Report of the OSS* (New York: Berkley Publishing, 1976), pp. 106–10; Simon Morioka, "Japanese Americans in the Service of their Country," Master of Arts Diss., Selwyn College, University of Cambridge, 1998, pp. 48–65. Among them was Issei artist Jun Atsushi Iwamatsu (pen name Taro Yashima). "Iwamatsu, Jun Atsushi," in *Encyclopedia of Japanese American History*; Leonard Rifas, "Taro Yashima: Pictures and Propaganda," *Nikkei Heritage* (Spring 2002): 15.

[48] Morioka, "Japanese Americans in the Service of their Country," pp. 52–54; Mattie E. Treadwell, *The Women's Army Corps*, U.S. Army in World War II (Washington, D.C.: Office of the Chief of Military History, 1954), p. 589; Brown, *Secret War Report*, p. 132.

[49] Army Service Forces Manual M–354, *Civil Affairs Handbook: Japan*, 8 vols. (Washington, D.C.: Army Service Forces, 1944–1945). See also *A Guide to O.S.S./State Department Intelligence and Research Reports, I, Japan and Its Occupied Territories During World War II* (Washington, D.C.: University Publications of America, 1977). Selected reports are available in Makoto Iokibe, ed., "The Occupation of Japan: U.S. Planning Documents, 1942–1945," Microfiche, Congressional Information Service, 1987, Bethesda, Md. See also Peter T. Suzuki, "Analyses of Japanese Films in Wartime Washington," *Asian Profile* 23, no. 5 (1995): 371–80.

Japanese.[50] These were translated into English and distributed to the top levels of the American government. FBIS senior staff included Dr. Chitoshi Yanaga from the University of California, Satoru Sugimura from Hawaii, and several Caucasians who had lived in Japan for extended periods. FBIS opened an office in Portland, Oregon, in 1941 and an office in San Francisco in 1942. However, most FBIS employees of Japanese ancestry stayed in Denver, where they monitored Japanese government broadcasts to its own people about the progress of the war. During 1944 a few Nisei were allowed to work for FBIS in Hawaii and Portland.[51] By the end of the war over fifty Nisei worked in the Portland office alone.

As American forces advanced in the Pacific, psychological warfare agencies moved closer to Japan to broadcast from locations such as Saipan, Guam, Manila, and mainland China. OSS Morale Operations had long hoped to operate closer to Japan. On 1 June 1945, it sent half its Issei and Nisei staff, twenty-seven in all, by troopship to India. They arrived outside Calcutta on 9 July. Five proceeded to Kunming, China, and the others were waiting for air transport when the war ended.[52]

After the capture of Saipan in July 1944, the Honolulu OWI set up a forward detachment there, including civilian Nisei Paul Toda, who volunteered for the assignment: "On Saipan he made himself invaluable as an interpreter in dealing with Japanese prisoners of war, as translator, as odd job man," his supervisor later wrote. "Nothing was too arduous or too menial for him."[53]

In the Philippines, in February 1945 MacArthur allowed OWI to begin propaganda broadcasts from Manila. Brig. Gen. Bonner F. Fellers, chief of the Southwest Pacific Area Psychological Warfare Board, called a conference to develop a coordinated plan for psychological warfare against Japan. Beginning in March 1945, the Psychological Warfare Board prepared and disseminated a newsletter, the *Rakkasan [Parachute] News*, for Japanese soldiers and the home islands. This weekly publication, written by Allied Translator and Interpreter Section (ATIS) Nisei with the help of Japanese prisoners of war, was widely read by Japanese troops in the final months of the war.[54]

In March 1945 Fellers asked ATIS for two Nisei to make radio broadcasts directly to the Japanese home islands. The ATIS executive officer assembled the Nisei, explained that they were looking for individuals with broadcast experience, and asked for volunteers. Much to his consternation, no one stepped forward. Col.

---

[50] The Foreign Broadcast Monitoring Service was renamed the Foreign Broadcast Intelligence Service in July 1942 and the Foreign Broadcast Information Service in 1946. Stephen Greene, "Nisei: Ears for the Government," *Common Ground* 7 (Autumn 1946): 17–20; Stephen C. Mercado, "FBIS against the Axis, 1941–1945," *Studies in Intelligence* (Fall/Winter 2001). MISLS also monitored Japanese shortwave radio for training purposes.

[51] Japanese American Citizens League, "They Work for Victory."

[52] Schonberger, "Dilemmas of Loyalty."

[53] Smith, *Americans from Japan*, p. 321.

[54] Sandler, *Cease Resistance*, pp. 208–10; Gilmore, *You Can't Fight Tanks with Bayonets*, pp. 109–11, 142, 157–58, 170–72.

Students at Fort Snelling monitor Japanese shortwave news broadcasts as part of their training.

Sidney F. Mashbir then spoke to the Nisei himself: "This is an extremely danger-ous thing to ask any Nisei to do. . . . I know that should your names become known dire vengeance will be wreaked upon your relatives in Japan. Not only that, but you will be the first Nisei to arrive in Manila and the Filipino guerrillas may mis-take you for Japanese in disguise and kill you. Therefore this job calls not only for ability and intelligence but nerve." Still no one volunteered. Lt. Gary Tsuneo Kadani finally explained that the Nisei were hesitant only "because none of us feels himself worthy or competent to carry out so important a mission, and none is so boastful or immodest as to believe that he is worthy of such a job." Instead Kadani selected ten candidates, of whom two were chosen: S.Sgt. Clifford P. Konno and Sgt. John Masuda. They became the first Nisei soldiers to enter Manila, where according to Mashbir "their services were outstanding." The Psychological War-fare Board soon requested additional Nisei, so in June 1945 MISLS sent M.Sgt. Masao Harold Onishi directly from Minnesota to Manila. Before the war, Onishi had worked as a Japanese-language announcer for KGMB in Hawaii.[55]

---

[55] Sidney F. Mashbir, *I Was an American Spy* (New York: Vantage, 1953), pp. 244–46; "Masao 'Harold' Onishi," *Hawaii Herald*, 2 Jul 93, pp. A–16 to A–17; *Yaban Gogai*, Sep–Oct 45, p. 5.

In February 1945 Captain Zacharias proposed a direct radio appeal to Japanese Army and Navy commanders. In early March the Office of Naval Intelligence brought him back to Washington, where he was assigned to the Psychological Warfare Branch (OP–16–W). There, he drew up a strategic psychological operations plan and in May 1945 began a series of broadcasts to Japan's top leadership, calling himself "an official spokesman."[56]

Other influential Americans urged the Roosevelt administration to use psychological warfare in hopes of averting a costly invasion of Japan. In April 1945 the chairman of the Senate Armed Services Committee, Senator Elbert D. Thomas (D-Utah), wrote to the president's chief of staff, Admiral William D. Leahy, urging such a campaign. Thomas spoke with authority, having served as a missionary in Japan and being the only member of the House or Senate who could read and speak the Japanese language. Leahy referred the senator to Captain Zacharias, whose plans were already well under way.[57]

ATIS began its own broadcasts to Japan on 19 July 1945, when Colonel Mashbir addressed a series of personal broadcasts directly to the Japanese people using OWI's facilities in Manila.[58] Japan was thus receiving radio broadcasts from several American agencies: OSS Morale Operations, the Office of War Information, the Office of Naval Intelligence (under Captain Zacharias), and ATIS (under Colonel Mashbir). Some of these agencies used social scientists to study the Japanese national character in search of exploitable vulnerabilities, assisted by a few civilian Issei and Nisei, but the Nisei role was generally circumscribed. Army field commanders used MIS Nisei in tactical psychological warfare. However, this pool of knowledge and talent was scarcely tapped. In any event, it is unclear whether the psychological warfare campaign against Japan had much effect.

Signals Intelligence

The Army and Navy developed impressive capabilities, codenamed MAGIC, one of the most closely held secrets of the war, to intercept Japanese radio communications, including Japanese diplomatic message traffic. The U.S. Army Signal Intelligence Service (SIS) located its code-breaking activities at Arlington Hall on

---

[56] Zacharias, *Secret Missions*, pp. 319–89, 399–424; Ellis M. Zacharias, "Eighteen Words That Bagged Japan," *The Saturday Evening Post* (17 November 1945): 17, 117–20; Ellis M. Zacharias, "How We Bungled the Japanese Surrender," *Look* (6 June 1950): 12–21. See also Ladislas Farago, *Burn after Reading* (New York: Pinnacle Books, 1961), and the review of Zacharias' book by his former colleague, Stephan T. Possony, in *Infantry Journal* (March 1947): 83–86. For later assessments, see Gar Alperovitz, *The Decision To Use the Atomic Bomb and the Architecture of an American Myth* (New York: Knopf, 1995), pp. 40–41, 394–404; William Craig, *The Fall of Japan* (New York: Dial Press, 1967), pp. 37–40; Richard B. Frank, *Downfall: The End of the Imperial Japanese Empire* (New York: Random House, 1999), pp. 220–21, 231–32; Winkler, *Politics of Propaganda*, pp. 136–48.

[57] *Dictionary of American Biography, Supplement Five, 1951–1955* (New York: Charles Scribner's Sons, 1977); Zacharias, *Secret Missions*, pp. 346–47.

[58] Mashbir, *I Was an American Spy*, pp. 281–82, 337–46, 354–68.

the outskirts of Washington, D.C., with an intercept station and technical training school at Vint Hill Farms near Warrenton, Virginia.[59] The Office of Naval Intelligence's counterpart to the SIS, OP–20–G, was at the Mount Vernon Academy in Washington, D.C.[60] To translate intercepted Japanese material, both organizations used language officers and Caucasian civilians such as Harold E. Zaugg, repatriated from Japan in 1942, and Virginia Aderholdt, a former teacher in Japan.[61] "Translation was the bottleneck of the MAGIC production line," historian David Kahn has written of the early years of the war. "Interpreters of Japanese were even scarcer than expert cryptanalysts. Security precluded employing Nisei or any but the most trustworthy Americans."[62]

Japanese radio messages, when decrypted, came in rōmaji syllables, rather than kanji characters. Rōmaji was easier to translate than kanji in some ways. In other ways it was more difficult, because one rōmaji syllable could refer to more than one Japanese word. Context would determine a word's intended meaning. As Commander McCollum explained: "The so-called translator in this type of stuff almost has to be a cryptographer himself. You understand that these things come out in the form of syllables, and it is how you group your syllables that you make your words. There is no punctuation. Now without the Chinese ideograph [kanji] to read from, it is most difficult to group these things together. That is, any two sounds grouped together to make a word may mean a variety of things."[63]

The problem of finding translators "was most acute in the case of Japanese, both because a knowledge of Japanese is rare in this country and because the volume of material to be translated was so great," SIS reported. "The only recourse was to train personnel from the very beginning."[64] SIS recruited the director of Japanese studies at Harvard University, Edwin O. Reischauer, in 1943 to find and train more Japanese translators. Assistant Secretary of War McCloy personally contacted the president of Harvard University to obtain Reischauer's services. Reischauer set up a Japanese-language school at Arlington Hall that eventually

---

[59] Carl Boyd, *Hitler's Japanese Confidant: General Oshima Hiroshi and Magic Intelligence, 1941–1945* (Lawrence: University Press of Kansas, 1993); Gilbert and Finnegan, *U.S. Army Signals Intelligence in World War II*; David Kahn, *The Codebreakers* (New York: Signet, 1973); Ronald Lewin, *The American Magic: Codes, Ciphers, and the Defeat of Japan* (New York: Farrar Straus Giroux, 1982); Donal J. Sexton, Jr., comp., *Signals Intelligence in World War II: A Research Guide* (Westport, Conn.: Greenwood Press, 1996); Ronald H. Spector, ed., *Listening to the Enemy: Key Documents on the Role of Communications Intelligence in the War with Japan* (Wilmington, Del.: Scholarly Resources Inc., 1988).

[60] W. J. Holmes, *Double-Edged Secrets: U.S. Naval Intelligence Operations in the Pacific during World War II* (Annapolis, Md.: Naval Institute Press, 1979); Edwin T. Layton, *"And I Was There": Pearl Harbor and Midway—Breaking the Secrets* (New York: William Morrow, 1985); Prados, *Combined Fleet Decoded*; Edward Van Der Rhoer, *Deadly Magic: A Personal Account of Communications Intelligence in World War II in the Pacific* (New York: Charles Scribner's Sons, 1978).

[61] Zaugg, *Sensei*, pp. 109, 115.

[62] Kahn, *The Codebreakers*, p. 27.

[63] Quote from Ibid.

[64] Quote from Gilbert and Finnegan, *U.S. Army Signals Intelligence in World War II*, p. 89.

trained 428 Caucasians. He received a direct commission to major in September 1943 and worked for the rest of the war as the liaison officer between SIS Special Branch and Arlington Hall.[65]

In the early years the available number of translators proved adequate to the task. However, when the volume of intercepted messages grew in 1944, they became overwhelmed. In January 1944 Australian soldiers discovered a set of Japanese codebooks on New Guinea that were photographed and sent to Arlington Hall. In the month before the Australians found the codebooks, Arlington Hall decrypted fewer than 2,000 Japanese Army messages. Two months later SIS decrypted more than 36,000. Soon 200,000 Japanese messages were waiting to be decrypted and translated.[66] The crisis apparently overcame previous SIS concerns about using Nisei for such sensitive work. On 27 January 1944, the SIS requested twenty-five Nisei from MISLS. School officials assembled a team under M.Sgt. Joe Yuzuru Masuda, a Kibei graduate of Crissy Field and an enlisted instructor. Only when their train left Minneapolis did the Nisei learn they were destined not for the Pacific, but for "some signal outfit in Virginia." Upon arrival at Vint Hill Farms Station, they were assigned to Detachment B–1–V, 2d Signal Service Battalion. At first their new commander, Maj. Gordon T. Fish, acted gruffly, as if he "detested being in command of a bunch of 'Japs.'" The Nisei learned that his eldest son had died while a prisoner of the Japanese in the Philippines. For his part, the major soon learned that the Nisei were Americans, not "Japs."[67] The Nisei got an even frostier reception from security officers, who insisted that any Nisei who had ever visited Japan or had relatives living there could not stay at Vint Hill Farms. Fourteen Nisei, including Sergeant Masuda, returned to Camp Savage. The school sent replacements under M.Sgt. Morio Nishita, another Crissy Field graduate and enlisted instructor. Despite the rocky start, Major Fish came to respect the Nisei, one of whom remembered him as "a gentleman, scholar, and a soldier who truly loved his men." In the spring of 1945 he sent two Nisei to the Signal Corps officer candidate school at Fort Monmouth, New Jersey.[68]

In June 1944 the school sent thirty more Nisei to Vint Hill. Altogether fifty Nisei were crammed into a poorly ventilated and -lighted building where they struggled with thousands of intercepted messages. The SIS gradually allowed the

---

[65] Edwin O. Reischauer, *My Life between Japan and America* (New York: Harper & Row, 1986), pp. 91–101; Gilbert and Finnegan, *U.S. Army Signals Intelligence in World War II*, pp. 89, 122; David Mead, "The Breaking of the Japanese Army Administrative Code," *Cryptologia* (July 1994): 199. Reischauer went on to a distinguished career after the war and served as ambassador to Japan from 1961 to 1966.

[66] Edward J. Drea, *MacArthur's Ultra: Codebreaking and the War against Japan, 1942–1945* (Lawrence: University Press of Kansas, 1992), p. 93; Gilbert and Finnegan, *U.S. Army Signals Intelligence in World War II*, p. 64.

[67] Ltr, Naomitsu Kitsuwa to Joseph Harrington, n.d. [1978], in Harrington Papers. Major Fish's son was probably Pvt. Robert L. Fish, who died in the Philippines on 20 February 1943.

[68] Harrington, *Yankee Samurai*, pp. 218, 267, 330; Mitsuo Mansho, in Tsukiyama et al., *Secret Valor*, pp. 106–07; Morio Nishita, MISNorCal Bio; Shigeo Shiraishi, in Tsukiyama et al., *Secret Valor*, p. 108.

Edward K. Kawamoto and other Nisei with the U.S. Army Signal Intelligence Service, Vint Hill Farms, Maryland

Nisei to try their hand at cryptanalysis, even though they had no special training for this line of work. The messages were mostly "commercial, industrial, or diplomatic communications," Mitsuo Mansho recalled. One message when translated mentioned a shipment of a mysterious "S X ore." Soon after, a brigadier general visited to compliment their work and singled out a particular message which had been relayed immediately to American submarines on patrol. Mansho later came to suspect that the interdicted shipment had been uranium ore.[69]

For more than a year the Nisei endured cramped and uncomfortable conditions at Vint Hill Farms, and their morale was often low. "Those of us who were unfortunate enough to have been assigned were short-changed by the military," one recalled. "We didn't expect to be pampered. Least the military could have done was to be fair with us."[70] They could see that Vint Hill Farms was clearly a sideshow to the main effort at Arlington Hall, where the Nisei were not allowed. During 1944 MISLS sent sixteen Caucasian officers to work at Arlington Hall, but not one Nisei.

[69] Mansho, in Tsukiyama et al., *Secret Valor*, p. 107. This may have been a reference to the solvent extraction (SX) method of separating uranium.

[70] Ltr, Kitsuwa to Harrington, [1978]. See also Ltr, Tatsuji Machida to Yutaka Munakata, 7 March 1945, requesting reassignment, Harrington Papers.

As the war progressed, other Nisei were assigned to tactical signals intelligence. The Army Air Forces assigned Nisei to its mobile radio squadrons. In January 1945 twenty-four Nisei were assigned to the 3795th Signal Intelligence Detachment, an experimental unit at Fort Monmouth, New Jersey. In July another twenty-four were assigned to the 4029th Signal Intelligence Service Detachment (Type C) at the Eastern Signal Corps Training Center, also at Fort Monmouth.[71] By war's end some 10,000 personnel were working in the Army's signal intelligence effort and 6,000 in the Navy's. Of these, perhaps a hundred were Nisei. Persistent suspicions of the Nisei prohibited their working in signals intelligence in more than a limited capacity.

Pacific Military Intelligence Research Section

Although Nisei were kept out of most signals intelligence work, translating captured documents was considered much less sensitive. The Nisei had proven valuable for translating captured documents near the front lines ever since the earliest campaigns. As Allied forces drew closer to Japan, the flow of captured documents threatened to overwhelm intelligence organizations. By the summer of 1944 the volume of documents being captured could be measured in tons. Field commanders established translation centers in each theater: ATIS in the Southwest Pacific; the Joint Intelligence Center, Pacific Ocean Areas (JICPOA), in the Central Pacific; the Southeast Asia Translator and Interrogation Center (SEATIC) in Southeast Asia; and the Sino Translation and Interrogation Center (SINTIC) in China. Even these could not keep pace. Many captured documents had little or no immediate value to theater commanders. The documents may have been routine or highly technical or may have had value only for strategic planning. Yet until late in the war the War Department had no translation section under its direct control. The small number of Nisei in the War Department G–2 Pacific Order of Battle Section could handle only occasional translation work. In June 1943 Colonel Rasmussen established a Translation Section under Yutaka Munakata using the fluctuating pool of graduates awaiting assignment at the school, but they did translations more for training value than for actual intelligence requirements.[72]

Maj. Gen. Clayton Bissell, who became the War Department G–2 in February 1944, felt that the War Department should have its own translation center. He knew that the Allies had the Military Intelligence Research Section (MIRS) in London, a joint translation center for German-language materials. In August 1944 he asked for Nisei translators to establish a similar center for Japanese-language transla-

---

[71] See Steve Sugano, Rocky Mountain Bio, pp. 57–58; Steve Sugano, MISNorCal Bio.

[72] MISLS, Addenda for: Projects Contemplated at MIS Language School, Savage, Minnesota, during the Period May 1–August 1, 1943, 29 Apr 43, Trng Grp, Ofc of the Dir of Intel G–2, RG 165, NARA; MISLS, "Training History of the Military Intelligence Service Language School," ann. 13, Translation Section, Unpubl Ms, 1946, CMH files; *MISLS Album*, p. 75.

Recent graduates at Fort Snelling worked in the translation pool while waiting for assignment.

tion.[73] On 6 September 1944, Maj. Sidney F. Gronich, who had helped establish MIRS in London, drove up to Camp Ritchie, Maryland, from Washington with five Nisei from the order of battle team to open the Pacific Military Intelligence Research Section (PACMIRS). MISLS sent seven Caucasian officers and twenty-four Nisei, including nine former instructors.[74]

Camp Ritchie was a small National Guard post nestled in the Blue Ridge Mountains two hours from Washington. In the summer of 1942 the War Department G–2 established the Military Intelligence Training Center there. The post provided a secure location where Nisei soldiers would be less conspicuous than in wartime Washington. The Nisei set up in a dilapidated warehouse that until recently had housed Italian prisoners of war. Capt. Lardner W. Moore was placed in charge of the translation work. Many of the Nisei were disappointed with stateside duty in a remote location. Gronich addressed their concerns forthrightly at the first meeting: "A great deal is going to be expected of you. You'll be asked to work far beyond your rank. Some of you certainly deserve commissions, all of

---

[73] MISLS memo, 18 Feb 44; After-Action Report, Pacific Military Intelligence Research Section (PACMIRS), sub: History and Organization of PACMIRS, Camp Ritchie, Maryland, 6 September 1944–14 August 1945; "History and Operation MIRS London and Washington Branches, 1 May 1943–14 July 1945," pp. 175–96, Unpubl Ms, n.d.; MID History.

[74] *Unsung Heroes*, pp. 23–26; Falk and Tsuneishi, *MIS in the War against Japan*, pp. 9–10, 30–31. Intervs, author with S. Phil Ishio, 18 Apr 95; with Arthur M. Kaneko, 25 Aug 95; with Joseph Milanowski, 30 Oct 87; with Yamane, 8 Dec 94. See also Eugene A. Wright Papers, NJAHS.

you higher rankings. I wish I could give you what you deserve. I cannot. I'm in no position to do so. But this isn't going to keep me from asking you to do what I feel each of you is capable of doing." [75]

At first PACMIRS was an extension of the order of battle section in the Pentagon. Several of the first Nisei to arrive from MISLS attended a four-week Pacific Order of Battle course in the Pentagon, where Major Reischauer's lectures on the history of Japan were especially popular. [76] However, General Bissell visited Camp Ritchie in October and issued new guidance: he wanted document translation, not order of battle work. With this revised mission PACMIRS went to work on 14 October.

That autumn intelligence requirements for the war against Japan began to change in significant ways. To support the strategic bombing campaign, the Army Air Forces needed intelligence on Japanese factories, railroads, and ports. The first B–29 raid against Japan was launched in June 1944 from bases in China; when American forces captured the Marianas, the XXI Bomber Command began building up forces there. However, existing intelligence on strategic, economic, and industrial targets was poor. On 1 November 1944, a lone B–29 flew over Tokyo on the first photoreconnaissance mission over the Japanese home islands. [77]

At Camp Ritchie, the Nisei settled down to their work. Sergeant Yamane, who had been in the Army since before Pearl Harbor, took a weekend pass to New York City to be married. When he returned, he found that PACMIRS had received some crates of Japanese documents, marked "no military significance," captured on Saipan several months earlier and sent to the Military Intelligence Training Center for training purposes. When Yamane began going through the crates in early December, one of the first documents he pulled out was a thick mimeographed item, "File of Proceedings of 1944 Liaison Conference of Chiefs of Ordnance Departments." This was the record of a meeting of top Japanese staff officers in May 1944 in Tokyo to review their country's munitions stocks and procurement programs. The document included inventories and statistical tables of all major weapons and munitions. [78] Yamane recognized the document's significance

---

[75] Quote from Pat Nagano, MISNorCal Bio.

[76] MID History, pp. 190–92; Records of the MIS Far East Intel School (Pacific Order of Battle School), RG 165, NARA. Reischauer published his lectures as Edwin O. Reischauer, *Japan: Past and Present* (New York: Knopf, 1946). See preface to Edwin O. Reischauer, *Japan: The Story of a Nation*, 3d ed. (New York: Knopf, 1981); Reischauer, *My Life*, p. 103.

[77] Kreis, *Piercing the Fog*, pp. 335–38, 364–71; U.S. Strategic Bombing Survey, *Summary Report (Pacific War)* (Washington, D.C.: U.S. Strategic Bombing Survey, 1946), pp. 112, 117; Kenneth P. Werrell, *Blankets of Fire: U.S. Bombers over Japan during World War II* (Washington, D.C.: Smithsonian Institution Press, 1996), pp. 102, 128–29.

[78] Interv, author with Yamane, 8 Dec 94; Harrington, *Yankee Samurai*, pp. 234–35; Kazuo E. Yamane, "World War II Experiences, Pentagon-Paris-Berlin," in Oguro, *Sempai Gumi*, pp. 106–13; Loni Ding, prod., *The Color of Honor*, documentary film, Vox Productions, 1987; 100th Infantry Battalion, "Remembrances," Unpubl Brochure, 100th Infantry Battalion 50th Anniversary Celebration, 1942–1992, 1992, pp. 171–72; Tsukiyama et al., *Secret Valor*, pp. 104–05; "Kazuo Yamane's Key Discovery," *Hawaii Herald*, 2 Jul 93, pp. A–19 to A–20.

and showed it to his superiors at once. Colonel Gronich responded by canceling all furloughs and assigning his best Nisei to translate it. Each day a staff car delivered that day's translations directly to the Pentagon. The full translation was published on 7 December 1944 as PACMIRS Special Report No. 1. The PACMIRS Nisei had hit a home run on their first at-bat.[79]

The volume of translation work raised issues of interagency coordination. Which service or agency should set translation priorities? Would PACMIRS give equal priority to documents of interest to the Navy and the Army Air Forces? In December 1944 representatives of the U.S. Army and Navy, British War Office, Australian and Canadian Armies, and the various Allied commands assembled in Washington for a Japanese document conference. After two weeks of discussion, they agreed to establish a new office to coordinate the flow of documents and establish priorities. As a result the Office of Naval Intelligence established the Washington Document Center in February 1945. Under the new procedures, all captured Japanese documents arriving in the United States were first processed by the center, which would review them and assign the translation either to PACMIRS or to the Far Eastern Branch of the Office of Naval Intelligence. The Office of Naval Intelligence borrowed several Nisei from PACMIRS to start its operation.[80]

Over the winter of 1944–1945 a sprinkling of combat veterans, including Caucasian team leaders such as Eugene Wright, John Anderton, and Lachlan Sinclair, was assigned to Camp Ritchie. Others found themselves assigned to PACMIRS by chance. For example, in March 1945 General Joseph W. Stilwell happened to visit Fort Sill, Oklahoma, where he noticed a Chinese American who had served on his staff in Burma. Capt. Won-Loy Chan, a graduate of Stanford University and later of MISLS, had spent twenty-three months in the China-Burma-India Theater as an intelligence officer. Stilwell greeted Chan with characteristic bluntness: "Charlie, what the hell are you doing here?" Chan began to explain, but Stilwell would not listen. "You don't belong here, Charlie," he said. Shortly afterward Chan received orders for PACMIRS, where he became the liaison officer with the center's translation customers.[81] Another returning veteran was Lt. S. Phil Ishio, who came to PACMIRS in June 1945 after two-and-a-half years in the Southwest Pacific.[82] The British and Canadian armies gave PACMIRS some of their best Japanese linguists. Canadian Nisei came to PACMIRS as translators when the Canadian Army began to train a few in 1945.[83] The chief of the translation group was a British officer, Lt.

---

[79] "Proceedings of Conference, Japanese Chiefs of Ordnance, Tokyo, May 1944," PACMIRS Special Rpt no. 1, 7 Dec 44; Willoughby, "The Character of Military Intelligence," pt. 2, pp. 196–97, in Folder 4, Box 3, Willoughby Papers, RG 23–B, MacArthur Memorial, Norfolk, Va. PACMIRS translations and reports can be found in the War Department G–2 Library ("P" File), Security Class Intel Ref Pubs, RG 165, NARA. See also Wright Papers, NJAHS.

[80] "Washington Document Center," pt. 8, in "Office of Naval Intelligence," pp. 894–99. Twenty-three boxes of WDC translations can be found in the records of the Chief of Naval Operations, RG 38, NARA.

[81] Won-Loy Chan, *Burma: The Untold Story* (Novato, Calif.: Presidio Press, 1986), p. 115.

[82] Interv, author with Ishio, 18 Apr 95.

[83] Ito, *We Went to War*, pp. 250–54.

Col. P. Pender-Cudlip, who had studied Japanese in London at the School of Oriental Studies and had been assigned as a language attaché in Tokyo from 1936 to 1939. He had then served with British Army intelligence in Singapore until it fell in 1942. This multinational group of talented Japanese linguists produced a steady flow of translations. In addition to translations of individual documents, they produced bulletins and reports on special topics and did special work as required, all of which was distributed to Allied headquarters.

Some PACMIRS Nisei later attended officer candidate school. Arthur M. Kaneko went to the infantry officer candidate school at Fort Benning, Georgia, in December 1944.[84] After his return in April 1945 as a new second lieutenant, whenever he served as officer of the day he took special pleasure in inspecting the prisoner of war officers' mess, where the German generals had to rise to attention each time he entered the room.[85]

Other Nisei found the routine wearing, and they chafed under their Caucasian officers. When Pat Nagano returned in July 1945 after a six-month absence, he noticed a distinct change in tone. Gronich, who had been promoted to colonel and was popular with the Nisei, had been transferred; and the Nisei felt they were no longer as trusted as before. In the early days they had been allowed to scan the documents to assess their intelligence value. Now they had to prepare word-for-word translations of every document the officers assigned to them.[86] The drudgery of translating dense technical materials took its toll on morale. In addition, the longer they worked, the more they resented their subordinate status. M.Sgt. George M. Koshi, a Nisei attorney who had worked in the Pentagon Order of Battle Section since 1943 and then at PACMIRS, wrote to a friend at MISLS: "We ought to be accustomed to working with Caucasian officers, by now, but when they head us only because they are Caucasians it really gets me down."[87] Many PACMIRS Nisei felt their contributions to the war effort were minimal at best. As the war dragged on they felt increasingly discouraged.

The Manhattan Project

In June 1943 the Military Intelligence Division's New York City branch requested Nisei for a special assignment. In August MISLS sent two Kibei, T4g. Kiyoshi Hirano and S.Sgt. Yutaka Namba.[88] Hirano had lived for eleven years in

---

[84] Interv, author with Kaneko, 25 Aug 95.

[85] See also Eugene Wright in *The Color of Honor*, Loni Ding, prod., and *Fifty Years of Silence*, Sheryl K. Narahara, prod. (San Francisco: Military Intelligence Service Club of Northern California/National Japanese American Historical Society, 1992); Arthur Kaneko in Harrington Papers.

[86] Nagano, "Lost Glory," MISNorCal Bio.

[87] Ltr, George M. Koshi, 16 September 1945, Harrington Papers.

[88] "Training History," ann. 2, p. 9; Harrington, *Yankee Samurai*, pp. 148, 152–54; Ltr, Kiyoshi Hirano to Lyn Crost Stern, 12 October 1992; Lyn Crost, *Honor by Fire: Japanese Americans at War in Europe and the Pacific* (Novato, Calif.: Presidio Press, 1994), pp. 285–87; *The Pacific War and Peace: Americans of Japanese Ancestry in Military Intelligence Service, 1941 to 1952* (San Francisco: Military Intelligence Service Association of Northern California/National Japa-

Japan, where he had graduated from high school with a teacher's certificate and had briefly taught school. Namba had lived in Japan and attended Meiji University. The two were assigned to the Morale Services Division of Army Service Forces, which published *Yank Magazine*. They worked on the nineteenth floor of an office building on Broadway in downtown Manhattan. Over the autumn and winter of 1943–1944, they prepared a Japanese-English dictionary, some language textbooks, and other miscellaneous translation work. At some point, probably early in 1944, a high-ranking Army officer interviewed Hirano and Namba in the Rockefeller Center. They were then instructed to report to an unmarked office upstairs from the Fulton Fish Market, where they were put to work translating Japanese technical documents and scientific papers on nuclear physics. Their supervisors stressed the need for absolute secrecy. The two Nisei did not even tell each other what they were working on. Hirano translated the confiscated New York branch office files of two Japanese businesses, Mitsui and Company and the Ogura Petroleum Company. The technical translation work was difficult, and "he was told to try to identify certain types and shapes of metals he'd never heard of before," as well as translate documents on metallurgy and polymerization. "Often it took a whole day of research to identify a single word," he recalled.[89]

Not until August 1945 did they learn that they had worked in support of the Manhattan Project, a closely guarded secret of the war effort and, like signals intelligence, protected by multiple layers of security. In the autumn of 1943 the director, Brig. Gen. Leslie R. Groves, pushed for better intelligence about German and Japanese atomic weapons programs. That December he sent the Alsos Mission, a scientific and technical intelligence team, to Italy. After the war, Americans learned that Japan's nuclear program was dwarfed by America's, but during the war Groves was concerned and asked his staff for any intelligence on possible Japanese developments.[90] The MIS Nisei played a small, indirect part in this effort by translating scientific, technical, and commercial documents that shed light on Japan's capabilities.[91]

---

nese American Historical Society, 1991), p. 21. Army Service Forces produced Japanese-language training materials such as TMs 30–341, 30–541, and 30–641. Hirano returned to MISLS in August 1944. In April 1945 MISLS sent three more Nisei to the New York Branch Office, Information and Education Division, Army Service Forces, for ninety days' temporary duty.

[89] *Unsung Heroes*, p. 27. *Pacific War and Peace* comments that "both men were never directly involved in the development and testing of the atomic bomb." The records of Japanese trading companies and banks seized in the United States at the start of the war can be found in the records of the Office of Alien Property Custodian, RG 131, NARA.

[90] Vincent C. Jones, *Manhattan: The Army and the Atomic Bomb* (Washington, D.C.: U.S. Army Center of Military History, 1985), pp. 280–91; John W. Dower, "'NI' and 'F': Japan's Wartime Atomic Bomb Research," in *Japan in War & Peace: Selected Essays* (New York: New Press, 1993), pp. 55–100.

[91] Kaoru Inouye, another MIS Nisei, learned after the war that one of his professors at the University of California, where he had majored in chemistry before the war, had requested him for the Manhattan Project. However, the War Department G–2 would not release him from his MIS assignment. Kaoru Inouye, MISNorCal Bio.

Army Map Service

The Army also needed maps for the war against Japan. From the outset the Army Map Service relied on maps and atlases from the Library of Congress and university collections, as well as maps captured during the fighting. When the war began, they sought to recruit individuals who could translate the thousands of place names on the Japanese maps; but they found that the pool of qualified translators was almost exhausted. In January 1943 the Army Map Service approached MISLS and requested MIS Nisei for translating work. Assistant Secretary McCloy personally approved the assignment of three MIS Nisei; school officials helped the Army Map Service select twenty civilians, many of them Nisei women from the camps. All were sent to Cleveland, Ohio, in May 1943 for this painstaking but important work.[92]

II Armored Corps Training Center

Another unusual assignment was teaching basic Japanese to the 1st Filipino Infantry, which activated in April 1942 with Filipino agricultural workers stranded in the United States when the war broke out. In the summer of 1943 the II Armored Corps established a special training center at Fort Ord and the Presidio of Monterey, California, to teach commando skills to selected Filipino officers and men. At that time the Western Defense Command did not allow persons of Japanese ancestry on the West Coast. Furthermore, hatred of the Japanese ran high in Filipino communities in the United States, so Nisei instructors would probably not have been acceptable to the Filipino troops. MISLS sent two Caucasian graduates to teach simple Japanese phrases and a few kanji characters.

In the spring of 1944 the War Department G–2, General Bissell, visited Monterey and met with the instructors. One of them, T.Sgt. Dempster P. Dirks, commented that foreign languages were better taught during times of peace, not in the midst of war. Furthermore, in his opinion the Presidio of Monterey would make an excellent setting for such a school. "I [wouldn't] put these buildings back in mothballs, this is an ideal location," Dirks suggested. "It's away from urban centers and relatively secluded. Operate in peacetime and teach several different languages." The general's response is not recorded, but Dirks proved prescient. After the war's end, MISLS moved to the Presidio of Monterey and expanded to train military linguists in dozens of languages for the postwar era.[93]

---

[92] Ltr, Col. William P. Scobey to Commander, Army Map Service, 19 February 1943, Class Ref-Sub File, 1940–1947, Ofc of Asst Sec of War, RG 107, NARA; "Training History," ann. 10, sec. IV(5); Blanche D. Coll et al., *The Corps of Engineers: Troops and Equipment* (Washington, D.C.: Office of the Chief of Military History, 1958), pp. 438–63; Office of the Chief Engineer, General Headquarters, Army Forces, Pacific, *Engineers of the Southwest Pacific*, vol. 3 (Washington, D.C.: Government Printing Office, 1950), pp. 75–78, 120–22, 199–201, apps.

[93] Dempster P. Dirks, in *MIS Club of Southern California Newsletter*, 1992. MISLS moved from Fort Snelling to the Presidio of Monterey in June 1946, was renamed the Army Language School in 1947, and later became the Defense Language Institute Foreign Language Center (DLIFLC).

Preparing for Military Government

As the war progressed, the United States developed plans for the occupation of Japan.[94] Although key policy issues such as the future status of the emperor were left unresolved, it was clear that military government over any Japanese territory would require a large number of Japanese-speaking personnel. In August 1943 the senior Army commander in Hawaii suggested using Nisei for occupation duties. "It occurred to me that a plan might be evolved to use many of these people in the rehabilitation and rule of Japan, once that country has been conquered," Lt. Gen. Robert C. Richardson wrote to McCloy. Could we not place educated Nisei, he suggested, "in minor key positions in Japan after the victory, with the thought of democratizing the people from which they sprang? This would serve a double purpose. It would assist materially in the Westernization of the Japanese, as these men would form a bridge between the mentality of their ancestors and modern American mentality and manners. Secondly, it would form an honorable outlet to educated American Japanese."[95] The War Department did not take up his proposal. In April 1944, when the Civil Affairs Division projected its requirements for 1,000 Japanese-speakers for the occupation, not even this high figure convinced planners to turn to the Nisei.[96]

Joseph C. Grew, former ambassador to Japan, consulted with Nisei leaders and visited MISLS several times. In September 1943, when Assistant Secretary McCloy asked him about using Nisei in the occupation of Japan, Grew responded with enthusiasm. John F. Aiso later remarked that the Nisei "had a great friend in Ambassador Grew."[97] Grew solicited Aiso's views about postwar Japan. In response, Aiso and his staff prepared a "blueprint study which publicly proposed such matters as the preservation of the emperor system, the agricultural land reform laws, and rewriting the Japanese constitution to eliminate the military's direct access to the throne and to guarantee the fundamental rights of the individual."[98] These proposals coincided with Grew's own thinking, and he arranged for Aiso to speak before a public forum in Chicago in November 1943 on "International Problems after the War." "The problem of Japan in the post-war

---

[94] Hugh Borton, *American Presurrender Planning for Postwar Japan* (New York: East Asian Institute, Columbia University, 1967); Eiji Takemae, *Inside GHQ: The Allied Occupation of Japan and Its Legacy* (New York: Continuum, 2002), pp. 201–14.

[95] Ltr, Robert C. Richardson to John J. McCloy, 13 August 1943, Robert C. Richardson Papers, Box 21, Hoover Institution Archives.

[96] Memo, WD G–1 for Chief of Staff, sub: Assignment of Citizens of Japanese Ancestry, 3 Apr 44, Tab E, Decimal 291.2, "Japanese," 1 Mar–Aug 44, WD G–1 Decimal Files, RG 165, NARA.

[97] Memo, Scobey for CS, 16 Sep 43, sub: Training of Loyal Japanese Americans for Civil Affairs Duties, in Folder: Scobey, Class Ref Sub Files, 1940–1947, Office of the Assistant Secretary of War (ASW), RG 107, NARA; John F. Aiso, "Observations of a California Nisei," Interv by Marc Landy, University of California at Los Angeles, 1971, pp. 79–80.

[98] John F. Aiso, Remarks to Military Intelligence Service Veterans' Reunion, Honolulu, 6 Sep 64.

world is beset with difficulties," explained the panel moderator while introducing Aiso. "Its solution needs all the wisdom we can muster. One source of knowledge, too often overlooked, is our native Americans of Japanese ancestry. Many are in the Army."[99] Aiso presented what he called "a few modest observations upon the reconstruction of Japan." His remarks, coordinated with the War Department Public Relations Office, called for ridding Japan of "insane militarism" but warned against abolishing the emperor system. He spelled out a reform agenda for Japan's constitution and legal, taxation, and education systems. He cautiously did not spell out any particular role for the Nisei. However, he boldly declared that "notwithstanding false reports from irresponsible quarters, the loss of our homes and the loss of economic security through compulsory war-time evacuation, our faith in America remains unshaken." Following this speech, Aiso apparently played no further role in postwar planning.[100]

In December 1943 the War Department took its first steps to train military government personnel for the "Asiatic theater." Language training loomed large in their worries. "[I]t is infinitely more important in a program for the Far East than for the Mediterranean-European theaters that recruitment and training for occupation be initiated well in advance of the event," warned one planning memorandum. "Familiarity in America with European languages and backgrounds, while not widespread, is nonetheless considerable; acquaintance with Far Eastern languages, institutions and points of view is practically nonexistent. Furthermore, the difficulties of imparting useful language and other relevant knowledge of the Far East are many times those of similar preparation for European areas." The memorandum, which did not mention the Nisei, asserted that "six months of intensive work in conversational Japanese is a bare minimum of useful instruction."[101]

The Office of the Provost Marshal General established Civil Affairs Training Schools at ten universities in 1944 and that July established a program at the University of Chicago to train Issei and Nisei civilians to become Japanese-language "informants," or language teachers. The Civil Affairs Division hoped to find 150 instructors but found only twenty-six who eventually taught introductory Japa-

[99] *New York Herald Tribune*, 18 Nov 43, pp. 18, 20; Tad Ichinokuchi, ed. *John Aiso and the M.I.S.: Japanese-American Soldiers in the Military Intelligence Service, World War II* (Los Angeles: Military Intelligence Service Club of Southern California, 1988), pp. 19–23.

[100] John F. Aiso, "Japan's Military System Must Be Crushed: Domestic and Economic Reforms Necessary," *Vital Speeches of the Day* (15 December 1943): 136–38; *New York Herald Tribune*, 18 Nov 43, pp. 18, 20; cited in *John Aiso and the M.I.S.*, pp. 19–23; Aiso, Speech, 6 Sep 64; Aiso, Speech, 12 Nov 66, printed in *Hokubei Mainichi*, n.d.; Interv, Aiso, 1970, pp. 79–80; Interv notes, Joseph Harrington with Aiso, 3 Jan 78. Aiso later made similar comments on the cost of the evacuation. *Yaban Gogai*, Dec 45.

[101] Cited in Harry L. Coles and Albert K. Weinberg, *Civil Affairs: Soldiers Become Governors* (Washington, D.C.: Office of the Chief of Military History, 1964), pp. 83–94. See also the call for language-qualified occupation personnel by anthropologist John Embree, "Military Occupation of Japan," *Far Eastern Survey* (20 September 1944).

nese to hundreds of military government officers.[102] The Navy established its own military government training programs at Columbia and Princeton.

In July 1944 the Civil Affairs Division established the Civil Affairs Holding and Staging Area (CASA) at Fort Ord, California.[103] In July 1944 five MIS Nisei were assigned to provide language instruction under 1st Lt. Suyeki Okumura, a Nisei lawyer, and M.Sgt. Paul Jun Sakai, a University of Washington graduate who had served with the 9th Infantry Division in North Africa in 1942–1943, before coming to MISLS as a language student.[104] The Nisei had no textbooks, so they improvised. They taught elementary Japanese phrases two hours per day, ten hours per week to the mostly junior Army and Navy officers. Some had received several months of Japanese instruction, but most had no previous exposure.

In December 1944 almost 1,000 more personnel arrived, bringing CASA's total strength to 1,124 and forcing the agency to relocate to the Presidio of Monterey in February 1945. MISLS sent seventeen more Nisei as instructors in January and ten more in April. In June 1945 another 234 officers arrived. In July CASA added Chinese-language classes in anticipation of landings on the coast of China. Capt. Quan H. Yuen, a Chinese American and the only officer to graduate from the MISLS Chinese course, taught the classes. CASA personnel also researched various aspects of Japanese government, economy, and society in preparation for the occupation. In February 1945 the Office of Strategic Services assigned a detachment of about sixteen professionals, many of whom were experts on Japan. They helped write various research reports and civil affairs manuals at the prefecture level.[105] By the summer of 1945 more than thirty MIS Nisei were training military government personnel in Monterey for the occupation of Japan. Others were training for occupation censorship duties at Fort Mason, San Francisco. Nine Nisei began a civil censorship training course in February 1945 and another twenty-five in July.

---

[102] History of Military Government Training: Operations of Japanese Informants Training School, File 4–4, MI, 46/1–1, vol. 2, CMH.

[103] "History of the Civil Affairs Holding and Staging Area, Fort Ord and Presidio of Monterey, California," Unpubl Ms, 1945, DLIFLC, Monterey, California; "Military Governors for Japan: Army Specialists Trained at Monterey," *Monterey Herald*, 17 Sep 45, p. 7; Arnold G. Fisch, Jr., *Military Government in the Ryukyu Islands, 1945–1950*, U.S. Army in World War II (Washington, D.C.: U.S. Army Center of Military History, 1988), pp. 15–19; Dorothy E. Richard, *United States Naval Administration of the Trust Territory of the Pacific Islands*, 3 vols. (Washington, D.C.: Office of the Chief of Naval Operations, 1957), 1: 54–61.

[104] Harrington, *Yankee Samurai*, pp. 12, 105. Sakai was not removed from his unit after Pearl Harbor, as were many other Nisei, and he sailed with the 9th Infantry Division for the invasion of North Africa in November 1942.

[105] "History of the Civil Affairs Holding and Staging Area," pp. 150–164.

Supreme Headquarters Allied Expeditionary Force

During the war, Japan maintained close diplomatic and commercial ties with Nazi Germany, which gave the Allies another valuable source of intelligence about both countries. For example, the Allies routinely intercepted the diplomatic cables of the Japanese ambassador to Berlin, *General Hiroshi Ōshima*, yielding invaluable insights into the Nazi high command. In the autumn of 1944, as Allied ground forces drew closer to Germany's borders, the War Department G–2 was eager to pick up any further intelligence from Japanese diplomats and businessmen in Central Europe.[106]

In case the Nazi government should suddenly surrender or collapse, General Dwight D. Eisenhower's Supreme Headquarters Allied Expeditionary Force (SHAEF) developed contingency plans for Operation ECLIPSE, a short-notice airborne assault on Berlin by the First Allied Airborne Army. In October 1944 PACMIRS alerted three MIS Nisei for possible deployment to Europe but shelved these plans when Allied forces stalled at Germany's border and the Germans launched a fierce counterattack in the Ardennes.[107] Not until January 1945 did Eisenhower's G–2 call for Japanese-language personnel. PACMIRS then sent three Nisei under Maj. John M. White, an experienced team leader and veteran of the Aleutians, and M.Sgt. Kazuo E. Yamane, who had discovered the Japanese Army ordnance plan. The four departed New York aboard a C–54. Upon arrival at Versailles on about 12 February they were assigned to the SHAEF G–2 Far Eastern Intelligence Section in the Trianon Palace Hotel, where SHAEF had its headquarters. At first the Nisei were told they would join a British commando unit to be inserted into Berlin ahead of the Russians. When this mission was scrubbed, the Nisei settled in with little to do other than visit Paris on pass. Otherwise, they waited in Versailles for the war to end.[108]

In the waning days of the war the Japanese embassy staff moved to Bad Gastein, a remote Austrian ski resort. When the German surrender finally came in May 1945, the 101st Airborne Division soon arrived and requisitioned the hotel in which the diplomats were staying. At first the diplomats refused to be evicted,

---

[106] Boyd, *Hitler's Japanese Confidant*; "Japanese in Europe as of 1 December 1944," 15 Jan 45, HRC Geog V Japan 201—Who's Who, CMH files.

[107] Kazuo E. Yamane, "World War II Experiences, Pentagon-Paris-Berlin," in Oguro, *Sempai Gumi*, pp. 106–13; Interv, author with Yamane, 8 Dec 94; Pat Nagano, "Lost Glory," MISNorCal Bio; Harrington, *Yankee Samurai*, pp. 271–73, 330–31. For Operation ECLIPSE, see Cornelius Ryan, *The Last Battle* (New York: Simon and Schuster, 1966), pp. 119–25.

[108] In some versions, for example, in Oguro, *Sempai Gumi*, pp. 112–13, Yamane claims his team deployed in October 1944. However, in the same account he says the German attack in the Ardennes (16 December 1944) had occurred "only a few weeks before our arrival." Pat Nagano recalled they left the United States shortly after 4 February 1945. Yamane's discharge certificate states he arrived in Europe on 12 February 1945; his certificate of appreciation from the SHAEF G–2 dates his assignment from 14 February 1945. Thus the February date appears more plausible. *Pacific War and Peace*, p. 69, repeats Yamane's error, as does Tsukiyama et al., *Secret Valor*, p. 105, and Crost, *Honor by Fire*, p. 283.

but by coincidence the division commander, Maj. Gen. Maxwell D. Taylor, had studied Japanese in Tokyo before the war as a language attaché. He appeared at the hotel and personally evicted the diplomats in their own language. The three MIS Nisei eventually helped guard these diplomats and other Japanese personnel. In July two of the Nisei escorted thirty-three Japanese diplomats to New York on board an ocean liner. The third, Yamane, returned soon afterward.[109]

Military Intelligence Training Units

During the first three years of the war the MIS Nisei proved their worth in combat and stateside sensitive intelligence assignments. With the invasion of Japan not far away, War Department leaders knew they would need even more Nisei in the MIS. However, during the winter and spring of 1945, war weariness was spreading throughout the United States. The Battle of Okinawa came as a sobering reminder of the high casualties certain to come with the invasion of Japan. It was an especially difficult time for individuals of Japanese ancestry in the United States. In December 1944 the government announced plans to allow them to return to the West Coast, but many local communities remained bitterly hostile. By one count, anti-Japanese bigotry sparked more than forty incidents of violence or intimidation on the West Coast in the first six months of 1945.[110]

Meanwhile, the casualty lists from the 442d Regimental Combat Team (RCT) were read with great sorrow in Japanese communities in Hawaii and on the mainland. In October–November 1944 the unit suffered over 1,400 casualties in six weeks in the Vosges Mountains. In April 1945 the unit returned to Italy and suffered over 1,000 casualties in just four weeks. The replacements coming to the unit were no longer volunteers, but younger Nisei draftees. Morale among the Nisei draftees in stateside training bases was poor. At Fort Meade, Maryland, several thousand waited for shipment overseas as individual replacements for the 442d RCT. Their morale began to show signs of deterioration as early as April 1945. When the war in Europe ended in May they were no longer needed as infantry replacements, so they just waited. In June MISLS selected 500 to begin Japanese-language training. But, at Fort Snelling, their morale only fell lower.[111] The lack of promotions and commissions was a common complaint, even though by early 1945 a few Nisei had received commissions through officer candidate schools and through battlefield commissions in both Europe and the Pacific. Nisei serving with

[109] "Nisei Sergeants Escort Captured Japan Diplomats," *Pacific Citizen*, 14 Jul 45; Nagano, MISNorCal Bio; Boyd, *Hitler's Japanese Confidant*, pp. 176–77. PACMIRS translated some Japanese documents captured in Europe. PACMIRS Limited Duty Accession Lists no. 1 (20 Jun 45) through 17 (27 Jul 45), "Summaries of Documents Bearing on the War in the Pacific Received by PACMIRS from the European Theater," Security Class Intel Ref Pubs, RG 165, NARA.

[110] Paul R. Spickard, *Japanese Americans: The Formation and Transformations of an Ethnic Group* (New York: Twayne, 1996), p. 127.

[111] Tamotsu Shibutani, *The Derelicts of Company K: A Sociological Study of Demoralization* (Berkeley: University of California Press, 1978), pp. 101–68.

other war agencies sometimes felt even worse. One Nisei assigned to the Office of Strategic Services in Washington, D.C., complained in a letter to a friend about prejudice, low pay, and security restrictions compared to conditions in the Army. "My past experience with the Army proves that the Army units including G–2 does not prejudice nisei due to heritage, or at least, many restrictions have been modified." In July 1945 he requested a discharge or transfer, declaring "I would rather fight and die under the rule where no prejudice or discrimination is practised."[112]

At this difficult time for the Nisei the War Department assigned them a new task, to pose as Japanese soldiers and train other American troops preparing for the invasion of Japan. The War Department faced an unprecedented challenge in 1945: redeploying millions of soldiers from Europe to the Pacific. The War Department wanted troops to receive an orientation on the characteristics of Imperial Japanese Army soldiers, because as a War Department press release explained it, "fighting the Japanese is different from fighting Germans." The War Department G–2 provided the training literature, including items such as a training circular on Japanese "character and training," written by Col. Charles N. Hunter of Merrill's Marauders. Army Ground Forces included an orientation on Japanese tactics, techniques, and weapons to be taught by Military Intelligence Training Units (MITUs) at three bases: Fort Meade, Maryland; Camp Hood, Texas; and Camp Roberts, California. Several MIS Nisei would be assigned to each MITU to demonstrate Japanese tactics and equipment by dressing up in Japanese Army uniforms, a task many Nisei found especially humiliating.[113]

The War Department had used Nisei soldiers to simulate Japanese soldiers at least once before. In October 1942 the War Department had selected two Nisei officers and twenty-six Nisei enlisted men from the 100th Infantry Battalion at Camp McCoy and sent them to Cat Island, Mississippi. The experiment was intended to determine if military dogs could be trained to sniff out Japanese soldiers in a subtropical field environment. The Nisei were shocked to learn they were to be guinea pigs. However, to the Nisei's relief, the dogs could not tell the difference between Nisei and soldiers of other races. Cat Island turned out to be easy duty; after six months the Hawaii-born Nisei rejoined the battalion and regaled their comrades with tales of the excellent fishing in the Gulf of Mexico.[114]

---

[112] Quote from Morioka, "Japanese Americans in the Service of their Country," p. 54.

[113] WD Press Release, 5 May 45, cited in John C. Sparrow, *History of Personnel Demobilization in the United States Army*, Department of the Army Pamphlet 20–210 (Washington, D.C.: Department of the Army, 1952), pp. 306–10; Robert R. Palmer et al., eds., *The Procurement and Training of Ground Combat Troops* (Washington, D.C.: Historical Division, Department of the Army, 1948), pp. 426–27, 623–47; WD Trng Circular 23, 28 May 45; "Soldiers Will Train GIs for Pacific War: Special Japanese American Training Teams Will Show Enemy Tactics to Troops," *Pacific Citizen*, 9 Jun 45, p. 1; "Special Nisei Teams Prepare GIs for Pacific War Conditions," *Pacific Citizen*, 4 Aug 45, p. 3; "'Know Your Enemy': MITU Shows the Way," *Fort Ord Panorama*, 3 Aug 45, p. 5.

[114] Thomas D. Murphy, *Ambassadors in Arms* (Honolulu: University of Hawaii Press, 1954), pp. 79, 92–93; Masayo Umezawa Duus, *Unlikely Liberators: The Men of the 100th and 442nd* (Honolulu: University of Hawaii Press, 1987), pp. 46–49; Raymond R. Nosaka, "Japanese Dog Bait," in *Japanese Eyes, American Heart*, pp. 155–57; Harrington, *Yankee Samurai*, p. 105. The Quarter-

In the spring of 1945 the Military Intelligence Training Center organized several MITUs, the first six graduating in late June. Eventually, the center organized twenty-nine MITUs using over 300 Nisei. In April MISLS sent the first thirty-four Nisei to Camp Ritchie for this training. In mid-June another 149 Nisei arrived from the replacement depot at Fort Meade to be "Saipan Joes."[115] Sixty-five combat veterans came from the 442d Regimental Combat Team in Italy, among them Pfc. Jesse M. Hirata, who was uncooperative. He had been in uniform since before Pearl Harbor, had fought with the 100th Infantry Battalion through Italy and France and had been awarded the Distinguished Service Cross. When he arrived at Camp Ritchie, "there was nothing to do except go to the movies and rent rowboats in the camp lake," he recalled. "They put us on KP, but we refused to work. I guess we felt we did our part in the war. MPs came, and we were ready to fight them, so they did not touch us."[116]

In July 1945 *Yank* magazine announced the orientation program, saying that American soldiers would learn about their new opponents through the eyes of an American Nisei named Joe: "How does it feel to be a member of the Jap armed forces? There's a guy here named Joe who can tell you from personal experience. A native American of Japanese descent, Joe spent several years in college in Japan just before the war and belonged to the Jap ROTC. Talking to him here in Washington you get a good picture of how the Jap Army and Navy stack up."[117]

MIS Nisei who were veterans of the war in the Pacific certainly had valuable insights to pass on, but most assigned to the MITUs were not Pacific veterans. The assignment raised uncomfortable issues. Many Nisei felt that playing Japanese soldiers was a humiliating reinforcement of racial stereotypes. After having fought hard to prove their loyalty, they asked themselves if the Army still thought of them as "Japanese" soldiers. "We were ordered to act the part of Japanese soldiers because we resembled them," S.Sgt. Hiroshi Sakai recalled, "although some of us expressed dissatisfaction to play this type of role."[118] M.Sgt. George M. Koshi, assigned to PACMIRS but not to the MITUs, worried about the Nisei in these units. "Most of them seem to be as disillusioned as many of us were," he wrote to a friend at Fort Snelling. "They were a little reluctant about talking [about] what is expected

---

master Corps established a war-dog reception and training center on Cat Island, Mississippi, in April 1943 and shipped a small detachment of dogs and handlers to the Southwest Pacific around this time. Erna Risch and Chester L. Kieffer, *The Quartermaster Corps: Organization, Supply, and Services*, 2 vols. (Washington, D.C.: Office of the Chief of Military History, 1955), 2: 323–37.

[115] Shibutani, *Derelicts of Company K*, pp. 172–79.

[116] Jesse M. Hirata, in *Japanese Eyes*, pp. 54–68. Another Nisei remembers seeing Nisei practicing at Camp Ritchie with Japanese uniforms and rifles. He "always remembered that scene, wondering how the young men felt about acting out the role of the enemy." Yoshiaki Fujitani, in *Japanese Eyes*, pp. 94–102.

[117] "Serving the Emperor," *Yank* (6 Jul 45): 16–17.

[118] Hiroshi Sakai, in Tsukiyama et al., *Secret Valor*, p. 103; S. Phil Ishio, in *Unsung Heroes*, pp. 27–28.

Two Nisei with a Military Intelligence Training Unit demonstrate a Japanese machine gun at Fort Ord, July 1945.

of them here, but I gathered that they are to be made into actors in the game of war. I presume that they will look pretty becoming in a different uniform."[119]

When the Nisei in the 442d Regimental Combat Team learned how the MIS Nisei were being used, they were very upset. Lyn Crost, a war correspondent covering the 442d RCT for the *Honolulu Star-Bulletin*, took the team's concerns to Secretary of the Interior Harold L. Ickes, who had responsibility for the War Relocation Authority: "Many [Nisei] told me they would rather go back into combat—anywhere—than have to dress up in Japanese uniforms and use Japanese weapons

---

[119] Ltr, George M. Koshi to Yutaka Munakata, 2 May 1945, in Harrington Papers.

in this training program.... They believe the use of Nisei for such work—particularly when they are required to copy Japanese enemy troops to the exact detail of even dress—will only serve to increase racial antagonism."[120]

The War Department G–2 defensively explained to Assistant Secretary of War McCloy that although Nisei would pretend to be Japanese soldiers, "one of the lessons" imparted by the training "is that Nisei in the American Army are Americans—as American as those of German, Italian, English or any other ancestry." The G–2 assured McCloy that "those few Nisei who had no interest in this type of duty were relieved" and praised the Nisei for the "spirit" they were showing. The G–2 denied "that doubt and hatred would be engendered."[121] A War Department spokesman pointed out to a Nisei newspaper correspondent "that the Japanese Americans [in the MITUs] were all volunteers because [the War Department] felt that it could not order these American citizens to play the distasteful role of the hated enemy."[122] The MITU training proceeded in July and August with Nisei playacting as Japanese soldiers before thousands of other American soldiers on bases across the country.

.   .   .

The MIS Nisei served in diverse noncombat roles, including those in the continental United States. Their role in the MITUs proved their versatility, even though they found it distasteful. Given the acute shortage of other Japanese-speaking Americans and the long time required for Japanese-language training, the MIS Nisei were invaluable in several fields, including prisoner of war operations, translation work, and strategic propaganda. They played a more indirect role in preparations for military government and for signals intelligence. Other civilian Issei and Nisei provided Japanese-language training. However, these stateside duties, although valuable, were not as important as serving overseas in the combat theaters to convince America of their loyalty. For many Nisei, being assigned to play Japanese soldiers was one more slap in the face and a reminder that even their wartime service had not changed their being perceived as more Japanese than American.

---

[120] Crost, *Honor by Fire*, pp. 269–71.

[121] Memo, Maj. Gen. Clayton Bissell to ASW, 24 Jul 45, sub: Use of Japanese-American Soldiers in Training, Trng Grp, Ofc of the Dir of Intel G–2, RG 165, NARA.

[122] "Special Nisei Teams Prepare GIs for Pacific War Conditions," *Pacific Citizen*, 4 Aug 45.

8

MIS Nisei in the
Campaigns of 1944

As the year 1944 opened, the United States and its Allies were on the offensive in the Pacific. Two years after Pearl Harbor, America's powerful land, sea, and air forces had seized the initiative and were driving toward the Japanese home islands. Allied intelligence capabilities matured rapidly to guide these campaigns. Japanese military dispositions and plans were becoming transparent to Allied commanders, who benefited from an ever-expanding torrent of intelligence. Every intelligence discipline—signals intelligence, aerial photography, coast watchers, guerrillas, captured documents, and prisoners of war—contributed to the overall picture. From the frontline rifle companies where the battle zone was measured in yards, up to MacArthur and Nimitz who reached across thousands of nautical miles, timely and accurate intelligence was the key to victory.

Nisei were integral to the intelligence effort. These onetime pioneers no longer had to prove themselves to skeptical or prejudiced Caucasian officers. During 1944 their numbers more than doubled to a thousand, and their work influenced every campaign. "Each one was as valuable as an infantry company," declared one intelligence officer in the China-Burma-India Theater.[1] Some Nisei were already seasoned veterans in the South and Southwest Pacific Theaters. During 1944 some

---

[1] Col. Gaspare F. Blunda, in Boyd Sinclair, "Valuable as a Company of Men," *Ex-CBI Roundup* (November 1951): 7.

returned stateside as a result of wounds or illness; others were selected for officer candidate school (OCS). Several were killed in action.

Nevertheless, the Nisei still found themselves trapped within the distinctive race hatred that was the hallmark of the Pacific War. Their compassion toward captured Japanese prisoners, all too rare on the front lines, could be justified on pragmatic grounds. But it also stemmed from a deep appreciation of what they had in common with their prisoners. The Nisei could never forget that even though they were American soldiers they "looked like the enemy."

By late 1943 the Combined Chiefs of Staff had approved a new plan for the defeat of Japan that called for three axes of attack: driving across the Central Pacific, pushing up from Southwest Asia toward the Philippines, and British Commonwealth forces in Southeast Asia recapturing Burma. America would meanwhile continue to support China and commence a long-range bombing campaign from bases in China and the Central Pacific.

South Pacific Area

The Solomon Islands Campaign moved north to Bougainville, where the 3d Marine Division landed at Empress Augusta Bay on 1 November 1943. The 37th Infantry Division followed a week later with their language team led by Capt. Gilbert B. Ayers and T3g. Dye Ogata. Ogata had been born in Washington State and grew up in Helena, Montana. He had taken over the team when its first leader was wounded on New Georgia. Japanese resistance on Bougainville at first was slight, but the American soldiers and marines were subjected to frequent attacks from the air. Shortly before sunrise on 16 November a Japanese bomb landed near Ogata, burying him in his own bunker. He clawed through the dirt to reach the surface. "Never worked faster in my life than I did for the next few moments," he told a reporter a few months later. "It may have been three minutes or ten. I don't know. All I knew was that the sky was up there somewhere and I was going to see it again before I gave up." Later that day the division commander presented him with the Purple Heart.[2]

On 5 December 1943, Capt. William Fisher brought another team of six Nisei to Bougainville with the XIV Corps headquarters. They interrogated prisoners, translated captured documents, and lectured troops on the importance of turning in prisoners and documents to G–2. Nisei such as T3g. Shigeru Yamashita flew

---

[2] "2d STR OC Buried Alive by Jap's Bomb," *Platoon Leader* [1944]; Joseph D. Harrington, *Yankee Samurai: The Secret Role of Nisei in America's Pacific Victory* (Detroit: Pettigrew Enterprises, 1979), pp. 167, 332; Interv, author with Dye Ogata, 30 Oct 87; Dye Ogata, Biography, Military Intelligence Service Club of Northern California (this and similar biographies hereafter cited as MISNorCal Bios). The Associated Press identified Ogata as "an Army specialist whose name and work are unmentionable because his job is an Army secret." *Los Angeles Times*, 20 Nov 43. In December 1943 the 37th Division language team was replaced by Susumu Toyoda's team. Interv, author with Susumu Toyoda, 12 Sep 96; Harrington, *Yankee Samurai*, pp. 173, 187–89. Ogata later attended officer candidate school at Fort Benning and was commissioned in December 1944.

*Ogata shows his teammates how he escaped after being buried, Bouganville,
November 1943.*

over Japanese positions in a light aircraft to broadcast surrender appeals over a
loudspeaker.[3] On 25 December the Americal Division language team arrived with
several Nisei from the first class at Crissy Field who had been serving in the South
Pacific since 1942. On 15 February the 3d New Zealand Division, accompanied by
several more Nisei, seized the Green Islands near Bougainville.[4] (*See Map 8.*)

---

[3] Jim Masaru Ariyasu, in David W. Swift, ed., "First Class," p. 13, Unpubl Ms, Mar 00, copy
in author's files; Stanley Sandler, *Cease Resistance, It's Good for You: A History of U.S. Army
Combat Psychological Operations* (Fort Bragg, N.C.: U.S. Army Special Operations Command,
1996), pp. 178–79.

[4] Harrington, *Yankee Samurai*, p. 183.

Nisei in the rear areas also faced hazards. One day Herb Maruyama, part of the XIV Corps language team, walked to a nearby river to wash his uniform and bathe, then walked back wearing only his skivvies and carrying his wet uniform over his arm. Before he could reach the safety of his tent he felt a bayonet at his back. Some American soldiers, mistaking him for a Japanese infiltrator, captured him and marched him straight to the prisoner of war stockade. When Captain Fisher, his commander, appeared at the stockade, he shouted: "Maruyama, what the hell are you doing?" and set him free at once.[5]

Also working at XIV Corps headquarters was Masami Tahira. Translating captured documents he found "enervating, and at times just stultifying—to put it plainly, tiresome, especially in the hot, tropical jungle. The humid surroundings were conducive to atrophy and debility." One diary entry he translated described the execution of a captured American pilot by beheading with a samurai sword. From that point onward, he "always carried an extra .45 caliber automatic pistol bullet in my pocket," Tahira recalled. "I saw to it that it didn't get wet, that it was oiled, cleaned, and shiny at all times. I knew it would do its grisly duty when I wanted it to."[6]

In late February 1944 the 37th Infantry Division language team interrogated a prisoner who warned them that the Japanese had planned an attack for Army Day, 10 March.[7] A few days later the Americal Division team translated a written order that identified 8 March as the attack date.[8] By one account, "the official reports of the Americal Division disclose that it was the work of the language detachment that largely was responsible for the divisional commander knowing well in advance where and approximately at what time and in what strength the Japanese would attack the division along the Torokina River near Bougainville."[9]

On 8 March T3g. Roy T. Uyehata was conducting a routine interrogation in the XIV Corps stockade when the Japanese prisoner unexpectedly asked him, "How can I get off this island?" Uyehata replied that it might take a few days. "I guess you know that you are going to be attacked at dawn of March 23," the prisoner said. Uyehata remembered this was *Shunki Koreisai*, a special holiday for the worship of the imperial ancestors.[10] He feigned indifference and told the prisoner that his commander already knew about it. But he quickly ended the session and

---

[5] Interv, author with Toyoda, 12 Sep 96; Harrington, *Yankee Samurai*, p. 190.

[6] Masami Tahira, in *Sempai Gumi*, ed. Richard S. Oguro (Honolulu: MIS Veterans of Hawaii, ca. 1981), pp. xx–xxvii; *The Pacific War and Peace: Americans of Japanese Ancestry in Military Intelligence Service, 1941 to 1952* (San Francisco: Military Intelligence Service Association of Northern California/National Japanese American Historical Society, 1991), pp. 139–45.

[7] Interv, author with Toyoda, 12 Sep 96; Susumu Toyoda, personal communication to author, 4 Oct 96; Harrington, *Yankee Samurai*, p. 188.

[8] Mac Nobuo Nagata, in Swift, "First Class," p. 10.

[9] War Department (WD) Press Release, 22 Oct 45, Japanese Evacuation Research Study (JERS), pt. 2, sec. 2, reel 20, frame 0037, Bancroft Library, University of California, Berkeley.

[10] Army intelligence officers already knew that "frequently Japanese military leaders choose festival or holiday dates to launch important attacks." See "Festivals and Holidays," *Intelligence Bulletin* 1, no. 3 (November 1942): 53–54.

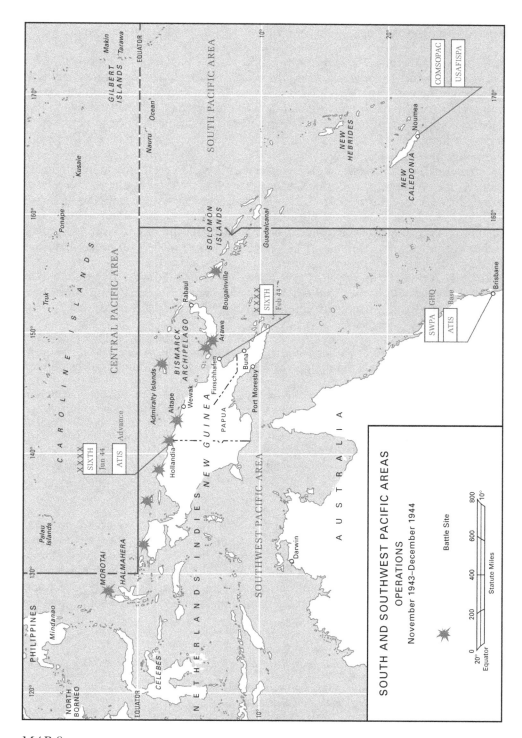

SOUTH AND SOUTHWEST PACIFIC AREAS
OPERATIONS
November 1943–December 1944

✴ Battle Site

| 0 | 200 | 400 | 600 | 800 |

Statute Miles

MAP 8

rushed the news to Captain Fisher, who sent a more senior interrogator, T.Sgt. Hiroshi Matsuda, to confirm the tip from a different prisoner. They then took the information directly to the corps commander, Maj. Gen. Oscar W. Griswold, who put all troops on alert and cancelled the open-air movies scheduled that evening. That night Japanese artillery opened up on the American positions and the newly completed airfields. A ground attack followed the next day. For the next two weeks Japanese soldiers repeatedly threw themselves against the American defenses at a cost to themselves of 5,500 dead and 3,000 wounded. The American lines held, with only light casualties.[11]

American commanders eagerly exploited all possible sources of intelligence. Nisei provided important information, as did photographic and signals intelligence. For example, Central Bureau in Australia intercepted a message from the Japanese 17th Army to Tokyo announcing plans for an attack on 22 March, which was passed to the American commander on Bougainville the day prior.[12] The attack did not occur on schedule, but on 23 March soldiers of the 37th Infantry Division found "a blood-smeared tactical map of the enemy 23rd Regiment showing what their intentions were for that night."[13] These confirmed the warning Uyehata had provided two weeks earlier, and the division commander ordered a full alert. Sgt. Susumu Toyoda, the Nisei team chief, described what happened next:

> Here was the prime opportunity to utilize the knowledge we acquired from the many months of study at MISLS. The language team worked feverishly to decode the vital message contained on the map. The initial interrogation was only the beginning of a multitude of "hot info" we were able to get.
>
> On the map, we found the disposition of the troops and its future plans. It stated on the map that the regiment would commence attacking at 2000. Preliminary information was sent to all commanders concerned and overlays were made to follow. The switch board in the Signal Corps section was busier than the one operating at the New York Stock Exchange. The corps commanding general was informed of the hot news and he immediately ordered all corps, division and independent artilleries to point their guns at the location of the enemy. At 1945 the barrage started with all guns firing simultaneously. The barrage was one of the heaviest laid on any impact area in the South Pacific.[14]

The Japanese assault came that night, but the Americans were ready and restored their lines within hours. The next morning patrols swept through a shell-pocked moonscape. A Nisei interrogator learned what had happened from a wounded Japanese soldier found in a shell hole: "They were just about to leave the area for the jumping-off line. Tears came out of his eyes as he related the fear and awe, and also how bitter it was that he was unable to fire even one shot against the

---

[11] Stanley A. Frankel, *The 37th Infantry Division in World War II* (Washington, D.C.: Infantry Journal Press, 1948), pp. 125–69.

[12] Ronald H. Spector, *Eagle against the Sun* (New York: Free Press, 1985), p. 456.

[13] Susumu Toyoda, personal communication to author, 4 Oct 96.

[14] *MISLS Album* (Minneapolis: Military Intelligence Service Language School, 1946), p. 103.

Americans." In despair he told the Nisei, "I came all the way from Kagoshima to fight the Americans, but you literally caught us with our pants down."[15]

The Japanese defeat was complete, and the Nisei had played an important part. Uyehata and Matsuda were awarded the Bronze Star. After the battle Captain Fisher wrote his parents to ask them to visit Uyehata's parents in the Poston camp. Fisher's parents informed Uyehata's parents that their son "had performed a very patriotic deed," though they "were not permitted to state the nature" of his accomplishments. Uyehata was convinced that he had saved a thousand American lives.[16] After the battle, Col. Kai E. Rasmussen visited Bougainville, where he met with the XIV Corps team and personally congratulated Uyehata on his achievement.[17]

Nisei sometimes made indirect contributions to signals intelligence. For example, among the prisoners captured on Bougainville was a Japanese Army radio operator. The Signal Intelligence Service (SIS) sent a captain to interrogate him, and Uyehata served as interpreter. The prisoner was familiar with the Japanese four-digit code, which American cryptographers had just begun to break. Even if the Americans could decipher the code, they had only limited success in matching the code groups to the specific words or units to which they corresponded. This prisoner had memorized the code groups for specific units. With Uyehata's assistance, the SIS captain gained valuable insights into the Japanese code system.[18]

After the battle of Bougainville, thousands of Japanese soldiers remained at large in the Solomon Islands. When the 25th Regimental Combat Team (RCT), composed of African American soldiers, was attached to the Americal Division for mopping-up operations, Nisei sometimes joined it on patrol. Leaflet drops continued for many months. Two Nisei received the Soldier's Medal for saving the life of a war correspondent who was being dragged out to sea by a riptide.[19] A few months later soldiers from Australia and New Zealand took over and continued the tedious and dangerous work of patrolling and tracking down cut-off units. In October 1944 the Allied Translator and Interpreter Section (ATIS) assigned two

---

[15] Ibid.; Interv, author with Toyoda, 12 Sep 96; John Miller, jr., *Cartwheel: The Reduction of Rabaul*, U.S. Army in World War II (Washington, D.C.: Office of the Chief of Military History, 1959), pp. 375–77.

[16] Interv, author with Roy T. Uyehata, 16 Nov 87; Stanley L. Falk and Warren M. Tsuneishi, eds., *MIS in the War against Japan* (Washington, D.C.: Japanese American Veterans Association, 1995), pp. 46–48; Roy T. Uyehata, in *World War II Reminiscences*, ed. John H. Roush, Jr. (San Rafael: California Department, Reserve Officers Association, 1995), pp. 257–60; Roy T. Uyehata, MISNorCal Bio; *World War II Times* (January, May 1988; January 1989).

[17] *Pacific War and Peace*, p. 33; Uyehata, in *World War II Reminiscences*, pp. 259–60; Uyehata, MISNorCal Bio.

[18] Roy T. Uyehata, "How We Broke the Japanese Four Digit Code," *World War II Times* (May 1988): 35. The four-digit army code was deciphered when a codebook was discovered in January 1944, but Allied cryptographers still did not know what each code group denoted. See Edward J. Drea and Joseph E. Richard, "New Evidence on Breaking the Japanese Army Codes," in *Allied and Axis Signals Intelligence in World War II*, ed. David Alvarez (London: Frank Cass, 1999), pp. 62–83; David Kahn, *The Codebreakers* (New York: Signet, 1973), p. 587.

[19] *Pacific Citizen*, 29 Jun, 28 Oct 44.

Nisei to the Australian 1st Division on Bougainville, where they spent the next seven months working with the Australians in mopping up.[20]

The battle of Bougainville marked the end of the South Pacific as a separate theater. American air, ground, and naval forces were reassigned to the Southwest Pacific or Central Pacific Theater. Most Nisei went to the Southwest Pacific. Tateshi Miyasaki, who had served since June 1942 on Guadalcanal, New Georgia, and Vella Lavella, went back to Idaho on furlough in May 1944. As his first order of business he got married, then he visited his mother who had been hospitalized for major surgery. The Army then sent him to Camp Shelby for basic training with the 442d RCT. He was soon transferred to Fort Snelling, where he became a language instructor.[21] Other Nisei from the South Pacific were selected for officer candidate school. Joe J. Yoshiwara and T. Hayashida were promoted to warrant officer. Masami Tahira volunteered for officer candidate school, in "any branch," he recalled, "so long as I could get out of this hot and uncomfortable pest hole." He was sent to the OCS in Brisbane in September 1944.[22]

Southwest Pacific Area

During 1943 General Douglas MacArthur's forces in the Southwest Pacific turned back Japanese advances, but the Japanese were still formidable foes. Papua New Guinea stretched out more than a thousand miles with its thickly forested, rugged mountains and its malarial lowlands. In 1944 MacArthur skillfully exploited intelligence to wage a war of operational maneuver to wrest the initiative from the Japanese commanders and take daring leaps along New Guinea's coast. The campaigns of 1944 sealed MacArthur's reputation as a master of the operational art.

By 1944 MacArthur's intelligence capabilities, including signals intelligence, aerial photography, translations, interrogation reports, and coast watchers and guerrillas operating in Japanese-controlled territory, had matured significantly. The largest single organization was ATIS in Brisbane. At the start of 1944 ATIS was staffed by about 150 Nisei, together with scores of other American Army and Navy personnel, with some Australian and British personnel. The number of Nisei doubled in the first half of the year. During 1944 ATIS received and examined 4,000 prisoners of war and translated 6,000 documents. Its files bulged with

---

[20] Allison B. Gilmore, *You Can't Fight Tanks with Bayonets: Psychological Warfare against the Japanese Army in the Southwest Pacific* (Lincoln: University of Nebraska Press, 1998), p. 70; Harrington, *Yankee Samurai*, pp. 189–90; Interv, author with Toyoda, 12 Sep 96; Interv, author with Robert R. Kimura, 9 Sep 96; Kimura, unidentified clipping, MIS Club of Southern California newsletter; Robert R. Kimura, in *The Saga of the MIS*, videotaped presentation, Los Angeles, 11 Mar 89; Harrington, *Yankee Samurai*, p. 231; Kimura, Joseph D. Harrington Papers, National Japanese Historical Society (NJAHS), San Francisco, Calif. Kimura and Matsumoto received Australian commendations. General Headquarters, Far East Command, *Operations of the Allied Translator and Interpreter Section, GHQ, SWPA*, Intelligence Series (Tokyo, Far East Command, 1948) (hereafter cited as ATIS History) app. 12, Decorations, Awards, and Commendations.

[21] Tateshi Miyasaki, in Swift, "First Class," p. 5.

[22] Masami Tahira, in Oguro, *Sempai Gumi*, p. 145.

*Allied Translator and Interpreter Section, Brisbane. The soldiers were
photographed from the rear to prevent their identification in case of capture.*

a staggering amount of data on every conceivable topic covering Japan's armed
forces, its soldiers, equipment, and tactics, patiently cross-indexed and updated
by a devoted army of clerical workers and intelligence analysts. From its printing
presses poured a steady stream of bulletins and technical reports, totaling more
than a million pages per month by the autumn of 1944.

For each combat operation ATIS sent teams of enlisted Nisei led by Caucasian
officers who worked at every level, regiment and division, corps and army, sharing
the hardships of the frontline soldiers. Some fell ill with malaria, dysentery, and
other hazards of the tropics; some were wounded or killed in action. In addition,
the Nisei constantly risked being mistaken for the enemy and were again regularly
assigned bodyguards. "I was bodyguard to an American of Japanese descent who
was risking his life to act as an interpreter for us," wrote a Caucasian soldier to
Time in February 1944. "He was a target for both Jap and American bullets. . . .
I wish to God that some of the people at home who say: 'Democracy is for the
white race only' could be made to go out and fight for it."[23] Commanders had
to ensure their troops were familiar with the Nisei. For example, when the 40th
Infantry Division was preparing for the New Britain landing, Moffett M. Ishikawa from San Jose, California, would meet with different units and tell them,
"Take a *good* look at me!"[24] Ironically, the first MIS Nisei to lose his life was not
killed by enemy action or friendly fire. S.Sgt. Ken Omura, a Seattle Kibei who

---

[23] Ltr to the Editor, *Time* (14 February 1944), reprinted in War Relocation Authority (WRA),
What We're Fighting For (Washington, D.C.: U.S. Department of the Interior, 1944), p. 7.

[24] Moffett M. Ishikawa, "Humor in Uniform," *Reader's Digest* (June 1958): 155.

had served with ATIS since September 1942, drowned on 19 March 1944 in the Admiralties.[25]

Col. Sidney F. Mashbir was the animating spirit behind ATIS, assisted by a handful of skilled Caucasian linguists such as Maj. John V. Shelton, Australian Imperial Force (AIF), chief of the Translation Section, and Maj. John E. Anderton as executive officer. Senior Nisei included three warrant officers, Sunao Phil Ishio, Gary Tsuneo Kadani, and Steve Shizuma Yamamoto. M.Sgt. George Kanegai was first sergeant. Continued growth for ATIS brought more problems. Mashbir and his staff became concerned about the declining language skills of recent graduates from Camp Savage. Tests administered to each arriving group showed "a steady diminution in the quality of the source material, inasmuch as an ever decreasing percentage of effective linguists is reaching this theater. This would seem to indicate that US potential resources are almost exhausted and that rigid control and economy in the distribution of linguists is imperative."[26] "When the linguists arrived from the Military Intelligence Language School," Mashbir wrote in his memoirs, "I was distressed to find that only a few were actually expert, and that as many as twenty-five percent were utterly unusable."[27] As a remedy he set up a training section for the incoming Nisei.

Japanese prisoners of war arrived in Australia in increasing numbers during 1944 as the tide of battle turned. They were interrogated by the Examination Section under Lt. Comdr. Samuel C. Bartlett, Jr., U.S. Naval Reserve, a Massachusetts district attorney who received the Legion of Merit on 14 July 1944 for his work.[28] But the Nisei brought more than cross-examination skills; they employed their knowledge of Japanese psychology and culture. Often, prisoners were interviewed multiple times; in this manner many were gradually won over to full cooperation.

Central Bureau was another intelligence organization that MacArthur relied upon heavily to guide his strategy. In 1942–1943 Central Bureau, working in cooperation with the Signal Intelligence Service at Arlington Hall, had struggled to extract intelligence from Japanese radio transmissions. In January 1944 Australian soldiers in New Guinea discovered a set of codebooks that retreating Japanese soldiers had buried. These codebooks were rushed to Brisbane and became crucial to breaking into Japanese Army code systems. From this point on, the trickle of signals intelligence became a flood.[29] Translation in Central Bureau was handled

---

[25] "Relatives Informed of Death of Sgt. Omura in New Guinea," *Pacific Citizen*, 1 Apr 44, p. 1; *Seattle Post Intelligencer* (5 April 1944), reprinted in WRA, *Nisei in the War against Japan* (Washington, D.C.: Department of the Interior, April 1945), p. 15; "Ken Omura, Ex-Seattleite, Drowned in New Guinea," *Seattle Times*, 13 Apr 44, p. 17. His cousin, Bill Hosokawa, published a remembrance in the *Pacific Citizen*, 6 Jan 45.

[26] ATIS, "Analysis of Linguistic Requirements," Unpubl Ms, 27 Jun 44, copy in author's files.

[27] Sidney F. Mashbir, *I Was an American Spy* (New York: Vantage, 1953), pp. 224–25.

[28] Ibid., pp. 226–30, 264–66.

[29] Edward J. Drea, *MacArthur's Ultra: Codebreaking and the War against Japan, 1942–1945* (Lawrence: University Press of Kansas, 1992), pp. 91–93; *The Quiet Heroes of the Southwest*

almost entirely by Caucasian linguists under Hugh Erskine, the son of missionary parents in Japan. Central Bureau occasionally borrowed Nisei from ATIS for
"special translations," but only one, Hawaii-born Clarence S. Yamagata, worked
in Central Bureau full-time.[30] Yamagata had graduated from the University of
California at Los Angeles in 1927 and then completed law school. Unable to find
work, he migrated to the Philippines and established a law practice in Manila,
where his clients included the Japanese embassy. When war broke out he worked
for the Philippine Department G–2 on Corregidor. Evacuated to Australia in April
1942, he joined Central Bureau as a cryptographic technician and translator. In
July 1944 he was commissioned a second lieutenant in the Signal Corps.[31]

Other valuable intelligence came from the Philippine guerrillas. Under the
direction of the Allied Information Bureau and later the Philippine Regional Section, thousands of Filipinos gathered information about the Japanese occupation
forces and passed it to Australia through clandestine radio links and small liaison
teams inserted by submarine. One important piece of intelligence arrived in Brisbane in the spring of 1944. On 31 March 1944, *Adm. Mineichi Koga*, commander of
the Japanese Combined Fleet Command, flew with his chief of staff, *Adm. Shigeru
Fukudome*, to Mindanao in the southern Philippines, where they encountered a
storm and crashed at sea. *Koga*'s aircraft disappeared in the dark, but *Fukudome*'s
splashed into the sea just off Cebu. Filipino fishermen plucked the admiral out of
the water and delivered him and his briefcase to the local guerrillas.[32] The local
Japanese commander soon learned that the guerrillas were holding a high-ranking prisoner. He pursued them and threatened retaliation if the captive was not
returned. The guerrilla commander, Lt. Col. John Cushing, an American mining engineer and reserve officer, radioed MacArthur's headquarters, which sent
a submarine to retrieve the documents. When the documents arrived in Australia
in early May, the Americans photographed them and rushed them back to Cebu,
where they were returned to the Japanese with *Fukudome*. The Japanese high command mistakenly concluded that the documents had not been compromised.

When Major Anderton at ATIS saw the documents, one in particular caught
his eye. It had a red cover with a dark "Z" across the front. Dated 8 March 1944,
the "Z-Plan" spelled out a new concept of operation for the Japanese Combined
Fleet. It detailed all naval forces available and how they would be used in the next
great showdown with the powerful American Navy. Colonel Mashbir assigned

---

Pacific Theater: An Oral History of the Men and Women of CBB and FRUMEL (Fort Meade, Md.:
National Security Agency, 1996); Drea and Richard, "New Evidence."

[30] ATIS History, p. 65.

[31] Clarence S. Yamagata, Biographical Summary, Unpubl Ms, 10 Feb 78, in Box 11, Harrington
Papers; *Quiet Heroes*, pp. 50–51; Harrington, *Yankee Samurai*, pp. 50–51; Richard Sakakida and
Wayne S. Kiyosaki, *A Spy in Their Midst: The World War II Struggle of a Japanese American Hero*
(Lanham, Md.: Madison Books, 1995), pp. 61–64, 90–93. Central Bureau awarded Yamagata the
Legion of Merit on 4 July 1945. No MIS Nisei received this award during the war.

[32] John Toland, *The Rising Sun: The Decline and Fall of the Japanese Empire, 1936–1945* (New
York: Random House, 1970), pp. 478–81; Steven T. Smith, *The Rescue* (New York: John Wiley and
Sons, 2001).

his top three Caucasian officers: Major Anderton, 1st Lt. Faubion Bowers, and Lt. Richard Bagnall, U.S. Navy. These officers prepared a rough translation and then brought in two Nisei, S.Sgt. Kiyoshi Yamashiro and T3g. Yoshikazu Yamada, to check their work. Mashbir personally turned the crank on the mimeograph machine to print twenty copies of the 22-page translation and sent a copy by air to Admiral Nimitz's headquarters in Hawaii. The very next day Mashbir appointed Yamashiro and Yamada as warrant officers.[33]

When a copy of the ATIS translation arrived in Hawaii, the fleet intelligence officer, Capt. Edwin T. Layton, U.S. Navy, fleet intelligence officer, faulted the ATIS translation, which he said "had been translated by someone unfamiliar with Japanese naval terminology" and retranslated the document himself. A few days later Joint Intelligence Center, Pacific Ocean Areas (JICPOA), printed the revised translation and distributed it to the fleet.[34] On 15 June Admiral Nimitz struck at the heart of Japan's defensive perimeter by attacking Saipan in the Marianas. As predicted in the captured Japanese plan, the Combined Fleet sallied into the open for the Battle of the Philippine Sea on 19–20 June. American naval commanders, in possession of the Japanese plans, inflicted a major defeat on Japanese naval power. The defeat was a blow from which Japan never recovered.[35]

Other captured documents proved useful. Major Anderton liked to tell the story, perhaps apocryphal, of an unusual document discovered on Guadalcanal which, when translated, turned out to be the schedule for a field brothel at Japanese headquarters at Rabaul. He claimed it even identified the separate hours and prices for officers and enlisted men. Fifth Air Force scheduled a strike for the time when the greatest number of senior officers would be visiting. After that, Anderton liked to say, "Japanese leadership at Rabaul was never the same."[36]

[33] ATIS Limited Distribution Translation no. 4, *"Z" Operation Orders*, 23 May 1944. (For a convenient listing of selected publications, see ATIS History, app. 9.) See also Harrington, *Yankee Samurai*, pp. 190–91, 195–97; Memo, Yoshikazu Yamada to Harrington, 18 Mar 78, Harrington Papers; Ted T. Tsukiyama, "Deciphering the 'Z-Plan,'" in *Secret Valor: M.I.S. Personnel, World War II Pacific Theater, Pre–Pearl Harbor to Sept. 8, 1951*, ed. Ted T. Tsukiyama et al. (Honolulu: Military Intelligence Service Veterans Club of Hawaii, 1993), pp. 55–57.

[34] W. J. Holmes, *Double-Edged Secrets: U.S. Naval Intelligence Operations in the Pacific during World War II* (Annapolis, Md.: Naval Institute Press, 1979), pp. 178–80; Edwin T. Layton, *"And I Was There!": Pearl Harbor and Midway—Breaking the Secrets* (New York: William Morrow, 1985), pp. 485–86; "Reminiscences of Rear Admiral Arthur H. McCollum," in *The Pacific War Remembered*, ed. John T. Mason (Annapolis, Md.: Naval Institute Press, 1986), pp.153–54; E. B. Potter, *Nimitz* (Annapolis, Md.: U.S. Naval Institute Press, 1976), pp. 295–96.

[35] According to the official ATIS History, the Z-Plan "proved to be of exceptional value and probably considerably shortened the war" (p. 47). See also WD Press Release, 22 Oct 45; *Pacific War and Peace*, p. 43; Tsukiyama et al., *Secret Valor*, pp. 55–57, 84–85; Michael Tsai, "The 'Z Plan,'" *Hawaii Herald*, 2 Jul 93; Lyn Crost, *Honor by Fire: Japanese Americans at War in Europe and the Pacific* (Novato, Calif.: Presidio Press, 1994), pp. 161–62.

[36] Harrington, *Yankee Samurai*, p. 228. Col. Elliott R. Thorpe, the Southwest Pacific Area (SWPA) chief of counterintelligence, relates a slightly different version. Elliott R. Thorpe, *East Wind, Rain: An Intimate Account of an Intelligence Officer in the Pacific, 1939–49* (Boston: Gambit, 1969), p. 147.

Brig. Gen. Charles A. Willoughby and Colonel Mashbir took a special interest in gathering information about Japanese war crimes. In April 1943 General Headquarters (GHQ) turned over to the theater counterintelligence officer "a large file of previously accumulated atrocity information." In April 1944 ATIS interrogated a captured Japanese Army civilian employee who had served in the Philippines in 1942–1943 and recorded in his diary details of atrocities and conditions the Allies had faced in Japanese prisoner of war camps. In July 1944 Willoughby established a War Crimes Investigation Board. Much of the evidence of Japanese war crimes came through the efforts of the ATIS Nisei.[37]

By 1944 the Counter Intelligence Corps (CIC) employed three Hawaii Nisei: the Bataan veteran M.Sgt. Arthur S. Komori, together with William T. Hiraoka and Sergeant Yamashiro. In March 1944 Komori was detailed to the Australian Department of Information, where he spent the next year monitoring Radio Tokyo and doing other translation work.[38]

The Allied air campaign in the Southwest Pacific drew upon expanding intelligence capabilities during 1944. The Fifth Air Force commander, Maj. Gen. George C. Kenney, was an avid consumer of ATIS reports, as well as "crash intelligence" from downed Japanese aircraft. Each crash site was investigated by special teams known as Air Technical Intelligence Units (ATIUs), later renamed Technical Air Intelligence Units (TAIUs). Nisei on the teams would translate data plates and documents found in the wreckage. The South Pacific Command formed a joint unit, Army-Navy Crash Intelligence, South Pacific Area, for the same purpose.[39]

Air commanders also realized the value of intercepting Japanese voice radio transmissions, and the Nisei played an important role in this. In 1943 the Army Air Forces developed a new unit, the "radio squadron, mobile," to conduct radio direction-finding and voice intercept operations.[40] In August 1943 the 1st Radio Squadron Mobile replaced the 138th Signal Radio Company on New Guinea in support of the Fifth Air Force. Not content to borrow Nisei from ATIS, in January 1944 the Air Staff requested a large number of linguists to be assigned to these units.

[37] ATIS History, pp. 47, 64; ATIS Research Rpt no. 72, "Japanese Violations of the Laws of War," 29 Apr 44; Mashbir, *I Was an American Spy*, pp. 234–37, 270; *A Brief History of the G–2 Section, GHQ, SWPA and Affiliated Units*, Intelligence Series (Tokyo: Far East Command, 1948), vol. 8, p. 38. Charles A. Willoughby and John Chamberlain quote from the captured diary in *MacArthur, 1941–1951* (New York: McGraw-Hill, 1954), pp. 157–60.

[38] Interv, Ann Bray with Arthur Komori, 1955; Harrington, *Yankee Samurai*, pp. 145, 245; Thorpe, *East Wind, Rain*, pp. 87–147; Duval A. Edwards, *Spy Catchers of the U.S. Army in the War with Japan* (Gig Harbor, Wash.: Red Apple Publishing, 1994), pp. 287–94; George Kiyoshi [Yamashiro] Sankey, "Areya, Koreye [This and That]," Unpubl Ms, excerpted in *Hawaii Pacific Press* (1 Dec 94): 56; George Sankey, MISNorCal Bio.

[39] George C. Kenney, *General Kenney Reports: A Personal History of the Pacific War* (New York: Duell, Sloan and Pearce, 1949). Kenney relied extensively on signals intelligence, which he could not mention in his memoirs. Michael J. Freeman, "Behind Enemy Lines!" *Airpower* (July 1994), describes the air technical intelligence unit assigned to the Southwest Pacific Area.

[40] John F. Kreis, ed., *Piercing the Fog: Intelligence and Army Air Forces Operations in World War II* (Washington, D.C.: Air Force History and Museums Program, 1996), pp. 361–63.

In response Camp Savage sent more than 200 Nisei for voice intercept training at MacDill Field, Florida. After four months the Nisei proceeded for advanced training to the Western Signal Aviation Unit Training Center at Camp Pinedale near Fresno, California, in the summer of 1944. They were among the first individuals of Japanese ancestry allowed to return to California since 1942. The exclusion orders were not lifted until December 1944.[41]

Twenty-five Nisei joined the 1st Radio Squadron Mobile at Hollandia on New Guinea in November 1944 and went into action in the Philippines in early 1945. Other Nisei joined the 7th Radio Squadron Mobile in the Markham Valley on New Guinea, which later moved to Morotai, an island in the Netherlands East Indies that could support airfields for the invasion of the Philippines. Other teams were assigned to the 6th Radio Squadron Mobile with the Tenth Air Force in China-Burma-India and the 8th Radio Squadron Mobile with the Twentieth Air Force on Guam. These Nisei provided valuable intelligence by listening in on Japanese pilots and air controllers as they conducted operations against Allied forces.[42]

The 1944 ground campaign in the Southwest Pacific was a series of daring landings on the New Guinea coast and the Bismarck Archipelago. In January 1944 ATIS sent a forward detachment to Sixth Army headquarters then at Finschhafen, led by WO Steve S. Yamamoto. Over several months Yamamoto single-handedly interrogated 3,100 prisoners of war and was awarded the Silver Star.[43] Each division was usually given six or seven Nisei for an operation. Other Nisei were sent on special missions. For example, in November 1943, when Sixth Army organized the Alamo Scouts, a special reconnaissance unit, they requested Nisei from ATIS.[44] Three volunteered; Richard Y. Hirata completed the rigorous training and went on to participate in several reconnaissance patrols in early 1944.[45]

Many Nisei actively sought combat duty, often for personal reasons. Colonel Mashbir told of "one of the less competent Nisei linguists" who repeatedly requested assignment to the front lines. Finally, the young Nisei showed Mashbir a letter from his Issei father, who was near death in an internment camp. Although the father was "a loyal subject of the Emperor," he acknowledged that his son was an American citizen and owed a great debt to the country of his birth. "This is my

[41] Kreis, *Piercing the Fog*, pp. 130–31; "Army Announces U.S. Soldiers of Japanese Ancestry Assigned to Central California Camp," *Pacific Citizen*, 26 Aug 44. One Nisei described his treatment by local civilians and his travels to Los Angeles. "Soldier Tells of Coast Experiences," *Pacific Citizen*, 7 Oct 44. About fifty Nisei joined the 8th RSM at Camp Pinedale in September 1944. *8th RSM: The Story behind the Flying Eight-Ball* (privately printed, 1946).

[42] Tsukiyama et al., *Secret Valor*, pp. 72–73, 77–81, 91; Ltrs, Ken Sekiguchi to Munakata, Harrington Papers, excerpted in *Yaban Gogai*, Aug 45; Ltr, Dempster P. Dirks to Roger Pineau, 11 August 1982, Correspondence, Box 13, Harrington Papers; Interv, Dawn E. Duensing with Yoichi Kawano and with James Sasami Okada, in *Americanism: A Matter of Mind and Heart*, vol. 1, *The Military Intelligence Service* (Maui, Hawaii: Maui's Sons and Daughters of the Nisei Veterans, 2001).

[43] Steve S. Yamamoto, in Swift, "First Class"; Sixth Army, General Orders No. 197, 18 Nov 44.

[44] "Alamo Scouts," *Intelligence Bulletin* (June 1946): 29–37.

[45] Interv, author with Richard Y. Hirata, 10 Sep 96.

Teiho Chena, Ted T. Tsukiyama, Thomas S. Goto, and Mark M. Akisada (left to
right) *with the 6th Radio Squadron Mobile in northeast India, late 1944*

dying command to you," the old man had written. "As your father, I demand that
to your death you be loyal to the United States; that you fight for the United States;
and, if necessary, that you die for the United States." At once Mashbir grasped the
Nisei's reason for requesting reassignment and gave his consent. "Within a very
few days," Mashbir wrote, the Nisei had "earned himself a combat decoration."[46]

Other ATIS Nisei had ample opportunity to serve in combat. In December
1943 MacArthur seized the western end of New Britain by landing the 1st Marine
Division at Cape Gloucester and the 112th Cavalry RCT at Arawe. Seven Nisei
served with the marine division under T.Sgt. Jerry Yoshito Shibata.[47] The Japanese fought hard; but equally difficult were heavy rain and winds, deep swamps,

---

[46] Mashbir, *I Was an American Spy*, pp. 249–50.

[47] Interv, U.S. Army Intelligence and Security Command with Harry K. Fukuhara; ATIS History, app. 12; Harrington, *Yankee Samurai*, p. 175. The 1st Marine Division G–2 staff included Maj.
Sherwood Moran, U.S. Marine Corps Reserve, a prewar missionary in Japan. Bernard C. Nalty,

and thick vegetation during four months in what the marines called the green inferno. One day on New Britain, one marine remarked to another: "I've been in a foxhole six months and I haven't seen a Jap. I don't know what one looks like." The second marine, who happened to be serving as bodyguard for a Nisei interpreter, replied, "I'll show you one for $5." The first marine handed over the money, and the bodyguard introduced him to the Nisei.[48]

The 112th Cavalry RCT came ashore at Arawe in the face of stiff Japanese resistance and heavy air attacks. T.Sgt. Yukitaka Terry Mizutari led the language team. Born in Hilo, Hawaii, and educated in Hawaii and Japan, Mizutari was popular with the other Nisei. He could play the ukulele and was a kendo master and excellent artist. He led his team with skill and courage. "Come on you fools," a teammate recalled hearing him mutter during a Japanese night attack on the command post. "You started this, and I am going to finish it."[49]

Meanwhile, on New Guinea, the 126th RCT was sent ashore 175 miles along the coast at Saidor on 2 January 1944 with another Nisei language team.[50]

In January 1944 the Fifth Air Force noticed that the Japanese seemed to have abandoned Los Negros, an island several hundred miles west of Rabaul. Signals intelligence predicted over 4,000 Japanese on the island, but American airmen could find no trace of them. MacArthur decided to send elements of the 1st Cavalry Division for a reconnaissance in force. On 29 February the 1st Cavalry Brigade landed and soon discovered there indeed were thousands of Japanese on the island.[51]

ATIS sent Capt. Paul W. Aurell and S.Sgt. Thomas T. Sakamoto with the lead elements. The brigade commander later signed a commendation for Sakamoto, describing how he "promptly and correctly interpreted captured enemy maps and documents [and] he submitted valuable reports to me on enemy unit identifications, strength of units, commanders' names, unit sectors, and the plans and intentions of enemy units."[52] Sakamoto may even have saved the general's life when American scouts detected some movement in tall grass about thirty yards from the brigade command post. The commanding general ordered Sakamoto to tell the Japanese to surrender. Sakamoto went forward with the task force S–2 and called out, but the Japanese answered with grenades and rifle fire. When the American soldiers returned fire, eighteen Japanese soldiers were killed or committed suicide, including the commander of the Japanese battalion defending the

---

Cape Gloucester: The Green Inferno (Washington, D.C.: Marine Corps Historical Center, 1994), p. 33.

    [48] "The Secrets Come out for Nisei Soldiers," *Los Angeles Times*, 20 Jul 82.

    [49] For Mizutari's actions on Arawe, see Howard I. Ogawa, "The Death of a Hero: This Is How Sgt. Mizutari Lived—And How He Died," *Pacific Citizen*, 20 Jan 45.

    [50] Interv, author with Harry T. Kubo, 11 Sep 96.

    [51] Kenney, *General Kenney Reports*, pp. 358–61; Willoughby and Chamberlain, *MacArthur, 1941–1951*, pp. 150–52; Drea, *MacArthur's Ultra*, pp. 99–104.

    [52] HQ, 1st Cav Bde, Commendation of ATIS no. 21, 14 Jun 44, 342.18–353, Assistant Secretary of War, RG 107, National Archives and Records Administration (NARA), Washington, D.C.

The 6th Infantry Division language team "captures" its team chief, Mizutari, in New Guinea, spring 1944. Harry K. Fukuhara is holding a captured Samurai sword.

airdrome. On the commander's body they found a copy of a field order for an attack on the American perimeter later that afternoon. The attack was thwarted, and Sakamoto was awarded the Bronze Star. The *Chicago Tribune* published the story and cited Sakamoto by name. Meanwhile, a copy of Sakamoto's commendation arrived at the War Department G–2. Brig. Gen. John Weckerling forwarded it to Assistant Secretary of War John J. McCloy with the comment that it indicated "the continuing and commendable work performed by Nisei interrogators and translators who were trained at the Military Intelligence Service Language School at Camp Savage."[53]

---

[53] Ltr, John Weckerling to John J. McCloy, 14 August 1944, with HQ, 1st Cav Bde, Commendation of ATIS no. 21, 14 Jun 44; ATIS History, p. 47; "California Japanese American Sergeant Cited for Action in Battle for Los Negros Island," *Pacific Citizen*, 15 Apr 44; "Reveal Husband of Cleveland Japanese Saved U.S. General," *Cleveland Press* (n.d.), reprinted in WRA, *Nisei in the War against Japan*, p. 11; *The Admiralties: Operations of the 1st Cavalry Division (29 February–18 May 1944)* (Washington, D.C.: War Department, Historical Division, 1945), p. 37; Mashbir, *I Was an American Spy*, p. 260.

In April 1944 MacArthur launched his boldest move yet, leaping hundreds of miles to bypass Japanese units along the New Guinea coast. Before the Japanese could recover, he pushed onward in July to reach New Guinea's western tip at Sansapor. In 100 days American ground troops advanced 1,300 miles. MacArthur's troops first landed at two weakly defended sites, Hollandia and Aitape.

Two divisions landed at Hollandia, each with a Nisei team. The team assigned to the 41st Infantry Division was led by two Caucasian officers and a senior Nisei, S.Sgt. John M. Tanikawa, A 42-year-old veteran of World War I, Tanikawa had served at Camp Savage as an instructor before requesting overseas duty.[54] Victory came swiftly at Hollandia, and captured documents were measured by the ton. A prisoner of war compound was filled with several thousand Japanese soldiers, who were guarded by special military police units that included Nisei interpreters. Maj. Gen. Robert L. Eichelberger, the I Corps commander, often personally interrogated Japanese prisoners with Nisei interpreters.[55] Sixth Army headquarters moved to Hollandia with the ATIS advance echelon, which included 41 officers and enlisted men. Several months later, in preparation for planned landings in the Philippines, ATIS sent an advance ATIS detachment to Hollandia, which grew into a miniature ATIS. By December 1944 it totaled 47 officers and 149 enlisted men.[56]

On 22 April 1944, the 163d RCT landed with a Nisei team to surprise the Japanese at Aitape. The landings at Hollandia and Aitape trapped thousands of Japanese soldiers, who turned to face the threat to their rear and fought their way back along the New Guinea coast. In July the Japanese launched desperate attacks along the Driniumor River. Weeks of fierce fighting resulted in the complete destruction of the Japanese forces. When Michael M. Miyatake joined the 112th Cavalry RCT to relieve another Nisei who had fallen ill, the appearance of the battlefield appalled him:

As we walked out of the area where the fighting had taken place, we had to step over hundreds of dead enemy bodies. Some were still grasping hand grenades, the pin already pulled. The slightest movement of a body could have set off an explosion at any moment.

The sight of blood-strewn bodies everywhere made me nauseated. I felt pity, then anger, and finally disgust to see so many young lives wasted. This was the first time I had witnessed the aftermath of combat. Walking through the area made me more determined than ever to get out of this mess alive and to let people know how pitiful and merciless the front could be.[57]

---

[54] Harrington, *Yankee Samurai*, p. 199.

[55] Interv, author with Paul T. Bannai, 11 Sep 96; Jay Luvaas, ed., *Dear Miss Em: General Eichelberger's War in the Pacific, 1942–1945* (Westport, Conn.: Greenwood Press, 1972), pp. 108–19, 122. Two language officers summarized the work of the 41st Infantry Division language teams at Hollandia in Ltr, James S. Mize and Robert L. Heilbroner to Colonel Rasmussen, 15 December 1944, Trng Grp, Ofc of the Dir of Intel G–2, RG 165, NARA. See also Edwards, *Spy Catchers*, pp. 134–39.

[56] ATIS History, pp. 27, 31, 34.

[57] *Japanese Eyes, American Heart: Personal Reflections of Hawaii's World War II Nisei Soldiers* (Honolulu: Tendai Educational Foundation, 1998), pp. 170–76.

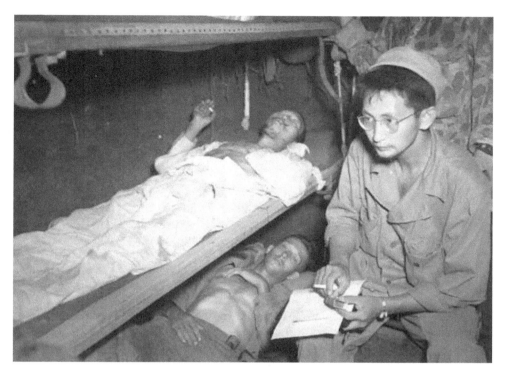

Fukuhara questions a wounded prisoner, Arawe, January 1944.

In May MacArthur pressed his advantage and landed more forces another hundred miles westward at Maffin Bay. After several days of tough fighting, GIs moved toward the high ground nicknamed Lone Tree Hill. The 6th Infantry Division went into action on 20 June, its initiation into combat. When the experienced Nisei team leader, T.Sgt. Harry K. Fukuhara, fell ill, Sergeant Mizutari took his place. Shortly after sundown on 23 June, the Japanese attacked toward the division command post where the Nisei worked. The fight became a wild melee, with bullets flying in all directions in the dark. The Nisei rolled out of their hammocks and grabbed their rifles. Mizutari took shelter behind a tree outside the intelligence tent, returned fire, and called on his teammates to do the same. As he rose to his knees to fire, he was hit in the chest. A teammate, Kiyoshi Fujimura, "felt something heavy fall on me. Realizing it was Terry, I sat up and cradled him in my arms all the while calling, 'Terry, Terry!' Then, I felt something warm on my hands and in front of my body. I felt a hole about a half inch in diameter near his chest—it was much larger in his back. I kind of sensed that he was dead.[58]

Mizutari was the first Nisei to die in combat in the Pacific. The citation for the posthumous Silver Star described how, "fully realizing the danger involved in moving from his concealed position, he rushed to a more strategic but vulnerable position in order to defend the men serving under him, thereby sacrificing his life." When Mizutari's team returned to Australia, they took up a collection and purchased a plaque to send to his family with a letter from Colonel Mashbir: "His record serves to exemplify the great work of the Nisei for their country to which cause he has given his life." In reporting Mizutari's death, the *Honolulu Advertiser* mentioned obliquely that his father was "at present on the mainland." In fact, his father was being held at a Department of Justice internment camp.[59]

On 27 May 1944, the 41st Infantry Division landed on Biak Island, off the New Guinea coast. Allied intelligence had once again underestimated Japanese strength, and the fight degenerated into a bitter struggle as the Americans tried to destroy the Japanese defenders dug into deep caves. On the second day soldiers discovered a roster of officers and noncommissioned officers from the principal defending force, the *222d Infantry Regiment*, which gave the attackers their first clear picture of the defending force.[60] The Japanese repeatedly counterattacked and held their ground for more than six weeks, delaying MacArthur's entire campaign. The Americans suffered about 400 killed in action and 2,000 wounded. Another 423 soldiers were hospitalized for psychoneurosis, and 6,811 became combat ineffective from various diseases. The Japanese defenders suffered 4,800 killed in action and thirteen captured, only one of whom was a combat soldier.[61]

The fighting on Biak inflamed American racial hatred. One witness was the famed aviator Charles A. Lindbergh, who arrived on 21 July to spend three weeks with a Fifth Air Force fighter group on Biak. What he saw and heard sickened and depressed him. "Sitting in the security and relative luxury of our quarters," he recorded in his journal, "I listen to American Army officers refer to these Japanese soldiers as 'yellow sons of bitches.' Their desire is to exterminate the Jap ruth-

---

[58] Kiyo Fujimura, "He Died in My Arms," in *John Aiso and the M.I.S.: Japanese-American Soldiers in the Military Intelligence Service, World War II*, ed. Tad Ichinokuchi (Los Angeles: Military Intelligence Club of Southern California, 1988), pp. 96–97; Interv, author with Hirata; Ogawa, "Death of a Hero." In Swift, "First Class," pp. 48–49, Kazuo Kozaki speculates that Mizutari may have been struck by friendly fire.

[59] 6th Inf Div, General Orders no. 28, 25 Jul 44; "Big Island's Dead, Wounded of Battle Fronts Are Listed," *Honolulu Advertiser*, 30 Jul 44, p. 9; WD Press Release, 22 Oct 45. The Defense Language Institute Foreign Language Center named an academic building in Mizutari's honor in 1980.

[60] ATIS History, p. 47.

[61] Robert L. Eichelberger, *Our Jungle Road to Tokyo* (New York: Viking, 1950), p. 153. The U.S. Army's official history reports that 220 Japanese were taken prisoner, most of them after organized resistance had ceased. Robert Ross Smith, *The Approach to the Philippines*, U.S. Army in World War II (Washington, D.C.: Office of the Chief of Military History, 1953), p. 392.

lessly, even cruelly. I have not heard a word of respect or compassion spoken of our enemy since I came here."[62]

Despite the setback on Biak, MacArthur moved his forces to seize Noemfoor Island, Sansapor, and finally, in September, Morotai in the Moluccas, over 200 miles west of New Guinea. Each time Nisei accompanied the landings to provide immediate tactical intelligence. Meanwhile, back at Hollandia and Brisbane, other Nisei worked to process the prisoners and captured documents. From January to September 1944 Allied forces had leapt over 1,300 miles and now held airfields within three hundred miles of the Philippines.

The dangerous work of clearing bypassed Japanese forces often fell to Australian units, which ATIS supported with Nisei language teams as well as the American units. "In the beginning, the Australians, like our own Navy, were loath to accept them at all," Colonel Mashbir later remarked, "so I simply had to get tough about it and told the Aussies it was Nisei or nothing. There just weren't enough Caucasians capable of doing intelligence work with the Australian divisions to go around."[63] Australian forces awarded numerous commendations to the Nisei "Yanks." However, by the end of 1944 American forces were moving to the Philippines and most Nisei assigned to Australian units returned to ATIS. The Australian director of Air Force Intelligence established a Japanese-language training program at Sydney University, where the first class of thirty-two Royal Australian Air Force enlisted students began training on 31 July 1944. The school's commanding officer was Flying Officer Max Wiadrowski, a prewar high school teacher who had studied Japanese privately before the war and had been assigned for a time to ATIS.[64]

Australia also assumed responsibility for most Japanese prisoners of war. By August 1944, 2,223 Japanese prisoners were in Australian custody, although they were outnumbered by almost 15,000 Italians and almost 1,600 Germans. Australia lacked sufficient linguists to supervise the Japanese prisoners. On 5 August 1944, 1,104 Japanese prisoners staged a breakout from Cowra Prisoner of War Camp in New South Wales. It took Australian forces more than a week to crush the rebellion and capture the escapees, of whom 234 were killed. Four Australians also lost their lives. Major Shelton was rushed from ATIS to assist in the investigation.[65]

Off-duty Nisei found wartime Brisbane a welcoming place, much as they had Minneapolis–St. Paul. For Nisei who had served in the forward areas, Australia

---

[62] Charles A. Lindbergh, *The Wartime Journals of Charles A. Lindbergh* (New York: Harcourt Brace Jovanovich, 1970), pp. 879–80; John W. Dower, *War without Mercy: Race and Power in the Pacific War* (New York: Pantheon, 1986), pp. 69–71.

[63] Mashbir, *I Was an American Spy*, p. 247; ATIS History, pp. 24–26; Interv, author with Yasuo Ace Fukai, 9 Sep 96. ATIS History, app. 12, lists twenty-four Australian commendations awarded to individual Nisei in 1944–1945.

[64] Colin Funch, *Linguists in Uniform: The Japanese Experience* (Australia: Japanese Studies Centre, Monash University, 2003), pp. 31–33, 51–75.

[65] Gavin Long, *Australia in the War of 1939–1945*, ser. 1, vol. 7, *The Final Campaigns* (Canberra: Australian War Memorial, 1963), app. 5; Funch, *Linguists in Uniform*, pp. 126–30.

seemed like a paradise. They spent their dollars freely in local restaurants and
taverns. A few managed to return home on leave. Kadani took the opportunity
of a stateside furlough to marry his sweetheart. The newlyweds spent Christmas
1944 with Kadani's parents in the Poston camp and spent New Year's with his
bride's parents in another camp, Gila River. In late 1943 Sergeant Komori returned
to Hawaii, which he had not seen since before the war, and visited Camp Savage
in Minnesota. However, he had found his true love in Australia. He married "an
Aussie Chinese girl," he recalled, "who was the first girl I had met in Australia in
1942. I had all day to court her, for my [radio] monitoring duties were at night."
Tom Takata was hospitalized with malaria he had contracted in New Guinea. During his long recovery he fell in love with Sylvia Joyce Look You, the daughter of a
Chinese doctor and an Australian woman. They married in August 1944.[66]

Two Nisei changed their names in Australia. California-born Arthur Katsuyoshi Ushiro changed his name to Arthur Robert Castle in April 1944 (*shiro* is the
Japanese word for "castle"). He changed his name, he later explained, "because
of the difficulty in spelling it and the desirability of 'Anglicizing' it because of his
present military duties." Yamashiro changed his last name to Sankey, a different
reading of the characters of his family name.[67]

Another change for ATIS was the arrival of ninety American servicewomen
from the Women's Army Corps (WAC) in May or June 1944. Australian servicewomen had worked for ATIS in clerical and other support capacities since its
beginning, but these were the first American women. Colonel Mashbir reported
that their arrival hurt morale: "Here were men who had lived through the rigors
of ten combat operations, who had lived under the most wretched and hazardous
conditions, and who were still T–5s. Suddenly they were forced to accept a group
of typists and stenographers in uniform, with the ranks of First Sergeant, Master
Sergeant, and T–3s, practically all of whom were senior to every single combat
soldier I had." However, because the Australian government would not permit its
servicewomen to leave the continent, the American forces had no choice but to
accept the American WACs as the campaign moved forward.[68]

Most Nisei enlisted men saw no promotions, but at least a few received commissions starting in 1944. On 22 April 1944, Colonel Mashbir awarded commissions to the three Nisei warrant officers, Phil Ishio, Gary Kadani, and Steve Yamamoto. Later that year he sent several others to officer candidate school in Brisbane,

---

[66] Harrington, *Yankee Samurai*, pp. 198, 226; Interv, Bray with Komori, 1955.

[67] "California Nisei Soldier [Ushiro] Seeks to Anglicize Name," *Pacific Citizen*, 1 Apr 44,
p. 1; Harrington, *Yankee Samurai*, p. 145. Several thousand Japanese in Hawaii changed their given
names during the war, but only a few changed their family name. Andrew Lind, *Hawaii's Japanese: An Experiment in Democracy* (Princeton: Princeton University Press, 1946), p. 143; Eileen H.
Tamura, *Americanization, Acculturalization, and Ethnic Identity: The Nisei Generation in Hawaii*
(Urbana: University of Illinois Press, 1994), pp. 169–71.

[68] Mashbir, *I Was an American Spy*, pp. 222–23; Mattie E. Treadwell, *The Women's Army Corps*,
U.S. Army in World War II (Washington, D.C.: Office of the Chief of Military History, 1954), pp.
410–23.

which produced at least six more Nisei second lieutenants by early 1945. However, not until the summer of 1945 was the ATIS table of allowances increased. Until then, ATIS was authorized fewer than forty lieutenants, which included the Caucasian team leaders trained at the Army Intensive Japanese Language School.[69]

Another burden for the ATIS Nisei was that of secrecy. Mashbir insisted on tight security and impressed the need on all personnel for pragmatic reasons. Each document published by ATIS bore this warning:

Captured documents and prisoners of war are sources of intelligence which the enemy can deny by disciplinary instruction if he becomes aware of the fact that reliable information is being obtained therefrom. Special care must, therefore, be taken to ensure the secrecy of this document.[70]

Despite the secrecy, the Nisei were in great demand. ATIS grew from 150 Nisei to 285 by the summer of 1944. In a June 1944 staff study, Mashbir requested 266 more within six months. In August the theater sent a memorandum to the War Department G–2, saying, "The services of Nisei in the various phases of Japanese language work in this theater have proved invaluable." However, Mashbir did not get all he requested. Eleven airborne-qualified Nisei arrived for the 11th Airborne Division that autumn, but no more Nisei arrived in the Southwest Pacific Theater until early 1945. Mashbir later complained that "we never succeeded in persuading anybody until just before the end of the war that that number would be needed, and, in fact, every request was turned down by higher authority."[71]

By the end of 1944 the Southwest Pacific Theater had developed an elaborate intelligence apparatus. The various intelligence disciplines were developed to a high degree and were staffed by thousands of military personnel. The resulting intelligence was disseminated, cross-referenced, and analyzed at all levels; combat commanders learned to rely on this intelligence for their tactical and operational plans. In much of this the ATIS Nisei played a vital role. "I am Mashbir's

---

[69] ATIS History, app. 3; Mashbir, *I Was an American Spy*, p. 250; "Intelligence Men Recount WW II Projects at Reunion," *Honolulu Star-Bulletin*, 2 Sep 68; Masami Tahira, in Oguro, *Sempai Gumi*, pp. 145–50. George Kanegai claims that in the spring of 1945 a commissioning board blackballed two Nisei who had anglicized their names. A board member told Kanegai, "Anybody who's ashamed of their Japanese name should not be commissioned." Interv, author with George Kanegai, 13 Sep 96, p. 23.

[70] ATIS History, p. 31; Mashbir, *I Was an American Spy*, pp. 237–38. In October 1945 Mashbir first revealed the existence of ATIS to the American press, calling it "a highly secret military organization." "U.S. Army Reveals Work of Nisei in Pacific," *Pacific Citizen*, 20 Oct 45, p. 1.

[71] Mashbir, *I Was an American Spy*, p. 224. In his unpublished memoir, Willoughby later claimed "some credit" for "sponsoring" the Nisei and recalled requesting 1,000 (p. 190). He wrote that MacArthur's chief of staff, Lt. Gen. Richard K. Sutherland, "readily agreed" but was "slightly amused" by the size of the request. "The Character of Military Intelligence," pt. 2, p. 190, Willoughby Papers from Gettysburg College, RG–23B, MacArthur Memorial, Library and Archives, Norfolk, Va.; Memo, GHQ SWPA to WD G–2, 5 Aug 44, 342.18, Asst Sec War, RG 107, NARA.

most avid reader," MacArthur once remarked. "In fact, I imagine I have read every word that he published." [72]

Central Pacific Area

The MIS Nisei who served in the Central Pacific fought a different kind of war. The theater featured predominantly naval battles waged in the air, on the surface, and under the sea to defeat the Japanese Combined Fleet and seize island strongholds to bring American power within striking distance of the Japanese home islands. For this Admiral Nimitz built up his intelligence staff to exploit multiple sources, especially intercepted naval radio communications. The centerpiece was JICPOA, an Army-Navy organization located in Makalapa near Nimitz's headquarters at Pearl Harbor. Brig. Gen. Joseph J. Twitty, a prewar Japanese-language attaché, was in command. Communications intelligence was handled by the Fleet Radio Unit, Pacific (FRUPAC).[73] Navy officials at all levels remained suspicious of all persons of Japanese ancestry, regardless of citizenship. For translators and interpreters the Navy relied upon Caucasian graduates of its language school at Boulder, Colorado. By early 1944 the JICPOA Translation Section had grown to over a hundred Navy language officers.[74] Other Japanese-language tasks in the Pacific Ocean Areas were performed by psychological warfare specialists. Tactical commanders used leaflets and loudspeakers to encourage surrender, but the campaigns to date had yielded only a handful of Japanese prisoners of war. In March 1944 Nimitz allowed the Office of War Information to establish a small office in Honolulu to help JICPOA develop leaflets. In June 1944 Nimitz established his own psychological warfare section.[75]

The battles of 1944 would require sustained ground combat operations (*Map 9*), and for this Nimitz needed more Army intelligence support. In the spring of 1944 the War Department G–2 offered to provide MIS Nisei to Navy Intelligence. In April and May 1944 two groups totaling some fifty Nisei left Camp Savage for Hawaii. For the first group of seventeen Hawaii Nisei it was a homecoming. On 10 May they began work on the top floor of a closed furniture store on Kapiolani

---

[72] Mashbir, *I Was an American Spy*, p. 240.

[73] Joint Intelligence Center, Pacific Ocean Areas, "Report of Intelligence Activities in the Pacific Ocean Areas," 15 Oct 45 (hereafter cited as JICPOA History), copy in author's files; *Military Intelligence in the Pacific, 1942–1946: Bulletins of the Intelligence Center, Pacific Ocean Area, and the Joint Intelligence Center, Pacific Ocean Area* (Wilmington, Del.: Scholarly Resources, S1661 [41 microfilm rolls], 1984). See also John Ashmead, *The Mountain and the Feather* (Boston: Houghton Mifflin, 1961).

[74] JICPOA History, pp. 40–45; W. J. Holmes, *Doubled-Edged Secrets: U.S. Naval Intelligence Operations in the Pacific during World War II* (Annapolis, Md.: Naval Institute Press, 1979), pp. 168–69.

[75] Ellis M. Zacharias, *Secret Missions: The Story of an Intelligence Officer* (New York: G. P. Putnam's Sons, 1946), pp. 323–24; Gilmore, *You Can't Fight Tanks with Bayonets*, p. 17; JICPOA History, pp. 31–32.

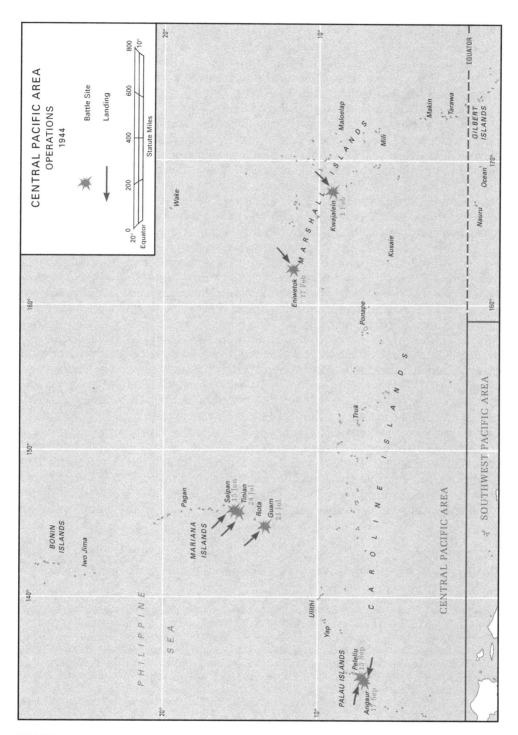

CENTRAL PACIFIC AREA
OPERATIONS
1944

⁕ Battle Site

→ Landing

Statute Miles
0   200   400   600   800
Equator
20°   10°

PHILIPPINE

SEA

BONIN
ISLANDS

Iwo Jima

Pagan

MARIANA
ISLANDS

Saipan
15 Jun
Tinian
24 Jul
Rota
Guam
21 Jul

Ulithi

Yap

PALAU ISLANDS
Peleliu
15 Sep
Angaur
17 Sep

CAROLINE ISLANDS

Truk

Ponape

Kusaie

Wake

Eniwetok
17 Feb

MARSHALL ISLANDS

Kwajalein
1 Feb

Maloelap

Mili

Nauru

Ocean

Makin

Tarawa

GILBERT
ISLANDS

EQUATOR

CENTRAL PACIFIC AREA

SOUTHWEST PACIFIC AREA

140°   150°   160°   170°   160°

20°   10°

MAP 9

Boulevard in "what was then a rather forlorn section of the city."[76] The annex had to be placed in Honolulu because the Navy would not relax its security rules against allowing Japanese on the base. Consequently, the Nisei lived and worked in this building, often taking their meals at a restaurant across the street because no mess hall was available to them.

The Translation Section was headed by Cmdr. John W. Steele, retired from the U.S. Navy. The JICPOA annex was headed by Maj. Glenn Brunner, U.S. Marine Corps Reserve, a Foreign Service officer who had served in Tokyo before the war; his executive officer, Maj. Lachlan M. Sinclair, had graduated from the first officer class at Camp Savage.[77] The annex included 5 Navy officers, 5 Army officers, and the 50 Nisei enlisted men. The Nisei were divided into three teams, each under a Nisei veteran of the Aleutian Islands Campaign. One, Nobuo Furuiye, was born on a Colorado truck farm. After graduating from a Denver high school, he had spent two years attending middle school in Japan. He had enlisted in January 1942 and served in Alaska. When he returned to the United States in late 1943, he was assured that he would not be sent overseas again. He made arrangements to have his fiancée released from the Jerome camp so they could be married in February 1944. Two months later he was sent to Hawaii and left his bride behind. The other two team leaders were Tadashi Ted Ogawa and Don C. Oka, both from the mainland and Aleutian veterans.[78] The Nisei made the most of living in wartime Honolulu. Almost 40 percent of Hawaii's prewar population was of Japanese descent. On weekends the Nisei soldiers could visit friends and relatives and were readily accepted into the local community. Ben I. Yamamoto had been born and raised in Pearl City and then trained at MISLS: "I couldn't believe my good fortune. Hawaii, after two and a half years on the mainland! . . . This was a good deal, giving us a chance to visit my family in Pearl City and enjoy local food. I even got carried away and got married."[79]

The work included translating captured diaries, notebooks, and occasional technical documents. "There was something unreal about our lives," wrote Donald Keene, a Boulder graduate assigned to the Translation Section. "We would spend most days translating diaries, letters, notebooks, and the like, but it was difficult to imagine that what we were doing was of any conceivable use to anybody. And

[76] Donald Keene, *On Familiar Terms: A Journey across Cultures* (New York: Kodansha, 1994), pp. 32–33. Keene was assigned to the JICPOA annex from September 1943 until March 1945.

[77] George Inagaki, Harrington Papers.

[78] Falk and Tsuneishi, *MIS in the War against Japan*, pp. 58–60, 99–100; "Rocky Mountain MIS Veterans Club Autobiographies," pp. 12–15, Unpubl Ms, ed. Kent T. Yoritomo, [1989], author's files (this and similar biographies hereafter cited as Rocky Mountain Bios); Don C. Oka, MISNorCal Bio; Don C. Oka, in *Saga of the MIS*; Sam Isokane, "JICPOA Annex Story," in Tsukiyama et al., *Secret Valor*, pp. 66–68. MIS Nisei in the Pacific Ocean Areas generally did not work in signals intelligence. However, Nobuo Furuiye reports having served for forty-five days in the autumn of 1944 aboard a Navy cruiser for "radio intercept duty." Falk and Tsuneishi, *MIS in the War against Japan*, p. 58.

[79] Ben I. Yamamoto, in Oguro, *Sempai Gumi*, pp. 67–77; *Japanese Eyes, American Heart*, pp. 177–85.

Nisei from the Joint Intelligence Center, Pacific Ocean Areas, celebrating New Year's, Honolulu, December 1944

there was the irritation of being under a commanding officer whom we disliked."[80] Another Navy language officer recalled how the captured documents came in boxes that were "permeated with that strange rich odor which you later came to recognize as the odor of the dead. The worst documents were drycleaned, but the odor became part of [the section]."[81] Some Nisei specialized in hand-written sōsho documents, but they sometimes handled printed materials as well. Oka's section spent several months translating a multivolume Japanese industrial directory that the XXI Bomber Command later used to target B–29 raids on the Japanese home islands. The Nisei also helped interrogate prisoners of war on Oahu, many of whom turned out to be Korean laborers.[82]

Despite the useful work of the JICPOA Nisei, their leaders had a low regard for their skill. "These Nisei, like most Nisei, are much handicapped by lack of educational background for this type of work, which calls for initiative and judgment in addition to language experience," Commander Steele told Comdr. Albert E. Hindmarsh, the director of the Navy's language school at Boulder, in January 1945. "In this group of 44 Nisei, only 1 had better than a high-school education. Consequently all the work of all Nisei has to be checked in detail by Boulder

---

[80] Keene, *On Familiar Terms*, p. 34.
[81] Ashmead, *The Mountain and the Feather*, p. 319.
[82] Gordon Cotler, "All in Favor Say 'Hai,'" *New Yorker* (9 April 1949): 100, describes Cotler's work with Japanese prisoners in Hawaii while assigned to JICPOA in the autumn of 1944. Cotler was a Caucasian graduate of the Army Intensive Japanese Language School and MISLS.

boys. . . . That is why Nisei are always organized as teams." Hindmarsh summarized the opinions of Navy intelligence officers in Hawaii toward the Nisei:

Almost unanimous is the view (all Navy circles and in Army groups who work directly
with Boulder graduates) that Nisei are too often limited in their usefulness; generally they
are short on English and/or Japanese, lack initiative and sense of responsibility, require
constant checking in their work (both spoken and written), suffer psychological handicaps
(many have asked to be kept out of advanced areas). There are a few notable exceptions to
these criticisms, but in general the attitude is that the Nisei are "better than nothing."[83]

These dismissive attitudes were in stark contrast to the acceptance of the Nisei
in the Southwest Pacific and may explain why the JICPOA annex never developed into anything like the highly praised Allied Translator and Interpreter Section. Army headquarters on Hawaii did not share the Navy's low estimation of the
Nisei. In addition to the volunteers for the 442d Regimental Combat Team and
the Military Intelligence Service, 600 Nisei soldiers served in Hawaii with the
1399th Engineer Battalion performing general construction work.[84] Concerning
their loyalty, the Hawaiian Department's assistant chief of staff for intelligence,
Col. Kendall J. Fielder, told a newspaper reporter in April 1944: "I have been in
charge of military intelligence activities here since June 1941, and am in a position
to know what has happened. There have been no known acts of sabotage, espionage, or fifth-column activities committed by the Japanese in Hawaii either on or
subsequent to Dec. 7, 1941."[85]

Not all MIS Nisei serving in the Central Pacific spent the war in Honolulu.
Some would prove themselves in combat. Until mid-1944 the War Department
had sent most MIS Nisei to the South Pacific and Southwest Pacific, about 385,
compared to only about 70 for the Central Pacific. After that the War Department
sent few additional Nisei to the Southwest Pacific. Instead, from May 1944 thru
April 1945, the War Department sent 160 Nisei to the Central Pacific. Most were
assigned to divisions or corps, leaving the 50 JICPOA Nisei to continue their
work unaided.

On 1 February 1944, soldiers and marines landed in the Marshall Islands. The
Nisei taught them simple Japanese phrases such as, "Throw down your weapons,"
"Sit down," and "Where is your regiment?" They even "produced a live drama

    [83] Office of the Chief of Naval Operations, "School of Oriental Languages," pp. 30, 34, Unpubl
Ms, Naval Historical Center, Washington, D.C.
    [84] These Nisei soldiers remained in Hawaii when the 100th Infantry Battalion departed in May
1942 and were assigned to the 1st Battalion, 370th Engineer Special Service Regiment, which was
redesignated the 1399th Engineer Construction Battalion on 21 March 1944. When Nisei eligibility for Selective Service was restored in 1944, the Army organized several other service units in
Hawaii with Nisei soldiers.
    [85] "Japanese-Americans in Hawaii," *Honolulu Advertiser*, 16 Apr 44. Colonel Fielder and Robert
C. Shivers, head of the FBI's Honolulu office, moderated the Navy's hostility to the large Japanese
population in Hawaii throughout the war. Tom Coffman, *The Island Edge of America: A Political
History of Hawaii* (Honolulu: University of Hawaii Press, 2003), pp. 59–102.

showing the right and wrong ways of processing and interrogating Japanese prisoners."[86] But the Americans took few prisoners alive. Before each assault, extensive naval gunfire and bombardment blasted the islands for days. When Mike Sakamoto went ashore on Eniwetok, he was staggered to see the island landscape littered with the ripped-apart bodies of its defenders. Moved to tears at his first vision of combat, he sang a Japanese song in their memory.[87]

The 7th Infantry Division faced stiff opposition when it assaulted Kwajalein, a major Japanese headquarters. A Caucasian soldier wrote to the *San Francisco Chronicle* praising the actions of a Nisei friend. He described how his friend had crawled into a slit trench armed only with a trench knife: "The enemy immediately started popping out of the other entrance with no desire to fight. From these prisoners our

Hachiya

interpreter learned of more—but I think what I've told is sufficient. Just take it from this G.I. that our interpreters have plenty of nerve and their services are invaluable."[88] The 7th Infantry Division's commanding general boasted of the Nisei to a war correspondent. The resulting story, published in February 1944, was the first official confirmation that Nisei were fighting in the Pacific.[89] After the battle the Nisei found large quantities of documents which they began to sort and translate. JICPOA sent several more Nisei to help with the enormous task, including T3g. Frank Tadakazu Hachiya, a Kibei from Hood River, Oregon. Hachiya spent the next five months on Kwajalein translating these materials. There, he met a fellow Oregonian, Monroe Sweetland, a small-town newspaper publisher. The two young men had much in common and enjoyed many long philosophical discussions. "There were bright tropical nights," Sweetland recalled, "when we sat out to talk of Oregon." Hachiya expressed his yearning "to return to 'the most beautiful valley in the world.' But he also knew what he was fighting for and he

[86] "Use of Nisei Saved GI Lives in Pacific," *Pacific Citizen*, 29 Sep 45, p. 1.

[87] Harrington, *Yankee Samurai*, pp. 182–83.

[88] Glenn W. M'Donald, Ltr to the Editor, *San Francisco Chronicle*, 16 Sep 44, reprinted in WRA, *What We're Fighting For*, pp. 20–21.

[89] "General Reveals Japanese Americans Took Part in Capture of Kwajalein Atoll," *Pacific Citizen*, 4 Mar 44.

knew especially well what he was fighting against—he understood both much better than most of us old-line Americans do."[90]

The next objective was the Marianas, an island group less than 1,500 miles from Japan. These included several islands needed as bases for future naval and air operations, such as the former U.S. naval station at Guam. Plans called for three Marine divisions and two Army divisions to seize Saipan, Tinian, and Guam. Saipan lay at the heart of the Japanese defenses, housing the *Japanese 31st Army* headquarters and 32,000 troops. Tens of thousands of Japanese civilians also lived in the islands, so American forces would for the first time encounter a large Japanese noncombatant population.

After weeks of bombardment the marines churned ashore on Saipan on 15 June 1944. In response, Japanese naval commanders carried out Operation A (A-GO), based on the compromised Z-Plan. The Japanese Combined Fleet and the U.S. Navy met in the Western Pacific between the Marianas and the Philippines. In this great air and sea battle the available forces on each side totaled more than twice those engaged in the Battle of Midway two years before. The Battle of the Philippine Sea became the largest carrier battle of the war. In addition to the Japanese plan, the Americans had another vital advantage: Navy language officers eavesdropped on the Japanese air coordinator's radio channel and guided American pilots to their targets. The result was the near-total destruction of Japanese naval air power, so great that the American pilots derisively called it the Great Marianas Turkey Shoot. When the battle ended, a staff officer on the flagship of Admiral Raymond A. Spruance, Commander, Central Pacific Force, suggested they shoot down the Japanese air coordinator as well. Capt. Arleigh A. Burke, U.S. Navy, chief of staff to the task force commander, vetoed the idea, saying, "You can't shoot that man down. He's done more good for the United States than any of us this day."[91] Victory in the Marianas was now assured, but weeks of bitter ground fighting remained.

Assault elements of the 27th Infantry Division followed the marines ashore on 16 June, followed the next day by division headquarters and T.Sgt. Timothy T. Ohta's language team. This was the language team's third assault landing but the first for their new officer, 2d Lt. Benjamin H. Hazard, Jr. In preparation for the landing, the team held orientation classes on how to handle prisoners of war and the importance of captured documents. The division's G–2 "walked into one

---

[90] Quoted in Martha F. McKeown, "Frank Hachiya: He Was American at Birth, and at Death," *Portland Oregonian*, 20 May 45.

[91] Ronald Lewin, *The American Magic: Codes, Ciphers, and the Defeat of Japan* (New York: Farrar Straus Giroux, 1982), pp. 255–56; "Reminiscences of Rear Admiral Arthur H. McCollum, U.S. Navy Retired," 2 vols., pp. 616–19, Unpubl Ms, 1970–1971, Naval Historical Center, Washington, D.C.; Mason, *Pacific War Remembered*, pp. 153–54. See also the memoir by Spruance's chief of staff, Carl J. Moore, "Command Decisions during the Battle of the Philippine Sea," in Mason, *Pacific War Remembered*, pp. 209–15. For a balanced assessment of American foreknowledge of Japanese plans, see Smith, *The Rescue*, pp. 256–88.

of these classes one day expecting to find 20 students; there were 120."[92] After the battle started other Nisei came from the JICPOA annex to support the marine divisions. The marine units also had Caucasian language officers from Boulder. Each marine battalion had Caucasian enlisted language specialists, graduates of the six-month Japanese course at Camp Elliott, California. For three weeks the soldiers and marines fought for every square foot of Saipan. Nisei provided valuable tactical support by translating captured documents on the spot and interrogating captured Japanese. In a humorous incident in an otherwise desperate battle, T3g. Nobuo Dick Kishiue watched in amazement as a Japanese Zero touched down on the Aslito airfield shortly after the Americans captured it. The Japanese pilot was hauled before Kishiue for interrogation. "When I asked why he had landed at Aslito," Kishiue recalled, "the pilot responded that he had taken off from Guam and thought the airfield was still in Japanese possession."[93]

Saipan was honeycombed with tunnels and caves, many of which contained desperate Japanese soldiers or frightened civilians. On 2 July T.Sgts. Ben Honda and George Matsui volunteered to enter some caves to encourage a large group of Japanese soldiers and civilians to surrender. Two Japanese soldiers attempted to use their weapons, and the accompanying American patrol promptly killed them. The two Nisei "succeeded in separating a large number of non-combatants from Japanese soldiers." For this Honda and Matsui were awarded the Bronze Star.[94]

The team chief, Sergeant Ohta, faced a similar situation:

> Word came in that a group of Japanese soldiers were holed up in a cave far down on a steep cliff facing the ocean. The sergeant was sent in a jeep, equipped with a loudspeaker, to the cliff but found that the jeep could not be brought close to the precipice.
>
> He tried shouting but the surf below drowned out his voice. Finally he found a fragile cliff ladder and climbed down alone and disappeared under a ledge where he could not be given protection by the Americans. A Japanese officer came out of the cave with a drawn revolver. He talked with the sergeant for several minutes, then suddenly turned and threw himself into the sea and drowned. But Sergeant Tim [Ohta] prevailed on two enlisted men to follow him up the ladder and surrender. He was awarded the Silver Star.[95]

Sgt. Jack Tanimoto swam through the surf to another cave where nine civilians were hiding. The civilians were willing to come out, but the entrance was under Japanese fire. Tanimoto held off the Japanese soldiers with a Browning Automatic Rifle until all civilians escaped unharmed. He also received the Silver Star.[96]

The Americans also used tactical psychological warfare on Saipan, beginning with massive leaflet drops before the landings.[97] These leaflets, supplied by the

---

[92] "Use of Nisei Saved GI Lives in Pacific."
[93] Falk and Tsuneishi, *MIS in the War against Japan*, p. 51.
[94] Crost, *Honor by Fire*, pp. 168–69.
[95] "Use of Nisei Saved GI Lives in Pacific."
[96] Ibid.
[97] Zacharias, *Secret Missions*, pp. 324–25.

Nisei interrogating Japanese prisoners, Saipan, July 1944

Office of War Information, were of limited effectiveness. After the battle T3g. Harold Nishimura wrote to the language school:

During the battle of Saipan I deeply felt the pressing need of suitable propaganda for certain situations. We had OWI's booklets and leaflets as in my previous campaign [Kwajalein] but their inappropriateness and childish composition has touched their pride and stirred them to further resistance.... I maintain that those who write propaganda must have actual experience in the fields to grasp the essence of effective propaganda by actual contact with new prisoners and documents.[98]

For three weeks the Japanese defenders fought back. American casualties climbed to 20 percent of committed units. However, the defeat of the Japanese fleet made the Japanese situation on Saipan hopeless. On 4 or 5 July soldiers of the 105th Infantry captured a Japanese Navy civilian.[99] T4g. Hoichi Kubo questioned him and learned of plans for an attack on 6 July. On that day Kubo accompanied a

---

[98] Ltr, T3g. Harold Nishimura to Col. Kai Rasmussen, 15 December 1944, Trng Grp, Ofc of the Dir of Intel G–2, RG 165, NARA.

[99] Interv, author with Hoichi Kubo and Benjamin Hazard, 30 Oct 87; Kubo, in *Japanese Eyes, American Heart*, pp. 278–82.

patrol and discovered a Japanese
sailor hiding in a narrow concrete
culvert. The sailor confirmed that
the Japanese were planning an
attack for that very night. He used
the word *gyokusai*, which Kubo
understood at once. More than a
banzai attack, gyokusai meant "to
smash the jewel," an all-out battle of mutual annihilation. Kubo
reported to his team leader, Lieutenant Hazard, who immediately
sent the message up the chain of
command so frontline units could
be warned.[100]

*Kubo comforts a child found alone in a
field in Saipan.*

Before sunrise the following
morning 5,000 Japanese threw
themselves against the 27th Infan-
try Division lines. Even with advance warning, the attack was devastating. Absorb-
ing horrific casualties, the Japanese sliced through two battalions that together lost
406 killed and 512 wounded. At the 105th Infantry, Kubo joined with headquarters
personnel who all fought as riflemen. When the sun came up the next morning, over
4,000 dead Japanese soldiers littered the battlefield. Quick action by the Nisei and
their commanders had averted catastrophic American losses.[101]

Other linguists who were not Nisei also played a role on Saipan. Two days
after the gyokusai, a marine enlisted linguist stumbled upon a small group of Japanese survivors of the attack. Pfc. Guy Gabaldon, a Mexican American, had been
adopted into a Japanese family in Los Angeles and grew up among Nisei friends.
When Gabaldon's foster parents were interned in 1942, he enlisted in the Marine
Corps and was eventually assigned to the 2d Marine Regiment intelligence section. The Japanese soldiers led him to a group of 800 Japanese soldiers and civilians hiding in caves, whom Gabaldon persuaded to surrender en mass. For this he
was awarded the Silver Star.[102]

---

[100] Philip A. Crowl, *Campaign in the Marianas*, U.S. Army in World War II (Washington, D.C.:
Office of the Chief of Military History, 1960), pp. 256–57; Edmund G. Love, *The 27th Infantry
Division in World War II* (Washington, D.C.: Infantry Journal Press, 1949), pp. 430–501; Holland
M. Smith, *Coral and Brass* (New York: Scribners, 1949), pp. 194–95.

[101] Hoichi Kubo, Military Bio, Unpubl Ms, author's files; Interv, author with Kubo and Hazard,
30 Oct 87; Hazard, personal communication to author, 22 Jan 97; Hazard, conference presentation,
18 Mar 00.

[102] The Marine Corps had sent Gabaldon to Camp Elliot, California, for Japanese-language
training, but he was removed for disciplinary problems. His story came to public attention in 1960,
when he was featured on the popular television program, *This Is Your Life*, followed by a Hollywood film, *Hell to Eternity* (Allied Artists, 1960). The Navy Department subsequently awarded
Gabaldon the Navy Cross. Guy Gabaldon, *Saipan: Suicide Island* (Saipan: G. Gabaldon, 1990);

Saipan was declared secure on 9 July, and JICPOA sent additional Nisei to help with the prisoners and captured documents. The marines also used three Hawaii-born Korean Americans to help with the thousands of Korean laborers whom the Japanese had brought to the islands.[103] Marine Maj. Gen. Holland M. Smith, the V Amphibious Corps commander, took a personal interest in the prisoners and captured documents. Through an interpreter Smith questioned captured Japanese officers and spoke with a captured Japanese medical officer about wounded prisoners. A captured Japanese officer told him firsthand of the suicide of *Lt. Gen. Yoshitsugu Saito*, who had ordered the gyokusai.[104]

Thousands of Japanese soldiers and civilians remained at large on the island even after the island was declared secure. For many, suicide took the place of death on the battlefield. Several thousand Japanese soldiers, sailors, and civilians on the northern end of the island killed themselves with grenades or other weapons or by leaping off the cliffs onto the rocks and sea below at Marpi Point. The Americans tried to stop the slaughter using loudspeakers to encourage surrender; but many Japanese chose death, sometimes in full view of the Americans. On 17 July Chief of Naval Operations Adm. Ernest J. King visited Saipan with Admiral Nimitz. Marpi Point, King recalled, was "the spot where the crowning horror of Japanese lunacy had taken place, . . . an orgy of self-destruction."[105]

On 26 July a patrol from the 105th Infantry was mopping up stragglers near Marpi Point when two Okinawan civilians crawled up over the sea cliff and approached with their hands raised. They told Kubo, who was accompanying the patrol, that they had escaped from a cave where Japanese soldiers were holding more than 100 civilians.[106]

Raul Morin, *Among the Valiant* (Alhambra, Calif.: Borden Publishing Co., 1966), pp. 232–33. Ronald Takaki lauds Gabaldon as "indeed a unique war hero—a Japanese-speaking, Mexican-American humanitarian soldier!" Ronald Takaki, *Double Victory: A Multicultural History of America in World War II* (Boston: Little, Brown, 2000), pp. 232–33.

[103] "Six Nisei Soldiers Win Citations on Saipan," *Pacific Citizen*, 12 Aug 44; Harrington, *Yankee Samurai*, pp. 182–83; Tsukiyama et al., *Secret Valor*, p. 82; "Navy Reveals Nisei 'Agents' Got Valuable Data for U.S.," *Pacific Citizen*, 6 Oct 45.

[104] Smith, *Coral and Brass*, pp. 5, 193, 198–99.

[105] Ernest J. King and Walter M. Whitehill, *Fleet Admiral King: A Naval Record* (New York: Norton, 1952), p. 564. See also Haruko Taya Cook, "The Myth of the Saipan Suicides," *MHQ* 7 (Spring 1995): 12–19; Crowl, *Campaign in the Marianas*, pp. 264–65; Dower, *War without Mercy*, pp. 249, 298–99; Robert Sherrod, *On to Westward: War in the Central Pacific* (New York: Duell, Sloan and Pearce, 1945); Toland, *Rising Sun*, pp. 588–90.

[106] Lt. Col. William M. Van Antwerp, 27th Infantry Division G–2, told Kubo's story to various audiences in 1944–1946. Memo, Van Antwerp to CG, 27th Inf Div, sub: Recommendation for Award of Distinguished Service Cross, 16 Aug 44, U.S. Army Forces Pacific & Predecessor Commands, RG 338, NARA. This resulted in the award of the Distinguished Service Cross by HQ USAFPAC General Orders No. 52, 18 Oct 44, as well as some press coverage: "Hawaiian Nisei Sergeant First To Receive DSC for Heroism in Central Pacific War Zone," *Pacific Citizen*, 13 Jan 45. "Use of Nisei Saved GI Lives in Pacific" refers to Kubo by first name only. William M. Van Antwerp, "How Sergeant Kubo Won the DSC," *Infantry Journal* (1946), gives the date of action as 23 July 1944.

The platoon leader gave Kubo permission to talk to the soldiers. Kubo, armed only with a pistol and some K-rations, climbed a hundred feet down a rope. While the patrol waited above, he disappeared into the cave. Two hours later he emerged with an amazing story. He had conversed with the desperate soldiers in the cave and shared a meal with them, contributing his own rations. As they sat around a bubbling rice pot, he gained their confidence and appealed to their sense of honor, the *bushido* code. The Americans did not fight civilians, he told them, so they should release the civilians. "I do not come here to discuss that you give yourselves up," he said. "I wish that you devote your considerations to releasing the civilians whom you are holding captive." Kubo told them: "You are the sons of Japanese parents. You were born in Japan and fight for your country, Japan. I am also the son of Japanese parents but I was born in the United States. The United States is my country and I fight for it. The United States has honored me by making me a sergeant." At this the Japanese soldiers bowed in respect (the highest ranking soldier present was a superior private). Furthermore, Kubo declared to them, his grandfathers had fought with the Imperial Japanese Army in the Russo-Japanese War in the famous 5th and 6th Divisions—better units than theirs, he added. He recited a classical Japanese proverb: "If I am filial, I cannot serve the emperor. If I serve the emperor, I cannot be filial."[107] This neatly explained his situation as a Nisei and his loyalty to America, the land of his birth.

Kubo told them that if they decided to release the civilians, they should come to the top of the cliff in two hours. With that he left the cave and climbed back up the cliff. Two hours later a small group appeared at the cliff top, soon followed by the others. In all, 9 soldiers and 122 civilians, including many women and children, surrendered. As the civilians climbed up, a shot rang out from a nearby cave and the American platoon leader fell dead. His body rolled over the cliff. Kubo "became mad with fury," according to a newspaper account. "He lined the nine [Japanese soldiers] up and for 15 minutes verbally lashed them unmercifully." He shouted:

Advocates for Americans of Japanese ancestry immediately recognized the potential value of Kubo's story. A *Chicago Times* reporter described how Kubo had "proved the quality of his Americanism." Keith Wheeler, "Sgt. Kubo Proves His Mettle in Danger," *Honolulu Star-Bulletin* (February 1945). The War Relocation Authority placed Wheeler's story on the first page of its collection of news clippings in April 1945. WRA, *Nisei in the War against Japan.*

Kubo's own recollections include Harrington, *Yankee Samurai*, pp. 207–10; Loni Ding, prod., *The Color of Honor*, documentary film, Vox Productions, 1987; Interv, author with Kubo and Hazard, 30 Oct 87; Crost, *Honor by Fire*, pp. 165–68; Kubo, "Military Biography," excerpted in *Japanese Eyes, American Heart*, pp. 278–82. The incident is also depicted in "A More Perfect Union," a permanent exhibit at the National Museum of American History in Washington, D.C.

[107] "*Chu naran to hossureba Ko narazu. Ko naran to hossureba Chu narazu.*" This saying is attributed to Taira Shigemori (1138–1179) during the civil wars of the later Heian period. Harrington, *Yankee Samurai*, pp. 209–10; Yasuko I. Takezawa, *Breaking the Silence: Redress and Japanese American Ethnicity* (Ithaca, N.Y.: Cornell University Press, 1995), p. 97.

"Someone shot that man who saved all of your lives! Is there not a samurai among you?" Driven to an emotional pitch himself, [he] finally incited such an emotional frenzy in the Japanese that they fought with each other to get down the cliff after the fallen US officer. And they fought with each other once again to bring his body back to the top.[108]

For his bravery, Kubo was awarded the Distinguished Service Cross, the highest award given to any Nisei in the Pacific Theater.

On Saipan, the Americans captured more than 1,700 Japanese soldiers, sailors, civilians, and Korean laborers, the largest number yet in the Central Pacific. There were so many that the Navy had to establish the rudiments of a military government. JICPOA could not supply enough Nisei interpreters, so the Army headquarters on Hawaii selected twenty Nisei then in basic training at Schofield Barracks (Selective Service had just resumed drafting Nisei) and flew them to Saipan with no further training.[109]

Because Saipan had been a major Japanese headquarters, the Americans also captured fifty tons of documents, a staggering volume. Dozens of Nisei and Caucasian linguists took weeks just to sift through the documents. Many documents were simply crated up and shipped to JICPOA, where tents had to be erected beside the main building to hold the rich intelligence harvest. From the files of the Imperial Japanese Navy Central Pacific Area Fleet Headquarters emerged a set of administrative orders that "contained a complete list of all vessels by classes, registries of vessels by home ports, statistical data and complement tables for all ships and the organization of divisions." Navy intelligence officers eagerly snapped up Japanese navigation charts. Also discovered was a digest of Japanese naval air bases that "contained sketches of all the principal naval air bases in Japan and her various possessions." When JICPOA could not handle the flow, the War Department quickly established a translation center, the Pacific Military Intelligence Research Section (PACMIRS) at Camp Ritchie, Maryland.[110]

Japan's defeat in the Philippine Sea and the loss of Saipan had an immediate impact in both Tokyo and Washington. *General Hideki Tojo* and his cabinet resigned on 18 July. Shortly afterward President Franklin D. Roosevelt met with MacArthur and Nimitz in Hawaii to finalize the plans for Japan's defeat.

To secure the Marianas, Nimitz seized Guam and the smaller island of Tinian. The III Amphibious Corps landed on Guam on 21 July to fight 18,500 Japanese defenders. Nisei teams went ashore with the 3d Marine Division and 1st Provisional Marine Brigade, backed by the 77th Infantry Division. Three weeks of fighting were required to eliminate Japanese resistance. As on Saipan, interpreters combed the islands to search out Japanese soldiers and civilians. They used the tools of tactical psychological warfare, leaflets and sound trucks, to

---

[108] "Use of Nisei Saved GI Lives in Pacific"; Harrington, *Yankee Samurai*, pp. 209–10; *Japanese Eyes, American Heart*, p. 282.

[109] Harrington, *Yankee Samurai*, p. 207; Smith, *Coral and Brass*, pp. 210–12.

[110] JICPOA History, pp. 43–44; Zacharias, *Secret Missions*, pp. 319–20; Holmes, *Doubled-Edged Secrets*, pp. 168–69, 194.

induce surrenders. A marine correspondent noted that this: "amounted to a new relationship between ourselves and our enemy—an incongruous relationship that bewildered a lot of our men. . . . To most of the Marines, who were used to seeing a fanatical enemy that preferred death to surrender, our new policy was at first puzzling." The marines outfitted an LCI landing craft with a public address system; for three days this "peace ship" sailed up and down Guam's rugged coast with three captured Japanese prisoners of war appealing to their fellow countrymen to surrender. Patrolling continued on land and along the coast for months. The use of Japanese prisoners of war to make surrender broadcasts grew more common as the war continued.[111]

On 24 July the 2d and 4th Marine Divisions jumped the short distance from Saipan to Tinian, where they confronted 8,000 Japanese defenders. JICPOA Nisei joined the fight on D+4. Once the island was declared secure, Don Oka led a Nisei team to assist with civil administration. One team member, Raymond Shogo Nagata, met a prisoner who was a Nisei from Hawaii and knew some people in common. The prisoner had been caught in Japan when war began and was conscripted. He had been a classmate of Nagata's sister in Hawaii; his brother-in-law had been Nagata's classmate.[112]

As soon as shore facilities could be repaired, the U.S. Pacific Fleet moved back into Guam and Nimitz soon moved his advance headquarters there as well. Army engineers began building airfields on Saipan, Guam, and Tinian. For the first time the Americans had air bases for the very-long-range bomber, the B–29, within range of the Japanese home islands. The first B–29 arrived on 12 October, and the first air attack against Japan was launched from Saipan on 24 November.

One more island chain remained to be seized before the Allies reached the Philippines. On 15 September the 1st Marine Division stormed ashore on the largest island in the Palaus, Peleliu. T.Sgt. Donald S. Okubo and two other Nisei landed on Peleliu with the third wave. They interrogated the few Japanese soldiers who were taken alive. "I was much more worried about the marines shooting me than the Japs. You know how those marines are: if they see anyone who even looks like the enemy they fire. Whenever I was on patrol I had to be escorted by half

---

[111] Alvin M. Josephy, Jr., "Some Japs Surrender," *Infantry Journal* (August 1945): 40–45; Alvin M. Josephy, Jr., *The Long and the Short and the Tall: The Story of a Marine Combat Unit in the Pacific* (New York: Knopf, 1946); Smith, *Coral and Brass*, pp. 221–22. Gordon Cotler described a similar incident in "Kobayashi," *The New Yorker* (26 August 1950): 54–57. In the television comedy series, *McHale's Navy* (1962–1966), the crew of the fictional PT–73 in the South Pacific included "Seaman Third Class Fuji Kobiaji, IJN," a friendly Japanese prisoner of war played by Yoshio Yoda.

[112] Isokane, "JICPOA Annex Story," pp. 66–68. Isokane adds that the prisoner had been "sent to the battle to gain intelligence data." After the war, Don Oka learned that his younger brother, Takeo Oka, who had been visiting Japan when war began, trained as a Japanese pilot and died during attacks on American forces in the Marianas. Harrington, *Yankee Samurai*, p. 211.

a dozen marines or I'd be a dead duck. Despite my Army uniform I was fired on several times."[113]

The 321st Infantry soon reinforced the marines on Peleliu, followed a few weeks later by the 323d Infantry. Both regiments brought their Nisei interpreters. On 25 October one Nisei, T4g. Masao Abe, was calling to Japanese soldiers hidden in a cave when he was wounded in the thigh and evacuated. Japanese resistance on Peleliu did not end until 27 November.[114]

Six miles away, the 81st Infantry Division landed on Angaur on 17 September, two days after the marines hit Peleliu. Ten Nisei under S.Sgt. James T. Kai had joined the division in Hawaii after coming directly from the school. They were accompanied by Maj. Lachlan M. Sinclair, the JICPOA executive officer. The Nisei interrogated prisoners, translated documents, and tried to persuade Japanese soldiers to surrender. Two Nisei were assigned to each regiment and four at division headquarters. Each was assigned two bodyguards. However, "soon after the operation started," the Army Ground Forces observer reported, "all Neisi [sic] were recalled to division CP since it was considered too hazardous to have them even as far forward as regiment. This worked well because [the] island was small."[115]

T4g. Robert K. Sakai, a Nisei from Riverside, California, had been a senior at the University of California when the war broke out. At division headquarters, he recalled, "mailbags full of captured documents piled up for sorting and translation. Some required on-the-spot translation; others were for later translation, and still others were sent to Joint Intelligence [Center], Pacific Ocean Area in Honolulu for careful analysis." He noticed that "if a Japanese prisoner was accosted by a Caucasian officer, even if the latter spoke fluent Japanese, the prisoner tended to freeze up, anticipating cruelty. If the captor had a Japanese face like himself, he visibly relaxed. Because of their brutally harsh training and the propaganda they had received about the cruelty of the Americans, Japanese prisoners were unprepared for considerate, humane treatment, which proved effective in interrogation." Other prisoners considered themselves to be dead and "reborn" and became quite willing to cooperate.[116] One day, while clearing caves, T4g. Shiuso Chojin saw

---

[113] "Honolulu Army Sergeant Storms Pacific Island Alone, Persuades Japanese Admiral To Surrender His Garrison," *Honolulu Advertiser*, 5 Oct 45; Harrington, *Yankee Samurai*, pp. 218–22; Tsukiyama et al., *Secret Valor*, pp. 64–65.

[114] 81st Infantry Division, "History of 313th Intelligence Service Organization," Unpubl Ms, ca. 1945, copy in author's files; Robert K. Sakai, in *Japanese Eyes, American Heart*, pp. 121–34. One enlisted Marine linguist on Peleliu, Earl F. Ziemke, later served as a historian with the Office of the Chief of Military History.

[115] "Observer's Report on 81st Infantry Division, Stalemate Operation, 30 August–25 September 1944," 2 October 1944, transmittal Ltr dtd 3 May 1945, 98–USFI–2.0, Box 1602, Entry 427, RG 407, NARA; William F. Aimone, "The Nisei and the CIC," *JAVA Newsletter*, March/April 2003, pp. 7–8. Major Sinclair later wrote to Colonel Rasmussen, seeking to be transferred from the JICPOA annex to a language team for an airborne unit. Ltr, Sinclair to Rasmussen, 10 December 1944, Trng Grp, Ofc of the Dir of Intel G–2, RG 165, NARA.

[116] Sakai, in *Japanese Eyes, American Heart*, p. 130.

another American soldier felled by a Japanese sniper. Chojin raced to him under fire, administered first aid, and helped drag him to safety. Chojin was awarded the Bronze Star for his heroism.

In just one year American forces in the Pacific Ocean Areas had driven over 1,500 miles closer to Japan, had penetrated the Japanese outer defense perimeter, and had crippled Japan's naval air power. American intelligence organizations were larger and more sophisticated than ever before, and MIS Nisei were now fighting with soldiers and marines in every campaign. However, racial hatred continued to fuel the conflict on both sides.

In January 1945 war correspondent Ernie Pyle arrived to cover the fighting in the Central Pacific. He had earned a reputation in Italy and France for honest reporting that reflected what the average soldier was thinking. In the Pacific, he sensed, Americans were fighting a different war; and this troubled him. He sensed that the average American's attitude toward the Japanese was very different from his attitude toward the Germans. Most Americans had never met a Japanese person and held stereotypical ideas accumulated through a century of prejudice. Pyle was honest enough to admit similar feelings himself.

In Hawaii, Pyle was taken to see Japanese prisoners of war in a stockade. The prisoners, he wrote, "give me a creepy feeling," as if not wholly human. He felt confused about the contradictory stories he was being told about the Japanese and worried about American efforts to analyze "the Jap psychology." Their stubborn resistance on Saipan, their willingness to face certain death, the suicidal kamikaze pilots, all had further hardened American attitudes against the Japanese. Pyle detected a hatred unlike anything he had seen in Europe.[117] For the MIS Nisei, this prejudice even as the tide was swinging in America's favor continued to make things difficult as they fought for their country.

China-Burma-India Theater

In 1943 the Allies established a unified command, the South-East Asia Command, under Lord Louis Mountbatten. The United States established the China-Burma-India Theater under Lt. Gen. Joseph W. Stilwell to bolster the British Commonwealth forces there, as well as to provide support to the Chinese Nationalists.[118] (*See Map 10.*) As in other theaters, intelligence was the key to victory. When Lt. Gen. William J. Slim took command of the British 14th Army in 1943, he complained, "We never made up for the lack of methodically collected intelligence or the intelligence organization which should have been available to us when the war

---

[117] Ernie Pyle, *Ernie's War*, ed. David Nichols (New York: Random House, 1986), pp. 366–73; Dower, *War without Mercy*, pp. 78, 82.

[118] Louis Allen, *Burma: The Longest War, 1941–1945* (New York: St. Martin's, 1985); Richard J. Aldrich, *Intelligence and the War against Japan: Britain, America and the Politics of Secret Service* (Cambridge: Cambridge University Press, 2000).

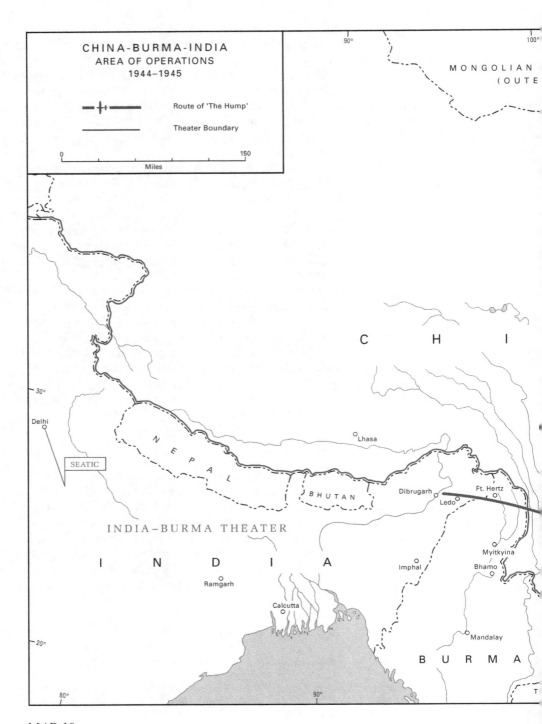

CHINA-BURMA-INDIA
AREA OF OPERATIONS
1944–1945

Route of 'The Hump'

Theater Boundary

0   150
Miles

90°   100°

MONGOLIAN
(OUTE

C   H   I

30°

Delhi

N E P A L   Lhasa

SEATIC

BHUTAN   Dibrugarh   Ft. Hertz
                                Ledo

INDIA–BURMA THEATER

I   N   D   I   A   Imphal   Myitkyina
                Ramgarh   Bhamo

        Calcutta

20°   Mandalay

80°   90°   B   U   R   M   A

MAP 10

REPUBLIC
(IA)

Peiping

Port Arthur Dairen

Tientsin

DIXIE MISSION

Yenan

Kaifeng

A

SINTIC

Hankow

Cheng-tu

Chungking

Changsha

Heng-yang

Kweiyang

Tuhshan

Kunming

Liuchow

Canton

Nanning

Hong Kong

Hanoi

FRENCH
INDOCHINA

HAINAN

Tsingtao

Nanking

Shanghai

K O R E A

Pusan

FORMOSA

PHILIPPINES

ATER

began."[119] American Nisei would play an important role in turning this around. For some, it would mean combat under the terrible conditions. For others, it meant the tedium of rear-area duties set amidst the fading splendor of British India.

The first MISLS graduate to arrive in India was not a Nisei, but a Chinese American, Lt. Won-Loy Chan. The Stanford graduate spoke Cantonese and had learned Japanese at Crissy Field and Camp Savage. In April 1943 he joined Stilwell's headquarters as an intelligence officer.[120] The State Department also sent political officers to the theater, among them John K. Emmerson, who had been assigned to the U.S. embassy in Tokyo in the 1930s and spoke Japanese. In July 1943 T.Sgt. Harry Katsuto Andow led ten Nisei by sea from Camp Savage to New Delhi, where they were assigned to the Joint Army-Navy Intelligence Collection Agency.[121] In October another team arrived by air under Lt. John D. McLaughlin and Sgt. Fusao Uchiyama, who had been recruited for MISLS from the 100th Infantry Battalion.[122]

Some Nisei were assigned to the British Commonwealth forces. Sgt. Roy T. Takai served with the British 4 Corps and 19th Division. Hiro Harold Nishimura served with the Indian 26th Division.[123] T3g. Eiichi "Eddy" Sakauye rescued a British captain in an Indian division under enemy fire in April 1944 and was awarded the Silver Star.[124] T4g. Henry Kuwabara served with the British 72d Infantry Brigade and was awarded the British Empire Medal.[125] In January 1944 Takai and Hiroshi Osako were sent to support British forces in Central Assam. When the Japanese attacked in March, Commonwealth forces in Imphal and Kohima were cut off for several weeks along with the American Nisei. "Although I've only been in this enchanted land of India for six months," Takai wrote to the *Pacific Citizen*, "I have already gotten a taste of war." He described the mortar, machine gun, and rifle fire and air raids close to the front lines.[126]

Stilwell took command of combined American and Chinese forces for the attack into northern Burma. (*Map 11*) In late December 1943 two Nisei joined

---

[119] William J. Slim, *Defeat into Victory: Battling Japan in Burma and India, 1942–1945* (London: Cassell, 1956), p. 221. One author disputes Slim's negative assessment of signals intelligence. Alan Stripp, *Codebreaker in the Far East* (New York: Oxford University Press, 1995), pp. 165–71. See also Douglas Ford, "'A Conquerable Yet Resilient Foe': British Perceptions of the Imperial Japanese Army's Tactics on the India-Burma Front, September 1942 to Summer 1944," *Intelligence and National Security* 18, no. 1 (Spring 2003): 65–90.

[120] Won-Loy Chan, *Burma: The Untold Story* (Novato, Calif.: Presidio Press, 1986).

[121] Sinclair, "Valuable as a Company of Men"; Interv, author with Roy T. Takai, 30 Oct 87; Roy T. Takai, MISNorCal Bio.

[122] Interv, author with Henry Kuwabara, 12 Sep 96.

[123] Interv, author with Takai, 30 Oct 87; Takai, MISNorCal Bio; Hiro Nishimura, *Trials and Triumphs of the Nikkei* (Mercer Island, Wash.: Fukuda Publishers, 1993), pp. 68–70.

[124] Sinclair, "Valuable as a Company of Men"; Ltr, Kimura to Munakata, 18 January 1945, Harrington Papers; Harrington, *Yankee Samurai*, pp. 140, 162, 249.

[125] "Nisei Officer Given the British Empire Award," *Pacific Citizen*, May 46; Harrington, *Yankee Samurai*, pp. 249, 344; *Pacific War and Peace*, p. 67.

[126] "Letters from Servicemen," *Pacific Citizen*, 3 Jun 44; Takai, MISNorCal Bio; Interv, author with Takai, 30 Oct 87; Fusao Uchiyama, Harrington Papers.

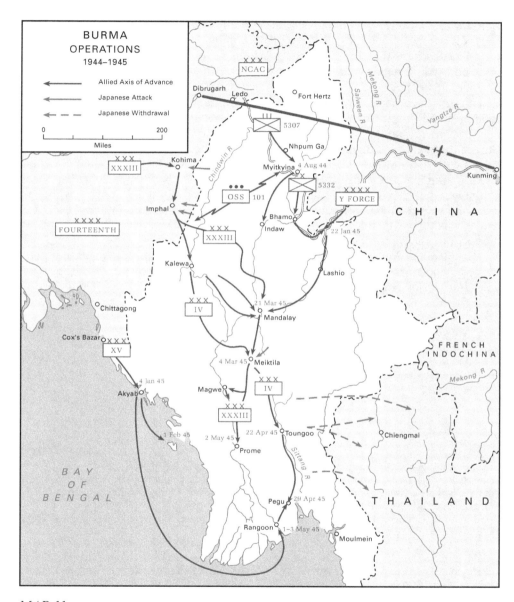

MAP 11

Lieutenant Chan in the G–2 section of the Northern Combat Area Command (NCAC). NCAC consisted of two Chinese divisions and a regiment-size American infantry unit, the 5307th Composite Unit (Provisional), which had arrived in India in October 1943. To command the unit Stilwell personally selected Brig. Gen. Frank D. Merrill, who had served as a language attaché in Tokyo before the war. Newsmen dubbed the unit Merrill's Marauders.[127]

Merrill knew that his Marauders would be operating deep behind enemy lines and would need some Japanese-speakers. In January 1944 he walked into Emmerson's office and began to reminisce about their days together in Tokyo. Warming to the subject, they began to sing familiar Japanese songs. "We stopped suddenly and Frank turned to me," Emmerson recalled. "Come along! I'm leaving for a secret camp in central India. This will be a special operation into the Burma jungle. You'll be great—to talk to the Japanese!"[128] Emmerson agreed but stayed with the Marauders only briefly. Fortunately, the War Department G–2 had already anticipated the need. In September 1943 MISLS selected fourteen Nisei volunteers, half of whom were Kibei, headed by Capt. William A. Laffin, who was born and raised in Japan by a Japanese mother and American father. The Nisei leader was Sgt. Edward Hideo Mitsukado, a court reporter from Hawaii. Half of the team members were college graduates.[129]

Because the Marauders would be operating behind enemy lines, assignment was especially risky for the Nisei if they should be captured alive. Before they went into action Stilwell visited the unit and happened to spot Sgt. Henry Hiroharu Gosho.

"Are you Chinese?" he asked.
"No, sir," replied Gosho.
"Are you Korean?"
"No, sir."
"Are you Filipino?"
"No, sir."

---

[127] *Merrill's Marauders (February–May 1944)*, American Forces in Action (Washington, D.C.: Military Intelligence Division, War Department, 1945); James E. T. Hopkins, *Spearhead: A Complete History of Merrill's Marauder Rangers* (Baltimore, Md.: Johns Hopkins University Press, 2000); Charles N. Hunter, *Galahad* (San Antonio, Tex.: Naylor, 1963); Charlton Ogburn, Jr., *The Marauders*, 2d ed. (New York: Harper and Brothers, 1959).

[128] John K. Emmerson, *The Japanese Thread: A Life in the U.S. Foreign Service* (New York: Holt, Rinehart and Winston, 1978), p. 150.

[129] Edgar Laytha, "Nisei," *CBI Roundup* (14 September 1944): 3, reprinted in *Pacific Citizen*, 14 Oct 44, p. 2; Sinclair, "Valuable as a Company of Men." See also Crost, *Honor by Fire*, pp. 117–33; Harrington, *Yankee Samurai*, pp. 184–85, 194–95, 201–02; Roland Kotani, "The Unsung Heroes: A Kibei in the Burma Jungle," *Hawaii Herald*, 6 Nov 81, reprinted in Oguro, *Sempai Gumi*, pp. 97–105; Thomas Tsubota, "From the 100th Battalion to Merrill's Marauders," in Tsukiyama et al., *Secret Valor*, p. 69; Akiji Yoshimura, "China-Burma-India: 14 Nisei and the Marauders (With Merrill's Marauders)," *Pacific Citizen*, 25 Dec 56 [1959?], reprinted in Oguro, *Sempai Gumi*, pp. 85–96, and in Ichinokuchi, *John Aiso and the M.I.S.*, pp. 85–94; Akiji Yoshimura and Howard Furumoto, Ltrs to the Editor, *The Burman News*, Feb 88, pp. 3–4.

"Don't tell me you're . . ."
"Yes, sir."

The general turned to a nearby officer and said, "Transfer that man to division headquarters and keep him there!" However, Gosho's unit quietly ignored Stilwell's order.[130] So often did he come under fire that his buddies named him Horizontal Hank, because of the many times he had to throw himself on the ground.

Merrill's Marauders entered combat in February 1944. The mountainous jungle was as much an enemy as the Japanese. Marching and fighting under harsh conditions without relief took a heavy toll on all soldiers, and scores of soldiers were evacuated for illness. At least four Nisei were evacuated for fever, exhaustion, or injury, one for a hernia from laboring under a heavy load.[131] The Nisei also carried the burden of proving their loyalty. One told a reporter: "I had a terrible feeling when the first Jap I had shot collapsed and expired with a heartbreaking 'Banzai!' on his lips, but my second shot came easy, the third even easier. I can't tell you exactly how many I have shot. It is very difficult to know in the jungle where everything melts into the background."[132]

Another Nisei with the unit was S.Sgt. Roy Hiroshi Matsumoto. Born near Los Angeles, he was a third-generation Japanese American, or Sansei, whose grandfather had immigrated to the United States. (He was, however, a member of the same age cohort as the Nisei generation.) Matsumoto had attended middle school in Japan before the war. His parents returned to Japan with his brothers and sisters but left Matsumoto in California to attend high school. In 1942 he had been interned in Jerome, Arkansas, where he volunteered for the Military Intelligence Service. In early March the Marauders discovered a Japanese telephone wire running through their position. Matsumoto climbed a tree and hooked up a field telephone to intercept the calls. He overheard a Japanese sergeant report that he had only three soldiers to guard an ammunition dump. The Americans attacked and destroyed the dump, and Matsumoto was later awarded the Legion of Merit.[133]

After marching and fighting through some of the toughest terrain in the world, the Marauders occupied blocking positions behind the veteran *Japanese 18th Division*. The 2d Battalion dug in around the village of Nhpum Ga with 600 men, including three Nisei. The Japanese surrounded the American battalion and attacked repeatedly for eleven days. So close were the Japanese that the Nisei could hear the Japanese officers shouting commands, which they quickly translated so the American soldiers could react in time. At night Matsumoto would crawl in front of American lines to eavesdrop on the Japanese soldiers. One night, he overheard preparations for a dawn attack, so he crawled back earlier than usual and made his report. The Americans quietly pulled back from their front lines in the dark and

---

[130] Emmerson, *The Japanese Thread*, pp. 160–61.
[131] Tsubota, "From the 100th Battalion to Merrill's Marauders," p. 69; Yoshimura, in Oguro, *Sempai Gumi*, p. 93.
[132] Laytha, "Nisei."
[133] *Merrill's Marauders*, pp. 39–40, 115.

Herbert Y. Miyasaki (left) *and Akiji Yoshimura with Merrill after the Battle of Nhpum Ga, 1 May 1944*

left their fighting positions booby trapped. When the Japanese attacked, the Americans caught them by surprise and cut them down. Japanese soldiers who fell into the American foxholes were killed by the booby traps. Just as the Japanese attack began to falter, Matsumoto stood up and shouted in his best command voice, "*Susume!* [Advance!]" The surviving Japanese leapt to their feet and rushed straight into the American fire. An American soldier called this "the all important outstanding contribution which I am convinced saved the lives of every man who survived the long tenacious defense of Nhpum Ga." According to the official report, "Sergeant Matsumoto became a legendary character overnight." The siege at Nhpum Ga was soon lifted.[134]

The Marauders were then sent to capture Myitkyina and its airfield from which the Japanese air forces threatened the airlift to China. Captain Laffin, now regimental S–2, led a Kachin patrol ahead of the main body to reconnoiter a route through sixty-five miles of mountainous jungle.[135] Following Laffin's reconnaissance party, the Marauders descended upon Myitkyina by surprise and on 17 May seized the airfield. Stilwell at once began to pour in reinforcements.[136] On 18 May Laffin took to the air in an L–5 liaison aircraft to reconnoiter the Japanese positions. As the plane lifted off, a Japanese Zero suddenly appeared and shot it down within sight of the end of the airstrip. All on board were killed. The Nisei were stunned by the loss of their team leader. The news "came as a great shock to me," recalled Akiji Yoshimura, "and the few minutes I was able to spend at his gravesite near the airstrip seemed a totally

---

[134] Maj. John M. Jones III, "Notes on Merrill Expedition, 1944," Unpubl Ms, JICA/CBI/SEA Branch, 27 Sep 44, copy in author's files; *Merrill's Marauders*, p. 86; Charles F. Romanus and Riley Sunderland, *Stilwell's Command Problems*, U.S. Army in World War II (Washington, D.C.: Office of the Chief of Military History, 1956), pp. 190–91; Warren T. Ventura, Ltr to Editor, *The Burman News*, May 90, p. 1; Harrington, *Yankee Samurai*, p. 194; Roy Matsumoto, Ltr to Editor, *The Burman News*, Feb 91, p. 8; Roy H. Matsumoto, "With Merrill's Marauders in Burma," in Falk and Tsuneishi, *MIS in the War against Japan*, pp. 62–64, 110–11.

[135] *Merrill's Marauders*, pp. 98–101, 106. The Kachins were a northern hill tribe equally opposed to the Burmese lowlanders and the Japanese occupiers.

[136] "Grads Aided in Saving Airfield," *Yaban Gogai*, Sep–Oct 45, p. 6.

inadequate tribute to a fine officer, leader and friend."[137] Team leadership fell to Sergeant Mitsukado.

The battle for the town lasted another eight weeks. Merrill's Marauders paid a terrible price. Most of the original Marauders were medically evacuated by air, including General Merrill and several Nisei such as Sergeant Gosho. While recuperating, Gosho took the opportunity to write to his twelve-year-old sister in an internment camp:

Right now I'm in an American hospital recovering and recuperating from my third attack of malaria, double hernia and intestinal ulcer. We were in Burma for four months fighting the Japs in the jungles and mountainsides. I had walked 860 miles, climbed hills that you practically had to crawl up, crossed and recrossed rivers 49 times. It rains quite a bit in Burma, and at times I slept wet, wet all day for weeks at a time.

Gosho also shared his thoughts on the special situation of Americans of Japanese ancestry:

For your sake I would want you to enter a real American school and live the American way. The life you are leading now [in a camp] is not the thing for you. You must live in America—'cuz you are all America by heart. Dad and mother must realize this and they do know it deep down in their hearts. Yes, Japan is a country of the past—her history ended on Dec. 7, 1941.[138]

Other Nisei were flown into Myitkyina. In July the Office of War Information sent a tactical psychological warfare team to broadcast surrender messages to Japanese soldiers using leaflets and loudspeakers.[139] One Nisei on the team, S.Sgt. Kenji Yasui, a Kibei from Los Angeles, learned to his distress that the Japanese division in the area came from Kyushu: It "was made up of men from the district where he had spent his youth. He expected momentarily to find his brother's body. He met a boyhood friend from his parental village while interrogating prisoners, and from him learned that the brother had been transferred to another division."[140]

As Japanese defenses crumbled, hundreds of Japanese soldiers attempted to flee across the Irrawaddy River. During mopping-up operations Yasui's team spotted some Japanese soldiers hiding on an island in the stream. With three Caucasian soldiers Yasui swam out to the island to persuade them to surrender. When he reached the island he called to the Japanese soldiers to assemble. Impersonating a Japanese officer, Yasui declared he needed them for a "special mission." Several

---

[137] Oguro, *Sempai Gumi*, p. 93; Frank Hawlett, "Heroic Death of Detroit Captain in Jungles of Burma Revealed," United Press, 23 May 44, reprinted in Oguro, *Sempai Gumi*, pp. 31–32; Hopkins, *Spearhead*, p. 536.

[138] "Nisei Writes Japan's Epitaph," *Chicago Sun*, 24 Sep 44, reprinted in *Pacific Citizen*, 21 Oct 44, p. 2; also reprinted in WRA, *Nisei in the War against Japan*, p. 5.

[139] Emmerson, *The Japanese Thread*, pp. 168–69.

[140] Hosokawa, *Nisei*, p. 299.

Japanese soldiers emerged from hiding, but two resisted and were killed by the Americans; another killed himself with a hand grenade. Yasui "announced he was a colonel and made them line up and execute close order drill," as John Emmerson described the scene. "Then he made them get in the river and swim across pushing a raft on which he stood with carbine aimed at them." Yasui brought in thirteen prisoners and was later awarded the Silver Star.[141]

The Americans and Chinese forces finally captured Myitkyina on 3 August. A few days later Sgt. Grant Jiro Hirabayashi paid a visit to Captain Chan, assistant G–2 with the Myitkyina task force: "Captain, you aren't going to believe this, but I've got about twenty female, I think Korean, POWs down at the center and I need help." These frightened young women were forced prostitutes, or "comfort women," for the Japanese Army. The Nisei showed them photographs of Japanese officers, but they learned little of value because the women spoke little Japanese. The last evening before the women were flown out to India, the Nisei threw a small going-away party. The Nisei sang American, Japanese, and Hawaiian songs accompanied by a guitar. The Korean women responded by singing the Korean folksong, "Arirang."[142]

Other Nisei in Burma served with Chinese units. While making surrender broadcasts from a liaison aircraft flying low over Japanese positions, S.Sgt. Frank T. Tokubo was twice shot down but landed safely in Chinese positions each time. On several occasions these Nisei were mistakenly captured by the Chinese, who had a deep hatred for the Japanese enemy. One Nisei captured by Chinese soldiers recalled that never in all his life had he talked so fast with sign language and wrote so many kanji to explain that they were *minkuo* (American) soldiers. He recalled that the shaken Nisei remained a pale green for the next three months or more.[143]

The fourteen Nisei with Merrill's Marauders in particular impressed senior American officers, starting with General Merrill himself: "As for the value of the Nisei group, I couldn't have gotten along without them. Probably few realize that these boys did everything that an infantryman normally does plus the extra work of translating, interrogating, etc., etc. Also, they were in a most unenviable position as to identity as almost everyone from the Japanese to the Chinese shot first and identified later."[144]

Merrill's comments were seconded by an observer from the Army Ground Forces who reported that the Nisei "have proven to be of great value to that organi-

[141] Ltr, John Emmerson to Colonel Rasmussen, 20 August 1944, Box 303, Entry 208, RG 165, NARA; Laytha, "Nisei"; Interv, Ken Akune with Kenji Yasui, 17 Jan 89.

[142] Chan, *Burma*, pp. 92–97; Harrington, *Yankee Samurai*, pp. 228, 241, 312.

[143] WD Press Release, 22 Oct 45; Sinclair, "Valuable as a Company of Men," p. 7; Harrington, *Yankee Samurai*, p. 242; "Sgt. Tokubo Reported Only Nisei Attached to Chinese Unit," *Pacific Citizen*, Jun 46.

[144] Sinclair, "Valuable as a Company of Men," p. 7.

zation. In every instance the men have been loyal and demonstrated great courage in carrying out their assignments."[145] The Marauders' unit historian wrote:

Some of the most valuable men in our outfit were the Nisei Japanese interpreters not with battalion and regimental headquarters but with a platoon in contact on the perimeter. The Japs talk loudly sometimes before they attack. On several occasions the Japanese interpreters told us exactly what the Japs were shouting and enabled us to get set for an attack from a certain direction. Once an interpreter caused the Japs to attack into a trap by shouting orders to them.[146]

All fourteen were awarded the Combat Infantryman Badge and Presidential Unit Citation. Four were awarded field commissions by December, including team leader Sergeant Mitsukado, who wrote to a friend that he was the "most surprised soldier" in Burma. "Wearing the bars feels great but I miss the company of the boys who went through hell with me. They're a great bunch." Three others returned to the United States to attend officer candidate school.[147]

The Nisei assigned to Merrill's Marauders also helped change the War Department's prohibition of any public notice of Nisei serving in the Military Intelligence Service. In May 1944 the headquarters of U.S. Army Forces in the China-Burma-India Theater requested an exception to policy from the Bureau of Public Relations in Washington:

Does stop still remain on Japanese-Americans serving in this theater? Lifting ban would appear desirable for following reasons:
1st, Morale of Nisei serving here would be raised if public recognition given them;
2nd, Might encourage better treatment of loyal Nisei;
3rd, Propaganda value against Japs;
4th, Nisei themselves realize chances they take at front lines and we doubt that treatment if captured, would be worse.
We would not release details of their intelligence activities but rather heroic action on their part at front lines.[148]

The War Department agreed. In September S.Sgt. Edgar M. Laytha, a member of the OWI team, published an article in *CBI Roundup* detailing the exploits of the Nisei in Burma. The *Pacific Citizen* ran excerpts on its front page, naming the

---

[145] Lt. Col. M. G. Crombez, 8 May 44, included in Memo, Col. W. H. Wood, sub: Nisei, OPD, 9 Jun 44, Trng Grp, Ofc of the Dir of Intel G-2, RG 165, NARA, reprinted in Tsukiyama et al., *Secret Valor*, pp. 15–16.

[146] Jones, "Notes on the Merrill Expedition, 1944."

[147] "Eddie Mitsukado, In Burma, Receives Field Commission," *Honolulu Advertiser*, 28 Jan 45, p. 4; "3 'Ears' of Merrill's Marauders Return to Fort Snelling as China-Burma Vets," *Minneapolis Morning Tribune*, 11 Jan 45.

[148] Radiogram, CG U.S. Army Forces, China, Burma, and India Rear Echelon, to War Department, 16 May 44, Class Ref Sub File, Asst Sec War, RG 107, NARA.

Nisei with Merrill's Marauders and others serving in the theater.[149] Kenji Yasui's bravery in tricking Japanese soldiers into surrendering also received widespread press coverage, and he was touted as the "Baby Sergeant York."[150] These became the first Nisei heroes of the war with Japan.

This publicity appeared in the autumn of 1944, an important time for Japanese Americans back home. For months the Secretary of the Interior had been urging President Roosevelt to close the camps, and the Supreme Court was nearing a decision to overturn the military exclusion orders from the West Coast. The 442d Regimental Combat Team began receiving extensive press coverage when it was committed to combat in Italy in June, but many Americans were not yet convinced of Nisei loyalty. *The Washington Post* published an editorial in September urging the War Department to release more details about the Nisei in the Pacific: "Nisei soldiers have played a vital and dramatic role in our succession of victories over the Japanese in the coral islands and steaming jungles of the Pacific theater of operations. Their knowledge of the Japanese language has been invaluable." The editorial acknowledged Hoichi Kubo's heroism on Saipan, as well as that of the Merrill's Marauders Nisei: "In Burma, according to men who have been their comrades there, the Nisei proved themselves particularly intrepid and helpful, venturing into the enemy lines and throwing them into confusion by speaking their language."[151]

The Merrill's Marauders Nisei became the best-known Nisei in the war against Japan. The War Relocation Authority used their story to impress other Americans with Nisei valor and loyalty. For example, in March 1945 the War Relocation Authority placed a story in the *Seattle Times* about Sergeant Gosho. The article cited a letter from a Caucasian sergeant:

The men of our platoon owe their lives to Sergt. Henry G[osho], a Japanese-American of Seattle. Hank (we call him Horizontal Hank because he's been pinned down so many times by Jap machine-gun fire) guided the machine-gun fire on our side which killed every Jap on that side.

The boys who fought alongside Hank agree that they never have seen a more calm, cool and collected man under fire. He was always so eager to be where he could be of the most use and effectiveness and that was most always the hot spot.[152]

---

[149] "Official Censorship Lifted on Participation of Nisei Soldiers on Burma Front against Japan," *Pacific Citizen*, 7 Oct 44; Laytha, "Nisei," p. 3; "Cite Japanese Americans on Burma Front," *Pacific Citizen*, 7 Oct 44; "Nisei Soldiers Aid Allied Victories on Burma Front," *Pacific Citizen*, 14 Oct 44, p. 2. Edgar M. Laytha, a journalist in the Far East before the war, wrote *The March of Japan* (New York: F. A. Stokes, 1936). He enlisted in April 1943, attended MISLS, and went to India with the OWI team. In the autumn of 1944 he parachuted into north Burma and disappeared. He was listed as missing in action.

[150] Editorial in *Twin Falls Times News*, Oct 44, reprinted in WRA, *Nisei in the War against Japan*, p. 7.

[151] WRA, *Nisei in the War against Japan*, p. 8.

[152] "Seattle Nisei Saves Platoon of Marauders," *Seattle Times*, 4 Mar 45, reprinted in WRA, *Nisei in the War against Japan*, p. 11; also cited in Emmerson, *The Japanese Thread*, p. 161.

Another Caucasian soldier wrote:

We of the Merrill's Marauders wish to boast of the Japanese-Americans fighting in our outfit and the swell job that they put up.... Many of the boys and myself especially, never knew a Japanese-American or what one was like—now we know and the Marauders want you to know that they are backing the nisei one hundred percent. It makes the boys and myself raging mad to read about movements against Japanese-Americans by some 4-F'ers back home. We would dare them to say things like they have in front of us.[153]

Another unconventional American unit, Office of Strategic Services (OSS) Detachment 101, fought in Burma without such publicity. The detachment began operations in January 1943 from a base camp in Assam by organizing hill tribes to conduct reconnaissance, sabotage, and the rescue of downed airmen.[154] Detachment 101 was the first element of the OSS to engage in combat operations against Japan, and for this it needed the language skills of the Nisei. OSS Director William J. Donovan was an early advocate for Nisei in the war effort and directed the recruitment of Nisei volunteers from Camp Shelby.[155]

OSS leaders in India did not wait for the Shelby Nisei but sought instead Nisei volunteers from the Southeast Asia Translation and Interrogation Center (SEATIC) and the Fourteenth Air Force. T5gs. Hideo Imai and Robert T. Honda volunteered in March 1944. Honda had served with Merrill's Marauders until evacuated for illness. The two Nisei parachuted into northern Burma and lived for months with the Kachin Rangers. "It was a rugged existence," Imai recalled. "We were supplied by air drops, food, books, clothes, ammunition, equipment.... Because of Jap agents among the tribes, we were forced to shift our command post continually. I had malaria several times and always suffered from dysentery."[156]

After eight months two other Nisei serving in India volunteered to take their places. T3g. Shigeto Ken Mazawa and T5g. Charles Y. Matsunaka were inserted into the Burmese jungle for:

Working in areas behind enemy lines and doing both language and radio intercept work. These two volunteered without any hesitation and took their jumps in fine form although having had no previous training in parachute jumping whatsoever. The para-

[153] Cited in Emmerson, *The Japanese Thread*, pp. 159–60.

[154] Richard Dunlop, *Behind Japanese Lines: With the OSS in Burma* (Chicago: Rand-McNally, 1979); William R. Peers and Dean Brelis, *Behind the Burma Road* (Boston: Little, Brown, 1963); James R. Ward, "The Activities of Detachment 101 of the OSS," in *The Secrets War: The Office of Strategic Services in World War II*, ed. George C. Chalou (Washington, D.C.: National Archives and Records Administration, 1992), pp. 318–27; Mary Previte, "Tad Nagaki," *Ex-CBI Roundup* (June 2002).

[155] Simon Morioka, "Japanese Americans in the Service of Their Country," Ph.D. Diss., Selwyn College, University of Cambridge, 1998, pp. 50–51.

[156] Sinclair, "Valuable as a Company of Men."

trooper who gave them instructions and who accompanied them on their jump flight told me that when their turns came to jump, they took off themselves with "no assistance."[157]

In October 1944 the original team of fourteen Nisei volunteers from Camp Shelby under 1st Lt. Ralph T. Yempuku arrived in the theater and was split up among several OSS activities. Yempuku and several other Nisei flew into Myitkyina in December to join Detachment 101 for the coming offensive to drive the Japanese from Burma.[158]

Allied intelligence organizations in India expanded rapidly in size and capability. One historian has counted twelve Allied intelligence organizations operating in the Southeast Asia Command. Most had a need for Japanese-language expertise. In May 1944 the Joint Intelligence Collection Agency in New Delhi was replaced by SEATIC, which was "established in order to pool the resources of British and US linguists." SEATIC was headed by Col. Allender Swift, a U.S. Army Japanese-language officer, and later by Col. Gaspare F. Blunda. SEATIC became the central pool for Nisei language personnel, similar to the Allied Translation and Interpreter Section in the Southwest Pacific.[159]

The British established a large prisoner of war compound near army headquarters at Red Fort in Old Delhi. This was also the location of Headquarters, Intelligence Bureau, and the Combined Services Detailed Interrogation Center. Dozens of Nisei helped with the interrogations, which sometimes produced valuable information. S.Sgt. Frank T. Tokubo spent five weeks interrogating prisoners from Nagasaki to glean details about the Mitsubishi aircraft factory located there. Other language work was done by British soldiers who had graduated from the Japanese program at the School of Oriental and African Studies in London or trained at the British intelligence school in Karachi.[160]

In this theater, Nisei were not used in signals intelligence, which was directed by the Wireless Experimental Center in Delhi and supported by Bletchley Park in Great Britain. Nevertheless, these cryptographers had good success against Japanese radio codes and used Caucasian translators.[161]

Life in the rear areas was enjoyable for the "Jap-Yanks," as the British called them, despite the difficult climate and the oppressive poverty. They came to enjoy

[157] Ibid.; WD Press Release, 22 Oct 45; Shigeto Mazawa, autobiography in Harrington Papers.

[158] Ralph Yempuku, "OSS Detachment 101, CBI Theater," in Tsukiyama et al., *Secret Valor*, pp. 75–76; Tomi K. Knaefler, *Our House Divided: Seven Japanese American Families in World War II* (Honolulu: University of Hawaii Press, 1991), pp. 88–95; Interv, Andrew Cox with Ralph Yempuku; Calvin Tottori, "The OSS Niseis in the China-Burma-India Theater," 2d ed., Unpubl Ms, 2001, copy in author's files.

[159] Sinclair, "Valuable as a Company of Men"; Harrington, *Yankee Samurai*, pp. 180–81, 215, 217; Funch, *Linguists in Uniform*, pp. 154–56.

[160] Harrington, *Yankee Samurai*, p. 226; Aldrich, *Intelligence and the War against Japan*, pp. 162, 167; Stripp, *Codebreaker in the Far East*, pp. 123–25, 139–44; Sadao Oba, *The "Japanese" War*, trans. Anne Kaneko (Sandgate, U.K.: Japan Library, 1995); Interv, author with Kuwabara, 12 Sep 96.

[161] Stripp, *Codebreaker in the Far East*, pp. 39–47.

being served afternoon tea by houseboys and having their "kit" maintained by servants. They could visit tourist sites such as the Taj Mahal. They also witnessed the waning days of the British Empire and scenes of unimaginable suffering such as the 1943 Bengal famine.

In the China-Burma-India Theater, the Tenth Air Force provided air support. In the spring of 1943 Maj. Sheldon M. Covell led a team of ten Nisei to the Air Intelligence School in Harrisburg, Pennsylvania, and then onward to the Tenth Air Force. However, Tenth Air Force needed more Nisei trained in low-level radio intercept. In December 1943 the Tenth Air Force commanding general wrote General Henry H. Arnold, Commanding General, U.S. Army Air Forces, for help: "The Japanese are great talkers over the radio [while in flight], but unfortunately we have no way of knowing what they are saying."[162] In response, MISLS sent twenty-five Nisei to MacDill Field, Florida, for special training, and then to Camp Pinedale, California. They arrived in India in October 1944 and joined the 6th Radio Squadron Mobile in Assam in January 1945.[163]

One Nisei went to a special assignment with the 1st Air Commando, which used fighters, bombers, transports, gliders, liaison planes, and even helicopters to provide air support to Merrill's Marauders, OSS Detachment 101, and the British long-range penetration groups known as the Chindits. Tom Shojiro Taketa was assigned early in 1944 and helped monitor Japanese radio communications.[164]

American Nisei played important roles in the China-Burma-India Theater, from SEATIC in Delhi to Merrill's Marauders, OSS Detachment 101, and British and Chinese combat units. The senior officer commanding Nisei in the theater, Colonel Blunda, gave them the highest praise:

Each one was as valuable as an Infantry company, despite the fact they were not combat troops. Many allied soldiers returned safely to their homes because the Nisei lighted the darkness in front of them by interrogating prisoners and translating documents. The value of the Nisei was that they supplied the missing link—understanding of the shades of meaning of the Japanese language—between the enemy and British and U.S. intelligence.[165]

The intelligence picture in China was more complex than in Burma and India. American intelligence agencies included the Sino-American Cooperative Organization (SACO), the OSS, and the Army's own theater G–2.[166] American plans for offensive operations in China suffered a major setback in April 1944, when Japanese forces smashed deep into China with the *Ichi-Gō* offensive. Chinese ground

---

[162] Quoted in Kreis, *Piercing the Fog*, p. 361.

[163] Ted Tsukiyama, "Radio Intelligence in CBI," in Tsukiyama et al., *Secret Valor*, pp. 72–73; Harrington, *Yankee Samurai*, p. 245.

[164] Harrington, *Yankee Samurai*, pp. 167, 224–25; "Jap-American Volunteer from Tule WRA Center Fights Nips in India," *Klamath Falls Herald and News*, n.d.; "Taketa Wins Bronze Star," *Yaban Gogai*, Sep–Oct 45, p. 4.

[165] Sinclair, "Valuable as a Company of Men," p. 7.

[166] Yu Shen, "SACO Re-Examined: Sino American Intelligence Cooperation during World War II," *Intelligence and National Security* 16, no. 4 (Winter 2001): 149.

troops were forced back throughout the country, and several American airfields were overrun. The Americans had no plans to commit ground troops on the Chinese mainland but clearly needed to bolster its intelligence capabilities. The G–2 for U.S. Forces China in Chungking was Col. Joseph K. Dickey, who had helped Colonel Rasmussen set up the Fourth Army Intelligence School at Crissy Field. Dickey was "the only key officer of the former Stilwell staff whom I had retained," wrote Lt. Gen. Albert C. Wedemeyer, who took command of American forces in China in October 1944, "and he had fully merited my confidence." In the spring of 1944 Dickey brought several Nisei to Chungking to form the Sino Translation and Interrogation Center (SINTIC). He was later joined by Maj. John A. Burden, a veteran of language work in the South Pacific. In December 1944 Burden wrote Rasmussen for his assistance in setting up a language section in Chungking. As a result, eight Merrill's Marauders veterans and several other Nisei were transferred there in early 1945.[167]

In the summer of 1944 General Stilwell sent a small observer mission to Chinese Communist headquarters in Yenan in northwest China.[168] The first group arrived on 22 July. A second contingent on 7 August included Major Burden and T4g. George I. Nakamura, a quiet Nisei from southern California and at twenty years old the mission's youngest member.[169] The Dixie Mission, as it was called, was directed to gather intelligence about the common Japanese enemy, as well as about the Chinese Communists. The Communists had excellent sources for military and political intelligence about Japan. Yenan was refuge to the head of the Japan Communist Party, *Susumu Okano* (*Sanzō Nosaka*). Exiled Japanese Communist leaders regularly received copies of the *Tokyo Asahi* daily newspaper in Yenan within ten days of publication. They also collected hundreds of Japanese prisoners of war and had considerable success in developing effective propaganda techniques.

In September 1944 Nakamura was joined by T4g. Shoso Nomura. In October the Office of War Information sent a third Nisei, T4g. Koji Ariyoshi, who had been a labor organizer and member of the American Communist Party before the war. Ariyoshi used his political background to establish a rapport with the Chinese and Japanese Communist leaders and filed reports on propaganda techniques and the future policies of the Japan Communist Party. *Okano* invited Ariyoshi and John

---

[167] Albert C. Wedemeyer, *Wedemeyer Reports!* (New York: Henry Holt, 1958), p. 351; Ltr, John A. Burden to Kai Rasmussen, 15 December 1944, Trng Grp, Ofc of the Dir of Intel G–2, RG 165, NARA; Interv, author with John A. Burden, 5 Dec 94.

[168] David D. Barrett, *Dixie Mission: The United States Army Observer Group in Yenan, 1944*, China Research Monographs no. 6 (Berkeley, Calif.: Center for Chinese Studies, 1970); Carolle J. Carter, *Mission to Yenan: American Liaison with the Chinese Communists, 1944–1947* (Lexington: University Press of Kentucky, 1997); John Colling, *The Spirit of Yenan: A Wartime Chapter of Sino-American Friendship* (Hong Kong: API Press, 1991); Maochun Yu, *OSS in China: Prelude to Cold War* (New Haven: Yale University Press, 1996).

[169] Intervs, author with George Nakamura, 6 Dec 94; with Sho Nomura, 10 Sep 96; and with Tosh Uesato, 21 Aug 95. Sho Nomura, in Ichinokuchi, *John Aiso and the M.I.S.*, pp. 106–24. After a month in Yenan, Burden returned to Chungking. Carter, *Mission to Yenan*, p. 155.

Emmerson to address the Japanese Emancipation League on Pearl Harbor Day, 7 December 1944. The two spoke about American democracy and freedom of speech. In particular Ariyoshi "told them about the nisei fighting for their country in spite of their Japanese ancestry." Ariyoshi's experiences in Yenan only reinforced his prewar political convictions. By his own testimony, "the main change was inside him. He came away a staunch partisan of the Chinese revolution."[170]

All sides used psychological warfare in China and Southeast Asia. The Japanese stressed the anticolonial nature of their policies and fostered subversion among Indian troops serving under British officers. The British exploited the hatred of the Kachin hill tribes toward the lowland Burmese. The British and Americans sought to undermine the morale of Japanese soldiers in the region. In 1943 the British Army hired the former owner of a Japanese-language print shop in San Francisco, Shigeki Oka, to print propaganda materials in Calcutta, such as the *Gunjin Shimbun [Soldier News]*.

The Office of War Information opened branch offices in New Delhi in 1942 and later in Bombay, Calcutta, and Karachi in India and Kunming and Chungking in China. In March 1944 nine Nisei arrived at the OWI compound in Ledo and at a tea plantation, Chota Powai, near Margherita. This marked a new phase in OWI's efforts. The OWI Nisei included Karl Yoneda, a Communist Party member, and leftists such as Koji Ariyoshi. Other team members included Chris Ishii, the talented graphic artist who designed the MISLS "gopher" emblem; Clarke Kawakami, who had worked for the *Dōmei* news service and was the son of the distinguished Issei journalist K. K. Kawakami; and S.Sgt. Edgar M. Laytha, a writer for the *Saturday Evening Post*.[171] The Ledo team began developing propaganda materials, including *Senjin Shimbun [Battlefront News]*. At first the Caucasians wrote leaflets for the Nisei to translate into Japanese. "How can I translate that?" Yoneda protested. "The Japanese just don't think that way!"[172] Eventually, the Caucasian officers let the Nisei share in the drafting.

---

[170] Emmerson, *The Japanese Thread*, p. 198; Koji Ariyoshi, *From Kona to Yenan: The Political Memoirs of Koji Ariyoshi*, ed. Alice M. Beechert and Edward D. Beechert (Honolulu: University of Hawaii Press, 2000); Hugh Deane, ed., *Remembering Koji Ariyoshi* (Los Angeles: U.S.-China Peoples Friendship Association, 1978). Ariyoshi's OWI reports from November 1944 to January 1945 were reprinted in U.S. Senate, Subcommittee to Investigate the Administration of the Internal Security Act and Other Internal Security Laws of the Committee on the Judiciary, *The Amerasia Papers: A Clue to the Catastrophe of China* (Washington, D.C.: Government Printing Office, 1970), vol. 2.

[171] Eleanor A. Sparagana, "The Conduct and Consequences of Psychological Warfare: American Psychological Operations in the War against Japan, 1941–1945," Ph.D. Diss., Brandeis University, 1990; Sandler, *Cease Resistance*, pp. 172–75; Emmerson, *The Japanese Thread*, p. 163; Harrington, *Yankee Samurai*, pp. 225–26, 249–50; Sinclair, "Valuable as a Company of Men"; Clarke Kawakami and Karl Yoneda, Harrington Papers.

[172] MIS Archival Collection and Harrington Papers, NJAHS; "Karl Yoneda—U.S. Soldier," *Peoples' World* (27 November 1945); Karl G. Yoneda, "A Brief History of U.S. Asian Labor," *Political Affairs* (September 1976); Karl G. Yoneda, *Ganbatte: Sixty-Year Struggle of a Kibei Worker* (Los Angeles: Asian American Studies Center, University of California at Los Angeles, 1983).

Serving in Burma with the Office of War Information were Kenji Yasui (left) *and Karl G. Yoneda* (second from right), *shown here displaying captured Japanese flags.*

After the fall of Myitkyina, scores of sick and wounded Japanese prisoners were flown to Ledo, where they were treated in the 20th General Hospital. Yoneda and the other OWI Nisei used the prisoners to develop more effective materials.[173] The long-range goal was to formulate a strategic policy to induce the ultimate surrender of Japan. "The metamorphosis which occurs in the mind of a Japanese prisoner of war," wrote Emmerson in August 1944, "suggests to us what may happen to the Japanese people." He concluded, "If we deal circumspectly with the

---

[173] "Karl Yoneda—U.S. Soldier"; Emmerson, *The Japanese Thread*, pp. 171–76; "Use of Japanese Prisoners of War," in *A Psychological Warfare Casebook*, ed. William E. Daugherty and Morris Janowitz (Baltimore: Johns Hopkins Press, 1958), pp. 198–201, 201–11; "Spot Interrogation of 31 POWs, Myitkyina, 28 Jul–4 Aug 44," copy in author's files; U.S. Office of War Information, India Division, "Psychological Warfare Operations to October 26, 1944," and U.S. Office of War Information, China Division, "Psychological Warfare Operations," in Historical Section, China-Burma-India Theater, "History of the China-Burma-India Theater, 21 May 1942 to 25 October 1945," Unpubl Ms, U.S. Army Center of Military History.

Japanese people, we can hasten internal collapse and prepare them for the consequences of their defeat."[174]

American forces prepared to renew the offensive in northern Burma in late 1944. That summer the War Department sent from the United States two infantry regiments: the 475th Infantry, which absorbed the surviving Merrill's Marauders veterans, and the 124th Cavalry, also an infantry regiment despite its designation. These were combined to form the 5332d Brigade (Provisional) and given the codename MARS Task Force. Dozens of Nisei, including some veterans of the Alaskan Theater, arrived to join these units and headquarters in the theater. Sgt. Kazuo Komoto led the 475th Infantry team, and Sgt. Kan Tagami led the 124th Cavalry team. When Toma Tasaki arrived in India that summer, two Marauder Nisei gave him some blunt advice: "Whatever you do, don't volunteer for Burma. It's rough."[175]

In October the Allies moved into northern Burma. The MARS Task Force was committed to action in December, while Commonwealth forces attacked farther south. Lieutenant Yempuku's OSS team renewed operations behind Japanese lines with the Kachin Rangers.[176] By the end of 1944, about 135 Nisei were assigned to the theater and were making important contributions to all these efforts. Stilwell's political adviser, Emmerson, wrote Colonel Rasmussen that summer to request more Nisei: "People are screaming for them."[177]

Leyte

In October 1944 the American axes of advance from the Central and Southwest Pacific converged in the central Philippines on the island of Leyte. For the 120 Nisei who served on Leyte, the battle would be their greatest test to date. By now some were combat veterans; a handful of them had been commissioned and were team leaders. Others were fresh from Camp Savage. Intelligence agencies, including ATIS in Brisbane and JICPOA in Hawaii, prepared for the return to the Philippines with photoreconnaissance of likely landing sites and detailed maps and special studies. Signals intelligence agencies in Australia, Hawaii, and Washington monitored Japanese communications for clues to troop dispositions and shipping. Philippine guerrillas provided vital intelligence. Intelligence agencies in the two theaters cooperated to an unprecedented degree.[178]

Leyte also became the first large-scale test of psychological warfare against Japan. ATIS amassed vast amounts of information through interrogations and

---

[174] Reprinted in *Amerasia Papers*, 2: 1747–49.

[175] Toma Tasaki, "Mars Task Force," in Tsukiyama et al., *Secret Valor*, p. 70.

[176] Yempuku, in Tsukiyama et al., *Secret Valor*, pp. 75–76; Harrington, *Yankee Samurai*, pp. 230–31, 242, 250; *Pacific War and Peace*, pp. 64–65; Interv, author with Kan Tagami, 7 Dec 94.

[177] Ltr, John Emmerson to Kai Rasmussen, 20 August 1944.

[178] Drea, *MacArthur's Ultra*, pp. 152–79; Ltr, Col. Joseph J. Twitty to Chief, Historical Section, Far East Command, 2 February 1948, cited in *A Brief History of G–2 Section, GHQ, SWPA, and Affiliated Units*.

translations of captured letters and diaries, and Colonel Mashbir indulged in amateur speculations about Japanese psychology.[179] In June 1944 MacArthur established the Psychological Warfare Branch under Brig. Gen. Bonner F. Fellers, who published the "Basic Military Plan for Psychological Warfare in the Southwest Pacific Area" on 2 August.[180] Mashbir detailed a Nisei warrant officer to Fellers and put Major Anderton in charge of the ATIS Philippine Islands Research Section. The Psychological Warfare Branch posted teams with Nisei to Sixth Army and the two army corps. The teams brought preprinted leaflets and mobile printing presses and during ten weeks of fighting blanketed Leyte with 700,000 leaflets.[181]

On 20 October the Nisei language teams went ashore with the assault elements of four divisions and two corps.[182] Maj. George Aurell led the Sixth Army team. His team sergeant, S.Sgt. Kazuo Kozaki, recalled: "We were kept busy all day and immediately. There were loads and loads of captured documents, although no prisoners were taken yet. I had to virtually wade through a pile of papers—operation orders, operation maps, manuals, magazines, books, paybooks, saving books, notebooks and diaries, handwritten or printed, official or private—to find out if there was any valuable information for our immediate use."[183]

Some Nisei saw direct combat. When the Japanese counterattacked the 7th Infantry Division, the Nisei "were a little bit heroic," a Caucasian sergeant recalled. "They would climb on board a Japanese tank going by, knock on the things, converse in Japanese, and as soon as the door popped open, they'd drop a hand grenade—boom!"[184]

On 25 October two more Sixth Army language detachments arrived on board a landing ship, tank, led by two Nisei second lieutenants, Steve Yamamoto and Phil Ishio, who had both served in ATIS since September 1942. Before they could unload, a Japanese bomb struck amidships, killing twenty-five soldiers and sailors. Eighty others were wounded, including two Nisei sergeants, Spady Ayato

---

[179] Mashbir, *I Was an American Spy*, pp. 226–32, 272–77.

[180] Gilmore, *You Can't Fight Tanks with Bayonets*; Sandler, *Cease Resistance*; Clayton D. Laurie, "The Ultimate Dilemma of Psychological Warfare in the Pacific: Enemies Who Don't Surrender and GIs Who Don't Take Prisoners," in *The U.S. Army and World War II: Selected Papers from the Army's Commemorative Conferences*, ed. Judith L. Bellafaire, U.S. Army in World War II (Washington, D.C.: U.S. Army Center of Military History, 1998).

[181] ATIS History, pp. 22–23; Mashbir, *I Was an American Spy*, p. 270; Gilmore, *You Can't Fight Tanks with Bayonets*, pp. 32–33, 154. The Philippine Islands Research Section was dissolved on 9 October 1944.

[182] Some sources report that Frank Hachiya parachuted into Leyte several weeks before the attack. Rep. Al Ullman, *Congressional Record* (11 Jun 63); Bill Hosokawa, *Nisei: The Quiet Americans* (New York: William Morrow, 1969), pp. 414–15; Oguro, *Sempai Gumi*, pp. 29–30. Taro Tsukahara told Joseph Harrington a similar story about Hachiya (Harrington Papers). I was unable to confirm this story, which seems unlikely.

[183] Kozaki, in Swift, "First Class," pp. 55–56.

[184] Studs Terkel, *"The Good War": An Oral History of World War Two* (New York: Pantheon, 1984), p. 23. This incident may have occurred on 20–21 October near Dulag, Leyte. See M. Hamlin Cannon, *Leyte: The Return to the Philippines*, U.S. Army in World War II (Washington: Office of the Chief of Military History, 1954), p. 128.

Koyama and Tsuneo "Cappy" Harada.[185] Koyama awoke some hours later on a sandy beach, stretched out in a row of dead sailors who had been taken ashore for burial. He could not feel anything on his left side, so he reached over with his right hand before losing consciousness again: "This single act of leaving my arm on my chest when others on both sides of me were laid side by side with their arms at their sides did indeed attract attention. I heard someone call out to a nearby chaplain who hurried over to my side to ask for my religion."

The chaplain reached for Koyama's identification tags and asked, "Buddhist?" Koyama shook his head no. The chaplain looked down at the tag again and said, "Looks like a B, but I guess it's a P," and recited the 23d Psalm. Koyama passed out, but survived.[186]

The landings on Leyte provoked the Imperial Japanese Navy to seek a decisive engagement. This became one of the great sea battles of the war, the Battle of Leyte Gulf. The Combined Fleet followed the basic strategy laid down in the Z-Plan. However, "the complete Japanese plan for the defense of the Philippines also was made known through the work of the language specialists from the Military Intelligence Service Language School long before our forces had landed on Leyte."[187] In the greatest naval engagement of the war, the American Navy crushed the Japanese battle fleet, which never again posed a serious threat. In desperation the Japanese turned to a terrible new tactic, aerial *kamikaze* attacks, which had a devastating effect on U.S. vessels and sailors. For most Americans, the kamikazes only reinforced the image of Japanese as fanatical and determined to fight to the bitter end.

Imperial Japanese Army headquarters decided to make Leyte the decisive battle to halt the relentless American advance toward the home islands. Despite the naval defeat, they poured in reinforcements, more than tripling troop strength on the island. Meanwhile, monsoon rains, thirty-five inches in six weeks, drenched the island, soaking everything and delaying vital airfield construction. As the two sides rushed troops to Leyte, the intelligence battle became crucial. For once, signals intelligence was not all revealing. For example, within days of the American landing, the Japanese high command shipped the 1st Division from Manchuria to Leyte, which "passed unnoticed by American codebreakers."[188] The first inkling came on 2 November when the XXIV Corps language team translated a captured

[185] Phil Ishio, "The New Guinea and Philippine Campaigns," in Falk and Tsuneishi, *MIS in the War against Japan*, p. 30.

[186] Spady A. Koyama, MISNorCal Bio; *Unsung Heroes: The Military Intelligence Service, Past-Present-Future* (Seattle: MIS-Northwest Association, 1996), pp. 49–51; Harrington, *Yankee Samurai*, pp. 240–41; Interv, author with Spady A. Koyama, 2 Nov 87. Koyama was evacuated to his home state of Washington, where he spent twelve months in the hospital, and was medically discharged. In 1947 he returned to active duty and accepted a commission. He remained on active duty until 1970.

[187] Adm. Thomas C. Kinkaid, in *Reports of General MacArthur*, 4 vols., U.S. Army in World War II (Washington, D.C.: U.S. Army Center of Military History, 1994), 1: 205; WD Press Release, 22 Oct 45.

[188] Drea, *MacArthur's Ultra*, p. 169.

operations order "revealing that the entire Japanese 1st Division had landed on Leyte on November 1 and that a 'grand offensive' would commence about mid-November."[189] On 4 November Nisei translated a captured operations order, dated 31 October, from the Japanese 16th Division.[190]

Nisei served at every level from regiment to Sixth Army, interrogating prisoners, translating captured documents, and using loudspeakers and leaflets to encourage surrenders. Most Nisei continued to serve under Caucasian officers, including some Navy Boulder graduates assigned to Army units. "It was hard for the Nisei interpreters" on Leyte, wrote Navy Lt. John Ashmead. "Only rarely did they become officers, and often enough their white officers knew less Japanese, certainly less spoken Japanese, than they did," even though the Nisei sometimes used "feminine or archaic words for war," having learned the language from their mothers and from Nisei instructors with no military experience.[191]

On 27 November the Japanese staged a daring airborne assault on the Buri airstrip; but the transport aircraft crashed, killing all the passengers. Nisei translated the documents found in the wreckage. A week later 350 Japanese paratroopers dropped out of the night sky in another attempt to capture the airstrip in a combined airborne/ground assault. The paratroopers sowed confusion by running up and down the strip using captured American weapons and allegedly shouting things such as "hello—where are your machine guns?" The attackers were finally tracked down and destroyed.[192]

Ishio, attached to Sixth Army headquarters, recalled:

I was awakened in the middle of the night and driven to the airfield to face the grim task of removing whatever documents could be found on the mangled and bloody bodies. A special light-proof tent had been put up for me to use. I spent the rest of the night translating the documents which I had picked up. It was extremely hot and close within the tent, and every sound outside seemed to be magnified ten-fold by my imagining that there would be a follow-up parachute drop. Actually, the orders which I translated called for another drop the next day, but this did not materialize.[193]

---

[189] Ibid., p. 170.

[190] ATIS History, p. 48; "The Character of Military Intelligence," pt. 2, p. 195, in Folder 4, Box 3, Willoughby Papers, RG 23–B, MacArthur Memorial. For similar examples see Language Detachment Report, encl 7, ann. 2, Leyte Historical Report of the 24th Infantry Division Landing Team.

[191] Ashmead, *The Mountain and the Feather*, p. 319. Ashmead served on Leyte with the 307th Headquarters Intelligence Detachment, assigned to XXIV Corps.

[192] Cannon, *Leyte*, pp. 297–305; Stanley L. Falk, *Decision at Leyte* (New York: Norton, 1966), pp. 259–70.

[193] Ishio, "The New Guinea and Philippine Campaigns," in Falk and Tsuneishi, *MIS in the War against Japan*, p. 30; Interv, author with Tsuneishi, 22 Aug 95; Harrington, *Yankee Samurai*, p. 250; Tom Masui, in Harrington Papers. Kenney described the captured papers in *General Kenney Reports*, p. 485.

The Americans held the Buri airstrip and pressed onward. The west coast port of Ormoc was captured by 10 December, cutting off further Japanese reinforcements. The Americans slowly squeezed the Japanese defenders, some of whom tried to escape to neighboring islands. The 77th Infantry Division language team led by T.Sgt. Shigeo Ito translated a document that told of a Japanese plan to move 600 soldiers to Ponson Island in Ormoc Bay. The convoy was intercepted and destroyed.[194]

At first the Americans took few prisoners, despite the pleas of intelligence officers. The 24th Infantry Division language team urged commanders to indoctrinate their troops and to offer "inducements (rewards, passes, money, etc.) to men in the front lines to take live prisoners. Too often, a Jap is killed because he is a Jap, a policy with which it is hard to disagree on emotional grounds, but one leading to a curtailment of valuable intelligence."[195] As the tide turned, prisoner numbers began to climb. T3g. Harold Nishimura, a veteran of the Aleutians and Saipan, served on Leyte with the 7th Infantry Division and wrote Colonel Rasmussen at Fort Snelling on 15 December, "I can assure that the morale of the enemy has changed since the beginning of this Pacific war."[196] Some prisoners held information of strategic value, such as one captured on 7 December who "had some knowledge of the Japanese balloon bombs that were appearing on the western coast of the United States."[197] In mid-December American infantrymen broke remaining Japanese resistance in the Ormoc Valley. At the 1st Cavalry Division's advance command post, the language team chief, Lt. William L. Dozier, interrogated prisoners of war nonstop for thirty-six hours. Sgt. Stanley S. Shimabukuro translated documents for fifty-one hours straight. The lieutenant praised Shimabukuro: "Captured letters and notebooks the *hakujin* [Caucasians] and Nisei could make no sense of, [Shimabukuro] could read," wrote Dozier, "even though parts of words were obscured by rain, sweat or blood."[198] About 65,000 Japanese soldiers fought on Leyte, but fewer than 400 became prisoners of war in the first ten weeks of battle, many of those sick or wounded. Over the next four months 439 more were captured.

The American victory on Leyte was costly. American casualties in ground combat amounted to 3,500 killed and 12,000 wounded, with another 2,800 naval and air casualties. In Europe, the situation appeared more hopeful. In September the War Department announced plans for partial demobilization to follow

---

[194] *Yaban Gogai*, Dec 45, p. 3.

[195] Language Detachment Report, encl 7, ann. 2, Leyte Historical Report of the 24th Infantry Division Landing Team. *Shōhei Ōoka* served with the Japanese Army on nearby Mindoro, where he was taken prisoner in December 1944 or January 1945. He described his experiences in the novel *Fires on the Plain* (New York: Knopf, 1957), and memoir, *Taken Captive: A Japanese POW's Story*, trans. and ed. Wayne P. Lammers (New York: John Wiley & Sons, 1996).

[196] Ltr, T3g. Harold Nishimura to Col. Kai Rasmussen, 15 December 1944, Trng Grp, Ofc of the Dir of Intel G–2, RG 165, NARA.

[197] ATIS History, p. 49.

[198] Harrington, *Yankee Samurai*, p. 255.

the defeat of Germany, but the defeat of Japan was not yet in sight. After three years American forces were not yet within striking distance of the Japanese home islands. They still had to take Luzon and major islands closer to Japan such as Iwo Jima and Okinawa. Every step was more costly than the last. The War Department estimated that two more years would be needed to break Japan's military power and invade the Japanese home islands in 1946 or later, supported by large numbers of troops shifted from Europe to the Pacific.

The end of Japanese resistance on Leyte provided a respite for some Nisei. Sergeant Kozaki had served in the Southwest Pacific since the spring of 1943 and had earned the Purple Heart on New Guinea. He was serving on Leyte with the team assigned to Sixth Army headquarters, where he attended a New Year's Eve dance party held by an African American regiment. As he walked in, "a couple of black soldiers came up to me, looking as if they were looking at a man from Mars."

"You Japanee?" one of them kept on asking me, shaking his head incomprehensibly, "And in de American Army?" After getting my somewhat irritated confirmation, the two men burst out laughing, clapping their hands and chanting: "A Japanee boy in de American Army." Soon dozens of black soldiers surrounded us, laughing and clapping their hands. . . . "Japanee boy! Japanee boy!" they chanted, dancing around me. They thought it was a huge joke. Perhaps it was. "Yeah, man! Yeah, man!" I shouted and started dancing with them.[199]

Frank Hachiya and the Hood River Incident

In late December 1944 American forces fanned out across Leyte to isolate and destroy small detachments of Japanese soldiers or persuade them to surrender. This process cost many additional American casualties.

On 30 December the 32d Infantry captured a prisoner and called for an interpreter. Frank Hachiya, acting team chief for the 7th Infantry Division, was slated to return to Hawaii but volunteered for one last combat mission. He had been born and raised in the farming community of Hood River, Oregon. Before the war his parents had sent him to Japan to attend Keio University in Tokyo. He returned to Oregon in 1941 for college but was drafted shortly after the war broke out. Even though his father was interned in the United States and his mother had remained in Japan, Hachiya volunteered for the language school. Earnest and articulate, he believed fervently in America and was eager to prove himself.

Hachiya hurried to the 32d Infantry's command post and interrogated the prisoner; but on the return trip, even though he was escorted by an American patrol, he was shot in the abdomen. The *New York Times* described what happened next:

Private Hachiya, mortally wounded though he was, could not lie there. The battalion wanted the information he had gathered. He must get back. So he crawled, bleeding and in agony, out of the valley and up the hill, through the grass and the scrub and around the

---

[199] Kazuo Kozaki, in Swift, "First Class," p. 61.

merciful protection of little hillocks. He was dying when he finally reached his lines. He made his report while they bound his wound.[200]

The field surgeons operated at once, but the bullet had torn through his liver. Most of the men in his regiment volunteered to give him blood transfusions, but he expired on 3 January 1945.[201]

Hachiya's death came to national attention at a critical moment for Americans of Japanese ancestry. On 17 December 1944, the War Department rescinded the exclusion orders that had kept Americans of Japanese ancestry away from the West Coast for over two years. The War Relocation Authority began to allow them to leave the camps for their homes, but the decision was not universally popular on the West Coast. Vigilante incidents were staged by people who did not want to see Japanese Americans return. On 29 November the American Legion post in Hood River, Hachiya's hometown, removed sixteen Nisei names from the county "roll of honor."

When Hachiya's death was announced, readers across the country immediately linked him to the Hood River incident. Americans of all races were outraged. The *Portland Oregonian* took up the cause, and the national press gave the story wide circulation. Even the national headquarters of the American Legion applied pressure on the local post. The *New York Times* editorial, titled "Private Hachiya, American," concluded: "Perhaps Private Hachiya never knew that the Legion post had dishonored him back home. Perhaps some day what is left of him may be brought back to this country for reburial among the honored dead."[202] In April 1945 the American Legion post reversed its stand and restored all names of Nisei servicemen from Hood River to the sign, this time including Frank Hachiya.[203]

---

[200] "Private Hachiya, American," *New York Times*, 17 Feb 45; *Pacific Citizen*, 2 Jun 45; "Snubbed Japanese Dies a Pacific Hero," *New York Times*, 16 Feb 45; Howard M. Moss, Ltr quoted in *Honolulu Star Bulletin*, ca. Jan–Feb 45; "Japanese American Soldier from Hood River Posthumously Awarded Silver Star Medal," *Pacific Citizen*, 5 May 45; *Pacific Citizen*, 2 Jun 45; Martha Ferguson McKeown, "Frank Hachiya: He Was American at Birth, and at Death," *Portland Oregonian*, 20 May 45; Harrington, *Yankee Samurai*, pp. 247–48; Oguro, *Sempai Gumi*, pp. 29–30.
Some have speculated that Hachiya was killed by American troops. See, for example, John F. Aiso, Speech at Twenty-fifth Reunion of MIS Nisei Veterans, 12 Nov 66; Hosokawa, *Nisei*, pp. 414–15; Oguro, *Sempai Gumi*, pp. 29–30; Edwards, *Spy Catchers*, p. 70. His team leader, Lt. Howard M. Moss, in a personal communication to the author on 5 August 2004, denied he was killed by American soldiers.
[201] The 7th Infantry Division posthumously awarded Hachiya the Silver Star. Some say he was recommended for the Distinguished Service Cross: Selective Service System, *Special Groups*, Special Monograph no. 10 (Washington, D.C.: Selective Service System, 1953), p. 141; Rep. Al Ullman (D-Oregon), *Congressional Record* (11 Jun 63); Hosokawa, *Nisei*, pp. 414–15; Oguro, *Sempai Gumi*, pp. 29–30. However, I have found no evidence for this. The Defense Language Institute Foreign Language Center named an academic building in his honor in 1980.
[202] "Private Hachiya, American," *New York Times*, 17 Feb 45; "Death of a Nisei," *Pacific Citizen*, 17 Feb 45. Hachiya's remains were later returned to Hood River, where he was reinterred with honors on 11 September 1948.
[203] Richard L. Neuberger, "The Nisei Come Back to Hood River," *Saturday Review of Literature* (10 August 1946), reprinted in *Readers Digest* (November 1946): 102–04. See also Alan K.

The MIS Nisei had an impact far beyond the battlefield. Sergeant Hachiya's loyal service, tragic death, and how these were interpreted back home served to demonstrate the broader significance of the contributions of the MIS Nisei. In Europe, the service of the 100th Infantry Battalion and 442d Regimental Combat Team demonstrated that the Nisei were prepared to fight and, if necessary, to die for their country. In the Pacific, the Nisei who fought against Japan showed a different dimension of loyalty. In the battle for acceptance at home, each was indeed "as valuable as an infantry company."

Ota, "Symbol of Protest: Oregon War Hero Honored," *Portland Oregonian*, May 80; Crost, *Honor by Fire*, pp. 205–08. Hachiya's name was not listed on the roll of honor because he had enlisted from Portland, where he had been attending college.

9

Fort Snelling, 1944–1945

By the summer of 1944 the Military Intelligence Service Language School (MISLS) had outgrown the facilities at Camp Savage and had graduated 1,400 soldiers, including 1,200 Nisei. In three years the school had grown from four instructors to more than ninety and from sixty students to 1,100, organized into fifty-two sections for the nine-month course. Col. Kai E. Rasmussen and a handful of other Caucasian officers headed the school; but the overwhelming majority of faculty, staff, and students was Nisei. At a time when the entire Japanese community on the West Coast had been forced into guarded camps and those in Hawaii remained under close surveillance, the War Department had organized a small group of Nisei to build the largest Japanese-language school in American history, an outstanding achievement of the Nisei generation.[1]

Three years into the war, the school faced increasing difficulties in recruiting enough qualified volunteers. The manpower solution came in January 1944 when the War Department reinstated Selective Service for the Nisei, primarily to meet requirements for combat replacements for the 100th Infantry Battalion and the 442d Regimental Combat Team (RCT) but also to meet growing requirements for language training. In early 1944 Rasmussen toured the South Pacific and returned with a renewed sense of urgency to expand the school's facilities.

---

[1] For basic sources on MISLS during 1944–1945, see those cited in Chapter Four, including MISLS, "Training History of the Military Intelligence Service Language School," Unpubl Ms, 1946, U.S. Army Center of Military History (CMH), and *MISLS Album* (Minneapolis: Military Intelligence Service Language School, 1946).

An opportunity arose in 1944 when the Seventh Service Command closed the reception center at Fort Snelling. Since 1942 Fort Snelling had provided the language school with administrative and logistical support and billets for the over-flow of students. Fort Snelling seemed more like the "real Army" to the Nisei com-pared to the wooden buildings at Camp Savage.[2] The school held one last gradu-ation ceremony at Camp Savage on 10 August 1944 and moved to Fort Snelling. Headquarters Company was awarded the Meritorious Service Unit Plaque for the move, but the civilian staff suffered at least one casualty when Technical Director John F. Aiso suffered a double hernia while moving his office.[3] Classes resumed on 21 August with 832 students.

The school remained under the direct control of the War Department G–2, which reorganized in June 1944. The Military Intelligence Division (MID) retained planning and policy functions, while operating functions went to the Military Intelligence Service (MIS). Also in 1944 Col. John Weckerling was promoted to brigadier general and named Deputy Assistant Chief of Staff for Intelligence. From his new position he could once again watch over the school he had founded. His superior, Assistant Chief of Staff for Intelligence Maj. Gen. Clayton L. Bis-sell, took a personal interest in the school and visited Fort Snelling several times to speak at graduation ceremonies.[4]

Spirit of the School

Soon after the school moved to Fort Snelling, Stone S. Ishimaru, a Nisei pho-tographer, captured the spirit of the school in a photo essay assignment for *Life* magazine. Most telling was a photograph of a Nisei color guard on Fort Snelling's historic parade ground. Ishimaru's photographs portrayed Americans of Japanese ancestry standing proudly in the heart of America.[5] The school's spirit in 1944 mirrored much of the Japanese American community. Much had changed since the dark days after Pearl Harbor. In Europe, the 100th Infantry Battalion and 442d

---

[2] Floyd E. Eller, "A Soldier Looks at History [Fort Snelling]," *Minnesota History* 24, no. 1 (March 1943): 1–10; Steve Hall, *Fort Snelling: Colossus of the Wilderness* (St. Paul: Minnesota Historical Society Press, 1987).

[3] Memo, MISLS, 27 Nov 44, with endorsements (approved 14 Dec 44). Headquarters Company was awarded a star for the subsequent six-month period, 27 November 1944–27 May 1945 (awarded 9 June 1945). Department of the Army Pamphlet 672–1, 6 Jul 61. Tad Ichinokuchi, ed., *John Aiso and the M.I.S.: Japanese-American Soldiers in the Military Intelligence Service, World War II* (Los Angeles: Military Intelligence Club of Southern California, 1988), p. 23; Interv, author with John F. Aiso, 1987.

[4] "A History of the Military Intelligence Division, 7 December 1941–2 September 1945," Unpubl Ms, copy in CMH files; Bruce W. Bidwell, "History of the Military Intelligence Division, Depart-ment of the Army General Staff," Unpubl Ms, 1959–1961, CMH files; Otto L. Nelson, Jr., *National Security and the General Staff* (Washington, D.C.: Infantry Journal Press, 1946), pp. 521–35.

[5] *Life* did not publish the photos. Ishimaru later published them privately. Stone S. Ishimaru, *Military Intelligence Service Language School, U.S. Army, Fort Snelling, Minnesota* (Los Angeles: TecCom Production, 1991); Stone S. Ishimaru, *Military Intelligence Service Language School, U.S. Army, Camp Savage, Minnesota* (Los Angeles: MIS Club of Southern California, 1992).

Nisei color guard, Fort Snelling, August 1944

RCT were winning public acclaim at such places as Cassino and Anzio. In October 1944 they were thrown into desperate battle in Southern France, where they suffered heavy casualties to liberate the "Lost Battalion." That summer the War Department removed Lt. Gen. John L. DeWitt from the Western Defense Command, the last obstacle to lifting the exclusion orders banning persons of Japanese ancestry from the West Coast. Meanwhile, the War Relocation Authority (WRA) was placed under the Department of the Interior, headed by New Dealer Harold L. Ickes, known to be a critic of the evacuation. The War Relocation Authority continued its leave clearance program from the camps; by the end of 1944 about one-third of the evacuees had been released for jobs or schooling. In December

1944 the War Relocation Authority announced plans to close the camps and the U.S. Supreme Court ruled that the federal government had "no authority to subject citizens who are concededly loyal to its leave regulations."[6] In Hawaii, the military governor lifted martial law in October 1944.

The driving force behind the school was Aiso, the 34-year-old Los Angeles Nisei attorney who directed day-to-day operations. Rasmussen was commandant, but the Nisei considered Aiso the true *kōchō-sensei*, or headmaster. To his closest colleagues he was a warm and inspirational leader; to others he was a demanding taskmaster. He believed the Nisei had a sacred mission:

Their common motivation was a burning desire to prove that a Nisei's belief in and devotion to the ideas of freedom and American institutions were stronger than the fortuitous ties of racial affinity. His self-assigned overall mission was to prove for all time to come that judging one's loyalty even in time of war on the basis of racial affinity and sympathetic affiliation alone was and is wrong.... And what better proof could he offer than to actively wage war directly against Japan.[7]

Rasmussen and the other Caucasian officers at the school held Aiso in high regard, as did other senior Army leaders and high government officials such as General Bissell and Joseph Grew, the former ambassador to Japan. Aiso returned the trust. "We are forever indebted to those who were in positions of leadership," Aiso later remarked, "who had faith in the AJA's [Americans of Japanese Ancestry] and without whose sponsorship we could never have had the chance to demonstrate our true qualities."[8]

Most younger Nisei students lacked Aiso's idealistic vision and gave a mixed response to his leadership. Many of the younger Nisei, especially those from Hawaii, saw Aiso as unnecessarily harsh and unbending: "We revered the man, respected his intelligence, feared his opinions, sought his counsel, but like all great public figures he was loved by many and yet disliked by some." The Nisei recognized in him a certain type of the older Nisei, conservative and accommodationist. Enlisted instructors often resented the cliquishness and special privileges of the civilian instructors, as well as Aiso's authority. After the war Aiso acknowledged these sentiments and apologized that "my personal immaturity and the restrictions of the military framework forced upon me by my superiors left much to be desired in the area of your personal comfort and welfare" and recognized what he called "my war-time role as the martinet."[9]

---

[6] *Ex Parte Endo*, 323 U.S. 283 (1944).

[7] John F. Aiso, remarks at Arlington National Cemetery, 2 Jun 63, in "Tributes to Japanese American Military Service in World War II," *Congressional Record* (11 Jun 63).

[8] John F. Aiso, Speech to MIS Veteran's Reunion, Honolulu, Hawaii, 6 Sep 64.

[9] Tad Ichinokuchi in *John Aiso and the M.I.S.*, p. 2; Ltr, John F. Aiso to MIS Veterans of Hawaii, 16 July 1962, in "MIS Reunion," a booklet distributed at a veterans' reunion in 1962; Aiso speech, 6 Sep 64.

In the spring of 1944 Bissell visited the school and was surprised at the extent of Aiso's authority over the faculty and students, even though Aiso was only a civilian. Bissell gave his support to commissions for the top civilians, but in the end only Aiso was commissioned. He pinned on major's gold oak leaves on 18 October 1944 and was named to the military position of Director of Academic Training. Henceforth Aiso's authority was unparalleled, although he noted that after his commissioning his relationship with Rasmussen "cooled off somewhat."[10]

Commissions for other instructors remained a sore point for the civilian instructors, whose students grew increasingly unwilling to accept civilian authority in the classroom. A school study later recommended commissions for division chairmen and at least half the instructors: "Problems of discipline among the student body would have been automatically solved. It would have added immeasurably to the prestige, dignity, and authority of the faculty."[11] Accomplishing the school's training mission grew ever more challenging as the war continued. The pioneering spirit of 1941 and 1942 had waned.

Colonel Rasmussen commissions Aiso as a major, October 1944.

Rasmussen grew increasingly concerned about student morale. According to school officials, "Many of the Nisei at Fort Snelling have had to teach or study with anxious hearts. Many had relatives in Relocation Camps in the Western States. After the Japanese were permitted to return from the Relocation Camps to the West Coast, incidents that caused much anxiety occurred." The Director of Personnel Procurement, Maj. Paul F. Rusch, recommended a Japanese Episcopalian minister, the Rev. Daisuke Kitagawa, whom he had known in Japan before the war. In July 1944 Rasmussen contacted Kitagawa who agreed to serve as the "unofficial civilian chaplain" to the Nisei soldiers at the school, working under the auspices of the Minneapolis Church Federation. Rasmussen also arranged religious services for the Buddhist students. The first service, held on 22 October

---

[10] *Yaban Gogai*, Nov 45; Kiyoshi Yano, "Participating in the Mainstream of American Life amidst Drawback of Racial Prejudice and Discrimination," in *John Aiso and the M.I.S.*, p. 17; John F. Aiso, "Observations of a California Nisei," Interv by Marc Landy, University of California at Los Angeles, 1971.

[11] "Training History," ann. 1, Academic Training, para 4e., p. 5.

1944 at Fort Snelling for fifty soldiers, was said to be the first Buddhist service ever held in an Army camp in the United States.[12]

Recruiting Students

More students came to the school than ever before. From December 1941 to the end of 1943, roughly 1,100 Nisei started language training. During 1944 the number of incoming students grew to 1,800. The number for 1945 was projected to reach 2,100. (*See Table 2.*) Actual school enrollment grew even faster as students for the nine-month course remained on the rolls longer.[13] Volunteers alone could no longer meet the swelling demand for language training and combat replacements for the 442d RCT. As a result the War Department authorized the resumption of Selective Service in early 1944. Selective Service reclassified the Nisei from IV–C to I–A; local boards began calling them up, beginning on the mainland in January 1944 and in Hawaii in April 1944. However, the new selectees did not begin to arrive at the school at once. Due to another change of policy, they attended basic training before language training. Others were inducted into the Enlisted Reserve Corps and then called to active duty as needed by the language school. The resumption of Selective Service also prompted a new wave of Nisei volunteers.

In the internment camps, the resumption of Selective Service precipitated a crisis similar to the registration crisis of 1943. Many Nisei were outraged and asked themselves how the U.S. government could incarcerate loyal American citizens and then subject them to conscription. While thousands of Nisei accepted registration and induction, more than 300 refused and were convicted for violating the Selective Training and Service Act.[14] This was a small number compared to the 50,000 conscientious objectors of all races jailed during the war, but most Nisei resisters cited the camps, not religious conviction, for their protest. A school report acknowledged a "resentment against relocation of their parents and discrimination against themselves." Observers noted that some in the camps scorned those who volunteered for Japanese-language training. Reverend Kitagawa described how "the parents of many [Nisei students] were exceedingly unhappy, in fact profoundly disturbed, to see their sons wearing the U.S. uniform and, of all things, being trained as 'spies' (as they thought of the intelligence service) against their

---

[12] War Department (WD) Press Release, 22 Oct 45; Daisuke Kitagawa, *Issei and Nisei: The Internment Years* (New York: Seabury Press, 1967), pp. 163–66; "Buddhist Service Held Recently in U.S. Army Camp," *Pacific Citizen*, 4 Nov 44.

[13] "Training History," ann. 10, Personnel Procurement Office, sec. IV.D., pp. 10, 15.

[14] Eric L. Muller, *Free To Die for Their Country: The Story of the Japanese American Draft Resisters in World War II* (Chicago: University Press of Chicago, 2001); Frank F. Chuman, *The Bamboo People: The Law and Japanese Americans* (Chicago: Japanese American Citizens League, 1981), pp. 252–61; "Draft Resistance," in *Encyclopedia of Japanese American History*, rev. ed., ed. Brian Niiya (New York: Facts on File, 2001). In 1947 President Truman pardoned all World War II draft resisters, including 265 Nisei.

own country, Japan. In various ways parents and the elders in the relocation centers were attempting to dissuade the Nisei from pursuing their training."[15]

In Hawaii, the recruiting problems were different. Because of labor shortages on the islands, employers often pressured their employees not to volunteer. Recruiters from the language school used "personal contacts with employers, civic clubs, newspapers, radio stations, educators plus publicity campaigns in Hawaii [that] pointed out the vital need for linguists."[16] Between early 1944 and the summer of 1945, about 1,400 Nisei from the mainland and about 1,000 more from Hawaii were selected for language training.

Another source of Nisei students was 800 soldiers assigned to service units on the mainland. Many had been repeatedly screened by language school recruiters but had low aptitude or language skills. School recruiters rescreened these soldiers and accepted many the second or third time around. The school also turned to another small group, alien Japanese who had been born in Japan but had come to America at an early age. They were often identical to the Nisei in outlook and schooling and "thoroughly Americanized." In early 1945 the War Department authorized the induction of alien Japanese volunteers.[17] Despite the pressing need for infantry replacements, the Military Intelligence Division had priority over all Nisei and alien Japanese selectees.[18]

By 1944 Nisei students arriving at Fort Snelling were quite different from their older brothers who had trained at Crissy Field and Camp Savage. On average the new students were younger and had less knowledge of the Japanese language. The average age for Nisei students at Camp Savage had been 24.5; but at Fort Snelling, that average fell to 22.9 years. Recruiters noted that prospective students' knowledge of kanji characters on average declined from 700 in 1943, to 300 in 1944, and to only 200 in 1945. Mainland Nisei, or "kotonks," had spent time in the internment camps where the use of the Japanese language was discouraged and language schools were forbidden. Hawaii Nisei, "Buddhaheads," were cockier and less accepting of the discipline of Army life. Friction between the two groups continued. One day an enlisted instructor from Hawaii, M.Sgt. George K. Hironaka, was interrupted on the first day of class by "an energetic Hawaiian," who asked him in pidgin: "Hey Sarge, you kinda talk like a kotonk, but you Hawaiian or wot?" Hironaka replied in perfect English, "Soldier, remember that regardless

[15] "Training History," p. 19; Kitagawa, *Issei and Nisei*, p. 163.

[16] "Training History," p. 19. On Selective Service and manpower problems in Hawaii, see Gwenfread Allen, *Hawaii's War Years, 1941–1945* (Honolulu: University of Hawaii Press, 1950).

[17] "Training History," ann. 10, sec. IV(2).

[18] Ltr, Adjutant General (AG), sub: Training and Assignment of Soldiers of Japanese Descent, 30 July 1944, Folder ASW 342.18, Enlistment, J. A. (Divisions), Formerly Security Class Corresp of John J. McCloy, 1941–1945, Record Group (RG) 107, National Archives and Records Administration (NARA); Ltr, AG, sub: Assignment of Americans of Japanese Ancestry, 16 June 1944, AGOC–E–B 210.31, Trng Grp, RG 165, NARA.

TABLE 2—SUMMARY OF STUDENT PERSONNEL FOR MISLS ACADEMIC TERMS AUGUST 1944–MARCH 1946[a]

Academic Term	Students Entered		Students Relieved[b]		Students Graduated			
	Officer	Enlisted	Officer	Enlisted	Officer	Date	Enlisted	Date
Aug 44		229	0	46	0		4 34 1 1 143 183	31 Jan 45 17 Feb 45 29 Mar 45 5 May 45 19 May 45
Aug 44 OCS	11	113	0	4	11	17 Feb 45	109	17 Feb 45
Sep 44	0	278	0	66	0		1 36 1 174 212	29 Mar 45 5 Apr 45 12 Jun 45 7 Jul 45
Dec 44	2 (1 AKA)	659	0	69	1 1 2	23 Jun 45 7 Jul 45	4 2 1 69 514 590	5 May 45 26 Jun 45 15 Jun 45 7 Jul 45 18 Aug 45
Dec 44 Chinese Division	7	54	6	21	1	7 Jul 45	8 23 2 33	5 Apr 45 7 Jul 45 23 Jul 45
Feb 45	2 (1 AEA)	377 (1 ACA) (1 AKA)	1	51	1	18 Aug 45	1 31 5 134 155 326	10 May 45 18 Aug 45 25 Aug 45 1 Sep 45 29 Sep 45
Mar 45 Special Officers' Class	13 (2 ACA)	0	3	0	10	19 May 45		
Apr 45	36 (17 AEA)		5		2 17 12 31	8 Aug 45 9 Aug 45 29 Sep 45		
Apr 45 OCS (AEA)		95		5			1 89 90	27 Aug 45 29 Sep 45
May 45	6	227	0	7	6	26 Oct 45	1 11 8 200 220	29 Aug 45 1 Sep 45 29 Sep 45 26 Oct 45

Table 2—Summary of Student Personnel for MISLS Academic Terms August 1944–March 1946[a]—Continued

Academic Term	Students Entered		Students Relieved[b]		Students Graduated			
	Officer	Enlisted	Officer	Enlisted	Officer	Date	Enlisted	Date
May 45 WAC		46 (1 ACA) (2 AEA)		5			2 39 41	2 Nov 45 16 Nov 45
Jul 45	10	334	1	11	9	26 Oct 45	1 285 1 36 323	29 Sep 45 26 Oct 45 7 Jan 46 2 Feb 46
Jul 45 Oral School	7 (1 AKA)	300 (2 AEA)		22	7	17 Nov 45	278	17 Nov 45
Aug 45 OCS	13	171	7	86	6	15 Dec 45	85	15 Dec 45
Sep 45	2	586 (1 AEA)	2	57			112 12 12 39 354 529	26 Oct 45 7 Jan 46 12 Jan 46 2 Feb 46 9 Mar 46
Oct 45 Oral School	2 (1 AEA)	309	1	41	1	19 Jan 46	268	19 Jan 46
Nov 45	10	407	(Still in School)					
Jan 46	13 (5 AEA) (1 Other)	283	(Still in School)					
Mar 46	1	290	(Still in School)					

ACA   American of Chinese Ancestry
AEA   American of European Ancestry
AKA   American of Korean Ancestry

Source: MISLS, "Training History of the Military Intelligence Service Language School," pp. 16–18, Unpubl Ms, 1946, U.S. Army Center of Military History (CMH).

Notes
a All Americans of Japanese Ancestry unless otherwise indicated. Figures are from existing available records, and slight inaccuracies are unavoidable.
b Includes those relieved for special assignment, academic reasons, CDD (Certificate of Disability for Discharge), etc.

of whether you are a 'Buddhahead' or 'Kotonk,' you're a soldier in the U.S. Army fighting for the same cause."[19]

The decline in maturity and language skills of Japanese American selectees resulted in a rising washout rate. The class that began in February 1944 at Camp Savage and then moved to Fort Snelling graduated in November with a 20 percent attrition rate. However, even the washouts were put to good use. "Many of those relieved were subsequently sent to Corps of Military Police to be trained for duty with PW Processing Teams." Classes that began that autumn saw attrition rates rise to 24 percent.[20] A postwar school report recommended higher admission requirements:

Wholesale and indiscriminate assignment of men to this school without regard to their background, inclination, and desire has tended to lower the over-all standard of the school and the graduate, to water the effectiveness of the instruction by dissipating the energies of the instructors, and to permit the entrance of undesirable elements thereby damaging the prestige of the school.[21]

Even the school's graduates in the field became concerned about the new students. A former enlisted instructor expressed his concerns in a letter to Yutaka Munakata in May 1945: "Too bad the quality of the men had fallen so low and after they get out to the front they are not able to tackle the work assigned to them. I suppose all cannot be efficient bi-linguists, but at least I hope they will be able to accomplish something and keep up the reputation others have earned for us."[22]

School Operations

The school's military leadership remained substantially as before. Rasmussen, the fatherly West Pointer, remained devoted to his Nisei students and treated them with respect. Col. Frank Hollingshead, a Coast Artillery officer like Rasmussen, became assistant commandant in 1944. The director of Personnel Procurement was Major Rusch, who had taught school in Tokyo for eighteen years. Maj. Fred B. Keller joined in 1944 as commander of the student battalion. In January 1945 a Women's Army Corps (WAC) officer, Capt. Jean Wiener, became the school's

---

[19] "Training History," ann. 10, sec. IV.D., p. 10; Masaharu Ano, "Loyal Linguists: Nisei of World War II Learned Japanese in Minnesota," *Minnesota History* 45, no. 7 (Fall 1977): 279, 282; George K. Hironaka, "Memoirs of an MISLS Instructor," in *Secret Valor: M.I.S. Personnel, World War II Pacific Theater, Pre–Pearl Harbor to Sept. 8, 1951*, ed. Ted T. Tsukiyama et al. (Honolulu: Military Intelligence Service Veterans Club of Hawaii, 1993), p. 61.

[20] "Training History," ann. 1, para. 6–6, p. 13.

[21] Ibid., para. 4a, p. 1. Other Army schools complained about the declining quality of students after 1943. See Robert R. Palmer et al., eds. *The Procurement and Training of Ground Combat Troops*, U.S. Army in World War II (Washington, D.C.: Historical Division, Department of the Army, 1948), p. 272.

[22] Ltr, George M. Koshi to Yutaka Munakata, 27 May 1945, in Joseph D. Harrington Papers, National Japanese Historical Society (NJAHS), San Francisco, Calif.

personnel officer. She earned the gratitude of the civilian instructors when she obtained pay for their months of overtime work retroactive to 1941.[23]

Aiso was assisted by several other West Coast Nisei who had worked together since 1941–1942. All were university graduates, and many had studied in Japan. Most lived with their wives near Fort Snelling and formed a close-knit group with Aiso at its center. Paul Tekawa, who replaced Aiso as technical director, had been a reporter for a Japanese-language newspaper. Yutaka Munakata, chief of the Translation Section, was an electrical engineer from the University of Washington. Shigeya Kihara had a master's degree in international politics from the University of California. Akira Oshida, chief of the research section, had earned a business degree at Meiji University and had been the public relations director for the Japanese pavilion at the 1939 Golden Gate International Exposition. The staff judge advocate was Capt. Walter T. Tsukamoto, the first Nisei to graduate from the Boalt Hall School of Law at the University of California. Before the war he had been active in the Japanese American Citizens League (JACL) and had served as national president from 1938 to 1940.

By 1944 the school had about thirty Nisei civilians on the faculty. Only four more were hired in 1944 and 1945. This small cadre worked together with top civilian administrators as a team. Few had any previous teaching experience. They learned under the watchful eyes of Aiso and his top assistants, working an average of fifteen classroom hours each week, plus other duties such as supervising study periods, grading exams, and developing new materials. According to a postwar report:

The faculty of the MISLS cannot be duplicated in the United States. With the many years of experience and training, there is not a more cohesive, effective, and wide awake unit to be found anywhere. Literally starting from scratch, the instructors have learned to teach the hard way, have perfected a system of training the thousands of linguists, and have worked out the administrative problem involved in a large institution such as this. The intelligence, ingenuity, and versatility of these instructors are the keystones of the successful language program.[24]

Top graduates, each handpicked by Aiso and his assistants, were held back as enlisted instructors to supplement the civilian faculty. Upon selection they were promoted to staff sergeant and within a few months to master sergeant. By the summer of 1945 their number had grown to over 100. During the war about 200 Nisei served as enlisted instructors.

From every walk of life and from every nisei community in the U.S. and Hawaii, have come these soldier instructors. "Fogey" men and new recruits, the nisei, the kibei, and even the issei; all have come, learned and graduated from the MISLS. From these graduates the best have been selected to serve as instructors. Against the express desires of

---

[23] "Training History," ann. 9, Personnel Office; *MISLS Album*, p. 67.
[24] "Training History," ann. 1, para. 3a.(2), p. 1.

many for assignments in the field and at the expense of Pacific theatre needs for these best qualified linguists, they were retained to help train others who were to follow in their footsteps.[25]

The school also used returning combat veterans such as 2d Lt. Dye Ogata, who had been language team chief for the 37th Infantry Division on Bougainville and then returned to the United States for officer candidate school (OCS). Upon commissioning, he was reassigned to MISLS. Other combat veterans, including some from the 100th Infantry Battalion and 442d Regimental Combat Team, visited the school to impart their field experiences.[26] However, most instructors had neither commissions nor combat experience to discipline and motivate their students, which became increasingly difficult to do as the war continued. School regulations stressed that instructors were in complete charge and "any orders issued by them will be accepted as orders of the Commandant."

In June 1945 the school selected thirty-three new enlisted instructors to handle the projected expansion of training. One of this group, Hitoshi G. "Ko" Sameshima, recalled that his fellow instructors as "a motley group of interesting, individualistic knowledgeable Nisei in the mid-20's to mid-30's age bracket."

Most of the class members, though bilingual, possessed primary and native fluency in Nihongo (Japanese language), whereas I was among the minority whose forté was English. The Kibei without exception were aces in Nihongo and all class members were intellectually high caliber. The Kibei were also well bred in Japanese culture and philosophy and could quickly shift to their Japanese thinking cap, a valuable intelligence asset, so I begrudgingly admitted.[27]

After the war many enlisted instructors distinguished themselves in other fields. Toshio George Tsukahira had a master's degree in history from the University of California at Los Angeles; after the war he became the highest ranking Japanese American in the Foreign Service.[28] Seattle-born S.Sgt. George Tsutakawa became perhaps the most distinguished Japanese American artist of his generation. Before the war he had attended the University of Washington School of Art. While stationed at Fort Snelling, he used his weekend passes to visit art museums

---

[25] Ibid., para 5a., p. 6.

[26] *MISLS Album*, pp. 88, 93, 98.

[27] Quote from Ko Sameshima, autobiography, 16 Apr 95, Unpubl Ms, Japanese American National Museum, Los Angeles, Calif.; Interv, author with Ko Sameshima, 10 Sep 96.

[28] Stanley L. Falk and Warren M. Tsuneishi, eds., *MIS in the War against Japan* (Washington, D.C.: Japanese American Veterans Association, 1995), pp. 9–10, 130–31. Toshio George Tsukahira was the author of *Postwar Development of Japanese Communist Strategy* (Cambridge, Mass.: MIT Press, 1954), and *Feudal Control in Tokugawa Japan: The Sankin Kotai System* (Cambridge, Mass.: Harvard University Press, 1966).

and galleries in Chicago, New York, and Boston. After the war he taught art at the University of Washington.[29]

The school sometimes found itself at odds with other government agencies over its skilled staff. For example, in 1944 the Office of the Provost Marshal General raised security objections to some of the civilian instructors. School officials were successful in fending off this bureaucratic attack: "The primary cause for objection to these men was the fact that they were kibei and had spent much time in Japan. Actually this was a great advantage in the efficient performance of their jobs. In addition they had been under surveillance for two or three years and no derogatory information had been compiled as to their loyalty." The Military Intelligence Division sided with the school and in February 1945 gave the commandant "full authority to employ Japanese Americans despite adverse recommendation by the Office of the Provost Marshal General."[30]

In 1944 the top enlisted instructors became division chairmen and were promoted to warrant officers.[31] Others were sent on special assignment. For example, in September 1944 the school sent nine enlisted instructors to the Pacific Military Intelligence Research Section at Camp Ritchie, Maryland.

New students arriving at Fort Snelling found a thriving school. Now housed in permanent facilities, the school had lost the air of harried improvising that had marked the converted aircraft hangar at Crissy Field and the former Civilian Conservation Camp at Camp Savage. The Nisei, especially those from Hawaii, were still surprised by the intense cold of the Minnesota winter. Not all incoming students could be accommodated in permanent barracks. Some were billeted in a temporary cantonment of poorly heated wooden huts. Ko Sameshima arrived from the Amache internment camp in December 1944. "It was especially morale shattering for me to be assigned quarters in a five-man tar-and-paper shack in a sector of rows of such shacks, lovingly referred to as 'the Turkey Farm.'" His bunkmates were Hawaii Nisei, "my first close contact. . . . As friendly as I attempted and wanted to be, I was made to feel an alien; . . . the reception verged on hostility." He was glad when he "moved out of the miserable environment of my quarters in the Turkey Farm shack" into permanent barracks. He excelled as a student and upon graduation was selected as an enlisted instructor.[32]

Despite the harsh winter weather, Minneapolis–St. Paul proved popular with the Nisei. The city offered plenty of opportunities for their off-duty time. A streetcar ran directly from Fort Snelling into downtown Minneapolis, where rail connections were good to Chicago and beyond. War Relocation Authority resettlement programs brought thousands of Japanese Americans to the Minneapolis–St. Paul metropolitan area. More than three hundred Nisei came from the camps to attend college in Minnesota. Job-placement agencies helped more than 1,000 Americans

---

[29] Martha Kingbury, *George Tsutakawa* (Seattle: University of Washington Press, 1990), esp. pp. 46–47, 143.

[30] "Training History," ann. 4, Intelligence Section, pp. 8–9.

[31] Ibid., ann. 1, para. 5, p. 3. During 1945 seven Nisei were appointed as warrant officers.

[32] Sameshima, autobiography.

Temporary barracks known as the Turkey Farm

of Japanese ancestry from the internment camps find work, including many young women. The USO kept up an active schedule of activities that brought the Nisei men and women together, and the chapel at Fort Snelling celebrated many Nisei weddings, often shortly before the grooms left for overseas.[33]

In addition to language training, students at the school received military training from the student battalion, commanded by Major Keller. Military training included physical training, road marches, weapons qualification, and other sub-

---

[33] The 1940 census counted thirty-seven persons of Japanese ancestry in Minneapolis–St. Paul. The 1950 census counted 905, which was a significant decline from the wartime peak. "A 1968 survey of metropolitan Nisei revealed that fully 50% had been stationed at Camp Savage or Fort Snelling or had a family member there." Michael Albert, "The Japanese," in *They Chose Minnesota: A Survey of the State's Ethnic Groups*, ed. June D. Holmquist (St. Paul: Minnesota Historical Society Press, 1981), pp. 558–71 (quote from p. 560); Bud Nakasone, "Japanese American Veterans of Minnesota," in *Unsung Heroes: The Military Intelligence Service, Past-Present-Future* (Seattle: MIS-Northwest Association, 1996), pp. 105–06; Al Tsuchiya, "Synopsis of a Minnesotan," *Nikkei Heritage* (Summer 2004): 16.

jects.[34] The battalion was also responsible for military discipline and routine supply and administrative functions.

The Nisei chafed at the very presence of Caucasian officer candidates. These graduates of the University of Michigan language program took the same course as the Nisei but received commissions when they graduated. In contrast, Nisei students were promoted to technician, fifth grade, after four months at Fort Snelling and upon graduation were normally promoted to technician, fourth grade (equivalent to sergeant), or technician, third grade (equivalent to staff sergeant). The Nisei, who often had better language skills, deeply resented being placed under officers they felt had been commissioned for no reason other than their race.

In the autumn of 1944 the avenues for Nisei commissions opened up as small numbers of Nisei from the school were sent to officer candidate school and returned as second lieutenants. About twenty attended OCS at Fort Benning, Georgia, in October 1944, among them T.Sgt. Edwin I. Kawahara, an enlisted instructor from Hawaii. In mid-1945 the group was sent to the field as language team leaders.[35]

Beginning in 1944, officer candidates from the Michigan program were placed in a new division, Division E. The third MISLS OCS class started in August 1944 with 11 officers and 113 officer candidates. The fourth class started in April 1945 with 14 officers, 93 officer candidates, and for the first time 16 Nisei officers.

The curriculum constantly evolved during the war. The biggest change was extending the course from six to nine months, starting with the February 1944 class. "The Snelling days were easier on studying," reported the school's album staff, "than the compressed training days at Savage."[36] Although each class lasted longer, new classes started more frequently. Crissy Field and Camp Savage had started five classes in thirty months. In the twelve months between August 1944 and July 1945, Fort Snelling started six regular classes and six classes for officer candidates and other special groups. By the summer of 1945 the school boasted 125 classrooms.

In August 1944 the first Fort Snelling class started with 229 Nisei enlisted students and 124 Caucasian officer candidates. In September another class started with 278 Nisei enlisted men. In December the largest class ever, with 659 Nisei enlisted men, began. By the end of the year the school had 1,081 students in training. New classes started in February, May, and July 1945. In the twelve months from August 1944 to July 1945, 2,400 Nisei started classes, almost twice the total student input of the previous three years combined.

As the school grew, the curriculum matured. The textbook series remained the Naganuma *Hyojun Nihongo Tokuhon*, or standard Japanese readers, as modified by the MISLS instructors. These were "graded texts [which] begin with a primer and range through seven books which include selections from Japanese

---

[34] *MISLS Album*, pp. 69–73.
[35] *Fort Snelling Bulletin*, Oct 44, cited in editorial, *Pacific Citizen*, 14 Oct 44; *Pacific Citizen*, 9 Dec 44; "Training History," ann. 1, para. 6–14, p. 40; Tsukiyama et al, *Secret Valor*, pp. 59–60.
[36] *MISLS Album*, p. 74.

elementary and middle school texts, essays, magazine articles, plays and advanced material in literary and epistolary Japanese." The curriculum also relied upon the four-volume heigo text prepared by the MISLS staff with its two-volume *Heigo Tokuhon* reader for military vocabulary. For reference the students carried the heavy Uyeda's *Daijiten* dictionary.[37]

Students were placed in sections of twenty with one instructor in permanent charge, although they were taught by several different teachers each day. The daily schedule was built around six fifty-minute periods from 0730 to 1620. Instructors monitored compulsory study periods from 1900 to 2100 four nights each week, plus examinations on weekends.

The basic principles of instruction varied little:

1. "Provision of maximum number of supervised contact hours," through "long and constant exposure to Japanese in every form," to cram three to six years of college-level instruction into nine months of intensive study.
2. "Specialization in a narrow military field," which increased over time. "The short time allotted ... coupled with reports from the field indicating that the scope of the language requirements there were limited exclusively to a narrow military field made it expedient to concentrate on military Japanese."
3. "Comprehension of the language and acquiring of fundamental technique."
4. "Insistence on the use of every possible media of instruction: visual, aural, oral, and through practice." This meant that "the students were deluged with Japanese every waking hour and through every means," such as films, native speakers, captured documents, and radio monitoring.
5. "Constant evaluation, revision and change of the curriculum, and teaching methods," because, as the faculty readily acknowledged, the school "was operated by amateurs." Graduates serving overseas "were able to point out those subjects that had helped them, what their own deficiencies were and were also able to send in pertinent suggestions based upon changed conditions in the field."[38]

Akira Oshida established the Research and Liaison Section, which maintained a collection of captured Japanese documents and a museum of Japanese weapons and equipment. Over time he built up a collection of 2,000 documents and maps: "In translation classes the trainees worked with captured documents still marked by the mud and rain of Guadalcanal, New Guinea or Saipan." Oshida worked hard to obtain current authentic Japanese materials from graduates in the field.[39]

Yutaka Munakata, head of the Translation Section, had been born in Washington but lived in Japan from ages three to twenty. He returned to Washington to attend an American high school and then the University of Washington, where he earned a bachelor of science degree in electrical engineering. The Translation Section employed recent graduates while they waited for their assignments, so

[37] *Ueda's Daijiten*, American ed. (Cambridge, Mass.: Harvard University Press, 1942); "Training History," ann. 1, para. 10c, pp. 16–17.
[38] "Training History," pp. 21–25.
[39] Ibid., ann. 6, History of J.O.B. [Japanese Order of Battle], and ann. 1, para. 4g., pp. 7–9.

Munakata became friendly with many of the students and asked them to keep in touch from overseas. As a result he received a steady stream of letters from the Southwest Pacific, Central Pacific, and China-Burma-India Theaters that included many valuable insights into how the Nisei were being employed in the field.[40]

In November 1944 Betty Hackett Uchiyama, wife of 2d Lt. Fusao Uchiyama, began publishing a mimeographed newsletter, called the *Yaban Gogai*, for the school's graduates. Although the school was no longer at Camp Savage, the "Savage Extra" reached out to its graduates across the Pacific.[41]

The school began specialized training as it grew. For example, it established a radio shack "for training students to become expert clear text wireless interceptors and radio monitors of Japanese broadcasts and wireless stations." Here, students learned to monitor Japanese news broadcasts in both rōmaji and kana. By mid-1945 the section had grown to eleven men, all licensed amateur radio operators. They monitored Japanese broadcasts for training purposes; but they also recorded, translated, and forwarded them to the War Department.[42] The school also established a propaganda writing course under James Oda, a prewar labor activist from California. The War Department knew of his left-wing background but allowed him to continue as an instructor.[43]

Since 1941 MISLS had taught only Japanese. The Military Intelligence Training Center at Camp Ritchie and other Army and Navy programs taught various other languages. In the autumn of 1944 MISLS established a Chinese language program, after other commands had established their own. That summer of 1944 Admiral Chester W. Nimitz identified a requirement for Chinese linguists for an attack on Formosa or the South China coast. In response U.S. Army Forces Middle Pacific in Hawaii established a Chinese language training center. MISLS supplied two Chinese American instructors and some curricular materials. By June 1945 the school in Hawaii was going strong with six officers and sixty enlisted trainees.[44]

MISLS had tried placing Chinese American soldiers in Japanese-language classes, beginning with fifty students in the summer of 1943 and twenty more a

---

[40] These letters can be found in the Harrington Papers. After the war Munakata remained on the staff of the language school, and after his death the Defense Language Institute named an academic building in his honor.

[41] "Training History," ann. 13, Translation Section, pp. 46–47. *Yaban* means "savage" or "barbarian"; *gogai* means "newspaper" or "extra." A partial set of *Yaban Gogai* may be found in Japanese Evacuation Research Study (JERS) microfilm, pt. 2, sec. 15, reel 85, frames 0091–.

[42] "Training History," ann. 1, para. 10c.(4), p. 18, and ann. 11, Radio Section; *MISLS Album*, p. 77; WD Press Release, 22 Oct 45; "Lid Off Radio Shack," in *Yaban Gogai*, Dec 45.

[43] "Training History," ann. 1, para. 9h., p. 12, and para. 10c.(10), p. 21; James Oda, *Heroic Struggles of Japanese Americans: Partisan Fighters from America's Concentration Camps* (Hollywood, Calif.: J. Oda, 1980); James Oda, *Secret Embedded in Magic Cables: The Story of a 101-Year-Old Japanese Communist Leader Who Served Japan, KGB, and CIA* (Northridge, Calif.: J. Oda, 1993), pp. 116–18, 128–30.

[44] U.S. Army Forces Middle Pacific (USAFMIDPAC), History of G–2 Section, pp. 23–24, Folder S–83, Trng Grp, RG 165, NARA; "Training History," ann. 10, sec. IV(6).

few months later. However, most Chinese American students could not keep up with the Nisei. The school learned that the ability to read Chinese characters was of little use in learning to read Japanese kanji because any resemblance between the two languages was superficial. Furthermore, school officials were convinced that "the problems connected with" Chinese students' studying Japanese "were primarily due to the low scholastic ability of the group."[45] Nevertheless, in 1944 the Military Intelligence Division directed MISLS to begin Chinese-language training. In December 1944 the school organized a Chinese Division, which grew to seven officer and fifty-four enlisted students. (*See Table 2.*)However, the attrition rate was high, almost 40 percent. Only one officer and thirty-three enlisted men graduated in July 1945; in mid-August they were shipped to Calcutta for the China Theater.[46]

Nisei in the Women's Army Corps

The Military Intelligence Division appeared reluctant to place Nisei women in language training. If the school's graduates were to be used on the battlefield as translators and interpreters at regiment and division level, so the reasoning probably went, then women would have to be excluded. In late 1943 the Women's Army Corps began recruiting Nisei but found few volunteers.[47] In July 1944 the War Department approved the recruitment of 100 Nisei women for language training, but recruitment remained difficult. In September 1944 Col. Kendall Fielder, G-2 of U.S. Army Forces Middle Pacific, "expressed pessimism on the number of female linguists who could be induced to join the WACs in Hawaii.... The two major factors in opposition to Hawaiian women volunteering for the Army appeared to be: 1) Parental influence opposed the girls' leaving the family. 2) Most boys did not approve of their sisters joining the WACs." Despite the colonel's pessimism, WAC recruiters enlisted twenty-six Nisei women in Hawaii and in January 1945 sent them to the mainland for training.[48] Overall, school officials reported that "the response of the Nisei women to the WAC recruiting program has been poor." Those with good language skills "are the so-called 'Japanese' or

---

[45] "Training History," ann. 10, sec. IV(6).

[46] See *MISLS Album*, p. 130. "Training History," ann. 1, para. 6–3(4), pp. 7–11, and para. 6–10(11), p. 15; ann. 5, Chinese Section; ann. 10, sec. IV(6).

[47] Mattie E. Treadwell, *The Women's Army Corps*, U.S. Army in World War II (Washington, D.C.: Office of the Chief of Military History, 1954); Brenda L. Moore, *Serving Our Country: Japanese American Women in the Military during World War II* (New Brunswick, N.J.: Rutgers University Press, 2003); *MISLS Album*, pp. 90–91, 131; *The Pacific War and Peace: Americans of Japanese Ancestry in Military Intelligence Service, 1941 to 1952* (San Francisco: Military Intelligence Service Association of Northern California/National Japanese American Historical Society, 1991), pp. 22–23. "Training History," pp. 14–15, 17, 19; ann. 1, para. 6–19, p. 17, para. 6–30, p. 20, and para. 9i., pp. 13–14; ann. 10.

[48] Allen, *Hawaii's War Years*, p. 291; "Training History," ann. 10; Historical Section, Office of the Provost Marshal General, "Monograph on History of Military Clearance Program," pp. 23–29, Unpubl Ms, CMH 4–4.1 AA.

Women's Army Corps students at choir practice, 1945

conservative element," and thus not interested in volunteering. Perhaps, they felt, a few might have worked as civil service employees.[49]

Nevertheless, the first Nisei WACs began reporting to the school in the autumn of 1944. They were assigned to the WAC detachment under Capt. Marian E. Nestor and initially worked in clerical positions on the school staff. On 28 May 1945, the first WAC class began with twenty-eight women students. As more women arrived, the class grew to forty-six.[50] The Nisei WACs proved to be as diverse and as capable as the male Nisei; many were college graduates. Tamie Tsuchiyama

---

[49] "Training History," ann. 1, para. 5c.(1), pp. 13–14.
[50] "WACs in Third Month of School," *Yaban Gogai*, Aug 45; Yaye Furutani Herman, "The WAC-MIS Experience," in *Unsung Heroes*, pp. 5–8.

had been enrolled in the doctoral program in anthropology at the University of
California when the war broke out. She worked as a field researcher for the Japanese Evacuation Research Study before enlisting in the Women's Army Corps and
being selected for language training.[51] The WAC class even included one Caucasian, Sgt. Rhoda Knudten, who had been born in Japan of Lutheran missionary
parents and had spent her entire life in Japan until coming to the United States to
attend college.

The Nisei WACs turned out to be excellent students. Major Rusch reported:
"Fully half of these women are qualified as secretaries and typists. The first ten
of the class are extremely expert as translators and interpreters of Japanese and
all of them are on par or a shade above par, in comparison with the Nisei male
linguists. . . . (Japanese women linguists have always been more diligent than male
students.)"[52]

The school leadership remained unconvinced, and Army officials in Hawaii
discouraged further recruiting efforts "unless the need for women was extremely
urgent." By the middle of 1945 school officials had concluded that all requirements for linguists could be filled by men. "In view of the fact that qualified male
linguists were available, the interest in the WAC program subsided, and additional
recruitment was abandoned. . . . It is believed that the time and energy spent in
connection with WAC recruitment was unproductive and that far greater results
could have been obtained had this effort been spent on the procurement of qualified male linguists."[53]

Graduate Assignments

The Military Intelligence Division centrally managed the assignment of MISLS
graduates, who remained in critically short supply throughout the war. The MID
Training Branch worked closely with the MISLS staff to decide where to send the
graduates; matching graduates to assignments remained problematic throughout
the war. Field commanders always wanted more, but the War Department could
fill only spaces identified on unit tables of organization. As far as War Department
personnel managers were concerned, by 1944 all authorized linguist spaces were
already filled. In fact, it appeared that all theaters were over strength by December
1944. This caused a major reassessment of language requirements. In January
1945 the General Bissell wrote "all War Department agencies whose plans envi-
sion the use of Japanese linguists," requesting that they inform him "of the nature

[51] Lane Ryo Hirabayashi, *The Politics of Field Work: Research in an American Concentration
Camp* (Tucson: University of Arizona Press, 1999), pp. 153–55.
[52] Ltr, Maj. Paul F. Rusch to Lt. Col. Mathewson, 13 October 1945, 091–300.6 (= Decimal 200),
G–2 OCCIO, Gen Corresp 1944–1945, GHQ SWPA/USAFPAC, RG 338, NARA.
[53] "Training History," ann. 10, sec. IV.(3), p. 5.

Graduates board a train for the port of embarkation and overseas assignment.

of such plans, the numbers and qualifications of linguists required with the best possible estimate of the dates on which such personnel will be required."[54]

The Navy Department reviewed its own language requirements at the same time. In January 1945 the head of the Boulder language school, Cmdr. A. E. Hindmarsh, flew to Hawaii to assess language officer requirements for the Central Pacific. Admiral Nimitz personally asked him for "all possible help" in obtaining 300 language officers for censorship duties during the occupation of Japan. The Joint Intelligence Center, Pacific Ocean Areas, with 44 Nisei and 261 Boulder graduates, requested 200 additional Boulder graduates. Nimitz' chief of military government complained that he had requested 400 Army Nisei but the War

---

[54] Memo, Trng Br to ACS, G–2, 12 Jan 45, MISLS Gen 1945, Trng Grp, RG 165, NARA; Ltr, ACS, G–2, to The Adjutant General, sub: Requirements for Officer and Enlisted Personnel Qualified as Japanese Linguists, 29 January 1945, File 291.2 Japs, 1–30 Jan 45, War Department G–1 Decimal Files, RG 165, NARA.

Department had cut this to 100 and none had yet arrived. He asked for at least 200 Navy language officers in the next eighteen months. Hindmarsh returned to the United States determined "to enroll [an] additional eight hundred Japanese-language officers between March and July 1945."[55]

While Army and Navy intelligence leaders in Washington looked at overall numbers, school officials at Fort Snelling built language teams tailored to each assignment. Teams assigned to an infantry division or corps usually had ten Nisei led by a staff sergeant as team leader, with six technicians, 4th class, and three technicians, 5th class. Whenever possible, each team included a balanced mix of Nisei strong in written Japanese, spoken Japanese, and the English language.

Assignment patterns shifted in 1944. By May of that year the Southwest Pacific Area had received its full allotment of Nisei linguists based on the number of divisions and corps headquarters. (*Chart 2*) The last combat division sent to that theater, the 11th Airborne Division, arrived in September 1944. In December 1944 and January 1945 the school sent two large groups of forty Nisei each to the Central and Southwest Pacific areas. In April 1945 the school sent another group of seventy Nisei to New Delhi to support the Allied drive into Burma and Malaya. However, from the summer of 1944 until the spring of 1945, most MISLS graduates were assigned in the continental United States, from the Army Air Forces to prisoner of war camps, the Signal Intelligence Service, and the Pacific Military Intelligence Research Section.[56]

At the school, this shift in assignment patterns led to a dramatic increase over the winter of 1944–1945 in the number of graduates awaiting assignment. Graduates usually received a two-week furlough before shipping out but then often waited for months at Fort Snelling. From February 1945 onward, the graduate pool hovered between 250 and 400 students, who were assigned to the Translation Section to keep their skills fresh.[57] In the spring of 1945 language requirements expanded rapidly as commanders prepared for the invasion of Japan. In May and June of 1945 the school sent 359 graduates to U.S. Army Forces Far East.

The school formed specialized teams as needed. In February 1945 the acting commandant, Colonel Hollingshead, asked 2d Lt. Wallace S. Amioka, a recent OCS graduate, if he would "be interested in leading a special team of Okinawa-descent enlisted men who had requested that [he] lead them." Amioka recalled, "Naturally I jumped at the chance."[58] Another Nisei student, Thomas H. Ige, had suggested the special team. He had grown up in Hawaii in an Okinawan village

[55] Office of the Chief of Naval Operations, "School of Oriental Languages," pp. 26–35, Unpubl Ms, Naval Historical Center, Washington, D.C.

[56] Military Intelligence Service Language School, Disposition of Graduates, Training Grp, Ofc of the Dir of Intel G–2, RG 165, NARA.

[57] "Training History," ann. 13.

[58] Interv, author with Wallace S. Amioka, 8 Dec 94; Wallace S. Amioka, Biography, Military Intelligence Service Club of Northern California (this and similar biographies hereafter cited as MISNorCal Bios); Wallace S. Amioka, remarks for panel discussion, 30 Oct 91; Tsukiyama et al., *Secret Valor*, pp. 97–98.

CHART 2—DISPOSITION OF ENLISTED NISEI MISLS GRADUATES, 1942–1945

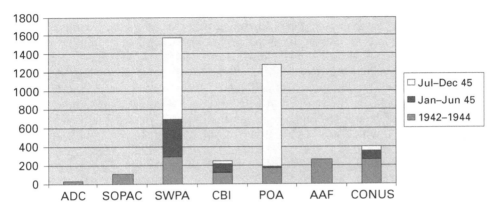

ADC	Alaska Defense Command
SOPAC	South Pacific
SWPA	Southwest Pacific Area
CBI	China-Burma-India
POA	Pacific Ocean Areas
AAF	Army Air Forces
CONUS	Continental United States

Source: Military Intelligence Service Language School, Disposition of Graduates, Trng Grp, Ofc of the Dir of Intel G–2, RG 165, NA.

and was fluent in the local dialect, very different from spoken Japanese. When the war began he had been a graduate student in economics at the University of Chicago and in March 1944 had enlisted for language training. After Camp Savage and basic training at Fort McClellan, he returned to Fort Snelling in January 1945. Observing how the war was drawing closer to Okinawa, he wrote the commandant to suggest that the school form a team of Okinawan-speakers. The commandant accepted and selected Amioka as team chief. The ten other members of the team were all Okinawans. Amioka, who did not speak the dialect, had to be tutored secretly by one of the Okinawans. The American assault on Okinawa began on 1 April 1945, and Amioka's team deployed soon after.[59]

---

[59] Joseph D. Harrington, *Yankee Samurai: The Secret Role of Nisei in America's Pacific Victory* (Detroit: Pettigrew Enterprises, 1979), pp. 285–86; Tsukiyama et al., *Secret Valor*, pp. 97–100; Thomas H. Ige, *Boy from Kahaluu: An Autobiography* (Honolulu: Kin Cho Jin Kai, 1989), pp. 78–80. Intervs, author with Amioka, 8 Dec 94, and with Thomas H. Ige, 5 Dec 94.

Other Japanese-Language Programs

Japanese-language programs for Caucasian personnel expanded alongside the MISLS program for Nisei soldiers. In the summer of 1944 the Army Japanese Language School at the University of Michigan at Ann Arbor graduated its third class. New classes began in May 1944, January 1945, and May 1945. Joseph K. Yamagiwa, an assistant professor at the university, directed about forty-five Issei and Nisei instructors. The program provided a basic foundation in the language to prepare students for the regular MISLS course.[60] Some students came to Ann Arbor from other Japanese-language programs in the Army Specialized Training Program (ASTP), which was terminated in 1944. Yamagiwa praised his students:

[They are] undoubtedly comprised of one of the best-selected units in the Army. High in their IQ and in the ratings received in the Army General Classification Tests, they are both proficient and articulate. Some are BIJ's; they were either "born in Japan" or have "been in Japan." In the [later] classes, a high percentage have come with extensive previous training amounting to as much as one year in various ASTP units. They consistently challenge the best efforts of the staff. Competition among the students is unusually keen.[61]

A few were already combat veterans. For example, Jacques Richardson started the ASTP Japanese class at Yale in early 1943 with 250 other students. When the ASTP was cancelled he was reassigned to an infantry division in France. He survived the fierce fighting in the Ardennes and managed to get himself reassigned to the Michigan program, where he resumed the study of Japanese in January 1945.[62]

Michigan classes began with the "oral-aural approach" and used only the spoken language for the first five or six weeks for "the fixing of pronunciation habits, the brute memorizing of phrases and sentences that are useful in everyday life, and the mimicking in unison of the pronunciation of instructors." This was followed by training in grammatical forms and speech patterns and finally the development of fluency in speaking. The pressures on the students were intense.[63]

---

[60] "Training History," ann. 3, The Army Japanese Language School: A Preliminary Report on the Academic Program; Joseph K. Yamagiwa, "The Japanese Language Programs at the University of Michigan during World War II," ch. 2, Unpubl Ms, 1946, Ann Arbor, Mich.; Grant K. Goodman, *America's Japan: The First Year, 1945–1946* (New York: Fordham University Press, 2005), pp. 10–11.

[61] "Training History," ann. 3, p. 9.

[62] Jacques Richardson, in Harrington Papers.

[63] "Training History," ann. 3, pp. 56–73 (quote from p. 59); Donald M. Richardson, "Random Recollections of the Second Class, AIJLS [Army Intensive Japanese Language School]," Unpubl Ms, Sep 88, author's files; Herbert Passin, *Encounter with Japan* (San Francisco: Kodansha, 1982). Lucian L. Rocke, Jr., reports that two students committed suicide during the time he attended the course. Lucian L. Rocke, Jr., in Harrington Papers. Goodman reports some suicides among Michigan graduates at Fort Snelling while he attended MISLS between August 1944 and February 1945. Goodman, *America's Japan*, p. 21. After the war some Michigan graduates became leading specialists in Japanese studies.

After graduation the officer candidates attended basic training and then reported to MISLS, which activated special OCS classes in February 1944, August 1944, April 1945, and August 1945, each with about a hundred Michigan graduates. Unlike the Nisei, the Caucasian students wore an OCS patch on their left pockets. Upon graduation, MISLS convened a commissioning board and most were commissioned as second lieutenants.

Yamagiwa also supervised other programs at the University of Michigan with the help of his assistant, Hide Shohara. These included the ASTP East Asia Area and Language Program with nineteen language instructors and 264 students. When the ASTP program concluded in September 1944, most of the instructors continued with the Civil Affairs Training School Far Eastern Program (Japan), which started in August 1944 with between nine and fifteen language instructors and 343 students.

The Navy School of Oriental Languages, University of Colorado at Boulder, expanded its enrollment as the war continued. By mid-1944 it had already graduated 600 Navy and Marine Corps language officers and had hundreds more in training. These students were midshipmen upon starting the course and received commissions before graduation. Navy Commander Hindmarsh was the driving force behind the school, interviewing students, recruiting faculty, and coordinating with Navy officials for future requirements. When the founding academic director, Florence Walne, resigned in September 1944 for health reasons, Glenn W. Shaw became director. By 1945 the school grew to 240 faculty members. Unlike the Army school at Fort Snelling, the Navy school used many Issei as instructors. In addition to the Japanese program, the school taught classes in Chinese, Malay, and Russian.

Boulder graduates streamed into the Pacific Ocean Areas, with more than two hundred serving in the Joint Intelligence Center, Pacific Ocean Areas, Translation Section and many others serving in active operations with the fleet and ashore. The translation work was tedious and exhausting, all the more so because "it was often difficult for them to discern any connection between their work and operations in progress," naval intelligence officer Cmdr. W. J. Holmes noted. He appreciated these naval reservists who labored in obscurity. When senior naval officers complained of their "unmilitary attitude," Holmes would respond: "Relax, we have always won our wars with a bunch of damned civilians in uniform anxious to get back to their own affairs, and we will win this one the same way."[64]

To meet expanding enrollment the Navy school opened a separate branch on 15 June 1945 at Oklahoma A&M, Stillwater, Oklahoma, under Navy Capt. John H. Morrill and academic director James H. McAlpine, a former missionary in

---

[64] W. J. Holmes, *Double-Edged Secrets: U.S. Naval Intelligence Operations in the Pacific during World War II* (Annapolis, Md.: Naval Institute Press, 1979), p. 169.

Japan who had taught at Boulder. Between June and August the Stillwater branch enrolled 700 students.[65]

The Marine Corps continued its own Japanese-language program for enlisted marines at Camp Elliott near San Diego, California. In December 1944 the school moved to Camp Lejeune, North Carolina. Although its graduates received only a few months' familiarization with simple printed materials such as field orders, they served down to regiment level on Guam, Iwo Jima, and Okinawa.

The British government also needed to train Japanese-language specialists: many of its Japanese-language officers had been captured at the beginning of the war in Hong Kong and Singapore. In 1944 Commonwealth forces went on the offensive in Burma and needed more linguists than ever before. The School of Oriental and African Studies in London expanded its Japanese program and in June 1944 began the Services General Purpose course, an eighteen-month integrated course for translators and interrogators. New classes started in 1944 and 1945 with a total of ninety-two students. The first class was scheduled to graduate in December 1945.[66]

The Canadian Army Language School, S–20, opened in Vancouver, British Columbia, in August 1943. At that time the Canadian government did not allow Nisei to serve in the armed forces and had evacuated 21,000 Japanese Canadians from British Columbia. The school's officer in charge was an over-age major, Arthur P. McKenzie, who had been born to missionary parents in Tokyo in 1889. "When the Nisei first met [him]," one student recalled, "they sat dumbfounded, listening to the *hakujin* [white] officer speak in eloquent Japanese much superior to their own. He had a good sense of humor and spelled his name in Japanese characters—*Asama Kenji*."[67]

In early 1945 Canada began to prepare a special force for the invasion of Japan, and in January 1945 the Ottawa government authorized the enlistment of Nisei as translators and interrogators. Major Aiso visited the first Nisei group in basic training in Brantford, Ontario, and administered language tests to fifty-two, rating only a quarter as good or excellent. He reported that their caliber "would correspond roughly to and favourably with the calibre of the Nisei students who are now being received by the Military Intelligence Service Language School in the United States under the compulsory draft system. . . . It became evident during the Interviews, that these men are keenly anxious to become good soldiers, and to

---

[65] Pauline S. McAlpine, *Diary of a Missionary* (Decatur, Ga.: Presbyterian Church in America, 1986).

[66] Sadao Oba, *The "Japanese" War*, trans. Anne Kaneko (Sandgate, U.K.: Japan Library, 1995).

[67] Roy Ito, *We Went to War: The Story of the Japanese Canadians Who Served during the First and Second World Wars* (Stittsville, Ontario: Canada's Wings, 1984), p. 214; Barry Broadfoot, *Years of Sorrow, Years of Shame: The Story of the Japanese Canadians in World War II* (Toronto: Doubleday, 1977); Patricia E. Roy, "The Soldiers Canada Didn't Want: Her Chinese and Japanese Citizens," *Canadian Historical Review* (September 1978): 341–58; Roy Ito Papers, NJAHS.

take whatever training may be necessary to increase their value as translators and interpreters."[68] One Canadian Nisei remembered Major Aiso's visit:

Major Aiso, stocky, trim, and neat in his American officers' uniform, informed the Canadians of the enviable records established by the 100th Infantry Battalion from Hawaii and the 442nd Regimental Combat Team. He described the Japanese language school at Fort Snelling and how the graduates were serving in many important positions in the US Army. He complimented the Canadians on the smartness of the platoon on the parade ground and said that all eyes at National Defence Headquarters in Ottawa were watching them and pulling for them.[69]

In April 1945 Aiso sent two American Nisei lieutenants, Dye Ogata and Ted Kihara, to help as instructors. Both were veterans of the South Pacific and had recently completed officer candidate school. They spent several months at the Canadian school. Ogata requested permission to bring his Nisei wife to Vancouver, but the Canadian government refused until Colonel Rasmussen made a personal appeal.[70]

Major Aiso visited Vancouver with Maj. John E. Anderton in June 1945, by which time the school had grown to 105 faculty, students, and staff. They praised the efforts of the staff but remarked that "operations are conducted under certain obvious difficulties and with limited and inadequate facilities. On the whole, it is surprising that the school has been able to develop to its present state under such circumstances." In July 1945 the first fifty Canadian Nisei arrived in Vancouver to join eighty Caucasian students already in training. The twelve-month course "was an extremely difficult one," one Nisei recalled. "Nervous breakdowns among the candidates were not uncommon." The top six Nisei joined the senior class, which had already been under way for nine months. In August they were assigned to a language team for the Canadian Army Pacific Force at Camp Breckinridge, Kentucky.[71]

Anderton toured other Allied language schools around the world to offer MISLS assistance. "It is considered essential," he wrote, "that the training efforts of these schools be integrated by exchange of technical information and training aids." His travels took him as far as Australia, where he visited the tiny Royal Australian Air Force Language School, which had only ten instructors, four of

---

[68] Ito, *We Went to War*, p. 209.

[69] Ibid., p. 208.

[70] Dye Ogata, personal communication to author, 30 Nov 91. Ogata and Kihara were joined by T.Sgt. T. Noguchi. Ito, *We Went to War*, p. 308.

[71] Ltr, Aiso and Anderton to G.O.C.-in-C. [General Officer Commander in Chief], Pacific Command (thru Commandant, S–20), sub: Report in re Visit to S–20 J.L.S., Pacific Command, with Observations on the Training of Personnel for Special Duties in the Canadian Pacific Force and Elsewhere, 9 June 1945, Trng Grp, RG 165, NARA; Ito, *We Went to War*, p. 212. Stanley W. Dziuban, *Military Relations between the United States and Canada, 1939–1945*, U.S. Army in World War II (Washington, D.C.: Office of the Chief of Military History, 1959), pp. 268–72. Canadians of Japanese ancestry were not permitted to return to British Columbia until 1949.

whom were on loan from ATIS. Nowhere else did he find a language school as large or efficient as MISLS at Fort Snelling, Minnesota.[72]

Training for the Invasion and Occupation

In early 1945 the War Department eased restrictions on publicity about the MIS Nisei. In January the War Department announced the award of the Distinguished Service Cross to Sgt. Hoichi Kubo for valor on Saipan the previous August. Other Nisei who fought with Merrill's Marauders received extensive press coverage around the same time. In March the War Relocation Authority held a press conference to focus on the MIS Nisei. The resulting story in the *Pacific Citizen* was entitled "Role of Japanese Americans in Pacific War Disclosed." In April the War Relocation Authority released a fifteen-page collection of news clippings, "Nisei in the War against Japan." Although the details remained sketchy, the MIS Nisei were no longer much of a secret.[73]

That spring the war in Europe was coming to a close. In April the Nisei were shocked by the death of President Franklin D. Roosevelt, the only president many could remember. While he had sanctioned the Japanese evacuation from the West Coast, he had also given Nisei the chance to prove their loyalty by serving in the armed forces. That spring and summer Nisei soldiers' families began leaving camp by the thousands to return to their former homes in the face of sporadic vigilante violence against their return. In June MISLS began granting special furloughs for students to assist their parents in leaving the camps.[74]

At Fort Snelling, more changes were coming as the school expanded and adapted to meet new demands. The school's leaders traveled away from the school more than ever before. Colonel Rasmussen kept a busy travel schedule in the spring and summer of 1945, leaving Colonel Hollingshead as acting commandant. Major Aiso spent a month in Ottawa advising the Canadian Army.

In the Pacific Theater, field commanders still complained that they did not have enough Nisei linguists and that recent graduates lacked the proficiency of their predecessors. In May 1945 an Army Ground Forces observer criticized the quality of MISLS graduates on Okinawa: "The need is felt here for good Nisei officers with Nisei enlisted men. The Nisei try hard, but don't seem to have the necessary military background to appreciate what tactical information is desired.

---

[72] Ltrs, Maj. John E. Anderton to MIS, sub: Visit to Royal Australian Air Force Language School, 10 July 1945; Maj. John E. Anderton to Deputy Director of Training, RAAF [Royal Australian Air Force], HQ, Melbourne, sub: Report in re Visit to Royal Australian Air Force Japanese Language School No. 3, School of Technical Training, Ultimo, Sydney, 12 July 1945. Both in Trng Grp, RG 165, NARA.

[73] "Hawaiian Nisei Sergeant First To Receive DSC [Distinguished Service Cross] for Heroism in Central Pacific War Zone," *Pacific Citizen*, 13 Jan 45; "Role of Japanese Americans in Pacific War Disclosed," *Pacific Citizen*, 10 Mar 45; War Relocation Authority, *Nisei in the War against Japan* (Washington, D.C.: Department of the Interior, 1945); "The Saga of 'Horizontal Hank' [Henry H. Gosho]: Seattle Nisei Fought Japanese in Burma's Jungle Warfare," *Pacific Citizen*, 19 May 45.

[74] "Training History," ann. 2, Admin Section, p. 7.

Merrill's Marauders veterans with Colonel Rasmussen, January 1945

They don't automatically get it, but have to be 'kept on the track' during interrogation by one of the G–2 officers."[75]

General Bissell, the War Department G–2, brushed aside such criticism: "The scarcity of qualified Japanese linguists is such that it is necessary to devote maximum time and effort to language instruction." They all received infantry basic training and "a minimum amount of general intelligence training...during the language course." He acknowledged that "this is insufficient to qualify the linguists to act independently as interrogators; but any further military training would be at the expense of language training, and the latter must be held paramount."[76]

That same spring, from Manila, Brig. Gen. Charles A. Willoughby requested 1,106 linguists for the coming invasion of Japan and Col. Elliott R. Thorpe

---

[75] Memo, Clayton L. Bissell to Charles A. Willoughby, 9 Jul 45, Folder: Trng Br Files, MISLS-General, 1945, Trng Grp, RG 165, NARA.

[76] Ibid.

requested 984 more for the Counter Intelligence Corps. Clearly, the school would have to accelerate the training process. One step was to reduce the course length from nine back to six months.[77] Even this was insufficient to meet the growing demand, so the school reintroduced an oral language course. The school had tried this in 1943, but results had been unsatisfactory. This time, faced with declining quality of recruits and rising demand from the field, the school had no choice. On 16 May 1945, Headquarters, U.S. Army Forces Pacific Ocean Area, requested permission to establish a language school in Hawaii that would have lower entrance requirements and less classroom time. In recent months this headquarters had recruited Nisei in Hawaii and sent them straight to Saipan and Okinawa with little or no language training.

On 31 May 1945, Colonel Rasmussen proposed instead that MISLS conduct a four-month oral language course. This started on 30 July as the Oral Language School with seven officers and 280 enlisted men, "from among men not qualifying for the regular course."[78] The minimum entrance requirement was "a conversational knowledge of the Japanese language, plus a slight knowledge of Kana." The new program, designated as Division F, "was a radical departure from the fundamental ideas of the MISLS," according to a postwar report, "where the emphasis was primarily on the training of men to work in the written Japanese and incidentally the oral linguist."[79] Many students for the Oral Language School came from a previously untapped source. Since the end of the war in Europe in May 1945, Nisei soldiers in the pipeline for the 442d RCT had been held in the replacement depot at Fort Meade, Maryland. In June over three hundred were selected for language training. They brought with them a smoldering resentment at their Army experience to date that was very different from that of the early 442d RCT volunteers. In the months to come they would become a source of discipline problems for the school.[80]

Other students came directly from the 442d RCT. When the War Department announced demobilization plans in September 1944, many Nisei in the 100th Infantry Battalion and the 442d RCT had enough points to return from overseas or be discharged. For example, 1st Lt. Masayuki "Spark" Matsunaga, a twice-wounded member of the 100th Infantry Battalion, came to Fort Snelling in October 1944. He was assigned as student company commander but spent most of his time speaking to public groups throughout the Midwest on behalf of the War Relocation Agency about the exploits of the 442d RCT. Another returning veteran, 2d Lt. Richard K. Hayashi, had attended the school as a student, served six months on a language team in the South Pacific, and then attended officer candidate school

---

[77] Memo, USAFFE [U.S. Army Forces Far East] G–2 to OCCIO, 18 Jun 45, Box G–1456, Gen Corresp, 1944–1945, 091–300.6, G–2 OCCIO, GHQ Southwest Pacific Area and U.S. Army Forces Pacific, RG 338, NARA; MID Memo 908 for Cmdt MISLS, 9 Jul 45, Trng Grp, RG 165, NARA. On the six-month course, see *MISLS Album*, p. 12; "Training History," ann. 1, para. 9i., p. 14.

[78] "Training History," ann. 1, para. 9i(1), pp. 14–15; ann. 10, para. IV(7).

[79] Ibid., ann. 1, para. 9i(2), pp. 14–15; ann. 10, p. 15.

[80] Tamotsu Shibutani, *The Derelicts of Company K: A Sociological Study of Demoralization* (Berkeley: University of California Press, 1978).

at Fort Benning. Upon commissioning, he was sent to the 442d RCT as a platoon leader. In May 1945 he was reassigned back to the language school.[81] Only weeks after the end of the war in Europe, MISLS recruiters visited Italy and selected 240 veterans from the 442d RCT who were granted forty-five days' leave before reporting to Fort Snelling.[82]

Matsunaga returned to Hawaii in July 1945 for discharge and wrote back to friends at Fort Snelling:

I often wish I were back there with the school. Somehow the driving spirit of the school as a whole seems to have a lasting effect on one who has been in any way connected with the school. I have met and talked with many graduates of the school, here in Hawaii, and found that they all seem to look back to the assignment at Camp Savage and Fort Snelling as the "good ole days."[83]

By the summer of 1945 the single focus of the school was training more linguists for the expected invasion and occupation of Japan. By 31 July 1945, the school had graduated 2,078 Nisei and hundreds of Caucasians. Almost as many students, 1,863, were still in training. The Nisei had a special motivation in their studies: to prove their loyalty. In John Aiso's words, "what better proof could [they] offer than to actively wage war directly against Japan."[84] The Military Intelligence Service gave them the chance to do just that.

[81] Richard K. Hayashi, MISNorCal Bio.
[82] "Training History," ann. 10, para. IV.E., p. 17; Thomas D. Murphy, *Ambassadors in Arms* (Honolulu: University of Hawaii Press, 1954), p. 271; Lyn Crost, *Honor by Fire: Japanese Americans at War in Europe and the Pacific* (Novato, Calif.: Presidio Press, 1994), p. 271.
[83] *Yaban Gogai*, Nov 45, p. 9; Murphy, *Ambassadors in Arms*, p. 275; Richard Halloran, *Warrior, Peacemaker, Poet, Patriot: A Portrait of Senator Spark M. Matsunaga* (Honolulu: Watermark, 2002). Matsunaga won election to the Hawaii territorial legislature in 1954, U.S. House of Representatives in 1962, and U.S. Senate in 1976.
[84] "Training History," ann. 1, para. 6–22, pp. 17–18; Memo, MID 908 to G–1, 31 Jul 45, Trng Grp, RG 165, NARA; John F. Aiso, Speech to MIS Veteran's Reunion, Honolulu, Hawaii, 6 Sep 64.

10

MIS Nisei in the Campaigns of 1945

As the year 1945 began, America had been at war for over three years. The U.S. Navy had already destroyed Japanese Navy and merchant fleet, and American bombers had begun an aerial campaign against Japan's cities and military facilities. Hundreds of thousands of Japanese soldiers had been killed or isolated with no hope of reinforcement or resupply. The liberation of the Philippines was under way. In the coming months the Military Intelligence Service (MIS) Nisei would exhibit their bravery and skill in the largest land campaigns yet seen in the region. As their numbers swelled, they refined their techniques until they became indispensable. At the same time, they recognized that the war would inevitably culminate in a massive amphibious invasion of the Japanese home islands, the land of their parents' birth.

By January 1945 the Military Intelligence Service Language School (MISLS) had already sent 1,050 Nisei graduates overseas. Two had died in action; several others had been severely wounded or died from nonbattle causes. One had been awarded the Distinguished Service Cross, dozens more the Silver Star and other decorations for valor. Nisei accompanied every Army and Marine division and corps, as well as Australian, New Zealand, British, and Chinese forces and served in rear-area intelligence centers in Hawaii, Australia, India, and the continental United States. War Department planners projected that the war would continue into 1946 and would draw upon forces redeployed from the European Theater after the expected defeat of Germany. In 1945 the MIS Nisei were to make their greatest contributions to victory.

Liberation of the Philippines

The battle for Leyte in the autumn of 1944 culminated in a stunning defeat for Japanese air, ground, and naval forces. General Douglas MacArthur's dramatic success was guided by skillful intelligence. By early 1945 about 400 Nisei were assigned to the Allied Translator and Interpreter Section (ATIS) under Col. Sidney F. Mashbir. Some of the Nisei had been overseas since 1942; more than a hundred had been reassigned to ATIS from the South Pacific. Mashbir now controlled all linguist assets in the Southwest Pacific Area. Advance ATIS was stationed in Hollandia with MacArthur's headquarters; Base ATIS remained in Brisbane, where ATIS had been established in September 1942. Since then ATIS had perfected battle-tested procedures for the speedy processing of captured documents and prisoners of war and dissemination of the resulting intelligence.[1]

ATIS assigned more than a hundred Nisei for the liberation of Luzon, which began with landings at Lingayen Gulf, southwest of Baguio, on 9 January 1945. (*Map 12*) Most of the previous fighting in New Guinea, the Admiralties, and the Solomons had been at regiment level and below. Now, on Luzon, Sixth Army deployed two corps abreast for the drive to Manila while Eighth Army landed the 11th Airborne Division south of the capital on 31 January. The campaign ultimately encompassed three corps headquarters and ten divisions. The MIS Nisei, a mixture of veterans and newcomers, performed the myriad tasks that had made them so valuable in earlier campaigns. They quickly translated captured documents to reveal Japanese plans and dispositions. One document captured on 19 January was a chart of Japanese radio frequencies that "was used by the I Corps signal officer to gain highly satisfactory results in the monitoring of Japanese radio communications." Another language team correctly identified and translated the Japanese general operation order for the defense of Luzon.[2]

MIS Nisei were assigned down to regiment level. On 3 February, when the 511th Parachute Infantry opened the main road to Manila from the south with a combat drop on Tagaytay Ridge, it was accompanied by the its four Nisei paratrooper-linguists.[3]

In three weeks the American units reached the outskirts of Manila, where Japanese defenders were determined to make the Americans fight block by block. Three American divisions that had become skilled in jungle warfare in the South

---

[1] "The Exploitation of Japanese Documents," ATIS Publication no. 6, 14 Dec 44, in General Headquarters, Far East Command, *Operations of the Allied Translator and Interpreter Section, GHQ, SWPA,* Intelligence Series, vol. 5 (Tokyo: Far East Command, 1948) (hereafter cited as ATIS History), app. 5. All U.S. Army personnel with ATIS were reassigned on 3 May 1944 to the Translator and Interpreter Service, U.S. Army Forces in the Far East. ATIS eliminated numerical designations for its advance echelons on 1 August 1944 but reinstated them on 18 April 1945, at which time division language teams were also given numerical designations. ATIS History, pp. 5, 28.

[2] Ibid., p. 48.

[3] George T. Ito, "Linguist-Paratroopers," *Voice of the Angels* (July 1996); Joseph D. Harrington, *Yankee Samurai: The Secret Role of Nisei in America's Pacific Victory* (Detroit: Pettigrew Enterprises, 1979), p. 263.

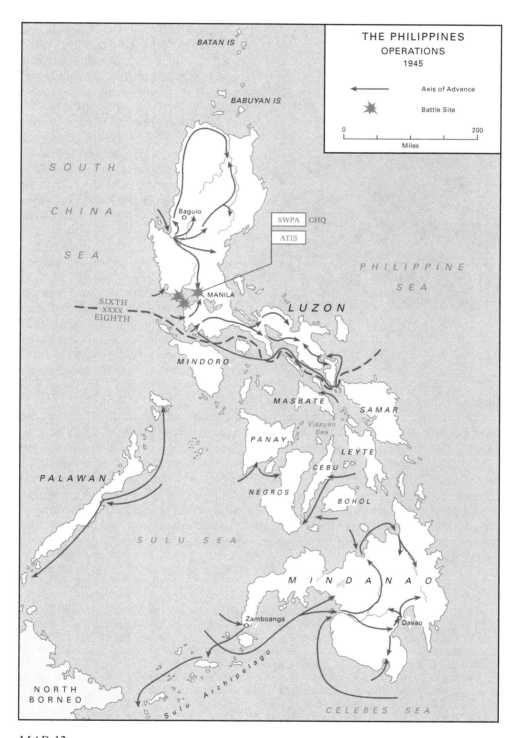

MAP 12

T4g. Henry Suzuki, Luzon, spring 1945

Pacific now had to learn urban warfare in the rubble of a city that had once sheltered 800,000 inhabitants. Nisei linguists were in the thick of the fighting, often at risk of being mistaken for Japanese soldiers by vengeful Filipinos embittered by years of harsh occupation and atrocities. In these challenging times the Nisei often had to use their wits as well as their language skill. On 4 February the 1st Cavalry Division liberated 3,500 civilian internees from Santo Tomas University, but Japanese soldiers held another 275 women and children hostage in one corner of the campus. Pvt. Kenji Uyesugi helped negotiate their release. Uyesugi, already a veteran of combat on Guam in support of the marines, found this a very different battlefield. The Japanese commander demanded safe passage in exchange for his hostages. The American commander reluctantly agreed, and Uyesugi stood aside as sixty-six Japanese soldiers marched away. The hostages were released as agreed.[4]

Other Nisei served in unfamiliar roles. Standing guard in Manila Bay was the island of Corregidor, which the Americans had to seize to open Manila's harbor. Sixth Army assigned the task to the 503d Parachute Regimental Combat Team (RCT). T3g. Harry M. Akune had accompanied the regiment on an amphibious landing on Mindoro during the previous December, after which the regimental commander asked him if he would join them for the combat jump onto Corregidor. Although Akune had no airborne training, he agreed. "The paratroopers treated me so well I felt that I was already a member of that elite group." Akune had time for only one practice jump, in which he injured his ankle. But he continued on the mission.[5]

---

[4] Robert Ross Smith, *Triumph in the Philippines*, U.S. Army in World War II (Washington, D.C.: Office of the Chief of Military History, 1963), pp. 251–52; Harrington, *Yankee Samurai*, p. 263; Wallace Moore, quoted in *Pacific Citizen*, 22 Dec 45, p. 5. Another Nisei, T3g. Bill Ishida, was awarded the Silver Star for fighting near Santo Tomas University. "Nisei Sergeant Decorated for Heroism in Battle for Manila," *Pacific Citizen*, 2 Jan 46.

[5] Jack Herzig, "Harry Akune's WWII Accomplishments Recognized," *Hokubei Mainichi* (9 January 1996); Harry Akune, in James Oda, *Secret Embedded in Magic Cables: The Story of a 101-Year-Old Japanese Communist Leader who served Japan, KGB, and CIA* (Northridge, Calif.: J. Oda, 1993), pp. 193–99; Akune presentation, in *The Saga of the MIS*, videotaped presentation,

On 16 February the 503d Parachute RCT surprised the Japanese defenders by jumping onto a small drop zone in a twenty-mile-an-hour wind that blew many troopers into the cliffs or off the island altogether, resulting in a 25 percent injury rate. When the time came, Akune jumped; but he landed badly and slid down an embankment. Bruised, shaken, and missing his carbine, he scrambled back up to the top of the hill, only to face "a whole line of guys, all pointing their guns at me!" Fortunately, one of them recognized Akune and they held their fire. Akune made his way to the command post and began translating the first documents captured. Within hours he was able to report two key pieces of intelligence: the Japanese commander had been killed as the assault began, and enemy strength was several times larger than expected. The Americans captured twenty Japanese soldiers, and Akune interrogated them as the battle continued. While he was interrogating one prisoner, the man attacked him. Fortunately, an American guard shot the prisoner and saved Akune's life.[6]

Manila was declared secure on 4 March, but the fight for Luzon was far from won. *General Tomoyuki Yamashita* divided his forces: one group retreated into the mountains south and east of Manila, and the other moved into the island's rugged north. Fighting continued for months. Meanwhile, the Americans began to build up a major logistical base in Luzon while assisting the Philippine people.

The Counter Intelligence Corps (CIC) was responsible for security in the liberated areas and handling Japanese infiltrators and suspected war criminals. In February 1945 CIC headquarters requested three dozen Nisei, but as late as April 1945 the 441st CIC Detachment still had only two, Arthur S. Komori and John Hiroshi Masuda. Komori recalled: "they had the chance of a lifetime to 'hang' Jap spies that were infiltrating Manila in civilian clothing. They were headed for sabotage, assassination of our leaders, and other subversive activities. I obtained many of their confessions and thus had the satisfaction of seeing them found guilty by court-martial."

Komori had first come to Manila in April 1941 as an undercover agent with another Hawaii Nisei, Richard M. Sakakida. Their mission had been to infiltrate the city's large Japanese civilian community for what was then called the Corps of Intelligence Police (CIP). Once war broke out, Komori was evacuated to Australia; but Sakakida and the rest of the CIP detachment fell into Japanese hands. Komori recalled:

Los Angeles, 11 Mar 89; Patrick K. O'Donnell, *Into the Rising Sun* (New York: Free Press, 2002), pp. 197–201.

[6] Harrington, *Yankee Samurai*, pp. 263–65; Herzig, "Harry Akune's WWII Accomplishments Recognized"; *Saga of the MIS*. Six Nisei, including George Kojima, were assigned to the 503d RCT in early 1945 as combat replacements, not as language specialists. However, the regiment used three as interpreters, even though they were not MISLS graduates. Kojima was wounded on Negros and spent three years in hospitals. Joseph D. Harrington Papers, National Japanese Historical Society (NJAHS), San Francisco, Calif.; "Nisei Paratroops in Action in Pacific," *Pacific Citizen*, 21 Jul 45.

After my escape, I wanted above all else to seek recognition for my "lost CIP." As the lone escapee, I wanted to hasten the day of their liberation. I was particularly miserable concerning the fate of Sakakida. I imagined with horror many a night of the tortures he would undergo if captured, since according to the Jap concept he was a traitor. . . . I often harped on the point of Sakakida's CIP mission and felt certain of his loyalty.

One CIC officer remarked that "Sakakida would be a more valuable man to him than would Gen. Yamashita, because of the knowledge Sakakida had of collaborationist activities in Manila." For months after the liberation of Manila, Komori could find no trace of Sakakida.[7]

The U.S. Army liberated thousands of other American soldiers and civilian internees who along with tens of thousands of Filipino soldiers and civilians had spent the war under atrocious conditions. Many more had died before liberation. MacArthur was particularly shocked to learn of a massacre of nearly 150 American prisoners of war on Palawan in December 1944 and feared that the Japanese might massacre their prisoners rather than let them fall into Allied hands. Mounting evidence of Japanese atrocities further inflamed hatred of the Japanese as a "cruel race." On 30 January 1945, American Alamo Scouts and rangers and Philippine guerrillas slipped behind Japanese lines to liberate 500 internees at Cabanatuan. On 24 February another raid liberated 2,147 internees at Los Baños.[8]

The Nisei in the Philippines were painfully aware that they faced racial hatred. Sgt. George I. Nakamura from Santa Cruz, California, had been a pre-med student at the University of California before the war. He had volunteered for the language school from a relocation camp in November 1942 against his father's wishes. In February 1945 he wrote to a former high school teacher in California:

One thing that I find amusing is that some of the Filipinos cannot understand why I am in the United States Army. "Gawds," they say, "what's a Jap doing in the division C.P.!" I try to explain how my folks have been in America for 35 years and that I'm an American born, educated and indoctrinated with American ideals but some of them seem dubious of it all. At least at first they seem bewildered.[9]

Racial hatred also engendered incidents more threatening than amusing. T3g. Iwao Roy Kawashiri and his language officer visited an American unit on Negros

---

[7] Interv, Ann Bray with Arthur Komori, 1955, p. 18, in Harrington Papers; Memo, 441st CIC Detachment, sub: Sakakida, Richard Motoso, 12 Nov 45; Arthur Komori, Biography, Military Intelligence Service Club of Northern California (this and similar biographies hereafter cited as MISNorCal Bios); Ted T. Tsukiyama et al., eds., *Secret Valor: M.I.S. Personnel, World War II Pacific Theater, Pre–Pearl Harbor to Sept. 8, 1951* (Honolulu: Military Intelligence Service Veterans Club of Hawaii, 1993), p. 35. All CIC detachments in the Southwest Pacific Area were consolidated into the 441st CIC Detachment on 25 June 1945.

[8] D. Clayton James, *The Years of MacArthur*, 3 vols. (Boston: Houghton Mifflin, 1975), 2: 512–13, 642–43; Robert L. Eichelberger, *Our Jungle Road to Tokyo* (New York: Viking, 1950), p. 206; E. Bartlett Kerr, *Surrender and Survival: The Experience of American POWs in the Pacific, 1941–1945* (New York: William Morrow, 1985), pp. 212–15.

[9] Ltr, George I. Nakamura to Mr. C. E. Fehliman, 26 February 1945.

in April or May 1945. (Kawashiri had graduated in April 1942 with the first class from Crissy Field and had served with the Americal Division for three years on Bougainville, Leyte, and Cebu.) The lieutenant went to the officers' mess tent, and Kawashiri got into the mess line for the enlisted men. Suddenly, a Philippine Scout pointed to Kawashiri and began shouting, "An enemy soldier!" The mess sergeant placed his hand on the Nisei's shoulder, and another Filipino soldier took the plate of food from his hands. Kawashiri quickly pulled out his dog tags and explained he was an interpreter from division headquarters, but the soldiers remained unconvinced. "The Philippine Scouts with their long machetes made me feel a bit nervous," Kawashiri recalled; and he began looking for his lieutenant, who appeared at a run. After that, Kawashiri always made sure he was accompanied by his language officer or another Caucasian.[10]

The campaign in the Philippines yielded thousands of Japanese prisoners of war, in part because the Americans employed psychological warfare to an extent not previously seen in the theater. Brig. Gen. Bonner Fellers established the theater Psychological Warfare Branch in June 1944 and in the spring of 1945 developed a comprehensive strategy for psychological warfare against Japan.[11] Colonel Mashbir also had a strong interest in psychological warfare and assigned several ATIS Nisei to work with captured Japanese prisoners of war (nineteen by May 1945) to develop leaflets. In March 1945 they developed a newspaper-style leaflet, the *Rakkasan [Parachute] News*, which was dropped in large quantities over Japanese-held areas of the Philippines and eventually over the Japanese home islands.[12]

In March the Psychological Warfare Branch asked ATIS for two Nisei to use as radio announcers. Mashbir asked for volunteers with broadcast experience, telling them:

This is an extremely dangerous thing to ask any Nisei to do. In fact, from the instant you leave here you will be traveling under a false name, because I know that should your names become known dire vengeance will be wreaked on your relatives in Japan. Not

---

[10] Iwao Roy Kawashiri, in "First Class," ed. David W. Swift, Jr., p. 13, Unpubl Ms, Mar 00, copy in author's files; Ltr, Roy Kawashiri to Joseph Harrington, 7 December 1977, Harrington Papers; Harrington, *Yankee Samurai*, p. 292. In January 1946 a group of Nisei linguists stationed in Manila complained of a "hostile attitude" and threats of violence from the Filipino population: "Army Will Act To Protect Nisei GIs in Philippines," *Pacific Citizen*, 19 Jan 46.

[11] ATIS History, pp. 63–64; USAFPAC, "Report on Psychological Warfare in the Southwest Pacific Area 1944–45," Record Group (RG) 4, Psychological Warfare, MacArthur Memorial, Library and Archives, Norfolk, Va.; "Basic Military Plan for Psychological Warfare against Japan with Appendices and Minutes of the Conference on Psychological Warfare against Japan, 7–8 May 1945," Bonner Fellers Papers, Hoover Institution Archives, Stanford University.

[12] Sample issues of *Rakkasan News* can be found in ATIS History, plate 13; Allison B. Gilmore, *You Can't Fight Tanks with Bayonets: Psychological Warfare against the Japanese Army in the Southwest Pacific* (Lincoln: University of Nebraska Press, 1998), p. 141. The *Rakkasan News* sometimes used cartoons from existing Japanese publications. One popular Japanese *manga* artist, Yokoyama Ryuchi, recognized his drawings in the American leaflets and after the war asked the U.S. Army for royalties. Haruko Taya Cook and Theodore F. Cook, *Japan at War: An Oral History* (New York: New Press, 1992), pp. 471–72.

only that but you will be the first Nisei to arrive in Manila and the Filipino guerrillas may mistake you for Japanese in disguise and kill you. Therefore this job calls not only for ability and intelligence but nerve.[13]

S.Sgt. Clifford P. Konno and Sgt. John Masuda volunteered and were flown from Brisbane to Manila. In June MISLS sent ten more Nisei directly from Minnesota led by enlisted instructors M.Sgts. Masao Harold Onishi and Yoshio Kenneth Harano.[14] Onishi had witnessed the first bombs falling on American soil. Born and raised in a fishing village close to Pearl Harbor, he had worked his way through the University of Hawaii as a Japanese-language announcer for KGMB in Honolulu. On 7 December 1941, he saw the Japanese airplanes strike Pearl Harbor. When the USS *Arizona* exploded and hot metal pieces landed in his yard, he threw his family into his car and drove away. "I looked out the car window and saw the flag of the Rising Sun on the planes. Then I realized it was Japan attacking us." He volunteered for the language school and upon graduation was held back as an instructor. Now he had a chance to speak directly to the Japanese people.[15]

Sixth Army established a central POW camp on Luzon, known as POW Camp No. 1, or LUPOW, near New Bilibid Prison outside Manila. Dozens of Nisei interpreters were assigned to interrogate over 5,000 prisoners and help with camp administration. Eighth Army established a similar camp on Leyte.[16] The Japanese prisoners had endured American firepower, the tropical environment, the self-destructive urges of their own leaders, little food, poor medical support, and the hatred of the Filipinos. The Nisei encountered a variety of other Japanese persons, soldiers and sailors, civilians (especially in the southern Philippines), as well as forced laborers and "comfort women" from Korea and Taiwan.

Many Japanese were surprised to meet the Nisei. One well-educated prisoner captured on Mindoro in January 1945 was a literary critic, *Shōhei Ōoka*, who spoke English. When a Nisei came to interrogate him, *Ōoka* was shocked. "I could hardly believe that I would meet a Japanese man in such excellent health at this place, only a few miles removed from where my outfit had been so ravaged by disease. Never did I feel more painfully the meaning of defeat than when I saw this man of Japanese blood dressed in an American uniform."[17]

---

[13] Sidney F. Mashbir, *I Was an American Spy* (New York: Vantage, 1953), p. 245.

[14] "Konno Gets Bars; Grads Hope To Broadcast from Tokyo," *Yaban Gogai*, Sep–Oct 45, p. 5.

[15] Masao Harold Onishi, MISNorCal Bio.

[16] Yoshito Iwamoto, in *MIS in the War against Japan*, ed. Stanley L. Falk and Warren M. Tsuneishi (Washington, D.C.: Japanese American Veterans Association, 1995), pp. 39–41. The ATIS History, p. 17, says that 5,410 prisoners were examined at New Bilibid up to 1 September 1945. After the war the LUPOW prisoner population peaked at 80,000.

[17] After the war *Ōoka* described the collapse of Japanese forces in the Philippines, his capture, and his imprisonment on Leyte. Ōoka Shōhei, *Taken Captive: A Japanese POW's Story*, trans. and ed. Wayne P. Lammers (New York: John Wiley & Sons, 1996), p. 34. He also drew upon his experiences to write a widely acclaimed novel, *Fires on the Plain* (New York: Knopf, 1957), and *Reite senki* [Military record of the Leyte operation] (Tokyo: Chūō Kōronsha, Shōwa, 1971).

Another prisoner, Japanese naval lieutenant *Kiyofumi Kojima*, had wandered the hills of northern Luzon for weeks trying to avoid Philippine guerrillas. When he finally surrendered to an American unit, he met his first Nisei, "a Japanese in an American uniform. I can't tell you how strange that felt. He questioned us, but this time in Japanese. Until then, I'd been using my very limited English." The Americans then took him to meet a Nisei first lieutenant: "He was unarmed. He took me to his own room. 'Mr. Kojima,' he asked me, 'would you like coffee or tea?' Coffee, I replied. Then he pulled out a bag of cookies. We'd been told it was our duty to endure privation to the moment of victory. We hadn't had such luxurious things for years. He just opened the bag and dumped them on the table. 'Go ahead,' he said. 'Please eat.'" The two "enemies" enjoyed a long conversation.

He informed me that his grandmother and grandfather lived in Hiroshima, and asked me what I thought of Nisei soldiers. Did I hate them? I realized he was genuinely worried about that, which was why he was being so kind to me. It gave me confidence. "You were born in America," I replied. "You're fighting for your country, America. I have no ill feelings about that." He was like me, and I did the same thing for my country. Then he told me about how Japanese-Americans were horribly ill-treated in America, that they were placed in camps, and still oppressed even though the outstanding record of the all-Nisei 442d Regimental Combat Team had changed the situation a little. We chatted until ten-thirty at night, and I learned that there were people who were suffering because they belonged to neither country.[18]

The Nisei's friendly approach won the prisoner's confidence. *Kojima* subsequently was transferred to Hawaii, where he helped monitor Japanese radio broadcasts and draft propaganda materials.

More intelligence came from captured documents, of which one collection was particularly noteworthy. The U.S. Navy found the heavy cruiser *Nachi*, the flagship of the Japanese Fifth Fleet, sitting on the bottom of Manila Bay where it had rested since being sunk in November 1944. In April 1945 Navy divers explored the wreck and found a complete library of all plans and orders issued by the Imperial Japanese Navy since 1941. Seventh Fleet requested an immediate translation, and ATIS assigned almost every officer to the task for six weeks. The resulting translations were later called "the most completely authentic exposition of current Japanese naval doctrine then in Allied hands, detailed information being included relative to the composition and command structure of the entire Imperial fleet."[19] Among them, for example, was the operational order for the Pearl Harbor attack.

---

[18] Cook and Cook, *Japan at War*, pp. 373–82. *Kiyofumi Kojima* tells the same story in *The Color of Honor*, documentary film, Loni Ding, prod., Vox Productions, 1987.

[19] ATIS History, p. 13; "Navy Operation Plans and Orders, 1941–1944, Recovered from CA NACHI," ATIS Limited Distribution Translations (LDT), no. 39, pts. 1–12, 22 Apr–18 Aug 45; ATIS History, pp. 13, 49–50; John Prados, *Combined Fleet Decoded: The Secret History of American Intelligence and the Japanese Navy In World War II* (New York: Random House, 1995), pp. 698–99; John Prados, "The Spies at the Bottom of the Sea," *MHQ* 6, no. 2 (Winter 1994): 39–47.

American soldiers were just as curious as the Japanese prisoners about the Nisei. In early 1945 2d Lt. Yoshikazu Yamada, a Nisei from Hawaii, met Sgt. Norman Mailer in the Philippines. Yamada was a University of Hawaii graduate and had been a graduate student at the University of Michigan until he was drafted in April 1941. In 1944 he was assigned to the 112th Cavalry RCT, where he earned a direct commission. Mailer, a Harvard graduate, had joined the regimental intelligence and reconnaissance platoon for the Luzon Campaign. He had dreams of writing the great novel of the war, which was published in 1948 as *The Naked and the Dead*. In it he describes an encounter between a Nisei lieutenant, "Tom Wakara," and a Navy language officer. Mailer portrays the Navy language officer as a blustering hypocrite, who tells another officer, "You know our Jap translators are overrated. I do all the work in our unit, of course I'm in charge, but Wakara isn't much help at all. I'm always having to correct his translations." The fictional Nisei, a sensitive and cultured Kibei, can read the captured diaries with more empathy than the officer, even though the Japanese philosophy seems ultimately futile to him. He also understands that he will never gain acceptance from Caucasians such as this naval officer. The Nisei is "a little tired of being treated as a freak," Mailer concludes. "He was alone, a wise man without a skin."[20]

Other Nisei wrestled with their sense of identity between the two cultures, sometimes in unexpected ways. T.Sgt. Masaji Gene Uratsu was assigned to the 158th Regimental Combat Team. A Kibei and graduate of the first class at Crissy Field, Uratsu had already earned a Bronze Star on New Guinea. A few days after landing on Luzon, the 158th RCT captured a huge supply dump "full of Japanese beer, sake, whiskey, Chinese medicinal wine, and all kinds of Japanese foodstuff." The language team held "a victory celebration of sorts, . . . a rip-roaring evening spent enjoying the spoils of war with our friends from headquarters," after which they stumbled into their cots. The next morning he awoke with "a terrific hangover." He rolled to the edge of his bunk and opened his eyes:

I happened to look down and there was a most ugly looking Japanese soldier staring at me. I had my gun, I had my machete within easy reach, but I knew that if I made even a slightest movement of muscle, he's gonna shoot me. So I thought Jesus Christ, there goes Gene Uratsu. But since I gotta go, I gotta remember this guy to the Devil or wherever I'm going.

So I took a good hard look at the guy. . . . And I looked at him again and I said I've seen this guy. I've seen this guy. . . . So again I looked at him. Then all of a sudden I realized I was looking at my own reflection.

He was looking into his shaving mirror that had fallen under his cot.[21]

[20] Norman Mailer, *The Naked and the Dead* (New York: Henry Holt, 1998), pp. 244–49. Yamada was assigned to the Air Corps in the Philippines in November 1941. He suffered a noncombat injury and was evacuated to Australia, where he was assigned to ATIS. Yamada later commented, "The story [in Mailer's novel] seems to parallel my own actual experience with a white lieutenant who was also a language officer." Tsukiyama et al., *Secret Valor*, p. 85.

[21] Masaji Gene Uratsu, in Swift, "First Class," pp. 20–21; Anthony Arthur, *Bushmasters* (New York: St. Martin's, 1987), p. 197; Masaji Gene Uratsu presentation, in *Saga of the MIS*.

The Luzon Campaign caused Sergeant Nakamura to reflect on his reasons for fighting. He had seen his friend and team chief, Sgt. Terry Mizutari, killed on New Guinea in June 1944. After visiting Manila on pass, he wrote home: "It's all wrecked now by the war, but I can see how it might have been in peacetime. Most of the buildings have been ruined either by artillery shells or bombs. There is so much waste connected with a war." [22] He celebrated his twenty-first birthday that May, but his teammates with the 6th Infantry Division still called him one of the "babies" of the outfit. The division continued fighting stubborn Japanese resistance in northern Luzon, and in June Nakamura wrote to his sister:

We have been more than just busy the last month and a half. Since coming to this new area we have had no day when we could relax and take it easy. It is the busiest we have been since coming overseas and it is more than I ever expected to see out here. Lately we have had so many prisoners that we just keep ourselves busy interrogating them all day long. Then we have to type up the reports so the day never seems to end. [23]

On 29 June a patrol from the 63d Infantry encountered some Japanese holdouts and called to division for an interpreter. Nakamura was chosen. Another Nisei later recalled that "usually we said our good-byes to all our teammates, knowing the ferocity of battle up front," but Nakamura "left that day without a word." When he reached the front lines, he found that the patrol had a small group of Japanese soldiers surrounded. Nakamura called for them to surrender to no avail. "Although he knew that he could be observed by the enemy, believing that they had not heard his calls, he crawled to within twenty-five yards of the emplacement, where he rose, exposing himself to view, and again called to the enemy encouraging them to surrender. The enemy's response was a single shot which fatally wounded [him]." The 6th Infantry Division awarded Nakamura the Silver Star posthumously. [24]

While the Sixth Army liberated Luzon, Eighth Army swept through the southern Philippines with five infantry divisions. Lt. Gen. Robert L. Eichelberger boasted that "in one forty-four-day time period alone these troops conducted fourteen major landings and twenty-four minor ones, thus rolling up an average of a landing every day and a half." [25]

The campaign began on 28 February, when the 186th Regimental Combat Team landed on Palawan, and culminated on 17 April with the landing on Mindanao, the second largest island in the Philippines and the location of its second largest city,

---

[22] Ltr, Nakamura, 14 May 1945, Historical Files, Defense Language Institute Foreign Language Center (DLIFLC), Monterey, Calif.

[23] Ltr, Nakamura, 7 June 1945, DLIFLC.

[24] HQ, 6th Inf Div, General Orders no. 139, 18 Jul 45; Kiyo Fujimura, "They Told Me 'G.I.' K.I.A.," in *John Aiso and the M.I.S.: Japanese-American Soldiers in the Military Intelligence Service, World War II*, ed. Tad Ichinokuchi (Los Angeles: Military Intelligence Service Club of Southern California, 1988), p. 95; Min Hara, in Ibid, p. 74; Nob Yamashita, "Fighting My Ancestors: The Autobiography of a Nisei," p. 22, Unpubl Ms, n.d. In 1980 DLIFLC dedicated an academic building to Nakamura on the Presidio of Monterey, California.

[25] Eichelberger, *Our Jungle Road to Tokyo*, p. 200.

Davao City. Mindanao held about 20,000 Japanese civilians and 43,000 Japanese troops. Wresting control of the island took two American divisions and thousands of Philippine guerrillas ten weeks at a cost of over 3,000 American casualties. The Nisei played a key role in Eighth Army operations. As a one-time intelligence officer, Eichelberger liked to interrogate prisoners himself with the help of a Nisei interpreter.[26] At regiment and division command posts, the Nisei translated documents, interrogated captured prisoners, and persuaded small groups of enemy soldiers to surrender.

Elsewhere in the South Pacific, hundreds of thousands of bypassed Japanese troops held out in New Guinea, the Solomons, Rabaul, and elsewhere, subsisting on whatever foods they could grow for themselves. During 1944 the Americans treated them to occasional bombing raids or guerrilla harassment but otherwise left them undisturbed. As American combat units shifted to the Philippines, the Australian government adopted a more aggressive strategy. After November 1944 the First Australian Army began to eliminate Japanese forces using three Australian divisions. As these Australian units took over from American units, they were often disappointed at the lack of intelligence from the Americans. For the most part, American units in the rear areas had not been patrolling aggressively. The Australians learned that "information of enemy strength and dispositions was extremely limited. Apart from the enemy forces immediately in front of them the Americans could supply very little information."[27] However, ATIS provided each Australian brigade with several American Nisei, a dozen of whom received Australian commendations.[28]

The Australian II Corps and 3d Division covered Bougainville and the Solomon Islands. When the Australians took over in October 1944, American intelligence officers assured them there were only 12,000 Japanese soldiers remaining on Bougainville. Australian intelligence officers revised this to 25,000. At the end of the war, the true number turned out to be 40,000.[29]

Bypassed Japanese forces could still be dangerous. As late as April 1945 the Japanese on Bougainville launched a surprise offensive against the Australians.[30] From the autumn of 1944 until the summer of 1945, about 2,100 Australian soldiers were killed or wounded in the Solomons. Life for Nisei with Australian units was seldom easy. They faced tropical diseases and the hazards of combat and missed the comradeship of their Nisei comrades. T4g. Robert T. "Rusty" Kimura from Sacramento, California, was assigned to Bougainville and would far rather have been assigned to an American outfit. The Australians offered him an Australian

---

[26] See Jay Luvaas, ed., *Dear Miss Em: General Eichelberger's War in the Pacific, 1942–1945* (Westport, Conn.: Greenwood Press, 1972), pp. 232, 245–46, 249–50, 282.

[27] Gavin Long, ed., *Australia in the War of 1939–1945*, ser. 1, vol. 7, *The Final Campaigns* (Canberra: Australian War Memorial, 1963), p. 611.

[28] ATIS History, app. 12, Decorations, Awards, and Commendations. Intervs, author with Paul T. Bannai, 11 Sep 96; with Yasuo Ace Fukai, 9 Sep 96; with Robert T. "Rusty" Kimura, 9 Sep 96.

[29] Long, *Final Campaigns*, pp. 100–103.

[30] Ibid., pp. 181–83.

A Nisei (with back to camera) *helps General Eichelberger question a Japanese soldier, Zamboanga, 10 March 1945.*

uniform, but he insisted on wearing his American uniform. It was seven long months before he saw ATIS again.[31]

On New Guinea, beginning in December 1944, the 6th Australian Division fought at Aitape and elsewhere. Over the next eight months 1,800 Australian soldiers were killed or wounded. Three Nisei were assigned to the 16th Brigade on New Guinea. The Australians gave the Nisei "Digger" campaign hats in place of the heavy American helmets, and the Nisei enjoyed the daily tea breaks. These Nisei "Yanks" proved their value many times over. One captured document, a Japanese operation order, gave the time and place for a submarine pickup off Aitape. The Nisei translated it, and the Australians intercepted and destroyed the submarine.[32]

---

[31] Interv, author with Kimura, 9 Sep 96.

[32] Richard Oguro, in *Sempai Gumi*, ed. Richard S. Oguro (Honolulu: MIS Veterans of Hawaii, ca. 1981), pp. 171–73.

On New Britain, the Australians bottled up the Japanese fortress of Rabaul, once the main objective for Allied operations in the region. American intelligence assured the Australians that only 38,000 Japanese Army personnel were inside. (The correct number turned out to be 93,000.) The 5th Australian Division took over operations on the island and gradually cleared Japanese from all but the eastern end, Rabaul itself. A Nisei, T5g. Larry Tamotsu Mizumoto, served for a while with the Australians on New Britain but suffered a breakdown and was evacuated for medical treatment.[33]

In May 1945 the Australian I Corps captured the oil-rich island of Borneo. Several American Nisei, including Paul T. Bannai, landed with the Australians. Bannai had been born in Colorado, where his father and grandfather were both coalminers, and had volunteered for language training from the Manzanar relocation camp. The Aussies outfitted him with an Australian uniform and the wide-brimmed Digger campaign hat.[34]

Sporadic fighting continued in the South Pacific long after organized resistance had been crushed. The African American 93d Infantry Division patrolled Morotai in the spring and summer of 1945, assisted by an ATIS Nisei team. On 2 August a patrol from the 93d Cavalry Reconnaissance Troop captured the Japanese colonel commanding the island. The division awarded Silver Stars to four patrol members, including Nisei T3g. Stanley J. Nakanishi.[35]

India-Burma and China

By early 1945 the United States had committed two infantry regiments and thousands of trainers, advisers, support units, and Army Air Forces elements to the China and India-Burma Theaters.[36] (*See Map 11.*) As Chinese and U.S. forces advanced in the north, British Commonwealth forces advanced from India and drove the Japanese from Burma. In February 1945 the Stilwell Road opened from Burma to China and American advisers prepared the Chinese Army for an offensive that would drive the Japanese Army to the coast. The XX Bomber Command flew B–29 Superfortresses from airfields in India and China to attack Japanese targets in Southeast Asia and Japan proper. By this time about 140 Nisei were already serving in the region; over the next six months another ninety joined them.

---

[33] Hawaii-born Mizumoto volunteered for the 442d RCT at age nineteen in 1943 and was selected instead for language training. One source states he was evacuated for a tropical disease, another says battle neurosis. He was hospitalized in Chicago, where he jumped off a bridge to his death on 8 July 1945. "Open Verdict Returned in Jap-American GI's Death," *Chicago Daily Tribune*, 10 Jul 45; "Wounded Nisei Soldier Plunges to Death in Chicago," *Pacific Citizen*, 21 Jul 45; *In Freedom's Cause* (Honolulu: University of Hawaii Press, 1949), p. 94.

[34] Interv, author with Paul T. Bannai, 11 Sep 96; Paul T. Bannai, MISNorCal Bio; Bannai presentation, in *Saga of the MIS*.

[35] Elliott V. Converse III, et al., *The Exclusion of Black Soldiers from the Medal of Honor in World War II* (Jefferson, N.C.: McFarland & Co., 1997), pp. 146, 159.

[36] In October 1944 the War Department (WD) divided the command into the China Theater and a separate India-Burma Theater.

George S. Harada, Arthur T. Morimitsu, and Tom Tsutsumi Tsunoda prepare to enter Burma with the 124th Cavalry Regimental Combat Team, part of the MARS Task Force, 19 December 1944.

Fifty worked in the Southeast Asia Translator and Interrogation Center (SEATIC) in New Delhi. Some lived like colonial pashas, with servants and travel opportunities. Others accompanied British and Indian divisions and psychological warfare teams on the front lines. Two dozen were assigned to the 6th Radio Squadron Mobile (RSM) monitoring Japanese air-ground radio traffic, "a routine, dull and unglamorous task, far from the field of battle," recalled one Nisei. "The most we suffered were dysentery and malaria." In diverse ways they made significant contributions to the Allied victory.[37]

Merrill's Marauders had proven at great cost that American ground forces could contribute to victory in Burma. The 5332d Brigade, or MARS Task Force, continued the push into northern Burma. The 475th Infantry made first contact with the Japanese in mid-December, and the 124th Cavalry entered the fight in mid-January. S.Sgt. Kazuo Komoto, a veteran of fighting in the Solomon Islands, led ten Nisei with the 475th Infantry. T.Sgt. Kan Tagami, a former MISLS enlisted

---

[37] Tsukiyama et al., *Secret Valor*, pp. 72–73. One Nisei, T.Sgt. Russell Takeo Fujino, was killed in Burma on 4 August 1945. He was not an MISLS graduate but had been sent to Burma in March 1945 with a U.S. Army medical unit. "Nisei Sergeant Reported Killed in Action in Burma," *Pacific Citizen*, 1 Sep 45.

instructor, led fifteen Nisei with the 124th Cavalry.[38] From January through March
the MARS Task Force, supplied only by air, maneuvered and fought over several
hundred miles of mountain ranges and treacherous rivers. Its members fought the
terrain, the climate, various illnesses, and on occasion, the enemy. One Nisei,
Arthur T. Morimitsu, recalled:

The one-month forced march in December over some of the roughest terrain in the world
took us through dense jungle growths, up narrow mountain passes eight thousand feet
high and swift streams that we forded waist-deep. Because of manpower shortage we also
ended up as probably one of the first Nisei muleskinners in the CBI. Hanging onto the lead
mule's tail helped on those steep terrains where we marched ten minutes and took five.
The pack mules carried weapons, ammo and other materiels [sic]. We carried our own
essentials—blanket, poncho, canteen, machete, trench shovel and carbine.[39]

"Before the first skirmish with the enemy," he recalled, "the Texans wondered
what we Nisei were doing in their outfit. After the first initial contact the entire
brass of the regiment crowded into our makeshift shelter at night to check out diaries and documents brought in by some of the troopers."[40]

Tagami remembered that at MISLS the Nisei had been taught: "Keep your
team together and don't go into combat because you're not supposed to be combat
trained." In Burma, this proved impossible, as Tagami and the other Nisei frequently volunteered for patrols. One time Tagami almost learned his lesson the hard way
when his reconnaissance patrol became surrounded and their Kachin irregulars
melted away. Tagami could hear the Japanese soldiers closing in on them as they
shouted "Go left, go left, they're over there." He relayed the Japanese commands to
the other members of the patrol, and they successfully eluded their pursuers.[41]

A few Nisei were attached to the Chinese New First Army. Sgt. Frank T.
Tokubo served with the Chinese until the capture of Lashio in March 1945. One
of his duties was to fly over Japanese lines in an L–5 liaison aircraft to broadcast
surrender messages through a loudspeaker. His aircraft was struck by ground fire
on two occasions, but each time it landed safely in Chinese positions. The Chinese
awarded Tokubo their equivalent of the Silver Star.[42] Other Nisei were attached to
the British Fourteenth Army. T4g. Samuel T. Harano, a Kibei from Hawaii, fought
from November 1944 with the Indian 19th Division, the first division to cross the

[38] Interv, author with Kan Tagami, 7 Dec 94; Interv, author with Toshio Uesato, 21 Aug 95;
"Waipahu Soldier [Toshi Uesato] Tells of Life with Mars Task Force in Burma," *Honolulu Advertiser*, 29 Apr 45.
[39] Arthur T. Morimitsu, MISNorCal Bio.
[40] Ibid. For another first-person account written in verse, see Toma Tasaki, "The Journey of the
Men of Mars," Unpubl Ms, n.d.
[41] Interv, author with Tagami, 7 Dec 94.
[42] "Sgt. Tokubo Reported Only Nisei Attached to Chinese Unit," *Pacific Citizen*, Jun 46; Harrington, *Yankee Samurai*, p. 249.

Irrawaddy. He then joined the Indian 5th Division, which led the final drive to Rangoon in April 1945.[43]

The Office of Strategic Services (OSS) had begun guerrilla operations in Burma in 1943, borrowing a few Nisei as needed from other commands. In November 1944 fourteen specially selected Nisei arrived to provide language support. Seven under 1st Lts. Junichi Buto and Ralph T. Yempuku were assigned to OSS Detachment 101, which numbered 131 officers, 418 American enlisted men, and some 9,000 native guerrillas principally from the Kachin tribes. The Nisei were assigned to small teams and often inserted by parachute into remote jungle camps behind Japanese lines. 1st Lt. Richard K. Betsui and four Nisei joined OSS Detachment 202 in Kunming, China; two others were assigned to New Delhi.[44]

Yempuku, a graduate of the University of Hawaii, had volunteered for the 442d RCT and volunteered a second time for the OSS. Soon after his arrival, he fell ill with malaria. When he recovered, he flew to OSS Detachment 101 headquarters at Myitkyina and then went forward to join a Kachin battalion in which half a dozen American officers led 150–200 lightly armed Kachin rangers. Yempuku was the only Japanese-speaker with the outfit and for a time even commanded a Kachin ranger company. Yempuku had three younger brothers living in Japan and often wondered as he prepared attacks on Japanese troops: "Jesus! What would happen if one of my brothers is in that convoy? What if my brother is among the prisoners I have to interrogate? . . . So much of war is placing personal feelings aside." He later learned that all three brothers had served in the Imperial Japanese Army, none in Burma.[45]

Detachment 101 saw its heaviest fighting in May and June 1945, killing 1,200 Japanese while losing 300 of its own. For this the unit was awarded the Distinguished Unit Citation. In July the detachment was inactivated and most of its personnel transferred to Kunming, where OSS Detachment 202 had set up a training camp for Chinese guerrillas. The detachment also inserted American teams behind Japanese lines in south China, including S.Sgt. Roy Matsumoto, a Merrill's Marauders veteran, who served near the French Indochina border.[46]

After the victory in Burma Lord Louis Mountbatten prepared to liberate Malaya and Singapore with amphibious landings set for early September. For this he would need even more Japanese linguists. In April 1945 "the British Chiefs of Staff Joint Intelligence Committee considered a report drawing attention to the lack of Japanese language personnel in South-East Asia Command," according to Japanese Canadian author Roy Ito. "SEATIC was short of trained linguists

[43] Samuel T. Harano, "My India-Burma Odyssey," Unpubl Ms.

[44] Calvin Tottori, "The OSS Niseis in the China-Burma-India Theater," 2d ed., Unpubl Ms, 2001, copy in author's files.

[45] Tsukiyama et al., *Secret Valor*, pp. 75–76; Tomi Kaizawa Knaefler, *Our House Divided: Seven Japanese American Families in World War II* (Honolulu: University of Hawaii Press, 1991), pp. 88–95; Interv, Andrew Cox with Ralph Yempuku, n.d.

[46] John Morozumi also served with the OSS in China. Harrington, *Yankee Samurai*, pp. 302–03.

and unable to function as a viable unit. The situation was considered desperate."[47] The first twelve Canadian Nisei arrived in Bombay on 21 April 1945, led
by Pvt. Albert Takimoto, a Canadian Nisei graduate of the University of British
Columbia. They were distributed among various British headquarters in India
and Burma, including psychological warfare units. Like the American Nisei, they
sought to fight for their country and prove their loyalty. Leaving for overseas
service "was a hard decision to make," one Canadian Nisei wrote his wife upon
arrival in India, "but I wanted all of us to be able to hold our heads up when we
walk the streets again."[48]

In China, American advisers worked to strengthen the Chinese Nationalist
Army. In return, American intelligence officers hoped to learn more about
Japanese forces in China. The G–2 of U.S. Forces in the China Theater was a prewar Japanese-language attaché, Col. Joseph K. Dickey, who had helped organize
the Fourth Army Intelligence School in 1941 and served as its director of training
until 1943. Working with Dickey in Chungking was Lt. Col. John Burden, who
had led the first group of Nisei to the South Pacific. In May 1945 Burden escorted
a high-ranking Japanese prisoner of war to the United States. While there, he visited MISLS and requested two Nisei who had served with him in the South Pacific,
T.Sgt. Tateshi Miyasaki and 2d Lt. Shigeo Yasutake. By that summer Burden had
about forty Nisei, including eight veterans of Merrill's Marauders, at the Sino
Interrogation and Translation Center (SINTIC). Six other Nisei were assigned to
Fourteenth Air Force.[49] In Chungking, Sergeant Tokubo and another Nisei were
placed in charge of a camp for 3,000 Japanese prisoners of war. Several Japanese
political exiles who had sought the protection of the Chinese government also
lived in Chungking.[50]

In early 1945 the Office of War Information (OWI) sent its psychological warfare team with eight Nisei from Ledo to Kunming and then to Chungking. T.Sgt.
Koji Ariyoshi was shocked at how the Nationalist Chinese were treating Japanese
prisoners of war in Kunming and a group of Korean comfort women who had been
captured with the Japanese, compared to how well the Chinese Communists were
treating Japanese prisoners being "re-educated" in Yenan. Nationalist government
officials refused his request to use one or two prisoners for propaganda work, as
the OWI had done in Burma. Another Nisei, T3g. Howard Furumoto, a veteran
of Merrill's Marauders, was assigned to OSS Detachment 203 in Chungking in
March to develop "black" propaganda. His clever fabrications included a patent

---

[47] Roy Ito, *We Went to War: The Story of the Japanese Canadians Who Served during the First
and Second World Wars* (Stittsville, Ontario: Canada's Wings, 1984), p. 163.

[48] Ito, *We Went to War*, p. 238. See also "Describe Departure of First Canadian Volunteers,"
Pacific Citizen, 14 Jul 45; "Canadian Nisei Troops Active in East Asia," *Pacific Citizen*, 24 Nov 45.

[49] Interv, author with John A. Burden, 5 Dec 94; Interv, Loni Ding with John A. Burden, 30 Sep
86, NJAHS; Tateshi Miyasaki, in Swift, "First Class"; Sohei Yamate, in *Japanese Eyes, American
Heart: Personal Reflections of Hawaii's World War II Nisei Soldiers* (Honolulu: Tendai Educational Foundation, 1998), pp. 299, 301–02.

[50] Harrington, *Yankee Samurai*, pp. 297–98.

medicine poster that exaggerated the disease risks for Japanese troops in China and a leaflet that "exposed" a nonexistent plot by Japanese militarists to depose the emperor. That summer he was given a field commission. In July a separate group of twenty-seven civilian Nisei arrived in Calcutta to develop propaganda for the OSS Morale Operations Branch; five proceeded to Kunming on 1 August.[51]

In mid-1945 the U.S. observer group in Yenan, the Dixie Mission, had three Nisei.[52] Two more arrived in July and August 1945. T4g. George I. Nakamura and T4g. Shoso Nomura had been in Yenan since the summer of 1944, doing Japanese order of battle under Ray Cromley, a *Wall Street Journal* correspondent in Tokyo before the war and now an OSS major. Sergeant Ariyoshi worked for the Office of War Information, studying propaganda techniques that the Communists were using to "re-educate" Japanese prisoners of war. He served as informal liaison with Japanese Communist leaders in exile in Yenan. He also met opponents of the Nationalists such as Madame Sun Yat-Sen (Soong Ch'ing-ling). "She seemed interested in the Nisei during our conversation," Ariyoshi recalled. "She knew a great deal about the evacuation and about the [100th Infantry Battalion and 442d RCT]. She was proud of the Nisei role in the war of liberation, as she called it. She said it was remarkable that my people were coming through the evacuation experiences with dignity and new strength."[53]

Central Pacific

In the Central Pacific, American forces continued on the most direct route to Japan, guided by powerful intelligence centers in Hawaii such as the Joint Intelligence Center, Pacific Ocean Areas (JICPOA), and the Fleet Radio Unit, Pacific (FRUPAC). Army officials in Hawaii lifted martial law in October 1944 but maintained surveillance of the local Japanese population using loyal Nisei such as Maj. Gero Iwai and Lt. Cmdr. Douglas T. Wada and the Nisei-dominated Emergency Service Committee.[54]

By early 1945 JICPOA numbered 500 officers and 800 enlisted men. MISLS had sent about 160 Nisei to the Central Pacific by this time. In January 1945 the school sent another forty and then ten more later that spring. Fifty Nisei worked for

---

[51] Koji Ariyoshi, *From Kona to Yenan: The Political Memoirs of Koji Ariyoshi*, ed. Alice M. Beechert and Edward D. Beechert (Honolulu: University of Hawaii Press, 2000), pp. 158–60; Interv, author with Howard Furumoto, 8 Dec 94; Howard Furumoto, "Black Propaganda," student paper, 1946, author's files; Howard Schonberger, "Dilemmas of Loyalty: Japanese Americans and the Psychological Warfare Campaigns of the Office of Strategic Services, 1943–45," *Amerasia Journal* 16, no. 1 (1990): 21–38.

[52] Intervs, author with George I. Nakamura, 6 Dec 94; with Shoso Nomura, 10 Sep 96; with Uesato, 21 Aug 95.

[53] Ariyoshi, *From Kona to Yenan*, pp. 156–57.

[54] Tsukiyama et al., *Secret Valor*, pp. 31–33; Interv, Ted Tsukiyama with Douglas T. Wada, 21 Mar 02; Gary Y. Okihiro, *Cane Fires: The Anti-Japanese Movement in Hawaii, 1865–1945* (Philadelphia: Temple University Press, 1991), pp. 195–276; Tom Coffman, *The Island Edge of America: A Political History of Hawaii* (Honolulu: University of Hawaii Press, 2003), pp. 59–105.

the JICPOA Translation Section in a former furniture store in downtown Honolulu. This section processed the large number of captured documents that included technical documents, nautical charts, administrative orders from the Japanese Navy, and data on Japanese industries. From the Marianas came crates of captured documents by the ton. Translators culled out documents of potential value and shipped the rest to the Pacific Military Intelligence Research Section in Camp Ritchie, Maryland. When Admiral Chester W. Nimitz established an advance headquarters on Guam in January 1945, JICPOA sent an advance intelligence center; the translation and interrogation sections remained in Hawaii. About thirteen JICPOA language officers, but no Nisei, went to Guam.[55] JICPOA attached Nisei to Army and Marine divisions and corps headquarters as needed for specific operations. These Nisei were assigned to "intelligence service organizations," each of which had up to seven officers and twenty enlisted men. By the summer of 1945 JICPOA had organized fifteen such teams.[56]

JICPOA assigned four intelligence service organizations for the assault on Iwo Jima (*Map 13*): one for the V Amphibious Corps and one for each Marine division. These teams included more than fifty Nisei. When the Nisei reported to Pearl Harbor for boarding, sentries stopped them at the gate because they looked Japanese. The Nisei were outraged, and some were angry enough to turn around. However, "cool heads prevailed," recalled M.Sgt. Don C. Oka. "We knew that, so far, we had done everything right in our duty to our country and weren't going to stop there. After some discussion and with the help of some of the Caucasian officers destined for the same ship, we were finally allowed to board. But only because those Caucasian officers escorted us."[57]

Several Nisei, including T5g. Terry Takeshi Doi, landed with the assault waves on 19 February 1945. Before the war, while living in Japan, Doi had been conscripted into the Imperial Japanese Army. He returned to the United States in 1941, only to learn that his American citizenship had been revoked because of his military service in Japan. While a student at MISLS in 1944, he had his citizenship restored so he could be assigned overseas. On Iwo Jima, Doi went "into cave after cave with only a flashlight and knife persuading many enemy soldiers to come out and surrender." He was awarded the Silver Star, and his language officer wrote to the judge who had restored his citizenship:

I know you'll be happy to know that Terry did one of the finest pieces of work possible. Doi was one of the first GIs to land on Iwo Jima. The limits of censorship prohibit details, but I can say Terry is one of the bravest and most capable men I have seen out here—that

---

[55] W. J. Holmes, *Double-Edged Secrets: U.S. Naval Intelligence Operations in the Pacific during World War II* (Annapolis, Md.: Naval Institute Press, 1979), pp. 197–99; Paul F. Boller, Jr., *Memoirs of an Obscure Professor and Other Essays* (Fort Worth: Texas Christian University Press, 1992), pp. 43–44.

[56] ATIS History, p. 29.

[57] Quote from Don C. Oka, MISNorCal Bio; Harrington, *Yankee Samurai*, pp. 279–80; *Saga of the MIS*.

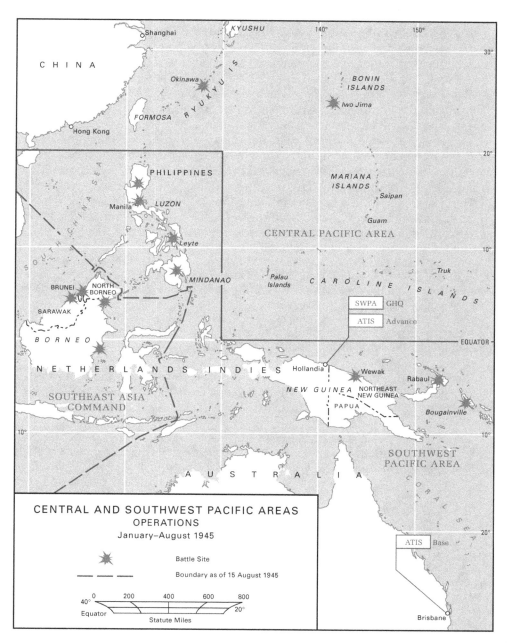

MAP 13

includes Marines as well as Army—and did not hesitate to put his life in great danger whenever it was felt that a useful military purpose would thereby be served.[58]

At least one MIS Nisei, Sgt. Mike Masato Deguchi, was wounded while fighting on Iwo Jima. While serving with the 8th Radio Squadron Mobile, he was seriously injured by a landmine and died soon after the end of the war.[59]

Another Nisei on Iwo Jima, T3g. James Yoshinobu, at forty-seven was one of the oldest serving MIS Nisei. This was his second war: he had served in the U.S. Army during the World War I. After that war he earned a degree in electrical engineering from Northwestern University; but, unable to find suitable employment in California, he operated a truck farm near Los Angeles before being interned in 1942. In December 1943 he brought his wife and five children out of the Rohwer internment camp to resettle in Chicago and then volunteered for language training. He landed with the 4th Marine Division and was also awarded the Silver Star.[60]

Ben I. Yamamoto had been assigned to the Byron Hot Springs interrogation center, but after thirteen months he requested an overseas assignment. He ended up with the 4th Marine Division on Iwo Jima:

I hit the beach on the fourth day and was greeted by a stack of dead Marines and a group of live ones sitting with blank stares. These gyrenes have had it—cracked. They were so gung ho on the transport but two or three nights on the front lines broke them. This was not an encouraging start for me.

We were assigned an area near the air strip, told to dig in and wait for orders. The first night's mortar barrage was a nightmare, some shrapnels landing too close for comfort. Yes, I did regret I didn't somehow stick it out at Byron.[61]

The accomplishments of the JICPOA Nisei were soon common knowledge back in Hawaii. The *Honolulu Star-Bulletin* praised them in an editorial on 1 March:

It hardly need be said that the Japanese Americans who face the enemy Japanese in this great Pacific battle face a special hazard. For them, if taken prisoner, there will be no mercy nor even an easy death. The least they can expect is prolonged torture. For they

---

[58] "Nisei Who Regained U.S. Citizenship Is War Hero," *Pacific Citizen*, 28 Apr 45; WD Press Release, 22 Oct 45.

[59] Oda, *Secret Embedded*, p. 73. Karl G. Yoneda claimed that Deguchi had been a fellow member of the Communist Party. Karl G. Yoneda, *Ganbatte: Sixty-Year Struggle of a Kibei Worker* (Los Angeles, Calif.: Asian American Studies Center, University of California at Los Angeles, 1983), p. 213.

[60] Harrington, *Yankee Samurai*, p. 277; WD Press Release, 22 Oct 45.

[61] Quote from Oguro, *Sempai Gumi*, pp. 70–72; Ben I. Yamamoto, MISNorCal Bio; *Japanese Eyes, American Heart*, pp. 180–82. See also "Henry Yokoyama: Nisei Recalls Historic Iwo Jima Battle," *Hawaii Herald*, 2 Jul 93, p. A–21; Public Media Video, "Return to Iwo Jima," videotaped presentation, 1985.

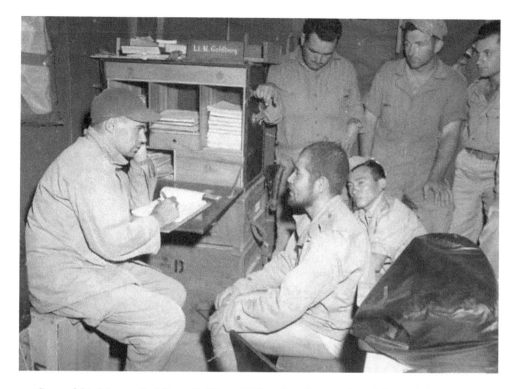

Second Lt. Manny Goldberg (left) *and T.Sgt. Ben Hirano* (third from right, seated)
question a prisoner, Iwo Jima, 25 March 1945.

would be regarded by the fanatical Japanese of the imperial forces, not merely as enemy combatants, but as traitors to Japan.[62]

Navy and Marine language officers from the Boulder School also served on the JICPOA teams. Marine units further relied upon enlisted marines from the Japanese-language courses at Camp Elliott and Camp Pendleton, California. For ship-to-shore radio nets the Marine Corps used Navajo Code Talkers. The Navajo had "Oriental" features like the Nisei, similarly risked being mistaken for the enemy, and were given bodyguards for their protection. A Marine signal officer later wrote, "The entire operation was directed by Navajo code.... Were it not for the Navajos, the marines would never have taken Iwo Jima."[63]

---

[62] Cited in *Pacific Citizen*, 31 Mar 45. See also "Japanese Americans Are Working with Marines in Iwo Jima Fight," *Honolulu Star-Bulletin*, 27 Feb 45.

[63] "Navajo Code Talkers," in *Native America in the Twentieth Century: An Encyclopedia*, ed. Mary B. Davis (New York: Garland, 1994); Bruce Watson, "Navajo Code Talkers: A Few Good

Nisei language team with the marines in the sands of Iwo Jima. Starting second from left: *Ben Kuwahara, George J. Kawamoto, Tamotsu Koyanagi, and two other Nisei.*

The marines declared Iwo Jima secure after twenty-six days, but fighting continued for months as soldiers and marines rooted out the remaining Japanese defenders from tunnels and caves. In April 1945 the 147th Infantry began mop-up operations and over the next two months killed 1,602 and captured 867 Japanese.[64] The Nisei continued to play a key role in this phase. One battalion commander told a reporter: "The Nisei were brought here for office work, and by golly, they've done better in the field than anyone. They're really good, no fooling. They try hard and they're smart—really interested in their jobs."[65]

Men," *Smithsonian* (August 1993): 34–42. Four Nisei may have served with Marine radio intelligence platoons on Iwo Jima and Okinawa for tactical voice intercept operations.

[64] Whitman S. Bartley, *Iwo Jima: Amphibious Epic* (Washington, D.C.: Headquarters, U.S. Marine Corps, 1954), pp. 190–93; George W. Garand and Truman R. Strobridge, *History of U.S. Marine Corps Operations in World War II,* vol. 4, *Western Pacific Operations* (Washington, D.C.: Historical Division, Headquarters, U.S. Marine Corps, 1971), pp. 703–04; Tsukiyama et al., *Secret Valor,* pp. 93–94.

[65] "Nisei Tells Japs in Iwo Caves: Come Out—Or Stay Forever," *Seattle Times,* 23 Apr 45, reprinted as "Nisei Helps Take 120 Iwo Jima Prisoners," *Pacific Citizen,* 28 Apr 45.

The Secretary of the Navy awarded the Navy Unit Commendation to all support units in V Amphibious Corps, including the JICPOA teams.[66] A more meaningful tribute came from Joe Rosenthal, an Associated Press photographer who electrified the country with his picture of the flag-raising on Mount Suribachi. Rosenthal spoke out forcefully against prejudice toward individuals of Japanese ancestry in America and called the recent Hood River incident a "crying shame":

All of those [Nisei] with whom I came into contact are anxious to prove their loyalty to this country. Often their anxiety is touching, for they volunteer for all sorts of dangerous missions.

Many have paid with their lives, and many more have been wounded. They have done an outstanding job for the allied cause and their heroism should be recognized. It has been recognized by the marine commanders where I saw them in action at Guam, Peleliu and Iwo.

Usually they work with headquarters in serving as interpreters. Armed with hand grenades at entrances to Jap pillboxes or caves, they often convince the enemy to surrender where American officers, lacking the proper diction of the Japanese language, would fail.

They work so close to the enemy on these missions that, along with the danger of being killed by Japs, they run the risk of being shot, unintentionally, by our own marines. From a distance it's hard to tell them from the enemy. Their dungarees soon become ragged in rough country and the similarity of their physical appearance makes their job that much tougher.[67]

Okinawa

As the marines fought for Iwo Jima, Nimitz's staff completed planning for Operation ICEBERG, a massive assault on Okinawa, the largest island in the Ryukyus and only 400 miles from Japan proper. (*See Map 14.*) Tenth Army would command the XXIV Corps and III Amphibious Corps, with four Army divisions and three Marine divisions. The campaign would feature the most extensive use of Nisei linguists to date, many of them in military government for the island's civilian population.[68]

---

[66] Bartley, *Iwo Jima*, pp. 242–43.

[67] "Jap-American Bravery Hailed by Camera Man," *Chicago Tribune*, Apr 45; War Relocation Authority (WRA), *Nisei in the War against Japan* (Washington, D.C.: Department of the Interior, 1945), p. 2; "Marine Generals Recognize Work of Nisei GIs in Pacific," *Pacific Citizen*, 14 Apr 45. The quotation is altered in *MISLS Album* (Minneapolis: Military Intelligence Service Language School, 1946), p. 115. Mineo Yamagata, a veteran of Saipan and Tinian, accompanied the 28th Marines to the summit of Suribachi and witnessed the famous flag-raising. Harrington, *Yankee Samurai*, p. 282. See also Ltr, Maj. Gen. Clayton Bissell to Col. Kai E. Rasmussen, 29 May 1945, copy in Richard K. Hayashi Collection, NJAHS.

[68] Arnold G. Fisch, Jr., *Military Government in the Ryukyu Islands, 1945–1950*, U.S. Army in World War II (Washington, D.C.: U.S. Army Center of Military History, 1988), pp. 15–29; Ted T. Tsukiyama, "The Battle of Okinawa Revisited," Unpubl Ms, n.d., author's files. Robert N. Colewell,

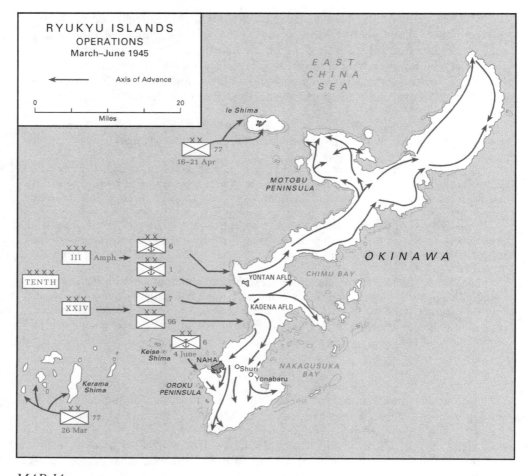

MAP 14

The Okinawan dialect posed special challenges for American forces. At Fort Snelling, MISLS formed a special team of Okinawan Nisei who spoke the Okinawan dialect.[69] On Leyte, the 96th Infantry Division language team included two brothers, Warren T. Higa and Takejiro Higa, born of Okinawan parents in Hawaii. When the boys were ages five and two, respectively, their mother took them to her home village in southern Okinawa, where they grew up and attended

---

"Intelligence and the Okinawa Battle," *Naval War College Review* (March–April 1985): 81–95. Colewell was chief of photo intelligence for Tenth Army.

[69] Interv, author with Thomas Ige, 5 Dec 94; Thomas H. Ige, *Boy from Kahaluu: An Autobiography* (Honolulu: Kin Cho Jin Kai, 1989), pp. 78–80; Okinawa Club of America, *History of the Okinawans in North America* (Los Angeles: Asian American Studies Center and Okinawa Club of America, 1988), pp. 450–51, 460–61.

school. They returned to Hawaii to avoid conscription into the Imperial Japanese Army or forced migration to Manchuria. In 1943 both brothers volunteered and were selected for language training.[70]

Sometime in November 1944 the XXIV Corps G–2 summoned T3g. Takejiro Higa: "The minute I entered the tent my heart nearly stopped beating as I saw hung before me a large blown-up map of the southern half of Okinawa. Chills ran up my spine as I realized the next target would be that part of Okinawa where I had lived for fourteen years and left merely six years before." The photo-interpreter officer showed him an aerial photo of the capital of Naha, but Higa could barely recognize the heavily bombed port. The officer then showed Higa a photograph of the village where Higa's parents had lived. "My hair stood up! For awhile I couldn't even open my mouth, I was so choked up." Higa put his eyes to the viewer and traced his finger over his grandfather's home and his relatives' houses (all still intact, he was relieved to see). The officer questioned him about the suspicious concrete structures that dotted the landscape. These were not fortifications, Higa explained, but traditional Okinawan tombs.[71] "It was a horrible feeling," Higa recalled. "Ever since the first day I saw the picture, every night I used to dream about my relatives. Every night, never miss. . . . I dreamed about my uncle, my cousins, and even my schoolmates."

In January 1945 forty Nisei arrived in Hawaii from Fort Snelling, but Tenth Army needed more than the school could provide. Consequently, U.S. Army Forces Middle Pacific selected about 165 Nisei with Japanese-language skills who been drafted but had not yet begun basic training. In February about seventy-five were formed into the Commander in Chief, Pacific Fleet (CINCPAC), 1st Provisional Military Government Interpreter Detachment, and attached to the assault forces. Once the invasion forces had departed Hawaii for Operation ICEBERG, the Army established the Allied Military Government Language School at Schofield Barracks in March for some 275 Nisei soldiers. In March and April 1945 more Hawaii Nisei were enlisted and rushed through the school. About ninety organized into the 6205th Interpreter Special Detachment flew to Okinawa between

---

[70] Interv, author with Takejiro Higa, 7 Dec 94; *"Aru Okinawa Hawaii Imin no Shinjuwan"* [One Okinawan Immigrant and Pearl Harbor], Unpubl Ms, 1991, author's files; Tsukiyama et al., *Secret Valor*, pp. 101–02; "Takejiro Higa: An Okinawan Caught in the Battle of Okinawa," *Hawaii Herald*, 2 Jul 93, p. A–24; *Japanese Eyes, American Heart*, pp. 291–302; Yuki Kikuchi, "The Pacific War of the Nisei in Hawaii," pp. 114–20, Unpubl English translation of a Japanese book, 1999. "Nisei Meets Father on Okinawa; Sgt. Higashi Received Special Training for Okinawa Invasion," photos in *Pacific Citizen*, 14 Jul 45. *Yaban Gogai*, Aug 45.

[71] See the photographs in Roy E. Appleman et al., *Okinawa: The Last Battle*, U.S. Army in World War II (Washington, D.C.: Department of the Army, Historical Division, 1948), p. 8; Chas. S. Nichol, Jr., and Henry I. Shaw, *Okinawa: Victory in the Pacific* (Washington, D.C.: Historical Branch, Headquarters, U.S. Marine Corps, 1955), p. 54. Both Japanese and American forces used the tombs for military purposes; local civilians used them for protection.

May and July 1945. A similar unit, the 6201st Interpreter Special Detachment, went to Saipan.[72]

The battle for Okinawa was marked by the most extensive psychological warfare yet in the Central Pacific. The Office of War Information borrowed Nisei from the JICPOA annex, together with trustworthy Japanese prisoners of war, to prepare propaganda leaflets. The leaflets were "based on twenty-five carefully developed themes. . . . The texts of the leaflets were reworked and reworded scores of times until the ideas and the language itself were intelligible to the average Japanese soldier." The illustrations "were designed to appeal to the Oriental sense of artistic values."[73] The JICPOA Psychological Warfare Branch printed and disseminated 5.7 million leaflets, including a weekly newspaper that was disseminated in Japan in the final months of the war.

Operation ICEBERG began on 26 March on the Kerama Islands, fifteen miles west of Okinawa, where the 77th Infantry Division with its Nisei team landed on Ie Shima against light opposition. On the third night of the battle, to the horror of the Americans, over 300 civilians killed themselves rather than surrender to the foreign invaders.[74] The 77th Infantry Division reloaded onto its transports and sailed away, grateful that its own casualties had been light.

The fates were not so kind when ten or more kamikazes attacked the convoy on 2 April. One crashed on the bridge of the USS *Henrico*, an assault transport carrying the 305th Infantry headquarters. The regimental commander and executive officer were killed outright. In all, forty-nine soldiers and sailors were dead or missing. Among the dead was a Nisei, T3g. Edwin Yukio Fukui. He had been born and raised in Tacoma, Washington, and was one of the first Nisei to enlist from Tule Lake in November 1942. Ie Shima was his third campaign with the 77th Division.[75]

On Easter Sunday, 1 April 1945, the assault waves came ashore on Okinawa expecting heavy resistance as on Iwo Jima. Instead they were met with an eerie silence. In Hawaii, the Tenth Army kept a forward command post ready to parachute onto the island with a team of airborne-qualified Nisei linguists under Sgt.

[72] Harrington, *Yankee Samurai*, pp. 314–15; U.S. Army Forces Middle Pacific (and Predecessor Commands), "History of G–2 Section, 7 December 1941–2 September 1945," 2 vols., pp. 217–18, Unpubl Ms, copy at U.S. Army Center of Military History; Ted T. Tsukiyama et al., eds., *Secret Valor*, rev. ed. (Honolulu: MIS Veterans Club of Hawaii, 2001), addendum, pp. 102(a)–(j); "Listening to Voices of the Past," *Honolulu Star-Bulletin*, 29 May 00.

[73] Edgar L. Jones, "Fighting with Words: Psychological Warfare in the Pacific," *Atlantic Monthly* (August 1945): 47–51.

[74] Appleman et al., *Okinawa: The Last Battle*, p. 58; Saburo Ienaga, *The Pacific War, 1931–1945* (New York: Pantheon, 1978), p. 185.

[75] Samuel E. Morison, *History of United States Naval Operations in World War II*, 15 vols. (Boston: Little, Brown, 1947–1952), 14: 176–77; Appleman et al., *Okinawa: The Last Battle*, p. 79; Harrington, *Yankee Samurai*, pp. 306–08; Roy Ito, Ltr from the field published in *Yaban Gogai*, Dec 45; "Nisei Gives Life for the U.S.," *Tacoma News Tribune*, 27 May 45; "Report Death of First Nisei GI on Okinawa," *Pacific Citizen*, 2 Jun 45.

Mits Usui. However, because of light opposition, the jump was canceled at H+4.[76] On Okinawa, the Nisei, some with CIC bodyguards, set about doing the tasks they had performed during previous campaigns: translating captured documents and interrogating the few prisoners.[77] On the third day one Nisei saved 250 Okinawans hiding in tombs in a ravine. According to a war correspondent who witnessed the incident, the unidentified Nisei entered a tomb and encountered an Okinawan woman, who lifted his helmet "to make sure he was of Japanese stock, then gasped and put a hand to her forehead in relief." Another Nisei told the correspondent:

[The civilians] are cooperating very well. This morning we had quite a time inducing a crowd to come out of a cave. They said they had been told they would be tortured with needles. Now they seem happy to be safe—from the way they are chipping in to clean up rubbish, wash clothes and make things livable. They are poor peasants for the most part—a pitiful lot who didn't expect kind treatment.[78]

When American soldiers found a detailed topographical map on the body of a dead Japanese artillery forward observer, Nisei worked through the night to translate it. American intelligence agencies had few maps of Okinawa's rugged terrain; aerial reconnaissance had not been possible until shortly before the invasion. The translated map was rushed to Hawaii, where JICPOA printed 12,000 copies for issue to every unit on Okinawa.[79] On 17 April the Tenth Army language team published another important translation, the *Japanese 32d Army* order outlining the basic plan of defense for Okinawa.[80] The Nisei also interrogated prisoners of war, but the Americans took an average of only four Japanese prisoners per day during the first ten weeks. One division G–2 told an observer: "The number of interrogators given to the division is

---

[76] Mits Usui, in *Saga of the MIS.*

[77] "Camp Savage 'Alumni' on Okinawa Boost State," *Minneapolis Star-Journal*, 24 Jul 45, reprinted in Oguro, *Sempai Gumi*, pp. 213–14; Duval A. Edwards, *Spy Catchers of the U.S. Army in the War with Japan* (Gig Harbor, Wash.: Red Apple Publishing, 1994), p. 247.

[78] "Japanese American Soldiers Take Part in Okinawa Invasion," *Pacific Citizen*, 14 Apr 45; "U.S. Army Utilizes Many Nisei Specialists in Okinawa Battles," *Pacific Citizen*, 5 May 45. On the experience of Okinawa's civilians, see Masahide Ota, "Re-examining the History of the Battle of Okinawa," in *Okinawa: Cold War Island*, ed. Chalmers Johnson (Encinitas, Calif.: Japan Policy Research Institute, 1999), pp. 13–37; Ishihara Masaie, "Memories of War and Okinawa," in *Perilous Memories: The Asia-Pacific War(s)*, ed. T. Fujitani et al. (Durham, N.C.: Duke University Press, 2001), pp. 87–106. For a firsthand description by an American doctor who was born in Japan and spoke Japanese, see Henry S. Bennett, "The Impact of Invasion and Occupation on the Civilians of Okinawa," *United States Naval Institute Proceedings* (February 1946): 263–75.

[79] Ichinokuchi, *John Aiso and the M.I.S.*, p. 79. On inadequate Allied maps, see Appleman et al., *Okinawa: The Last Battle*, p. 14; Nichols and Shaw, *Okinawa: Victory in the Pacific*, pp. 19–21; and Benis M. Frank and Henry I. Shaw, Jr., *History of U.S. Marine Corps Operations in World War II*, vol. 5, *Victory and Occupation* (Washington, D.C.: Headquarters, U.S. Marine Corps, 1968), pp. 78–79.

[80] Headquarters, U.S. Army Forces Pacific Ocean Areas, Observers Rpt: The Okinawa Operation, 15 Jun 45, p. 18, Combined Arms Research Library, Fort Leavenworth, Kans.; Appleman et al., *Okinawa: The Last Battle*, p. 92; Ichinokuchi, *John Aiso and the M.I.S.*, p. 79.

T.Sgt. Hiroshi "Bud" Mukaye (left) *and S.Sgt. Ralph Minoru Saito* (center), *7th Infantry Division, question a Japanese sailor, Okinawa, 17 June 1945.*

hopelessly inadequate. Each battalion commanding officer needs one. The G–2 stated that a thousand instances could be cited where lives could have been saved if prisoners could have been interrogated right at battalion." [81]

After the initial landings, the XXIV Corps wheeled right to face the main Japanese defenses on the south end of the island. Soon the Americans found themselves stalled in brutal World War I–style fighting. Heavy rains turned the soil into a quagmire, and the soldiers faced the most intense Japanese artillery concentrations they had ever seen. On the evening of 18 April the corps language team received a captured Japanese forward observer's chart that showed all Japanese artillery and heavy mortar positions in their sector. Knowing that an American attack was set for the next morning, Lt. Benjamin Hazard and his Nisei worked straight through the night to translate the chart. They finished two hours before the

---

[81] Rpt, Army War College, sub: Report on the Okinawa Operation, 1 May 45, Trng Grp, Ofc of the Dir of Intel G–2, RG 165, National Archives and Records Administration (NARA).

attack, and Hazard delivered the translation to the corps assistant G–2. However, the attack went on as scheduled with three American divisions—the 7th, 27th, and 96th Infantry Divisions—attacking on line. The result was disastrous; at no point did the Americans break through. The corps lost 720 dead, wounded, and missing in a single day. When the corps commander found out about the captured map, he was furious and told Hazard that had he known about the map he would have called off the attack.[82]

Not all casualties came from enemy fire. One day two Nisei with the 7th Infantry Division were cleaning their carbines when one accidentally discharged and grazed Toshimi Yamada. When he limped to the aid tent for treatment, he requested a Purple Heart. When the surgeon told him that the wound had to result from Japanese action, Yamada responded, "Well, what the hell do *you* call the guy?" The surgeon still refused, saying it had to be caused by an *enemy* Japanese. "Well, he's sure as heck my enemy *now!*" Yamada did not have long to wait for his Purple Heart: a few days later he was wounded while flushing Japanese soldiers out of a cave.[83]

On 16 April the 77th Infantry Division seized Ie Shima, an island near Okinawa. Sgt. Vic Nishijima with the division language team saw "an elderly private" walking toward a minefield on the first or second day and "bawled him out." Only later did he learn that this was the famous war correspondent Ernie Pyle. On 18 April Pyle was killed by a Japanese machine gun.[84] Three days later Tenth Army declared Ie Shima secure and the Nisei stepped up their efforts to persuade isolated groups of Japanese soldiers and civilians to surrender. At one point Nishijima coaxed 150 civilians from a single cave. In the early morning light of 23 April T4g. Mitsuo "Mits" Shibata saw another group of civilians approach American lines. He jumped up, waved his arms, and shouted to them. In an instant he fell mortally wounded, probably killed by a fellow American soldier who mistook him for Japanese. Shibata, a veteran of the Aleutians and the South Pacific, was the second member of the division's language team to die in three weeks.[85] Teammate T.Sgt. Shigeo Ito wrote to his friends in the language school: "After losing two of our buddies, the team almost went to pieces. It certainly was hard to

---

    [82] Appleman et al., *Okinawa: The Last Battle*, pp. 184–207; Falk and Tsuneishi, *MIS in the War against Japan*, pp. 54–57; Harrington, *Yankee Samurai*, p. 335.

    [83] Harrington, *Yankee Samurai*, pp. 309–10. Two Marine Corps enlisted linguists were killed on Okinawa. Ltr, Calvin Dunbar to author, 11 July 1999, author's files.

    [84] "Private 'Bawled Out' by Nisei Sergeant Was Ernie Pyle," *Pacific Citizen*, 21 Jul 45; Harrington, *Yankee Samurai*, pp. 323–24.

    [85] Harrington, *Yankee Samurai*, p. 325. By a later account, Shibata was "shot in error by a BAR-wielding GI as he sought to rescue some civilians." "America's Superb Secret Human Weapon in World War II," Brochure, Presidio of San Francisco Army Museum, 1 Nov 81; see also Ichinokuchi, *John Aiso and the M.I.S.*, p. 81. A visiting newspaper publisher heard that two Nisei had been killed by American troops while taking prisoners. "Noted U.S. Publisher Says Japanese Americans Faced Double Hazard in Pacific," *Pacific Citizen*, 15 Sep 45, p. 2. He was probably referring to Fukui and Shibata, only one of whom was killed by friendly fire. See also Michael Sakamoto, interview notes by Joseph Harrington, NJAHS.

take. We finally pulled ourselves together and I believe the eight of us did the work of 11 men. Yes, we felt that spiritually the two of the boys are still with us, and so we decided to finish our mission without any additional aid."[86]

Most language teams on Okinawa were led by Caucasian Army or Navy lieutenants. One Boulder graduate, Marine 1st Lt. Spencer V. Silverthorne, earned the Silver Star on 13 June by persuading fifty-six Japanese to surrender.[87] Tensions between the Nisei and their Caucasian officers were common. The Army language officers had trained alongside the Nisei, but the Navy officers often had no contact with the Nisei until assigned to a team. The JICPOA final report later commented, "It frequently happened that the two types of language personnel were in competition, or openly working against each other, largely as a result of misunderstandings which could easily have been avoided."[88]

Some Navy officers earned the respect of the Nisei. During the fighting Lt. Donald Keene, U.S. Navy Reserve, took over the 96th Infantry Division language team. It was, he later admitted, "the first time in my life [I had] a group of men in my command." Before the war Keene had studied at Columbia University and had a gift for the Japanese and Chinese languages. When he took over the team, "at first I was obliged to demonstrate (as usual) that I really could read and speak Japanese, but it did not take long to become friends."[89] One Nisei on the XXIV Corps team, T.Sgt. Warren Tsuneishi, had been a student at the University of California before the war and was of a similar scholarly bent. Tsuneishi and Keene developed mutual respect and enjoyed long conversations about the nature of loyalty, especially for the Kibei. Tsuneishi explained to the Caucasian officer "what it meant to be an American fighting in the Army against the country of my parents."[90]

Organized Japanese resistance finally collapsed in June, and the surviving Japanese soldiers began to surrender in large numbers. On 20 June the Americans took a record 977 prisoners. At one point Tatsuo Elmer Yamamoto went into a cave and persuaded 350 Japanese to surrender. In July 2d Lt. Wallace S. Amioka led a combat patrol into a remote area to locate a Japanese colonel and his staff; when

---

[86] *Yaban Gogai*, Dec 45.

[87] *History of the Sixth Marine Division* (Washington, D.C.: Infantry Journal Press, 1948), pp. 157, 189; Roger V. Dingman, "Language at War: U.S. Marine Corps Japanese Language Officers in the Pacific War," *Journal of Military History* 68 (July 2004): 875–81.

[88] Joint Intelligence Center, Pacific Ocean Areas, "Report of Intelligence Activities in the Pacific Ocean Areas," 15 Oct 45, p. 45 (hereafter cited as JICPOA History), copy in author's files. Warren Higa felt the navy language officers compared favorably to the Army's Michigan graduates. Harrington, *Yankee Samurai*, p. 328.

[89] Donald Keene, *On Familiar Terms: A Journey across Cultures* (New York: Kodansha, 1994), pp. 49–50.

[90] Warren Tsuneishi, Ltr to the Editor, *New York Times*, 14 Mar 94; Interv, author with Warren Tsuneishi, 22 Aug 95; Harrington, *Yankee Samurai*, p. 341. Another Navy language officer on Okinawa was Kenneth Lamott, who had been born in Japan. After the war he became a writer and editor. His first novel portrayed the relationship between a Caucasian language officer and a Nisei sergeant in a prisoner of war camp on Okinawa. Kenneth Lamott, *The Stockade* (Boston: Little, Brown, 1952).

Nishijima (right) *and a captured Japanese soldier* (left) *used to make surrender appeals, Aka Shima*

the colonel was discovered, he tried to escape and was shot by the patrol members. Soon more than 7,000 Japanese soldiers were in American hands and Tenth Army had to establish large holding compounds for the prisoners alongside camps for the dislocated civilians. On Saipan and Guam, similar mopping-up efforts continued for many months.[91]

The rising surrender rate was in part due to tactical psychological warfare developed by the Office of War Information with the Nisei and trusted Japanese prisoners. This proved to one observer that "Japanese troops can be reached by propaganda weapons as well as bullets and flamethrowers." Without such weapons,

---

[91] Harrington, *Yankee Samurai*, pp. 310–11, 343–45; Shelly Mydans, "Guam Holdouts Give Up," *Life* (9 July 1945): 67–70; "Tinian Experiment," Yank (3 August 1945): 10–11; Gordon Cotler, "Kobayashi," *New Yorker* (26 August 1950): 54–57; Gordon Cotler, "A Sort of Detective Story," *New Yorker* (9 February 1952): 88–93.

Amioka (in front with helmet), *guided by a Japanese prisoner, leads an American patrol to the hiding place of a senior Japanese commander, Okinawa, 10 July 1945.*

he concluded, Americans must "be prepared to continue the Pacific war until the majority of the vast numbers of remaining Japanese troops have been killed."[92]

These mopping-up operations could be as dangerous as active combat. T4g. Thomas H. Ige was wounded by a landmine while attached to an African American antiaircraft battalion on the Kerama Islands. The Hawaii-born Ige had been a graduate student in economics at the University of Wisconsin before the war. He volunteered for language training and joined the Okinawan-speaking team. While on the Kerama Islands, he "made it a point to mingle freely with both sides [African American and Caucasian], eating my meals with each group on an alternating basis."[93] On 27 July he accompanied a patrol led by an African American lieutenant to look for more Japanese and was severely wounded when the point man stepped on a landmine. Ige's bodyguard, an African American from

[92] "Jap Surrenders Are Increasing—Psychological Warfare Proves Effective," *Life* (9 July 1945); quote from Jones, "Fighting with Words"; Stanley Sandler, *Cease Resistance, It's Good for You: A History of U.S. Army Combat Psychological Operations* (Fort Bragg, N.C.: U.S. Army Special Operations Command, 1996), pp. 210–18; JICPOA History, p. 31.

[93] Ige, *Boy from Kahaluu*, p. 85.

Schenectady, New York, wrote Ige's wife in Minneapolis to tell her that her husband had been wounded.[94]

On Okinawa, the American troops encountered an unprecedented humanitarian crisis. At one point during the fighting on Okinawa, the 96th Infantry Division team rounded up 1,500 civilians in a single surrender. (On Saipan, by comparison, only a few thousand Japanese civilians had been taken.)[95] Tenth Army had plans for humanitarian assistance and military government, but these plans were quickly overwhelmed. Many civilians, injured, ill, exhausted, and terrified, fled their homes. Between one-tenth and one-fourth of all civilians died. By the end of the fighting the military government was responsible for the care and feeding of 200,000 civilians. The Island Command started with seventy-five Japanese linguists and within weeks received another ninety-five. The Counter Intelligence Corps faced an equally severe shortage and in some cases used Okinawans who spoke some English.[96]

Lieutenant Amioka's Okinawan-speaking team arrived toward the end of April; Army and Navy authorities in Hawaii continued to search for other Nisei who spoke Japanese, even recruiting from among discharged or convalescing veterans of the 100th Infantry Battalion. Among these was Pfc. Thomas Taro Higa, an original member of the battalion. He had been born in Hawaii to Okinawan parents who sent him to their home village to be raised by his grandparents. He returned, was drafted, and ended up in the 100th Infantry Battalion. When MISLS recruiters visited the battalion in 1942, Higa was not among those selected for language training: "I think that most of us did not respond to the recruitment because we felt a certain mental agony in engaging in interpreting activities against Japan, our grandfather's country, even for the sake of assisting the country of our birth. . . . Many Nisei felt less mental agony in going to the European front and fighting against the Germans."[97]

Higa fought the Germans in Italy and was wounded at Cassino in January 1944. He returned to the United States for treatment. Upon recovery he toured the United States for the War Relocation Authority to tell the American public about the Nisei fighting in Europe.[98] When the battle for Okinawa began, he helped

---

[94] Ibid., pp. 87–88. Many years later, while serving as administrative assistant to Senator Daniel K. Inouye, Ige stood on the Lincoln Memorial as Rev. Martin Luther King, Jr., delivered his famous "I Have a Dream" speech in 1963. Ige, *Boy from Kahaluu*, pp. 153–55.

[95] *Yaban Gogai*, Aug 45.

[96] Fisch, *Military Government in the Ryukyu Islands*, pp. 45–60; Appleman et al., *Okinawa: The Last Battle*, pp. 415–19; Edwards, *Spy Catchers*, p. 243. The refugees included numerous Taiwanese and Korean laborers, as well as a number of Korean comfort women. Ige, *Boy from Kahaluu*, pp. 82–83.

[97] "Pfc. Higa Reports Okinawa Civilians Get Kind Treatment from U.S. Military Government," *Pacific Citizen*, 28 Jul 45; quote from Thomas Taro Higa, *Memoirs of a Certain Nisei (Aru Nisei No Wadachi), 1916–1985* (Kaneohe, Hawaii: Higa Publications, 1988), p. 160.

[98] "Nationwide Speaking Tour Outlined for 100th Veteran: Pfc. Higa Tells Issei of Conditions Faced by Japanese Americans," and Saburo Kido, "Timely Topics," *Pacific Citizen*, 9 Sep 44. On the War Relocation Authority's 1944–1945 public relations campaign, see Thomas D. Murphy,

organize a relief campaign in Hawaii for the Okinawan civilians. The Hawaiian Department G–2, Col. Kendall J. Fielder, personally asked Higa to go to Okinawa. Higa agreed and arrived on 25 April to join other Nisei in coaxing Okinawan civilians out of hiding. He went into caves twelve different times, he recalled, and was successful all but once. Even so, his main effort continued to be organizing civilian relief efforts.[99]

Okinawan-speaking Nisei became adept at spotting Japanese deserters among the refugees. Recalled one Nisei:

The ability of most of our team members to speak the Okinawan dialect proved most helpful in interrogation of Japanese prisoners. This was especially valuable and effective in separating out the Japanese soldiers masquerading as Okinawan civilians. A few basic questions to them in the Okinawan dialect immediately unmasked their disguise. Very few Japanese soldiers could understand, much less speak, the dialect. They would be embarrassed when unmasked and, thereafter, would be in a more cooperative mood.[100]

In June the *Japanese 32d Army*'s senior operations officer was identified while trying to pass himself off as a civilian refugee. Captured by the 96th Infantry Division and questioned by George Inagaki, he revealed that the *32d Army* chief of staff had ordered several key staff officers to infiltrate the refugees and attempt to return to Japan to report on the battle to the Imperial General Headquarters.[101]

The war was bringing the Nisei closer to their parents' homes: several found family members on Okinawa. T4g. Seiyu Higashi had been born in California but raised on Okinawa. Upon graduation from middle school in 1937, he had returned to Los Angeles and had not seen his father since. They were reunited in Naha on 21 June, and the cheerful photograph appeared in newspapers across the United States.[102] Even Ernie Pyle reported that he had met a farmer who had lived in Hawaii for a time and whose Nisei son was serving in the U.S. Army.[103] Takejiro Higa met his 7th/8th grade teacher soon after coming ashore with the 96th Infantry Division. "Neither of us could say much in that very emotional encounter," he

---

Ambassadors in Arms (Honolulu: University of Hawaii Press, 1954), pp. 274–79. Another wounded Nisei veteran who served as a spokesman for the WRA in the autumn of 1944 was Capt. Spark M. Matsunaga, who later became a U.S. senator from Hawaii.

[99] Another recuperating 100th Infantry Battalion veteran, Walter Kajiwara, was sent to Saipan to help round up Japanese stragglers. Harrington, *Yankee Samurai*, pp. 313–14.

[100] Ige, *Boy from Kahaluu*, pp. 80–81; Edwards, *Spy Catchers*, p. 249.

[101] Harrington, *Yankee Samurai*, p. 341; Thomas M. Huber, *Japan's Battle of Okinawa, April–June 1945* (Fort Leavenworth, Kans.: Combat Studies Institute, 1990), p. 114. The interrogation report of *Col. Hiromichi Yahara* proved helpful to the writing of the U.S. Army's official history of the battle; he later published his own account. Hiromichi Yahara, *Okinawa Kessen* [Battle of Okinawa] (Tokyo: Yomiuri shimbunsha, 1972).

[102] "Nisei GI Finds Dad on Okinawa," *Minneapolis Morning Tribune*, 6 Jul 45, reprinted in Oguro, *Sempai Gumi*, p. 215; "Sgt. Higashi Received Special Training for Okinawa Invasion," *Pacific Citizen*, 14 Jul 45. Jiro Arakaki also found his father. "Jiro Arakaki: Okinawa," *Hawaii Herald*, 2 Jul 93, p. A–30; Jiro Arakaki, MISNorCal Bio.

[103] Ernie Pyle, *Ernie's War* (New York: Random House, 1986), p. 409.

Higashi reunited with his father, Okinawa, 21 June 1945

recalled. A few weeks later he met two classmates who did not recognize him wearing an American uniform. Without disclosing his identity, he questioned them closely and surprised them with his detailed knowledge of their village and school. Finally he asked them if they remembered a classmate named Takejiro Higa. They admitted they did but said that he had returned to Hawaii before the war. Higa "looked them straight in the face" and shouted in their dialect: "Goddammit, don't you recognize your own classmate?" The two Okinawans burst into tears and stammered, "Now, knowing that our own classmate is on the other side, we believe our lives will be saved." Higa recalled that "the three of us grabbed each other's shoulders and had a cry."[104]

---

[104] Interv, author with Higa, 7 Dec 94; *"Aru Okinawa Hawaii Imin no Shinjuwan"*; "Unforgettable Encounters: Battle of Okinawa," in Tsukiyama et al., *Secret Valor* (1993 ed.), pp. 101–02;

Another first was the discovery of significant numbers of American Nisei on Okinawa. This forced the U.S. government and Japanese American community leaders to confront the uncomfortable issue of how to handle American citizens of Japanese ancestry who had remained in Japan and Japanese-controlled areas during the war. In June 1945 the Japanese American Citizens League (JACL) ran the first editorials and commentaries on the question in the *Pacific Citizen*. Ironically, before the landings the Japanese government had also been suspicious of the American Nisei among the Okinawan population and had spread rumors of spy activities, including allegations that the Americans may have infiltrated Nisei into Okinawa by submarine before the landings.[105]

The War Department sent one unusual Nisei to assist with military government. Before the war Masaji Marumoto had graduated from Harvard Law School and had practiced law in Honolulu. After Pearl Harbor he had served as liaison between military government and law enforcement in Hawaii and the local Japanese community. He had enlisted in 1943 and in May 1945 was commissioned into the Judge Advocate General's Corps. He arrived on Okinawa on 25 June. For five weeks he crisscrossed the island in a jeep "to locate and interview civilians with leadership background, who were willing to participate" in an American-sponsored assembly of prominent Okinawans. His list of local leaders was accepted by the American authorities; the Provisional Advisory Assembly held its first meeting in Ishikawa on 15 August as Okinawa's first step toward self-government after three generations of Japanese rule.[106]

On 18 June, as the American victory was almost complete, a Japanese shell killed the Tenth Army commander, Lt. Gen. Simon B. Buckner. However, organized Japanese resistance soon ended and Buckner was replaced by General Joseph W. Stilwell. Stilwell was well acquainted with Nisei soldiers, having commanded them before the war in the 7th Infantry Division and again in the China-Burma-India Theater. The situation of the Nisei soldiers was on his mind even on Okinawa. On a visit to the 27th Infantry Division he congratulated Sgt. Hoichi Kubo on his Distinguished Service Cross and told him that "the boys of Merrill's Marauders send their regards." One day Sgt. Nobuo Dick Kishiue, also with the 27th Infantry Division, was setting up a prisoner of war collecting point at a crossroad. A jeep pulled up and out climbed Stilwell, who struck up a conversation with the Nisei. Kishiue recalled that the general "fully understood the work that we were trying

"Takejiro Higa: An Okinawan Caught in the Battle of Okinawa," *Hawaii Herald*, 2 Jul 93, p. A–24; *Japanese Eyes, American Heart*, pp. 291–302; Kikuchi, "The Pacific War of the Nisei in Hawaii," pp. 114–20.

[105] For example, see Bill Hosokawa's column in *Pacific Citizen*, 23 Jun 45; Larry Tajiri, "Nisei USA," *Pacific Citizen*, 14 Jul 45. For rumors of infiltration by submarine, see Ota, "Re-examining the History of the Battle of Okinawa." I have seen no evidence that Nisei in fact were infiltrated.

[106] Masaji Marumoto, "Okinawa Revisited: A Look at Past, Future," *Honolulu Sunday Star-Bulletin and Advertiser*, 14 Feb 71; Fisch, *Military Government in the Ryukyu Islands*, p. 105; Coffman, *Island Edge of America*, pp. 61–66; Tsukiyama, "Battle of Okinawa Revisited," pp. 41–42.

to do." [107] Later that autumn Stilwell expressed his sense of outrage at the treatment of persons of Japanese ancestry in California. Speaking to a correspondent with the G.I. newspaper, *C.B.I. Roundup*, he declared with characteristic bluntness:

> You're damned right, those Nisei boys have got a place in the American heart—now and forever.... I say we soldiers ought to form a pick-axe club to protect the Japanese-Americans who fought with us in this war. Yes sir, a pick-axe club. Any time we see any bar-fly commando picking on any of these kids or in any way discriminating against them, we ought to bang them over the head with a pick-axe, and I'm willing to be the charter member of such a club....
>
> We cannot allow a single injustice to be done these Nisei without defeating the very purposes for which we fought this whole war.... These Nisei have bought an awful big chunk of America with their own blood. [108]

Army Air Forces

The Army Air Forces had more than 200 MIS Nisei assigned in the Pacific by 1945. However, the most famous Nisei with the Army Air Forces was not in the MIS. Shortly after Pearl Harbor, Nebraska-born T.Sgt. Ben Kuroki had enlisted and flew thirty missions in Europe as a gunner, including the costly Ploesti Raid on 1 August 1943. [109] In 1944 he returned to the United States to a hero's welcome and toured the country on behalf of the War Relocation Authority and the Japanese American Citizens League to publicize Nisei contributions to the war effort. Early in 1945 he was reassigned to the Pacific, where he flew twenty-seven missions against Japan as a B–29 turret gunner with the 313th Bombardment Wing. For these later missions the Army Air Forces awarded him a second Oak Leaf Cluster for his Distinguished Flying Cross. [110]

---

[107] Hoichi Kubo, "Military Biography," p. 14, Unpubl Ms, 1996, copy in author's files; Nobuo Dick Kishiue, in Falk and Tsuneishi, *MIS in the War against Japan*, p. 52; Nobuo Dick Kishiue, MISNorCal Bio.

[108] *CBI Roundup* (11 October 1945); paraphrased in *Pacific Citizen*, 8 Dec 45; Bill Hosokawa, *Nisei: The Quiet Americans* (New York: William Morrow, 1969), pp. 414. Stilwell returned to the United States and, from his new position as Sixth Army commander, continued his campaign for justice for the Nisei. On 8 December 1945, he presented the posthumous Distinguished Service Cross to the sister of a Nisei soldier who had served with the 442d RCT. The Santa Ana, California, ceremony was attended by several Hollywood personalities including Ronald Reagan, who as President of the United States signed the Civil Liberties Act of 1988 granting redress to Japanese Americans who were affected by wartime relocation and internment.

[109] Another Nisei, Sgt. Rodney Higashi, served as chief engineer and gunner with a B–24 squadron that was sent to the Fifth Air Force in early 1944. "Japanese American Gunner Flies 150 Combat Missions against Japanese in Pacific," *Pacific Citizen*, 26 May 45. The Air Corps enlisted a few other Nisei before Pearl Harbor.

[110] Ralph G. Martin, *Boy from Nebraska: The Story of Ben Kuroki* (New York: Harper & Brothers, 1946); "Sgt. Ben Kuroki Reported in Action on Pacific Front," *Pacific Citizen*, 17 Mar 45; "Sgt. Ben Kuroki Completes 27 Combat Missions in Superfort over Japanese Territory," *Pacific Citizen*, 11 Aug 45; "Sgt. Ben Kuroki Awarded DFC [Distinguished Flying Cross] at B–29 Base," *Pacific Citizen*, 13 Oct 45; Arthur A. Hansen, "Sergeant Ben Kuroki's Perilous 'Home Mission':

Unlike Kuroki, Nisei in the MIS serving with the Army Air Forces were kept
out of the public eye. By January 1945 about 265 Nisei had been assigned to air
intelligence functions. Dozens served on technical intelligence teams with Fifth,
Seventh, Tenth, Thirteenth, and Twentieth Air Forces, specializing in gathering
information from downed Japanese aircraft and captured aviation equipment. The
Technical Air Intelligence Unit–Southwest Pacific Area language team was led by
Lt. Ernest J. Silver, the only Air Corps officer to graduate from MISLS. One of the
Nisei on his team, Robert K. Fukuda, had taken preflight training at the University
of Hawaii in 1940–1941 but was not allowed to take flying lessons at that time,
he believed because of secret restrictions that prohibited Americans of Japanese
ancestry from such training.[111]

Perhaps a hundred others were assigned to the 1st, 6th, 7th, and 8th RSMs in
the Philippines, India-Burma, and the Marianas. These special units listened to
Japanese air-to-ground radio communications. Beginning in 1944 each squadron
was assigned about twenty-five Nisei. Sgt. Ted T. Tsukiyama, who served in India-
Burma with the 6th RSM, described his duties:

We intercepted Japanese air force air-ground radio communications between fighter
planes and tower at Japanese airfields in Northern Burma. Nisei on three-man radio intercept teams (four hours on, eight hours off, around the clock) monitored Japanese air traffic at six airfields. We recorded all Japanese air-ground radio traffic on old-fashioned
recorder rolls, translated, and sent them in to air force G–2 to analyze the Japanese flight
activity, number and types of aircraft, as well as message content. Fighter pilots utilized
code names. . . . The towers maintained their own identity, and all conversation was in
uncoded voice. The Japanese had no idea they were being monitored![112]

The duty was tedious. If the Japanese were not active in a certain area or the
radio reception was poor, there was little for the Nisei to do. One Nisei in the
Philippines with the 7th RSM complained in August 1945: "The majority of us are
corporals with no hope of a raise, as long as we're in this squadron. . . . [A] transfer
to the ground force G–2 is virtually nil, and frankly in my opinion I think we're
'screwed.' " Another Nisei wrote to express his agreement:

He did a good job of explaining our plight. Our life has been mixed with disgust, regret,
disillusionment, excitement, fun and sorrow. We couldn't do any good in the 1st Radio
Squadron, yet we were refused transfers. Seven fellows "piloted" two 1/2-ton trucks

Contested Loyalty and Patriotism in the Japanese American Detention Centers," in *Remembering
Heart Mountain: Essays on Japanese American Internment in Wyoming*, ed. Mike Mackey (Powell,
Wyo.: Western History Publications, 1998), pp. 153–75.

[111] Michael J. Freeman, "Behind Enemy Lines," *Airpower* (July 1994): 10–23, 44–55; Fukuda,
private communication to author, 5 Sep 01.

[112] Tsukiyama et al., *Secret Valor* (1993 ed.), pp. 72–73. On Okinawa, Navy language officers
performed similar radio monitoring duties to warn of kamikaze attacks: Holmes, *Double-Edged
Secrets*, pp. 207–08.

while seven others were night watchmen on transport planes. Promotions too, have been lacking for us.

A few weeks later the first writer replied:

[Enemy radio activity] was at minimum and ... reception, was very poor due to our position and more often than not the voice came in very weak and garbled plus the intense artificial and manmade interference that we had to contend with. As a result of these factors, the voice section was soon relegated to minor import—and not thru the fault of the Niseis. ... It is now a good year and half since I have had anything to do with the language and bitterly feel that for all practical purposes we may as well never have attended the school.[113]

Even tedious assignments could be dangerous on occasion. Yukio Tamura was shot through the lung by a Japanese sniper while serving on Palawan Island with the 7th RSM.[114] When Twentieth Air Force B–29s began attacking Japanese cities, MIS Nisei flew along to protect the aircraft from Japanese air defense networks by monitoring Japanese radio circuits.[115] In the spring of 1944, XX Bomber Command had begun using Nisei on missions against targets in Southeast Asia and Formosa. Sergeant Komoto, who had been wounded in New Georgia in 1943, and Sgt. Masaharu Okinaka were awarded the Air Medal, although the press release identified them only as radio operators. Other Nisei flew with the XXI Bomber Command in the Marianas and were awarded Bronze Stars for combat missions.[116]

In December 1944 the 8th RSM arrived in Guam with about fifty Nisei to support the strategic bombardment of Japan. They became part of RAGFOR, the Army-Navy Radio Analysis Group (Forward). At first, B–29s simply recorded Japanese radio transmissions during the bombing raids, then after each mission the Nisei would listen to and translate the tapes. In the spring of 1945 ten Nisei began to fly along with B–24 "ferret" missions to monitor communications in real time. The RAGFOR officer in charge later praised these Nisei: "Jap voice for air-ground communications was close to a virgin field, and one which the 8th RSM was almost alone endeavoring to exploit. Records and transcripts of voice activity

---

[113] Ken Sekiguchi, Ltr from the field published in in *Yaban Gogai*, Aug 45, p. 7; Kaz Oshiki, Ltr from the field published in *Yaban Gogai*, Sep–Oct 45, p. 9; Ltr, Ken Sekiguchi to Yutaka Munakata, 9 September 1945, Harrington Papers. An edited version of Sekiguchi's letter was reprinted in *Yaban Gogai*, Sep–Oct 45, p. 6.

[114] Harrington, *Yankee Samurai*, p. 283; Interv, Dawn E. Duensing with James Sasami Okada, in *Americanism: A Matter of Mind and Heart*, vol. 1, *The Military Intelligence Service* (Maui, Hawaii: Maui's Sons and Daughters of the Nisei Veterans, 2001); Ibid., pp. 143–44, 150–51.

[115] John F. Kreis, ed., *Piercing the Fog: Intelligence and Army Air Forces Operations in World War II* (Washington, D.C.: Air Force History and Museums Program, 1996), pp. 297–347; Kenneth P. Werrell, *Blankets of Fire: U.S. Bombers over Japan during World War II* (Washington, D.C.: Smithsonian Institution Press, 1996), pp. 190–92.

[116] *Pacific Citizen*, 16, 23 Jun 45; Tsukiyama et al., *Secret Valor* (1993 ed.), p. 91.

during B–29 missions were provided by the XXI Bomber Command. Nisei operators were continually provided for ferret missions."[117]

B–29s dropped propaganda leaflets as well as bombs. By early 1945 Guam-
based JICPOA language officers used prisoners of war to develop warning leaflets
for the XXI Bomber Command.[118] In July 1945 the Psychological Warfare Branch
in Hawaii began a "city" leaflet campaign. Each leaflet announced: "These leaflets are being dropped to notify you that your city has been listed for destruction
by our powerful air force."[119]

Sgt. John Okada from Seattle served with the 8th RSM. He later recalled how
he would sit "smoking in the belly of a B–24 on his way back to Guam from a
reconnaissance flight to Japan. His job was to listen through his earphones, which
were attached to a high-frequency set, and jot down air-ground messages spoken
by Japanese-Japanese in Japanese planes and in Japanese radio shacks." On one
such flight he talked with a Caucasian lieutenant who was shocked to learn that
Okada's family was interned. "Hell's bells," said the lieutenant, "if they'd done
that to me, I wouldn't be sitting in the belly of a broken-down B–24 going back to
Guam from a reconnaissance mission to Japan." Okada replied, "I got reasons."
"They could kiss my ass," exclaimed the lieutenant. "I got reasons," was all Okada
replied. For most MIS Nisei, their reasons, though sometimes difficult to explain,
were never far from their minds.[120]

Preparing for Operation OLYMPIC

By mid-summer 1945 organized Japanese resistance had ended on Okinawa
and in the Philippines. Japan's Navy lay on the bottom of the sea; her cities lay in
ruins. America was gathering its strength for the invasion of the Japanese home
islands beginning in early November. Operation OLYMPIC, the invasion of the
southern island of Kyushu, would involve more troops, ships, and aircraft than the
Normandy invasion. MacArthur's plans called for Sixth Army to command three
Army corps and one Marine amphibious corps with thirteen divisions. Meanwhile,
a million troops would redeploy from Europe to the Pacific. In early August Lt.
Gen. Courtney H. Hodges secretly arrived in Manila with an advance party from
First Army to prepare for Operation CORONET, the follow-on landing on the Kanto
Plain set for the spring of 1946.

The War Department G–2 was already deeply involved in planning the utilization of Japanese linguists for the coming invasion. As early as 28 December

---

[117] "Report of Mission to Pacific Ocean Areas RAGFOR and Associated Activities at Guam, 27
March 1945," Special Research History 133 (SRH–133); Memo, Lt. Cmdr. Robert B. Seaks, OIC,
RAGFOR, n.d., sub: Performance of 8th Radio Squadron Mobile, reproduced in "The Story Behind
the Flying Eight Ball [8th RSM]," p. 40, Unpubl Ms, [1945?], author's files; Tsukiyama et al., *Secret
Valor* (1993 ed.), p. 83.

[118] Boller, *Memoirs of an Obscure Professor*, pp. 44–49.

[119] Sandler, *Cease Resistance*, pp. 220–21.

[120] John Okada, *No-No Boy* (Rutherford, Vt.: Tuttle, 1957), p. xi.

1944, Army and Navy intelligence chiefs had convened the Washington Document Conference to deal with the flood of captured Japanese documents pouring in from Pacific battlefields. All Pacific Theater intelligence staffs were represented along with the British War Office and the Australian and Canadian Armies. The conference called for the United States to establish a joint Army-Navy center to receive and allocate incoming documents, "after theatre exploitation." The new organization, named the Washington Document Center, commenced operations in February.[121]

The conference further recommended that one headquarters control all language personnel in the Pacific. In April 1945 the Joint Chiefs of Staff reorganized the Pacific commands, making MacArthur commander of all ground forces and Nimitz commander of all naval forces. In response to this realignment the War Department G–2 gave MacArthur's command, redesignated as U.S. Army Forces in the Pacific, authority to review and coordinate all requests for Army Japanese linguists. For the invasion of Japan ATIS gained authority over all MIS Nisei for the first time, including those formerly assigned to JICPOA and those arriving from language training.[122] Colonel Mashbir advised Maj. Gen. Charles A. Willoughby that 4,000 additional Nisei would be required for the invasion. Willoughby objected, "Well, I'm not going to stand for any such God-damned thing as that." Mashbir replied: "Well, General, I don't give a damn whether you do or not. Frankly if we don't have these linguists, somebody is going to be tried by court-martial and I'm going to be God-damned sure it isn't me." Mashbir did not get all 4,000, but from May to July 1945 MISLS shipped 1,073 graduates to U.S. Army Forces in the Pacific.[123]

In preparation for the invasion, ATIS moved from Brisbane to Manila. In March, Advance ATIS sent one officer and three enlisted men from Hollandia to Manila, where they took over part of the Philippine Racing Club in the Santa Ana district. Base ATIS left Brisbane on 4 June, after almost three years in Australia. Personnel, files, and equipment were loaded onto three Liberty ships. The main body departed on 17 June and arrived on 5 July in Manila harbor, which was jammed with vessels waiting to discharge their cargo. The Nisei went to work and

---

[121] After-Action Report, Pacific Military Intelligence Research Section (PACMIRS), sub: History and Organization of PACMIRS, Camp Ritchie, Maryland, 6 September 1944–14 August 1945, p. 6; "Office of Naval Intelligence," p. 894, United States Naval Administration in World War II, 16 parts in 4 vols., Unpubl Ms, n.d., U.S. Naval Historical Center, Washington, D.C.

[122] ATIS History, p. 28; WD, Ltr, MID 908, 23 April 1945. On 8 August ATIS issued an instruction that assigned all Army Japanese linguists to the Translator and Interpreter Service, General Headquarters. ATIS SOPI [Standing Operating Procedure Instructions] no. 4, Policy and Procedure Concerning the Use of Language Personnel and the Processing of Prisoners of War and Captured Documents in the Pacific, 8 Aug 45. Fifteen JICPOA intelligence service organizations, each with up to seven officers and twenty enlisted men, were transferred to ATIS on 30 August 1945. ATIS History, p. 29.

[123] Interv, D. Clayton James with Col. Sidney F. Mashbir, 1 Sep 71, p. 12, D. Clayton James Collection, RG 49, MacArthur Memorial; Covert Warfare, 12 vols. (New York: Garland, 1989), vol. 2.

Allied Translator and Interpreter Section at the Santa Ana Racecourse, Manila.
In July and August 1945 ATIS was augmented by hundreds of recent MISLS
graduates and the 5225th Women's Army Corps Detachment.

had unloaded and uncrated most of their equipment by 1 August. Hundreds more recent MISLS graduates arrived directly from Minnesota. ATIS was also augmented by the 5225th Women's Army Corps Detachment with about 150 women, including a few Nisei, none of them MISLS graduates.[124]

The arrival of hundreds of Nisei in Manila aroused public curiosity. Mashbir recalled:

The night the personnel arrived, thousands of Filipinos thronged the gates and even climbed the walls to see what, as the Filipino major [commanding the guard force] explained to me, were thought to be the "Japanese prisoners." I told him they were not Japanese prisoners, but American soldiers. He looked at me blankly, until I had to explain to him.

"This officer," I said, "is Irish-American, that officer is German-American, you are Filipino-American, and these are *Japanese*-Americans."

Again he looked blank, but finally light began to dawn.

"Are they American citizens?" he asked.

"Yes," I replied, "they are American citizens."

---

[124] Mattie E. Treadwell, *The Women's Army Corps,* U.S. Army in World War II (Washington, D.C.: Office of the Chief of Military History, 1954), pp. 433, 435; ATIS History, p. 12; Brenda L. Moore, *Serving Our Country: Japanese American Women in the Military during World War II* (New Brunswick, N.J.: Rutgers University Press, 2003), p. 116.

Whereupon, after a lengthy harangue in Tagalog, he succeeded in dispersing the crowd. However, the next morning found an equally large crowd outside the gates. I asked the major what they wanted this time.

"They have come to see the American citizens," he said.[125]

One Nisei who arrived with ATIS, Howard Yasumaro Uno, met his older brother, Kazumaro "Buddy" Uno, in Manila. Before the war Buddy had worked in southern California as a journalist and was well-known to some of the ATIS Nisei. He had left California for the Far East during the Depression and had spent the war years in Manila working for a Japanese radio station. At the war's end he had been captured by the Filipino guerrillas. Howard visited his brother in New Bilibid Prison soon after his arrival. Colonel Mashbir hoped to film their encounter, "sensing the terrific drama that could occur from what I believed would be the first confrontation of brothers on opposite sides in the Pacific Theater." However, shortly after their initial meeting, Howard was unloading a ship when he "stepped backward into an open hatch, fell, and broke his back." The two brothers did not meet until much later.[126]

Planning for the coming invasion put great pressure on intelligence. Aerial and submarine reconnaissance increased, and intelligence staffs collected and produced intelligence at a frantic pace. Kyushu was extensively photographed and mapped, but few Japanese prisoners of war had recent knowledge of Kyushu, where the Japanese troop buildup was worrying top-level planners. Japanese troop strength on the island had grown from 150,000 to 600,000 in the first half of 1945. To track the buildup, intercepted radio communications, not the sorts of intelligence that ATIS could provide, played the most important role. On 29 July General Willoughby issued a sober assessment and declared, "We are in a race against time." The buildup was a "threatening development," and he warned that "if this development is not checked it may grow to a point where we attack on a ratio of one to one which is not the recipe for victory."[127]

---

[125] Mashbir, *I Was an American Spy*, p. 256; ATIS History, p. 35. T3g. Saburo Kubota arrived in Manila toward the end of June as part of a shipment of about 200 Nisei. As they "rode railroad flatcars to the replacement center," he recalled "young Filipino boys throwing stones at us yelling, 'Haponese,' when we passed through the villages." Tsukiyama et al., *Secret Valor* (1993 ed.), p. 90.

[126] Mashbir, *I Was an American Spy*, p. 248 (gives Howard Uno's first name as "Roy"); "Report Buddy Uno Interned by U.S. Troops near Manila," *Pacific Citizen*, 25 Aug 45, p. 1; Yuji Ichioka, "The Meaning of Loyalty: The Case of Kazumaro Buddy Uno," *Amerasia Journal* 23, no. 3 (1997): 45–71, esp. notes 52 and 54.

[127] *Reports of General MacArthur*, 4 vols., U.S. Army in World War II (Washington, D.C.: U.S. Army Center of Military History, 1994), 1: 395–43; Barton J. Bernstein, "The Alarming Japanese Buildup on Southern Kyushu, Growing U.S. Fears, and Counterfactual Analysis: Would the Planned November 1945 Invasion of Southern Kyushu Have Occurred?" *Pacific Historical Review* 68, no. 4 (November 1999): 561–609; Edward J. Drea, *MacArthur's Ultra: Codebreaking and the War against Japan, 1942–1945* (Lawrence: University Press of Kansas, 1992), pp. 202–23; Edward J. Drea, "Previews of Hell," *MHQ* 7, no. 3 (Spring 1995): 74–81; Richard B. Frank, *Downfall: The End of the Imperial Japanese Empire* (New York: Random House, 1999), pp. 197–213; Douglas

As preparations continued for the invasion, the War Department made changes to personnel policies affecting the Nisei. Many Nisei had long hoped in vain for
officer commissions and watched with resentment as their Caucasian classmates
were appointed second lieutenants upon graduation from language training. In
fact, the problem of obtaining commissions was not confined to the Nisei, and
frontline units struggled with persistent shortages of combat leaders throughout
the war. Not until the autumn of 1944 did the War Department allow theater commanders to grant field commissions. MacArthur's headquarters delegated that
authority to Sixth and Eighth Armies in May 1945.[128] By the spring of 1945 several ATIS Nisei had gained their commissions through officer candidate school or
field commissions. From India to Okinawa, several other MIS Nisei also won field
commissions that spring and summer.

With the end of the war in Europe the War Department announced a rota-
tion system for "high-point" men and discharges for some, but declared the MIS
Nisei essential personnel. A few of the longest-serving MIS Nisei were allowed
to return to the States that spring and summer on 45-day furloughs. One lucky
Nisei, S.Sgt. Minoru Masukane, had served in Australia, New Guinea, and the
Philippines since April 1943. When he arrived in San Francisco on 5 May 1945 for
a 45-day furlough, a personnel officer reviewing his records determined that he
already had eighty-seven points, enough for immediate discharge. On 14 May he
took off his uniform and never returned to ATIS.[129]

In Manila, two other Nisei preparing for furloughs were also being considered
for commissions. The day before their planned departure the personnel warrant
officer asked them to delay for three or four days to receive their commissions.
One replied bluntly: "Do I look like officer material? I'm going on home." The
other, S.Sgt. Richard S. Oguro, was more interested in getting back to Hawaii
in time for his wedding. He made an obscene suggestion as to what the warrant
officer could do with the second lieutenant's bars. The next day the two Nisei
hopped on an airplane and arrived in Hawaii two days later. Neither was ever
commissioned.[130]

.   .   .

MacEachim, *The Final Months of the War with Japan: Signals Intelligence, U.S. Invasion Plan-
ning, and the A-Bomb Decision* (Washington, D.C.: Center for the Study of Intelligence, 1998);
John R. Skates, *The Invasion of Japan: Alternative to the Bomb* (Columbia: University of South
Carolina Press, 1994), pp. 134–47.

   [128] Walter Krueger, *From Down Under to Nippon* (Washington, D.C.: Combat Forces Press,
1953), pp. 324–25; Robert R. Palmer et al., *The Procurement and Training of Ground Combat
Troops*, U.S. Army in World War II (Washington, D.C.: Department of the Army, Historical Division, 1948), pp. 152–57. The 442d RCT began granting direct commissions in the autumn of 1944.
To cite a well-known example, S.Sgt. Daniel K. Inouye was commissioned in December 1944.

   [129] "First Nisei Soldier Wins Discharge on Point System," *Pacific Citizen*, 26 May 45; "Nisei
Discharged on Points Returns to Home in California," *Pacific Citizen*, 9 Jun 45.

   [130] Oguro, *Sempai Gumi*, pp. 174–75.

The momentum toward the culminating point of the war continued regardless of the actions of any individuals. On 26 July 1945, Allied leaders meeting in Potsdam demanded Japan's unconditional surrender. "The alternative for Japan is prompt and utter destruction." That seemed a fair description of what Japan was already suffering, but on 28 July the Japanese government rejected these latest demands.[131] On Luzon, Sixth Army and its subordinate units continued planning for the invasion, now barely ninety days away. In Kunming, China, the OSS drew up plans to parachute special teams into Japan with Nisei interpreters to disrupt Japanese defenses, even though Lieutenant Yempuku, already a veteran of behind-the-lines OSS missions in northern Burma, told his superiors, "No way could it succeed or could we survive."[132] Another Nisei, T.Sgt. Robert Oda, learned he was to be put ashore by submarine near Wakayama on the Inland Sea with two trusted Japanese prisoners of war to report on weather and beach conditions.[133]

All the American soldiers dreaded the high casualties certain to accompany any invasion. Secretary of War Henry L. Stimson said of the troops redeploying from Europe: "These men were weary in a way that no one merely reading reports could readily understand." President Harry S. Truman told his top advisers that "he had hoped there was a possibility of preventing an Okinawa from one end of Japan to the other."[134]

The Nisei shared this apprehension. Some felt a special dread, now that the fighting was about to reach Japan proper. Most Japanese immigrants to America came from the southern parts of Japan, which meant that many had relatives still living in the area. One such Nisei was T4g. Nob Yamashita, who served with the 6th Infantry Division from New Guinea to Luzon and saw his team chief, Terry Mizutari, killed at Aitape in June 1944. Yamashita came to know another teammate, George Nakamura, "pretty good" on their thirty-day voyage from San Francisco to New Guinea, but Nakamura had died just as the Luzon Campaign seemed finished. "Tragically, the intelligence wasn't even needed," Yamashita lamented. "The surrounding areas were all secure. The colonel just wanted to question [some prisoners] for what little they knew. . . . MIS personnel weren't supposed to be expendable like that." Yamashita stopped taking his atabrine tablets, contracted malaria, and was hospitalized in July. By the time he was released, his unit was preparing for Kyushu, where his American-born sister and other relatives

---

[131] William Craig, *The Fall of Japan* (New York: Dial Press, 1967), pp. 66–68; Frank, *Downfall*, pp. 232–39.

[132] Tsukiyama et al., *Secret Valor* (1993 ed.), p. 76.

[133] Harrington, *Yankee Samurai*, pp. 354–55. However, Robert Oda's memoir states that his mission was to land on Kyushu, not Wakayama. Robert Oda, in Harrington Papers. Reconnaissance in the Inland Sea may have been part of a strategic deception plan, Operation PASTEL, designed to fool the Japanese into thinking the initial invasion site was the island of Shikoku. See Thomas M. Huber, *PASTEL: Deception in the Invasion of Japan* (Fort Leavenworth, Kans.: Combat Studies Institute, 1988), pp. 5–6; Lance Q. Zedric, *Silent Warriors of World War II: The Alamo Scouts behind Japanese Lines* (Ventura, Calif.: Pathfinder Publishing, 1995), pp. 241–43.

[134] Frank, *Downfall*, pp. 126–27, 143; Michael D. Pearlman, *Unconditional Surrender, Demobilization, and the Atomic Bomb* (Fort Leavenworth, Kans.: Combat Studies Institute, 1996).

were living. "I had a feeling of fear. I had a fear of shooting women and children that were supposedly training to attack us when we hit the beach in Kyushu. I thought maybe I could shoot myself in the leg and claim that in cleaning my carbine I accidentally shot myself in the leg, thinking that the chamber was empty. That would let me avoid hitting the beach."[135]

Many of the other Nisei felt the same way. 2d Lt. Harry K. Fukuhara had been overseas for more than two years and had won the Bronze Star with Oak Leaf Cluster and a battlefield commission. As an "old" master sergeant at age twenty-five, he had been accorded considerable respect; now he was just another second lieutenant. "I was suffering from battle fatigue and I had been hospitalized several times with malaria. I was physically and emotionally exhausted." He had not heard from his mother and brothers in Hiroshima since the war began.[136]

In early August, Fukuhara went directly to Colonel Mashbir with two other long-serving Nisei from I Corps language teams. As Mashbir recalled, "three of my best Nisei officers" requested permission to speak to him. They came in, sat down, and he offered them cigarettes.

Finally the senior, after a great deal of hesitation, started to talk. "Sir," he said, "we would each like to be relieved from the division to which he is assigned and transferred to another combat division...." This was extremely unusual. I was accustomed to having them take their assignments and carry them out without question, without remark. I knew that when three of them from three different divisions in one corps came with such a request, there must be something behind it far out of the ordinary.[137]

The three Nisei explained that their parents had come from the same sectors that had been assigned to their divisions. They themselves had attended university in Japan and feared that if they were recognized their families would be mistreated. "They made it perfectly clear, by insistent repetition, that they had no reluctance whatever to participate in the invasion of Japan, but that if it could be done they preferred to be attached to divisions which were not going into their native province." Mashbir acknowledged their concerns and promised to look into the matter. He then ordered his subordinates to identify the native province of each Nisei under his command so that, "where necessary," they could be transferred "unobtrusively... to divisions which were due to attack other parts of Japan."[138] The invasion was less than three months away.

---

[135] Yamashita, "Fighting My Ancestors," p. 22. In September 1945 the 6th Infantry Division was sent to occupy Korea; Yamashita served there until December 1945, when he was sent home and discharged.

[136] Interv, Harry Fukuhara, U.S. Army Intelligence and Security Command, 5 Jun 90; Harry Fukuhara, "The Return," Nikkei Heritage (Fall 1995): 12.

[137] Mashbir, I Was an American Spy, p. 252. Torao Pat Neishi, who also had relatives in Hiroshima, accompanied Fukuhara to the meeting. Interv, Sheryl Narahara with Torao "Pat" Neishi, 1992, NJAHS.

[138] Mashbir, I Was an American Spy, p. 252.

11

MIS Nisei
and the Surrender of Japan,
August–September 1945

Startling news swept around the world on 6 August 1945: a single bomb of hith-erto unimaginable power had leveled Hiroshima in southern Japan. The Japanese people struggled for the right word. Their language simply lacked words to describe what had happened. Some used the word *pika*, a flash (of lightning), or *pika-don*, flash-boom. The U.S. government called it an atomic bomb. The MIS Nisei already knew the Japanese word *bakudan*, bomb. So they looked up the word for atomic, *genshi*, and combined it to form *genshi-bakudan*, literally atomic bomb.[1]

2d Lt. Harry K. Fukuhara, like many of the MIS Nisei, had family members living in Hiroshima. In fact, before the war he had attended school in the city. Now stationed in the Philippines, he delivered the news to the Japanese prisoners of war near Manila:

I told them that a new bomb called the atomic bomb, equivalent to thousands of tons of TNT, had been dropped on Hiroshima on August 6, and that one single explosion had

---

[1] Richard B. Frank, *Downfall: The End of the Imperial Japanese Empire* (New York: Random House, 1999), pp. 264–65; Stanley L. Falk and Warren M. Tsuneishi, eds., *MIS in the War against Japan* (Washington, D.C.: Japanese American Veterans Association, 1995), pp. 34–38. See also Allan S. Clifton, *Time of Fallen Blossoms* (New York: Knopf, 1951), p. 49. Clifton, an Australian linguist, served near Hiroshima in 1946 with the British Commonwealth Occupation Force.

completely wiped out the entire city of Hiroshima and that it had been erased from the surface of the earth. I told them nothing living had survived and that all human and animal life was non-existent. I further elaborated that no vegetation, plant life or trees would grow there and people would not be able to live there for at least 100 years, due to radiation. When I told them that, they were silent—either they did not believe me or else the information was beyond their comprehension. I know that I did not want to believe it myself.[2]

Three days later the Twentieth Air Force dropped a second bomb on Nagasaki. A rumor that Japan was about to surrender swept through American service personnel throughout the Pacific. When the news hit Manila, it touched off six hours of delirious celebration; similar celebrations erupted on Guam, in Honolulu, and elsewhere. On Okinawa, a Japanese guerrilla commander saw the night sky fill with tracers and wondered if it was the grand Japanese counterattack he had been hoping for; but his scouts reported that the Americans seemed to be celebrating. On 10 August came radio reports that Tokyo had accepted the Potsdam Declaration demanding unconditional surrender. The rumors were true.[3]

The Nisei were jubilant that the fighting had finally ended, but the way it ended hit them hard. More than for other Americans, the war's ending was bittersweet. Half of all Japanese immigrants to the United States came from Hiroshima and the neighboring prefectures. Many Nisei, like Fukuhara, still had relatives in the area; some Nisei had lived and attended school there before the war. Fukuhara recalled his feelings upon hearing of the Hiroshima bombing:

My frame of mind . . . was one of shock and relief. . . . I was shocked because Hiroshima was where I had lived before the war and where my mother and three brothers were still living. I was relieved because we would not be participating in the long-dreaded invasion. . . . For the first few days I kept thinking: Why? Why did they drop it on Hiroshima? . . . The more I thought about it, the more depressed I became. My thinking degraded to the point that I blamed myself—that they had died because I had volunteered to fight against them.[4]

Another Nisei officer, 2d Lt. George S. Taketa, knew from interrogating prisoners in Manila that Japan could not hold out much longer, so he felt the atomic bombings were unnecessary: "What the hell are we doing? Why kill additional people? We didn't have to; the war was going to end. Then a couple of days later

---

    [2] Harry Fukuhara, "The Return," *Nikkei Heritage* (Fall 1995): 12–13; Loni Ding, prod., *The Color of Honor*, documentary film, Vox Productions, 1987; Interv, John P. Finnegan with Harry Fukuhara, 5 Jun 90, U.S. Army Intelligence and Security Command, Fort Belvoir, Va.
    [3] John Toland, *The Rising Sun: The Decline and Fall of the Japanese Empire, 1936–1945* (New York: Random House, 1970), p. 852; Louis Allen, *The End of the War in Asia* (London: Hart-Davis, 1976); Robert J. C. Butow, *Japan's Decision To Surrender* (Stanford, Calif.: Stanford University Press, 1954); William Craig, *The Fall of Japan* (New York: Dial Press, 1967, 1979); Frank, *Downfall*; Stanley Weintraub, *The Last Great Victory: The End of World War II, July/August 1945* (New York: Dutton, 1995).
    [4] Fukuhara, "The Return."

they dropped one over Nagasaki. And that really shook us. I said, 'Geez, what the hell is going on? Here another hundred thousand killed. . . .' It was a terrible thing; I wouldn't do it to a dog. . . . It just made us sick."[5]

On the other side of the world, Nisei stationed with the 442d Regimental Combat Team (RCT) in Italy also expressed mixed feelings. One expressed the consensus of millions of American soldiers when he told a correspondent, "Those goddamn bastards! They cost us plenty at Pearl Harbor. It's time they paid for it." Other Nisei remained silent, "still trying to comprehend what an atomic bomb could do."[6] S.Sgt. Mike Masaoka, the regimental public relations officer and a leading Japanese American Citizens League (JACL) spokesman, described the atomic bombs as "the ghastly and unnecessary *coup de grâce*." He recalled, "Reporters came to our camp for comment. How did we feel about Japan's surrender? We were elated. The war was over, wasn't it?" The atomic bomb, he felt, "was a helluva weapon. It was just too damned bad that civilians had to be killed—we had seen too much of that in Italy and France. But if it shortened the war, we were glad we had this new weapon rather than the other guys."[7]

Army commanders in the Pacific shared the Nisei's feelings. General Douglas MacArthur was reportedly "appalled and depressed" by the atomic bombings and felt there was no military justification for their use. "Probably no living man has seen as much of war and its destruction as I had," he later wrote. "My abhorrence reached its height with the perfection of the atomic bomb."[8] Maj. Gen. Charles A. Willoughby, MacArthur's G–2, knew that Japan had been on the verge of collapse and was seeking to negotiate. "There was then no reason to use the Atom bomb and give the show away that we had perfected the most revolutionary weapon in modern history. MacArthur was not consulted; he was merely presented with a fait accompli." Brig. Gen. Bonner Fellers, MacArthur's chief of psychological warfare, felt much the same way.[9]

---

[5] George S. Taketa, in David W. Swift, Jr., ed., "First Class," pp. 8–9, Unpubl Ms, Mar 00, copy in author's files.

[6] Lyn Crost, *Honor by Fire: Japanese Americans at War in Europe and the Pacific* (Novato, Calif.: Presidio Press, 1994), p. 288. For similar reactions, see Paul Fussell, "Thank God for the Atomic Bomb," *The New Republic* (26 August 1991).

[7] Mike Masaoka, *They Call Me Moses Masaoka: An American Saga* (New York: William Morrow, 1987), p. 182.

[8] Douglas A. MacArthur, *Reminiscences* (New York: Time, 1964), p. 347.

[9] Gar Alperovitz, *The Decision To Use the Bomb and the Architecture of an American Myth* (New York: Knopf, 1995), pp. 350–52; Barton J. Bernstein, in *Judgment at the Smithsonian*, ed. Philip Nobile (New York: Marlowe & Co, ca. 1995), p. 142. Charles A. Willoughby, "The Character of Military Intelligence," pt. 2, p. 197, Unpubl Ms, Charles A. Willoughby Papers, Record Group (RG) 23B, MacArthur Memorial, Library and Archives, Norfolk, Va. ATIS coordinator Colonel Mashbir and CIC chief General Thorpe both avoided mention of the atomic bombings in their memoirs. Sidney F. Mashbir, *I Was an American Spy* (New York: Vantage, 1953); Elliott R. Thorpe, *East Wind, Rain: An Intimate Account of an Intelligence Officer in the Pacific, 1939–49* (Boston: Gambit, 1969). For other soldier responses, see J. Glenn Gray, *The Warriors: Reflections on Men in Battle* (New York: Harper and Row, 1973), pp. 238–39.

For some Nisei the war's end meant new beginnings. For example, Sgt. Akira Nakamura had already been on Okinawa for five months by August 1945. Just before going overseas, he had been married in the Fort Snelling chapel. On Okinawa, he had survived several close calls; at one point an American bullet struck his helmet and left a dent, "a slight headache, ringing of his ears and wounded pride." But he had survived. A few days after the Hiroshima bombing, he received a cablegram informing him that his wife had given birth to a daughter in Minneapolis on 6 August. He searched through the ruins of an Okinawan distillery, "found a clay urn filled with well-aged sweet potato whiskey," and brought it back to the language detachment, where his Nisei buddies helped him celebrate the birth of his first child.[10]

For several days after the atomic bombings the relentless pounding of Japan continued by air and sea. The Twentieth Air Force paused its B–29 raids after 10 August, but land-based aircraft of the Fifth and Seventh Air Forces and carrier aircraft and surface units from the Third Fleet continued to blast Japanese targets. "Never before in history had one nation been the target of such concentrated air power."[11] The Psychological Warfare Board continued its radio broadcasts twelve hours per day and dropped up to 2 million copies per week of the *Rakkasan News* on Japan and Japanese troop concentrations around the region. Col. Sidney F. Mashbir broadcast personal appeals to Japanese leaders on 9 and 13 August. On the night of 13–14 August, B–29s dropped 5 million leaflets over the Tokyo area. Prepared by the Joint Intelligence Center, Pacific Ocean Areas (JICPOA), and the Office of War Information, the leaflets gave the texts of the Japanese note accepting the Potsdam Declaration, as well as the American Secretary of State's reply, which the Japanese government had not yet released to its own people.[12]

On 15 August Radio Tokyo carried a special broadcast to the Japanese people. Speaking to the nation for the first time, the emperor addressed his "good and loyal subjects" in traditional courtly language. "Despite the best that has been done by everyone," he explained, "the war situation has developed not necessarily

---

[10] Akira Nakamura, Biography, Military Intelligence Service Club of Northern California (this and similar biographies hereafter cited as MISNorCal Bios); Akira Nakamura, in "Rocky Mountain MIS Veterans Club Autobiographies," Unpubl Ms, ed. Kent T. Yoritomo, [1989], author's files (this and similar biographies hereafter cited as Rocky Mountain Bios).

[11] Quote from *Reports of General MacArthur*, 4 vols., U.S. Army in World War II (Washington, D.C.: U.S. Army Center of Military History, 1994), 1: 442; Samuel E. Morison, *History of United States Naval Operations in World War II*, 15 vols. (Boston: Little, Brown, 1947–1952), 15: 447–50.

[12] Wesley F. Craven and James L. Cate, eds., *The Army Air Forces in World War II*, 7 vols. (Chicago: University of Chicago Press, 1950), 5: 732; Craig, *Fall of Japan*, pp. 168–69; Toland, *Rising Sun*, pp. 829–30; General Headquarters, Far East Command, *Operations of the Allied Translator and Interpreter Section, GHQ, SWPA*, Intelligence Series, vol. 5 (Tokyo: Far East Command, 1948) (hereafter cited as ATIS History), p. 63; Josette H. Williams, "The Information War in the Pacific," *Studies in Intelligence* 46, no. 3 (2002). Captain Zacharias believed that this final leaflet campaign caused "a delay in acceptance of surrender" and incited a last-minute revolt. Ellis M. Zacharias, *Secret Missions: The Story of an Intelligence Officer* (New York: G. P. Putnam's Sons, 1946), pp. 386–87.

to Japan's advantage." He announced Japan's acceptance of the Allied terms and called upon his subjects to accept peace by "enduring the unendurable and suffering what is insufferable."[13] Allied psychological warfare units spread the emperor's words throughout the region as propaganda leaflets and voice recordings.

MacArthur's headquarters began to implement its contingency plan, Operation BLACKLIST, for the sudden surrender of Japan. The 11th Airborne Division in southern Luzon was alerted for immediate movement to Japan, and the Army Air Forces assembled hundreds of transport aircraft to move the division to Japan by way of Okinawa. The division would have the honor of being the first American soldiers to land in Japan. The division already had an experienced Nisei language team. In addition, the 306th Counter Intelligence Corps (CIC) Detachment under Capt. John H. Norton was assigned ten more Nisei, Military Intelligence Service Language School (MISLS) graduates recently arrived in the Philippines.

In forty-eight hours the division moved the 800 miles from Luzon to Okinawa. On 12 August in the gathering dusk a transport aircraft arrived at an airfield near Naha carrying thirty soldiers from division headquarters, including most of the 306th CIC Detachment and the ten new Nisei. Shortly before their arrival the airfield had been subjected to a kamikaze attack and ships in the harbor had sent up thick clouds of obscuring smoke. The airfield, which sat on a bluff overlooking the ocean, was blacked out. Twice the pilot tried to land. On the third attempt the plane crashed into the cliff short of the runway and killed everyone on board.[14]

This was the largest loss of life to the MIS during the entire war. An 11th Airborne Division officer described the accident in a letter to Fort Snelling:

Just prior to leaving for Okinawa for staging, we received a group of replacements, and they were all men fresh out of the states. They arrived at our Hqs a day and a half before we flew to Okinawa. . . . It was a terrible shock to all of us. These men, whose names and

---

[13] The emperor's address has been variously translated. For one version, see Ted T. Tsukiyama et al., eds., *Secret Valor: M.I.S. Personnel, World War II Pacific Theater, Pre–Pearl Harbor to Sept. 8, 1951* (Honolulu: Military Intelligence Service Veterans Club of Hawaii, 1993), pp. 78–81. Compare with text given in *Reports of General MacArthur*, 1: 444–45, 2: 727–28, plate 167; Toland, *Rising Sun*, pp. 838–39; Craig, *Fall of Japan*, pp. 209–12; John W. Dower, *Embracing Defeat: Japan in the Wake of World War II* (New York: Norton, 1999), pp. 33–39.

[14] Duval A. Edwards, *Spy Catchers of the U.S. Army in the War with Japan* (Gig Harbor, Wash.: Red Apple Publishing, 1994), p. 241; William B. Simpson, *Special Agent in the Pacific, WWII: Counterintelligence—Military, Political, and Economic* (New York: Rivercross Publishing, 1995), pp. 107–12. Simpson was a member of the 306th CIC Detachment. He flew to Okinawa on the afternoon of 12 August and learned of the crash the next morning. The 441st CIC headquarters in Tokyo was later named for Captain Norton. The crash was first reported in *Pacific Citizen*, 8 Sep 45. At Fort Snelling, the *Yaban Gogai* printed nine names in its September–October 1945 issue and added the tenth name and additional details in the November issue. T4g. Iwao Iijima described the crash in a letter dated 23 August 1945. Hawaii War Records Depository, Reel 26–A, Hamilton Library, University of Hawaii at Manoa. See also E. M. Flanagan's account, "The Occupation of Japan," *Army* (August 1995): 48–58.

faces I had not as yet familiarized myself with, came without records or papers of any kind, and the identifying of them was difficult.[15]

Two other Nisei died in the frenzy of activity after the Japanese surrender. S.Sgt. Shoichi S. Nakahara had enlisted in June 1943 from Hilo, Hawaii. He had been an excellent student at MISLS, attended voice-intercept training in Florida, and then was assigned to the 1st Radio Squadron Mobile (RSM). On 13 August he was returning from Manila when his jeep was involved in an accident near San Fernando. An Army chaplain who had served with MISLS at Camp Savage conducted his memorial service.[16] On Okinawa, Pvt. Masayuki Ishii died in a vehicle accident on 19 August. The twenty-year-old had enlisted in Hawaii in April 1945, had attended basic training at Schofield Barracks, and had been sent directly to Okinawa with the 1st Provisional Military Government Detachment.[17]

In the tumultuous days following the Japanese surrender, Colonel Mashbir commissioned about 100 Allied Translator and Interpreter Section (ATIS) Nisei on 18 August and promoted 600 Nisei enlisted men by one grade. As Mashbir recalled:

Jubilation was the order of the day when the first one hundred were sworn in as lieutenants. This number finally reached the one-hundred-and-fifty mark because of vacancies that then occurred in the combat divisions, which had also been awarded a T/O.... Any other group on earth would have taken Manila apart, because seven hundred promotions in two days is not a thing that a bunch of soldiers will pass over lightly. But the Nisei received this news with the same dignity and reserve with which they had received bad news in the past.[18]

As early as the autumn of 1943 Mashbir had begun sending Nisei to officer candidate school in Australia and pressed for an increase in authorizations for language officers. The planned invasion of Japan made that possible, and the War Department issued a new table of allowances for ATIS effective 29 July. The authorized number of lieutenants jumped from 38 to 300, while that for captains and above jumped from 26 to 116. Enlisted authorizations more than tripled, from

---

[15] *Yaban Gogai*, Nov 45.

[16] Ibid. Sep–Oct 45, p. 3; *In Freedom's Cause* (Honolulu: University of Hawaii Press, 1949), p. 103; Tsukiyama et al., *Secret Valor*, p. 91.

[17] *Freedom's Cause*, p. 55.

[18] Mashbir, *I Was an American Spy*, p. 250. The exact number of Nisei commissioned at this time is not clear, as some Nisei on detached service were also promoted at about the same time. "Report Battlefield Commissions for 200 Pacific Nisei," *Pacific Citizen*, 1 Sep 45. One photo of the ATIS ceremony shows forty to fifty Nisei. Benjamin Obata, who was commissioned at this time, recalls sixty or seventy. Interv, author with Benjamin Obata, 21 Aug 95. ATIS History, p. 59, asserts, "To date [1948], ATIS has obtained direct commissions for eighty United States Army enlisted linguists."

ATIS Nisei becoming second lieutenants, Manila, 18 August 1945

419 to 1,377. As a result ATIS held officer selection boards for the new authorizations; three weeks later Mashbir swore in the new lieutenants.[19]

A few high-point Nisei were reluctant to accept commissions, which would
require them to remain on active duty for an indefinite period. Those who accepted
had plenty of reason for "dignity and reserve": Some felt that the commissions
were too long in coming. When Thomas Sakamoto was recruited for the Fourth
Army Intelligence School in the summer of 1941, then Capt. Kai E. Rasmussen
had promised him a commission. He had watched Caucasian students pin on lieutenant's bars upon graduation while their Nisei classmates who often had better
language skills graduated with sergeant's stripes. Not until June 1945 did Sakamoto receive a field commission. Now the Army was handing out commissions
even to Nisei who had never spent a day in combat. "It was wholesale," wrote
S.Sgt. Clifford Konno to a friend at Fort Snelling. "The WD [War Department]
decided that we needed a little more rank in Japan or something."[20]

The Japanese Surrender

On 11 August General MacArthur was appointed Supreme Commander for
the Allied Powers to accept the Japanese government's surrender in Tokyo and

---

[19] ATIS History, app. 3.
[20] Ltr, Clifford Konno, 19 September 1945, Joseph D. Harrington Papers, National Japanese
Historical Society (NJAHS), San Francisco, Calif.

to direct the military occupation of Japan and southern Korea. Other Allied commanders were directed to accept the surrender of Japanese armed forces, each in his respective area: Lord Louis Mountbatten in Southeast Asia, Generalissimo Chiang Kai-shek in China, and the Soviet High Command in Manchuria and northern Korea. (*See Map 15.*) Overnight MacArthur's headquarters switched from planning for the invasion to planning for an unopposed occupation. On 12 August General Willoughby formed an advisory committee of experts on Japan to aid MacArthur and the general staff. Mashbir provided Maj. John E. Anderton as the executive officer for the committee and assigned dozens of experienced Nisei to GHQ staff sections. Meanwhile, hundreds more recent MISLS graduates arrived in Manila and were assigned new duties. By 1 September ATIS counted over 1,300 Nisei. All would be needed in the months ahead.[21]

As the emperor's speech was being broadcast in Japan, MacArthur's signal center in Manila sought to establish the first-ever direct radio contact with the Japanese high command by sending plaintext messages in kana, rōmaji, and English to the main Japanese commercial teletype station: "Tokyo from Manila: We have an urgent message for you." They tried several known frequencies, but no Japanese station would respond. After several hours GHQ gave them a longer message detailing the procedures for discussions, but there was still no answer. After ten hours of what MacArthur's official report called "exasperating and suspicious delays," a Tokyo station responded. Thus, in the early hours of 16 August Manila and Tokyo began to exchange technical messages in English about the surrender talks.[22]

MacArthur demanded that the Japanese send a delegation to Manila. From the outset, language problems caused some minor incidents. The first message directed the Japanese to send a delegation to Ie Shima near Okinawa and directed that the Japanese planes be marked with green crosses. However, the Japanese language has several words for "green," so the American translators wrote "green" and added "the color of grass."[23] On 19 August two Japanese bombers displaying green crosses arrived at Ie Shima. They were met by a large crowd of American soldiers and reporters, among them several Nisei. Sgt. Hoichi Kubo with the 27th Infantry Division on the island recalled 7 December 1941, when he had witnessed Japanese aircraft attacking Wheeler Field on Oahu. He had later fought on Makin, Majuro, Saipan, and Okinawa. For valor on Saipan he was awarded the Distinguished Service Cross and was the only MIS Nisei to receive this award. He had witnessed the war's beginning and now was witnessing its end.[24]

---

[21] Willoughby, "Character of Military Intelligence," pt. 2, p. 201.

[22] Craig, *Fall of Japan*, pp. 217, 228–29; *Reports of General MacArthur*, vol. 1 supplement, p. 12; "Surrender on the Air," *Military Review* (May 1946): 31–39; Jacques Kunitz, "Sequel to Surrender on the Air," *Signals* 1, no. 2 (November–December 1946).

[23] Mashbir, *I Was an American Spy*, p. 287; John E. Anderton, in Willoughby, "Character of Military Intelligence," pt. 2, p. 203.

[24] Joseph D. Harrington, *Yankee Samurai: The Secret Role of Nisei in America's Pacific Victory* (Detroit: Pettigrew Enterprises, 1979), p. 349; Interv, author with Hoichi Kubo, 30 Oct 87.

Lt. Gen. Torashiro Kawabe, vice chief of the Imperial Army General Staff, and the Japanese delegation stepped down from their aircraft. A Nisei officer instructed them to move to the American C–54 transport aircraft for the flight to Nichols Field near Manila. Lt. Warren S. Munzenmeyer flew with them to Manila as interpreter for the flight crew. The Caucasian MISLS graduate had taught before the war at the American School in Japan. Willoughby met the delegation at Nichols Field, backed by Mashbir, several Caucasian interpreters, and two Nisei, 2d Lt. Thomas T. Imada and 2d Lt. George Kenichi Kayano, who had been commissioned only the day before. Imada recorded his excitement in a letter home:

Today will be one of the Red Letter days for me in the Army. Only last evening I was commissioned as a 2d Lieutenant in the Army of the United States. . . . This was to be our first assignment as officers. Only in an Army of the United States could a Nisei be given such an important task.[25]

The Japanese delegation climbed into waiting staff cars, with one American linguist riding in each. *Kawabe* got into the lead car with Willoughby and Mashbir. Willoughby, trying to be friendly, asked *Kawabe* in what language he would like to converse. *Kawabe* shrewdly suggested they use German. *Kawabe* had studied in Germany and knew that Willoughby was of German birth.[26]

Over the next few days the Nisei found some opportunities for small talk with the Japanese. *General Kawabe* had brought a Nisei of his own, *Sadao Roy Otake,* who spoke fluent English and Japanese. A graduate of New York University, *Otake* had been in Japan when the war broke out. He was drafted into the Japanese Army and was now a second lieutenant. He was astonished to learn that among the American guards was his brother-in-law, Sojiro Takamura from Hawaii. "Look me up in Japan," *Otake* told him. At another point a Nisei interpreter tried to strike up a conversation with a Japanese official by asking: "When the Japanese attacked Hawaii, why didn't they land?" The Japanese officer did not respond. Another Nisei, T4g. Raymond H. Katayama, asked a Japanese officer if the atomic bomb had indeed destroyed Hiroshima. "Hiroshima hasn't been destroyed," the officer replied. "It has vanished from the face of the earth."[27]

---

[25] *Yaban Gogai,* Sep–Oct 45; WD Press Release, 22 Oct 45; "Japanese Surrender Envoys Escorted by Nisei Officers," *Pacific Citizen,* 25 Aug 45; Mashbir, *I Was an American Spy,* pp. 250–51.

[26] Craig, *Fall of Japan,* pp. 237–49 (quote on p. 242); Transcript of U.S.-Japanese meetings in Manila, 19–20 Aug 45, Folder #15, Box 24, Papers of Lt. Gen. Richard K. Sutherland, U.S. Army, 1941–1945, RG 30, MacArthur Memorial; "The Japs Get MacArthur's Orders," *Life* (3 September 1945): 23–27; John E. Anderton, in Willoughby, "Character of Military Intelligence," pt. 2, pp. 200–22; ATIS History, pp. 35–37; *Reports of General MacArthur,* 1: 447–50; Mashbir, *I Was an American Spy,* pp. 278–99; Edwards, *Spy Catchers,* p. 246; Toland, *Rising Sun,* pp. 857–61; George Kenichi Kayano, MISNorCal Bio; Harvey Watanabe, in Falk and Tsuneishi, *MIS in the War against Japan,* pp. 42–44; Harvey Watanabe, personal communication to author, 19 May 03.

[27] Falk and Tsuneishi, *MIS in the War against Japan,* pp. 42–44; Toland, *Rising Sun,* p. 860; Hawaii quote from Craig, *Fall of Japan,* p. 242; Hiroshima quote from *Yank* (28 September 1945).

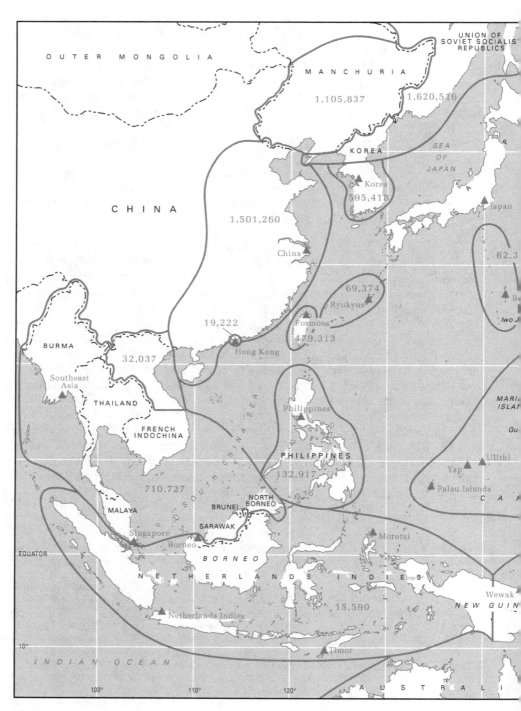

MAP 15

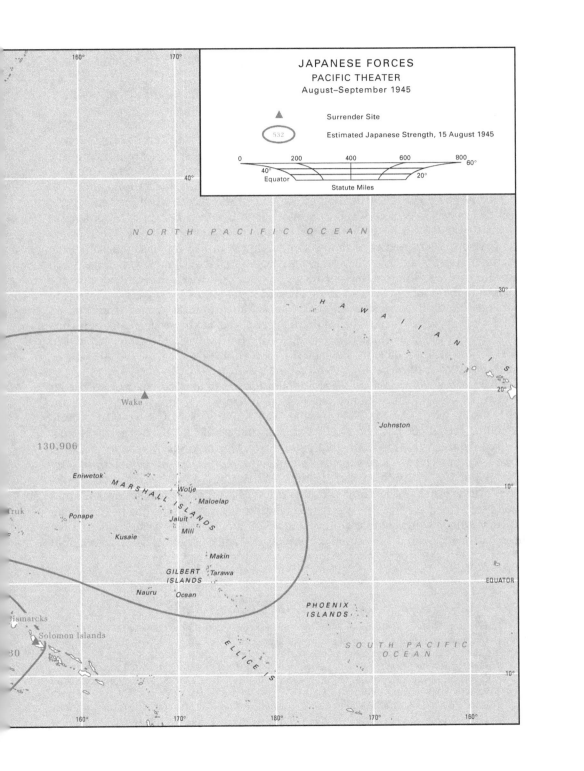

JAPANESE FORCES
PACIFIC THEATER
August–September 1945

▲   Surrender Site

532   Estimated Japanese Strength, 15 August 1945

Statute Miles

160°   170°   40°   60°

N O R T H   P A C I F I C   O C E A N

H A W A I I A N   I S

30°

Wake ▲

Johnston

20°

130,906

Eniwetok

M A R S H A L L   I S L A N D S

Wotje

10°

Maloelap

Truk

Ponape

Jaluit

Mili

Kusaie

Makin

GILBERT ISLANDS Tarawa

Nauru   Ocean

EQUATOR

PHOENIX ISLANDS

Bismarcks

Solomon Islands

E L L I C E   I S

S O U T H   P A C I F I C   O C E A N

30

10°

160°   170°   180°   170°   160°

The Americans presented the Japanese delegates with directives from Washington translated into Japanese. A few days before the meeting, Mashbir selected Sgt. Kiyoshi Hirano to review the draft translations. Hirano, a California-born Nisei, had been educated in Japan and for a time had taught middle school there before returning to America in 1939. At first Hirano declined on grounds that his Japanese was not good enough to translate such important documents. Mashbir insisted: "Sergeant Hirano, you were a school teacher in Japan according to your service record. You have the best background in Japanese education among the group here. Someone has to do this very important job to end the war. Please do your duty." Hirano worked straight through three nights to finish the assignment.[28]

During the conference Imada and Kayano worked with Mashbir and several other Caucasian interpreters and translators. The Japanese delegates brought documents that the ATIS Nisei worked around the clock to translate.[29] On the second day differences erupted over the proper language to use for the emperor in the instrument of surrender. In the version presented to the delegates, which had been translated in Washington, the Japanese pronoun "I" was used for the emperor rather than the imperial "we." The Japanese delegates were upset at such insulting language. Mashbir suggested that they could substitute the proper word and he would clear it with MacArthur.[30] On 20 August the Japanese delegates returned to Japan with the agreed upon documents. In Manila, the ATIS Nisei worked in shifts for ten straight days to translate the surrender terms and the initial occupation directives.

GHQ had developed a contingency plan for the sudden collapse or surrender of Japan. Operation BLACKLIST called for Eighth Army to occupy Tokyo and northern Honshu, while the Sixth Army and III Amphibious Corps were to occupy the south. The Tenth Army on Okinawa contributed the XXIV Corps for Korea. Meanwhile, the VII Amphibious Force sent two Marine divisions to North China ports. The Americans were suspicious that the Japanese might lure them in only to slaughter them or poison their leaders. Willoughby described "the enormous initial military risks of landing with token forces on the Japanese mainland, into a colossal armed camp.... All possible landing areas, in the event of American armed landing, were completely organized by the Japanese Army and each of these had the potentiality of another Okinawa." Using Okinawa as "a completely

---

[28] Harrington, *Yankee Samurai*, p. 348; Crost, *Honor by Fire*, p. 289. As a precaution, all translations were marked "This is an unofficial translation." English was considered the official language for the surrender directives. Mashbir, *I Was an American Spy*, p. 289.

[29] Translator and Interpreter Section, "Documents Submitted to the SCAP by the Japanese Mission To Negotiate Surrender, Manila, 19 August 1945," Folder 6, Box 23, U.S. Army Forces, Pacific, RG 4, MacArthur Memorial; ATIS History, p. 13.

[30] Toland, *Rising Sun*, p. 859; Craig, *Fall of Japan*, pp. 246–47; Mashbir, *I Was an American Spy*, pp. 304–10; D. Clayton James, *The Years of MacArthur*, 3 vols. (Boston: Houghton Mifflin, 1970–1985), 2: 779.

authentic yardstick," he predicted over 700,000 American casualties, "had we gone in shooting."[31]

In the first weeks of the occupation Caucasian language officers, rather than MIS Nisei, were entrusted with several critical tasks, including the initial landings, the surrender ceremony, and MacArthur's first meeting with the emperor. On 28 August American minesweepers led the Third Fleet into Tokyo Bay, and the same morning sixteen C–46 transports landed at the Atsugi naval air station southwest of Tokyo carrying Col. Charles P. Tench from G–3, GHQ, and 150 Army Air Forces communication specialists. They landed without incident and in forty-five minutes established radio communications with Okinawa. Local Japanese officials began preparing the airfield for the 11th Airborne Division, scheduled to arrive on 30 August with its own team of Nisei linguists. The 4th Marines would land the same day at the Yokosuka naval base.[32] The Atsugi advance party included Maj. Faubion Bowers, one of ATIS's top Caucasian linguists, but no Nisei. Bowers had lived in Tokyo before the war and was one of the first Caucasians to graduate from Camp Savage. He interpreted for the discussions between Tench and the Japanese officers, but the Japanese provided their own English interpreters as well.[33]

2d Lt. Thomas Sakamoto flew into Atsugi on 30 August with a press pool of American correspondents to cover MacArthur's triumphal arrival:

The morning was dark and overcast, with low-hanging clouds. Our plane flew towards our destination with great confidence, for we were to be among the first to land in Japan. But I was filled with anxiety as I did not know what was awaiting us.

The next few hours passed uneventfully, until suddenly in the distance an eerie shadow of a huge mountain appeared. It was Mt. Fuji. As we flew over its peak, I reminisced about a mere eight years earlier when, as a student in Japan, a classmate and I had climbed Fuji-san. How little did I realize then that I would be seeing Mt. Fuji again under a totally different circumstance. I had always pictured Mt. Fuji as a majestic snow-capped mountain, but today it looked only like a dark ghostly figure, perhaps reflecting the tragic defeat of Japan.

---

[31] Charles A. Willoughby, "Occupation of Japan and Japanese Reaction," *Military Review* (June 1946): 3–4.

[32] Col. C. T. Tench, "Advance Party: Mission Surrender," *Infantry Journal* (August 1946): 30–36; Craig, *Fall of Japan*, pp. 285–90; Harrington, *Yankee Samurai*, p. 353. Hayami Russ Sato accompanied the 11th Airborne Division advance party to Atsugi. He recalls the date as 25 August, but this is incorrect. Hayami R. Sato, MISNorCal Bio, Rocky Mountain Bio. Although not assigned to the 11th Airborne Division, S.Sgt. Kazuo Komoto also landed with the division at Atsugi. WD Press Release, 22 Oct 45; *Pacific Citizen*, 8 Sep 45.

[33] Interv, D. Clayton James with Faubion Bowers, RG 49, D. Clayton James Collection, MacArthur Memorial; Falk and Tsuneishi, *MIS in the War against Japan*, pp. 11–13, 89–91, 94; Faubion Bowers, "Japan, 1940–1949: A Tumultuous Time Remembered," *Japan Society Newsletter*, Oct 95, pp. 4–7. Some sources report that S.Sgt. Hideo Ihara from the 1st Radio Squadron Mobile landed at Atsugi on 28 August for "a special mission," perhaps to monitor Japanese military communications. Tsukiyama et al., *Secret Valor*, p. 91; WD Press Release, 22 Oct 45.

Then between the breaks in the clouds, we could see the neatly laid out pattern of rice fields and the thatched farmhouses sporadically dotting the landscape below. Soon we descended and taxied onto a runway, as if awakening from a dream. This was Atsugi airfield on August 30, 1945.[34]

Crowds of Americans and Japanese gathered near the airfield to greet MacArthur, who held a press conference on the tarmac. Sakamoto was startled to meet among the fifty Japanese correspondents in the crowd a high school classmate: Jimmy Wada from Hawaii, who had gone to Japan to attend Meiji University. When the war broke out, he was attached to the Imperial Navy. Sakamoto gave his friend all the K-rations he had brought with him. That same day Admiral Chester W. Nimitz landed at Yokosuka accompanied by at least one JICPOA Nisei, T.Sgt. Robert Oda.[35]

On 2 September Colonel Mashbir escorted the Japanese delegates on board the USS *Missouri* in Tokyo Bay for the surrender ceremony. Three Nisei were on board that day. Sakamoto, who was still escorting the American correspondents, watched as *Foreign Minister Mamoru Shigemitsu* hobbled on his wooden leg before a silent, hostile audience:

Every available space was occupied by sailors. The atmosphere was one of celebration. But this festive moment abruptly turned to silence as the Japanese delegation arrived. They were stripped of their samurai swords. One could hear a pin drop. The delegation was left standing for fifteen minutes, subject to hostile staring. If there was ever a scene that brought to me how sad a defeated nation can be, this was it. Of the total surrender ceremony, this fifteen minutes of cruel silence and abusive staring impacted me more than any other portion of the ceremony. I recalled then my four years of high school education in Japan, of once proud *Yamato Damashii* (Japanese spirit), *Bushido* (Way of the Samurai) mentality of the Japanese military, and as a Nisei of my parents' pride in those things Japanese, now vanished at that moment on the deck of the *Missouri* in a total defeat and disgrace for the Japanese people and the nation.[36]

---

[34] Interv, David Swift with Thomas Sakamoto, in Swift, "First Class"; *The Saga of the MIS*, videotaped presentation, Los Angeles, 11 Mar 89; Thomas Sakamoto, "Witness to Surrender," *Nikkei Heritage* (Winter 2003): 8–9.

[35] Interv, author with Thomas Sakamoto, 16 Nov 87; *Saga of the MIS*; WD Press Release, 22 Oct 45; Harrington, *Yankee Samurai*, pp. 354–55. At least two other Nisei lieutenants, 2d Lts. Yoshito Fujimoto and Kay I. Kitagawa, traveled with MacArthur's advance echelon. GHQ, Travel Orders, 28 Aug 45.

[36] Thomas Sakamoto, biographical statement, 1 Nov 96, author's files; *Saga of the MIS*; Thomas Sakamoto, "News of the Century: Japan's Surrender & Hiroshima, September 1945," *Nikkei Heritage* 7, no. 3 (Fall 1995): 10–11; Interv, author with Sakamoto, 16 Nov 87; Sakamoto, "Witness to Surrender," pp. 8–9; Mashbir, *I Was an American Spy*, pp. 332–34. Sources differ on other Nisei on board that day. Kayano identifies Jiro Yukimura. Kayano, MISNorCal Bio. Duval Edwards identifies Noboru Yoshimura. Edwards, *Spy Catchers*, p. 262. Saburo Kubota identifies Thomas Imada, in Tsukiyama et al., *Secret Valor*, p. 90. Shigeya Kihara identifies Kiyoshi Hirano. "Fifty Years of the Yankee Samurai," Unpubl Ms, Mar 90, author's files. Another source identifies Kazu Yoshihashi. War Relocation Authority Photo no. 464, Bancroft Library, University of California, Berkeley. Roy

*MacArthur meets with the Japanese press corps upon his arrival in Japan,
30 August 1945. Sakamoto* (upper right) *serves as press escort.*

With the surrender, small numbers of Nisei began to enter Japan with combat
units or on special assignments. M.Sgt. Arthur S. Komori entered Tokyo Bay with
the first American ship as personal interpreter for Brig. Gen. Elliot R. Thorpe,
chief of counterintelligence. Lt. Kay Kitagawa went ashore as Fleet Admiral William F. Halsey's personal interpreter. When the 1st Cavalry Division rolled into
Tokyo on 8 September, it was accompanied by its Nisei language team.[37]

Numerous combat divisions and corps headquarters, each with its Nisei language team, poured into Japan over the next several weeks. Several Nisei were
detailed to the Navy, which needed to secure the cooperation of the Japanese Navy
for clearing minefields and seizing shore facilities. In the largest such operation,

---

Uyehata identifies Thomas Sakamoto, Noby Yoshimura, Jiro Yukimura, Thomas Imada, and Kaz
Yoshihata. Roy Uyehata, "MIS Chronology, 1940–1999," Unpubl Ms, 1999, author's files.

[37] Arthur Komori, MISNorCal Bio; Tsukiyama et al., *Secret Valor*, p. 35; Harrington hints
that Komori worked undercover at this time. Harrington, *Yankee Samurai*, p. 350; *Yaban Gogai*,
Sep–Oct 45.

beginning on 22 September, thirty-two American minesweepers and thirty-three Japanese minesweepers cleared a two-mile-wide channel for 150 miles through the Inland Sea.[38] The V Amphibious Corps got a firsthand look at Japanese defenses on Kyushu that would have awaited Operation OLYMPIC when it landed in September with Nisei teams from JICPOA. Sgt. Don Oka was attached to the 5th Marine Division when it moved to Sasebo on 22 September and then onward to Nagasaki. His mission was to "release all Japanese political prisoners, locate all downed U.S. planes and the whereabouts of all surviving airmen."[39] At Aomori, the northernmost port on Honshu, the 81st Infantry Division landed on 18 September. On the first day some Japanese men walked around 2d Lt. Robert K. Sakai and asked themselves in Japanese, "Who is this Asian-looking person dressed in an American military uniform? He must be Chinese or Korean."[40]

Freeing Allied prisoners of war was an urgent concern. When the Americans arrived, POW camps in Japan held about 32,000 Allied prisoners. In the Philippines, thousands of former prisoners of war and civilian internees told horrifying stories of great suffering and atrocities. Intelligence channels picked up indications that the Japanese might execute prisoners rather than relinquish them. These concerns were well grounded. When the U.S. Navy bombarded Wake Island in October 1943, the Japanese executed 96 American civilian prisoners held there since December 1941. In December 1944 the Japanese commander on Palawan Island in the Philippines executed 150 American prisoners when he thought the island was about to be retaken. The Potsdam Declaration had warned that "stern justice shall be meted out to all war criminals, including those who have visited cruelties upon our prisoners."[41] In the last months of the war military authorities made plans for the rapid recovery of prisoners of war and internees, and camps were identified from the air. When the surrender came, Twentieth Air Force bombers and Navy carrier aircraft dropped food and medical supplies into the camps. The liberated prisoners were brought to Yokohama and then moved onward to Guam, Saipan, or Manila. Thousands of Allied POWs and internees were also released in China and Southeast Asia.

In a few instances the Nisei helped the Recovered Personnel Detachments make arrangements with camp officials. Sgt. Ichiro James Ito reported that his team would "inquire with camp officials, go over train schedules, inquire about

---

[38] Morison, *History of United States Naval Operations*, 15: 12–14.

[39] Don C. Oka, MISNorCal Bio; Henry I. Shaw, Jr., *The United States Marines in the Occupation of Japan* (Washington, D.C.: Headquarters, U.S. Marine Corps, 1969); Benis M. Frank and Henry I. Shaw, Jr., *History of U.S. Marine Corps Operations in World War II*, vol. 5, *Victory and Occupation* (Washington, D.C.: Headquarters, U.S. Marine Corps, 1968); Charles R. Smith, *Securing the Surrender: Marines in the Occupation of Japan* (Washington, D.C.: Headquarters, U.S. Marine Corps, 1997).

[40] *Japanese Eyes, American Heart: Personal Reflections of Hawaii's World War II Nisei Soldiers* (Honolulu: Tendai Educational Foundation, 1998), p. 132.

[41] *Reports of General MacArthur*, vol. 1 supplement, pp. 89–116; Gavan Daws, *Prisoners of the Japanese: POWs of World War II in the Pacific* (New York: William Morrow, 1994); ATIS Research Rpt no. 86, 24 Aug 44 (see ch. 3, note 53).

the route and act as interpreters for officers." In areas where Allied prisoners had been forced to work as slave laborers, he wrote, "coal mining officials made us guests in private clubs and hotels. After talking to some of the people here I found that there were no signs of resentment in their speech or actions; only the quiet aloofness shown to all strangers."[42] From a camp near Tokyo, marines liberated one unusual prisoner, Sgt. Frank Fujita, Jr. He had been born and raised in Texas by his Japanese father and Caucasian mother. Upon the outbreak of the war he had been on Java in the Netherlands East Indies with a Texas National Guard artillery battalion when they were captured in March 1942.[43]

In the first few weeks only a few dozen MIS Nisei arrived in Japan, most assigned to combat units. Those few were stretched thin to meet critical requirements, together with even fewer Caucasian linguists. All too often this shortage forced American commanders to rely on interpreters provided by the Japanese government. Three weeks after MacArthur's arrival, when the emperor requested a private meeting, the Imperial Household Agency supplied the interpreter. Major Bowers waited outside the meeting, but his services were not needed.[44]

Regional Surrenders

The surrender of Japanese Army and Navy forces in the home islands was swiftly accomplished. However, several million other Japanese soldiers and sailors were spread throughout the Asia-Pacific region. Within a few days of the emperor's announcement, armies that had been locked in a deadly embrace from the Burmese highlands to Pacific atolls laid down their arms. Two million Japanese soldiers remained in China and Manchuria and almost a million in Korea. Another million soldiers were scattered from Burma through the Netherlands East Indies to New Guinea. A quarter million were stranded from the Gilberts and Marshalls to the Bonins and the Ryukyus.[45] Imperial General Headquarters sent out radio messages on 16 August to its regional commands, ordering them to cease fighting; the Imperial Household Agency sent imperial princes to Manchuria, China,

---

[42] *Yaban Gogai*, Nov 45, pp. 5, 8.

[43] "Sgt. Fujita, Only Nisei Taken Prisoner by Japanese in Pacific Fighting, Reported Liberated," *Pacific Citizen*, 22 Sep 45; Frank Fujita, *Foo! A Japanese-American Prisoner of the Rising Sun* (Denton: University of North Texas Press, 1993). Another Nisei, Frank Fujino, was said to have been captured on Bataan but escaped and later joined the 442d RCT. "Nisei Survived Death March on Bataan, Lost a Leg in Rescue of Lost Battalion," *Pacific Citizen*, 29 Mar 47, p. 1.

[44] Herbert P. Bix, *Hirohito and the Making of Modern Japan* (New York: HarperCollins, 2000), pp. 541–51; *Yaban Gogai*, Sep–Oct 45, p. 3; Dower, *Embracing Defeat*, pp. 292–97; Fabion Bowers, "Japan, 1940–1949: A Tumultuous Time Remembered," *Japan Society Newsletter*, Oct 95, pp. 4–7; Faubion Bowers, "The Late General MacArthur, Warts and All," *Esquire* (January 1967): 90.

[45] *Reports of General MacArthur*, vol. 1, pp. 459–60, plate 134, and vol. 1 supplement, plate 48; Meirion Harris and Susie Harris, *Soldiers of the Sun: The Rise and Fall of the Imperial Japanese Army* (New York: Random House, 1991), pp. 444–72.

and Southeast Asia to ensure compliance. In other areas, the Allies had to inform isolated Japanese detachments that the war had ended.[46]

On 19 August MacArthur's headquarters directed that no formal surrenders be held anywhere until he had completed the ceremony in Tokyo Bay, which complicated local surrenders throughout the region. Not until 2 September did the Imperial General Headquarters send out General Order no. 1 (drafted by American planners), ordering all Japanese armed forces to lay down their weapons.[47] During these weeks suspended between war and peace, the Nisei were needed everywhere. They transmitted the emperor's speech to isolated Japanese detachments by leaflet, radio, and loudspeaker in a dramatic intensification of psychological warfare. They accompanied Allied troops to disarm Japanese forces. They arranged the surrender ceremonies with their myriad administrative and logistical details. Parlays had to be arranged, radio links established, information about troop dispositions exchanged, and minefields cleared.

In each region, the Allied troops first had to contact local Japanese commanders. In some cases, the Japanese had not yet received word of the surrender through their chain of command and feared an Allied ruse. In many cases, the Allies provided copies of the emperor's rescript. Some Japanese commanders refused to deal with the Allies and killed themselves rather than endure such humiliation. Commanders on both sides would sometimes arrange local ceasefires, which held until formal surrender ceremonies could be held, sometimes weeks later. The Nisei played an essential role in all these talks. Areas such as Korea, French Indochina, and the Netherlands East Indies contained a volatile mix of Japanese troops, nationalist forces, and former colonial forces. In some areas, the Allies retained Japanese troops and local authorities for months after the surrender, making the situation even more chaotic and dangerous. In other areas, Allied or indigenous forces wreaked terrible vengeance on Japanese soldiers. Everywhere, the local population suffered from famine, diseases, destruction, and displacement.

Southeast Asia

After the United States withdrew its combat troops from the Southeast Asia Command in the spring and summer of 1945, 150–200 Nisei remained in New Delhi with the Southeast Asia Translation and Interrogation Center (SEATIC).[48]

---

[46] *Reports of General MacArthur*, vol. 1, p. 446, and vol. 2, pt. 2, pp. 742–45, 748–55; Frank, *Downfall*, pp. 326–29. Bix, *Hirohito*, cites CINCPAC-CINCPOA, Bulletin no. 164–45, 15 Aug 45.

[47] Supreme Commander for the Allied Powers, Government Section, *Political Reorientation of Japan, September 1945 to September 1948*, 2 vols. (Washington, D.C.: Government Printing Office, 1949).

[48] Earl Louis Mountbatten, *Post Surrender Tasks: Section E of the Report to the Combined Chiefs of Staff by the Supreme Allied Commander South-East Asia, 1943–45* (London: Her Majesty's Stationery Office, 1969); Bisheswar Prasad, ed., *Official History of the Indian Armed Forces in the Second World War, Post-War Occupation Forces: Japan and South-East Asia* (India: Orient Longmans, 1958); S. Woodburn Kirby, ed., *The War against Japan*, 5 vols. (London: Her Majesty's Stationery Office, 1969), vol. 5; Allen, *End of the War in Asia*; Peter Dennis, *Troubled Days of Peace: Mountbatten and South East Asia Command, 1945–1946* (New York: St. Martin's, 1987).

They were joined by Canadian Nisei trained at the Canadian Army language school in Vancouver, twelve of whom arrived in April 1945.[49] Lord Mountbatten's forces had been preparing for the invasion of Malaya, Operation ZIPPER, scheduled for September; American Nisei already had been assigned to British and Commonwealth units for the assault. However, Operation ZIPPER was superseded by hasty plans to seize Japanese-held Southeast Asia following the surrender. Adding to Mountbatten's worries, at the last minute the Combined Joint Chiefs moved the boundary line between his theater and MacArthur's, transferring most of Southeast Asia and Indonesia to Mountbatten. In September 1945 Mountbatten rushed his forces to take possession of former British, French, and Dutch colonies and conduct what the British called Recovery of Allied Prisoners of War and Internees.[50]

On 27 August Allied and Japanese representatives met in Rangoon for regional surrender talks. Serving as interpreters were two newly commissioned Nisei, 2d Lts. Teichiro Hirata and Joe Amaki. Hirata wrote to friends at Ft. Snelling:

In early August, just prior to the surrender, I was flown to Kandy, Ceylon, to await the word to cease fire. Then in late August I was fortunate in drawing an assignment to the surrender negotiations held in Rangoon, Burma.... [S]everal of the Nisei boys ... were scattered about along the Malay Peninsula, and some were sent to Java, [Hong Kong], [Bangkok], and Saigon.[51]

Singapore, the site of Britain's humiliating 1942 defeat, was selected for the surrender ceremony on 12 September. A local surrender agreement was signed on 4 September, and British troops landed the following day. On 9 September assault troops, accompanied by six Canadian Nisei, landed on the Malay Peninsula. American 2d Lt. Kan Tagami, a veteran of the MARS Task Force, accompanied the 34th Indian Corps into Kuala Lumpur. About fifteen American Nisei remained with Commonwealth forces in Malaya and Singapore to assist with the surrender and demobilization of Japanese forces.[52]

Commonwealth forces pushed into the southern half of French Indochina, arriving in Saigon on 8 September. As an interim measure the British commander ordered the Japanese commander to maintain law and order; but the British soon found themselves caught between French officials and the Vietnamese nationalists, the Vietminh. Iwao Kumabe, attached to the British, was in Saigon in late

---

[49] Roy Ito, *We Went to War: The Story of the Japanese Canadians Who Served during the First and Second World Wars* (Ontario: Canada's Wings, 1984), pp. 235–79.

[50] Kirby, *War against Japan*, 5: 243–49, 532–41; William J. Slim, *Defeat into Victory: Battling Japan in Burma and India, 1942–1945* (London: Cassell, 1956), pp. 531–32. The territory was formally transferred from the Southwest Pacific Area to the Southeast Asia Command on 2 September.

[51] *Yaban Gogai*, Dec 45, p. 5; Allen, *End of the War in Asia*, p. 119. For a description of local surrender negotiations in Burma from the Japanese perspective, see Allen, *End of the War in Asia*, pp. 3–13.

[52] Interv, author with Kan Tagami, 7 Dec 94; Kirby, *War against Japan*, 5: 271–73; Henry Hideo Kuwabara, MISNorCal Bio.

September when "shooting broke out. We were told to prepare against any attack, and our barracks were barricaded. . . . The rebels had barricaded the roads to the airport, and put up posters that the police tore down."[53]

British authorities in Saigon with Nisei assistance also investigated war crimes. Kumabe helped interrogate the *Kempeitai* (Japanese military police) chief for South Indochina, which took three weeks. Kumabe himself remained in Saigon until February 1946. Sam T. Kikumoto flew to Saigon to aid in investigating the treatment of American prisoners of war held in Indochina. He spent six months in Saigon helping to interrogate *Kempeitai* members who had abused or killed Americans.[54] French troops arrived in October. Most Americans had left by the end of the year, the Nisei involved in war crimes investigations among the last to leave.[55]

The Netherlands East Indies presented similar problems. Indonesian nationalist leader Achmed Sukarno proclaimed the Indonesian Republic on 17 August, weeks before the arrival of Allied troops, and obtained arms from the Japanese Army. The Netherlands government dispatched a lieutenant governor, who arrived at Southeast Asia Command headquarters at Kandy on 1 September. Mountbatten later reported that the official "[gave] me no reason to suppose that the reoccupation of Java would present any operational problem, beyond that of rounding up the Japanese."[56]

The first Allied force sent to the Netherlands East Indies was Force 136 "Mastiff," which parachuted to liberate Allied prisoners of war on 8 September. The Royal Navy arrived at Batavia (Jakarta) on 16 September and immediately requested troops to maintain order; two Indian divisions were dispatched. All this required close work with Japanese commanders and units, which required linguists. Second Lt. Gil Ryo Arai accompanied the British forces to Java, while T.Sgt. Paul T. Bannai assisted Australian forces with surrenders in Bali, Java, and the former Portuguese colony of Timor. By early 1946 all American Nisei had been withdrawn from the South-East Asia Command.[57]

China

In the months before the surrender, Japanese troops began withdrawing from southern China and Chinese nationalist forces advanced toward the coast. With the

---

[53] Allen, *End of the War in Asia*, pp. 96–131; Kirby, *War against Japan*, 5: 297; Harrington, *Yankee Samurai*, pp. 358–59.

[54] Harrington, *Yankee Samurai*, pp. 357–58; Interv, Dawn Duensing with Sam T. Kikumoto, in *Americanism: A Matter of Mind and Heart*, vol. 1, *The Military Intelligence Service* (Maui, Hawaii: Maui's Sons and Daughters of the Nisei Veterans, 2001).

[55] Ronald H. Spector, *Advice and Support: The Early Years, 1941–1960*, U.S. Army in Vietnam (Washington, D.C.: U.S. Army Center of Military History, 1983), pp. 64–73; Robert D. Schulzinger, *A Time for War: The United States and Vietnam, 1941–1975* (New York: Oxford University Press, 1997), pp. 19–22.

[56] Kirby, *War against Japan*, 5: 311.

[57] Intervs, author with Tagami, 7 Dec 94, and with Paul T. Bannai, 11 Sep 96; Paul T. Bannai, MISNorCal Bio.

support of 30,000 American advisers with the U.S. Forces China Theater and Chinese Combat Command, Chinese forces were poised to launch a major offensive in the south. Guerrilla units under the Sino-American Cooperative Organization passed through Japanese-held areas to reach Nanking (Nanjing), Canton (Guangzhou), Peking (Beijing), and Shanghai. In late July Lt. Gen. Albert C. Wedemeyer and Chiang Kai-shek agreed that American troops would seize China's coastal cities in the event of a sudden Japanese collapse and hold them until nationalist troops could arrive. When the surrender came, 3 million Japanese soldiers remained in China and Manchuria. On 10 August the Joint Chiefs of Staff sent Wedemeyer a new directive for the China Theater and authorized Chiang Kai-shek to accept the surrender of all Japanese forces in China. After the Japanese surrender, Admiral Nimitz provided a marine amphibious corps with two divisions.[58]

In the north, the Soviet Union abruptly broke its long truce and attacked on 9 August. More than a million Soviet soldiers swept into Manchuria and northern China and seized Sakhalin Island and the northern half of Korea. The Red Army gave the Kwantung Army no chance to surrender. Instead it was completely shattered, losing about 80,000 killed.[59]

Dozens of Nisei were serving in China, about forty with the Sino Translation and Interrogation Center (SINTIC) in Chungking. Perhaps six others were assigned to the Fourteenth Air Force. Others worked for the Office of War Information. Five were in Yenan with the Dixie Mission. A few were parceled out to Chinese guerrilla forces with the Office of Strategic Services (OSS). Other language personnel included some Chinese-American graduates of the MISLS Chinese-language program. For example, in August the school sent thirty Chinese-language graduates to China at the urgent request of the China Theater. Nisei in China worked under two experienced American language officers, Col. Joseph K. Dickey and Lt. Col. John Burden.

Immediately after the surrender announcement OSS Detachment 202 conducted rescue missions for Allied prisoners of war in eight camps in China, Korea, Hainan Island, and Formosa. Individual Nisei were assigned to most teams, including several of the original fourteen Nisei selected for the OSS in 1943. One team went to Manchuria in search of senior Allied prisoners held by the Japanese, including the defeated commanders of the Philippines and Singapore, Maj. Gen. Jonathan M. Wainwright and British General Arthur E. Percival, respectively.

Six OSS operatives parachuted near the Hoten prison camp outside Mukden on the morning of 16 August after a long B-24 flight from Sian (Xian) in north-central China. Cpl. Fumio Kido was the team's lone interpreter. They were met by Japanese soldiers with fixed bayonets and a Japanese sergeant who barked

---

[58] Albert C. Wedemeyer, *Wedemeyer on War and Peace*, ed. Keith E. Eiler (Stanford, Calif.: Hoover Institution Press, 1987), pp. 133–54; Albert C. Wedemeyer, *Wedemeyer Reports!* (New York: Henry Holt, 1958).

[59] Alvin D. Coox, *Nomonhan: Japan Against Russia, 1939*, 2 vols. (Stanford, Calif.: Stanford University Press, 1985), 2: 1059–74; David M. Glantz, *August Storm: Soviet Tactical and Operational Combat in Manchuria, 1945* (Fort Leavenworth, Kans.: Combat Studies Institute, 1983).

a command at the Americans. Kido interpreted: "He says to kneel down." The sergeant demanded to know who they were. Kido explained that the war was over and they had come to bring aid to the prisoners, but the sergeant was skeptical. A Japanese officer approached to question Kido. "He seemed only interested in knowing whether I was Japanese or not," Kido recalled. "I replied that I was of Japanese ancestry but that I was an American and an American soldier."[60]

After a long wait, another Japanese officer arrived and apologized, saying that the news of the surrender had just reached Mukden. The officers took the Americans to their headquarters to wait for further instructions. The Japanese were especially confused about Kido, who overheard a Japanese officer telephone his higher headquarters to ask, "We have an American-born Japanese here. What do we do with him?" He could not hear the answer on the other end. Later that day they met a *Kempeitai* colonel, who produced a bottle of American whiskey and conversed with them in excellent English. When Kido asked where he had learned his English, the colonel explained he had spent some time in Hawaii.[61]

The following morning Japanese officials allowed the team to visit the prison camp, where they liberated over a thousand prisoners. Wainwright and Percival flew to Tokyo just in time for the surrender. One of the other senior American prisoners, Maj. Gen. George M. Parker, recommended the OSS team for the Distinguished Service Cross:

From my personal observation and experience based on three years close contact with the Japanese Army, I feel certain that the lives of all the members of [the] party were in grave danger during the greater part of August 16th. Any misunderstood action on the part of one of the Americans would not only have resulted in quick death to that individual and mass punishment to the others, but in the failure of the attempt to contact the prisoners.[62]

One week later the first Soviet troops arrived in Mukden, and Kido feared they would treat him as a Japanese soldier. He quickly memorized some simple Russian phrases such as *"Nyet Nipponaky soldat!"* ["No Japanese soldier!"].[63]

Capt. John K. Singlaub led another OSS team on 27 August to Hainan Island, where 356 Australian and Dutch soldiers and sailors were being held. The lone Nisei interpreter was Lt. Ralph Yempuku. Yempuku had never jumped before, Singlaub recalled, "but did not hesitate to volunteer." They jumped from five or six hundred feet. When Yempuku's parachute opened, a buckle hit him in the face and split open

---

[60] Calvin Tottori, "The OSS Niseis in the China-Burma-India Theater," 2d ed., p. 42, Unpubl Ms, 2001, copy in author's files.

[61] Craig, *Fall of Japan*, pp. 221–28; Roger Hilsman, *American Guerrilla* (Washington: Brassey's, 1990), pp. 232–52; Fumio Kido, MISNorCal Bio; Harrington Papers. Craig states that the Japanese soldiers struck Kido, but Kido later denied this.

[62] Memo, Maj. Gen. George M. Parker to CG, U.S. Army Forces, China Theater, 1 Sep 45, app. to Kido, MISNorCal Bio. The China Theater awarded to all American members of the OSS rescue teams the Soldier's Medal, not the Distinguished Service Cross. HQ, U.S. Forces, China Theater, General Order no. 211, 4 Nov 45, in Harrington Papers.

[63] Kido, MISNorCal Bio, p. 6.

his chin. He hit the ground hard with blood streaming down his face. But he had no time to worry about that: in minutes trucks arrived and disgorged nervous Japanese soldiers who approached the team with fixed bayonets. From the opposite direction, Chinese farm laborers rushed over to see what was happening.

Singlaub made a quick decision. He spun around with his back to the advancing Japanese soldiers and told Yempuku to interpret: "Stop right there." Yempuku translated: "The major commands, stop right there!" Then Singlaub spun around and shouted in an angry voice, "Turn those troops around. Face the Chinese civilians. You will protect these supplies from them." Yempuku translated in the same tone of voice. The Japanese lieutenant hesitated, and then he too made a decision. He turned his troops around to face the approaching Chinese laborers. "We had won the first engagement of this strange campaign," Singlaub recalled.[64]

The OSS sent other teams to POW camps elsewhere in China, Korea, and Formosa. S.Sgt. Dick S. Hamada accompanied a team that landed near Peking on 17 August, where they found four survivors of the 1942 Doolittle bombing raid on Tokyo.[65]

In the aftermath of the Japanese surrender, the U.S. headquarters in the China Theater moved forward from the wartime capital of Chungking to Shanghai on the coast. In these weeks the language section did heavy translation work. Most Nisei flew onward to Nanking, the capital of Japanese-occupied China. Colonel Burden attended the formal surrender ceremony on 9 September at Whampoa, the Central Military Academy in Nanking.[66]

Meanwhile, the III Amphibious Corps seized key points on the China coast, recalling the marines' long service in China before the war. The corps chief of staff and G–2 were both former Chinese-language attachés. Navy language officers, aided by a few Nisei, did most of the work of liaison with local Japanese officials. The 1st Marine Division advance party arrived at Tientsin on 24 September and conducted a surrender ceremony on 6 October for 50,000 Japanese soldiers. The 6th Marine Division landed at Tsingtao on 11 October and conducted a local surrender ceremony on 25 October. The situation on the ground grew more complicated by the day because the nationalists controlled the cities while the Communists controlled the countryside. During October the Fourteenth Air Force flew 50,000 nationalist troops into the area. The marines accepted local surrenders, maintained order, and facilitated the repatriation of hundreds of thousands of Japanese soldiers and civilians, as well as many Koreans, Okinawans, and Taiwanese. Eventually the III Amphibious Corps repatriated more than 500,000 Japanese and

---

[64] John K. Singlaub, *Hazardous Duty: An American Soldier in the Twentieth Century* (New York: Simon & Schuster, 1991), pp. 71–101; Craig, *Fall of Japan*, 278–84. Singlaub was a captain but on this mission wore major's rank insignia.

[65] Tottori, "OSS Niseis." For an account of the liberation of another camp, see Mary Previte, "Ted Nagaki," *Ex-CBI Roundup* (June 2002).

[66] Ho Ying-Ch'in, "Accepting the Surrender and Taking-Over Conditions," *China Handbook, 1937–1945* (New York: Macmillan, 1947), pp. 764–67; Allen, *End of the War in Asia*, pp. 219–56; John Burden autobiography, Unpubl Ms, 1992, copy in author's files.

Koreans.[67] Nisei John Noguchi accompanied the 1st Marine Division to Chang-zhou and eventually sailed to Sasebo as escort for a returning Japanese battalion. Among the returning Japanese soldiers he discovered an American-born Nisei whom Noguchi had known when they were students together at San Francisco State College. His friend had been caught in Japan at the start of the war, was drafted into the Japanese Army, and spent three years stationed in China.[68]

In North China, the marines found that their greatest problems came not from the defeated Japanese soldiers but from the clash between Chinese factions. General Order no. 1 had directed Japanese forces in China to surrender to Chiang Kai-shek, which left the Communists out of the picture. Soon the marines were pulling joint duty with Japanese soldiers to protect key areas from the Chinese Communists. The marines and nationalists even used some Japanese Army units in fighting against Communist guerrillas. According to the official Marine Corps history, "the [Japanese] China Expeditionary Army reversed its wartime role and became a quasi-ally of the National Government." The last Nisei were withdrawn by the end of 1946 and the bulk of marine forces by early 1947.[69]

Other Nisei were scattered throughout China on special assignments. The China Theater headquarters sent a small team with one Nisei to T'aiyuan in Shansi Province in North China to observe the surrender of 60,000 Japanese troops of the North China Area Army.[70] Three other Nisei joined a U.S. advisory group for Formosa. Toshio Uesato flew to Taihoku (Taipei) on Formosa in mid-November to help repatriate Japanese troops. Six weeks later he accepted a civilian position in the SCAP Civil Intelligence Section in Tokyo. He took the civil service job in part because he wanted to search for his older brother, a University of Hawaii graduate who had been studying at Waseda University when war broke out. He later learned that he had been conscripted and died of malaria on Bougainville in April 1944.[71]

The U.S. Army had maintained its liaison mission to the Chinese Communists in Yenan, though the relationship had noticeably cooled. In July 1945 Col. Ivan D. Yeaton, a former U.S. military attaché to Moscow, took command of the Dixie Mission. He was impressed with the three Nisei already there, two of whom, Koji Ariyoshi and George I. Nakamura, had received field commissions that spring. In August two more Nisei arrived.

Yeaton considered Ariyoshi the most important man on the Dixie Mission "because the Communists trusted him and gave him free access to their compound."[72] Ariyoshi had been in Yenan since October 1944 and was genuinely

---

[67] See Donald Keene's letters in Otis Cary, ed., *From a Ruined Empire: Letters—Japan, China, Korea, 1945–46* (San Francisco: Kodansha, 1975); Donald Keene, *On Familiar Terms: A Journey across Cultures* (New York: Kodansha, 1994), pp. 58–68.

[68] John Noguchi, MISNorCal Bio, Rocky Mountain Bio.

[69] Frank and Shaw, *Victory and Occupation*, pp. 521–650 (quote on p. 532).

[70] Arthur T. Morimitsu, in Falk and Tsuneishi, *MIS in the War against Japan*.

[71] Intervs, author with Toshio Uesato, 21 Aug 95, and with George I. Nakamura, 6 Dec 94.

[72] Carolle J. Carter, *Mission to Yenan: American Liaison with the Chinese Communists, 1944–1947* (Lexington: University Press of Kentucky, 1997), p. 202.

impressed with the Communists and their political work with Japanese prisoners. The Americans, he recalled, "were generally favorably impressed by the broad participation in government by the people of all classes, reduced land rent, clean government, active resistance against the Japanese invaders, and the educational program that reached the peasant masses who were generally neglected in the Nationalist areas." Ariyoshi also had good relations with the small group of Japanese Communists in Yenan, including *Sanzō Nosaka.*[73]

In September 1945 Ariyoshi flew to Chungking, where he reported to Wedemeyer on the strength of Communist forces: "What China needs is not Nationalist domination but good clean government and democracy. Such a government must be broadly representative." Wedemeyer sent him to Ambassador Patrick J. Hurley, to whom he delivered the same assessment. Hurley responded angrily and shook his finger in Ariyoshi's face: "Young man, you have been fooled by Communist propaganda! I am the only American who has not been fooled by Communist propaganda!"[74] Deeply discouraged at America's China policy, Ariyoshi flew back to Yenan, where he stayed a few months longer. When General George C. Marshall visited Yenan in March 1946, Ariyoshi accompanied him. He was discharged in China and briefly worked for the State Department before finally leaving China in July 1946.[75]

When news of the Japanese surrender reached the former British possession of Hong Kong, the British internees took matters into their own hands, established a provisional government using former colonial officials, then radioed Allied forces to announce they had liberated themselves. The British government dispatched a naval task force from Subic Bay in the Philippines and accepted the provisional surrender on 3 September.[76]

The surrender ceremony took place on 16 September in the gracious old Peninsula Hotel. The OSS observer team included Lieutenant Yempuku. By strange coincidence, one of the interpreters for the Japanese delegation was Yempuku's younger brother, Donald. Both had been born in Hawaii and were graduates of McKinley High School. When war broke out, Donald was still living in Japan. He renounced his U.S. citizenship and found work with the *Dōmei* news and the military press bureau as a translator. When he entered the crowded hotel lobby, he spotted his older brother wearing an American uniform. "I knew it was Ralph right away," he recalled, "Immediately, I was happy he was alive. But almost in

---

[73] Koji Ariyoshi, *From Kona to Yenan: The Political Memoirs of Koji Ariyoshi*, ed. Alice M. Beechert and Edward D. Beechert (Honolulu: University of Hawaii Press, 2000), pp. 124–25, 150–51 (quote from pp. 150–51).

[74] Ariyoshi, *From Kona to Yenan*, pp. 174–78.

[75] Upon returning to the United States, Ariyoshi wrote a memoir; but in 1947 his New York publisher rejected it. Ariyoshi later published it himself in installments in the *Honolulu Record*, a progressive weekly he edited. In 1951 he and six others were arrested under the Smith Act. He was convicted of "conspiring to teach and advocate the overthrow of the government by force," but this was later overturned.

[76] Kirby, *War against Japan*, 5: 283–88; Allen, *End of the War in Asia*, pp. 251–56; Morison, *History of United States Naval Operations*, 15: 5.

the same breath, I was embarrassed because he was on the side of the enemy." He decided not to approach his brother, who did not notice him. The brothers finally met several months later in Japan. "This time, we shook hands," Donald recalled. "Japanese, you know, never show much emotion. We didn't discuss the war. I felt that we were all fortunate to have come out alive."[77]

In northern Indochina, the situation was explosive. The Japanese Army had overthrown the Vichy colonial regime in March 1945, so the Japanese surrender left a power vacuum. Ho Chi Minh, the Vietnamese nationalist leader, declared himself president of "free Vietnam" on 16 August. The OSS inserted a team on 22 August with a Nisei interpreter, T.Sgt. Alvin Toso. This team liberated 300 Allied prisoners but could not control the area without reinforcement. The Viet Minh seized power in Hanoi on 2 September and declared a provisional government. To seize territory and disarm the Japanese soldiers, Chiang Kai-shek sent across the border 80,000 men accompanied by American advisers, who reached Hanoi in mid-September. French troops did not arrive until early October. Several Nisei were assigned to the advancing Chinese, including Tom Haga, who took a train from Kunming to the Indochina border at the end of August. Another Nisei, 2d Lt. Clarke H. Kawakami, was picked for the mission because he spoke French, but he asked George I. Nakamura to take his place. Nakamura had just returned to Chungking after eleven months in Yenan for a commissioning board. Kawakami wanted to go to Japan, not Indochina, as quickly as possible. Shortly before he had left Japan in 1941, he had married a Japanese actress. Now he was anxious to return and find her. Nakamura won his commission, agreed to take Kawakami's place, and soon found himself in Hanoi.[78]

Following the Japanese surrender in Hanoi in late September, the Nisei helped arrange the evacuation of all Japanese troops to Formosa and then on to Japan. But first the U.S. Navy had to clear Haiphong Harbor of Japanese mines. For this Toshi Uesato was assigned to a U.S. Navy destroyer to obtain information from the Japanese Navy on their sea mines in the area. Throughout October and November he interviewed Japanese naval officers and helped translate their charts for the American naval officers. All Americans were withdrawn from northern Indochina by December 1945, and the Chinese troops departed the following spring.[79]

Central Pacific

Scattered across the Central Pacific, more than a quarter-million Japanese soldiers and sailors were slowly wasting away on bypassed islands while American forces were stronger than ever and backed by powerful intelligence. JICPOA in Hawaii, grown to 544 officers and 1,223 enlisted men, produced 2 million printed sheets of intelligence each week. On Guam, the Advance Intelligence Center

---

[77] Tomi Kaizawa Knaefler, *Our House Divided: Seven Japanese American Families in World War II* (Honolulu: University of Hawaii Press, 1991), pp. 85–87.
[78] Interv, author with G. Nakamura, 6 Dec 94.
[79] Intervs, author with Uesato, 21 Aug 95, and with George Nakamura, 6 Dec 94; George I. Nakamura, MISNorCal Bio; Spector, *Advice and Support*, pp. 51–73.

provided direct support to Nimitz and his combat commanders. More than 200 Nisei were assigned to JICPOA. Some worked in the JICPOA Annex in downtown Honolulu, while others served with Army and Marine divisions and corps. JICPOA was also staffed with several hundred Navy and Marine language officers from the Navy's Oriental Language School in Boulder, Colorado.[80]

JICPOA conducted psychological warfare operations with the Office of War Information using leaflets and voice broadcasts to induce surrenders on bypassed islands. In May 1945 the Psychological Warfare Section established a special stockade on Oahu for Japanese prisoners of war assisting the program. After the Japanese surrender these efforts were increased.[81]

Within weeks of the Japanese surrender, this massive theater intelligence infrastructure was dismantled. Nimitz had no responsibilities for the occupation of Japan or Korea, so JICPOA and its translation annex were closed and the intelligence specialists, including the Nisei, were reassigned or demobilized. Several Nisei were dispatched to help with local surrenders. Some were deployed for the Navy Technical Mission to Japan or the U.S. Strategic Bombing Survey.[82]

In the war's closing days, T3g. Don S. Okubo was patrolling the Marshall Islands in a Navy landing craft, using a loudspeaker to call out to stragglers. Sometimes cooperative prisoners of war made the broadcasts under his supervision. Okubo had fought with the 1st Marine Division on Peleliu, which he considered his "most dangerous assignment."

I was much more worried about the marines shooting me than the Japs. You know how those marines are: if they see anyone who even looks like the enemy they fire. Whenever I was on patrol I had to be escorted by half a dozen marines or I'd be a dead duck. Despite my army uniform I was fired on several times.[83]

A few days after Japan's surrender, Okubo was sent to Mille Atoll to negotiate the surrender of the Japanese headquarters there. Late in the afternoon he went ashore alone, only to learn that the admiral's headquarters was on another island. By the time he reached the second island, night had fallen; so the whaleboat that brought him there cautiously pulled up to the dark landing. The Japanese guards

---

[80] On the end of the war in the Pacific Ocean Areas, see CINCPAC-CINCPOA, Rpt of Surrender and Occupation of Japan, 11 Feb 46; Morison, *History of United States Naval Operations*, 15: 3–6; Frank and Shaw, *Victory and Occupation*, pp. 449–63; Dorothy E. Richard, *United States Naval Administration of the Trust Territory of the Pacific Islands*, 3 vols. (Washington, D.C.: Government Printing Office, 1957), vol. 2. For a list of seventy-five major islands that remained under Japanese control, see Memorandum to the Press, 18 Aug 45, in *Navy Department Communiqués 601–624* (Washington, D.C.: U.S. Navy), pp. 71–73.

[81] Joint Intelligence Center, Pacific Ocean Areas, "Report of Intelligence Activities in the Pacific Ocean Areas," 15 Oct 45, p. 32 (hereafter cited as JICPOA History), copy in author's files.

[82] Rpt of Intelligence Activities; ATIS History, p. 29; Sam Setsuo Isokane, "Nisei Men of JICPOA Annex," Unpubl Ms, n.d.

[83] "Honolulu Army Sergeant Storms Pacific Island Alone, Persuades Japanese Admiral To Surrender His Garrison," *Honolulu Advertiser*, 5 Oct 45.

held their fire and took Okubo to their lieutenant, who told the lone Nisei that it was too late to disturb the admiral. The Nisei insisted that his commander had ordered him to deliver the message personally to his Japanese counterpart that the war had ended and to ask the Japanese commander to surrender his forces. The Japanese lieutenant relented and took Okubo to the cave where the admiral was sleeping. Okubo met with the admiral for two hours before obtaining his promise to surrender. The next morning the whaleboat returned to take Okubo back to the command ship. As a result of his solo mission, more than 1,000 Japanese sailors and soldiers on the atoll surrendered on 22 August in the first mass surrender in the Central Pacific. For his valor Okubo was promoted to master sergeant and awarded the Bronze Star.[84]

In the Bonin Islands, the marines had captured Iwo Jima; but 40,000 Japanese remained on other islands in the chain. The Americans and Japanese held surrender talks on Chichi Jima on 31 August; the surrender ceremony was held on 3 September. However, because of the large number of Japanese soldiers and their dispersal throughout the chain, the Americans did not take possession of the other islands until 13 December.

In the Ryukyu Islands, the Americans declared Okinawa secure in June; but 105,000 Japanese soldiers and sailors remained at large throughout that chain. On 7 September the Tenth Army commander, General Joseph W. Stilwell, accepted their surrender, with Sergeant Oda serving as his interpreter. The surrender did not bring an end to the overwhelming problems in the Ryukyus. In mid-September a powerful typhoon hit Okinawa, and another hit a few weeks later. Soldiers, prisoners of war, and refugees all suffered as their tent cities and improvised shelters were destroyed by the wind and rain. Scores of Nisei worked with military government officials to relieve the civilian suffering.[85]

Following the surrender, small groups of Japanese soldiers continued to hide in Okinawa's rugged terrain. In mid-September Sgt. Tim Ohta and a bodyguard went looking for one group of holdouts. The two Americans went as far as they could together, then Ohta "ventured alone into Japanese-held territory and disappeared into the rocks." A short while later he returned with two Japanese officers who agreed to surrender the forces under their command. Three days later Ohta, his bodyguard, and a Marine officer drove two trucks to the agreed-upon location. The bodyguard recalled the scene: "It was dawn, with mist still in the valley. I expected we'd be early and that the Japanese soldiers would wander down from the hills during the day. The scene which greeted us was unforgettable: the Japanese stood at attention in battalion formation, ... fairly well dressed, their weapons neatly stacked, and silent as we approached." The Marine officer was "clearly

---

[84] Atoll Commander, Majuro, Commendation, 10 Dec 45, author's files; "Honolulu Army Sergeant"; Tsukiyama et al., *Secret Valor*, pp. 64–66; Steve Lum, "Donald Okubo's Amazing Story," *Hawaii Herald*, 2 Jul 93, p. A–23. Okubo's Bronze Star was upgraded to the Silver Star in 2001.

[85] Harrington, *Yankee Samurai*, pp. 354–55; Akira Nakamura, MISNorCal Bio. Tenth Army was inactivated on 15 October 1945, and responsibility for the Ryukyus passed to Army Forces Western Pacific.

A Nisei sergeant (second from right) *assists as* Lt. Gen. Yoshio Tachibana *surrenders 40,000 Japanese in the Bonin Islands, USS* Dunlap, *3 September 1945.*

taken aback at this scene, . . . [and] left in one truck to get more transportation." Ohta, his bodyguard, and the remaining truck driver stayed behind to guard the 250 Japanese soldiers. Ohta had thought to bring four cartons of cigarettes, which he presented to the Japanese colonel for his men. "Each soldier stepped forward, saluted, took his cigarette and returned to the ranks—an amazing display of discipline in a defeated army." When the marine returned with more trucks, the surrender proceeded without incident. Ohta was awarded the Silver Star.[86]

On Guam and Saipan in the Marianas, American soldiers guarded tens of thousands of Japanese prisoners. On Saipan, one refugee camp alone held 18,000 civilian detainees. Japanese prisoners on Guam "sobbed loudly, waving their hands and showing great and visible grief when they heard Hirohito's radio address on the empire's surrender."[87]

---

[86] Edwards, *Spy Catchers*, pp. 249–50.

[87] Tom O'Brien, "Camp Susupe," *Yank* (22 June 1945); quote from *Yaban Gogai*, War Extra, Aug 45.

T3g. Jiro Arakaki (right) *helps an Army intelligence officer* (center) *question a senior Japanese officer, Yonakunajima, Ryukyus, 7 October 1945.*

In the Carolines and the Marianas, 130,000 Japanese soldiers and sailors remained under the command of the *Japanese 31st Army* and *Fourth Fleet.* After U.S. Navy bombers dropped surrender leaflets on Truk, American pilots spotted white crosses spread out on the island's runways. On 30 August surrender negotiations using JICPOA Nisei were held aboard an American destroyer. The night before the surrender, the intelligence officer handed T3g. Sam Setsuo Isokane the American general's prepared speech to translate into Japanese. Isokane had left his dictionary back in Hawaii; nevertheless, he worked through the night to prepare a translation, which the naval intelligence officer read out loud the next morning. The formal surrender ceremony with two Nisei interpreters was held on 2 September. The next day Isokane sailed to Rota, where he interpreted as 3,000 Japanese surrendered.[88]

---

[88] CINCPOA Press Releases no. 244, 2 Sep 45, and no. 247, 3 Sep 45; Tsukiyama et al., *Secret Valor*, p. 67; Isokane, "Nisei Men of JICPOA Annex."

T3g. William Hiromu Wada (third from left) interprets for Vice Adm. Frank J. Fletcher during surrender talks on the USS Panamint, *flagship of the North Pacific Force, 9 September 1945.*

On nearby Yap Island, five Hawaii Nisei persuaded 7,000 Japanese troops and civilians to surrender.[89] On 31 August 2,500 Japanese surrendered on Marcus Island with the help of Nobuo Furuiye. In the final months of the war he had served on Iwo Jima, where he was wounded by mortar fire, worked with refugees on Saipan, and interpreted at a war crimes trial on Guam. Soon after the Marcus surrender he was attached to the Navy Technical Mission in Sasebo.[90] On Wake Island, Larry Watanabe helped a Marine general negotiate the surrender of 1,262 emaciated Japanese defenders on 4 September.[91]

On 31 August the North Pacific Fleet set sail from the Aleutians for northern Japan. Two Nisei, T3g. Hiromu William Wada and T3g. Laurence Mihara, sailed with Admiral Frank J. Fletcher on his flagship, the USS *Panamint.* When they reached Japanese waters, a Japanese pilot came aboard to guide them through the heavily mined strait between Honshu and Hokkaido. The pilot brought his own interpreter, a Canadian Nisei who spoke English well. The Americans arrived at the Ominato naval base on 6 September. On 9 September Wada interpreted as

---

[89] Tsukiyama et al., *Secret Valor*, p. 67; Gwenfread Allen, *Hawaii's War Years, 1941–1945* (Honolulu: University of Hawaii Press, 1950), p. 273; Harrington, *Yankee Samurai*, p. 355.

[90] Falk and Tsuneishi, *MIS in the War against Japan*, pp. 58–60; Nobuo Furuiye, MISNorCal Bio; *Yaban Gogai*, Nov 45, p. 8.

[91] S. E. Smith, ed., *The United States Marine Corps in World War II* (New York: Random House, 1969), pp. 923–29; Morison, *History of United States Naval Operations*, 15: 5.

Fletcher accepted the surrender. Soldiers from the Eighth Army did not arrive in that part of Japan until 25 September.[92]

The JICPOA Nisei also had an indirect influence on the status of Japanese Americans in the United States. In October the Japanese American Citizens League called upon the Navy to allow Japanese Americans to enlist, something the service had resisted during the war. In response the new Chief of Naval Operations, Admiral Nimitz, declared that Japanese Americans had "served with distinction in the ... Pacific Ocean Areas and elsewhere," and lifted the Navy's wartime ban on Japanese American enlistments.[93]

Korea

The mission to take control of the southern half of Korea was given to the XXIV Corps. Because of Korean hostility toward the Japanese, 1st Lt. Benjamin H. Hazard, but no Nisei, accompanied the reconnaissance party. Hazard was an experienced language officer and veteran of fighting on Saipan and Okinawa. When the first twenty Americans landed on 6 September outside Seoul, a Japanese battalion was in formation on the Kimpo airfield to greet them. Hazard interpreted, and the Japanese helpfully provided their own English-speakers.

Nisei language teams accompanied the units that landed at Inchon on 8 September. About thirty Nisei were assigned to XXIV Corps headquarters; smaller teams were attached to the divisions, military government, and the CIC. T.Sgt. Warren Tsuneishi landed with the corps team. "I felt personally a sense of trepidation," he wrote a few days later:

As I waited for my turn to go down the cargo net, and then ashore, I thought that Korea, after forty-odd years of Japanese misrule and oppression, would not be the healthiest spot in the world for us. ... I was afraid that, like Americans, the Koreans would be unable to differentiate between Japanese-Japanese, whom they have good reason to hate, and Japanese-Americans; nor would they be able to comprehend how completely American birth and life in the United States have made us. I felt, however, that perhaps we would be able to convince them with our bad manners, our hit-and-miss spoken Japanese, and our general inability to act like the polite and docile—and at times cruel—Japanese.[94]

---

[92] "North Pacific Fleet Occupies Ominato," in *U.S. Naval Institute Proceedings* (October 1945): 1245; Morison, *History of United States Naval Operations*, 15: 7; Bill Wada, "My Two Year Experiences and Impressions on the Aleutian Islands," MISNorCal Bio.

[93] "Nimitz Declares Nisei GIs Have Served with Distinction in Pacific Forces," *Pacific Citizen*, 10 Nov 45; "Disclose Administrative Order Issued Opening Enlistments in Any Branch of Naval Service," *Pacific Citizen*, 17 Nov 45; "Nisei Accepted by Navy as Ban Lifted," *Pacific Citizen*, 5 Jan 46; Bill Hosokawa, *JACL in Quest of Justice: The History of the Japanese American Citizens League* (New York: William Morrow, 1982), p. 309. On 15 August 1945, Nimitz outlawed "the use of insulting epithets in connection with the Japanese as a race or as individuals." *Time* (10 September 1945): 5; quote from Frank, *Downfall*, p. 330.

[94] Ltr, Warren Tsuneishi, 12 September 1945, in Cary, *From a Ruined Empire*, p. 27.

Six-hundred-thousand Japanese soldiers remained in Korea, and the colonial administration continued as it had since 1910. Japanese was the language of administration and education. The Japanese had used thousands of Korean laborers throughout Asia and the Pacific. North of the 38th Parallel, the Red Army was pouring into the country. As in other places, the Americans found it convenient to use Japanese troops and the colonial police to maintain order, much to the outrage of the local population. In this confusing situation the Nisei proved their value. They worked with the Japanese command and civilian officials, as well as with Japanese-speaking Korean leaders. Japanese soldiers were gradually removed to Cheju Island off the southern coast and then repatriated to Japan.

For some Nisei, occupation duty in Korea was a welcome respite. T4g. Nob Yamashita arrived with the 63d Infantry, which was posted to Kunsan, a Japanese naval base on the southwest coast. The California-born Nisei had served with the 6th Infantry Division in New Guinea and Luzon, earning the Combat Infantryman Badge and suffering from malaria and dengue fever. He had seen two teammates killed during the war, Terry Mizutari in New Guinea and George I. Nakamura in the Philippines. In Kunsan, Japanese merchants greeted him with open arms and found him a comfortable room with a Japanese family. "So began the best seven weeks or so of my time in the service. It made up for all the bum deals I had before. . . . It was wonderful compared to New Guinea and the Philippines." His duties were minimal, and he spent most evenings soaking in the Japanese bath and sitting around the stove talking, smoking, dining on fresh fruits, and sipping sake, "which I did not drink much of." In November his replacement arrived, a recently commissioned Nisei lieutenant. Yamashita knew the lieutenant had no combat experience, so he asked how he had earned a commission. The lieutenant said simply that he had an IQ over 110 and had tended bar at GHQ's noncommissioned officers' club. "I guess," Yamashita reflected, "as with other things, the boys down at GHQ got the goodies first, and hardly any came down to us in the field. . . . Anyway, I wonder how my replacement turned out." Soon afterward Yamashita boarded a transport for home.[95]

The Philippines

When the war ended, the Philippines was the staging area for three-quarters of a million American service members. More than a thousand Nisei were assigned to ATIS or different combat units. Prisoner of war camps held tens of thousands of Japanese on Leyte and Luzon. One camp on Luzon held a thousand Formosan laborers. T4g. Toshio Ichikawa took a psychological warfare team to the camp and spoke for two hours to convince them "that Japan had actually surrendered." When they finally understood him, they cheered noisily. He reported they were

---

[95] Nob Yamashita, "Fighting My Ancestors: The Autobiography of a Nisei," pp. 22–25, 29, Unpubl Ms, n.d.

especially happy when he told them "that Formosa will soon belong to China," after fifty years of Japanese rule.[96]

Japanese soldiers responded to the surrender news with much less enthusiasm. In September 1945 tens of thousands of Japanese soldiers remained in the hills and jungles. In northern Luzon, *General Tomoyuki Yamashita* remained at large with 60,000 troops. After the emperor's announcement, the 32d Infantry Division made contact with *Yamashita*'s staff by dropping a written message from a low-flying liaison aircraft. Around this time an American patrol ran into a thirty-man Japanese patrol. The Nisei linguist with the patrol, S.Sgt. Kiyo Fujimura,

boldly approached them and informed them of the cessation of hostilities while his men watched from a distance. However, due to lack of radio communication with Japan, they were skeptical and unconvinced. So Kiyo returned and told his men that he'll have to bring them over to convince them thoroughly. His patrol would not trust Japanese coming in fully armed, so he went back again, did some fast talking, and got them to come in without their weapons. Kiyo said that he finally convinced them when he threatened to wire Japan and bring one of their princes.[97]

Surrender talks with *Yamashita* began on 24 August. On 2 September *Yamashita* and his staff walked out of the hills into American custody. He formally surrendered his command the following day at the former residence of the U.S. high commissioner at Camp John Hay, Baguio.[98] The Sixth Army G–2, Col. Horton V. White, personally interrogated *Yamashita* and several other senior Japanese officers at Bilibid Prison. Lt. Gen. Walter Krueger later wrote that "General Yamashita expressed astonishment at the complete, detailed information which Sixth Army had of his military situation throughout the campaign."[99]

Farther south, from the Netherlands East Indies to the Solomon Islands, a quarter-million Japanese soldiers and sailors surrendered to Australian forces. On Bougainville, Australian light aircraft dropped 230,000 leaflets announcing Japan's surrender. After some difficult negotiations, a surrender ceremony was held at Torokina on 8 September and the Japanese troops concentrated in new

---

[96] *Yaban Gogai*, Dec 45, pp. 6, 10.

[97] Quote from Min Hara, in *Only What We Could Carry: The Japanese American Internment Experience*, ed. Lawson F. Inada (Berkeley, Calif.: Heyday Books, 2000), p. 361; Nob Yamashita, in *Saga of the MIS*; "General Yamashita's Troops Surrender to 'Captain' Kiyo Fujimura," in *John Aiso and the M.I.S.: Japanese-American Soldiers in the Military Intelligence Service, World War II*, ed. Tad Ichinokuchi (Los Angeles: Military Intelligence Service Club of Southern California, 1988), pp. 140–41. For this, Fujimura was awarded the Silver Star.

[98] *Reports of General MacArthur*, 1: 461, 464–65. ATIS History says his surrender was "negotiated entirely by ATIS personnel" (p. 37). H. W. Blakeley, *32d Infantry Division in World War II* (Madison, Wis.: Thirty-Second Infantry Division History Commission, [1955]), pp. 266–75; William H. Gill, *Always a Commander: The Reminiscences of Major General William H. Gill* (Colorado Springs: Colorado College, 1974), pp. 98–104; Robert L. Eichelberger, *Our Jungle Road to Tokyo* (New York: Viking, 1950), pp. 255–58.

[99] Walter Krueger, *From Down Under to Nippon* (Washington, D.C.: Combat Forces Press, 1953), pp. 325–28.

camps. In New Guinea, *Lt. Gen. Hatazo Adachi* surrendered on 13 September. On Morotai, Japanese soldiers surrendered to the African American 93d Infantry Division with help from the division's Nisei team. When Australian General Sir Thomas Blamey held the Borneo surrender ceremony on 9 September, the final count included 36,700 military and 5,000 civilians. In the former Portuguese colony of Timor, Nisei Paul T. Bannai helped with surrender at Koepang on 11 September. The largest surrender ceremony in the region was held in Rabaul on 6 September on the British aircraft carrier HMS *Glory*. When Australian troops landed at Rabaul several days later, they found 80,000 Japanese military personnel and 21,000 civilians, far more than previously estimated.[100]

The end of the war in the Pacific was the culmination of three years of active service for the MIS Nisei, during which they had developed specialized combat intelligence skills and served in numerous campaigns from Burma to the Pacific Islands. With the Japanese surrender came challenges that called for their language and cultural skills in new and unexpected ways.

---

[100] Interv, author with Bannai, 11 Sep 96; ch. 23, "After the Ceasefire," in *Australia in the War of 1939–1945*, ser. 1, vol. 5, *The Final Campaigns*, ed. Gavin Long (Canberra: Australian War Memorial, 1963), Sources disagree on some surrender ceremony dates. See *Reports of General MacArthur*, 1: plate 133.

12

MIS Nisei and the
Early Occupation of Japan,
September 1945–February 1946

American troops entered Japan with apprehension, unsure how they would be received by their former enemies. On the other side, the Japanese people feared the American soldiers. The worst fears on both sides soon evaporated; the Japanese people cooperated with the American occupiers to restore their country, its economy, and society. "Whatever the causes of this cooperativeness," writes American historian Edwin O. Reischauer, later ambassador to Japan, "there can be no denying that it was the single most important factor in the history of the occupation, accounting in large part for the degree of success we had in Japan."[1]

The MIS Nisei were an important factor in achieving this unprecedented cooperation between once bitter enemies. From the first landings, Nisei served as liaisons between military government officers and Japanese officials. They helped dismantle the instruments of Japanese military power and repatriate millions of Japanese servicemen from overseas. They helped censor civil communications and assisted with war crimes investigations and trials. They worked in an astonishing variety of roles to guarantee a peaceful and ultimately successful occupation during which former enemies became close allies. The work of the Nisei in the initial months of the occupation laid the foundation for all that was to follow.

---

[1] Cited in D. Clayton James, *The Years of MacArthur*, 3 vols. (Boston: Houghton Mifflin, 1970–1985), 3: 8.

Fort Snelling

The occupation demanded linguists just as urgently as had combat operations, perhaps even more so. The principal source was the Military Intelligence
Service Language School (MISLS) at Fort Snelling, Minnesota. When the war
ended, the school had 160 instructors and more than 1,800 students in training
for the impending invasion. At Fort Snelling, the initial reaction to the war's end
was similar to that of Americans everywhere: shock and relief. At first the atomic
bombings left instructors and students feeling numb as they anxiously listened to
radio broadcasts. Then on Friday, 9 August, came news that Japan had accepted
the Potsdam Declaration. The following Sunday the school held baccalaureate
services followed by a picnic and outdoor dance. On the evening of 14 August
came President Harry S. Truman's announcement that the Japanese had surrendered. The students were jubilant; one quipped, "Hurray! The bastards quit! We
go home!" Shigeya Kihara recalled that the older Nisei reacted more somberly,
"saddened by our ambivalent background." Students were confined to post for the
remainder of the day to prevent any "incidents." That night the beer flowed freely
and more than a few students ended up in the guardhouse. That same evening the
St. Paul radio station recorded a five-minute interview with two Nisei veterans
from the school, T.Sgt. Kazuhiko Yamada and T.Sgt. Kaoru Nishida, for nationwide broadcast over the NBC network. Colonel Rasmussen cancelled classes for
15 August and ordered a memorial service in the field house followed by a battalion parade attended by hundreds of civilians from Minneapolis–St. Paul. Students
were given 24-hour local passes. Classes resumed on Friday, 17 August.[2]

On Saturday, 18 August, the school held its largest commencement ever, with
552 graduates. The guest speaker, Maj. Gen. Clayton Bissell, the War Department
G–2, praised the work of previous graduates. Their job was just beginning, he told
them, because many combat-experienced Nisei would be returning home. "We
must have replacements so the men that have been over there two and three years
and who have the necessary 85 points can come back."[3] The school published
orders for more than 700 Nisei, including recent graduates and holdovers from
earlier classes awaiting assignment. Maj. John F. Aiso, director of academic training, led more than 500 by train to Los Angeles, where they boarded transport ships
and proceeded on a twenty-day voyage to Manila, during which the surrender
ceremony on the USS *Missouri* took place.[4]

---

[2] *Yaban Gogai*, Aug 45; Tamotsu Shibutani, *The Derelicts of Company K: A Sociological Study
of Demoralization* (Berkeley: University of California Press, 1978), p. 221 (student quote); Kihara
quote from Joseph D. Harrington, *Yankee Samurai: The Secret Role of Nisei in America's Pacific
Victory* (Detroit: Pettigrew Enterprises, 1979), p. 351.

[3] *Pacific Citizen*, 1 Sep 45; *Yaban Gogai*, Sep–Oct 45, p. 2; Shibutani, *Derelicts of Company K*,
pp. 260–61. Shibutani gives Bissell the pseudonym Jonathan Wilson.

[4] Kaoru Inouye, Biography, Military Intelligence Service Club of Northern California, p. 5 (this
and similar biographies hereafter cited as MISNorCal Bios).

Aiso took a brief leave of absence in Southern California and returned to Minnesota for some of the most trying months in the school's history. "For most army organizations," stated a school official a few weeks later, "VJ-Day meant the beginning of curtailment of activities and a slackening to a peacetime tempo. For the Military Intelligence Service Language School, it spelled just the opposite—heavier loads and a faster gait."[5] Graduations rushed by one after the other. On 1 September, before classes had been scheduled to finish, 134 students were assigned to civil censorship. On 29 September another 155 Nisei enlisted men graduated with 111 Caucasian officers and officer candidates. New students poured in, over 400 each month until December. In the first seven months after the surrender, the school took in 1,875 new students. By 15 October student enrollment peaked at 1,936. In November and December alone the school shipped 1,097 enlisted graduates to Japan. Regular classes no longer received the full nine-month course but graduated after six. One regular course began on 30 July with 253 students; it was hurried through in three months, with most students graduating on 26 October. "Speed up" sections received four months' training at most. A special oral course began on 30 July with 307 students; 285 graduated on 17 November. A special officer candidate class began on 27 August with 184 Caucasian students. Many students were discharged before graduation, resulting in a 50 percent attrition rate; only 91 graduated on 15 December.

General Bissell took a personal interest in keeping the language school in operation, and he knew that skilled instructors would be needed more than ever. On 29 September he returned to address another graduation and praised the enlisted instructors:

Theirs was pure hard work. They took it and carried it through—I'm proud of them. Many of them would have looked forward to travel, see action, but they remained. I'm asking that they keep their shoulder to the wheel a little longer. If the 3,700 linguists now overseas are to come back, someone has to replace them. That means more work for the instructors. They are the heart and soul of this school—their job is not yet done.[6]

The faculty was indeed the heart and soul of the school. The staff revamped the curriculum by dropping military topics in favor of general language usage, speaking skills, civil affairs, Japanese government, and administration. The school continued to publish its mimeographed newsletter, *Yaban Gogai*, through the end of the year to keep in touch with its far-flung graduates, who in turn submitted scores of letters from the field. The special Chinese-language classes continued in support of the occupation forces in China, and in October the school began a Korean-language class with eight students under a Korean American officer, Lt. Calvin Kim.

---

[5] War Department (WD) Press Release, 22 Oct 45.
[6] *Yaban Gogai*, Sep–Oct 45.

Most of all, the instructors held the school together during a period of great strain. The rapid demobilization threw the entire War Department into turmoil. Disgruntled soldiers around the globe became the subject of congressional and press attention. For Americans of Japanese ancestry, the strains were even greater. Families on the mainland were reemerging from the internment camps and picking up the pieces of their lives. In some cases they were met with prejudice and harassment by white neighbors who were not pleased at their return. In Europe, the 442d Regimental Combat Team (RCT) remained in northern Italy guarding German prisoners of war until the spring of 1946. Some high-point men returned home, and a few came to MISLS for retraining.

The school continued to absorb hundreds of Nisei selectees from training centers. At Fort Meade, Maryland, more than a thousand Nisei replacements waited for assignment to Europe. Recruiters from the school visited in June and August and selected 850 for language training. In September recruiters visited fifteen other Army posts and selected another 600 Nisei. In July, August, and September the Army headquarters in Hawaii shipped 800 Nisei to the mainland for basic training and language training.[7]

The school instructors and cadre redoubled their efforts to keep the new students in line now that the war had ended. Robert T. Matsushita, nineteen, was enlisted from Hawaii that July, attended basic training, and arrived at Fort Snelling in November:

Boy! Our company commander was a 100th Battalion man. Oh, he was strict! Very strict! He was from Hawaii also. He wanted us to really shape up and be a good soldier. I remember he was strict with us. Without that, I'd never be a good soldier. . . . [Capt. Kiyoshi Kuramoto] was from Honolulu. Some of the boys seemed to dislike him because he was very serious about haircuts. We used to have those long . . . sideburns. He didn't like them. If we had sideburns, there's no weekend passes for you. Quite a few of our boys didn't get weekend passes because they kept their sideburns long. He wanted all crew top, real GI haircut.[8]

The Nisei from Fort Meade with lower language aptitude were grouped in Company K in the temporary wooden huts of the "Turkey Farm." Disobedience and violence became common, to the despair of the instructors and staff. At one point Aiso assembled the company and threatened to withhold their weekend passes: "I am not at all pleased with your conduct. There have been too many derelictions in this division. . . . You have a job to do; I expect you to do it. I hold all

---

[7] MISLS, "Training History of the Military Intelligence Service Language School," ann. 10, Personnel Procurement Office, Unpubl Ms, 1946, U.S. Army Center of Military History (CMH), and Gen Records, 1943–1945, Military Intelligence [Service] Language School, Fort Snelling, Minn., Records of the Army Staff, Record Group (RG) 319, National Archives and Records Administration (NARA).

[8] Interv, Dawn Duensing with Robert Matsushita, in *Americanism: A Matter of Mind and Heart*, vol. 1, *The Military Intelligence Service* (Maui, Hawaii: Maui's Sons and Daughters of the Nisei Veterans, 2001).

the officers and noncommissioned officers under me strictly responsible for your conduct." His speech had little impact on the disgruntled students. According to one, after this incident, Aiso "came to symbolize all the pettiness and anything else obnoxious that took place." The anger, bitterness, and occasional brawls continued.[9] One student in the company later wrote:

Company K was blamed for virtually all the violence that broke out at Fort Snelling in the autumn of 1945. Actually, fewer than a half dozen members of the unit were involved. As a general atmosphere of gloom and futility settled over the company, a small band of disgruntled Hawaiians was able to give vent to its pent-up hostility—first within the company and later against outsiders.[10]

War Department policy on demobilization shifted repeatedly, which caused uncertainty in the ranks. Many European veterans from the 100th Infantry Battalion and the 442d Regimental Combat Team arrived at Fort Snelling for language training, only to be discharged. When Bissell returned for another graduation on 15 December, fewer than one in five graduates agreed to remain in service and many OCS candidates turned down commissions. Bissell gave them a stern lecture: "While others were dying overseas," he said, they "had stayed home in comfortable barracks, had the 'best food when civilians went without,' and had the 'best teachers,' and a good education." His words had little effect.[11]

One school official lamented "the present unsettled conditions of both the faculty and student body":

Uncertainty as to their future in the Army, as to their further needs as linguists and especially as to the future status of the school have contributed to the general unrest. Due to the absence of a clearly defined plan in regard to the future of the school and the kaleidoscopic changes occasioned by the shifts in the Army policy since VJ Day, the training section has been forced to revise the program and improvise from day to day. The fast dropping requirements for discharge have taken toll of our best and most experienced enlisted instructors month after month. This loss has had to be made up by digging deeper and deeper down into the barrel. The later replacements have dropped not alone in ability but in maturity and in the conviction that this job is essential. Ill-trained and poorly oriented instructors have not the quality of leadership and stability so necessary in training these new recruits. These constant changes in the curricula and in instructors have further undermined the morale of the students already shaken by the general letup after the cessation of hostilities.[12]

---

[9] Shibutani, *Derelicts of Company K*, pp. 269–70. Shibutani gives Aiso the pseudonym Robert Kawashita. Shibutani took detailed field notes during his military service, which became the basis for this book.

[10] Ibid., p. 284. For another view on Company K, see Interv, author with Susumu Toyoda, 12 Sep 96. Toyoda was school battalion adjutant in 1945.

[11] Shibutani, *Derelicts of Company K*, pp. 323–24. On demobilization and soldier morale after V-J Day, see John C. Sparrow, *History of Personnel Demobilization in the United States Army* (Washington, D.C.: Government Printing Office, 1952).

[12] "Training History," ann. 1, Academic Training, para. 3–b–3, p. 3.

Poor morale was exacerbated by the departure of longtime administrators. The director of personnel procurement, Maj. Paul Rusch, left for Japan with two other officers who had been repatriated in 1942.[13] In October Col. Kai E. Rasmussen took extended leave to visit Germany and his native land, Denmark, where his parents still lived. A few months later he was named military attaché to Oslo, Norway.[14]

Major Aiso requested release from active duty but instead received orders for Japan. He stepped down as director of academic training on 1 October and handed over the position to one of the senior instructors, Tsutomu Paul Tekawa. In his farewell letter to the students, Aiso praised Rasmussen and the instructors, but warned of "an indication of slacking on the part of some students now that the war is over." He admonished them that "what may result, can nullify all that the former graduates have accomplished in the past four years."[15] In November he wrote to the school's graduates overseas that the faculty was "battling the spirit of disintegration that demobilization in general has contagiously spread[;] they are still holding the line making strategic retrograde movements to meet the new post V-J Day students and conditions."[16]

Over the winter and spring of 1945–1946 the War Department considered what to do with the school. Fort Snelling was scheduled for closure, so the school needed to find a new home. The War Department offered it to General Douglas MacArthur's headquarters in Tokyo, but a restriction on overseas tour lengths meant that students could not attend language training and then complete a full tour. In the spring of 1946 Rasmussen learned that the Presidio of Monterey, California, was vacant and scheduled for closure. Knowing that many of the students and instructors were from the West Coast, Rasmussen made a bid for the post: it was taken off the closure list. The school held one final graduation in May 1946 and moved to Monterey.

Another sign of change at the school was the presence of women soldiers in the classrooms. Forty-six students from the Women's Army Corps (WAC) started a six-month oral proficiency course in May 1945. Most were Nisei, but the group included several Caucasians and Chinese Americans and was commanded by a Caucasian officer, Capt. Marian E. Nestor. Forty-one graduated in November; half went to Camp Ritchie, Maryland, to work at the Pacific Military Intelligence Research Section, where they were housed at the "presidential retreat" in the Catoctin Mountains. Some of these were later transferred to Fort Holabird, Maryland,

---

[13] *Yaban Gogai*, Sep–Oct 45. See also Rusch's mimeographed letters from Tokyo in Paul Rusch File, Joseph D. Harrington Papers, National Japanese American Historical Society (NJAHS), San Francisco, Calif.

[14] *Yaban Gogai*, Sep–Oct 45.

[15] Ibid., Nov 45.

[16] Ibid., Dec 45. John F. Aiso, "Observations of a California Nisei," Interv by Marc Landy, University of California at Los Angeles, 1971. His transfer was delayed when a predeployment medical examination disclosed a double hernia that had to be repaired before overseas deployment. He departed for Japan in January 1946.

The first women MISLS graduates to deploy overseas, January 1946. Among them were eleven Japanese Americans, a Chinese American, and Sgt. Rhoda V. Knudten, all from the MISLS Women's Army Corps detachment.

for more translation duty.[17] Three remained at Fort Snelling as instructors, "much to the delight of the EMS [enlisted men]," according to the school album.[18]

Thirteen women selected for occupation duty flew to Tokyo on 23 January 1946. This group included 11 Nisei, 1 Caucasian, and 1 Chinese American. They were surprised to learn that MacArthur's headquarters had not been notified of their arrival. They also learned that the War Department had just announced that all WACs would be returned from overseas as soon as possible. The director of the Women's Army Corps had ordered all WACs removed from the Pacific Theater by 1 January 1946. Of the 5,000 women who had served in the Southwest Pacific Area during the war, only 200 were allowed into Japan as War Department civilians. As a consequence, the thirteen language school graduates were invited to

---

[17] Among the Nisei WACs assigned to PACMIRS was Tamie Tsuchiyama. Lane Ryo Hirabayashi, *The Politics of Field Work: Research in an American Concentration Camp* (Tucson: University of Arizona Press, 1999), pp. 153–55.

[18] *MISLS Album* (Minneapolis: Military Intelligence Service Language School, 1946), p. 91.

accept immediate discharges and were offered one-year contracts as War Department civilians. All of them remained in Tokyo as civilian employees.[19]

The end of the war caused the closure of most other Japanese-language training programs. At the University of Michigan, Prof. Joseph K. Yamagiwa headed a
program that had trained 975 Caucasian officer candidates since early 1943. When
the war ended, forty-six Issei and Nisei instructors were teaching 300 students
to prepare them for the regular course at Fort Snelling. Six other instructors had
been working since June on a large translation project for the Office of the Provost
Marshal General, which ended in October. In September Yamagiwa reported that
the end of the war had "unsettled the morale of a small section of the student body
and necessitated a stiffening of standards to separate those who are weak either in
their schoolwork or in their conviction that the work must be carried on."[20] In one
incident a group of students staged an "apparently innocent college prank" and
"managed to raise a Japanese flag on the campus flag pole in such a way that it
could not be lowered." Shortly afterward they published an anonymous manifesto
explaining "that the flag-raising was undertaken ... in order to call attention to the
restrictions placed on them, ... and including a long list of complaints," most of
which "were laid at the feet of the 'incompetent' officers and noncommissioned
officers who were in charge of the daily routines."[21] Yamagiwa left in November to join the U.S. Strategic Bombing Survey; the War Department terminated
the Michigan program on 22 December with one class only halfway through the
course. The last two classes hastily wrapped up their courses and, bypassing the
usual eight-week basic training, were sent directly to Fort Snelling to begin the
MISLS course in mid-January.[22]

The Navy School of Oriental Languages at the University of Colorado continued its programs at Boulder, which by now included instruction in Chinese and
Russian as well as Japanese. A new branch had opened in June 1945 with 700 students at Oklahoma A&M College in Stillwater, Oklahoma, under Navy Capt. John
H. Morrill and Dr. James H. McAlpine, a former missionary and senior instructor

[19] Mattie E. Treadwell, *The Women's Army Corps,* U.S. Army in World War II (Washington,
D.C.: Office of the Chief of Military History, 1954), pp. 456–60; Brenda L. Moore, *Serving Our
Country: Japanese American Women in the Military during World War II* (New Brunswick, N.J.:
Rutgers University Press, 2003), pp. 124–31; Yaye (Furutani) Herman, in *Unsung Heroes: The
Military Intelligence Service, Past-Present-Future* (Seattle: MIS-Northwest Association, 1996),
pp. 5–8; Kenji Murase, "More Than Mannequins: Nisei Women in the WACs," *Nikkei Heritage*
(Winter 2003): 10–11; Photo in *Pacific Citizen,* 26 Jan 46.
[20] "Training History," ann. 3, The Army Japanese Language School: A Preliminary Report.
[21] Edward E. Jones and Harold B. Gerard, *Foundations of Social Psychology* (New York: John
Wiley & Sons, 1967), pp. 8–12. Jones was among the pranksters.
[22] Joseph K. Yamagiwa, "The Japanese Language Programs at the University of Michigan during World War II," ch. 2, Unpubl Ms, 1946, Ann Arbor, Mich.; "Training History," ann. 9, Personnel Office.

at Boulder. The school closed on 30 June 1946. Between the two locations the school had 240 faculty members. Both branches closed in the summer of 1946.[23]

Other Japanese-language training programs continued for a time; but on 21 August 1945, the War Department abruptly closed all Civil Affairs Training Schools except the one at the University of Virginia. All 678 remaining students were slated for Japan following their brief language instruction.[24] The Marine Corps' Japanese-language school at Camp Lejeune, North Carolina, closed in December 1945.

The Canadian Army Japanese Language School (S–20) had about fifty students (Nisei and Caucasians combined) in training in Vancouver when the war ended. On the day of the surrender the students gathered in the assembly hall to hear a radio address by British Prime Minister Clement Attlee. One Canadian Nisei later recalled:

There was no jubilation, no shouting, no expressions of joy; the Nisei had mixed feelings. There was relief that the war was over, but with millions of others, they shared feelings of horror and revulsion, a sharper understanding of the utter obscenity of war. One atom bomb could indiscriminately kill thousands of men, women, and children. It was no longer war in the accepted sense; it was the slaughter and destruction of a nation. Nonetheless, the S–20 students were disappointed that they had come so far but were denied actual service on the battlefield. They had no glowing military service record to display in their quest to be called Canadians. Perhaps it was enough that they had volunteered for service, the ultimate test of citizenship and loyalty.[25]

The school held a brief ceremony, which "concluded with the national anthem and three cheers for the king." The students were dismissed, and "most Nisei headed quietly for dinner in Chinatown."[26] A few graduates were shipped to the Southeast Asia Command, others to the Pacific Military Intelligence Research Section (PACMIRS) in Maryland. In November 1945 the school relocated to Ambleside Camp in West Vancouver. Another class graduated in March 1946 with ten Caucasians and four Nisei and the final class in June 1946 with twenty-eight Nisei. Shortly before the students completed their final examinations, the government announced there would be no further overseas postings; the remaining students were granted discharges. In all, the school graduated forty-eight Canadian Nisei. A Canadian Army report concluded, "there is no doubt that they would have

---

[23] Office of the Chief of Naval Operations, "School of Oriental Languages," Unpubl Ms, Naval Historical Center, Washington, D.C.; Pauline S. McAlpine, *Diary of a Missionary* (Decatur, Ga.: Presbyterian Church in America, 1986). Morrill had escaped from Corregidor in 1942. John H. Morrill and Pete Martin, *South from Corregidor* (New York: Simon and Schuster, 1943).

[24] *Army and Navy Register* (25 August 1945): 1.

[25] Roy Ito, *We Went to War: The Story of the Japanese Canadians Who Served during the First and Second World Wars* (Stittsville, Ontario: Canada's Wings, 1984), p. 224.

[26] Ibid.

made a valuable contribution to the Allied land war effort against Japan had larger numbers of them been enlisted sooner."[27]

In the continental United States, by August 1945 hundreds of MISLS graduates were serving at various locations. Camps for Japanese prisoners were scattered around the country. Some Nisei soldiers, often those who did not perform well in language training, were assigned to the military police units guarding the camps.[28] In September the Civil Affairs Staging Area in Monterey hastily closed and its students and staff were deployed or discharged. The handful of Nisei language instructors was reassigned.

At Vint Hill Farms in rural Virginia, more than sixty Nisei worked for the Signal Security Agency. By the spring of 1945 the Military Intelligence Division was already consolidating all signals intelligence activities: "Experience has demonstrated that most Japanese military traffic now intercepted in the Pacific and Far East can be forwarded to Arlington Hall Station, decoded, translated, evaluated and disseminated to operational headquarters more quickly than the same processes can be performed within any theater."[29] For several difficult weeks in August and September 1945, as Japanese officials negotiated surrender terms, the airwaves were alive with Japanese radio traffic. The Nisei at Vint Hill Farms helped translate these intercepts in support of Arlington Hall. "As Japan's legions stacked their arms in surrender," writes historian Edward Drea, "the former great stream of military radio communications declined to a trickle, mainly directing units to burn codebooks and cryptanalytic paraphernalia." Nevertheless, American code breakers continued to read Japanese diplomatic traffic with its embassies and consulates for some time after the surrender. Some Vint Hill Farms Nisei were discharged in November and December; the last left in February 1946.[30] When the war ended, another twenty-five Nisei were attending voice intercept training at Fort Monmouth, New Jersey; but they returned to Fort Snelling, and most were sent to Japan.[31]

---

[27] Ibid., p. 278.

[28] *Yaban Gogai*, Aug 45.

[29] Memo, MID for Chief of Staff, sub: Centralized Control of Signal Intelligence Activities for War against the Japanese, 1 Jun 45 (SRH–169), in *U.S. Army Signals Intelligence in World War II: A Documentary History*, ed. James L. Gilbert and John P. Finnegan, U.S. Army in World War II (Washington, D.C.: U.S. Army Center of Military History, 1993), p. 219.

[30] Edward J. Drea, *MacArthur's Ultra: Codebreaking and the War against Japan, 1942–1945* (Lawrence: University Press of Kansas, 1992), p. 225; Richard B. Frank, *Downfall: The End of the Imperial Japanese Empire* (New York: Random House, 1999), pp. 221–51, 326–30; Ronald Lewin, *The American Magic: Codes, Ciphers and the Defeat of Japan* (New York: Farrar Straus Giroux, 1982), pp. 290–91; Ted T. Tsukiyama et al., eds., *Secret Valor: M.I.S. Personnel, World War II Pacific Theater, Pre–Pearl Harbor to Sept. 8, 1951* (Honolulu: Military Intelligence Service Veterans Club of Hawaii, 1993), p. 108; Ltr, Naomitsu Kitsuwa to Joseph Harrington, ca. 1977, Joseph D. Harrington Papers, NJAHS.

[31] Susumi Hidaka, in "Rocky Mountain MIS Veterans Club Autobiographies," Unpubl Ms, ed. Kent T. Yoritomo, [1989], author's files (this and similar biographies hereafter cited as Rocky Mountain Bios).

Immediately after the surrender the Signal Security Agency deployed a Target Intelligence Committee team to Japan. Capt. Clarence S. Yamagata, who had worked in Central Bureau since 1942, entered Tokyo with the team on 8 September. But the Japanese cryptographers had covered their tracks very well. Central Bureau members visited the Japanese signal corps headquarters, but all codebooks and cryptological equipment were gone. They did find several copies of a Japanese translation of Herbert O. Yardley's controversial 1931 book, *The American Black Chamber*, which had revealed that the American government had read Japanese diplomatic messages during the Washington Conference in 1921.[32]

Another forty-five Nisei were working at PACMIRS. Among them were some of the best, most experienced Japanese linguists, including Maj. John E. Anderton from the Allied Translator and Interpreter Section (ATIS), Capt. Won-Loy Chan from Burma, 1st Lt. Sunao Phil Ishio from ATIS, M.Sgt. George M. Koshi from MISLS, 2d Lt. Dye Ogata from the South Pacific, 1st Lt. Toshio G. Tsukahira from MISLS, and Lt. Col. Eugene A. Wright from the South Pacific serving as deputy chief. By the summer of 1945 PACMIRS was sitting on a mountain of Japanese documents. PACMIRS had received about 120,000 original documents, but most were useless. Only about 10 percent "were found to contain new or useful information. Highly skilled linguists have to be used for the scanning of all documents, both valuable and worthless, [leading to] the waste of man-hours involved in dealing with the useless material received."[33] Some of the documents, including some German-language documents pertaining to Japan, came by an indirect route from Europe after the German surrender. The translators found the work dull and exhausting. Morale declined further after Lt. Col. Sidney F. Gronich, the first PACMIRS chief, was reassigned to the European Theater in July and was replaced by Col. Sidney P. Marland, the former operations officer of the 43d Infantry Division. Twenty-one Nisei WACs from MISLS were assigned in December.

PACMIRS worked closely with the Washington Document Center. On 29 August the War Department G–2 and the Office of Naval Intelligence convened the Washington Document Conference to coordinate "the handling and exploitation of Japanese documents." The attendees agreed that an advance echelon should be sent to Japan to gather strategic intelligence, especially relating to the Soviet Union. The advance echelon of nearly a hundred personnel (including between twenty-five and fifty Nisei) left for Tokyo in October; the main body arrived on 29 November. Full-scale operations began on 4 December with about seventy-five

---

[32] *The Quiet Heroes of the Southwest Pacific Theater: An Oral History of the Men and Women of CBB and FRUMEL* (Fort Meade, Md.: National Security Agency, 1996), pp. 51–52; Robert C. Christopher, "When the Twain Met," in *The Occupation of Japan: The Grass Roots Level*, ed. William F. Nimmo (Norfolk, Va.: General Douglas MacArthur Foundation, 1992). On Yardley's book and its reception in Japan, see David Kahn, *The Codebreakers* (New York: Signet, 1973), pp. 179–81. For similar activities of the Target Intelligence Committee in Europe after the German surrender, see James Bamford, *Body of Secrets* (New York: Doubleday, 2001), pp. 7–19.

[33] After-Action Report, PACMIRS, sub: History and Organization of PACMIRS, Camp Ritchie, Maryland, 6 September 1944–14 August 1945, p. 26.

Nisei, including some detailed from ATIS. The teams spread out across Japan to search for the records of government ministries and other agencies. For example, Koshi helped search the underground facilities of the Imperial General Headquarters in Nagano Prefecture. 1st Lt. Arthur M. Kaneko helped recover Imperial General Staff studies on Manchuria and the Soviet Far East. In more than four months the Washington Document Center team "screened, processed, packed, and shipped 419,064 documents from Japan."[34]

Several Nisei who went to Japan with these teams stayed on to work for the Tokyo War Crimes prosecution section as civilian interpreters or monitors, including Koshi, a graduate of Denver Law School. Others, such as Kaneko, returned to Washington and set about translating Japanese intelligence documents about the Soviet Far East. PACMIRS closed in 1946; the Washington Document Center was absorbed into the Central Intelligence Group, which later became the Central Intelligence Agency.

One year after Japan's surrender, the War Department had only one remaining Japanese-language training program, the Military Intelligence Service Language School, in its new home at the Presidio of Monterey. In 1947 the school expanded to include more than two dozen languages and was renamed the Army Language School.

Nisei Arrive in Japan

The initial landings and formal surrender ceremony were followed by weeks of frantic activity as American combat units poured into defeated Japan. Outside Tokyo, the 11th Airborne Division landed at Atsugi Airfield followed closely by the 27th Infantry Division. The 1st Cavalry Division landed at Yokohama and on 8 September became the first American unit to enter Tokyo, accompanied by its Nisei language team.[35] Over the next several weeks ten divisions and six corps arrived in Japan. Each division and corps was accompanied by a team of Nisei linguists, who were needed everywhere at once. The commanding general of Eighth

---

[34] *Unsung Heroes*, pp. 23–26; General Headquarters, Far East Command, *Operations of the Allied Translator and Interpreter Section, GHQ, SWPA*, Intelligence Series, vol. 5 (Tokyo, Far East Command, 1948), p. 72 (hereafter cited as ATIS History); Interv, author with Arthur M. Kaneko, 25 Aug 95; Y. Kono, MISNorCal Bio; George M. Koshi, "My Experience in Japan with the Occupation Forces," MISNorCal Bio; Ltr, George M. Koshi to Yutaka Munakata, 9 Nov 45, Harrington Papers, NJAHS. In 1949 the CIA transferred 3,450 cubic feet of captured records from the Washington Document Center (WDC) to the National Archives. James W. Morley, "Check List of Seized Japanese Records in the National Archives," *Far Eastern Quarterly* 9, no. 3 (May 1950). After the peace treaty was signed in 1951, the Japanese government sought their return. In 1957–1958, with a Ford Foundation grant, the Library of Congress microfilmed 400,000 pages and returned the originals to Japan. Various scholars have used these files, such as MISLS graduate George O. Totten III, whose book *The Social Democratic Movement in Prewar Japan* (New Haven, Conn.: Yale University Press, 1966) was based on Home Ministry files.

[35] S.Sgt. George Chuman was reported to have been the first MIS Nisei to enter Tokyo. *Pacific Citizen*, 13 Oct 45.

Army personally appealed to Maj. Gen. Charles A. Willoughby for more Nisei "of the type I would want to use personally for confidential discussions," General Robert L. Eichelberger wrote his wife. "He had already sent me 16, varying from captains to sergeants."[36] Until the arrival of ATIS from Manila, the Nisei remained in short supply:

During the months of October, November, and December 1945, the acute need for trained linguistic personnel for duty with the Occupation Forces in Japan became apparent to everyone. Requisitions for large numbers of linguists to deal with surrender problems throughout the entire Pacific area were also received. ATIS was hard-pressed to fill the many demands for linguistic talent.[37]

Lt. Charles Tatsuda, Tokyo, November 1945. This watercolor by Cecil Calvert Beall was printed in Collier's Magazine, *24 November 1945.*

Finding sufficient linguists was critical. Unlike the occupation of Germany, in Japan "the language barrier alone represented an effective bar to administration," as the Supreme Commander of the Allied Powers (SCAP) official history put it, because the military government operated through established governmental mechanisms at all levels.[38] The widely read study of Japanese national character, published by anthropologist Ruth Benedict in the early months of the occupation, opened with a strongly worded assertion of this cultural and linguistic gap: "The Japanese were the most alien enemy the United States had ever fought in an all-out struggle. In no other war with a major foe had it been necessary to take into account such exceedingly different habits of acting and thinking."[39] Now the U.S. Army needed the Nisei to help govern Japan in peace.

Many Americans who had studied Japanese found it a difficult language. In March 1946 the U.S. Education Mission to Japan called for national language reform: "The need for a simple and efficient medium of written communication

---

[36] Jay Luvaas, ed., *Dear Miss Em: General Eichelberger's War in the Pacific, 1942–1945* (Westport, Conn.: Greenwood Press, 1972), p. 301.

[37] ATIS History, p. 67.

[38] *Reports of General MacArthur*, 4 vols., U.S. Army in World War II (Washington, D.C.: U.S. Army Center of Military History, 1994), vol. 1 supplement, pp. 2, 4.

[39] Ruth Benedict, *The Chrysanthemum and the Sword: Patterns of Japanese Culture* (Boston: Houghton Mifflin, 1946), p. 1.

is well recognized, and the time for taking this momentous step is perhaps more favorable now than it will be for many years to come."[40] A Navy language officer with the SCAP Information Section expressed similar frustration and advocated reform that would make for more efficient government and reduce illiteracy. The Japanese language was so complicated even for the Japanese themselves that "this difficulty must have slowed down Japan's war effort in ways which it is hard for us even to begin to imagine." The Japanese language, he wrote, "hastened the fall of Japan by veiling military and technical operations in a linguistic fog."[41] But like it or not, Japan could be ruled only using the medium of the Japanese language as it existed.

During the war the Nisei occasionally had been considered for a possible role in the occupation of Japan. In September 1942, during the debate within the War Department on the enlistment of Japanese American volunteers, Edwin O. Reischauer argued:

Such a unit might prove an invaluable asset in lessening the inevitable animosity of the Japanese populace for us and our troops. If liberal numbers of Japanese Americans were to be among the troops of occupation we may station in Japan or were to be among the units which receive the surrender of the Japanese armies, the bitterness of the defeat would be alleviated slightly and cooperation with the victor nations would seem more possible to the Japanese.[42]

In November 1943 John Aiso, then the chief instructor at MISLS, described some of the policies implemented two years later. However, Nisei were rarely invited to help formulate occupation policy and were not trained at the Military Government School or the Civil Affairs Training Schools.[43] In May 1945 film director Orson Welles picked up the theme and suggested that the Nisei were "in an enviable position to bring the democratic gospel to the land of their ancestors." Larry Tajiri, editor of the *Pacific Citizen*, responded that "Nisei Americans are far more eager to see democracy work in the Hood River and San Joaquin valleys of the western coast than in acting as missionaries for democracy in Japan." Tajiri conceded that Nisei would "be able to render a valuable service, especially

---

[40] Herbert Passin, *Society and Education in Japan* (New York: Columbia University, 1965), p. 280.

[41] John Ashmead, Jr., "A Modern Language for Japan," *Atlantic Monthly* (January 1947): 68–72.

[42] Takashi Fujitani, "The Reischauer Memo: Mr. Moto, Hirohito, and Japanese American Soldiers," *Critical Asian Studies* 33, no. 3 (2001): 379–402 (quote from p. 402).

[43] John F. Aiso, "Japan's Military System Must Be Crushed," *Vital Speeches of the Day* (15 December 1943); Aiso, Speech, 12 Nov 66, printed in *Hokubei Mainichi*, n.d.; see also Aiso speech, 1964. Another Nisei may have helped to develop occupation policies: John M. Maki had been an instructor at the University of Washington before the war and served with the Office of War Information from 1943 to 1945. After the war he earned a Ph.D. in political science from Harvard University and became a scholar of Japanese constitutional law. John M. Maki, *Japanese Militarism: Its Cause and Cure* (New York: Knopf, 1945), and *Government and Politics in Japan: The Road to Democracy* (New York: Praeger, 1962).

as linguists." But he reminded his readers that using them for the occupation would require an "extensive project of training Nisei Americans for reconstruction work."[44]

Immediately after Japan's surrender the War Department declared its intent to use the Nisei. On 18 August Bissell told hundreds of Nisei graduates at Fort Snelling:

The need for language students is even greater now than when you first entered the school under war conditions.... The Nisei of this school will be absolutely essential to the successful occupation of Japan and to the winning of the peace. Just as the former graduates served as the vital connecting link between Allied soldiers and the Japanese in combat, the Nisei will serve as the language bridge between the Allied occupation forces and the 80,000,000 people of Japan.[45]

Aiso also suggested that Nisei might be well suited for occupation duty: "Perhaps the heartaches caused by the spiritual and material destruction wrought by evacuation will better fit us for the tasks of reconstruction by a better understanding of the feelings of the millions of innocent men, women, and children caught unmercifully in the ravages of this 'most-civilized' holocaust, World War II."[46]

Many Nisei were eager to serve in the occupation, but many combat veterans opposed the idea. In September several Nisei serving with the 25th Infantry Division on Luzon poured out their frustrations in a letter to the *Pacific Citizen*: "We are sick of people calling us non-combatants. We are also slighted when you refer to us as the men to reorganize the New Japan. We have done our bit. Now you do yours. We want to get back home to our loved ones just as badly as our Caucasian brothers in arms."[47]

Regardless of the opinions and feelings of individuals, the occupation needed large numbers of linguists. For the first two months after the surrender, hundreds of replacements from Fort Snelling continued to arrive in Manila. From June thru August 1945, MISLS shipped 1,073 enlisted Nisei to Manila, including one group of 536 who arrived in early September on board the AP *Kinkaid*. That November a new table of allowances authorized ATIS to grow to 2,667.

The influx of replacements and discharge of veterans caused constant turmoil for ATIS in Manila. "Adding to the difficulties of effective operation in this critical period," according to an ATIS report, "many of the most experienced linguists of the Section were removed from ATIS for duty with various GHQ [General Headquarters] staff sections which experienced an immediate demand for on-the-spot

[44] Orson Welles, in *New York Post*, 18 May 45; Larry Tajiri, "Nisei and Post-War Japan," *Pacific Citizen*, 26 May 45.

[45] *Pacific Citizen*, 1 Sep 45; *Yaban Gogai*, Sep–Oct 45, p. 2; Shibutani, *Derelicts of Company K*, pp. 260–61. Shibutani gives Bissell the pseudonym Jonathan Wilson.

[46] *Yaban Gogai*, Dec 45.

[47] Ltr to the Editor, *Pacific Citizen*, 22 Sep 45.

translators and interpreters."[48] While they waited for movement to Japan, the Nisei continued to translate thousands of pages of captured documents and to interrogate Japanese prisoners of war. The replacements needed testing and remedial training. In September and October ATIS published translations of thirty-three different enemy publications. Adjacent to the racetrack, ATIS set up a small POW holding area for special prisoners. One ATIS Nisei, Kaoru Inouye, a thirty-year-old chemist and graduate of the University of California, was one of the replacements who arrived in Manila in September. He especially enjoyed

the opportunity to talk to [these] POW's, many of whom were high executives/technical personnel of Japanese firms operating in PI [the Philippine Islands] and members of the Japanese Consular Service besides Army and Navy officers. An interesting discussion was held with a Captain of the aircraft carrier used for bombing Pearl Harbor. The discussion disclosed dissension between the Japanese Army and Navy, lack of logistics for invasion of Hawaii, miscalculation of war effort of United States, denouncing the use of English language, and use of Nisei's as linguist.[49]

On 27 September ATIS sent an advance party with Advance Echelon, General Headquarters, which arrived in Tokyo on 3 October. GHQ took over the *Dai-Ichi* building, former headquarters of the *Eastern District Army Command* next to the imperial palace. The office building included a 735-room hotel; one ATIS Nisei, 2d Lt. Harvey H. Watanabe, became the de facto manager of the hotel and liaison to its Japanese staff. Nearby stood another large office building, headquarters of Japan's major shipping line, *Nippon Yusen Kaisha* (*NYK*). ATIS took over the lower three stories for office space and used the upper four for billets and messes. Like most of Tokyo's office buildings, its central heating plant had been removed for scrap metal; so the Nisei used temporary oil stoves for the approaching winter. The ATIS main body arrived on two transport vessels on 15 and 16 November and completed unloading on 1 December. Nearly 2,000 American Nisei set up shop in the heart of Tokyo.[50]

The ATIS Nisei quickly became integral to military government at the working level. General Willoughby, MacArthur's chief of intelligence and one of the most important leaders in the occupation, continued to control ATIS during the occupation. ATIS reorganized to reflect its new duties. Australian Maj. John Shelton continued to head the Translation Section. The Nisei shifted from translating captured documents to translating civilian materials such as the letters, postcards, and telegrams that thousands of Japanese private citizens had sent directly to General MacArthur. In December 1945 Shelton established the Letters Subsection to translate these materials. According to a language officer in the section, they "were

---

[48] *Yaban Gogai*, Sep–Oct 45, p. 9; ATIS History, pp. 13, 29, 77.

[49] Inouye, MISNorCal Bio, pp. 5–6.

[50] Harvey H. Watanabe, personal communication to author, 19 May 03; ATIS History, ch. 9, Occupation Activities; Grant K. Goodman, *America's Japan: The First Year, 1945–1946* (New York: Fordham University Press, 2005).

The Allied Translator and Interpreter Section occupied the NYK *building, shown here from across the Imperial Palace moat.*

mostly expressions of gratitude for the Allied victory, for the orderly Occupation, and for the anticipated future democracy of Japan under MacArthur's guidance. . . . A number of letters contained intelligence of various kinds, i.e., information on 'war criminals' and their nefarious activities and/or their whereabouts, data on hidden arms caches, reports of ultranationalists political activities which the writers saw as inimical to Japan's nascent democracy, etc."[51]

Another task for the Translation Section was to prepare a summary of the daily press. "Each morning, when General MacArthur arrived at his office on the fifth floor of the *Dai-Ichi* building, on his desk would be a full English translation of all editorials and of a wide selection of articles from the Japanese press of the previous evening and that same morning. Such a project, as you might well imag-

---

[51] Grant K. Goodman, "The Grass Roots in Tokyo: A Language Officer Remembers," in Nimmo, ed., *Occupation of Japan*, p. 148; Goodman, *America's Japan*, pp. 52–60; John W. Dower, *Embracing Defeat: Japan in the Wake of World War II* (New York: Norton, 1999), pp. 227–29; ATIS History, p. 70; Sodei Rinjiro, ed., *Dear General MacArthur: Letters from the Japanese during the American Occupation* (Lanham, Md.: Rowman & Littlefield, 2001).

ine, entailed around the clock translation and, in those bad old days, mimeographing."[52] In February 1946, when Maj. Gen. Courtney Whitney and the Government Section wrote a new constitution for Japan, ATIS supplied translators.[53]

Upon arrival in Tokyo, ATIS underwent rapid change. The wartime coordinator, Col. Sidney F. Mashbir, was awarded the Distinguished Service Medal and departed for the United States on 8 December: "The war had ended; my small share had been contributed," he recorded in his memoirs. "I had no wish to be a *gauleiter* [Nazi-style "district leader," or petty dictator] in a conquered country."[54] Over the next two years ATIS was commanded subsequently by five officers, beginning with Col. Harry I. T. Creswell, author of a widely used Japanese-English military dictionary.[55] Four other colonels commanded ATIS for brief periods: Harold Doud, I. G. Walker, Eric H. F. Svensson, and Archibald W. Stuart. Stuart had been assistant commandant of MISLS from 1942 to 1944.[56]

MacArthur's headquarters was changing as well. In April 1945 GHQ, Southwest Pacific Area, had become GHQ, U.S. Army Forces Pacific, and now included forces previously under U.S. Army Middle Pacific. In August 1945 ATIS dissolved its Allied Land, Naval, and Air Force subelements; the remaining American portion was renamed the Translator and Interpreter Service. Twenty-one British, Australian, and New Zealand officer linguists remained, some as War Department civilians (such as Shelton, who headed the Translation Section until 1948). On 1 January 1946, GHQ, U.S. Army Forces Pacific, became GHQ, Far East Command. ATIS was officially inactivated as of 30 April 1946, and the organization continued as the Translator and Interpreter Service (TIS), GHQ, Far East Command.

The early months of the occupation were marked by high turnover among American personnel in Japan. As soon as units arrived in Japan, they began sending veterans home, starting with those with the highest points. Recent draftees arrived to take their places. At the end of December, Sixth Army was relieved of occupation duties in the southern half of Japan and Eighth Army took over military government for the entire country. (*Map 16*) American troop strength peaked in January 1946 at 240,000 before declining sharply. This drawdown affected the Nisei as well. At first they were declared to be critical personnel. Then in mid-

---

[52] Goodman, "Grass Roots in Tokyo," p. 148.

[53] Min Hara, in *John Aiso and the M.I.S.: Japanese-American Soldiers in the Military Intelligence Service, World War II*, ed. Tad Ichinokuchi (Los Angeles: Military Intelligence Service Club of Southern California, 1988), p. 75, reprinted in *Only What We Could Carry: The Japanese American Internment Experience* (Berkeley, Calif.: Heyday Books, 2000), p. 362; James, *Years of MacArthur*, 3: 119–39; Dower, *Embracing Defeat*, p. 380.

[54] Sidney F. Mashbir, *I Was an American Spy* (New York: Vantage, 1953), p. 347. Five other Caucasian officers on the ATIS staff, but no Nisei, received the Legion of Merit. ATIS History, app. 12.

[55] Harry I. T. Creswell et al., *A Dictionary of Military Terms, English-Japanese, Japanese-English* (Chicago: University of Chicago Press, 1942).

[56] Eric H. F. Svensson later wrote a dissertation about the occupation, "The Military Occupation of Japan: The First Years Planning, Policy Formulation, and Reforms," Ph.D. Diss., University of Denver, 1966.

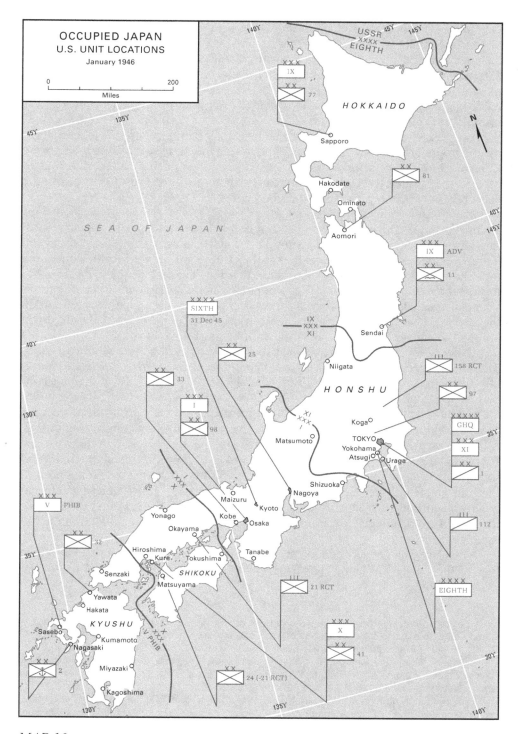

MAP 16

October 1945 this was reversed. Some Nisei were offered three-month furloughs to reenlist; others were awarded commissions, while still others were discharged in Japan and accepted civil service positions. ATIS personnel strength peaked at 250 officers and 1,700 enlisted personnel; these numbers declined sharply in the months that followed. By the spring of 1946 the authorized strength for ATIS was reduced to 809, almost two-thirds of which was now in civilian positions (301 military, 508 civilian).[57]

The Nisei were anxious to return home. Many had families still in the internment camps. The War Relocation Authority was intent upon closing all camps by December 1945 except for Tule Lake, which remained open a few months longer. Many Nisei wanted to help their parents return home to the West Coast or resettle elsewhere after three years behind barbed wire.

Most Nisei were curious about Japan, just as most Japanese were curious about the Nisei. During the war rumors had been widespread in Japan that all Japanese living in America had been killed. The Nisei dispelled these rumors and thereby helped allay Japanese fears that the Americans would kill their men and rape their women. Most Nisei discovered that the Japanese people were friendly toward them. One reported: "GI's are popular wherever they go. Especially those who can speak Japanese. Whenever they stop to talk with a Japanese civilian on the street, passersby gather around, and in no time, 30 or 40 form a tight circle around the conversationalists, bending an intent and pleased ear."[58]

Other Nisei reported that some Japanese looked down on the American Nisei. Major Aiso reported that the Nisei "were coolly received at first," but "were gradually being received more cordially by the Japanese people." He remained concerned about moral lapses among the occupation troops, and especially the Nisei. "It was most unfortunate that a few Nisei were abusing their positions as occupation personnel and had marred the good name of the Nisei by committing unlawful and disagreeable acts against the Japanese people." Historian John Curtis Perry concluded that "the level of expectation for *nisei* was extremely high, indeed impossible to achieve. Japanese expected *nisei* to be sensitive to the nuances of their ancestral culture. Because they looked Japanese, ... they were expected to behave accordingly. Naturally they did not, and they were resented for it. That the *nisei* were privileged to be among the victors seemed especially galling to the Japanese."[59]

Most Nisei had never seen Japan before, so the occupation gave them a chance to visit their ancestral land.[60] For Kibei, who had lived in Japan before the war, it

---

[57] For an unflattering firsthand portrait of the early days of Nisei replacements that arrived at Camp Zama in January 1946, see Shibutani, *Derelicts of Company K*, pp. 364–410.

[58] "People in Japan Show Friendly Attitude toward Nisei GIs," *Pacific Citizen*, 12 Jan 46.

[59] Kiyoshi Yano, "Participating in the Main Stream of American Life," in Ichinokuchi, *John Aiso and the M.I.S.*, pp. 24, 29; John C. Perry, *Beneath the Eagle's Wings: Americans in Occupied Japan* (New York: Dodd, Mead & Co., 1980), pp. 172–73.

[60] For firsthand impressions of Japan by Caucasian language officers in the early occupation, see Otis Cary, ed., *From a Ruined Empire: Letters—Japan, China, Korea, 1945–46* (San Francisco:

Sgt. J. Kenneth Iwagaki visits his parents in July 1945, shortly after their return to San Jose, California, from the Heart Mountain camp.

was a chance to rediscover a dramatically changed country. Many Nisei used the occupation to search out family and schoolmates, some traveling to the devastated city of Hiroshima. Most Japanese emigrants to the United States came from Hiroshima and neighboring Yamaguchi Prefectures.

The first Nisei to visit Hiroshima after the bombing was probably the Hawaii-born journalist Leslie Nakashima, who had spent the war years in Japan. Before the war he had worked for the *Honolulu Star-Bulletin* and had been a member of the territorial legislature. When war broke out he had been working in Tokyo for the United Press. On 22 August 1945, he hastened to Hiroshima to search for his mother. A few days later he filed a story, his first with an American newspaper

Kodansha, 1975); John Ashmead, "The Japs Look at the Yanks," *Atlantic Monthly* (April 1946): 86–91.

since 1941. "I was dumbfounded at the destruction before me. . . . What had been a city of 300,000 had vanished." He found his mother, who had been weeding a relative's vegetable garden on the outskirts of the city on the day of the bombing. When she saw the flash, she threw herself face down on the ground and heard "a terrific explosion." She arose to see tall columns of white smoke rising "from all parts of the city, high into the sky." She ran home, "because she didn't know what would happen next."[61]

On 9 September 2d Lt. Thomas Sakamoto escorted a group of American correspondents to Hiroshima, where they visited the Red Cross hospital. "Even after fifty years, I find it very difficult to fully describe my feelings and emotions of that day. . . . Lying in every available space were not combat soldiers, but defenseless women, children and elderly Japanese. . . . As a Japanese American, I was really shaken up—to think that these defenseless people were subjected to that kind of cruelty by one bomb, transforming their lives, body, and totally disfiguring their faces[,] was hard to take."[62]

On 2 October 2d Lt. Harry Fukuhara went on pass to Hiroshima to look for his family. He found their home, its windows shattered and glass shards imbedded in the walls inside. He found his mother and sister safe, but his older brother had been on the way to work when the bomb struck and was to die of acute radiation sickness within the year.[63]

Capt. Ralph Yempuku was eligible for a discharge but reenlisted for the Counter Intelligence Corps so he could search for his family:

First chance I got, I headed for Hiroshima. I didn't know the country. All I knew was that my parents lived on a tiny island called Atatashima near Hiroshima City. The train official had never heard of the place. When I got to Hiroshima City, I was shocked—there was nothing there but devastation. The whole city was wiped out. I thought my parents really must be dead. I left Hiroshima City thinking that.

But later, I decided to try again. This time, I went further into Hiroshima. I asked people along the way and finally found a man who said he could take me out to Atatashima in his skiff.

Night had fallen when I got to Atatashima. When my mother answered my knock, she didn't know who I was until I said "Okasan" [mother]. My father almost had another

[61] "Nisei Reporter Says Atomic Bomb Wiped Out Hiroshima," *Pacific Citizen*, 1 Sep 45. During the war Nakashima worked at Radio Tokyo for *Dōmei*. In early September he identified the California-born Nisei *Iva Ikuko Toguri d'Aquino* to American correspondents as Tokyo Rose. Clifford Uyeda, "Also Born on the Fourth of July: The Story of 'Tokyo Rose,'" *Nikkei Heritage* (Summer 1994): 4–8, 14–16.

[62] Quote from Thomas Sakamoto, "News of the Century: Japan's Surrender & Hiroshima, September 1945," *Nikkei Heritage* 7, no. 3 (Fall 1995); Interv, author with Thomas Sakamoto, 16 Nov 87; *The Saga of the MIS*, videotaped presentation, Los Angeles, 11 Mar 89.

[63] Harry Fukuhara, MISNorCal Bio; Harry Fukuhara, "The Return," *Nikkei Heritage* (Fall 1995): 12–13; Harry Fukuhara, "My Story, 50 Years Later," *Nikkei Heritage* (Winter 2003): 12–13; "For Family Living in Japan: Brothers Split by War and Circumstance," *San Francisco Chronicle*, 5 Aug 95.

stroke. They were convinced that I had died because of all the weird propaganda that they had heard about the slaughter of the nisei.[64]

Frank Tokubo found his parents and five brothers alive near Hiroshima. He learned that his family had been ostracized because the whole community knew that one of their sons was serving in the U.S. Army. To counter this shame, one of his younger brothers had volunteered for the *Tokko-tai*, or kamikaze corps; however, he had not gone on a mission before the war had ended.[65]

Lt. Steve Shizuma Yamamoto landed in September with Sixth Army and helped set up its headquarters in the ancient capital of Kyoto. In December he rode the train to Hiroshima to look for his father and stepmother. "Early in the morning I got off at the local station out in the country. I was in uniform and had a duffle bag with me." A young man loaned him a bicycle so he wouldn't have to carry his bag.

I went along the road toward the homestead. In the distance I see the womenfolks sweeping in their front yards, and as I approached closer everybody disappears. When I got to my dad's homestead, nobody comes out. I holler, '*Ohayō!*' [Good morning!]. Nobody comes out. So I waited. Slowly my aunt opened the *shoji* [sliding door], peered out, recognized me and said, '*Oh, Shizuma-san desuka*'? [Oh, is it Shizuma?] That was the reaction I got when I visited Hiroshima. Everybody was afraid of Americans in uniform.[66]

In Italy, veterans with the 442d Regimental Combat Team also reenlisted for occupation duty. A front-page story in the *Pacific Citizen* of 20 October 1945 told of one such 442d RCT veteran who reenlisted for the "opportunity to search the atomic ruins of Hiroshima for his aged mother."[67]

Counter Intelligence Corps, War Crimes Trials, and the Purge

At the very beginning of the occupation the Counter Intelligence Corps (CIC) moved to the forefront, from having small detachments with each combat division to becoming a major force in the occupation. In June 1945 the 441st CIC Detachment absorbed the small, individual detachments. It had few Nisei assigned at that time, among them M.Sgt. Arthur S. Komori, personal interpreter for the theater CIC chief, Brig. Gen. Elliott Thorpe. In the summer of 1945 the Military Intelligence Training Center at Camp Ritchie, Maryland, organized a special CIC class

---

[64] Tomi Kaizawa Knaefler, *Our House Divided: Seven Japanese American Families in World War II* (Honolulu: University of Hawaii Press, 1991), pp. 93–94. Yempuku learned that his four brothers all survived the war.

[65] Harrington, *Yankee Samurai*, pp. 226, 353.

[66] Interv, David W. Swift, Jr., with Steve Yamamoto, in David W. Swift, Jr., ed., "First Class," Unpubl Ms, Mar 00, copy in author's files.

[67] Masayo Umezawa Duus, *Unlikely Liberators: The Men of the 100th and 442nd* (Honolulu: University of Hawaii Press, 1987), pp. 230–31; "Nisei GI Will Seek Mother in Hiroshima Ruins," *Pacific Citizen*, 20 Oct 45.

of eighty Nisei who were individual replacements from Fort Meade, Maryland. None was an MISLS graduate, but all reportedly had at least fair speaking ability in Japanese.[68]

After the surrender CIC personnel rushed into Japan, their mission to protect occupation forces and investigate war crimes. In December the theater CIC head-quarters, the 441st CIC Detachment, installed itself in the former headquarters building of the *Kempeitai*, the Japanese military police.[69] Thorpe soon became known as "the most feared man in Japan." Once the CIC arrived, Thorpe later wrote, "the biggest problem was to spread as thinly as possible the limited number of our Japanese-speaking agents."[70]

War crimes investigations called for tact, as the CIC soon learned. On MacAr-thur's first day in Tokyo, he gave Thorpe a simple mission: "Thorpe, have your people arrest General [Hideki] Tojo and lock him up." On 11 September CIC agents drove to the house where the former prime minister was staying (he had stepped down in July 1944). When the general saw the American soldiers, he shot himself before they could arrest him. CIC agents learned that it was better to sum-mon individuals using Japanese officials, rather than approaching them directly. *Tojo* recovered to face trial.[71]

Like the other occupation forces, the CIC was hampered by hasty demobiliza-tion. Komori left Japan in November 1945 to return home to Hawaii. At the same time several Caucasian language officers, including former members of the school staff from Fort Snelling such as Lt. Col. Paul R. Rusch and Col. Archibald W. Stuart, transferred to CIC. ATIS assigned more Nisei to CIC, but CIC leaders com-plained of their weak language proficiency. Mashbir responded that they would

---

[68] *Covert Warfare*, vol. 2 (see below), dates this to 1 August, but Joseph Y. Kurata recalls that it began in May and graduated in late July. *Covert Warfare*, 12 vols. (New York: Garland, 1989), vols. 2, 11; "Counter Intelligence in Occupied Japan," in *MIS in the War against Japan*, ed. Stanley L. Falk and Warren M. Tsuneishi (Washington, D.C.: Japanese American Veterans Association, 1995), pp. 79–83; George S. Ishida, "CIC in Yokohama, 1945 to 1953," in Tsukiyama et al., *Secret Valor*, pp. 118–19. *The Pacific War and Peace: Americans of Japanese Ancestry in Military Intel-ligence Service, 1941 to 1952* (San Francisco: Military Intelligence Service Association of Northern California/National Japanese American Historical Society, 1991), p. 78, refers to about a hundred Nisei in training at Camp Ritchie in the spring of 1945.

[69] *A Brief History of the G–2 Section, GHQ, SWPA and Affiliated Units*, Intelligence Series (Tokyo: Far East Command, 1948), pp. 117–18; George S. Ishida, in Tsukiyama et al., *Secret Valor*, pp. 118–19.

[70] Elliott R. Thorpe, *East Wind, Rain: An Intimate Account of an Intelligence Officer in the Pacific, 1939–49* (Boston: Gambit, 1969), pp. 184, 193. See also *Reports of General MacArthur*, vol. 1 supplement, pp. 231–67; General Headquarters, Far East Command, *Operations of the Civil Intelligence Section, SCAP*, Intelligence Series, vol. 9 (Tokyo: Far East Command, 1948); Duval A. Edwards, *Spy Catchers of the U.S. Army in the War with Japan* (Gig Harbor, Wash.: Red Apple Publishing, 1994); William B. Simpson, *Special Agent in the Pacific, WWII: Counterintelligence—Military, Political, and Economic* (New York: Rivercross Publishing, 1995), pp. 113–206. Simpson was assigned to the 11th Airborne Division as a CIC special agent from August 1945 to April 1946.

[71] Thorpe, *East Wind, Rain*, p. 184.

Nisei special agents with the Counter Intelligence Corps, Yokohama, 1946

have to make do with what they had: "Practically all of ATIS old and experienced linguists have been returned or are being returned in the very near future to the United States under the point system. Linguists now available at ATIS are nearly all hastily and incompletely trained and inexperienced personnel just recently arrived from the United States."[72]

CIC's mission soon broadened to include civil intelligence. When Thorpe returned to the United States in February 1946, Willoughby brought CIC under his own direct control, something he had never been able to do during the war. Willoughby thus became more powerful than ever. CIC soon became involved in the search for Communists in Japan, including Communist infiltration of repatriates, the Japan Communist Party, and the Soviet spy ring led by Richard Sorge, who had been arrested in 1941 and executed in 1944.[73]

---

[72] Memo, ATIS GHQ ADVON to CIS, 30 Nov 45, G–2, OCCIO, Gen Corresp, 1944–1945, 091–300.6 (Decimal 200), GHQ, Southwest Pacific Area and U.S. Army Forces Pacific, RG 338, NARA.

[73] Eiji Takemae, *Inside GHQ: The Allied Occupation of Japan and Its Legacy* (New York: Continuum, 2002), pp. 161–68; *Reports of General MacArthur*, vol. 1 supplement, pp. 256–67. See the 441d CIC Detachment report on the Sorge case from early 1946, in *Covert Warfare*, vol. 7.

When American forces arrived in Japan, the U.S. government was determined to hold Japanese leaders to account for war crimes. As many as seventy Nisei were involved in war crimes work, playing critical roles as translators, interpreters, and investigators. Their job was not easy; in the interval between Japan's surrender and the arrival of American forces, Japanese military and civilian officials engaged in the systematic destruction of potentially incriminating records. As a result, the prosecution had to build its cases on wartime intelligence and postwar interrogations. Fortunately, ATIS had begun focusing on gathering war crimes evidence as early as 1943.[74]

The first major trial was held not in Tokyo, but in Manila for *General Tomoyuki Yamashita* beginning in late October 1945. Six or eight Nisei were assigned as interpreters under Navy language officer Lt. Cmdr. Samuel C. Bartlett. Two others served on the defense team and fifteen on the prosecution team. Nisei working on the trial had the opportunity to meet the defendant, who at one point consented to have his photograph taken with them. "I am glad to know you men have fought for the country of your birth," *Yamashita* told them. "That is the way it should be. You are American citizens. Therefore, you should fight for the United States."[75]

American prosecutors in Manila received timely assistance when Richard M. Sakakida emerged from the mountains in northern Luzon in September 1945. After the fall of Corregidor in 1942, the Corps of Intelligence Police had lost track of the Hawaii-born undercover agent. At last they learned that he had been held for six months in a POW camp in 1942–1943 and had suffered torture in Bilibid Prison. But he had managed to win the confidence of the Japanese, who employed him in the staff judge advocate section inside the Japanese Army headquarters from March 1943 to the end of the war. He secretly used his position whenever possible to help American and Filipino prisoners, who later described how he would slip food to them and do other small kindnesses. The Japanese held trials for Filipinos accused of being guerillas, but "the trials were highly superficial with only weak attempts made to simulate fairness," Sakakida later wrote, and the Filipinos were often sentenced to death. "Occasionally, I was forced to fill in as an interpreter at the trials. About all I could do was to tone down some of the replies of those being accused so that the Japanese wouldn't be so harsh on them." He later described how he had passed secrets to Philippine guerrillas and assisted them in other ways that would surely have cost his life if discovered.[76]

---

[74] For example, see ATIS Research Rpt no. 72, "Japanese Violations of the Laws of War," 29 Apr 44.

[75] Quote from "Honolulu Realty Broker [Tad Tadashi Yajima] Recalls Days as Interpreter at Yamashita's Trial," *Honolulu Advertiser*, ca. 1957; "Snelling GIs Take Part in Yamashita Case," *Yaban Gogai*, Dec 45, p. 1; Ichinokuchi, *John Aiso and the M.I.S.*, pp. 125–27, 142–50; Sueo Ito, Rocky Mountain Bio.

[76] Quote from Richard Sakakida and Wayne S. Kiyosaki, *A Spy in Their Midst: The World War II Struggle of a Japanese American Hero* (Lanham, Md.: Madison Books, 1995), pp. 151, 152; "Mission in Manila—The Sakakida Story," video, 1994; Ann Bray, "Undercover Nisei," in *Military Intelligence: Its Heroes and Legends* (Arlington Hall Station, Va.: U.S. Army Intelligence and Security Command, 1987), pp. 29–45.

T.Sgt. Tadao Ichinokuchi (left) *with* Yamashita, *on trial for war crimes, Manila, November 1945.* Yamashita *was convicted and executed in February 1946.*

In late 1944, when *Yamashita* left Manila for northern Luzon, Sakakida accompanied the judge advocate section into the mountains. As the situation deteriorated he became separated from his section; in September 1945 he finally was reunited with American forces but had suffered from dysentery, malaria, beriberi, and an untreated abdominal wound from a mortar fragment. At first the CIC investigators were suspicious because he had worked for the Japanese, but they soon satisfied themselves as to his loyalty. Sergeant Komori, who by then had moved on to Tokyo with General Thorpe, vouched for his former colleague. He "felt certain of [Sakakida's] loyalty. I was glad when General Willoughby took my word for it."[77] The CIC restored Sakakida as a special agent and promoted him to master sergeant. His insider knowledge of Japanese occupation activities in the Philippines proved immediately useful to the prosecutors. He testified against a member of *Yamashita*'s staff on 15 November 1945.

Following the *Yamashita* trial, most Nisei involved in the trial moved to Japan for further trials in Tokyo and Yokohama. Trials continued in Manila for lesser

[77] Quote from Interv, Ann Bray with Arthur S. Komori, 1955, pp. 11–12.

defendants. In all, the United States held 97 trials in the Philippines for 215 Japanese defendants, which resulted in 195 convictions and 92 death sentences. Sakakida remained in Manila for eighteen more months working on war crimes investigations and sometimes found himself investigating Japanese officers with whom he had worked during the war. At one point he identified the *Kempeitai* officers responsible for his torture:

Looking frightened and guilty, my former torturers prostrated themselves on the ground as if ready to accept any punishment I chose to inflict upon them. But by now I was far too removed from the rage I had felt while in their control; the war was over, and I had no desire to return to bitter hatred and killing. As soldiers in combat we had all done what was required of us. . . . I was ready to let bygones be bygones.[78]

In January 1946 MacArthur announced the formation of the International Military Tribunal for the Far East. Already, on 1 December 1945, ATIS had established war crimes echelons in Tokyo and Manila to support the trials. Dozens of Nisei served as translators, interpreters, and investigators. Proceedings began in May 1946 against twenty-eight Class A defendants, high military and civilian government leaders, in the former Army Ministry building in Tokyo.[79] The trials, which lasted until 1948, presented unusual challenges. War crimes trials were a new experience for the Nisei, who worked with investigators, prosecutors, and defense attorneys. Japanese documents captured during the war were translated by ATIS Nisei and introduced as evidence. Other evidence came from interrogations of thousands of witnesses and suspects. The trials brought to light some of the war's most horrifying events, including abuse of prisoners, forced labor, executions, cannibalism, and human experimentation. Several of the most proficient Nisei interpreters, including several enlisted instructors from Fort Snelling, served as courtroom monitors. In Tokyo, the courtroom was equipped with the latest technology for simultaneous interpretation, similar to that used at the Nuremberg trials and the United Nations conference in San Francisco. Japanese nationals worked as interpreters, while the American Nisei monitored to ensure accuracy. The Nisei worked under intense pressure. Controversies could erupt over the correct interpretation of a single word, potentially a life-and-death issue for the defendant. Japanese journalists were present in the courtroom and paid close attention to the interpretation. Many Nisei viewed the trials with mixed feelings and like many other Americans had doubts about what they considered "victor's justice."

---

[78] Sakakida, *A Spy in Their Midst*, pp. 186–87.
[79] Arnold C. Brackman, *The Other Nuremberg: The Untold Story of the Tokyo War Crimes Trials* (New York: William Morrow, 1987); Dower, *Embracing Defeat*, pp. 443–84; James, *Years of MacArthur*, 3: 93–108; Richard H. Minear, *Victors' Justice: The Tokyo War Crimes Trial* (Princeton, N.J.: Princeton University Press, 1971); Philip R. Piccigallo, *The Japanese on Trial: Allied War Crimes Operations in the East, 1945–1951* (Austin: University of Texas Press, 1979); Yuki Tanaka, *Hidden Horrors: Japanese War Crimes in World War II* (Boulder, Colo.: Westview Press, 1996); Jeanie M. Welch, *The Tokyo Trial: A Bibliographic Guide to English-Language Sources* (Westport, Conn.: Greenwood Press, 2001).

A Nisei sergeant (standing at right center) *interprets at a war crimes tribunal in Japan in early January 1946.*

As Thorpe later expressed it, "We wanted blood, and by God, we had blood."[80] Even MacArthur wrote that "the principle of holding criminally responsible the leaders of the vanquished in war was repugnant to me" and distanced himself from the proceedings. Despite such feelings, the Nisei performed their duties with dedication and skill.[81]

Nisei also helped conduct hundreds of trials of Class B and Class C defendants in Yokohama, where Eighth Army established the Yokohama Interrogation Center on 10 October 1945. Most of these trials involved accusations of brutality toward Allied prisoners of war. Australian Capt. G. J. Moses, one of ATIS's best Caucasian language officers, commanded dozens of ATIS Nisei, who worked closely with the

---

[80] Cited in Dower, *Embracing Defeat*, p. 452.
[81] Ken K. Aiba, "MIS in War Crimes Trials," in *Unsung Heroes*, pp. 15–21; *Pacific War and Peace*, pp. 76–77.

CIC to develop evidence for the prosecution.[82] More than 300 trials were conducted in Yokohama between 1945 and 1949. Twenty-six Nisei worked as investigators, eighteen as interpreters, and fifty in the interpreter-translator section. In April 1946 six Nisei serving in Japan for the Washington Document Center took civilian jobs on these trials. George M. Koshi, an attorney from Colorado, took a discharge in Japan to become a defense attorney with the Eighth Army judge advocate section. Ken K. Aiba became chief investigator for the defense section.[83]

Other Nisei worked at Sugamo Prison, where the defendants were confined. One Nisei guard was Sohei Yamate from Hawaii, who had served for six months in Kunming, China: "To my relief, my Japanese-language skills were never really tested.... At times, I can hardly believe that at the young age of twenty, I was handing out orders to former generals, admirals, ambassadors, and prime ministers. Given my Hawaiian upbringing, I was never good at honorifics."

When *General Tojo* was confined in Sugamo Prison following his suicide attempt, Yamate was assigned to monitor the general's family visits. The twenty-year-old Yamate used the direct approach and asked the general not to try to kill himself again because Yamate would be held responsible. *Tojo* told him not to worry. Yamate could see that the general was "a beaten man," especially, Yamate felt, when the general heard how poorly the Nisei spoke the Japanese language; it was only then that the general "finally realized that he had lost the war."[84]

The United States and its Allies held other war crimes trials throughout the region. The U.S. Navy conducted forty-seven trials on the Pacific Islands, principally on Guam and Kwajalein. The United States held eleven trials in China, including one trial in Shanghai for the killers of some American airmen. China, the Philippines, Australia, Britain, France, and the Netherlands conducted separate trials. The Australians alone tried over 900 Japanese. Canadian Nisei with Commonwealth forces served in war crimes investigations and trials in Java, Singapore, and Hong Kong. One Canadian Nisei, Sgt. Tadashi Ode, who graduated from the Canadian language school in September 1945, was assigned to the prosecution section for the International Military Tribunal for the Far East.[85]

---

[82] ATIS History, p. 66.

[83] George M. Koshi, MISNorCal Bio. Koshi continued legal work in Japan for many years and later published a handbook of Japanese criminal law, *Japanese Legal Advisor: Crimes and Punishments* (Rutland, Vt.: Charles E. Tuttle Co., 1970).

[84] Quote from Tsukiyama et al., *Secret Valor*, p. 112; *Japanese Eyes, American Heart: Personal Reflections of Hawaii's World War II Nisei Soldiers* (Honolulu: Tendai Educational Foundation, 1998), pp. 328–34; Ichinokuchi, *John Aiso and the M.I.S.*, pp. 142–50, 151–55.

[85] Cary, *From a Ruined Empire*, pp. 196–217; Ito, *We Went to War*, pp. 256–72; Timothy Maga, "'Away from Tokyo': The Pacific Islands War Crimes Trials, 1945–1949," *Journal of Pacific History* 36, no. 1 (2001): 37–50. Jeannie M. Welch, "Without a Hangman, Without a Rope: Navy War Crimes Trials after World War II," *International Journal of Naval History* 1, no. 1 (April 2002). One prisoner in Hong Kong was Canadian Nisei *Kanao Inouye* from Kamloops, British Columbia. He had moved to Japan in 1935 at age nineteen and in 1944–1945 worked as an interpreter for the *Kempeitai*. He was charged with twenty-seven acts of cruelty committed as part of Japanese interrogations and was convicted and hanged in 1947.

T.Sgt. Donald S. Okubo (front right) *interprets at a war crimes trial, Kwajalein Atoll, 21 November 1945. A Japanese warrant officer* (kneeling) *demonstrates how an American prisoner had been executed by beheading.*

Related to the war crimes trials was the purge of leading Japanese civilian leaders. This was also one of the most controversial aspects of the occupation. Shortly after MacArthur arrived in Japan, he ordered Thorpe to draw up a list of top military and civilian leaders to put on trial. Many Americans demanded that the emperor be removed from the throne and tried as a war criminal, but MacArthur decided to retain him. Brig. Gen. Bonner Fellers, one of MacArthur's most trusted lieutenants, worked behind the scenes to protect the emperor with the aid of Maj. John E. Anderton from ATIS.[86]

In February 1946 MacArthur removed the Civil Intelligence Section from investigating war criminals and directed it to continue the purge. That same month Major Aiso arrived from Fort Snelling and was assigned to the Civil Intelligence Section as a legal assistant. Despite his humble birth in Southern California, Aiso was well connected with many Japanese leaders under consideration for the purge. To cite just one example, when the emperor paid his first visit to MacArthur on 27

---

[86] Herbert P. Bix, *Hirohito and the Making of Modern Japan* (New York: HarperCollins, 2000), pp. 567–68; Dower, *Embracing Defeat*, pp. 277–330.

September 1945, the Japanese diplomat *Hidenari Terasaki* served as the emperor's personal interpreter. Aiso and *Terasaki* had shared a room in the early 1930s at Brown University, where Aiso was attending on a Japanese government scholarship. (*Terasaki* also had a connection with MacArthur's inner circle: his wife Gwen was Bonner Feller's cousin.) In 1926–1927, when Aiso was sixteen, his parents had sent him to a special school in Japan for the children of Japanese diplomats returning from overseas, where he befriended other future officials. After graduating from Brown and the Harvard School of Law, he went back to Japan in 1936, this time as an attorney for a New York law firm. From 1936 to 1939 he did legal work in Tokyo, Shanghai, and Mukden for the British-American Tobacco Company and got to know many Japanese businessmen.

By 1946 much had changed. Aiso had spent the intervening years as the senior Nisei in MISLS and now was wearing the uniform of an officer in the U.S. Army. Aiso avoided his former contacts and benefactors out of consideration for his position and theirs. It was his aim, he later said, "to enforce the purge with fairness, justice, and humanity." However, he clashed with Col. Charles L. Kades, chief of the government section. Kades freely admitted that he had "no knowledge whatsoever about Japan's history or culture or myths. . . . I was blank on Japan, except of course I knew about the atrocities that had occurred during the war and I was aware of their expansion into China and Southeast Asia." Aiso recalled that "Colonel Kades seemed to lack an understanding of the true nature of the Japanese people and was unduly harsh in literal enforcement [of] decrees against the Japanese." In particular Aiso was "very much opposed [to] the mechanical method of screening which was applied," such as membership in certain societies.[87]

Deeply discouraged, Aiso left Japan after his twelve-month tour. In February 1947 he returned to Los Angeles to resume his law practice, which the war had interrupted six years earlier. There, much of his legal work involved helping Issei and Nisei returning to the Los Angeles area from wartime internment. He was replaced in the Civil Intelligence Section by another Nisei lawyer, Maj. Walter T. Tsukamoto, who had served as national president of the Japanese American Citizens League during the critical years 1940–1942.[88]

The war crimes trials also drew attention to the fact that thousands of American Nisei had spent the war in Japan and that many had worked for the Japanese armed forces, government, or war industries. This publicity threatened to aggra-

---

[87] Kades quote from Dower, *Embracing Defeat*, p. 223; Aiso quotes from Aiso, "Observations of a California Nisei," p. 88.

[88] Aiso, "Observations of a California Nisei"; Interv, Loni Ding and Eric Saul with John F. Aiso, 1986, NJAHS; Interv, author with John F. Aiso; Yano, "Participating in the Main Stream," in Ichonokuchi, *John Aiso and the M.I.S.*, pp. 4–32. See also John Aiso, "Japan as Observed from MacArthur's Headquarters," *Rafu Shimpo*, ca. 22 Mar 47, cited in Ichinokuchi, *John Aiso and the M.I.S.* Upon transfer to the Officer Reserve Corps in 1947, Aiso was promoted to lieutenant colonel. In 1953 Governor Earl Warren named Aiso to the Los Angeles municipal court, making him the first Japanese American to serve on a state bench on the mainland. Ironically, in 1942, as California attorney general, Warren had been instrumental in the evacuation of all individuals of Japanese ancestry from the state.

vate the long-standing prejudice on the American West Coast against the Japanese, just as thousands of Japanese Issei and Nisei were returning from the War Relocation Authority camps. In October 1945 American authorities arrested *Iva Ikuko Toguri d'Aquino*, a California-born Nisei who been in Japan at the outbreak of the war. She had become one of more than a dozen English-language radio announcers for Radio Tokyo's overseas service known by the collective nickname Tokyo Rose. She was released in 1946 without trial but was rearrested in 1948 and brought to San Francisco, where she was convicted of treason after a sensational trial. The *Pacific Citizen* commented that "race prejudice is a definite factor in the trial." In another case, California-born *Tomoya Kawakita* was accused of having mistreated Allied prisoners of war. He had gone to Japan in 1939 and worked as an interpreter for a Japanese company that used Allied prisoners. When he returned to Los Angeles in 1946, he was identified by a former prisoner of war, convicted of eight counts of treason, and given a death sentence, which was later commuted to life imprisonment.[89]

Other Occupation Duties

In the early days of the occupation the Nisei became essential to the day-to-day function of military government and throughout the country. Their duties most often took the form of liaison with Japanese local government officials to supervise the carrying out of SCAP directives. The first order of business in each city and prefecture was to establish working relationships with local officials. In what must have been repeated hundreds of times, Ben I. Yamamoto arrived in Sasebo in late September 1945 with a U.S. Navy headquarters to help inventory Japanese naval munitions stockpiles. At first he carried a .38 cal. revolver:

After all, we did not know how we would be received by the natives. I packed my six-shooter with me the first two days and was careful not to let any Japanese get behind me. It was an awkward, uncomfortable relationship, with some of the Japanese men casting embarrassing glances at my gun. These people didn't look dangerous at all; in fact, they looked much like the Issei back home. On the third day I left my firearms at home. They reacted beautifully. They warmed up to me and worked more enthusiastically. We shared our lunch with each other and played volleyball during our breaks, among other things.[90]

---

[89] Frank F. Chuman, *The Bamboo People: The Law and Japanese Americans* (Chicago: Japanese American Citizens League, 1981), pp. 288–95; "d'Aquino, Iva Ikuko Toguri," and "Kawakita v. United States," in *Encyclopedia of Japanese American History*, rev. ed., ed. Brian Niiya (New York: Facts on File, 2001). For the impact of the Tokyo Rose trial on postwar Japanese American communities, see David K. Yoo, *Growing Up Nisei: Race, Generation, and Culture among Japanese Americans of California, 1924–1949* (Urbana: University of Illinois Press, 2000), pp. 174–79 (quote from p. 177).

[90] *Japanese Eyes, American Heart*, p. 184; Richard S. Oguro, ed., *Sempai Gumi* (Honolulu: MIS Veterans of Hawaii, ca. 1981), pp. 74–75.

A Nisei captain (left) *and another U.S. Army officer* (right) *question a Japanese shipmaster transporting repatriates to Japan.*

The Nisei helped with another urgent task, the repatriation of 3.5 million Japanese soldiers and sailors and 3 million civilians stranded overseas when the war ended. The SCAP G–2 supervised this vast undertaking. The Japanese had to be controlled, cared for, and shipped home. The effort dragged on for several years, particularly for the Japanese captured by the Soviets in Manchuria. As with the rest of the occupation, SCAP worked through existing Japanese agencies. In this case, the War and Navy Ministries were transformed into the First and Second Demobilization Ministries. (They merged into a single Demobilization Board on 1 July 1946.) To develop an orderly process, SCAP held a conference on repatriation in January 1946. Weather and the availability of shipping determined the rate of return. Shipment from the ice-bound ports in the Soviet Far East was delayed until the autumn of 1946. SCAP designated four principal ports of entry—Sasebo, Hakata, Maizuru, and Hakodate—where American intelligence personnel screened returning Japanese. (*Map 17*) Repatriates of special interest were interrogated at a Central Interrogation Center established in June 1946.[91]

SCAP simultaneously supervised a massive return flow of civilians from Korea, Formosa, and other parts of Japan's former empire. On the southern island of Kyushu, V Amphibious Corps was particularly busy supervising this two-way

---

[91] *Reports of General MacArthur*, vol. 1 supplement, pp. 149–93; ATIS History, pp. 72–74; Dower, *Embracing Defeat*, pp. 48–64.

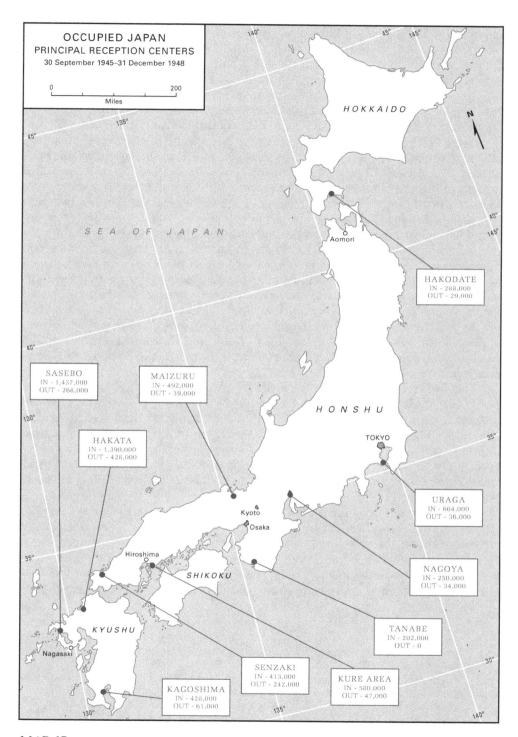

OCCUPIED JAPAN
PRINCIPAL RECEPTION CENTERS
30 September 1945–31 December 1948

0   200
Miles

HOKKAIDO

N

SEA   OF   JAPAN

Aomori

HAKODATE
IN - 288,000
OUT - 29,000

SASEBO
IN - 1,437,000
OUT - 268,000

MAIZURU
IN - 492,000
OUT - 39,000

HONSHU

TOKYO

HAKATA
IN - 1,390,000
OUT - 428,000

URAGA
IN - 664,000
OUT - 36,000

Kyoto

Osaka

Hiroshima

NAGOYA
IN - 250,000
OUT - 34,000

SHIKOKU

KYUSHU

TANABE
IN - 202,000
OUT - 0

Nagasaki

SENZAKI
IN - 413,000
OUT - 242,000

KAGOSHIMA
IN - 428,000
OUT - 61,000

KURE AREA
IN - 580,000
OUT - 47,000

MAP 17

repatriation. By the end of November 1945 over 700,000 Japanese had returned from overseas through Kyushu ports, while 273,276 Koreans, Chinese, and Okinawans had departed through the same ports. Inevitably, frictions occurred between the various groups. Kure on the Inland Sea was the repatriation point for Korean workers returning to the peninsula. In December 1945 rioting broke out there between Korean workers and Japanese sailors. Nisei from the X Corps language detachment were called out to help control the rioting.[92]

In the Philippines, Prisoner of War Camp No. 1 south of Manila held 60,000–80,000 Japanese prisoners. After the surrender, ATIS organized the Luzon Prisoner of War (LUPOW) team with perhaps 100 Nisei to assist the military police in controlling the massive camp. Some were MISLS graduates, but some were shipped directly from Hawaii with no language training. T.Sgt. Yoshito Iwamoto was assigned to the LUPOW records section, where he "spent most of [his] spare time looking for Nisei who been drafted into the Japanese army," including his two older brothers "who had been stranded in Japan and drafted." He later learned they were not sent to the Philippines; one had served in Malaya and the other in Manchuria.[93] Nisei and Caucasian language officers sometimes got to know individual Japanese prisoners of war and agreed to carry messages to their families in Japan. When the Americans were subsequently assigned to Japan, they searched out the prisoners' families and brought word of their sons and husbands still alive in prisoner of war camps. In one instance, 2d Lt. Tad Yajima, who had served in *General Yamashita*'s trial, paid a courtesy call to the general's widow in Kamakura a few months after his execution.[94]

The first repatriation ship to depart the Australian-controlled areas was a Japanese aircraft carrier that left Rabaul on 28 February 1946 with 2,658 men on board. Through June 1946 thirty-seven ships departed from Rabaul with a total of 90,909 Japanese personnel. In the southern Philippines, where Japanese immigrants had settled peaceably before the war, officials deported "practically everyone who looked Japanese and their Filipino wives with their half-Japanese small children. Other families were split up."[95] The extensive prewar Japanese population in the Philippines virtually disappeared.

Little noticed among the millions of Japanese returning to Japan were 8,000 from America. Most were Issei, but more than 1,000 were Nisei. Starting in December 1944, these Nisei at Tule Lake for varying reasons had accepted a U.S. government offer to renounce U.S. citizenship. At the end of the war many petitioned to withdraw their renunciations and fought deportation, but the government persevered. The first group arrived in Japan on 10 December 1945 to

[92] Inouye, MISNorCal Bio.

[93] *Yaban Gogai*, Dec 45, p. 5; Yoshito Iwamoto, in Falk and Tsuneishi, *MIS in the War against Japan*, pp. 39–41; Harrington, *Yankee Samurai*, p. 353.

[94] Cary, *From a Ruined Empire*, p. 217; "Honolulu Realty Broker Recalls Days as Interpreter."

[95] George Totten, in Falk and Tsuneishi, *MIS in the War Against Japan*, pp. 34–38.

face an uncertain future in a devastated and unfamiliar land that many of them had never seen.[96]

The last major repatriation program to get started and the last to be completed was from the Soviet Far East. It began with a trickle in the autumn of 1946, but this was soon halted by the onset of winter weather. It restarted in April 1947 and continued on and off through the early 1950s, eventually totaling about 700,000. The American intelligence officials subjected these repatriates to special scrutiny to detect signs of Communist indoctrination and to identify former Japanese Army officers who could provide information of intelligence value about Soviet forces and facilities in the region.[97]

MIS Nisei performed a surprising variety of other duties, such as serving with the U.S. Strategic Bombing Survey, in the early months of the occupation. The War Department established the survey in late 1944 to investigate the effectiveness of the aerial campaigns against Germany and Japan. Teams of experts worked in Germany for several months after the surrender. In August 1945 President Truman directed a similar study for Japan. The advance party arrived in Japan on 4 September 1945 and by the end of the month numbered several hundred. The survey requested fifteen volunteers from ATIS in the Philippines, including several from the Army Air Forces radio squadrons mobile. More Nisei joined after ATIS arrived in Tokyo.[98] Lt. Col. David W. Swift, one of two Caucasians to graduate from Crissy Field in 1942, joined as head of the logistics section. Several Navy language officers served as well.[99] Nisei accompanied survey teams to examine bomb damage and to help conduct thousands of interviews. In just a few months the teams gathered data for over a hundred reports on various topics. Most personnel returned to the States by the end of 1945, and the survey released several reports over the following year. *Japan's Struggle To End the War* (1 July 1946) concluded based on extensive interviews that Japan would have surrendered "in all probability prior to 1 November 1945," even without the atomic bombings. *The Effects of Atomic Bombs on Hiroshima and Nagasaki* (30 June 1946) was the first technical study of the bombings.

[96] Michi Weglyn, *Years of Infamy: The Untold Story of America's Concentration Camps* (New York: Morrow Quill, 1976), pp. 229–65; "Renunciation of Citizenship," in *Encyclopedia of Japanese American History*.

[97] Y. Kono, MISNorCal Bio; *Pacific War and Peace*, pp. 80–82; Allen H. Meyer, "Repatriation at the Grass Roots Level," in Nimmo, *Occupation of Japan*, pp. 101–15. For an early example of intelligence on Soviet forces, see GHQ, FECOM [Far East Command], MI [Military Intelligence] Section, GS [General Staff], ATIS, ATIS Bulletin no. 1, 15 Jan 47, based on 817 military and civilian interrogations.

[98] Intervs, Dawn Duensing with Yoichi Kawano and James Sadami Okada, in *Americanism: A Matter of Mind and Heart*; David MacIsaac, *Strategic Bombing in World War II: The Story of the United States Strategic Bombing Survey* (New York: Garland, 1976); U.S. Army Air Force, Assistant Chief of Staff, Intelligence, *Mission Accomplished: Interrogations of Japanese Industrial Military and Civil Leaders of World War II* (Washington, D.C.: Government Printing Office, 1946).

[99] Swift, "First Class," pp. 293–97; Ltrs by Frank Turner in Cary, *From a Ruined Empire*.

Harvard Professor of Psychiatry Alexander H. Leighton came to Japan with the Strategic Bombing Survey's Morale Division. A self-appointed expert on Japanese psychology, Leighton had studied Japanese internees in Poston and then worked in the Office of War Information. T.Sgt. Yasuo Baron Goto and M.Sgt. Keith Kaneshiro, together with several other non-MIS Nisei, served as translator-analysts for Leighton. In December 1945 he traveled to Hiroshima "to study the feelings and attitudes of the survivors" and published his impressions in *The Atlantic Monthly.*[100]

The Joint Intelligence Center, Pacific Ocean Areas (JICPOA), sent another special survey team, the Naval Technical Mission to Japan (NAVTECHJAP) to gather "intelligence in which the Ground Forces and Air Forces would not normally be vitally interested but which to the U.S. Navy was of inestimable value." The group arrived shortly after the surrender. One Nisei with the mission was Nobuo Furuiye, one of the first Nisei assigned to the JICPOA annex and a veteran of Iwo Jima, where he had been wounded by mortar fragments. He helped inventory Japanese armaments on Kyushu. While in southern Japan, he took the opportunity to visit relatives and classmates in Kumamoto; he departed in November 1945 to return to his native Colorado. NAVTECHJAP eventually published 185 reports on Japanese naval equipment and other naval topics.[101]

Dr. Karl T. Compton, president of the Massachusetts Institute of Technology and leader of the Office of Scientific Research and Development, led a Scientific and Technical Survey Mission to Japan with two handpicked Nisei. Second Lt. Yoshikazu Yamada, a combat veteran with the 1st Cavalry Division and 112th Cavalry Regimental Combat Team, had been a graduate student in chemistry at the University of Michigan before the war. Fumio Yagi had earned his Ph.D. in mathematics from the Massachusetts Institute of Technology and was working at Fort Snelling when the war ended.[102]

Research into Japanese wartime science and technology continued during the occupation. An MIS Nisei, Kaoru Inouye, had been a chemistry major at the

---

[100] Alexander H. Leighton, "That Day at Hiroshima," *Atlantic Monthly* (October 1946): 85–90; Alexander H. Leighton, *The Governing of Men: General Principles and Recommendations Based on Experience at a Japanese Relocation Camp* (Princeton, N.J.: Princeton University Press, 1945); quote from Alexander H. Leighton, *Human Relations in a Changing World: Observations on the Use of the Social Sciences* (New York: E. P. Dutton & Co., 1949). Leighton's account appeared shortly after John Hersey's influential account was published in *The New Yorker* (31 August 1946).

[101] Ltr, Col. Joseph J. Twitty to Chief, Historical Section, Far East Command, 2 February 1948, Folder 1, Box 17, RG 23, Charles A. Willoughby Papers, MacArthur Memorial, Library and Archives, Norfolk, Va.; Nobuo Furuiye, Rocky Mountain Bio; Falk and Tsuneishi, *MIS in the War against Japan*, pp. 58–60; *Unsung Heroes*, pp. 94–95. For NAVTECHJAP reports, see *Reports of the U.S. Naval Technical Mission to Japan*, Microfilm Pub 2, Oct 94, Operational Archives, U.S. Naval Historical Center, Washington, D.C.

[102] Karl T. Compton, "If the Atomic Bomb Had Not Been Used," *Atlantic* (December 1946); Donald M. Richardson, comp., "Random Recollections of the Second Class, AIJLS [Army Intensive Japanese Language School], aka the Second OCS Class, MISLS, Fort Snelling, Minn," p. 34, Unpubl Ms, Sep 88, author's files. Navy language officers also assisted. Sherwood Moran described visits to Japanese factories in his letter of 30 September 1945 in Cary, *From a Ruined Empire.*

*The Civil Censorship Detachment employed hundreds of Japanese civilians,
shown here on the ground floor of the NYK building.*

University of California. He was discharged in the summer of 1946 and took
a civilian job with the 5250th Technical Intelligence Detachment investigating
Japan's chemical warfare research activities. As part of his work, he interrogated
key Japanese scientific personnel returning from Soviet prison camps in Manchuria.[103] In the Philippines, the Army Air Forces Technical Air Intelligence Unit
rebuilt and tested Japanese aircraft that had been abandoned at Clark Field, many
still in operating condition. About 145 aircraft were shipped to the Technical Air
Intelligence Center in Washington, D.C. In the unit were Lt. Ernest Silver, the
only Japanese-language officer in the Army who was also an aviator, and Floyd
Yamamoto, a graduate of University of Washington who had worked for Showa
Aircraft Company in Japan before the war.[104]

Another urgent task was imposing civil censorship of newspapers, magazines,
and books, as well as letters and telegrams. In early September MISLS selected 149
Nisei enlisted men and twenty-three officers before graduation and sent them to a
short course in civil censorship at Fort Mason in San Francisco. Because they were
all awarded sergeant's stripes, they were nicknamed the Zebra Platoon.[105] Over the
next few months the school sent thirteen more Nisei enlisted men and sixty-two

[103] Kaoru Inouye, MISNorCal Bio; Sheldon H. Harris, *Factories of Death: Japanese Biological Warfare, 1932–1945, and the American Cover-Up*, 2d rev. ed. (New York: Routledge, 2002).
[104] Robert K. Fukuda, personal communication to author, 5 Sep 01.
[105] Kojiro Kawaguchi, "The Story of the Zebra Platoon," Unpubl Ms, author's files.

officers for censorship duties. From Hawaii came fourteen Nisei women trained for censorship who arrived in Japan on 1 November 1945.[106] The Civil Censorship Detachment employed hundreds of Japanese nationals who worked under the supervision of American Nisei. Some of the local hires came from the estimated 15,000 American-born Nisei who had spent the war in Japan. The detachment's mission was the "close scrutiny of every newspaper, radio script, movie scenario, dramatic production, book, magazine, and pamphlet in Japan."[107] Caucasian language officers, including Maj. Faubion Bowers, also worked in censorship. He took a special interest in traditional *kabuki* theater and befriended many actors. In 1947 he took a civilian job as theater censor and used this position to shield *kabuki* from its detractors and aid its revival.[108]

MIS Nisei also played a role in writing the war's history. Initially, American interest in the Japanese side of the war stemmed from the demands of prosecuting war crimes. This soon turned to a broader historical interest. Researching the history of the war was hampered by the lack of documentation on the Japanese side. For example, a complete set of Imperial General Headquarters army orders and directives covering the war years 1937–1945 was not discovered until 1949. The captured records that ATIS had accumulated took on greater significance because the other intelligence centers such as JICPOA and PACMIRS closed down shortly after V-J Day. As early as 1 December 1945, ATIS published two historical reports, *Japan's Decision To Fight*, "solely based on documentary evidence held at ATIS, GHQ, prior to 1 January 1945," and *The Pearl Harbor Operation*.[109] The Strategic Bombing Survey interrogations of Japanese leaders similarly filled more gaps in the documentary record.

In October 1945, GHQ directed the collection and exploitation of Japanese military history records and directed Japanese authorities to establish a historical bureau and prepare a history. General Willoughby took charge and named as chief of the Historical Investigation Section Col. Frederick Munson, who had

---

[106] "Original Women 'M.I.S.' Linguists Were Dept of the Army Civilians," *M.I.S. Veterans Newsletter* [Hawaii], Sep–Oct 03, p. 3.

[107] *Reports of General MacArthur*, vol. 1 supplement, pp. 232–33, 236–41 (material cited from p. 236); Kawaguchi, MISNorCal Bio; Dower, *Embracing Defeat*, pp. 405–40. Takemae, *Inside GHQ*, pp. 110–11. According to Dower, *Embracing Defeat*, pp. 619–20, note 10, "Since much of the translating work on which GHQ relied was conducted by Nisei to whom Japanese was a second language, more than a little Japanese resentment concerning inaccurate or incomplete communication with the conquerors became directed against these second-generation Japanese-Americans. These ethnic tensions comprise a sensitive and generally unexplored subtheme in the occupation."

[108] Faubion Bowers, "Japan, 1940–1949: A Tumultuous Time Remembered," *Japan Society Newsletter*, Oct 95, pp. 4–7; Faubion Bowers, *Japanese Theater* (New York: Hermitage House, 1952); Shiro Okamoto, *The Man Who Saved Kabuki: Faubion Bowers and Theatre Censorship in Occupied Japan* (Honolulu: University of Hawaii Press, 2001).

[109] Jerome Forrest and Clarke H. Kawakami, "General MacArthur and His Vanishing War History," *The Reporter: The Political Yearbook 1952* (New York: Fortnightly Publishing Company, 1953), p. 138; ATIS, "Japan's Decision To Fight," ATIS Research Rpt no. 131, 1 Dec 45; ATIS, "The Pearl Harbor Operation," ATIS Research Rpt no. 132, 1 Dec 45.

Nisei and local Japanese women at a weekly dance, Tokyo, September 1946

been military attaché in Tokyo in 1941. On 17 October Munson sent to the Japanese military his first questionnaire about the Pearl Harbor attack.

In the autumn of 1946 Willoughby launched two major historical efforts directed by Gordon W. Prange, a professor of history from the University of Maryland. One project was a history of MacArthur's campaigns in the Southwest Pacific with a supplement on the military phase of the occupation. A separate volume written by former Japanese Army and Navy officers covered the Japanese side. *Lt. Gen. Torashiro Kawabe*, who had conducted the surrender negotiations in Manila, became chief of the Japanese Section of the GHQ Historical Division. The Nisei joined this historical effort as translators, interpreters, and research assistants. The Japanese volume was translated into English under Nisei 2d Lt. Clarke H. Kawakami, chief American editor. Kawakami was the son of the well-known Issei author K. K. Kawakami, who had written extensively before the war on the relations between Japan and America. Lieutenant Kawakami had served with the MIS in Burma and China.[110]

. . .

In the years that followed, the Nisei became a language bridge between America and Japan, as General Bissell had predicted. Thousands continued to serve until the occupation ended in 1952, and many continued to work for the U.S. government in Japan long after that. What had begun in 1941 with sixty Nisei soldiers and four civilian instructors at Crissy Field on the Presidio of San Francisco had influenced the course of war and peace for both countries in the years that followed and in ways they never could have imagined.

---

[110] Publication of all volumes was suspended when MacArthur left Tokyo in 1951. Willoughby used portions for Charles A. Willoughby and John Chamberlain, *MacArthur, 1941–1951* (New York: McGraw-Hill, 1954); MacArthur used the material in Douglas MacArthur, *Reminiscences* (New York: Time, 1964). Forrest and Kawakami, "General MacArthur and His Vanishing War History," pp. 126–42; James, *Years of MacArthur*, 3: 668–69. The U.S. Army Center of Military History first published the volumes in 1966, after MacArthur's death. Takemae, *Inside GHQ*, pp. 165–66; S. Daito and H. Takahashi, "Postwar Trends and Developments in the Study of Military History in Japan," *Mededelingen van de Sectie Militaire Geschiedenis*, 14 (1991): 74–81.

Epilogue

MIS Nisei and History

The story of the Military Intelligence Service (MIS) Nisei emerged at the end of the war, but it was overshadowed by better-known stories about their brothers in the 100th Infantry Battalion and 442d Regimental Combat Team (RCT) in Italy and France. The first significant news story about the MIS Nisei originated from the 27th Infantry Division on Okinawa, based on information provided by the division G–2, Lt. Col William K. Antwerp, and former language team leader, 1st Lt. Benjamin Hazard. In mid-September 1945 the North American Newspaper Alliance carried this story of Nisei bravery on Makin, Saipan, Eniwetok, and Okinawa. The story opened with a sweeping claim: "The war in the Pacific would have been far more costly and thousands more American lives would have been lost had it not been for the Nisei—American Japanese—serving with the United States Army." One officer told the reporter, "These men are too valuable to risk in the front lines, but it's all we can do to restrain them from getting into the thick of it every time." Hazard spoke proudly of the ten Nisei on his team, led by S.Sgt. Tim Ohta. Sgt. Hoichi Kubo earned the Distinguished Service Cross on Saipan; two of the Nisei earned the Silver Star. "Men in the 27th Division will stare at you unbelievingly when you tell them that there were some people and some newspapers in the U.S. that violently opposed the use of Nisei in the Pacific. 'Are those people crazy?' the soldiers will ask. 'Only God knows how many of us are alive today only because we had these marvelous guys with us.'"[1]

---

[1] "Nisei Saved U.S. Thousands of Lives in Pacific Theater," *Seattle Times*, 18 Sep 45; "Use of Nisei Saved GI Lives in Pacific," *Pacific Citizen*, 29 Sep 45. The story identified the Nisei by first name only. Hoichi Kubo (identified only as "Sergeant Hoichi") was mistakenly said to have been awarded the Distinguished Service Cross posthumously.

A few weeks later, shortly before the arrival of the Allied Translator and Interpreter Section (ATIS) advance party in Tokyo, Col. Sidney F. Mashbir for the first time disclosed ATIS's existence to the press and presented staggering statistics about the millions of pages translated and the thousands of prisoners interrogated. But in his eyes the biggest story was the loyalty and bravery of the Nisei: "No group in the war had as much to lose. Capture would have meant indescribable horror to them and their relatives in Japan." In later years Mashbir continued to tell the MIS Nisei story, writing about the Nisei in *The Saturday Evening Post* in 1948. In his memoirs he concluded, "The United States of America owes a debt to these men and to their families which it can never fully repay." But the American public soon forgot these stories.[2]

In Tokyo, Maj. Gen. Charles A. Willoughby ordered the preparation of a ten-volume history of intelligence in the Southwest Pacific Area to document the achievements of the Allied Translator and Intelligence Service, the Allied Intelligence Bureau, the Counter Intelligence Corps, and other agencies that had been under his purview. The ATIS volume, completed in 1948, detailed the many contributions of the Nisei and included samples of typical products; but it was marked restricted and never released to the general public.[3]

Back in Minnesota, the language school told the story from its perspective as soon as wartime restrictions were removed. Col. Kai E. Rasmussen held a press conference on 22 October 1945 at Fort Snelling and issued a lengthy press release about the school and its graduates. Local newspapers ran stories that were reprinted in the Japanese American press.[4] The school's newsletter, *Yaban Gogai*, trumpeted the press conference under the headline, "MISLS Secrecy Lifted— WD [War Department]," and began, "The veil of secrecy which had cloaked the activities of the Military Intelligence Service Language School for the past four years, was lifted Monday, 22 October." The press release itself outlined the basic story and gave many valuable details about the Nisei. In the words of the anonymous author, "Never before in history did one army know so much concerning its

---

[2] The Associated Press story about Mashbir's press conference appeared in the *Pacific Citizen*, 20 Oct 45. Quote from Sidney F. Mashbir, *I Was an American Spy* (New York: Vantage, 1953), p. 242; Sidney F. Mashbir, "I Was an American Spy," *Saturday Evening Post*, 27 Mar, 3 Apr 48.

[3] General Headquarters, Far East Command, *Operations of the Allied Translator and Interpreter Section, GHQ, SWPA*, Intelligence Series, vol. 5 (Tokyo, Far East Command, 1948) (hereafter cited as ATIS History).

[4] The War Department (WD) Press Release, 22 Oct 45, was in three parts: Part 1, "The Military Intelligence Service Language School"; Part 2, "Nisei Linguists—Eyes and Ears of Allied Pacific Forces"; Part 3, "Army Japanese Linguists in Training." Japanese Evacuation Research Study (JERS), pt. 2, sec. 2, reel 20, frame 0037, Bancroft Library, University of California. The story was covered in the *St. Paul Dispatch*, 22, 23, 24 Oct 45; *Minneapolis Star-Journal*, 22 Oct 45; *Minneapolis Morning Tribune*, 23 Oct 45; and *Pacific Citizen*, 27 Oct, 3 Nov, 22 Dec 45. The authorship of the press release is unknown, but was most likely prepared by the MISLS staff. A different version, probably a draft, can be found in Trng Grp, Ofc of the Dir of Intel G–2, Record Group (RG) 165, National Archives and Records Administration (NARA).

enemy prior to actual engagement as did the American army during most of the Pacific campaign."[5]

This initial publicity was only the beginning. Over the winter and spring of 1945–1946, the school's staff prepared a lengthy administrative history of the school and its various departments; however, this remained unpublished.[6] The school also published an illustrated album in about June 1946, shortly before the school left Fort Snelling. The album was prepared under editor Lt. Richard K. Hayashi and art editor and designer M.Sgt. Tom Okamoto. Hayashi was one of the few Nisei to have served in both the MIS and the 442d RCT. Okamoto, a commercial artist, had worked at Disney Studios before the war.[7]

Another way to commemorate the MIS history was through forming veterans' groups. As MIS Nisei veterans returned to their homes, they joined groups such as the American Legion and Veterans of Foreign Wars, often opening their own Nisei posts. In June 1946 Honolulu attorney Masaji Marumoto and six other Nisei in Hawaii formed the MIS Linguists Associates, the first veteran's association specifically for MIS Nisei.[8]

With the end of the war and loosening of secrecy restrictions, individuals began to evaluate MIS Nisei contributions to victory. In 1945 the War Relocation Authority asked the War Department to publicize the wartime contributions of the Nisei, including those in the MIS, to counter public opinion on the West Coast, which remained hostile to the Nisei. The two agencies cooperated in an aggressive public relations campaign to promote acceptance of the Issei and Nisei. The War Department sent a few MIS officers on lecture tours to educate the public about the MIS Nisei. Lt. Col. Wallace H. Moore, who had fought with Nisei in the Pacific, undertook a sixty-day speaking tour in the autumn of 1945.[9] In January 1946 General Willoughby returned to the United States, speaking to the press at each stop. In Hawaii, San Francisco, and New York, he had high praise for the

---

[5] *Yaban Gogai*, Nov 45, p. 1. WD Press Release, 22 Oct 45. The "never before" statement was later attributed to General MacArthur or General Willoughby, but I have seen no evidence of this. In 1946 Weckerling revised the press release for submission as an article to the *Infantry Journal*. It was declassified in February 1948 but not published at that time. In 1971 he provided a copy to an MIS Nisei veterans' group, who published it in the *Hokubei Mainichi*, 27 Oct–5 Nov 71, and reprinted it in booklet form. John Weckerling, "Japanese Americans Play Vital Role in United States Intelligence Service in World War II" (1946), first printed in *Hokubei Mainichi*, 27 Oct–5 Nov 71, reprinted as a pamphlet.

[6] MISLS, "Training History of the Military Intelligence Service Language School" Unpubl Ms, with annexes, 1946, U.S. Army Center of Military History (CMH). Another copy may be found in General Records, 1943–1945, Military Intelligence [Service] Language School, Fort Snelling, Minn., Records of the Army Staff, RG 319, NARA.

[7] *MISLS Album* (Minneapolis: Military Intelligence Service Language School, 1946), pp. 84–85, 124; Richard K. Hayashi, Biography, Military Intelligence Service Club of Northern California (this and similar biographies hereafter cited as MISNorCal Bios).

[8] "MIS Reunion," a booklet distributed at a veterans' reunion in 1962; Ted T. Tsukiyama et al., eds., *Secret Valor: M.I.S. Personnel, World War II Pacific Theater, Pre–Pearl Harbor to Sept. 8, 1951* (Honolulu: Military Intelligence Service Veterans Club of Hawaii, 1993), p. 22.

[9] Talk given by Lt. Col. Wallace H. Moore, 3 Nov 45, JERS Papers, pt. 2, sec. 15.

MIS Nisei. In Hawaii, he expressed concern about reports of discrimination on the West Coast:

The nature of Nisei service, from an intelligence point of view, represented the greatest single contribution to the Pacific war. . . .
Language detachments (of Nisei) were placed with every division, corps, and army in the Pacific. The division detachments, of course, accompanied the division in action. They bore their share of losses, awards and decorations. Their loyalty was never questioned. Had they been captured, they ran an even greater risk than the rank and file of other American troops.
In spite of the 2,000 to 3,000 Nisei used, 40 percent of whom were Hawaii-born, there has been no single case of disloyalty or ill-feeling. They did their job quietly, and with great efficiency. . . .
I have been employing several thousand Nisei since 1942, and feel morally obligated to report on them.[10]

A few months later one of the top Caucasian language officers in ATIS, Lt. Col. John E. Anderton, told a reporter that Willoughby "has said that the war would have lasted at least two years longer if it were not for the Nisei boys." Bradford Smith, chief of the Honolulu branch of the Office of War Information, published a book in 1948 about Americans of Japanese ancestry. In discussing the MIS Nisei, Bradford wrote: "General Charles Willoughby, MacArthur's Chief of Staff for Intelligence, says their work shortened the war by two years." Colonel Rasmussen echoed these sentiments: "The use of thousands of Japanese Americans in the Pacific shortened the war considerably and saved the lives of thousands of American soldiers and billions in American Dollars."[11] Colonel Mashbir, writing about the ATIS Nisei in *The Saturday Evening Post* in 1948, made the same point: "I know that their faithful service to the United States saved many thousands of American lives and shortened the war by months." Had it not been for the Nisei, the war "would have been a far more hazardous, long-drawn-out affair. . . . At a highly conservative estimate, thousands of American lives were preserved and millions of dollars in matériel were saved as a result of their contribution to the war effort." At a memorial service for Nisei soldiers at Arlington National Cemetery, Mashbir "declared it would be impossible to determine how many hundreds of American lives and how many billions of dollars were saved due to the intelligence supplied by the Nisei in the ATIS."[12]

---

[10] "AJA Service in Pacific Termed Greatest Single Contribution by Willoughby," *Hawaii Times*, 22 Jan 46. Sentence order changed for clarity.
[11] "Role of Japanese American Linguists in Pacific Campaign Described by Army Officer," *Pacific Citizen*, 11 May 46; "Nisei Lauded for Skillful War Intelligence Work in Pacific," *Honolulu Advertiser*, 9 May 46; Bradford Smith, *Americans from Japan* (Philadelphia: J. B. Lippincott, 1948), p. 325.
[12] Mashbir, "I Was an American Spy"; Mashbir, *I Was an American Spy*, p. 242; "High Praise Paid Nisei at Arlington," *The Washington Post*, 31 Oct 49.

Great as Nisei contributions to victory may have been, their contributions to the subsequent peace were even greater and just as hard to measure. In February 1946 Willoughby told a New York audience that without the Nisei, "the occupation job in Japan could not have been accomplished on the ground of language difficulties alone. . . . The result would have been utter chaos, and recent history shows that nothing acceptable to democratic tastes ever emerged from national wreckage."[13]

The Japanese recognized the importance of the Nisei as well. Several years into the occupation, even the emperor found a way quietly to express his appreciation. The occasion arose during one of the many attacks by the American press against General Douglas MacArthur for his policy toward the emperor. MacArthur later complained in his memoirs of a "vehement press and radio campaign within the United States [at the start of the occupation] against retention of the Emperor. . . . [Reporters and commentators] were now insisting that Hirohito and his family, and the complete Japanese government, be stamped out." This hostility continued for years. In April 1949 the weekly newsreel, "The March of Time," requested permission to film the emperor. MacArthur considered the request an invasion of privacy and decided to send a private message to the emperor that he could decline this latest request.[14]

One evening MacArthur's aide-de-camp summoned 1st Lt. Kan Tagami, the general's personal language officer, and told him to convey MacArthur's message to the emperor in person. California-born Tagami was a combat veteran of Burma, where he had earned a field commission. His Japanese was excellent from six years' schooling in Japan before the war. In the 1920s he had once set eyes on Hirohito, then prince regent, while changing trains at a railway station near his school. The children were called out of class and told to bow their heads when the prince regent alit from his carriage. But the young American boy had lifted his head and caught a glimpse of the young Hirohito. It would be twenty more years before he saw the emperor again.

That evening Tagami crossed to the palace from the Dai-Ichi Building and was ushered into the emperor's presence. No one else was there, not even members of the imperial household. Tagami was no longer a schoolboy but a U.S. Army officer. He gave MacArthur's message to the emperor, who listened politely and answered, "I will do what is appropriate." With that, Tagami began to leave, but the emperor motioned for him to stay. "Tagami, where are your father and mother from?" Tagami responded, from Hiroshima. The emperor thanked him and all the Nisei then serving in the occupation: "Your Japanese ability has truly made the

---

[13] "General Tells of Nisei Service in Pacific War," *Pacific Citizen*, 16 Feb 46. See also *Yaban Gogai*, Dec 45, and *Pacific Citizen*, 26 Jan 46.

[14] Douglas MacArthur, *Reminiscences* (New York: Time, 1964), p. 320. For MacArthur's troubles with the press in 1949, see D. Clayton James, *The Years of MacArthur*, 3 vols. (Boston: Houghton Mifflin, 1970–1985), 3: 261–64.

government's work much easier. The Nisei are a bridge across our two countries. Thank you very much."[15]

.   .   .

The accomplishments of the MIS Nisei remained little known after the war. While their brothers who served in the 100th Infantry Battalion and 442d Regimental Combat Team enjoyed public acclaim, the MIS Nisei remained true to their wartime pledge of secrecy, their service known to but a few. Maj. Gen. Clayton Bissell lauded their proud silence. On 29 September 1945, the War Department G–2 visited Fort Snelling for a graduation ceremony. His advice to the graduates was straightforward: "If you Japanese-Americans are ever questioned as to your loyalty, don't even bother to reply. The magnificent work of the graduates of the Military Intelligence Service Language School in the field has been seen by your fellow Americans of many racial extractions. Their testimony to your gallant deeds under fire will speak so loudly that you need not answer."[16]

The MIS Nisei took pride in their "gallant deeds under fire" and their service as a language bridge between America and Japan. Their ability to speak the Japanese language stemmed from their immigrant parents, long afternoons in after-school language classes, and, for the Kibei, from schooling in Japan. They learned from their instructors at Crissy Field, Camp Savage, or Fort Snelling and then went out to prove their loyalty, courage, and skill on many battlefields. They served their country, brought honor to their families, and ultimately turned enemies into friends.

---

[15] "A Conversation with the Emperor," in *Japanese Eyes, American Heart: Personal Reflections of Hawaii's World War II Nisei Soldiers* (Honolulu: Tendai Educational Foundation, 1998), pp. 315–20; Interv, author with Kan Tagami. Tagami served on MacArthur's personal staff from November 1946 until April 1951. Tagami's meeting with the emperor probably occurred sometime between the autumn of 1948 and the spring of 1949. Fukuhara places it in early April 1949.

[16] Quote from WD Press Release, 22 Oct 45. Reproduced with slight variations in *Yaban Gogai*, Sep–Oct 45, p. 2; *Yaban Gogai*, Dec 45, p. 9; *MISLS Album*, p. 115.

Bibliography

Libraries and Archives

Amherst College Archives and Special Collections, Amherst, Mass.
- John J. McCloy Papers

Combined Arms Research Library, Fort Leavenworth, Kans.

Hoover Institution Library and Archives, Stanford, Calif.
- Dr. John A. Burden Papers
- Kay I. Kitagawa Papers
- Frederick P. Munson Papers
- General Robert C. Richardson, Jr., Papers
- Henri H. Smith-Hutton Papers
- William M. Van Antwerp Papers

Japanese American National Museum, Los Angeles, Calif.

MacArthur Memorial, Library and Archives, Norfolk, Va.
- Record Group (RG) 3, Records of Headquarters, Southwest Pacific Area
- RG 4, Records of General Headquarters, U.S. Army Forces, Pacific
- RG 5, Records of General Headquarters, Supreme Commander for the Allied Powers
- RG 23, Papers of Maj. Gen. Charles A. Willoughby
- RG 27, National Security Agency/Central Security Service Cryptologic Documents from World War II
- RG 49, D. Clayton James Collection

National Archives and Records Administration, Washington, D.C.
- RG 107, Records of the Office of the Secretary of War
- RG 165, Records of the War Department General and Special Staffs
- RG 210, Records of the War Relocation Authority
- RG 319, Records of the Army Staff
- RG 337, Records of Headquarters, Army Ground Forces
- RG 407, Records of the Adjutant General's Office
- RG 457, Records of the National Security Agency/Central Security Service

National Archives and Records Administration–Pacific Region, San Bruno, Calif.
- RG 181, 12th Naval District

National Japanese American Historical Society, San Francisco, Calif.
- Joseph D. Harrington Papers
- Richard Hayashi Collection
- Judge Eugene A. Wright Papers
- Military Intelligence Service of Northern California Biographies (cited as MISNorCal Bios). *These are more than a hundred short biographies or autobiographies of MIS Nisei compiled during the late 1980s and early 1990s from various sources. Roy T. Uyehata provided copies to author.*

Naval Historical Center, Washington, D.C.

U.S. Army Center of Military History, Washington, D.C.

U.S. Army Military History Institute, Carlisle Barracks, Pa.

University of California, Bancroft Library, Berkeley, Calif.
- Japanese Evacuation Research Study

University of Maryland, University Libraries, College Park, Md.
- Gordon W. Prange Collection

Interviews

Interviews by Author

Abe, Victor H.	Kanegai, Yoshio George	Sakamoto, Thomas T.
Aiso, John F.	Kaneko, Arthur M.	Sameshima, Hitoshi G.
Amioka, Wallace S.	Kawamoto, Yukio	Shimoyama, Isao
Bannai, Paul T.	Kimura, Robert T.	Tagami, Kan
Burden, Dr. John A.	Koyama, Spady A.	Takabayashi, George H.
Fujikawa, John	Koyanagi, Tamotsu	Takai, Roy T.
Fukai, Yasuo Ace	Kubo, Harry T.	Takao, Frank T.
Furumoto, Howard	Kubo, Hoichi Bob	Toyoda, Susumu
Hara, Minoru	Kuwabara, Henry	Tsuneishi, Warren M.
Hazard, Benjamin H.	Milanoski, Joseph J.	Uesato, Toshi
Higa, Takejiro	Nakamura, George I.	Usui, Mitsuo
Hirata, Richard Y.	Nomura, Shoso	Uyehata, Roy T.
Honke, Robert K.	Obata, Benjamin T.	Yamane, Kazuo E.
Ige, Thomas H.	Ogata, Dye	Yoshihashi, Taro
Ishio, Sunao Phil	Okubo, Don S.	

Other Interviews

Aiso, John F., Interv by Loni Ding, 1986, National Japanese American Historical Society.
———. "Observations of a California Nisei" (1971). Transcript of oral history conducted in 1970 by Marc Landy. Collection 300/83. Department of Special Collections, Charles E. Young Research Library, University of California, Los Angeles.

Bowers, Faubion, Interv by D. Clayton James, 18 Jul 71, MacArthur Memorial, Library and Archives.

Duensing, Dawn E., ed. and comp., *Americanism: A Matter of Mind and Heart*, vol. 1, *The Military Intelligence Service*. Maui: Maui's Sons and Daughters of the Nisei Veterans, 2001.

Kihara, Shigeya, Interv by Donald McCabe, 19 Jul 91, Defense Language Institute Foreign Language Center.

———. Interv by Stephen A. Haller, 21 Jan 94, Golden Gate National Recreation Area, National Park Service (courtesy of Stephen Haller).

Mashbir, Sidney F., Interv by D. Clayton James, 1 Sep 71, MacArthur Memorial, Library and Archives.

Munson, Frederick P., Interv, 5 Mar 75, Hoover Institution Library and Archives.

Takao, Eric. Intervs with thirty-seven MIS Nisei veterans, 1993 (courtesy of Frank T. Takao).

Wada, Douglas T., Interv by Ted T. Tsukiyama, 21 Mar 02 (courtesy of Ted Tsukiyama).

Yasui, Kenny, Interv, 17 Jan 89.

MIS Veterans' Accounts

Ariyoshi, Koji. *From Kona to Yenan: The Political Memoirs of Koji Ariyoshi*, ed. Alice M. Beechert and Edward D. Beechert. Honolulu: University of Hawaii Press, 2000.

Falk, Stanley L., and Warren M. Tsuneishi, eds. *MIS in the War against Japan*. Washington, D.C.: Japanese American Veterans Association, 1995.

Goodman, Grant K. *America's Japan: The First Year, 1945–1946*. New York: Fordham University Press, 2005.

Harrington, Joseph D. *Yankee Samurai: The Secret Role of Nisei in America's Pacific Victory*. Detroit: Pettigrew Enterprises, 1979.

Higa, Thomas Taro. *Memoirs of a Certain Nisei (Aru Nisei no Wadachi), 1916–1985*. Kaneohe, Hawaii: Higa Publications, 1988.

Ichinokuchi, Tad, ed. *John Aiso and the M.I.S.: Japanese-American Soldiers in the Military Intelligence Service, World War II*. Los Angeles: Military Intelligence Service Club of Southern California, 1988.

Ige, Thomas H. *Boy from Kahaluu: An Autobiography*. Honolulu: Kin Cho Jin Kai, 1989.

Japanese Eyes, American Heart: Personal Reflections of Hawaii's World War II Nisei Soldiers. Honolulu: Tendai Educational Foundation, 1998.

Nishimura, Hiro. *Trials and Triumphs of the Nikkei*. Mercer Island, Wash.: Fukuda Publishers, 1993.

Oda, James. *Heroic Struggles of Japanese Americans: Partisan Fighters from America's Concentration Camps*. Hollywood, Calif.: J. Oda, ca. 1980.

———. *Secret Embedded in Magic Cables: The Story of a 101-Year-Old Japanese Communist Leader Who Served Japan, KGB, and CIA*. Northridge, Calif.: J. Oda, 1993.

Oguro, Richard S., ed. *Sempai Gumi*. Honolulu: MIS Veterans of Hawaii, ca. 1981.

The Pacific War and Peace: Americans of Japanese Ancestry in Military Intelligence Service, 1941 to 1952. San Francisco: Military Intelligence Service Association of Northern California/National Japanese American Historical Society, 1991.

Roush, John H., Jr., ed. *World War II Reminiscences*. San Rafael, Calif.: Reserve Officers Association of the United States, California Department, 1995.

Sakakida, Richard M., and Wayne S. Kiyosaki. *A Spy in Their Midst: The World War II Struggle of a Japanese-American Hero*. Lanham, Md.: Madison Books, 1995.

Swift, David W., Jr., ed. "First Class." Unpubl Ms, 2000, copy in author's files.

Swift, David W., Sr. *Ninety Li a Day*, ed. David W. Swift, Jr. Social Life Monographs, vol. 69. Taipei: Chinese Association for Folklore, 1975.

Tasaki, Toma. "The Journey of the Men of Mars." Unpubl Ms, n.d.

Tottori, Calvin. "The OSS Niseis in the China-Burma-India Theater," 2d ed. Unpubl Ms, 2001, copy in author's files.

Tsukiyama, Ted. T., et al., eds. *Secret Valor: M.I.S. Personnel, World War II Pacific Theater, Pre–Pearl Harbor to Sept. 8, 1951*. Honolulu: Military Intelligence Service Veterans Club of Hawaii, 1993; rev. ed., 2001.

Unsung Heroes: The Military Intelligence Service, Past-Present-Future. Seattle: MIS-Northwest Association, 1996.

Yoneda, Karl G. *Ganbatte: Sixty-Year Struggle of a Kibei Worker*. Los Angeles: Asian American Studies Center, University of California at Los Angeles, 1983.

Yoritomo, Kent T., ed. "Rocky Mountain MIS Veterans Club Autobiographies." Unpubl Ms, ca. 1989 (cited as Rocky Mountain Bios).

Official Histories

The Admiralties: Operations of the 1st Cavalry Division (29 February–18 May 1944). American Forces in Action. Washington, D.C.: War Department, Historical Division, 1945.

Appleman, Roy E., et al. *Okinawa: The Last Battle*. U.S. Army in World War II. Washington, D.C.: Department of the Army, Historical Division, 1948.

Bartley, Whitman S. *Iwo Jima: Amphibious Epic*. Washington, D.C.: Headquarters, U.S. Marine Corps, 1954.

Cannon, M. Hamlin. *Leyte: The Return to the Philippines*. U.S. Army in World War II. Washington, D.C.: Office of the Chief of Military History, 1954.

The Capture of Makin, 20–24 November 1943. American Forces in Action. Washington, D.C.: War Department, Historical Division, 1946.

Cline, Ray S. *Washington Command Post: The Operations Division*. U.S. Army in World War II. Washington, D.C.: Office of the Chief of Military History, 1951.

Coles, Harry L., and Albert K. Weinberg. *Civil Affairs: Soldiers Become Governors*. Washington, D.C.: Office of the Chief of Military History, 1964.

Coll, Blanche D., et al. *The Corps of Engineers: Troops and Equipment*. Washington, D.C.: Office of the Chief of Military History, 1958.

Conn, Stetson, Rose C. Engelman, and Byron Fairchild. *Guarding the United States and Its Outposts*. U.S. Army in World War II. Washington, D.C.: Office of the Chief of Military History, 1964.

Craven, Wesley F., and James L. Cate, eds. *The Army Air Forces in World War II*, 7 vols. Chicago: University of Chicago Press, 1948–1958.

Crowl, Philip A. *Campaign in the Marianas*. U.S. Army in World War II. Washington, D.C.: Office of the Chief of Military History, 1960.

————, and Edmund G. Love. *Seizure of the Gilberts and Marshalls*. U.S. Army in World War II. Washington, D.C.: Office of the Chief of Military History, 1955.

Dexter, David. *Australia in the War of 1939–1945*, ser. 1, vol. 6, *The New Guinea Offensives*. Canberra: Australian War Memorial, 1961.

Dziuban, Stanley W. *Military Relations between the United States and Canada, 1939–1945*. U.S. Army in World War II. Washington, D.C.: Office of the Chief of Military History, 1959.

Fisch, Arnold G., Jr. *Military Government in the Ryukyu Islands, 1945–1950*. U.S. Army in World War II. Washington, D.C.: U.S. Army Center of Military History, 1988.

Frank, Benis, and Henry Shaw, Jr. *History of U.S. Marine Corps Operations in World War II*, vol. 5, *Victory and Occupation*. Washington, D.C.: Historical Division, Headquarters, U.S. Marine Corps, 1968.

Garand, George W., and Truman R. Strobridge. *History of U.S. Marine Corps Operations in World War II*, vol. 4, *Western Pacific Operations*. Washington, D.C.: Historical Division, Headquarters, U.S. Marine Corps, 1971.

General Headquarters (GHQ), Far East Command. *Operations of the Allied Translator and Interpreter Section, GHQ, SWPA*. Intelligence Series. Tokyo: Far East Command, 1948, vol. 5.

————. *Operations of the Civil Intelligence Section, SCAP*. Intelligence Series. Tokyo: Far East Command, 1948, vol. 9.

Greenfield, Kent R., et al. *The Army Ground Forces: The Organization of Ground Combat Troops*. U.S. Army in World War II. Washington, D.C.: Department of the Army, Historical Division, 1947.

Hough, Frank O., Verle E. Ludwig, and Henry I. Shaw, Jr. *The History of the U.S. Marine Corps in World War II*, vol. 1, *Pearl Harbor to Guadalcanal*. Washington, D.C.: U.S. Marine Corps, 1958.

Jones, Vincent C. *Manhattan: The Army and the Atomic Bomb*. Washington, D.C.: U.S. Army Center of Military History, 1985.

Lee, Ulysses. *The Employment of Negro Troops*. U.S. Army in World War II. Washington, D.C.: Office of the Chief of Military History, 1966.

Lewis, George G. *History of Prisoner of War Utilization by the United States Army, 1776–1945*. Washington, D.C.: Government Printing Office, 1955.

Long, Gavin. *Australia in the War of 1939–1945*, ser. 1, vol. 7, *The Final Campaigns*. Canberra: Australian War Memorial, 1963.

MacGregor, Morris J., Jr. *Integration of the Armed Forces, 1940–1965*. Washington, D.C.: U.S. Army Center of Military History, 1981.

Merrill's Marauders (February–May 1944). American Forces in Action. Washington, D.C.: War Department, Military Intelligence Division, 1945.

Military Intelligence Service Language School. "Training History of the Military Intelligence Service Language School," Unpubl Ms, U.S. Army Center of Military History, 1946.

Miller, John, jr. *CARTWHEEL: The Reduction of Rabaul*. U.S. Army in World War II. Washington, D.C.: Office of the Chief of Military History, 1959.

————. *Guadalcanal: The First Offensive*. U.S. Army in World War II. Washington, D.C.: Department of the Army, Historical Division, 1949.

Milner, Samuel. *Victory in Papua*. U.S. Army in World War II. Washington, D.C.: Office of the Chief of Military History, 1957.

MISLS Album. Minneapolis: Military Intelligence Service Language School, 1946.

Morison, Samuel E. *History of United States Naval Operations in World War II*, 15 vols. Boston: Little, Brown, 1947–1952.

Morton, Louis. *Strategy and Command: The First Two Years*. U.S. Army in World War II. Washington, D.C.: Office of the Chief of Military History, 1962.

Mountbatten, Earl Louis. *Post Surrender Tasks. Section E of the Report to the Combined Chiefs of Staff by the Supreme Allied Commander South-East Asia, 1943–45*. London: Her Majesty's Stationery Office, 1969.

Nichol, Chas. S., Jr., and Henry I. Shaw. *Okinawa: Victory in the Pacific*. Washington, D.C.: Historical Branch, Headquarters, U.S. Marine Corps, 1955.

Office of the Chief Engineer, General Headquarters, Army Forces, Pacific. *Engineers of the Southwest Pacific 1941–1945*, vol. 6, *Airfield and Base Development*. Washington, D.C.: Government Printing Office, 1951.

Palmer, Robert R., et al., eds. *The Procurement and Training of Ground Combat Troops*. U.S. Army in World War II. Washington, D.C.: Department of the Army, Historical Division, 1948.

Papuan Campaign: The Buna-Sanananda Operation (16 November 1942–23 January 1943). American Forces in Action. Washington, D.C.: War Department, Historical Division, 1945.

Prasad, Bisheshwar, ed. *Official History of the Indian Armed Forces in the Second World War, Post-War Occupation Forces: Japan and South-East Asia*. India: Orient Longmans, 1958.

Reports of General MacArthur, 4 vols. U.S. Army in World War II. Washington, D.C.: U.S. Army Center of Military History, 1966, 1994.

Richard, Dorothy E. *United States Naval Administration of the Trust Territory of the Pacific Islands*, 3 vols. Washington, D.C.: Government Printing Office, 1957.

Risch, Erna, and Chester L. Kieffer. *The Quartermaster Corps: Organization, Supply, and Services*, 2 vols. Washington, D.C.: Office of the Chief of Military History, 1955.

Romanus, Charles F., and Riley Sunderland. *Stilwell's Command Problems*. U.S. Army in World War II. Washington, D.C.: Office of the Chief of Military History, 1956.

————. *Time Runs Out in CBI*. U.S. Army in World War II. Washington, D.C.: Office of the Chief of Military History, 1959.

Smith, Robert Ross. *The Approach to the Philippines*. U.S. Army in World War II. Washington, D.C.: Office of the Chief of Military History, 1953.

————. *Triumph in the Philippines*. U.S. Army in World War II. Washington, D.C.: Office of the Chief of Military History, 1963.

Sparrow, John C. *History of Personnel Demobilization in the United States Army*. Department of the Army Pamphlet 20–210. Washington, D.C.: Department of the Army, 1952.

Stacey, C. P. *Six Years of War: The Army in Canada, Britain and the Pacific*. Official History of the Canadian Army in the Second World War. Ottawa: Edmond Cloutier, 1955.

Stockman, James R. *The Battle for Tarawa*. Washington, D.C.: Headquarters, U.S. Marine Corps, 1947.

Treadwell, Mattie E. *The Women's Army Corps*. U.S. Army in World War II. Washington, D.C.: Office of the Chief of Military History, 1954.

War Relocation Authority. *The Evacuated People: A Quantitative Description*. Washington, D.C.: Government Printing Office, 1946.

———. *WRA: A Story of Human Conservation*. Washington, D.C.: Government Printing Office, 1946.

Western Defense Command. *Final Report: Japanese Evacuation from the West Coast, 1942*. Washington, D.C.: Government Printing Office, 1943.

Woodburn, Kirby S., ed. *The War against Japan*, 5 vols. London: Her Majesty's Stationery Office, 1957–1969.

Zimmerman, John L. *The Guadalcanal Campaign*. Washington, D.C.: U.S. Marine Corps, 1949.

Other Works

Agard, Frederick B., et al. *A Survey of Language Classes in the Army Specialized Training Program*. New York: Commission on Trends in Education, Modern Language Association, 1944.

Albert, Michael. "The Japanese," in *They Chose Minnesota: A Survey of the State's Ethnic Groups*, ed. June D. Holmquist. St. Paul: Minnesota Historical Society Press, 1981.

Aldrich, Richard J. *Intelligence and the War against Japan: Britain, America and the Politics of Secret Service*. Cambridge: Cambridge University Press, 2000.

Allen, Gwenfread. *Hawaii's War Years, 1941–1945*. Honolulu: University of Hawaii Press, 1950.

Allen, Louis. *Burma: The Longest War, 1941–1945*. New York: St. Martin's, 1985.

———. *The End of the War in Asia*. London: Hart-Davis, 1976.

Alperovitz, Gar. *The Decision To Use the Bomb and the Architecture of an American Myth*. New York: Knopf, 1995.

The Amerasia Papers: A Clue to the Catastrophe of China. Washington, D.C.: Government Printing Office, 1970, vol. 2.

Angiolillo, Paul F. *Armed Forces' Foreign Language Teaching: Critical Evaluation and Implications*. New York: Vanni, 1947.

Ano, Masaharu. "Loyal Linguists: Nisei of World War II Learned Japanese in Minnesota." *Minnesota History* 45, no. 7 (Fall 1977): 273–87.

Arthur, Anthony. *Bushmasters*. New York: St. Martin's, 1987.

Ashmead, John. "The Japs Look at the Yanks." *Atlantic Monthly* (April 1946): 86–91.

———. "A Modern Language for Japan." *Atlantic Monthly* (January 1947): 68–72.

———. *The Mountain and the Feather*. Boston: Houghton Mifflin, 1961.

Bailey, Beth, and David Farber. *The First Strange Place: Race and Sex in World War II Hawaii*. Baltimore: Johns Hopkins University Press, 1992.

Bamford, James. *Body of Secrets*. New York: Doubleday, 2001.

Barbeau, Arthur E., and Florette Henri. *The Unknown Soldiers: Black American Troops in World War I*. Philadelphia, Pa.: Temple University Press, 1974.

Barrett, David D. *Dixie Mission: The United States Army Observer Group in Yenan, 1944*. China Research Monographs no. 6. Berkeley, Calif.: Center for Chinese Studies, 1970.

Bath, Alan H. *Tracking the Axis Enemy: The Triumph of Anglo-American Naval Intelligence*. Lawrence: University Press of Kansas, 1998.

Bellafaire, Judith L., ed. *The U.S. Army and World War II: Selected Papers from the Army's Commemorative Conferences*. U.S. Army in World War II. Washington, D.C.: U.S. Army Center of Military History, 1998.

Benedict, Ruth. *The Chrysanthemum and the Sword: Patterns of Japanese Culture*. Boston: Houghton Mifflin, 1946, 1989.

Bennett, Henry S. "The Impact of Invasion and Occupation on the Civilians of Okinawa." *United States Naval Institute Proceedings* (February 1946): 263–75.

Bergerud, Eric. *Touched with Fire: The Land War in the South Pacific*. New York: Penguin, 1996.

Bernstein, Barton J. "The Alarming Japanese Buildup on Southern Kyushu, Growing U.S. Fears, and Counterfactual Analysis: Would the Planned November 1945 Invasion of Southern Kyushu Have Occurred?" *Pacific Historical Review* 68, no. 4 (November 1999): 561–609.

Bidwell, Bruce W. *History of the Military Intelligence Division, Department of the Army General Staff: 1775–1941*. Frederick, Md.: University Publications of America, 1986.

Bird, Kai. *The Chairman: John J. McCloy, The Making of the American Establishment*. New York: Simon & Schuster, 1992.

Bishof, Günter, and Robert L. Dupont, eds. *The Pacific War Revisited*. Baton Rouge: Louisiana State University Press, 1997.

Bix, Herbert P. *Hirohito and the Making of Modern Japan*. New York: HarperCollins, 2000.

Bixler, Margaret T. *Winds of Freedom: The Story of the Navajo Code Talkers of World War II*. Darien, Conn.: Two Bytes Publishing, 1992.

Bleakley, Jack. *The Eavesdroppers*. Canberra, Australia: AGPS Press, ca. 1991.

Blegen, Theodore C. *Minnesota: A History of the State*. Minneapolis: University of Minnesota Press, 1963.

Blum, John M. *V Was for Victory: Politics and American Culture during World War II*. New York: Harcourt Brace Jovanovich, 1976.

Boller, Paul F., Jr. *Memoirs of an Obscure Professor and Other Essays*. Fort Worth: Texas Christian University Press, 1992.

Boritt, Gabor, ed. *War Comes Again: Comparative Vistas on the Civil War and World War II*. New York: Oxford University Press, 1995.

Borton, Hugh. *American Presurrender Planning for Postwar Japan*. New York: East Asian Institute, Columbia University, 1967.

———. *Japan Since 1931: Its Political and Social Developments*. New York: Institute for Pacific Relations, 1940.

Bosworth, Allan R. *America's Concentration Camps*. New York: Bantam, 1968.

Bowers, Faubion. *Japanese Theater*. New York: Hermitage House, 1952.

Boyd, Carl. *Hitler's Japanese Confidant: General Oshima Hiroshi and MAGIC Intelligence, 1941–1945*. Lawrence: University Press of Kansas, 1993.

Brackman, Arnold C. *The Other Nuremberg: The Untold Story of the Tokyo War Crimes Trials*. New York: William Morrow, 1987.

Brinkley, Alan. "Minister without Portfolio." *Harper's* (February 1983): 31–46. Reprinted in Alan Brinkley. *Liberalism and Its Discontents*. Cambridge, Mass.: Harvard University Press, 1998, pp. 177–209.

Broadfoot, Barry. *Years of Sorrow, Years of Shame: The Story of the Japanese Canadians in World War II*. Toronto: Doubleday, 1977.

Brown, Anthony C., ed. *The Secret War Report of the OSS*. New York: Berkley Publishing, 1976.

Buchanan, Daniel C. *Inari: Its Origin, Development, and Nature*. Tokyo: Asiatic Society of Japan, 1935.

Budiansky, Stephen. "Truth Extraction." *Atlantic Monthly* (June 2005): 32–35.

Burton, Jeffery F., et al. *Confinement and Ethnicity: An Overview of World War II Japanese American Relocation Sites*. Publications in Anthropology 74. Tucson: Western Archeological and Conservation Center, National Park Service, 1999.

Butow, Robert J. C. *Japan's Decision To Surrender*. Stanford, Calif.: Stanford University Press, 1954.

California: A Guide to the Golden State. American Guide Series. New York: Hastings House, 1939.

Calvocoressi, Peter, Guy Wint, and John Pritchard. *Total War*, vol. 2, *The Greater East Asia and Pacific Conflict*, rev. 2d ed. New York: Pantheon, 1989.

Cardozier, V. R. *Colleges and Universities in World War II*. Westport, Conn.: Praeger, 1993.

Carter, Carolle J. *Mission to Yenan: American Liaison with the Chinese Communists, 1944–1947*. Lexington: University Press of Kentucky, 1997.

Cary, Otis, ed. *Eyewitness to History: The First Americans in Postwar Asia*. San Francisco: Kodansha International, 1984, 1995.

Chalou, George C., ed. *The Secrets War: The Office of Strategic Services in World War II*. Washington, D.C.: National Archives and Records Administration, 1992.

Chandonnet, Fern, ed. *Alaska at War, 1941–1945: The Forgotten War Remembered*. Anchorage: Alaska at War Committee, 1995.

Chin, Frank. "Come All Ye Asian American Writers of the Real and the Fake," in *The Big Aiiieeeee!: An Anthology of Chinese American and Japanese American Literature*, ed. Jeffery P. Chan et al. New York: Meridian, 1991, pp. 1–92.

Chinn, Thomas W. *Bridging the Pacific: San Francisco Chinatown and Its People*. San Francisco: Chinese Historical Society of America, 1989.

Choy, Peggy. "Racial Order and Contestation: Asian American Internees and Soldiers at Camp McCoy, Wisconsin, 1942–1943," in *Asian Americans: Comparative and Global Perspectives*, ed. Shirley Hune et al. Pullman: Washington State University Press, 1991, pp. 87–102.

Chuman, Frank F. *The Bamboo People: Japanese-Americans, Their History and the Law*. Chicago: Japanese American Citizens League, 1981.

Clear, Warren J. "Close Up of the Jap Fighting Man." *Infantry Journal* (November 1942): 16–23.

Clifton, Allan S. *Time of Fallen Blossoms*. New York: Knopf, 1951.

Coffman, Tom. *The Island Edge of America: A Political History of Hawaii*. Honolulu: University of Hawaii Press, 2003.

Cohen, Theodore. *Remaking Japan: The American Occupation as New Deal*. New York: Free Press, 1987.

Colewell, Robert N. "Intelligence and the Okinawa Battle." *Naval War College Review* (March–April 1985): 81–95.

Colling, John. *The Spirit of Yenan: A Wartime Chapter of Sino-American Friendship*. Hong Kong: API Press, 1991.

Controvich, James T. *The Central Pacific Campaign, 1943–1944: A Bibliography*. Westport, Conn.: Meckler, 1990.

Converse, Elliott V., III, et al. *The Exclusion of Black Soldiers from the Medal of Honor in World War II*. Jefferson, N.C.: McFarland & Co., 1997.

Cook, Haruko Taya. "The Myth of the Saipan Suicides." *MHQ* 7 (Spring 1995): 12–19. Reprinted in Robert Cowley, ed. *No End Save Victory: Perspectives on World War II*. New York: G. P. Putnam's Sons, 2001.

———, and Theodore F. Cook. *Japan at War: An Oral History*. New York: New Press, 1992.

Coox, Alvin D. *Nomonhan: Japan against Russia, 1939*. Stanford, Calif.: Stanford University Press, 1985, vol. 2.

Corbett, P. Scott. *Quiet Passages: The Exchange of Civilians between the United States and Japan during the Second World War*. Kent, Ohio: Kent State University Press, 1987.

Cotler, Gordon. "All in Favor Say 'Hai.'" *New Yorker* (9 April 1949).

———. "Kobayashi." *New Yorker* (26 August 1950): 54–57. Reprinted in William E. Daugherty. *A Psychological Warfare Casebook*. Baltimore: Operations Research Organization, 1958.

———. "The Parker Brothers at Antipolo." *New Yorker* (22 April 1950).

———. "A Sort of Detective Story." *New Yorker* (9 February 1952): 88–93.

Craig, William. *The Fall of Japan*. New York: Dial Press, 1967; Penguin, 1979.

Creswell, Harry I. T., et al. *A Dictionary of Military Terms, English-Japanese, Japanese-English*. Tokyo: Kaitakusha, 1937; Chicago: University of Chicago Press, 1942.

Crost, Lyn. *Honor by Fire: Japanese Americans at War in Europe and the Pacific*. Novato, Calif.: Presidio Press, 1994.

Cullum, George W. *Biographical Register of the Officers and Graduates of the U.S. Military Academy at West Point, New York, Since Its Establishment in 1802*, vol. 7, supplement, 1920–1930, ed. William H. Donaldson. Chicago: Lakeside Press, 1931.

Curtin, Patricia A. "Press Coverage of the 442nd Regimental Combat Team (Separate-Nisei): A Case Study in Agenda Building." *American Journalism Review* 12, no. 3 (Summer 1995): 225–41.

Daito, S., and H. Takahashi. "Postwar Trends and Developments in the Study of Military History in Japan." *Mededelingen van de Sectie Militaire Geschiedenis* 14 (1991): 74–81.

Daniels, Roger. "Japanese America, 1930–1941: An Ethnic Community in the Great Depression." *Journal of the West* (October 1985): 35–49.

————. *The Politics of Prejudice: The Anti-Japanese Movement in California and the Struggle for Japanese Exclusion*, 2d ed. Berkeley: University of California Press, 1977.

————. *Prisoners without Trial: Japanese Americans in World War II*. New York: Hill and Wang, 1993.

————, ed. *American Concentration Camps: A Documentary History of the Relocation and Incarceration of Japanese Americans, 1941–1945*, 9 vols. New York: Garland, 1989.

————, et al., eds. *Japanese Americans: From Relocation to Redress*, rev. ed. Seattle: University of Washington Press, 1991.

Davis, Goode, Jr. "Proud Tradition of the Marines' Navaho Code Talkers." *Marine Corps League* (Spring 1990): 16–26.

Daws, Gavan. *Prisoners of the Japanese: POWs of World War II in the Pacific*. New York: William Morrow, 1994.

Deane, Hugh, ed. *Remembering Koji Ariyoshi: An American GI in Yenan*. Los Angeles: U.S.-China Peoples Friendship Association, 1978.

Dear, I. C. B., ed. *The Oxford Companion to World War II*. New York: Oxford University Press, 1995.

Dennis, Peter. *Troubled Days of Peace: Mountbatten and South East Asia Command, 1945–1946*. New York: St. Martin's, 1987.

Dingman, Roger V. "Language at War: U.S. Marine Corps Japanese Language Officers in the Pacific War." *Journal of Military History* 68 (July 2004): 853–83.

Dorwart, Jeffery M. *Conflict of Duty: The U.S. Navy's Intelligence Dilemma, 1919–1945*. Annapolis, Md.: Naval Institute Press, 1983.

Doud, Harold. "Six Months with the Japanese Infantry." *Infantry Journal* (January–February 1937). Reprinted in Paul W. Thompson et al., eds. *How the Japanese Army Fights*. New York: Penguin, 1942.

Dower, John W. *Embracing Defeat: Japan in the Wake of World War II*. New York: Norton, 1999.

————. *Japan in War and Peace: Selected Essays*. New York: New Press, 1993.

————. *War without Mercy: Race and Power in the Pacific War*. New York: Pantheon, 1986.

Drea, Edward J. "'Great Patience Is Needed': America Encounters Australia, 1942." *War & Society* (May 1993): 21–51.

————. *MacArthur's Ultra: Codebreaking and the War against Japan, 1942–1945*. Lawrence: University Press of Kansas, 1992.

————. "Previews of Hell." *MHQ* 7, no. 3 (Spring 1995): 74–81.

————. *In the Service of the Emperor: Essays on the Imperial Japanese Army*. Lincoln: University of Nebraska Press, 1998.

————, and Joseph E. Richard. "New Evidence on Breaking the Japanese Army Codes," in *Allied and Axis Signals Intelligence in World War II*, ed. David Alvarez. London: Frank Cass, 1999, pp. 62–83.

Dulles, Foster R. *Yankees and Samurai: America's Role in the Emergence of Modern Japan*. New York: Harper & Row, 1965.

Dunlop, Richard. *Behind Japanese Lines: With the OSS in Burma*. Chicago: Rand-McNally, 1979.

Duus, Masayo Umezawa. *Unlikely Liberators: The Men of the 100th and 442nd*. Honolulu: University of Hawaii Press, 1987.

Edwards, Duval A. *Spy Catchers of the U.S. Army in the War with Japan*. Gig Harbor, Wash.: Red Apple Publishing, 1994.

Eichelberger, Robert L. *Our Jungle Road to Tokyo*. New York: Viking, 1950.

Eisenhower, Dwight D. *Crusade in Europe*. Garden City, N.Y.: Doubleday & Co., 1948.

Elisséeff, Serge, and Edwin O. Reischauer. *Elementary Japanese for University Students*. Cambridge, Mass.: Harvard-Yenching Institute, 1941.

Elisséeff, Serge, Hugh Borton, and Edwin O. Reischauer, eds. *A Selected List of Books and Articles on Japan in English, French, and German*. Washington, D.C.: Committee on Japanese Studies, American Council of Learned Societies, ca. 1940.

Eller, Floyd E. "A Soldier Looks at History [Fort Snelling]." *Minnesota History* 24, no. 1 (March 1943): 1–10.

Embree, John F. "Military Occupation of Japan." *Far Eastern Survey* (20 September 1944).

———. *Suye Mura: A Japanese Village*. Chicago: University of Chicago Press, 1939.

Emmerson, John K. *The Japanese Thread: A Life in the U.S. Foreign Service*. New York: Holt, Rinehart and Winston, 1978.

Escue, Lynn. "Coded Contributions: Navaho Talkers and the Pacific War." *History Today* (July 1991).

Farago, Ladislas. *The Broken Seal: "Operation Magic" and the Secret Road to Pearl Harbor*. New York: Random House, 1967.

Federal Records of World War II, 2 vols. Washington, D.C.: Government Printing Office, 1951.

Feis, Herbert. *The Road to Pearl Harbor: The Coming of the War between the United States and Japan*. Princeton, N.J.: Princeton University Press, 1950; New York: Atheneum, 1967.

Finnegan, John P., and Romana Danysh. *Military Intelligence*. Army Lineage Series. Washington, D.C.: U.S. Army Center of Military History, 1998.

Fischer, Ernest F., Jr., *Guardians of the Republic: History of the Noncommissioned Officer Corps of the U.S. Army*. New York: Ballantine, 1994.

Flynn, George Q. *The Draft, 1940–1973*. Lawrence: University Press of Kansas, 1993.

Ford, Douglas. "'A Conquerable Yet Resilient Foe': British Perceptions of the Imperial Japanese Army's Tactics on the India-Burma Front, September 1942 to Summer 1944." *Intelligence and National Security* 18, no. 1 (Spring 2003): 65–90.

Forrest, Jerome, and Clarke H. Kawakami. "General MacArthur and His Vanishing War History." *The Reporter: The Political Yearbook 1952*. New York: Fortnightly Publishing Company, 1953.

Frank, Richard B. *Downfall: The End of the Imperial Japanese Empire*. New York: Random House, 1999.

———. *Guadalcanal*. New York: Random House, 1990.

Frankel, Stanley A. *The 37th Infantry Division in World War II*. Washington, D.C.: Infantry Journal Press, 1948.

Freeman, Michael J. "Behind Enemy Lines!" *Airpower* (July 1994).

Fuchs, Lawrence H. *Hawaii Pono, "Hawaii the Excellent": An Ethnic and Political History*. Honolulu: Bess Press, 1961.

Fujita, Frank. *Foo! A Japanese-American Prisoner of the Rising Sun*. Denton: University of North Texas Press, 1993.

Fujitani, Takashi. "The Reischauer Memo: Mr. Moto, Hirohito, and Japanese American Soldiers." *Critical Asian Studies* 33, no. 3 (2001): 379–402.

Funch, Colin. *Linguists in Uniform: The Japanese Experience*. Australia: Monash University, Japanese Studies Centre, 2003.

Gabaldon, Guy. "Saipan: Suicide Island." Saipan: G. Gabaldon, 1990.

Garfield, Brian. *The Thousand Mile War: World War II in Alaska and the Aleutians*. Garden City, N.Y.: Doubleday, 1969.

Gilbert, James L., and John P. Finnegan, eds. *U.S. Army Signals Intelligence in World War II: A Documentary History*. U.S. Army in World War II. Washington, D.C.: U.S. Army Center of Military History, 1993.

Gill, William H. *Always a Commander: The Reminiscences of Major General William H. Gill*. Colorado Springs: Colorado College, 1974.

Gilmore, Allison B. *You Can't Fight Tanks with Bayonets: Psychological Warfare against the Japanese Army in the Southwest Pacific*. Lincoln: University of Nebraska Press, 1998.

Glantz, David M. *August Storm: Soviet Tactical and Operational Combat in Manchuria, 1945*. Fort Leavenworth, Kans.: Combat Studies Institute, 1983.

Goodwin, Doris K. *No Ordinary Time: Franklin & Eleanor Roosevelt: The Home Front in World War II*. New York: Simon & Schuster, 1994.

Grassick, Mary. *Fourth Army Intelligence School: Historic Furnishings Report*. Harpers Ferry, W.Va.: National Park Service, 1999.

Gray, J. Glenn. *The Warriors: Reflections on Men in Battle*. New York: Harper and Row, 1973.

Greene, Stephen. "Nisei—Ears for the Government." *Common Ground* (Autumn 1946): 17–20.

Greenwood, John T. "The U.S. Army Military Observers with the Japanese Army during the Russo-Japanese War (1904–1905)." *Army History* (Winter 1996): 1–14, 16.

Hafford, William E. "The Navaho Code Talkers." *Arizona Republic* (February 1989): 36–44.

Hall, R. Cargill, ed. *Lightning over Bougainville: The Yamamoto Mission Reconsidered*. Washington, D.C.: Smithsonian Institution Press, 1991.

Hall, Steve. *Fort Snelling: Colossus of the Wilderness*. St. Paul: Minnesota Historical Society Press, 1987.

Haller, Stephen A. *The Last Word in Airfields: A Special History Study of Crissy Field, Presidio of San Francisco, California*. San Francisco: National Park Service, 1994.

Halloran, Richard. *Warrior, Peacemaker, Poet, Patriot: A Portrait of Senator Spark M. Matsunaga*. Honolulu: Watermark, 2002.

Hamilton, James W., and William J. Bolce, Jr. *Gateway to Victory*. Stanford, Calif.: Stanford University Press, 1946.

Hamm, Diane L. "Undercover Nisei," in *Military Intelligence: Its Heroes and Legends.* Arlington Hall Station, Va.: U.S. Army Intelligence and Security Command, 1987.

Hansen, Arthur A. "Sergeant Ben Kuroki's Perilous 'Home Mission': Contested Loyalty and Patriotism in the Japanese American Detention Centers," in *Remembering Heart Mountain: Essays on Japanese American Internment in Wyoming*, ed. Mike Mackey. Powell, Wyo.: Western History Publications, 1998, pp. 153–75.

Harries, Meirion, and Susie Harries. *Soldiers of the Sun: The Rise and Fall of the Imperial Japanese Army.* New York: Random House, 1991.

Harris, Sheldon H. *Factories of Death: Japanese Biological Warfare, 1932–1945, and the American Cover-Up*, rev. ed. New York: Routledge, 2002.

Hawaii's Own: Picture Story of 442nd Regiment, 100th Battalion and Interpreters. Honolulu: L. H. Sakamoto, 1946.

Hayashi, Brian M. *Democratizing the Enemy: The Japanese American Internment.* Princeton, N.J.: Princeton University Press, 2004.

Hays, Otis, Jr. *Alaska's Hidden Wars: Secret Campaigns on the North Pacific Rim.* Fairbanks: University of Alaska Press, 2004.

Henderson, Harold G. *The Bamboo Broom: An Introduction to Japanese Haiku.* Boston: Houghton Mifflin, 1934.

———. *Handbook of Japanese Grammar.* Boston: Houghton Mifflin, 1943.

Hersey, John. *Into the Valley: A Skirmish of the Marines.* New York: Knopf, 1943; New York: Shocken, 1989.

Herzig, John A. "Japanese Americans and MAGIC." *Amerasia Journal* 11, no. 2 (Fall/Winter 1984): 47–65.

Hewes, John E., Jr. *From Root to McNamara: Army Organization and Administration, 1900–1963.* Washington, D.C.: U.S. Army Center of Military History, 1975.

Hill, Max. *Exchange Ship.* New York: Farrar & Rinehart, 1942.

Hilsman, Roger. *American Guerrilla.* Washington, D.C.: Brassey's, 1990.

Hirabayashi, Lane Ryo. *The Politics of Field Work: Research in an American Concentration Camp.* Tucson: University of Arizona Press, 1999.

History of the Sixth Marine Division. Washington, D.C.: Infantry Journal Press, 1948.

Hit the Beach: Your Marine Corps in Action. New York: Wm. H. Wise, 1948.

Ho, Ying-Ch'in. "Accepting the Surrender and Taking-Over Conditions," in *China Handbook, 1937–1945.* New York: Macmillan, 1947, pp. 764–67.

Hoffman, Jon T. *From Makin to Bougainville: Marine Raiders in the Pacific War.* Washington, D.C.: U.S. Marine Corps Historical Center, 1995.

Hogan, David W. *U.S. Army Special Operations in World War II.* U.S. Army in World War II. Washington, D.C.: U.S. Army Center of Military History, 1992.

Holmes, W. J. *Double-Edged Secrets: U.S. Naval Intelligence Operations in the Pacific during World War II.* Annapolis, Md.: Naval Institute Press, 1979.

———. "Naval Intelligence in the War against Japan, 1941–45: The View from Pearl Harbor," in *New Aspects of Naval History*, ed. Craig L. Symonds et al. Annapolis, Md.: Naval Institute Press, 1981.

Hopkins, James E. T. *Spearhead: A Complete History of Merrill's Marauder Rangers.* Baltimore: Johns Hopkins University Press, 2000.

Hosokawa, Bill. *JACL in Quest of Justice: The History of the Japanese American Citizens League*. New York: William Morrow, 1982.

———. *Nisei: The Quiet Americans*. New York: William Morrow, 1969.

———. "Our Own Japanese in the Pacific War." *American Legion Magazine* (July 1964).

———. *Thirty-Five Years in the Frying Pan*. New York: McGraw-Hill, 1978.

Houston, Jeanne Wakatsuki, and James D. Houston. *Farewell to Manzanar*. New York: Houghton Mifflin, 1973.

Huber, Thomas M. *Japan's Battle of Okinawa, April–June 1945*. Fort Leavenworth, Kans.: Combat Studies Institute, 1990.

———. *PASTEL: Deception in the Invasion of Japan*. Fort Leavenworth, Kans.: Combat Studies Institute, 1988.

Hunter, Charles N. *Galahad*. San Antonio, Tex.: Naylor, 1963.

Hutchison, Kevin D. *World War II in the North Pacific: Chronology and Fact Book*. Westport, Conn.: Greenwood Press, 1994.

Ichihashi, Yamato. *Japanese in the United States: A Critical Study of the Problems of the Japanese Immigrants and Their Children*. Stanford, Calif.: Stanford University Press, 1932.

Ichioka, Yuji. "The Meaning of Loyalty: The Case of Kazumaro Buddy Uno." *Amerasia Journal* 23, no. 3 (1997): 45–71.

Ienaga, Saburō. *The Pacific War, 1931–1945*. New York: Pantheon, 1978.

In Freedom's Cause. Honolulu: University of Hawaii Press, 1949.

Inada, Lawson Fusao, ed. *Only What We Could Carry: The Japanese American Internment Experience*. Berkeley, Calif.: Heyday Books, 2000.

Inouye, Daniel K. *Journey to Washington*. Englewood Cliffs, N.J.: Prentice-Hall, 1967.

Inouye, Frank T. "Immediate Origins of the Heart Mountain Draft Resistance Movement," in *Remembering Heart Mountain: Essays on Japanese American Internment in Wyoming*, ed. Mike Mackey. Powell, Wyo.: Western History Publications, 1998, pp. 121–39.

Iriye, Akira. *Pearl Harbor and the Coming of the Pacific War*. New York: St. Martin's, 1999.

Irons, Peter. *Justice at War: The Story of the Japanese American Internment Cases*. New York: Oxford University Press, 1983.

Ishihara, Masaie. "Memories of War and Okinawa," in *Perilous Memories: The Asia-Pacific War(s)*, ed. T. Fujitani et al. Durham, N.C.: Duke University Press, 2001, pp. 87–106.

Ishimaru, Stone S. *Military Intelligence Service Language School, U.S. Army, Camp Savage, Minnesota*. Los Angeles: MIS Club of Southern California, 1992.

———. *Military Intelligence Service Language School, U.S. Army, Fort Snelling, Minnesota*. Los Angeles: TecCom Production, 1991.

Ishio, S. Phil. "The Nisei Contribution to the Allied Victory in the Pacific." *American Intelligence Journal* (Spring/Summer 1995): 59–67.

Ito, Roy. *We Went to War: The Story of the Japanese Canadians Who Served during the First and Second World Wars*. Stittsville, Ontario: Canada's Wings, 1984.

James, D. Clayton. *The Years of MacArthur*, 3 vols. Boston: Houghton Mifflin, 1970–1985.

Jeffreys-Jones, Rhodri, and Andrew Lownie, eds. *North American Spies: New Revisionist Essays*. Lawrence: University Press of Kansas, 1991.

Jeffries, John W. *Wartime America: The World War II Home Front*. Chicago: Ivan R. Dee, 1996.

Jones, Edgar L. "Fighting with Words: Psychological Warfare in the Pacific." *Atlantic Monthly* (August 1945): 47–51.

Jones, Edward E., and Harold B. Gerard. *Foundations of Social Psychology*. New York: John Wiley & Sons, 1967.

Josephy, Alvin M., Jr. *The Long and the Short and the Tall: The Story of a Marine Combat Unit in the Pacific*. New York: Knopf, 1946.

———. "Some Japs Surrender." *Infantry Journal* (August 1945): 40–45.

Kahn, David. *The Codebreakers: The Story of Secret Writing*. New York: Signet, 1973; rev. ed., New York: Scribner, 1996.

———. "The Intelligence Failure of Pearl Harbor." *Foreign Affairs* (Winter 1991/92): 138–52.

———. "The United States Views Germany and Japan in 1941," in *Knowing One's Enemies: Intelligence Assessment before the Two World Wars*, ed. Ernest R. May. Princeton: Princeton University Press, 1984, pp. 476–501.

Kawano, Kenji. *Warriors: Navajo Code Talkers*. Flagstaff, Ariz.: Northland Publishing Co., 1990.

Keefer, Louis E. "Birth and Death of the Army Specialized Training Program." *Army History* (Winter 1995): 1–7.

———. *Scholars in Foxholes: The Story of the Army Specialized Training Program in World War II*. Jefferson, N.C.: McFarland, 1988.

Keene, Donald. *On Familiar Terms: A Journey across Cultures*. New York: Kodansha, 1994.

Kennedy, David M. *Freedom from Fear: The American People in Depression and War, 1929–1945*. New York: Oxford University Press, 1999.

Kennedy, M. D. *The Military Side of Japanese Life*. Boston: Houghton Mifflin, 1923.

Kenney, George C. *General Kenney Reports: A Personal History of the Pacific War*. New York: Duell, Sloan and Pearce, 1949.

Kerr, E. Bartlett. *Surrender and Survival: The Experience of American POWs in the Pacific, 1941–1945*. New York: William Morrow, 1985.

King, Ernest J., and Walter M. Whitehill. *Fleet Admiral King: A Naval Record*. New York: Norton, 1952.

Kitagawa, Daisuke. *Issei and Nisei: The Internment Years*. New York: Seabury Press, 1967.

Kitano, Harry H. L. *Japanese Americans: The Evolution of a Subculture*, 2d ed. Englewood Cliffs, N.J.: Prentice-Hall, 1976.

———, and Roger Daniels. *Asian Americans: Emerging Minorities*, 2d ed. Englewood Cliffs, N.J.: Prentice-Hall, 1995.

Knaefler, Tomi Kaizawa. *Our House Divided: Seven Japanese American Families in World War II*. Honolulu: University of Hawaii Press, 1991.

Koch, Scott A. "The Role of U.S. Army Military Attachés between the World Wars." *Studies in Intelligence* (Winter 1994): 53–57.

Koshi, George M. *Japanese Legal Advisor: Crimes and Punishments*. Rutland, Vt.: Charles E. Tuttle Co., 1970.

Krammer, Arnold. "Japanese Prisoners of War in America." *Pacific Historical Review* (February 1983): 67–91.

———. *Nazi Prisoners of War in America*. New York: Stein and Day, 1979.

Kreis, John F., ed. *Piercing the Fog: Intelligence and Army Air Forces Operations in World War II*. Washington, D.C.: Air Force History and Museums Program, 1996.

Krueger, Walter. *From Down Under to Nippon*. Washington, D.C.: Combat Forces Press, 1953.

Kumamoto, Bob. "The Search for Spies: American Counterintelligence and the Japanese American Community, 1932–1941." *Amerasia Journal* 6 (1979): 45–75.

LaFeber, Walter. *The Clash: U.S.-Japanese Relations throughout History*. New York: Norton, 1997.

Lagerquist, Syble. *Philip Johnston and the Navajo Code Talkers*. Billings, Mont.: Council for Indian Education, 1983.

Lamott, Kenneth. *The Stockade*. Boston: Little, Brown, 1952.

Laytha, Edgar. *The March of Japan*. New York: F. A. Stokes, 1936.

Layton, Edwin T. *"And I Was There": Pearl Harbor and Midway—Breaking the Secrets*. New York: William Morrow, 1985.

Leary, William M., ed. *We Shall Return: MacArthur's Commanders and the Defeat of Japan, 1942–1945*. Lexington: University Press of Kentucky, 1988.

Lee, Loyd E., ed. *World War II in Asia and the Pacific and the War's Aftermath, with General Themes: A Handbook of Literature and Research*. Westport, Conn.: Greenwood Press, 1998.

Leighton, Alexander H. *The Governing of Men: General Principles and Recommendations Based on Experience at a Japanese Relocation Camp*. Princeton, N.J.: Princeton University Press, 1945.

———. *Human Relations in a Changing World: Observations on the Use of the Social Sciences*. New York: E. P. Dutton & Co., 1949.

Lewin, Ronald. *The American MAGIC: Codes, Ciphers and the Defeat of Japan*. New York: Farrar Straus Giroux, 1982.

Lind, Andrew. *Hawaii's Japanese: An Experiment in Democracy*. Princeton: Princeton University Press, 1946.

Lindbergh, Charles A. *The Wartime Journals of Charles A. Lindbergh*. New York: Harcourt Brace Jovanovich, 1970.

Linderman, Gerald F. *The World within War: America's Combat Experience in World War II*. New York: Free Press, 1997.

Linn, Brian M. *Guardians of Empire: The U.S. Army and the Pacific, 1902–1940*. Chapel Hill: University of North Carolina Press, 1997.

Liu, F. F. *A Military History of Modern China, 1924–1949*. Princeton, N.J.: Princeton University Press, 1956.

Lory, Hillis. *Japan's Military Masters: The Army in Japanese Life*. New York: Viking, 1943.

Loureiro, Pedro A. "'Boulder Boys': Naval Japanese Language School Graduates," in *New Interpretations in Naval History*, ed. Randy C. Balano and Craig Symonds. Annapolis, Md.: Naval Institute Press, 2001, pp. 366–88.

————. "Japanese Espionage and American Countermeasures in Pre–Pearl Harbor California." *Journal of American–East Asian Relations* 3, no. 3 (Fall 1994): 197–210.

Love, Edmund G. *The 27th Infantry Division in World War II*. Washington, D.C.: Infantry Journal Press, 1949.

————, ed. *Dear Miss Em: General Eichelberger's War in the Pacific, 1942–1945*. Westport, Conn.: Greenwood Press, 1972.

Lynn, John A. *Battle: A History of Combat and Culture*. Boulder, Colo.: Westview Press, 2003.

McAlpine, Pauline S. *Diary of a Missionary*. Decatur, Ga.: Presbyterian Church in America, 1986.

MacArthur, Douglas. *Reminiscences*. New York: McGraw-Hill, 1964.

MacDonnell, Francis. *Insidious Foes: The Axis Fifth Column and the American Home Front*. New York: Oxford University Press, 1995.

MacEachim, Douglas. *The Final Months of the War with Japan: Signals Intelligence, U.S. Invasion Planning, and the A-Bomb Decision*. Washington, D.C.: Center for the Study of Intelligence, 1998.

MacIsaac, David. *Strategic Bombing in World War II: The Story of the United States Strategic Bombing Survey*. New York: Garland, 1976.

MacKenzie, S. P. "The Treatment of Prisoners of War in World War II." *Journal of Social History* 66, no. 3 (September 1994): 487–520.

McMichael, Scott R. *A Historical Perspective on Light Infantry*. Fort Leavenworth, Kans.: Combat Studies Institute, 1987.

McMillan, George. *The Old Breed: A History of the First Marine Division in World War II*. Washington, D.C.: Infantry Journal Press, 1949.

McNaughton, James C. "Japanese Americans and the U.S. Army: A Historical Reconsideration." *Army History* 59 (Summer–Fall 2003): 4–15.

————. "Nisei Linguists and New Perspectives on the Pacific War: Intelligence Race, and Continuity," in *The U.S. Army and World War II*, ed. Judith L. Bellafaire. U.S. Army in World War II. Washington, D.C.: U.S. Army Center of Military History, 1998, pp. 371–81.

————. "Training Linguists for the Pacific War, 1941–1942," in *The U.S. Army and World War II*, ed. Judith L. Bellafaire. U.S. Army in World War II. Washington, D.C.: U.S. Army Center of Military History, 1998, pp. 129–45.

————. Kristen E. Edwards, and Jay M. Price. "'Incontestable Proof Will Be Exacted': Historians, Asian Americans, and the Medal of Honor." *Public Historian* 24 (Fall 2002): 11–33.

McWilliams, Carey. *Prejudice: Japanese-Americans, Symbol of Racial Intolerance*. Boston: Little, Brown, 1944.

Maga, Timothy. "'Away from Tokyo': The Pacific Islands War Crimes Trials, 1945–1949." *Journal of Pacific History* 36, no. 1 (2001): 37–50.

Mailer, Norman. *The Naked and the Dead*. New York: Rinehart and Company, 1948; Henry Holt, 1998.

Maki, John M. *Government and Politics in Japan: The Road to Democracy*. New York: Praeger, 1962.

———. *Japanese Militarism: Its Cause and Cure*. New York: Knopf, 1945.

Manchester, William. *Goodbye, Darkness: A Memoir of the Pacific War*. New York: Dell, 1980.

———. "The Man Who Could Speak Japanese." *American Heritage* (December 1975): 36–39, 91–95.

Marchio, James D. "Days of Future Past: Joint Intelligence in World War II." *Joint Force Quarterly* (Spring 1996): 116–23.

Marshall, S. L. A. *Battle at Best*. New York: Pocket Books, 1965.

———. *Bringing Up the Rear: A Memoir*, ed. Cate Marshall. San Rafael, Calif.: Presidio Press, 1979.

Martin, Ralph G. *Boy from Nebraska: The Story of Ben Kuroki*. New York: Harper & Row Brothers, 1946.

Masaie, Ishihara. "Memories of War and Okinawa," in *Perilous Memories: The Asia-Pacific War(s)*, ed. T. Fujitani et al. Durham, N.C.: Duke University Press, 2001, pp. 87–106.

Masaoka, Mike. *They Call Me Moses Masaoka: An American Saga*. New York: William Morrow, 1987.

Mashbir, Sidney F. *I Was an American Spy*. New York: Vantage, 1953.

———. "I Was an American Spy." *Saturday Evening Post*, 27 Mar, 3 Apr 48.

Mason, John T., ed. *The Pacific War Remembered*. Annapolis, Md.: Naval Institute Press, 1986.

Matthew, Robert J. *Language and Area Studies in the Armed Services: Their Future Significance*. Washington, D.C.: American Council on Education, 1947.

Mead, David. "The Breaking of the Japanese Army Administrative Code." *Cryptologia* (July 1994): 193–203.

Mercado, Stephen C. "FBIS against the Axis, 1941–1945," *Studies in Intelligence* 11 (Fall/Winter 2001).

———. "Japanese Army Intelligence Activities against the United States, 1921–1945." *Studies in Intelligence* 38, no. 2 (Summer 1994): 49–55.

Michener, James A. *Tales of the South Pacific*. New York: Macmillan, 1947.

Minear, Richard H. *Victors' Justice: The Tokyo War Crimes Trial*. Princeton, N.J.: Princeton University Press, 1971.

Minnesota: A State Guide. American Guide Series. New York: Hastings House, 1938, rev. ed. 1954.

Moore, Brenda L. *Serving Our Country: Japanese American Women in the Military during World War II*. New Brunswick, N.J.: Rutgers University Press, 2003.

Moore, Jeff M. "JICPOA: Joint Intelligence during WW II." *Military Intelligence* (July–September 1995): 35–39.

Morimoto, Toyotomi. *Japanese Americans and Cultural Continuity: Maintaining Language and Heritage*. New York: Garland, 1997.

Morin, Raul. *Among the Valiant*. Alhambra, Calif.: Borden Publishing Co., 1966.

Morioka, Simon. "Japanese Americans in the Service of their Country." Master of Arts Diss., Selwyn College, University of Cambridge, 1998.

Morrill, John H., and Pete Martin. *South from Corregidor*. New York: Simon and Schuster, 1943.

Muller, Eric L. *Free To Die for Their Country: The Story of the Japanese American Draft Resisters in World War II*. Chicago: University Press of Chicago, 2001.

Murayama, Milton. *All I Asking for Is My Body*. Honolulu: University of Hawaii Press, 1988.

Murphy, Thomas D. *Ambassadors in Arms*. Honolulu: University of Hawaii Press, 1954.

Murray, Williamson, and Allan R. Millett. *A War To Be Won: Fighting the Second World War*. Cambridge, Mass.: Harvard University Press, 2000.

Myer, Dillon S. *Uprooted Americans: The Japanese Americans and the War Relocation Authority during World War II*. Tucson: University of Arizona Press, 1971.

Nadler, Scott E. *The Evolution of Foreign Language Training in the Armed Forces*. Washington, D.C.: Defense Language Institute, 1972.

Nakahata, Yutaka, and Ralph Toyota. "Varsity Victory Volunteers: A Social Movement." *Social Process in Hawaii* (November 1943): 29–35.

Nalty, Bernard C. *Cape Gloucester: The Green Inferno*. Washington, D.C.: U.S. Marine Corps Historical Center, 1994.

Native America in the Twentieth Century: An Encyclopedia, ed. Mary B. Davis. New York: Garland, 1994.

Nelson, Otto L., Jr. "The Organization of G–2 in World War II." *Infantry Journal* (September 1946): 32–37.

———. *National Security and the General Staff*. Washington, D.C.: Infantry Journal Press, 1946.

Niiya, Brian, ed. *Encyclopedia of Japanese American History*, rev. ed. New York: Facts on File, 1993, 2001.

Nimmo, William F., ed. *The Occupation of Japan: The Grass Roots Level*. Norfolk, Va.: General Douglas MacArthur Foundation, 1992.

Nobile, Philip, ed. *Judgment at the Smithsonian*. New York: Marlowe & Co., ca. 1995.

Oba, Sadao. *The "Japanese" War*, trans. Anne Kaneko. Sandgate, U.K.: Japan Library, 1995. Originally published as *Senchu London Nihongo Gakko*. Tokyo: Chuokoron-Sha, 1988.

O'Brien, David J., and Stephen S. Fugita. *The Japanese American Experience*. Bloomington: Indiana University Press, 1991.

O'Brien, Robert W. *The College Nisei*. New York: Arno Press, 1978.

Odo, Franklin S. *No Sword To Bury: Japanese Americans in Hawai'i during World War II*. Philadelphia: Temple University Press, 2004.

O'Donnell, Patrick K. *Into the Rising Sun*. New York: Free Press, 2002.

Ogburn, Charlton, Jr., *The Marauders*, 2d ed. New York: Harper and Brothers, 1959.

Okada, John. *No-No Boy*. Rutherford, Vt.: Tuttle, 1957. Reprint, Seattle: University of Washington Press, 1979.

Okamoto, Shiro. *The Man Who Saved Kabuki: Faubion Bowers and Theatre Censorship in Occupied Japan*. Honolulu: University of Hawaii Press, 2001.

Okihiro, Gary Y. *Cane Fires: The Anti-Japanese Movement in Hawaii, 1865–1945*. Philadelphia: Temple University Press, 1991.

Okinawa Club of America. *History of the Okinawans in North America*, trans. Ben Kobash-
igawa. Los Angeles: Asian American Studies Center and Okinawa Club of America,
1988.

Omura, James. "Japanese American Journalism during World War II," in *Frontiers of Asian
American Studies: Writing, Research, and Commentary*, ed. Gail M. Nomura et al.
Pullman: Washington State University Press, 1989.

O'Neill, William L. *A Democracy at War: America's Fight at Home and Abroad in World
War II*. New York: Free Press, 1993.

Ōoka, Shōhei. *Fires on the Plain*. New York: Knopf, 1957.

———. *Taken Captive: A Japanese POW's Story*, trans. and ed. Wayne P. Lammers. New
York: John Wiley & Sons, 1996.

Ōtani, Isao. *Japan Bōi: Nikkei Amerikajintachi no Taiheiyō Sensō* [Japan Boy: A Japanese
American during the Pacific War]. Tokyo: Kadokawa Shoten, 1983.

O'Toole, G. J. A., ed. *The Encyclopedia of American Intelligence and Espionage*. New
York: Facts on File, 1988.

Packard, Wyman H. *A Century of U.S. Naval Intelligence*. Washington, D.C.: Office of
Naval Intelligence/Naval Historical Center, 1996.

Parker, Frederick D. *A Priceless Advantage: U.S. Navy Communications Intelligence and
the Battles of Coral Sea, Midway, and the Aleutians*. United States Cryptologic History, ser. IV, World War II, vol. 5. Fort Meade, Md.: Center for Cryptologic History,
National Security Agency, 1993.

Passin, Herbert. *Encounter with Japan*. San Francisco: Kodansha, 1982.

———. *Society and Education in Japan*. New York: Columbia University, 1965.

Paul, Doris A. *The Navaho Code Talkers*. Bryn Mawr, Pa.: Dorrance and Co., 1973.

Pearlman, Michael D. *Unconditional Surrender, Demobilization, and the Atomic Bomb*.
Fort Leavenworth, Kans.: Combat Studies Institute, 1996.

Peers, William R., and Dean Brelis. *Behind the Burma Road: The Story of America's Most
Successful Guerrilla Force*. Boston: Little, Brown, 1963.

———. "Intelligence Operations of OSS Detachment 101." *Studies in Intelligence* (Summer 1960).

Pei, Mario A. *Languages for War and Peace*, 2d ed. New York: Vanni, 1945.

Perras, Galen R. *Stepping Stones to Nowhere: The Aleutian Islands, Alaska, and American
Military Strategy, 1867–1945*. Toronto, Canada: UBC Press, 2003.

Perry, John C. *Beneath the Eagle's Wings: Americans in Occupied Japan*. New York: Dodd,
Mead & Company, 1980.

*Personal Justice Denied: Report of the Commission on Wartime Relocation and Internment
of Civilians*. Seattle: University of Washington Press, 1997.

Piccigallo, Philip R. *The Japanese on Trial: Allied War Crimes Operations in the East,
1945–1951*. Austin: University of Texas Press, 1979.

Pineau, Roger. "The Death of Admiral Yamamoto." *Naval Intelligence Professionals Quarterly* (Fall 1994): 1–5.

Pogue, Forrest C. *George C. Marshall*, 4 vols. New York: Viking, 1963–1987.

Portner, Stuart. "The Japanese-American Combat Team." *Military Affairs* (Fall 1943):
158–62.

Potter, E. B. *Nimitz*. Annapolis, Md.: U.S. Naval Institute Press, 1976.

Prados, John. *Combined Fleet Decoded: The Secret History of American Intelligence and the Japanese Navy in World War II*. New York: Random House, 1995.

———. "The Spies at the Bottom of the Sea." *MHQ* 6, no. 2 (Winter 1994): 39–47.

———. "U.S. Intelligence and the Japanese Evacuation of Guadalcanal, 1943." *Intelligence and National Security* (April 1995): 294–305.

Prange, Gordon W. *At Dawn We Slept: The Untold Story of Pearl Harbor*. New York: McGraw-Hill, 1981.

———. *Pearl Harbor: The Verdict of History*. New York: McGraw-Hill, 1986.

Putney, Diane T. "The U.S. Military Intelligence Service: The ULTRA Mission," in *ULTRA and the Army Air Forces in World War II*, ed. Lewis F. Powell. Washington, D.C.: Office of Air Force History, 1987.

Pyle, Ernie. *Ernie's War*, ed. David Nichols. New York: Random House, 1986.

The Quiet Heroes of the Southwest Pacific Theater: An Oral History of the Men and Women of CBB and FRUMEL. Fort Meade, Md.: National Security Agency, 1996.

Rademaker, John A. *These Are Americans: The Japanese Americans in Hawaii in World War II*. Palo Alto, Calif.: Pacific Books, 1951.

Rearden, Jim. *Cracking the Zero Mystery*. Harrisburg, Pa.: Stackpole, 1990.

Reischauer, Edwin O. *Japan: Past and Present*. New York: Knopf, 1946.

———. *Japan: The Story of a Nation*, 3d ed. New York: Knopf, 1981.

———. *My Life between Japan and America*. New York: Harper & Row, 1986.

Robinson, Greg. *By Order of the President: FDR and the Internment of Japanese Americans*. Cambridge, Mass.: Harvard University Press, 2001.

Rodriggs, Lawrence R., ed. *We Remember Pearl Harbor: Honolulu Civilians Recall the War Years, 1941–1945*. Newark, Calif.: Communications Concepts, ca. 1991.

Rosenberg, Emily S. *A Date Which Will Live: Pearl Harbor in American Memory*. Durham, N.C.: Duke University Press, 2003.

Rosenman, Samuel I., comp. *The Public Papers and Addresses of Franklin D. Roosevelt*, 13 vols. (New York: Random House, 1938–1950).

Roy, Patricia E. "The Soldiers Canada Didn't Want: Her Chinese and Japanese Citizens." *Canadian Historical Review* (September 1978).

Sakamaki, Kazuo. *I Attacked Pearl Harbor*, trans. Toru Matsumoto. New York: Young Men's Christian Association Press, 1949.

Sandler, Stanley. *Cease Resistance, It's Good for You: A History of U.S. Army Combat Psychological Operations*. Fort Bragg, N.C.: U.S. Army Special Operations Command, Directorate of History and Museums, 1996.

Sano, Iwao Peter. *One Thousand Days in Siberia: The Odyssey of a Japanese-American POW*. Lincoln: University of Nebraska Press, 1997.

Sarasohn, Eileen Sunada, ed. *The Issei, Portrait of a Pioneer: An Oral History*. Palo Alto, Calif.: Pacific Books, 1983.

Schonberger, Howard. "Dilemmas of Loyalty: Japanese Americans and the Psychological Warfare Campaigns of the Office of Strategic Services, 1943–45." *Amerasia Journal* 16, no. 1 (1990): 21–38.

Schrijivers, Peter. *The GI War against Japan: American Soldiers in Asia and the Pacific during World War II*. New York: New York University Press, 2002.

Schulzinger, Robert D. *A Time for War: The United States and Vietnam, 1941–1975*. New York: Oxford University Press, 1997.

Selective Service System. *Selective Service as the Tide of War Turns*. Third Report of the Director of Selective Service, 1943–1944. Washington, D.C.: Selective Service System, 1945.

———. *Special Groups*. Special Monograph no. 10. Washington, D.C.: Selective Service System, 1953.

Sexton, Donal J., Jr., comp., *Signals Intelligence in World War II: A Research Guide*. Westport, Conn.: Greenwood Press, 1996.

Shaw, Henry I., Jr. *The United States Marines in the Occupation of Japan*. Washington, D.C.: Headquarters, U.S. Marine Corps, 1961, 1969.

Shellum, Duane R. *America's Human Secret Weapon* (Minneapolis, Minn.: Minnisei Printers, 1977).

Sherrod, Robert L. *On to Westward: War in the Central Pacific*. New York: Duell, Sloan and Pearce, 1945.

Shibutani, Tamotsu. *The Derelicts of Company K: A Sociological Study of Demoralization*. Berkeley: University of California Press, 1978.

Shirey, Orville C. *Americans: The Story of the 442d Combat Team*. Washington, D.C.: Infantry Journal Press, 1946.

Simpson, William B. *Special Agent in the Pacific, WWII: Counterintelligence—Military, Political, and Economic*. New York: Rivercross Publishing, 1995.

Sinclair, Boyd. "Valuable as a Company of Men." *Ex-CBI Roundup* (November 1951).

Singlaub, John K. *Hazardous Duty: An American Soldier in the Twentieth Century*. New York: Simon and Schuster, 1991.

Skates, John Ray. *The Invasion of Japan: Alternative to the Bomb*. Columbia: University of South Carolina Press, 1994.

Sledge, E. B. *With the Old Breed at Peleliu and Okinawa*. Novato, Calif.: Presidio Press, 1981. Reprint, New York: Oxford University Press, 1990.

Slim, William J. *Defeat into Victory: Battling Japan in Burma and India, 1942–1945*. London: Cassell, 1956. Reprint, New York: Cooper Square, 2000.

Smith, Bradford. *Americans from Japan*. Philadelphia: J. B. Lippincott, 1948.

Smith, Charles R. *Securing the Surrender: Marines in the Occupation of Japan*. Washington, D.C.: Headquarters, U.S. Marine Corps, 1997.

Smith, Holland M. *Coral and Brass*. New York: Scribners, 1949.

Smith, S. E., ed. *The United States Marine Corps in World War II*. New York: Random House, 1969.

Smith, Steven T. *The Rescue*. New York: John Wiley and Sons, 2001.

Sodei, Rinjiro, ed. *Dear General MacArthur: Letters from the Japanese during the American Occupation*. Lanham, Md.: Rowman & Littlefield, 2001.

Sparagana, Eleanor A. "The Conduct and Consequences of Psychological Warfare: American Psychological Warfare Operations in the War against Japan, 1941–1945." Ph.D. Diss., Brandeis University, 1990.

Spector, Ronald H. *Advice and Support: The Early Years, 1941–1960*. U.S. Army in Vietnam. Washington, D.C.: U.S. Army Center of Military History, 1983.

————. *Eagle against the Sun: The American War with Japan*. New York: Free Press, 1985.

————, ed. *Listening to the Enemy: Key Documents on the Role of Communications Intelligence in the War with Japan*. Wilmington, Del.: Scholarly Resources, 1988.

Spickard, Paul R. *Japanese Americans: The Formation and Transformations of an Ethnic Group*. New York: Twayne, 1996.

Stephan, John J. *Hawaii under the Rising Sun: Japan's Plans for Conquest after Pearl Harbor*. Honolulu: University of Hawaii Press, 1984.

————. "Hijacked by Utopia: American Nikkei in Manchuria." *Amerasia Journal* 23, no. 3 (Winter 1997–1998).

Stouffer, Samuel A., et al. *The American Soldier*, vol. 1, *Adjustment during Army Life*. Princeton, N.J.: Princeton University Press, 1949.

Straus, Ulrich. *The Anguish of Surrender: Japanese POWs of World War II*. Seattle: University of Washington Press, 2003.

Stripp, Alan. *Codebreaker in the Far East*. New York: Oxford University Press, 1995.

Strong, Edward K. *The Second-Generation Japanese Problem*. Stanford, Calif.: Stanford University Press, 1934.

Strong, George V. *Common Chinese-Japanese Characters*. Yokohama: Kelly and Walsh, ca. 1911.

Suzuki, Peter T. "Analyses of Japanese Films in Wartime Washington." *Asian Profile* 23, no. 5 (1995): 371–80.

————. "Ruth Benedict, Robert Hashima and *The Chrysanthemum and the Sword*." *Research: Contributions to Interdisciplinary Anthropology* 3 (1985): 55–69.

Svensson, Eric H. F. "The Military Occupation of Japan: The First Years Planning, Policy Formulation, and Reforms." Ph.D. Diss., University of Denver, 1966.

Takaki, Ronald. *Double Victory: A Multicultural History of America in World War II*. Boston: Little, Brown, 2000.

————. *Strangers from a Different Shore: A History of Asian Americans*. Boston: Little, Brown, 1989.

Takemae, Eiji. *Inside GHQ: The Allied Occupation of Japan and Its Legacy*. New York: Continuum, 2002.

Takezawa, Yasuko I., *Breaking the Silence: Redress and Japanese American Ethnicity*. Ithaca, N.Y.: Cornell University Press, 1995.

Tamura, Eileen H. *Americanization, Acculturalization, and Ethnic Identity: The Nisei Generation in Hawaii*. Urbana: University of Illinois Press, 1994.

Tanaka, Yuki. *Hidden Horrors: Japanese War Crimes in World War II*. Boulder, Colo.: Westview Press, 1996.

Tateishi, John. *And Justice for All: An Oral History of the Japanese American Detention Camps*. New York: Random House, 1984.

Taylor, Maxwell D. *Swords and Plowshares*. New York: W. W. Norton, 1972.

tenBroek, Jacobus, et al. *Prejudice, War, and the Constitution*. Berkeley: University of California Press, 1954.

Terkel, Studs. *"The Good War": An Oral History of World War Two*. New York: Pantheon, 1984.

Thorpe, Elliott R. *East Wind, Rain: An Intimate Account of an Intelligence Officer in the Pacific, 1939–49.* Boston: Gambit, 1969.

Toland, John. *The Rising Sun: The Decline and Fall of the Japanese Empire, 1936–1945.* New York: Random House, 1970.

Totten, George O., III. *The Social Democratic Movement in Prewar Japan.* New Haven: Yale University Press, 1966.

Towle, Philip, et al., eds. *Japanese Prisoners of War.* New York: Hambledon, 2000.

Tsukahira, Toshio George. *Feudal Control in Tokugawa Japan: The Sankin Kotai System.* Cambridge, Mass.: Harvard University Press, 1966.

———. *Postwar Development of Japanese Communist Strategy.* Cambridge, Mass.: MIT Press, 1954.

Tuchman, Barbara W. *Stilwell and the American Experience in China, 1911–1945.* New York: Macmillan, 1970.

"Use of Japanese Prisoners of War," in *A Psychological Warfare Casebook*, ed. William E. Daugherty and Morris Janowitz. Baltimore: Johns Hopkins University Press, 1958, pp. 201–11.

Uyeda, Clifford. "Also Born on the Fourth of July: The Story of 'Tokyo Rose.'" *Nikkei Heritage* (Summer 1994): 4–8, 14–16

Van Antwerp, William M. "How Sergeant Kubo Won the DSC." *Infantry Journal* (1946).

Van Der Rhoer, Edward. *Deadly Magic: A Personal Account of Communications Intelligence in World War II in the Pacific.* New York: Charles Scribner's Sons, 1978.

Votaw, John F. "United States Military Attachés, 1885–1919: The American Army Matures in the International Arena." Ph.D. Diss., Temple University, 1991.

Warner, Denis, and Peggy Warner, with Sadao Seno. *The Sacred Warriors: Japan's Suicide Legions.* New York: Van Nostrand Reinhold, 1982.

Watkins, T. H. *Righteous Pilgrim: The Life and Times of Harold L. Ickes, 1874–1952.* New York: Henry Holt, 1990.

Watson, Bruce. "Navaho Code Talkers: A Few Good Men." *Smithsonian* (August 1993): 34–43.

Weckerling, John. "Japanese Americans Play Vital Role in United States Intelligence Service in World War II." [1946]. Printed in *Hokubei Mainichi*, 27 Oct–5 Nov 71, and reprinted as a pamphlet.

———. "The Japanese Language Detail." *Cavalry Journal* (May–June 1932): 31–34.

Wedemeyer, Albert C. *Wedemeyer Reports!* New York: Henry Holt, 1958.

———. *Wedemeyer on War and Peace*, ed. Keith E. Eiler. Stanford, Calif.: Hoover Institution Press, 1987.

Weglyn, Michi. *Years of Infamy: The Untold Story of America's Concentration Camps.* New York: Morrow Quill, 1976.

Weigley, Russell F. "The Role of the War Department and the Army," in *Pearl Harbor as History: Japanese-American Relations, 1931–1941*, ed. Dorothy Borg and Shumpei Okamoto. New York: Columbia University Press, 1973, pp. 165–88.

Weinberg, Gerhard L. *A World at Arms: A Global History of World War II.* New York: Cambridge University Press, 1994.

Weintraub, Stanley. *The Last Great Victory: The End of World War II, July/August 1945.* New York: Dutton, 1995.

Welch, Jeanie M. *The Tokyo Trial: A Bibliographic Guide to English-Language Sources*. Westport, Conn.: Greenwood Press, 2001.

———. "Without a Hangman, Without a Rope: Navy War Crimes Trials after World War II," *International Journal of Naval History* 1, no. 1 (April 2002).

Werrell, Kenneth P. *Blankets of Fire: U.S. Bombers over Japan during World War II*. Washington, D.C.: Smithsonian Institution Press, 1996.

Wickware, Francis S. "The Japanese Language." *Life* (7 September 1942). Reprinted as "Honorable Mistake—The Japanese Language." *Readers Digest* (October 1942): 55–57.

Williams, Josette H. "The Information War in the Pacific." *Studies in Intelligence* 46, no. 3 (2002).

Willoughby, Charles A., and John Chamberlain. *MacArthur, 1941–1951*. New York: McGraw-Hill, 1954.

Winkler, Allan M. *The Politics of Propaganda: The Office of War Information, 1942–1945*. New Haven, Conn.: Yale University Press, 1978.

Winton, John. ULTRA *in the Pacific: How Breaking Japanese Codes & Cyphers Affected Naval Operations against Japan, 1941–45*. Annapolis, Md.: Naval Institute Press, 1993.

Wohlstetter, Roberta. *Pearl Harbor: Warning and Decision*. Stanford, Calif.: Stanford University Press, 1962.

Wolf, Thomas P. "McCloy, John Jay, Jr.," in *American National Biography*, ed. John A. Garraty and Mark C. Carnes. New York: Oxford University Press, 1999.

Wong, K. Scott. "War Comes to Chinatown: Social Transformation and the Chinese of California," in *The Way We Really Were: The Golden State in the Second World War*, ed. Roger W. Lotchin. Urbana: University of Illinois Press, 2000, pp. 164–86.

Yahara, Hiromichi. *Okinawa Kessen* [Battle of Okinawa]. Tokyo: Yomiuri Shimbunsha, 1972.

Yamagiwa, Joseph K. *Modern Conversational Japanese*. New York: McGraw-Hill, 1942.

Yamazaki, Toyoko. *Futatsu no Sokoku* [Two Homelands], 3 vols. Tokyo: Shinchosha, 1983.

Yoo, David K. *Growing Up Nisei: Race, Generation, and Culture among Japanese Americans of California, 1924–1949*. Urbana: University of Illinois Press, 2000.

Yu, Maochun. *OSS in China: Prelude to Cold War*. New Haven: Yale University Press, 1996.

Yu, Shen. "SACO Re-Examined: Sino American Intelligence Cooperation during World War II." *Intelligence and National Security* 16, no. 4 (Winter 2001): 149–74.

Zacharias, Ellis M. *Secret Missions: The Story of an Intelligence Officer*. New York: G. P. Putnam's Sons, 1946.

Zaugg, Harold E. *Sensei, the Ultra American: From Missionary Teacher to Wartime Translator*. Manhattan, Kans.: Sunflower University Press, 1995.

Zedric, Lance Q. *Silent Warriors of World War II: The Alamo Scouts behind Japanese Lines*. Ventura, Calif.: Pathfinder Publishing, 1995.

Zeiler, Thomas W. *Unconditional Defeat: Japan, America, and the End of World War II*. Wilmington, Del.: Scholarly Resources, 2004.

Zumwalt, James. "Our Parents Told Us, 'This Is Your Country.'" *Parade Magazine* (26 May 96).

Film and Video

Beyond Barbed Wire. Mac and Ava Picture Productions, 1997.

The Color of Honor. Vox Productions, 1987.

Fifty Years of Silence: The Untold Story of Japanese American Soldiers in the Pacific Theater, 1941–1952. National Japanese American Historical Society, 1992.

Go For Broke. Metro-Goldwyn-Mayer, 1951.

Mission in Manila: The Sakakida Story. National Japanese American Historical Society, 1994.

Nisei Soldier: Standard Bearer for an Exiled People. Vox Productions, 1983.

Prejudice and Patriotism: The Story of Japanese American Military Intelligence Service. National Japanese American Historical Society, ca. 2000.

A Tradition of Honor. Go for Broke Educational Foundation, 2002.

Uncommon Courage: Patriotism and Civil Liberties. Bridge Media, 2001.

Index

China-Burma-India Theater—continued
    surrenders of Japanese forces
        China, 398–404
        Southeast Asia, 396–98
Chindits, 287
Chinese Americans
    at Fourth Army Intelligence School, 52
    Japanese Americans compared, 5, 8
    military government training, 227
    at MISLS, 97n, 142–43, 315–16, 399
    Nisei confused with, 73, 113
Chinese Exclusion Act of 1882, 8
Chinese-language programs, 315–16
Chinese Nationalist Army, 348
Chinese New First Army, 346
Choctaws used as Code Talkers, 179
Chojin, T4g. Shiuso, 272–73
CIC. See Counter Intelligence Corps.
Citizenship, American
    dual citizenship of Nisei, 11
    Issei ineligibility for, 8
    Nisei losing and regaining, 12n, 115, 350
    Nisei renouncing, 450–51
Civil Affairs Holding and Staging Area
    (CASA), 227, 424
Civil Affairs Training Schools (CATS), 159,
    226, 323, 423
Civil censorship in occupied Japan, 453–54
Colleges and universities. See also California
    at Berkeley, University of; Colorado,
    University of; Columbia University;
    Harvard University; Michigan, Univer-
    sity of; Oklahoma A&M College;
    Pennsylvania, University of; Princeton
    University; Virginia, University of;
    Washington, University of.
    ASTP language programs, 153–57
    independent language programs, 158
    military government language training at,
    159–60
Collins, Maj. Gen. J. Lawton, 73
Colorado, University of, 58–59, 70, 150–52,
    168, 323, 422–23. See also Navy School
    of Oriental Languages; Office of Naval
    Intelligence (ONI).
Columbia University, 119, 159, 362
Combat Infantry Badge, Nisei awarded, 83,
    187, 193, 283, 411
Combat Intelligence Center, Noumea, New
    Caledonia, 172, 174
Comanche used as Code Talkers, 179
Commander in Chief, Pacific Fleet (CINCPAC),
    1st Provisional Military Government
    Interpreter Detachment, 357

Commissions. See also Caucasians, as leaders
    of language teams.
    Aiso, 116, 131
    anglicized names, supposed blackballing
    of Nisei with, 257n
    AIJLS graduates, 323
    ATIS personnel, 182, 256–57, 384–85, 434
    in the field, 376, 378, 387
    Merrill's Marauders Nisei, 283
    MIS Nisei graduates, 130–31
    MISLS instructors, 116, 303
    morale of draftees due to lack of, 229–30
    Navy V–12 precommissioning program,
    153, 156
    Office Candidate School, MIS Nisei
    attending, 131, 176–77, 222, 242, 313
    Sakamoto, Thomas, 26
Communism, 126, 209, 211, 288–89
Communist Chinese, 288–89, 348–49, 377,
    399, 402–04
Communist Japanese, 288–89, 439, 451
Company K at Fort Snelling, 418–19
Compton, Karl T., 452
Continental U.S., MIS Nisei serving in,
    195–233
    II Armored Corps Training Center, 224
    Army Map Service, 224
    interrogation of POWs, 203–07
    Manhattan Project, 222–23
    military government, 225–27
    Military Intelligence Division (MID),
    198–201
    Military Intelligence Training Units,
    229–33
    Pacific Military Intelligence Research
    Section, 218–22, 228
    Pacific Order of Battle Section, 200–203
    psychological warfare, 207–14
    Signal Intelligence Service, 200, 214–18
Coordinator of Information (later Office of
    Strategic Services), 59, 207, 208
Cornell University conference of Japanese-
    language teachers, 1941, 24, 29
CORONET. See Operations.
Corps of Intelligence Police, 20. See also
    Counter Intelligence Corps.
    language training school, 23
    Philippines, surveillance of Japanese
    community in, 20
    prisoners of war from, 335–36
Cory, 1st Lt. Ralph, 69
Counter Intelligence Corps (CIC), 20. See
    also Corps of Intelligence Police.
    306th CIC, 383

Printed in the USA
CPSIA information can be obtained
at www.ICGtesting.com
LVHW082232300424
778982LV00040B/1158